THE LIFE OF ROBERT BURNS

ROBERT BURNS

From the original miniature painted in
1795 probably by Alexander Reid, in the
collection of Mr. Oliver R. Barrett

THE LIFE OF
ROBERT BURNS

BY

FRANKLYN BLISS SNYDER

ARCHON BOOKS
1968

LIBRARY OF CONGRESS CATALOG CARD NUMBER: 68-16336
PRINTED IN THE UNITED STATES OF AMERICA

TO
W. D. S.

PREFACE

To TELL the story of Burns's life as truthfully as possible, discriminating between verifiable fact and unsubstantiated anecdote, has been my purpose in writing this biography.

While engaged in this pleasant task I have had the assistance of many persons. Friendly students, and colleagues both at Northwestern and elsewhere, have read portions of the manuscript, and have suggested not a few improvements. Professor Ney McMinn has read it all, and has laid me under a heavy debt of gratitude. Mr. Theodore W. Koch, University Librarian at Northwestern University, has been my steadfast ally in collecting Burnsiana; had it not been for his interest in the whole matter, the book would not have been undertaken. Mr. Septimus Pitt, City Librarian of Glasgow, Mr. David Dunlop, his assistant, and Mr. Lauriston Sharp, Assistant Librarian at the University of Edinburgh, deserve more than a passing word of thanks for the help they gave me during the summer of 1930. Mr. J. C. Ewing, Editor of the *Burns Chronicle*, has not only responded to requests for information in the way which has endeared him to students of Burns the world over, but has called to my attention several facts of which I should otherwise have been ignorant.

Mr. Oliver R. Barrett of Chicago has been generous with his permission to reproduce interesting items in his Burns collection; Mr. John Gribbel of Philadelphia has furnished me with a photostat of Burns's Excise commission, reprinted in the Appendix.

To Mr. G. W. Shirley, Librarian of the Ewart Public Library at Dumfries, and Professor J. De Lancey Ferguson of Western Reserve University, my obligations are of a sort that can hardly be stated. Mr. Shirley has read the entire manuscript, and has

PREFACE

put at my disposal a large amount of material culled from the collections in the Ewart Library. I have tried to acknowledge specific examples of my indebtedness to him at appropriate places in the text; no footnotes, however, could indicate the extent of his friendly and penetrating criticism. Professor Ferguson has been my unfailing court of final appeal in disputed or debatable matters. He has sent me more new material than one has a right to expect from anybody, and has supplied me with an advance set of the proofs of his own definitive edition of Burns's letters, without which this biography could not have been written. Only he and I will ever know how much I owe him!

To The National Council of Learned Societies I am grateful for a grant to cover part of the expense connected with the preperation of this book.

FRANKLYN BLISS SNYDER.

Northwestern University,
Evanston, Illinois.

CONTENTS

CHAPTER | | PAGE

I BURNS'S AYRSHIRE — 3
   1 The "Lay of the Land" — 4
   2 The Chief Towns — 6
   3 A Land of Farmers — 12
   4 Church and State — 18
   5 Education — 29

II THE EARLY YEARS — 32
   1 Alloway — 32
   2 Mount Oliphant — 45

III LOCHLIE AND IRVINE — 64

IV MOSSGIEL — 96
   1 Life on the Farm — 96
   2 Mauchline: The Town and Its Inhabitants — 102
   3 Three Lovers of Burns — 118

V THE KILMARNOCK VOLUME — 149
   1 The Making of the Book — 149
   2 Omissions from the Volume — 157
   3 The Published Poems — 166

VI EDINBURGH: THE FIRST WINTER — 186
   1 "Auld Reekie" — 186
   2 New Friendships — 194
   3 The 1787 Edition — 220

VII VACATION TOURS: AN INTERLUDE — 235

VIII EDINBURGH: THE SECOND WINTER — 256
   1 "Auld Reekie" Again — 256
   2 Burns and *The Scots Musical Museum* — 258
   3 Clarinda — 263
   4 The Excise Appointment — 274
   5 The Return to the Farm — 278
   6 Jean Armour Again — 282

CONTENTS

CHAPTER   PAGE

IX   ELLISLAND   294
      1   THE FARM   294
      2   FAMILY PROBLEMS   302
      3   THE EXCISEMAN   314
      4   TWO ELLISLAND FRIENDSHIPS   321
      5   INTELLECTUAL INTERESTS   334
      6   BURNS'S HEALTH   343
      7   FAREWELL TO ELLISLAND   346

X   DUMFRIES   354
      1   THE TOWN OF DUMFRIES   355
      2   DUMFRIES EXPERIENCES   361
      3   NEW FRIENDS   373
      4   THE DUMFRIES EXCISEMAN   394
      5   LITERARY WORK   406
      6   THE END OF THE STORY   426
      7   AFTERWARDS   436

XI   THE MAN AND THE POET   442
      1   BURNS THE MAN   444
      2   BURNS THE POET   459

APPENDIX
  A. BIBLIOGRAPHICAL NOTES   477
      1   GENERAL BIBLIOGRAPHIES   477
      2   THE MOST IMPORTANT BIOGRAPHIES, BIO-
          GRAPHICAL STUDIES, AND EDITIONS   478
      3   SOURCE MATERIAL FOR SCOTTISH ECCLESIASTI-
          CAL AND ECONOMIC HISTORY   496

  B. POEMS BY SAUNDERS TAIT   498

  C. THE ELLISLAND LEASE   503

  D. BURNS'S EXCISE COMMISSION   507

INDEX   511

ILLUSTRATIONS

ROBERT BURNS		*Frontispiece*
		PAGE
BURNS'S AYRSHIRE		5
WILLIAM BURNES'S COTTAGE AT ALLOWAY		35
MAUCHLINE		105
A PLAN OF THE CITY OF EDINBURGH	*Facing*	186
THE BACK CAUSEWAY, MAUCHLINE		285
BILL FROM MATTHEW MORISON, MAUCHLINE	*Facing*	300
BILL FROM PETER HILL, EDINBURGH	*Facing*	334
TAILOR'S BILL FROM NICHOL RAE, DUMFRIES	*Facing*	360
THE MILL VENNEL, DUMFRIES, 1802		367
MANUSCRIPT OF AULD LANG SYNE	*Facing*	420
LETTER TO JOHN CLARK WRITTEN AT BROW, 16 JULY 1796	*Facing*	428

LIST OF ABBREVIATIONS

The following works, frequently quoted in the text, are referred to in the footnotes by the abbreviations here listed:

[CURRIE, DR. JAMES], *The Works of Robert Burns with an Account of his Life.*
London, 1803. 4 vols.
All references are to this 1803 edition, unless otherwise specified.
Cited as Currie.

CHAMBERS, ROBERT, *The Life and Works of Robert Burns.*
New York, 1859. 4 vols.
Cited as Chambers.

DOUGLAS, WILLIAM SCOTT, *The Works of Robert Burns.*
Edinburgh, 1877–1879. 6 vols.
Cited as S. D.

EDGAR, ANDREW, *Old Church Life in Scotland.*
Paisley, 1885; 1886.
Cited as Edgar.

WALLACE, WILLIAM, *The Life and Works of Robert Burns,* edited by Robert Chambers, revised by William Wallace.
Edinburgh, 1896. 4 vols.
Commonly referred to as "The Chambers-Wallace Burns."
Cited as C. W.

HENLEY, W. E., and HENDERSON, T. F., *The Poetry of Robert Burns.*
Edinburgh, 1896–1897. 4 vols.. The Centenary Edition.
Cited as H. H.

FERGUSON, J. DE LANCEY, *The Letters of Robert Burns.*
Oxford, 1931. 2 vols.
Cited as *Letters.*

THE LIFE OF ROBERT BURNS

CHAPTER I

BURNS'S AYRSHIRE

LIFE in the Ayrshire of Burns's youth was not in any sense English; it was not even British; it was distinctly and definitely Scottish. Between the Scotsman of 1760 and his English contemporary there lay the gulf of six centuries of political and religious antagonisms, a gulf made manifest, even so late as the close of Burns's life, in striking differences in language, law, literature, and general manner of living. To be sure, the Union of 1707 had thrown a narrow and somewhat unstable bridge across this chasm. But following the Union had come the two rebellions of 1715 and 1745—rebellions which were aimed primarily at re-establishing the House of Stuart on the English throne, but which were also expressive of a widespread regret over the absorption of the Scottish body politic by its southern neighbor. And though the economic advantages resulting from the Union did something to ameliorate the bitterness engendered by six hundred years of rivalry, the gulf separating the two peoples was still virtually unbridged when Burns was born in 1759. So far as national culture was concerned, Scotland was still independent of her partner in the Union.

Some knowledge of this Scottish mentality and culture is essential for an understanding of Burns's work and life; for despite the national and—at its best—universal appeal of his poetry, much of it is definitely and specifically local. It grew directly out of Burns's daily experiences in Ayrshire, out of the life which he himself lived; and in so far as the poet ever had any specific audience or body of readers in mind, it was written for the delectation of his friends and neighbors. "The Holy Fair" can not be read in a vacuum, insulated from the world of Ayrshire Presbyterianism; "The Twa Dogs" and "The Auld Farmer's Salutation to his Mare" gain immeasurably in poignancy when one considers that Burns knew the life of the tenant farmer as well, say, as Whittier knew the life of the village shoemaker; and when one reminds oneself, as best one can, of how life must have appeared to parish minister or upland farmer. This first chapter, then, will not be concerned with Burns himself, but will paint the background and furnish the necessary stage setting for the drama of his career.

1

THE "LAY OF THE LAND"

Ayrshire, the section of Scotland most intimately associated with Burns's early years, lies in the southwestern part of the kingdom, at the point where the waters of the Irish Sea first narrow themselves into the Firth of Clyde. In shape, it may be likened to a somewhat irregular triangle, the base extending north and south along the coast for approximately sixty miles. Half way up this base line is the county town of Ayr, lying beside the mouth of the river from which both town and shire were named. Twenty-five miles east of Ayr, in the Cumnock Hills, is the apex of the triangle. To the northeast lie the counties of Renfrew and Lanark; to the southeast, Dumfries, Kirkcudbright, and Wigtown. To the west is the Irish Channel, across which on a clear day one may see the rugged island hills of Arran and the rocky triangle of Ailsa Craig. Slightly more than eleven hundred square miles of rolling uplands and pleasantly variegated river valleys lie within these boundaries. Four years before Burns's birth there were fifty-nine thousand persons living in the shire, which means an average density of population twice that of the State of Vermont in 1930. There are no mountains, such as one finds in the Highlands; to the east the hills shoulder their way up to an elevation of two thousand feet. Except in these somewhat bleak eastern uplands, it is a good land for farmer

[4]

or dairyman or poet; yes, for miner too, since coal and iron lie
in abundance beneath the surface of the soil. But the winters
are long, and when the December gales blow in from the North
Atlantic one has need of a stout heart and close-wrapped plaid
of homespun to exclude the chill.

Some readers have found it hard to understand why Burns,

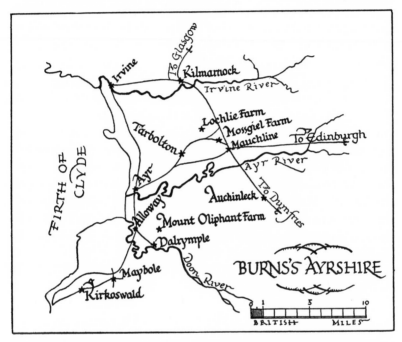

who spent his youth thus almost within constant sight of the sea,
remained so untouched by its power. But it is clear to any
student of his verse that the rivers which have cut their tree-
bordered channels from the hilly eastern slopes to the seacoast
played a large part in his experience. Turn to any map of Scotland and you will see them: to the north the Irvine, beside which
had grown up the fishing village and seaport to which the river
had given a name, and the inland town of Kilmarnock, home of
spinners and weavers. Next come two streams which Burns's
verse has made known wherever his fame has spread—the Ayr,

[5]

a very considerable little river, and "Bonnie Doon," spanned at Alloway by the single arch of the old bridge. To the south, less important, but still not unknown to the reader of the lyrics, flow the Stinchar and the Girvan. They are small enough streams as they slip quietly westward beneath the sunshine of a July afternoon; but see them in March, big with the melting snows of the hill country, or in September, swollen into a "spate" by the equinoctial rains, and you realize that fording them would be a venturesome task for even an experienced horseman, and that only the stoutest of bridges, built in the good old manner, could withstand the swirling rush of their brown waters.

It is perhaps worth reminding ourselves, while we still have their relative positions in mind, that three of these rivers formed the boundaries of the old districts into which Ayrshire had once been divided. The names appear not infrequently in Burns's verse, albeit they have disappeared from the modern maps. North of the Irvine lay Cunninghame; southwest of the Doon was Carrick, Robert Bruce's earldom. Between the Irvine and the Doon lay Kyle, Burns's own land, which in turn was sub-divided by the Ayr into the northern Kyle Stewart and the southern King's Kyle.

2

THE CHIEF TOWNS

In the middle of the eighteenth century three towns promised to become the chief centers of this pleasant district: Irvine, Ayr, and Kilmarnock. Ayr, the smallest of the three, had in the year 1755 a population of 2564; Kilmarnock, the largest, boasted 4403 in the same census. Each had a distinct history and flavor. And the manner of living, the civilization, of these typical Ayrshire towns, was as important an element in Scottish culture as the mode of living followed on the farm.

Least important of the three to the student of Burns was Irvine, where the poet was to spend some months learning the flaxdresser's trade, and to meet Richard Brown, the sailor, who became one of his most intimate friends. A fishing town, lying not directly on the coast itself, but on the north bank of the river Irvine, the village was not of the sort to charm the youthful poet. Long clusters of sand dunes, interminable mudflats covered at high tide but exposed by the receding ebb, and broken-down wharves where fishing smacks unloaded their catch,—all these told of Irvine's proximity to the sea, but brought little of its romance into the life of the vicinity. The town itself consisted of a miscellaneous collection of storehouses, flax-dressing shops, and solidly built residences of the simplest sort, clustering close to the long main street which ran through the village from northwest to southeast. A stone bridge, new in 1746, connected Irvine with Fullerton on the south bank of the river. Such was the Irvine of Burns's youth—an unpretentious little town, the home of flaxdressers and fishermen. The fact that only two Scottish ports outranked Irvine in the amount of tonnage entered and cleared is an indication that Scottish sea-faring was not prospering, and that at this date the most characteristic elements of Scottish life were not to be found on the coast.

Of far greater significance in Burns's life than Irvine, and of more interest to the student, was the county-town, Ayr,

> Auld Ayr, wham ne'er a town surpasses
> For honest men and bonie lasses.

Here, indeed, the poet may be said to have grown up; for Alloway, his birthplace, was but two miles to the south, and Mount Oliphant and Lochlie, to which his father successively moved the family during the lad's youth, both lay within ten miles of Ayr Cross.

The greater the pity, then, from some points of view, that virtually everything associated with the old town has disappeared, and that except for the two bridges, and probably a single public house, there is little which the visitor of today can surely connect with the town which Burns knew.

[7]

Old traditions still persist, however; as for instance the legend that here Sir William Wallace in 1297 burned to death five thousand of his southern foemen, revelling in the Ayr granaries; nor has time dimmed the glory of Robert Bruce, the scene of whose first campaign against Wallace's conqueror was the neighboring district of Carrick, and whose title to the Scottish throne was recognized by a special session of Parliament sitting at Ayr in 1315. Here, too, in 1651 General Monk built one of his chain of forts, and garrisoned it with four hundred and ninety foot and a hundred horse—grim veterans of Worcester and Dunbar, charged with keeping peace in this turbulent corner of the kingdom. All this and much more concerning the history of Ayr Burns knew and gloried in; all this has come down unchanged from his day. But physically the town of Burns's youth is no more.

The river still winds its way through the town, however, and the Auld Brig, extensively repaired twenty years ago, still lifts its four masonry arches over the brown water, and stands sturdily against the spring freshets. The "drowsy dongeon clock" of the Tolbooth has been silent for a century. Wallace Tower, which in Burns's day was a square, rock-built donjon forty feet high, standing prominently above the thatched roofs of the town and displaying the second of the two town clocks, this also has gone, replaced by a more pretentious structure. "Ratton Key," which Burns called a "small landing place" on the river bank, has disappeared, together with the larger quay, both superseded by the piers of the modern seaport at the mouth of the river. The High Street rambles pleasantly along as it did a century and a half ago; but the townsfolk who picked their way warily between the mud holes in the old cobblestone pavement would never recognize the modern business street, with its trams and cinemas, as its successor. The Tam o' Shanter Inn of today is probably a genuine relic of Burns's time, and gives one a fair sample of the characteristic town architecture of 1760. It is a low, box-like, two-storeyed house of stone, overcast with plaster. A small-paned window flanks the single door on either side; two more windows huddle close under the eaves of the thatched roof. Behind the thick walls the "ingle" still "bleezes;" but life outside moves more noisily and more swiftly than in the days when Tam and Souter Johnny foregathered here, or when Burns himself, after selling his father's farm produce at market or fair, stopped to warm himself by the fire before mounting his horse for the ten mile ride back to Lochlie.

In such houses—few of them over a single storey high, many built not of stone but of puddled clay and straw—dwelt the burghers of the ancient town. They were lawyers, physicians, merchants, and workers at many crafts, who plied their trades busily during the week, and on Sundays gathered in the parish church to listen to Dr. Dalrymple, whom the poet's father admired, and who baptized young Robert the day after he was born, or to Dr. M'Gill, whose prosecution for heresy was later to arouse Burns's wrath. On market days there was a bustle of activity as the farmers rode in to barter grain for a bolt of cloth or side of well-tanned leather; and when a fair was on, the little town could scarce find room for the visitors—Highlanders with their droves of black cattle; fishermen from the villages along the seacoast, trading salt herring for oatmeal; gypsies with their horses for sale; itinerant peddlers, vagabonds, hawkers of ballads, a recruiting sergeant with his drummer, and all the picturesque human elements in the pageantry of small town holiday life. But the fair came only four times a year; and when the last Highlander had straggled back to Argyllshire, and an opportune thunderstorm had washed the litter from the streets into the river, life soon resumed its wonted placidity.

Not the sort of town to charm a lad with the variegated show of society or industry or trade; but a town rich in historic traditions, unashamed of its industry and frugality, and inhabited for the most part by intelligent and thoughtful folk, who took pride in their burgh school, and saw to it that only a learned and godly minister occupied the pulpit of the parish church.

Eleven miles northeast of Ayr is Kilmarnock. When Burns was born, forty five hundred persons, more or less, were living there, weaving cloth for bonnets and hose, making the rough Kilmarnock carpets that all Scotland knew, or stitching locally tanned leather into boots and shoes, and enjoying a comfortable if unpretentious economic independence. There was little that was impressive, and nothing that was beautiful in the physical aspect of the town. A quarter of a mile northeast of the Market Cross, where the life of the burgh centered, was the High Church, the oldest and for many years the only establishment of the Church of Scotland in Kilmarnock. A few rods southwest of the Cross stood the second, or Low Church. A mile northeast rose the ruins of Dean Castle, ancient seat of the Earls of Kilmarnock, which had been destroyed by fire in 1735, and never restored. Except for these structures, and the Tolbooth or Town House built in 1711, there was little in the Kilmarnock of 1760 to attract the casual traveller as he rode through the town on his way to Glasgow, twenty miles to the northeast. Narrow and ill-paved streets, low houses crowded suffocatingly close to one another, formed a prospect monotonous and uninviting. There were good trout in the Irvine river, to be sure; and good ale was to be had at two pence a Scotch pint—the equivalent of two English quarts—at nearly two score of public houses. But the town as a whole was dreary and unattractive; the sort of place through which one hurries on the way to a more congenial stopping point for the night.

But to judge the temper of Kilmarnock folk—or of their neighbors in Ayr, for that matter—by the physical appearance of the town, would be rash and unfair. Beneath the somewhat drab exterior there pulsed a life which ever since the Reformation had been keenly sensitive to the momentous questions of religion and politics. The artisans who spent toilsome days at their looms were the people who had saved Presbyterianism from extinction during the persecutions of Charles II, and more important, had secured for themselves the right to worship their God in the manner their consciences bade.

The victory had not been won without bloodshed. Here in Kilmarnock, in 1666, had been set up the heads of John Ross and John Shields, executed for their opposition to Episcopalianism. Into Kilmarnock in 1667, after the battle of Pentland Hills, had ridden General Dalziel with his dragoons, to fine the town fifty thousand merks for its share in the rising, and to terrorize the inhabitants by his brutality. Twelve years later, when the battle of Bothwell Bridge had marked another luckless attempt of the Covenanters to resist the armed forces of the sovereign, six men from Kilmarnock were transported for complicity in the affair, to perish as captives under hatches when the prison ship was wrecked on the Orkney shoals. Here in the spring of 1683 John Nisbet was hanged in the market place as a rebel, to be honored by an inscription in the Low Church burying ground which makes clear the temper of his fellow townsmen:

Here lies John Nisbet, who was taken by Major Balfour's party, and suffered at Kilmarnock, 14 April, 1683, for adhering to the Word of God and our Covenants.

Nor did the passing of time altogether soften the stern temper of the Kilmarnock Presbyterians. In 1764, when the Earl of Glencairn, exercising his right as patron, presented the Reverend William Lindsay as his nominee for the ministry of the Low Church, the second ministry of the Burgh, such a riotous assembly gathered to protest against the unpopular selection that both preacher and noble patron were glad to escape without severe bodily harm.

Life in Kilmarnock during Burns's youth may have been quiet and uneventful enough in most respects; but one had only to touch that life on the vital matter of loyalty to old ideals, to discover that sombre-coated Covenanters still walked the streets of the old town, and that John Knox still ruled the hearts of its inhabitants. All this Burns knew; it was part of the Ayrshire tradition. Nor could the young poet well forget that the last Earl of Kilmarnock had ridden out from this quiet town in 1745 to join Prince Charlie, only to be left wounded on Culloden

[11]

field, and to lay down titles and wealth and life itself beneath the headsman's axe on Tower Hill.

Small wonder, then, that Burns, farmer though he was, found Ayr and Kilmarnock of abundant and constant interest. Here lived people whom he loved, and some whom he disliked. Here were friends to whom he could show a scrap of newly written verse, with whom he could spend a happy evening of talk over the ale, and from whom he could count on aid and comfort in an emergency. Here were people who read books, and had books to lend to an ambitious youngster. Here was a cross-section of Scottish life, seen against a background rich in memories and traditions. And here was John Wilson with his printing press, destined to focus the eyes of the world on Kilmarnock by publishing Burns's first volume.

3

A LAND OF FARMERS

Except for the relatively few thousands thus engaged in the occupations of townsfolk, and the still fewer who suffered in the serfdom of the coal pits, Burns's Ayrshire contemporaries earned their living, as the poet was to do for many years, by working the soil. But the person who travels through Ayrshire today, or knows its fame as the home of a prized breed of cattle, will have difficulty in visualizing the conditions that existed at the middle of the eighteenth century, or in realizing the hardships attendant upon being "A farmer upon the Carrick border."

In the first place, only a few persons were actual free-holders; everyone else was a renter, and rents were high; so high, indeed, that until the latter part of the century they constituted a severe drain upon even the most productive soil. For example, when in 1765 the poet's father, William Burnes,[1] leased the farm of Mount Oliphant, seventy acres of not too fertile ground, he paid forty pounds a year for the first six years, and forty-five pounds a year for the second six years of the term—which amounts to an annual charge of over twelve shillings per acre. In 1777, when he removed to the larger farm at Lochlie, the rental was twenty shillings a year for each of its one hundred and twenty acres of upland soil.[2] Again, when Burns himself rented Ellisland, in March, 1788, his lease required annual payments of fifty pounds for the first three years, and seventy pounds for the remainder of the seventy-six year term. Of course, as every one knows, William Burnes was driven into bankruptcy by his Lochlie agreement; his son found Ellisland a ruinous bargain. But the fact that the two men, both experienced farmers, should have been willing to undertake such burdensome charges, is indicative of a general situation. It is perhaps true that these examples are extreme ones; both Burns and his father paid for poor land what would have been fair rental for the best. But it seems indisputable that farm values in southern Scotland were unwarrantably inflated during much of Burns's life; and that except when war-time scarcity sent the prices of farm products to unexpectedly high levels, these heavy rentals laid a severe and at times a crushing burden on the Ayrshire farmer.

If rentals were high, however, wages for farm laborers were disproportionately low. An unmarried plowman, at the middle of the century, expected about three pounds per year, with lodgings furnished in the dark and ill-ventilated garret or loft, and an allowance of meal for his food. By 1790 the average pay of such servants had risen to seven pounds, the exact amount Robert and Gilbert Burns were allowed out of the family treasury at Lochlie and Mossgiel. Married laborers received somewhat more, and might be given, or allowed to build, a small hut or cot in which to shelter their families.

So far as housing conditions were concerned, one has but to examine the cottage at Alloway in which Burns was born in order to see a typical small farm house of that time and place. In the idiom of the day, it was a "clay bigging," one storey high, fashioned by William Burnes himself from the soil of the vicinity, and covered with a heavy roof of thatch. In outside

[13]

dimensions it measured seventy-seven by eighteen feet. The cottage itself, or living quarters, occupied the southern end of the building, and comprised only two chambers: the kitchen, or but, and the room, or ben. Next to the cottage was the stable, or byre, with stalls for four or five cows and two horses; finally, at the northern end of the building, was the barn or granary. Roof and walls were continuous throughout; two partitions were all that divided the building into its three sections. According to some opinion the only entrance to the building, in Burns's day, was through the barn, which opened into the byre, which in turn connected with the cottage. Other authorities have it that the doors of the present edifice are, like the windows, approximately those of the building of 1759, and that the cottage had its own outer doorway. No one really knows.

There is a similar uncertainty concerning the location of the highway in 1759, and its position with relation to the house. The road of today runs southeast of the cottage; it may have occupied the same position in William Burnes's time, for the description of his plot of land, as it appears in the feu-record, states that it is bounded on the southeast by the "road from Slaphouse to the bridge of Doon." [3] This road was laid out about 1750, and took the place of one which ran much nearer the seacoast. On the other hand, there is a persistent tradition that the highway in 1759 ran directly in front of the cottage, so that William Burnes had to cross the road whenever he went to his garden plot. The earliest picture of the cottage, drawn on the spot in 1801 by W. Score, seems to confirm this tradition—but one can not be certain.

In 1800 the house itself was thus described by Gilbert Burns:

The house consisted of a kitchen in one end, and a room in the other, with a fireplace and chimney. . . . My father had constructed a concealed bed in the kitchen, with a small closet at the end, of the same materials with the house, and, when altogether cast over, outside and in, with lime, it had a neat, comfortable appearance, such as no family of the same rank, in the present improved style of living, would think themselves ill-lodged in. [4]

[14]

Such was the home of an industrious, ambitious Scottish nursery-man and small farmer in 1759. When this same farmer later moved to Mount Oliphant, his house differed in only a few respects from the cottage which he had built for his bride. It was probably slightly larger; more stone and timber would presumably have been used in the construction; there was a low attic where children or servants could sleep; the byre and barn were perhaps separate buildings, and not merely parts of one single structure.

Within such homes life moved on a plane of simple democracy, the farmer and his family setting themselves off in no way from the dairy-maid and unmarried plowman. The entire group met at a common table, joined in the manifold labors of seedtime and harvest, gathered peat in the winter, and spent the long evenings of the dark months spinning or weaving the cloth that an itinerant tailor would fashion into clothing, or making shoes and harness out of carefully hoarded leather. Always the head of the family would be mindful of the duty laid upon him by custom and church law, the obligation to instruct both servants and children in scripture and catechism, and to examine them concerning their spiritual state. Of books there would certainly be a few in such a home, laid carefully on a shelf above the reach of childish fingers: the "big ha' Bible" in a place of honor, and near it Dr. Thomas Boston's *Fourfold State*, or Stackhouse's *History of the Bible*, or Poole's invaluable *Annotations*. No light reading this, but sternly edifying, proper for a race of men and women bred in the tradition of Calvin and John Knox.

When one turns from conditions within the house to the varied activities of the fields, one discovers that Burns lived at a time when Scottish agriculture was undergoing drastic and salutary changes. The most characteristic and possibly most vicious feature of the old system, the "run-rigg" method of cultivation, under which the arable land was divided into a series of strips of ground, or riggs, separated from one another by wide ditches, the riggs being plowed and seeded in triennial rotation,—this

[15]

had at last been virtually abandoned in the lowlands. Instead of having the use of one rigg in each of, say, a dozen locations, the farmer might now have all his land in one parcel, and might cultivate it as he himself wished, without regard to the whims or superstitions of his neighbors. Then, too, the immemorial habit of leasing land for only two or three years had given place to a system of longer tenure, under which there was an incentive for the farmer to improve his holdings. Fields were no longer left unenclosed, undrained, and unfertilized. Under the stimulus of the "Society of Improvers of Knowledge of Agriculture," which had been founded in 1723, Scotsmen were encouraged to experiment with English methods; and in general the experiments succeeded. Where formerly the farmer had trusted to tradition or incantation as his sole guide, he began now to read and to think. His cattle improved in quality; his crops doubled and trebled in value. Instead of contenting himself with grey oats and "bere," the poorest form of barley, yielding only two or three seeds at harvest for each one planted in the spring, he learned the value of other and better grain, as well as of turnips and potatoes. He bought more and better farming tools, and used them more intelligently. To be sure, Burns's plow was a clumsy affair, which demanded four horses and at least two men for its proper manipulation. Such an invaluable adjunct as the threshing mill did not come into general use till after Burns had given up farming entirely. The poet, like his father, threshed his grain on the barn floor, and swung a flail such as one of the Covenanters might have carried into battle in lieu of a pike. But he no longer slowly ground his grain by hand; instead of the old "knocken bere," or crushed barley, he now had a clean and uniform meal, ground at one of the mills that had become general about the middle of the century.

But despite such improvements Burns and his neighbors had still to contend with their age-old enemy, a rigorous climate. Frosts and snow as late as May, sleet storms in September, made the season short and the harvest ever uncertain. And though seed had been good and the summer propitious, if the grain

[16]

were not garnered before the first autumnal gale swept in from the ocean, an entire year's crop might be ruined over night.

Even when the end of "hairst" saw the grain safe under cover, or piled into stacks in the yard, the farmer of 1760 was still handicapped by lack of an easily accessible market for the part of his crops not needed at home. Roads were unbelievably bad, and wheeled vehicles moved only with the utmost difficulty over the unkept trails fit hardly for horsemen. As a result, a farmer wishing to sell part of his crop carried it to market in panniers slung over his horse's back, or dragged it, still more toilsomely, on a crude sledge. Shortly after the middle of the century Lord Cathcart, an enterprising Ayrshire landowner, offered to supply his tenants with carts,—only to have the proffered vehicles declined as useless. The Turnpike Act of 1751 ultimately wrought a great improvement in the state of the highways, and the farmer profited most by the change. But the betterment was slow; and during Burns's youth the situation was almost as bad, even in Ayrshire, as it was to remain over most of the Highlands till well past the end of the century.

The building of good roads did not bring about an immediate improvement in the conditions of travel or in the distribution of the mails. The bi-weekly stage connecting Edinburgh and Glasgow, which ran first in 1749, averaged less than four miles an hour, nor was it possible to improve upon this speed till 1780. As late as 1782, William Creech—who was later to be Burns's Edinburgh publisher—could record it as a marvel that at last a person could make the round trip between Edinburgh and London in a week. No stage of any sort ran between Glasgow and London till 1788. The mails, which were carried by post boys on horseback, were even more leisurely than the stages; in 1790 it still took four days for an Edinburgh letter to reach London. But by the close of Burns's life letters moved with reasonable swiftness from one to another of the one hundred and sixty-four Scottish post offices; and though the charges were high, the service was rather more certain than in England at the same time. And inevitably, as means of transportation and communication improved, the farmer shared in the general economic betterment, till by the close of the century the prosperity of the Ayrshire farmer was well established.

4

CHURCH AND STATE

The average Scotsman of 1760 took little interest in the civil government. If he were a Highlander, and a near relative of the chieftain, he probably grumbled over the abolition of the hereditary jurisdictions, which, with the right of pit and gallows, had been swept out of existence in 1748. If he were a Lowlander with Jacobite ancestry, he thought back somewhat wistfully to the days before the Union, passed his glass of wine across his goblet of water when drinking the King's health, and enjoyed his measure of happiness without much further concern over governmental problems. If he were a Lowlander and a Whig, or in any way connected with the great Clan Campbell, he thanked God for the House of Hanover, and accepted with unquestioning gratitude whatever was done for Scotland by King George's ministry. During much of Burns's life the actual ruler of Scotland was Henry Dundas, first Lord Melville, who was successively Solicitor General for Scotland, Lord Advocate, and Keeper of the Signet in Scotland, and for three decades the most influential person in the kingdom. He not only distributed the royal patronage throughout Scotland, but was virtually in control of the election machinery by which Scottish members of the two houses of Parliament were chosen, and was not uncommonly referred to as "the uncrowned King of Scotland." But except when Dundas once introduced a bill into Parliament removing certain restrictions from Roman Catholics, it was only an occasional Ayrshireman who took much notice of his actions.

Of course Burns himself, especially during the last seven years of his life, felt a keen interest in both local politics and international developments. But Burns was far more sensitive to such matters, far more accessible to ideas, than most of his contemporaries, who as a rule lived reasonably within the law that had come down to them from the past, grumbled at—and evaded—the ever-increasing excise duties, and worried themselves no further about the state.

And, indeed, why should they? When the Scottish Parliament had finally been persuaded to ratify the Union of 1707, the nation—so thought many a patriotic Scot—had ceased to exist. The Rose had at last triumphed over the Thistle; and though forty-five members of the House of Commons and a dozen elected Peers journeyed laboriously to each session of Parliament as Scottish delegates, they represented only a meagre fraction of the population, and—what was worse—did all they could to free themselves from the "Scotticisms" at which their English colleagues were wont to jibe.[5] Even in Ayrshire, where there were more qualified freeholders than in any other county, there were so late as 1782 only two hundred and five persons entitled to vote,—and this for a population of sixty-five thousand. The average at this time for the thirty-three counties of the kingdom was only eighty voters per county. Small wonder, then, that the Scotsman of Burns's youth was relatively unconcerned with the government under which he lived, and that the student of the Scottish social order can pass swiftly over that phase of his problem.[6]

As compensation, however, for the slight voice accorded him in the civil government, this Scotsman had one great institution still in his control, and over its problems he spent the laborious days that an American of the same era might have devoted to politics. Established Presbyterianism, the national Church of Scotland, which Knox had placed in its position of supremacy, and for which the Covenanters and their sons had fought not with words alone but with pikes and muskets as well, this beloved Church had risen to its greatest power at the close of the seventeenth century, when the ministers had been the real rulers of Scotland, and the General Assembly made the only laws that were sure of enforcement. The first part of the eighteenth century saw the Church divided by schismatics and challenged by heretics; from 1750 to 1770, however, it was again firmly intrenched in power, and even to the end of Burns's life it was probably the most potent single influence in the daily existence of an Ayrshireman.   Furthermore, it was in the southwestern counties of Scotland, in Burns's own country, that the ecclesiastical domination had been most complete; from the same localities, moreover, had come the first and most significant mutterings of theological rebellion.[7]   Hence it arose that the Church, which had molded the very soul of Scotland, was to touch Burns's life at many points, and strongly to influence his poetic output.   Indeed, till one understands something of the history, the organization, and the doctrine of the Church of Scotland, one can read but little of Burns with intelligent appreciation.

The historical narrative can be compressed into a few sentences.   Presbyterianism, which Knox had built on the wreckage of Catholicism, and which in 1643 seemed on the point of becoming the established church polity of England as well as of Scotland, had been superseded in 1661 by Episcopalianism, to which the Scots were antagonistic.   The attempt to impose it upon them had occasioned the bloody years of persecution, when the Covenanters, driven from manse and meeting house, held their conventicles in the fields, or lurked in the glen till Claverhouse's raiding party of dragoons should have given over the search.   In 1688 Episcopalianism in turn gave place to a Presbyterianism which had been both strengthened and embittered by the sufferings of the preceding generation.   Retribution was swift.   In 1690 the General Assembly was commissioned by Parliament to "try and purge out all inefficient and scandalous and erroneous ministers by due course of ecclesiastical process and censure."   Then followed what has been called the Presbyterian Inquisition, in the course of which six hundred of the nine hundred active clergymen of Scotland were dismissed from their parishes, often on the flimsiest of charges, and not infrequently with the accompaniment of mob violence.   Only in the north of the kingdom, where Presbyterianism had never found a secure foothold, and in some parts of the eastern shires, were the Episcopal clergy permitted to remain at their duties. In 1694, however, the General Assembly was curbed by a more moderate Parliament, and the days of bitterest strife came to an end.   And, indeed, there was little reason for continuing the purgation.   By the turn of the century the Church was unchallenged in its supremacy, and though it was destined to be divided by internal dissensions, it no longer feared attack from without.

Into the history of the many secessions that were to mark the next hundred and fifty years, it would be unprofitable to go. Petty disagreements concerning the relation of the Church to the State, concerning psalmody and ritual, interpretation and patronage, grew swiftly into open dissension, and led to separation.   But it is to be remembered that the Church as a whole became steadily more liberal, and that the seceders were in virtually every case persons who left the establishment in order to return to the Church of the "good old days."   Thus in 1737 there was formed a schismatic party, a powerful organization of what the world today would call fundamentalists, which in turn was divided ten years later into the Associate Synod and General Associate Synod.   Similarly, from the Associate Synod were formed the two groups familiar to readers of Burns's satires, and popularly known as "Old Lights" and "New Lights."   The former constituted the most stubborn and unprogressive wing of Presbyterianism; the latter represented a more liberal element.

Despite such disruptions, however, the essential character of Scottish Presbyterianism remained unchanged.   A mellowing of temper as the passing years dimmed the memory of persecution, a gradual relaxation of the bonds in which the Church held its members, a steady if at times imperceptible liberalizing of creedal interpretations—these were the inevitable developments of the second half of the eighteenth century.   But just as Scottish Episcopalianism of the seventeenth century had resembled Presbyterianism in every important respect save in its recognition of Bishops, who were offensive because they symbolized the royal interference in spiritual affairs, so the Presbyterianism of

1780 resembled that of 1688. All branches of the Church gloried in the same history, made use of approximately the same organization, and rested upon the same Calvinistic tenets as the foundation stones of their belief.

The organization of the Church, as it existed in the middle of the eighteenth century, was a model of simplicity. At the bottom of the pyramid was the parish, the smallest organized area, served, except in relatively few instances, by one church and one minister. In 1755 there were eight hundred and ninety such parishes in Scotland. Time had been when each parish chose its own minister; but after the restoration of patronage in 1712 the system changed to such an extent that virtually every parish had a patron who nominated, or "presented," the minister of his choice. Not all such persons were acceptable to the church members, and many a dissenting meeting house was built in protest against an unpopular presentation. But a wise patron guarded against embarrassment to himself and his nominee by ascertaining the wishes of the parish before making the formal presentation. Once installed, the minister held his charge for life, except as he might be called to a more desirable living, or dispossessed for immorality or heresy.

The confidential counsellors of the minister, and his assistants in the onerous task of caring for the spiritual welfare of the parish, were the elders. They collected and disbursed the offerings for the poor, ministered to the sick, scrutinized candidates for church membership, and, most important of all, as members of the Kirk Session examined all persons accused of misconduct.

This Kirk Session, or lowest form of ecclesiastical court, was the agency through which the Church made its power felt most directly. In every parish the minister and two or more elders composed the Session,—a tribunal which was supposed to meet at least once a week, to give thought to the spiritual affairs of the parish. The Session kept the membership roll, the minutes of its own meetings, and the official registers of baptisms, marriages and burials. To it were summoned persons suspected—

or accused—of many sorts of misconduct. The Session could fine a man for pulling kail on Sunday; it could sentence fornicators to stand on the "cutty stool" and be publicly rebuked by the minister during service; it could recommend to the Presbytery the infliction of the "lesser excommunication"—temporary suspension from the Sacrament of the Lord's Supper—upon anyone who neglected its summons, or proved contumacious when he appeared, as well as upon persons convicted of serious offenses. It would pry into every man's home, and rebuke him for his ways; it granted certificates of good character to persons moving to another parish, or withheld them from such as had incurred its displeasure. It was the Kirk Session that ordered Burns and Jean Armour to be publicly rebuked; it was from "Daddy" Auld, as presiding member of the Session, that Burns received the promise of his certificate of bachelorhood; it was the Kirk Session of Mauchline, composed of Auld, Fisher, and Sillar, that took cognizance of Gavin Hamilton's errors—and occasioned "Holy Willie's Prayer"! By the inherent qualities of its procedure it turned every parish into a hotbed of gossip, encouraged spying, and made all evils known abroad. In a static community it had enormous influence, but the ills it caused were almost as serious as those it sought to cure. Thus it came about that though the Kirk Session did indeed represent the power and dignity of the Church in every Scottish hamlet, it degenerated into a medium of ecclesiastical tyranny which ultimately provoked even sober conservatives to protest, and brought forth derisive laughter from the ungodly who delighted in Burns's satires.

As links between the Parish at the bottom, and the General Assembly at the top of the Church organization, stood the Presbytery and the Synod. The Presbyteries, of which in 1755 there were sixty-nine, were composed of a varying number of contiguous parishes. As delegates to the meetings of the Presbytery to which it belonged each parish sent its minister and one elder, and before the court of clergy and laymen thus established came all appeals from decisions of the Kirk Session. Unable to act except upon matters which had already been before a Session, the Presbytery considered these appeals with meticulous care, and reviewed at length the evidence concerning the contumacy of a Jacobite laird who had snapped his fingers at the Session, or a servant girl who had refused to name the father of her illegitimate child. Not infrequently the Presbytery reversed the findings of the Session, as witness the case of Gavin Hamilton before the Presbytery of Ayr.[8] When justice seemed to have been done in the lower court, however, it was in the power of the Presbytery to inflict upon a culprit the dreaded "greater excommunication." Prior to 1690 this sentence brought upon the offender not only ecclesiastical censure but also the civil penalties of outlawry and confiscation of lands and goods; latterly it was restricted to debarring the offender permanently from the Lord's Supper, handing him over officially to Satan, and rendering him anathema throughout orthodox Scotland.

Either party to a case before the Presbytery might appeal to the next highest judicature, the Synod. Of these there were fifteen in 1755, each composed of from two to eight adjacent Presbyteries, and consisting of every member of all the Presbyteries within its boundaries. Cases of petty scandal rarely reached the ears of these tribunals. The time of a Synod was better occupied in considering problems of theological interpretation, or in listening to the defence of a minister whom the Presbytery had found guilty of heresy, than in reviewing evidence which had already been spread in unpleasant detail on the records of the two lower courts.

Above the Synods was the General Assembly, the Supreme Court of the Church of Scotland, which met annually in Edinburgh, and in a real way took the place of the old Scottish Parliament. To it came commissioners from the Presbyteries, from Royal Burghs, and from the Universities; from its decisions there was no appeal, save—in theory but rarely in practise, and then only on lay matters,—to Parliament. This was no petty tribunal concerned with the tattle of village gossip, but a most potent, grave, and reverend assemblage of the leading

[24]

clergy and laity of Scotland. On its rolls were peers, lords of session, baronets, lairds, and the foremost members of the Scottish Bar, as well as those ministers whose influence and reputation made them known throughout the land. And always it must be remembered that this was no divinely constituted oligarchy, inflicting its will upon a voiceless people; this was no College of Cardinals, but a representative assembly, sensitive to public opinion throughout the Church, and reflecting in its decisions and utterances the will of the people who constituted its electorate.

Such, in brief, was the organization of the Church in which Burns was baptized. But the secret of the power which that Church wielded is not to be discovered through any study of ecclesiastical machinery. The soul of the Church was its creed; the rest was mere body.

The student of this creed will be led back at least to 1536, when Calvin published the first edition of his *Institutes*. Here is to be found the Genevan's sternly logical elaboration of his doctrine of predestination: the two-fold decree of God foreordaining part of the human race to eternal happiness, and the remainder to eternal damnation. Through no merits of their own are these happy ones elected for salvation; equally with those foreordained to punishment do they share the guilt of Adam's sin. God's grace alone saves the elect from unending punishment; God's grace expressed through the atoning sacrifice of His Son. Here too is to be found Calvin's doctrine of the Lord's Supper, interpreting it as a symbolic institution, and rejecting the perplexing doctrine of transubstantiation so fundamental to the Romanist. Here also appear the principles of ministerial equality and lay representation. Here, in short, in the sinewy Latin of the *Institutes*, are the germinal ideas from which were to spring all the varying shades of Calvinistic creeds.

But Calvin and the *Institutes* of 1536 were far removed from "Daddy" Auld and his fervent assistant "Holy Willie." Closer to them stood John Knox, whose body rested beneath a stone in St. Giles's church-yard, but whose fiery spirit lived on in the *Scotch Confession of Faith*.[9]   In this confession Calvin's fundamental doctrines reappear, expressed in the sturdy idiom of Edinburgh, and driven home with a zeal which the reader may call that of a saint or a fanatic, as he pleases.   "We firmly propose to abide to the end in the confession of this our faith," Knox and his colleagues had written at the close of their prefatory letter; that they and their successors had done so, the deeds and records of two centuries bore witness.

Still closer to Burns and his contemporaries was the Solemn League and Covenant of 1643, a political as well as a religious document; an international agreement which brought Scottish aid to the English Parliamentary forces, which at least opened the way towards making Presbyterianism the recognized church polity of the three kingdoms, and which enabled Scottish commissioners to sit at Westminster and to take a large part in preparing the Confession and Catechisms which bore the name of that Assembly.

To be sure, the Solemn League and Covenant was burned by the hangman in Westminster Hall in 1661, and for three decades thereafter the Covenanters suffered persecutions which recalled the days of Bloody Mary.   But the spirit that had descended from Calvin and Knox was not to be subdued.   The Church lived on, and the creed which had found its most famous expression in the publications of the Westminster Assembly was still the creed of orthodox Scotland when Burns was born.

The critic of this epoch of Scottish theology will do well to recall that the very authors of these memorable documents foresaw some of the dilemmas which might perplex their successors.   "The doctrine of this high mystery of predestination," they had written, "is to be handled with special prudence and care."[10]   And, indeed, when the reader of today undertakes to grasp the full import of the time-honored phrases, he finds himself repeatedly baffled.   Predestination—original sin—election —reprobation—these are the shibboleths by which one tests one's fitness for the task.   And if one finds it hard to reconcile predestination with free will, or to avoid making God himself the author of sin, one may turn to Jonathan Edwards, whom eighteenth century Scotland esteemed more highly than did his own parishioners at Northampton, and still remain perplexed.

But one need not be particular in criticism, for Calvinism, impressive, logical, clever, as it all was, bore within itself the seeds of its own undoing. The uncompromising creed that pronounced all mankind deserving of hell-fire because of Adam's sin, that opened Heaven only to the small company of the elect, chosen by God without much regard to their merits, and closed it to all others, no matter how saintly their lives,—this creed was bound to be challenged. It came into sharp conflict with human experience; it denied what seemed to be true; it affirmed—both of God and man—what men believed to be false. And challenged it was, long before Burns had made sport of the

> Orthodox, orthodox,
> Wha believe in John Knox.

As might have been expected, it was the universities, especially the University of Glasgow, which blew the heretic blast that disconcerted the orthodox and at the same time strengthened them in their resolution to maintain the good old faith unadulterated. John Simson, Professor of Divinity at Glasgow from 1708 to 1729, was accused of heresy, and in May of 1717 was found by the General Assembly to have "vented some opinions not necessary to be taught in divinity." Twelve years later he was suspended from teaching in the University, but was allowed to retain his salary and other emoluments—an indication of the changing temper of the times. Similarly, Archibald Campbell, appointed Professor of Church History in St. Andrews in 1730, found himself under attack because of his book *Apostles no Enthusiasts*. He was charged before the Assembly with Pelagianism, but was acquitted in March, 1736, to the regret of the "Marrow men." [11] But it was the lectures of Francis Hutcheson, Professor of Moral Philosophy at Glasgow from 1729 till his death in 1746, which carried to a high conclusion the work begun by Simson. Whoever came in contact with Hutcheson testified to the remarkable influence which he wielded. Adam Smith

[27]

was one of his devoted pupils; Hume consulted him on moral and ethical problems. Not far removed, philosophically, from Shaftesbury, and preaching a mild form of Presbyterianism which in effect differed but little from the Deism then popular, Hutcheson avoided unnecessary offence to any party, and built up a school of liberal ministers, whose "moral gospel" became increasingly popular as the years passed. Indeed it is not too much to call Hutcheson the real founder of the liberal movement that had grown to such alarming proportions by the time Burns wrote his satires.

It was inevitable that so able a man as Hutcheson should do much towards tempering the rigorous Calvinism of 1692. But even had there been no softening of the old creed, that creed would still have deserved no scant praise at the hands of the historian. It was a creed which brought home to every man the eternal distinction between sin and righteousness, and which placed every man face to face with his Creator and Judge. It bade each person search the Scriptures for revelations of God's will, and scrutinize his own heart for signs of his future condition. It opened the gates of Heaven to the regenerate, and held up before the sinner the certainty of a Hell with which there was no temporizing. There was nothing equivocal about this creed, nothing sentimental. And it was essentially a democratic creed, admitting no ranks or orders, either among clergy or laity. A man might be duke or cotter, laird or plowman, during the week; but on the Sabbath he took his place in the Kirk as a freeman of a state that looked to no earthly potentate as sovereign.

It was in this world of Calvinistic tenets and Presbyterian influence that Burns grew to manhood. Though his own religious belief was far different from that of his thoroughly orthodox contemporaries, it is noteworthy that his satire was directed not primarily against a creed which he could not accept for himself, but rather against the ignorant or intolerant or hypocritical professors of that creed. He could hardly have made his respect for one phase of the old order more clear than in the lines which the critics of that order are inclined to overlook,—

The Solemn League and Covenant
Now brings a smile, now brings a tear.
But sacred Freedom, too, was theirs:
If thou'rt a slave, indulge thy sneer.

5

EDUCATION

It would perhaps be an exaggeration to say that the Scottish concern over education was due largely to Presbyterianism, which made it incumbent on each church member to read the Bible for himself, and to follow the sermons of his minister in an intelligently critical mood. But it is no exaggeration to say that in many instances the primary purpose of elementary education, during the seventeenth and early eighteenth centuries, was religious instruction; and that when the pupils had learned to read the Bible and Catechism, they had mastered the chief items of the curriculum. Certainly it was the Church which had been responsible for the notable Acts of Parliament of 1633 and 1643, ordering the establishment of a public school in each parish of Scotland. Unfortunately, however, there had been no money to maintain the schools thus laudably decreed. Not till 1696 did Parliament even attempt to provide for the salaries and living quarters of the teachers. Even as late as 1735 reports to the Presbytery of Ayr showed twelve parishes in that relatively prosperous section of the Lowlands to be entirely without organized schools. But it is notable that the seventeenth century provided Scotland with an admirable plan for popular education, a plan superior to anything then in existence elsewhere in Europe. National poverty alone kept the plan from being put into execution.[12]

By the time of Burns's youth, however, the situation was far from discouraging. Parish schools, taught by young men of no meagre ability, were to be found throughout the Lowlands, and their scope was not limited to the elements of Calvinistic theology. In the large centers, such as Dumfries, or Ayr, or Kilmarnock, the burgh schools or academies offered an admirable preparation for any one of the four universities. And even when the combination of poverty and bad roads made it difficult for parents to send their children to school, there was always the possibility of employing a tutor for the youngsters of a few neighboring households. This young man would probably be a candidate for the ministry; he would ask only a meagre wage— a shilling a quarter for each pupil; he would meet his students in an empty barn or granary; and he would be qualified to teach the rudiments of Latin, French, and music, as well as the fundamental "Three R's." When Burns's father and his friends thus engaged John Murdoch, they were doing no more than was being done at the same time in many parts of southern Scotland, and that had been done by ambitious farmers as well as by lairds and gentry for nearly a century.

On the whole, the Ayrshire lad of 1759 stood an admirable chance of receiving at least the beginnings of an education, and of growing up in association with "reading people." Had Burns been born in the Highlands, the situation might have been different. There might have been no friendly rivalry in the art of letter writing, no buying of volumes from an Edinburgh bookseller, no Ellisland library association, no study of French and Latin. But in the land of Burns's youth these things came naturally to the children of an intelligent and devout farmer, who desired that his sons should learn wisdom even as he desired that they should follow after righteousness.

This popular concern over education, second only to the popular regard for religion, must always be remembered as a vastly important factor in Burns's intellectual environment. Not alone in Edinburgh did he find an audience capable of appreciating the full point of his satiric thrusts. His world of humble farmers and townsfolk was a world hospitable to ideas, and habituated to the thoughtful if at times acrimonious discussion of ideas. Consequently the environment in which he grew up shaped his poetic work along lines that made it appeal far more widely than could have been the case had he not been subject to the tonic influence of an intelligently critical body of readers.

All in all, then, Ayrshire was a good place in which to grow to manhood. Physically, it was a pleasant land. There was enough urban life to relieve the inevitable monotony of the farm; and the situation of the farmer, though still unsatisfactory, tended to become steadily better as the years passed. It was a land rich in historic memory and tradition; a land where the Kirk had won most unquestioned sway and been most sharply challenged. It was hospitable to a rebellious genius such as Burns, and certain to have made any young man of genius something of a rebel. It was tenacious of inherited beliefs, but not unfriendly to the new ideas which threatened what still remained of the old social and intellectual stagnation. And especially during the latter half of the eighteenth century, when the jostle and clash of conflicting theories were most pronounced, especially at that time Ayrshire was a good place in which to be born and to live and to write poetry.

[1] Thus he always spelled his name.

[2] By 1784 rentals of from 25 to 45 shillings per acre were not uncommon in Ayrshire and Perthshire.

[3] James M'Bain, *Burns' Cottage*, Glasgow, 1904, p. 18. A facsimile of Campbell's deed to Burnes appears at pages 16 and 17. M'Bain traces the history of the land and cottage from 1757 to 1904.

[4] Currie, I, 378 f.

[5] See Sir John Sinclair's *Observations on the Scottish Dialect*, London, 1782, a book published to help Scotsmen Anglicize their speech.

[6] An interesting account of the "laws and government" of Scotland may be found in William Guthrie's *New Geographical, Historical and Commercial Grammar*, London, 1770, pp. 64 ff. This was one of the books that William Burnes borrowed for the use of his children.

[7] The Lollards of Kyle had caused trouble to the establishment even before the Reformation.

[8] See below, Chapter IV, p. 110.

[9] Formally ratified August 17, 1560. See Philip Schaff, *Creeds of Christendom*, New York, 1878; 3 vols.; I, 681.

[10] *Ibid.*, III, 610.

[11] E. Fisher's *Marrow of Modern Divinity*, London, 1645, was the text book of the most orthodox branches of the Church. "Marrow men" in time came to be synonymous with conservatives.

[12] Burgh schools, however, had existed in many instances in continuation of those established by the Roman Catholic Church, salaries being paid and schoolhouses furnished by the Town Councils.

CHAPTER II

THE EARLY YEARS

1

ALLOWAY

THE clerk of the Ayr and Alloway Kirk Session had been recording baptisms, marriages, and burials in the parish for several years before the January day when William Burnes appeared to announce the birth and baptism of his first child. The formula that he used on such occasions was brief but adequate; why waste words when a mere statement of fact was all that church law demanded? Accordingly his entry concerning the most memorable event he was ever to have the honor of recording differed in no respect from the scores of others that he had already inscribed in his carefully guarded volumes. This was his phrasing:

Robert Burns, lawful son to William Burns, in Alloway, and Agnes Broun, his spouse, was born January 25, 1759; bapd. 26, by Mr. William Dalrymple. Witnesses: John Tennant and Jas. Young.

When the ink was dry, he closed the book and went about his business, as a good clerk was supposed to do.

Interestingly enough, the clerk of the session spelled the family name as it was probably pronounced in Ayrshire, and as the poet was before long to spell it, but not as the father would have spelled it had he made the entry himself. "Robert Burnes," he would have written; for that had been the name of his father, a tenant farmer in Kincardineshire, seventy miles northeast of Edinburgh on the coast of the North Sea. He had been a man of rather more than average ability, this grandfather of the poet,—concerned over the education of his children, prosperous enough to have silver spoons on his dining table though towards the close of his life he found himself in financial difficulties, and so skilful a tiller of the soil that the Earl Marishal probably employed him, as a young man, as gardener at Inverugie Castle, in Aberdeenshire. Such at any rate is the statement credited to Burns by John Ramsay of Ochtertyre, who further records the poet as saying that his grandfather was "plundered and driven out in the year 1715."[1] Whether or not this Robert Burnes actually was "out" in 1715 can hardly be determined. Obviously he may have been, for the Earl Marischal was a faithful adherent of the Stuarts, and raised a force of his tenants for service under the Old Pretender. Equally certain is it that Burns chose to believe that the grandfather whose name he bore had fought and suffered in the lost cause. In the autobiographical letter to Dr. Moore he wrote, "My forefathers rented land of the famous, noble Keiths of Marshal, and had the honor to share their fate."[2] Again, to Lady Winifred Maxwell Constable, a sturdy Jacobite, he wrote, "Though my Fathers had not illustrious Honors and vast Properties to hazard in the contest; though they left their humble cottages only to add so many units more to the unnoted croud that followed their Leaders; yet, what they could they did, and what they had they lost."[3]

Such was the tradition which the poet cherished, and which explains, in part at least, the enthusiasm with which he later composed or revised Jacobite lyrics.

Neither grandfather nor father seems to have been involved in the Forty-five. The former was still tenant of Clochanhill, and, just before the Rebellion broke out, leased two other adjacent farms with the hope that by adding to his lands he might be able to make a fair living for himself and his family. That the family was looked upon with some suspicion, however, during the years following Culloden, may possibly be deduced from the fact that William Burnes in 1748 felt impelled to secure a certificate from three Kincardineshire landholders, to the effect

[33]

that he was "the son of an honest farmer in this neighbourhood," and "a very well-inclined lad himself." [4]   On the other hand, this certificate may have been nothing more than what any young man about to venture into the world for the first time would have been glad to take with him as testimonial and identification.

The doubt concerning the significance of this certificate is characteristic of the uncertainty which enwraps the whole problem of the Jacobitism of Burns's forebears.   All that can be said with assurance is that the poet treasured the belief that his family in some way had been connected with the lost cause.   Definite evidence, however, is lacking.

In any case this "well-inclined lad," son of the Earl Marischal's gardener, had been born in the parish of Dunottar, Kincardineshire, on November 11, 1721.   Like his father he developed some skill as a gardener, and may have been apprenticed to the trade.   Till he was twenty-seven years old he lived near home; but in 1748 his father, ruined in his ambitious farming schemes by the Rebellion, became bankrupt, and the household was broken up.   William Burnes, with a brother Robert who had been bred as a mason, left Kincardineshire in search of work. Half a century later his son Gilbert wrote thus to Mrs. Dunlop:

I have often heard my father describe the anguish of mind he felt when he parted with his elder brother Robert on the top of a hill, on the confines of their native place, each going off his several way in search of adventures, and scarcely knowing whither he went.   My father undertook to act as gardener and shaped his course to Edinburgh, where he wrought hard when he could get work, passing through a variety of difficulties.   Still, however, he endeavoured to spare something for the support of an aged parent, and I recollect hearing him mention his having sent a bank-note for this purpose, when money of that kind was so scarce in Kincardineshire that they hardly knew how to employ it when it arrived. [5]

At Edinburgh Burnes discovered that his gardener's talents were in demand.   "Landscaping" was coming into fashion; "The Meadows," now a public park on the south side of the

WILLIAM BURNES'S COTTAGE AT ALLOWAY

From an unpublished pen and ink drawing by Adrian de Friston

town, was being laid out; here for a time at least he found congenial employment. But by 1750 he was ready to leave the city. This time he journeyed westward to Ayrshire, to work at his trade for the Laird of Fairlee, and subsequently for the Crawfords of Doonside. Before long he had decided to set up for himself as a nurseryman, to build a house, and to marry. Consequently he "feued," or leased in perpetuity, from Dr. Campbell of Ayr, seven and a half acres of land in Alloway. The nursery scheme was not destined to prosper. But Dr. Fergusson, an Ayrshireman who had amassed enough wealth in his London practise to retire and purchase an estate in his native country, gave Burnes employment as head gardener on his estate of Doonholm, which was not far distant from the plot of ground at Alloway. The work left Burnes sufficient leisure so that in the summer and autumn of 1757 he built a two-roomed clay cottage on his holding, and thus definitely established himself as a member of the community. Here, immediately after his marriage on December 15, 1757, he and his bride Agnes Broun, or Brown, began their life together.

There had never been any taint of Jacobitism in the family history of the young wife. On the contrary, the Brouns of Ayrshire, tenant farmers for many generations, had been orthodox Presbyterians, and some of them had suffered in the cause of the Covenant. Two of the Cumnock branch of the family had barely escaped the headsman's axe after Bothwell Bridge in 1683; another, in 1685, had been stood up in front of a wall by Claverhouse's firing party and shot, while his wife and children had been forced to look on as spectators.

Gilbert Broun, father of the poet's mother, was for many years tenant of the 160 acre farm of Craigenton, in the parish of Kirkoswald, where Agnes, his first child, was born on March 17, 1742. She was the eldest of six children. When her mother died she found herself, though only ten years old, burdened with the responsibilities of the entire household. Two years later, however, her father remarried, and Agnes was sent off to live with a grandmother who had herself known the persecutions of the "bloody years." In her retentive memory the girl early stored away a generous assortment of old songs and ballads; she learned to read the Bible before she was ten; she never learned to write, even her own name; she sang, after the country fashion, with enthusiasm and no inconsiderable skill. Her temper was not always under perfect control. But she became skilful in all the arts of the housewife, and was able, when need arose, to help even in the arduous labor of the threshing floor.

Just when Agnes Broun and William Burnes first met, one can not say; possibly it was at the Maybole fair of 1756 that the tall, dark, grave, and somewhat taciturn nurseryman from Alloway fell under the fascination of the vivacious, red-haired, and brown-eyed girl whom he was to marry. Each had been in love before, and Agnes had once been engaged to a plowman on her grandmother's farm. But all memories of other attachments seem soon to have been forgotten, and the two lived together in an ideal companionship till the death of William Burnes on February 13, 1784.[6]

Such, in the briefest compass, was the immediate ancestry of Robert Burns.[7] One searches his family history in vain for any signs of genius; one finds many indications, however, that both the Brouns and Burneses were substantial folk, the best sort of tenant farmers and tradesmen, loyal to the faiths in which they had been reared, devoutly religious, industrious, thrifty, able to endure hardships without whimpering, and intensely devoted to the members of their family circles. It is an easy guess that the poet's personal charm came to him from his mother; his tenacity of purpose, amounting at times to stubbornness, and his tendency to melancholia, were more suggestive of his father. On the father's side, be it remembered, the Burneses were newcomers to Ayrshire; the mother's family had been there at least since the battle of Bannockburn. The father's family was of Saxon origin; in the mother's veins, though her name was probably Norman, there may have been some lingering traces of the Celtic blood which undoubtedly survived in Ayrshire after it had disappeared from the eastern sections of the island, and which some critics have considered—mistakenly, as it seems—responsible for the lighter and more joyous elements in Burns's poetry.[8]

Thirteen months after William and Agnes Burnes had been married, their first child, Robert, was born. The exact date, as the world knows, was January 25, 1759. The story is widely current that when the baby was but a few days old a northwest storm so damaged the roof of the cottage that mother and child had to be carried off through the night to a nearby farmhouse. The most authoritative account of what happened is to be found in Gilbert's letter to Dr. Currie, printed for the first time in Currie's 1803 edition:

When my father built his "clay biggin," he put in two stone-jambs, as they are called, and a lintel, carrying up the chimney in his clay-gable. The consequence was, that as the gable subsided, the jambs, remaining firm, threw it off its centre; and, one very stormy morning, when my brother was nine or ten days old, a little before daylight, a part of the gable fell out, and the rest appeared so shattered, that my mother, with the young poet, had to be carried through the storm to a neighbour's house, where they remained a week, till their own dwelling was adjusted.[9]

This is one of the few incidents of Burns's earliest days that have come down to us in dependable form, and one which, viewed in the light of what was to follow, it has been easy to call symbolic. But the tradition that Burns himself in after years cited it as an indication that fate destined his whole life to be tempestuous, seems not to have originated till long after his death. And, indeed, Robert's own comment on the incident was that the wind "blew handsel in" on him.

When the baby was one day old he was baptized by his father's pastor and friend, the Reverend William Dalrymple. The minister who thus signalized Burns's affiliation with the established Church had been preaching in Ayr since December, 1746.

For the first ten years he had held the second or junior ministry of the parish; in June of 1756, however, he had been preferred to the first ministry. It was to his sermons that William Burnes listened each Sabbath, sermons that confirmed the poet's father in his own liberal theology, although they were not radical enough to subject their author to prosecution for heresy.

With this incident of the baptism the authenticated records of Burns's infancy come to a close. We know, to be sure, that a second son, Gilbert, was born in the cottage on September 28, 1760, and two sisters, Agnes and Anabella, on September 30, 1762 and November 14, 1764, respectively.[10] Other specific information concerning the household of William Burnes during these early years is entirely lacking.

But it is not hard to imagine the life of William Burnes's children. That they were healthy youngsters, and the father and mother skilful in the art of bringing them safely through the precarious early years, is abundantly proved by the fact that all seven of the children were living till November, 1785, when the death of the youngest son John, who was then sixteen years old, first broke the family circle. Growing up within two miles of the county town, Ayr, in a cottage close to the road to Maybole and the south, they must have stared with childish interest at the picturesque pageantry of the highway which linked their little plot of ground to the unknown world beyond the horizon. That the two oldest, Robert and Gilbert, sometimes rode in with their father to market or fair, is as certain as that they found a pleasant playground along the tree-bordered banks of the Doon, half a mile to the south. Inevitably they must have followed their mother about the work of her little dairy, driving the three or four cows in from pasture, and helping, as farm children can, in the work of the byre. When inclement weather sent them into the cottage for warmth and shelter, there was Betty Davidson, widow of a cousin of their mother's, ready to entertain them with what Robert afterwards called "the largest collection in the country of tales and songs concerning devils, ghosts, fairies, brownies, witches, warlocks, spunkies, kelpies, elf-candles, dead-lights, wraiths, apparitions, cantraips, enchanted towers, giants, dragons, and other trumpery;" [11]—tales which could well be localized in the near-by churchyard of "Alloway's auld haunted kirk."

There is no evidence that during the first five or six years of Burns's life he appeared to be other than an average youngster, though less likely, perhaps, than the average lad to forget what he had heard. "At these years," he wrote later, "I was by no means a favourite with anybody. I was a good deal noted for a retentive memory, a stubborn, sturdy something in my disposition, and an enthusiastic idiot piety. I say idiot-piety because I was then but a child." [12] A normal boy he seems to have been, growing up in a more than normally favorable home environment, developing a will of his own, and learning easily from both books and experiences.

The boy's formal education began during this Alloway period. His father may have been, as Burns later put it, a man of "stubborn, ungainly integrity, and headlong, ungovernable irrascibility," but he saw to it that his boys had their chance at the learning which every Scotsman coveted for his sons.

It was "a person by the name of Campbell" [13] who had the honor of serving as Burns's first master. His school was at Alloway Miln, or Mill, a mile or so from the family cottage. Here during the early months of 1765 Robert and Gilbert were "grounded a little in English." [14] Campbell, however, found the schoolmaster's desk uncongenial, and abandoned it a few months later for a position as master of the Workhouse in Ayr. It was then that William Burnes took the lead in securing a tutor for his sons and those of four neighboring families, and had the good fortune to find John Murdoch to fill the position.

Murdoch had been born in Ayr on March 25, 1747, and was thus not quite twelve years older than his pupil Robert. He was a well-read young man, who had been through the burgh school at Ayr, gone on to Edinburgh to finish his studies, and in 1755 had returned to his native town to look for a school. [15] His own account of the manner of his employment and of his educational technique is at once characteristic and picturesque, and altogether worthy of being reprinted:

In 1765, about the middle of March, Mr. W. Burnes came to Ayr, and sent to the school, where I was improving in writing, under my good friend Mr. Robinson, desiring that I would come and speak to him at a certain inn, and bring my writing-book with me. This was immediately complied with. Having examined my writing, he was pleased with it,—(you will readily allow he was not difficult,) and told me that he had received very satisfactory information of Mr. Tennant, the master of the English school, concerning my improvement in English and in his method of teaching. In the month of May following, I was engaged by Mr. Burnes, and four of his neighbours, to teach, and accordingly began to teach the little school at Alloway, which was situated a few yards from the argillaceous fabric above-mentioned.[16] My five employers undertook to board me by turns, and to make up a certain salary, at the end of the year, provided my quarterly payments from the different pupils did not amount to that sum.

My pupil, Robert Burns, was then between six and seven years of age; his preceptor about eighteen. Robert, and his younger brother Gilbert, had been grounded a little in English before they were put under my care. They both made a rapid progress in reading, and a tolerable progress in writing. In reading, dividing words into syllables by rule, spelling without book, parsing sentences, &c, Robert and Gilbert were generally at the upper end of the class, even when ranged with boys by far their seniors. The books most commonly used in the school were, the *Spelling Book*, the *New Testament*, the *Bible*, *Mason's Collection of Prose and Verse*, and *Fisher's English Grammar*. They committed to memory the hymns, and other poems of that collection, with uncommon facility. This facility was partly owing to the method pursued by their father and me in instructing them, which was, to make them thoroughly acquainted with the meaning of every word in each sentence that was to be committed to memory. By the by, this may be easier done, and at an earlier period, than is generally thought. As soon as they were capable of it, I taught them to turn verse into its natural prose order; and sometimes to substitute synonimous expressions for poetical words, and to supply all the ellipses. These, you know, are the means of knowing that the pupil understands his author. These are excellent helps

[42]

to the arrangement of words in sentences, as well as to a variety of expression.

Gilbert always appeared to me to possess a more lively imagination, and to be more of the wit, than Robert. I attempted to teach them a little church-music. Here they were left far behind by all the rest of the school. Robert's ear, in particular, was remarkably dull, and his voice untunable. It was long before I could get them to distinguish one tune from another. Robert's countenance was generally grave, and expressive of a serious, contemplative, and thoughtful mind. Gilbert's face said, *Mirth, with thee I mean to live;* and certainly, if any person who knew the two boys, had been asked which of them was most likely to court the muses, he would surely never have guessed that Robert had a propensity of that kind.[17]

In his autobiographical letter Burns passed over this phase of his education with only a casual reference, but he recorded in some detail the effect which his early reading had upon him:

The earliest thing of composition that I recollect taking pleasure in was *The Vision of Mirza,* and a hymn of Addison's, beginning, "How are thy Servants blest, O Lord." I particularly remember one half-stanza which was music to my boyish ears—

For though in dreadful whirls we hung,
High on the broken wave—

I met with these pieces in *Mason's English Collection,* one of my school-books. The two first books I ever read in private, and which gave me more pleasure than any two books I ever read again, were, *The Life of Hannibal,* and *The History of Sir William Wallace.*[18] Hannibal gave my young ideas such a turn, that I used to strut in raptures up and down after the recruiting drum and bag-pipe, and wish myself tall enough that I might be a soldier; while the story of Wallace poured a Scottish prejudice into my veins which will boil along there till the flood-gates of life shut in eternal rest.[19]

Gilbert's account was more specific:

Under Mr. John Murdoch we learned to read English tolerably well, and to write a little. He taught us too the English grammar. I was too young to profit much from his lessons in grammar; [20] but Robert made

[43]

some proficiency in it, a circumstance of considerable weight in the unfolding of his genius and character; as he soon became remarkable for the fluency and correctness of his expression, and read the few books that came in his way with much pleasure and improvement; for even then he was a reader when he could get a book.[21]

Out of the accounts of Robert, Gilbert, and Murdoch, there emerge two not insignificant facts: first, even at the age of six or seven Burns was an eager reader; and second, the school-books on which he sharpened his youthful wits were purely English, and might have turned whatever literary talents he then possessed into English, not Scottish, channels. It will be worth while to recall the list, as Murdoch gave it: *The Spelling Book; The New Testament; The Bible;* Masson's *Collection of Prose and Verse;* Fisher's *English Grammar.* Good solid provender, this, but containing nothing to suggest to the student the existence of a vernacular literary tradition. It was a matter of course that the Bible should play a large part in the education of an Ayrshire boy in 1765; that Burns read it thoroughly all his life is made clear by the aptness and frequency of the Biblical quotations and allusions throughout his mature work. Neither is it to be wondered at that a spelling book and grammar found their places on Murdoch's desk.[22] The *Collection of Prose and Verse* was of a different stamp, however; its use would indicate that Murdoch was ambitious to lead his pupils beyond the rudiments, and introduce them to what it is not unfair to call English literature. It was the work of Arthur Masson (not Mason, as Burns wrote), and contained selections from Shakespeare, Milton, Dryden, Addison, Thomson, Gray, Akenside, and Shenstone, besides odds and ends of less readable verse; an assortment of moral, didactic, and historical prose; and a number of Mrs. Elizabeth Rowe's *Moral Letters.*[23] The influence which this book exerted on Burns can hardly be overstated. He memorized much of the poetry, and used Mrs. Rowe's letters as models for many of his own "literary" attempts in prose. And—more important—he shaped his standards of value in conformity with those which he found exemplified in Masson's anthology.

[44]

Thus one sees Burns, a lad of six or seven years already noted for his retentive memory, early brought in contact with the very English writers whose influence was later to appear in much that he himself produced.   At the same time Betty Davidson was entertaining him with her tales of "devils, ghosts, fairies,"—in fitting contrast to the decorous pabulum provided by Murdoch, and more in keeping with the popular tradition.   When, twenty years later, such astonishingly different poems as "Hallowe'en" and "Man was Made to Mourn" were to appear in Burns's first volume, the two sorts of seeds sown in the boy's mind during his earliest school days had merely borne their natural fruit.

2

MOUNT OLIPHANT

Towards the close of 1765 William Burnes found the cottage at Alloway too small for his steadily growing family.   Accordingly he approached Provost Fergusson, by whom he was still employed as gardener, with the proposal to lease Fergusson's seventy acre farm of Mount Oliphant, two miles southeast of Alloway, which had just become vacant.   This was precisely the sort of step which any ambitious tiller of the soil would have approved.   But to succeed in the new project Burnes would need far more in the way of farm stock than he had required at Alloway; to purchase this stock he must have cash, and virtually all of his capital was tied up in the Alloway grounds and cottage. Unable at the moment to dispose of these holdings, he turned to Fergusson for assistance, and found that his new landlord would lend him the necessary hundred pounds.   So the greatest obstacle to Burnes's plan was immediately removed.   Incidentally, the fact that Fergusson not only accepted him as a tenant, but readily advanced a considerable sum of money, is good evidence of Burnes's reputation for industry and integrity.

The lease on Mount Oliphant was for twelve years—from

Martinmas (November 11), 1765, to Martinmas, 1777. There was a so-called "freedom in the lease" at the end of six years, when the tenant might remove; if he failed to do so, he was held for the remainder of the term. The rental was forty pounds annually for the first half of the term, and forty-five pounds for the second.[24] Though the tenant had the right to use the soil of the new farm on and after Martinmas, 1765, he could not take possession of the buildings till Whitsun of 1766, at which time the family left the "clay bigging" at Alloway, and began eleven years of life in the new home.

For two years Robert and Gilbert continued, intermittently, to attend the little school at Alloway, till Murdoch himself left the neighborhood. But though this tie with the Alloway days remained thus unbroken for a considerable time, in all other respects the family life changed somewhat radically. William Burnes was no longer a gardener subsisting on a small but regular wage from his employer, but a tenant farmer, burdened with a considerable debt at the outset of his experiment, and under the necessity of himself performing the heavy labors of the farm till his boys should be able to assist him. Servants, according to Gilbert, there were none. Instead of living beside the busy highway, virtually within sight of the roofs and chimneys of Ayr, the family now found itself in relative isolation, shut off from the friendly converse of passers-by. Even today the inquisitive motorist finds himself some distance from the main highway before he reaches the group of buildings that stand on the site of the old farm. "Nothing," says Gilbert, "could be more retired than our general manner of living at Mount Oliphant; we rarely saw any body but the members of our own family. . . . My father was for some time almost the only companion we had."[25]

Furthermore, the new farm proved stubbornly unproductive. When one remembers that Gilbert later called it "Almost the very poorest soil I know of in a state of cultivation,"[26] one wonders at the inexperience which prompted William Burnes to undertake so unprofitable a bargain, and which subjected his

family to unaccustomed hardships.[27] "We lived very sparingly," wrote Gilbert:

For several years butcher's meat was a stranger in the house, while
all the members of the family exerted themselves to the utmost of their
strength, and rather beyond it, in the labours of the farm. My brother,
at the age of thirteen, assisted in threshing the crop of corn, and at fifteen
was the principal labourer on the farm, for we had no hired servant, male
or female. The anguish of mind we felt at our tender years under
these straits and difficulties was very great. To think of our father
growing old (for he was now above fifty) broken-down with the long-
continued fatigues of his life, with a wife and five other children,[28] and
in a declining state of circumstances, these reflections produced in my
brother's mind and mine sensations of the deepest distress. I doubt not
but the hard labour and sorrow of this period of his life, was in a great
measure the cause of that depression of spirits with which Robert was so
often afflicted through his whole life afterwards. At this time he was almost constantly afflicted in the evenings with a dull headache, which, at a
future period of his life, was exchanged for a palpitation of the heart,
and threatening of fainting and suffocation in his bed, in the night-time.[29]

It should not be inferred that William Burnes made any ab-
normal demands on his sons when first the family moved to
Mount Oliphant, or for some years thereafter. On the contrary Robert and Gilbert, as we have seen, continued for two
years to attend Murdoch's school at Alloway; when Murdoch
left the neighborhood, late in 1767 or early in 1768, the father
himself took up the duties of schoolmaster. But let Gilbert tell
the story:

"My father . . . conversed familiarly on all subjects with us as if
we had been men, and was at great pains, while we accompanied him
in the labours of the farm, to lead the conversation to such subjects as
might tend to increase our knowledge, or confirm our virtuous habits.
He borrowed Salmon's *Geographical Grammar*[30] for us, and endeavoured to make us acquainted with the situation and history of the different
countries in the world; while, from a book-society in Ayr, he procured
for us Durham's *Phisico and Astro-Theology*, and Ray's *Wisdom of
God in Creation*, to give us some idea of astronomy and natural history.

[47]

Robert read all these books with an avidity and industry scarcely to be equalled. My father had been a subscriber to Stackhouse's *History of the Bible*, then lately published by John Meuros in Kilmarnock: from this Robert collected a pretty competent knowledge of ancient history: for no book was so voluminous as to slacken his industry, or so antiquated as to damp his researches. A brother of my mother, who had lived with us some time, and had learned some arithmetic by our winter evening's candle, went into a bookseller's shop in Ayr, to purchase *The Ready Reckoner, or Tradesman's Sure Guide*, and a book to teach him to write letters. Luckily, in place of *The Complete Letter-Writer*, he got by mistake, a small collection of letters by the most eminent writers, with a few sensible directions for attaining an easy epistolary style. This book was to Robert of the greatest consequence. It inspired him with a strong desire to excel in letter-writing, while it furnished him with models by some of the first writers in our language.[31]

The books which William Burnes thus brought to the attention of his sons are still interesting volumes. To turn their pages is to realize with startling vividness what it meant to live in the atmosphere of even liberally inclined Scottish Presbyterianism of 1765. Guthrie's *Geographical Grammar*,[32] which Robert mentions in connection with Salmon's, is a compendious volume that treats in a not uninteresting manner "the present state of the several kingdoms of the world," and to which the student of today may profitably turn for information concerning the "population, inhabitants, customs, and manners" of Scotland during Burns's life.

When one opens Derham's two volumes,[33] one finds oneself confronted by the well-known teleological arguments for the existence of God. "The Heavens declare the Glory of God, even to the Heathen World, so manifestly are they the Handy-Work of God."[34] Thus Derham stated his conclusions in an anticipatory summary of the second work. The reader who turns the pages that follow will find himself entertained by a succinct *resumé* of the popular astronomy of the day; he will be conscious, however, that the author's chief interest is theological, and not scientific.

[48]

John Ray's *Wisdom of God*[35] was an earlier and more widely read document of the same sort, in which the distinguished naturalist summoned all creation to the witness-stand to give testimony concerning the divine Creator. Even the "ugly, creepin', blastit wonner" which Burns was later to apostrophize is included:

Here, by the by, I can not but look upon the strange instinct of this noisome and troublesome creature the louse, of searching out foul and nasty clothes to harbour and breed in, as an effect of divine providence, designed to deter men and women from sluttishness and sordidness, and to provoke them to cleanliness and neatness.[36]

Thomas Stackhouse's *History of the Bible*[37] is a work of a different sort. It is, fundamentally, a re-telling of the Bible story in rather vivid eighteenth century prose, and not in any sense a history of the Bible. To the Biblical narrative, however, have been subjoined what the title-page aptly describes as "Answers to most of the controverted questions, dissertations upon the most remarkable passages, and a connection of profane history all along. To which are added notes, explaining difficult texts, rectifying mis-translations, and reconciling seeming contradictions." All in all, it is an impressive document, and well illustrates the theological scholarship of the day. It is, furthermore, extremely readable, and contains a considerable amount of valuable information upon many subjects germane to the principal narrative. When William Burnes subscribed to the 1765 Edinburgh reprint[38] he brought into the Mount Oliphant farm house a work which any intelligent Scotsman would have been glad to put before his sons as part of their educational material. Like Ray's and Derham's works, however, and like the volumes which Murdoch had used as text-books in his Alloway school, it was purely English. Indeed, it is obvious that all the early formal educational influence to which Burns was subjected, both secular and religious, tended to Anglicize him, so far as language and literary style were concerned. Had his native genius been less strong, it might easily

[49]

have been warped entirely out of its destined orbit, and rendered as insipid as that of his contemporary Michael Bruce.

Few records other than those concerned with the education of Robert and Gilbert survive from these early years at Mount Oliphant. Two little vignettes of the family life are preserved in Gilbert's narrative, however, and may well be incorporated in this account. The first is of importance only as it shows William Burnes to have been solicitious concerning the education of his daughters as well as of his sons:

It was I think not over two years after [1766] that Murdoch, our tutor and friend, left this part of the country, and there being no school near us, and our little services being useful on the farm, my Father undertook to teach us arithmetic in the winter evenings by candle-light, and in this way my two eldest sisters got all the education they received.[39]

The second, also recorded by Gilbert, has been often reprinted and commented upon, but seems significant enough to be reproduced again:

I remember a circumstance that happened at this time, which, though trifling in itself, is fresh in my memory, and may serve to illustrate the early character of my brother. Murdoch came to spend the night with us, and to take his leave when he was about to go into Carrick. He brought us a present and memorial of him, a small compendium of English Grammar, and the tragedy of *Titus Andronicus*, and by way of passing the evening, he began to read the play aloud. We were all attention for some time, till presently the whole party was dissolved in tears. A female in the play (I have but a confused recollection of it) had her hands chopt off, and her tongue cut out, and then was insultingly desired to call for water to wash her hands. At this, in an agony of distress, we with one voice desired that he would read no more. My father observed, that if we would not hear it out, it would be needless to leave the play with us. Robert replied that if it was left he would burn it. My father was going to chide him for this ungrateful return to his tutor's kindness, but Murdoch interposed, declaring that he liked to see so much sensibility; and he left *The School for Love*, a comedy (translated I think from the French), in its place.[40]

Except for these two glimpses into the family life of Mount Oliphant, the extant records are silent so far as the intimate human relationships are concerned. One knows without being told that by 1771, when the last of the seven children had been born, the farm house was almost as crowded as had been the cottage at Alloway, and this despite the fact that there was a loft, or upstairs room, where the older boys slept. One knows, too, that Robert and Gilbert worked over-much at the tasks of the farm, and that by the summer of 1772 they had become such valuable assistants that only one could be spared at a time for a little further schooling. Once again one turns to Gilbert for the narrative, though it is a casual remark of Murdoch's which dates the episode definitely:

My brother was about thirteen or fourteen, when my father, regretting that we wrote so ill, sent us week about during a summer quarter, to the parish school of Dalrymple, which, though between two and three miles distant, was the nearest to us.[41]

Dalrymple, which lay south and east of Mount Oliphant, was a pleasant village on the Doon river. Here Burns met James Candlish, son of the local blacksmith, and afterwards lecturer in medicine in Edinburgh, whom he subsequently addressed as "my ever dear old acquaintance,"[42] and whom he still later designated as "the earliest friend except my only brother that I have on earth, &'one of the worthiest fellows that ever any man called by the name of Friend."[43] In other respects the weeks at Dalrymple seem to have come and gone without making any great impression upon the thirteen year old student of penmanship.

By the summer of 1773 Murdoch was back in Ayr, a master in the English school. Again William Burnes sent Robert away for further training at the hands of a man for whom he had a sincere respect. Murdoch afterwards wrote:

Robert Burns came to board and lodge with me, for the purpose of revising English grammar, etc., that he might be better qualified to instruct his brothers and sisters at home. He was now with me day and

[51]

night, in school, at all meals, and in all my walks. At the end of one week I told him, that, as he was now pretty much master of the parts of speech, etc., I should like to teach him something of French pronunciation, that when he should meet with the name of a French town, ship, officer, or the like, in the newspapers, he might be able to pronounce it something like a French word. Robert was glad to hear the proposal, and immediately we attacked the French with great courage.

Now there was little else to be heard but the declension of nouns, the conjugations of verbs, etc. When walking together, and even at meals, I was constantly telling him the names of the different objects, as they presented themselves, in French; so that he was hourly laying in a stock of words, and sometimes little phrases. In short, he took such pleasure in learning, and I in teaching, that it was difficult to say which of the two was most zealous in the business; and about the end of the second week of our study of the French, we began to read a little of the *Adventures of Telemachus*, in Fenelon's own words.[44]

For only three weeks could the boy be spared from the farm; but when he returned to Mount Oliphant he brought with him a French Dictionary, a grammar, and *Télémaque*, as well as Ruddiman's famous *Rudiments of the Latin Tongue*, which he seems to have purchased on the advice of Murdoch's friend Robinson, writing-master in Ayr. Gilbert says that he continued the study of French after returning home, and that in a short time he could "read and understand any French author in prose." That Burns ultimately became moderately proficient in French is obvious from his later correspondence. The Latin, however, did not prosper.

Thus it was, during the early years at Mount Oliphant, that Burns made an irregular but nevertheless successful start towards the liberal education which he ultimately won for himself. Clearly it was no exaggeration when he wrote, "Though I cost the schoolmaster some thrashings, I made an excellent English scholar, and against the years of ten or eleven, I was absolutely a critic in substantives, verbs, and particles." [45]

At the same time Burns's theological or religious education was not being overlooked. The Bible had been one of his earliest school-books; he read it to such good purpose that John Tennant, a fellow pupil in Murdoch's Alloway school, later said that Burns "had the New Testament more at command than any other youth ever known" [46] to him. The books that came into the family home were, as we have seen, predominantly religious in import and influence. And always there was the poet's father ready at hand with religious advice and instruction, eager to bring up his children in the way they should go.

To the fact that the father, William Burnes, was distinctly liberal in his theology, may fairly be attributed some of his son's later defections from orthodoxy. The father never went as far as the son was to go, in his departure from the old creeds. But he found pleasure in Dr. Dalrymple's mild questionings of the sterner Calvinistic tenets, such as the doctrine of election, and in his suggestion that any penitent sinner might look forward to the joys of Heaven. Hence when William Burnes compiled the *Manual of Religious Belief*,[47] which in his home supplemented if it did not supplant the Westminster Catechism, he leaned far over to the side of the moderates whose "moral gospel" was becoming increasingly offensive to the orthodox. No one can be entirely certain how much of the little pamphlet is the work of Burnes, and how much is the work of Murdoch; but whatever the situation as regards authorship, William Burnes accepted the result, put his name to it, and taught his sons by it. There is no trace of Arminian heresy in the booklet; it is, however, definitely not Calvinistic. Thus it came about that the poet grew up in an atmosphere of relatively liberal theology, and acquired, quite literally at his father's knee, a creed out of which it was not difficult to evolve the Deistic belief of his more mature life.

The story of the later years at Mount Oliphant includes three or four incidents already well known, but not unimportant. It was in his "fifteenth autumn," [48] according to his own statement, which would place the affair in the autumn of 1773, that Burns's hard and somewhat hum-drum existence was brightened by the advent of "love and poesy." His own narrative is a familiar

[53]

one—concise, characteristic, and worth being quoted once again:

This kind of life, the chearless gloom of a hermit, with the increasing toil of a Galley-slave, brought me to my sixteenth year, a little before which period I first committed the sin of rhyme. You know our country custom of coupling a man and a woman together as partners in the labors of harvest. In my fifteenth autumn my partner was a bewitching creature who just counted an autumn less. My scarcity of English denies me the power of doing her justice in that language,[49] but you know the Scotch idiom,—She was a bonie, sweet, sonsy lass.—In short, she altogether unwittingly to herself, initiated me into a certain delicious passion, which, in spite of acid disappointment, gin-horse prudence, and bookworm Philosophy, I hold to be the first of human joys, our chiefest pleasure here below. . . . Among her other love-inspiring qualifications, she sung sweetly; and 'twas her favourite Scotch reel that I attempted to give an embodied vehicle in rhyme. . . . Thus with me began love and poesy, which at times have been my only, and till within this last twelve-month, have been my highest enjoyment.[50]

The only literary result of this experience was the song "Handsome Nell"—the "bewitching creature's" name was Nelly Kilpatrick—which the poet entered in his first Commonplace Book, together with some rather inflated strictures upon it, and the statement that it was composed "in a wild enthusiasm of passion."[51] One searches the stanzas in vain for any foreshadowing of genius; on the other hand, it is clear that the young rimester had a not inaccurate ear; and, what is more significant in view of his future accomplishment, it was a definite tune, a "favorite Scotch reel," that furnished the starting point for the versifier. Thus at the very beginning of Burns's poetical career the combination of love, hard labor, and a scrap of music, resulted in a song. If the poetry was to be of a different and more memorable sort later on, this basic formula for Burns's lyrical composition was not to be greatly altered to the end of his writing days.[52]

At the same time that this new experience was widening the

horizon of Burns's existence, the work of the farm was weighing heavily upon him, and the domestic outlook growing steadily less promising. He afterwards wrote:

My father's generous master [53] died; the farm proved a ruinous bargain; and to clench the curse, we fell into the hands of a Factor, who sat for the picture I have drawn of one in my tale of "Twa Dogs." [54] My father was advanced in life when he married. I was the eldest of seven children; and he, worn out by early hardship, was unfit for labor. My father's spirit was soon irritated, but not easily broken. There was a freedom in his lease in two years more, and to weather these, we retrenched expenses. We lived very poorly. I was a dexterous ploughman for my years, and the next eldest to me was a Brother, who could drive the plough very well, and help me to thrash. A novel-writer might perhaps have viewed these scenes with some satisfaction; but so did not I. My indignation yet boils at the threatening, insolent epistles from the Scoundrel Tyrant, which used to set us all in tears. [55]

In other words, poverty, hard labor, and illness, were now familiar visitors at Mount Oliphant. By 1775, when Robert was sixteen years old, there were nine mouths to be fed from the yield of seventy stony acres tilled by one adult invalid and two immature boys. Small wonder that the boy who bore the brunt of the labor found himself broken in health, and subject, all the rest of his life, to physical and nervous disorders which trace back to these hard years.

Characteristically, however, the father would not acknowledge himself defeated by fate, nor abate his efforts to give at least one of his sons still further opportunity towards an education. In the summer of 1775 [56] William Burnes again sent Robert away from home to continue his schooling, this time to Kirkoswald, thirteen miles southwest of Ayr, and about two miles from the sea. Burns's own statement may indicate that he was looking forward to work other than that of the farm: "I spent my seventeenth summer a good distance from home, at a noted school, on a smuggling coast, to learn mensuration, surveying, dialling, &c, in which I made a pretty good progress." [57]

Two considerations seem to have prompted the choice of Kirkoswald for this educational adventure. In the first place, Hugh Rodger, parish schoolmaster, was a man of considerable local reputation as a teacher of "mensuration" and "dialling."[58] He was much in demand, locally, as a surveyor. Any young man contemplating this as his calling would have been glad to enroll among Rodger's scholars. Furthermore, Burns's maternal uncle Samuel Broun lived on a farm only a mile from Kirkoswald village, and seems to have offered board and lodging to his nephew during the time he was studying with Rodger.[59] Either of these facts would have been warrant enough for choosing the Kirkoswald school.

The weeks spent under Rodger's tutelage had little effect upon Burns's intellectual development. He was not intended for mathematics. But in another respect the experience was a broadening one. His one story needs but little amplifying:

I made greater progress in the knowledge of mankind. The contraband trade was at this time very successful;[60] scenes of swaggering riot and roaring dissipation were as yet new to me, and I was no enemy to social life. Here, though I learned to look unconcernedly on a large tavern-bill, and mix without fear in a drunken squable, yet I went on with a high hand in my geometry till the sun entered Virgo, a month which is always a carnival in my bosom; a charming Fillette, who lived next door to the school, overset my trigonometry, and set me off in a Tangent from the sphere of my studies. I struggled on with my sines and cosines for a few days more; but stepping out to the garden one charming noon to take the sun's altitude, I met my angel,

> Like Proserpine, gathering flowers,
> Herself a fairer flower,—

It was in vain to think of doing any more good at school. The remaining week I staid I did nothing but craze the faculties of my soul about her, or steal out to meet with her. And the two last nights of my stay in the country, had sleep been a mortal sin, I was innocent.[61]

All of which, when properly evaluated, means that the young man found himself in different company from that to which he had been accustomed at Mount Oliphant, and that for a second time he thought himself to be in love. That he took much part in "scenes of swaggering riot," or himself incurred large tavern bills, is impossible. He had no money to spend in such ways.

The affection for Peggy Thompson, who "overset" his trigonometry, seems to have been something more than a passing whim. To her Burns afterwards presented a copy of his Kilmarnock volume with a poetic inscription beginning:

> Once fondly lov'd, and still remember'd dear.

He thought well enough of the quatrains, despite their lugubrious sentimentalism, to have them copied in the first volume of the Glenriddell MSS., and to append to them, in his own hand, this note:

> 'Twas the girl I mention in my letter to Dr. Moore, where I speak of taking the sun's altitude.—Poor Peggy! Her husband is my old acquaintance, & a most worthy fellow.—When I was taking leave of my Carrick relations intending to go to the West Indies, when I took farewell of her, neither she nor I could speak a syllable.—Her husband escorted me three miles on my road, & we both parted with tears.[62]

The experience was virtually empty of results, so far as poetry was concerned.

Of the myths and legends which have grown up around Burns's Kirkoswald experience, most of which may be found recorded—with appropriate disclaimers—in Chambers-Wallace,[63] this only need be said: they have no real bearing on the story of his life and work, they rest on the most unsubstantial of evidence, and may best be entirely disregarded.

More attention should be paid to Burns's own statement concerning the fondness for letter writing which he developed at this time. Following the account of the weeks at Kirkoswald, he wrote:

> I returned home very considerably improved. My reading was enlarged with the very important addition of Thomson's and Shenstone's

[57]

works. I had seen mankind in a new phasis, and I engaged several of my schoolfellows to keep up a literary correspondence with me. This last helped me on much in composition. I had met with a collection of letters, by the wits of Queen Ann's reign, and I pored over them most devoutly. I kept copies of any of my own letters that pleased me, and a comparison between them and the composition of most of my correspondents, flattered my vanity. I carried this whim so far, that though I had not three farthings worth of business in the world, yet every post brought me as many letters as if I had been a broad plodding son of daybook and ledger.[64]

This frank statement was hardly needed to convince one of Burns's pride in his letter-writing ability. When he cared to, he wrote admirable prose, and was obviously pleased with the result. It is equally clear that his epistolary style owed much to the early eighteenth century English tradition. But without these statements by Burns himself we should not have realized how early in life his passion for well-ordered words made itself felt, or how consciously he strove after excellence in writing. He was no ordinary farm lad, content to eat and sleep when the day's work was at an end; the fact that he seemed destined to a lifetime of manual labor was never allowed to interpose a barrier between him and the pleasures of the intellectual life. What he says, however, concerning the amount of his correspondence, must be understood as the perhaps pardonable exaggeration of a recognized man of letters looking back upon the events of his youth. That Burns's correspondence grew to the size he suggests, is clearly impossible. There was not money enough in the family with which to pay the postage.[65]

The family remained at Mount Oliphant till Whitsun, 1777, when Robert was a few months more than eighteen years old. Between the Kirkoswald experience in the summer of 1775 and the departure from the farm that had supported them for eleven years, there is little to record, except that the agent into whose hands Provost Fergusson's affairs had come, pressed William Burnes for his arrears of rental, and that the family looked forward eagerly to the termination of the lease and escape from the "ruinous bargain." There was little time or inclination for poetry; two or three scraps of song, and possibly a few lines of blank verse, are the entire surviving literary product of these last years.

Looked at as a whole, however, the Mount Oliphant period was notable in at least three respects. First, it was during these eleven years that Burns acquired what it is not unfair to call the beginnings of a liberal education. Of formal schooling, to be sure, there had been but little, and that little sadly interrupted. From 1765 to 1767 he had attended—intermittently—Campbell's or Murdoch's elementary schools at Alloway; the summer of 1772 saw him spending a few weeks in Dalrymple brushing up on penmanship and grammar; the summer of 1773 brought three weeks with Murdoch at Ayr, during which he began French and Latin; the summer of 1775 introduced him to various sorts of mathematics at Kirkoswald. Little enough, judged by modern standards! But the obvious truth is that Burns's education was almost entirely self-acquired. He was a lad of unusual native ability and ambition; his memory was phenomenal. He had the good fortune to be guided by an intelligent and sympathetic master, and to live in a home where learning was highly esteemed. He was an eager reader, and that at an age when most boys are fully content with their primers; to the end of his life he continued to read—voraciously, intelligently. With him the educational process was a continuing process, till by the time of his thirty-seventh birthday he had made himself master of a very considerable field of history, theology, mathematics, philosophy, and literature.

Even before the Mount Oliphant period came to an end he had read more than is generally recognized. In addition to the Bible and elementary school texts, Hamilton of Gilbertfield's version of *Wallace*, and (probably) the *Tea-Table Miscellany*, he knew something at least of Shakespeare, Milton, Dryden, Thomson, Gray, Akenside, and Shenstone; more of Pope, Addison, and eighteenth century letter writers; he had acquired at least an introduction to history, theology, and contemporary philosophy. He had dipped into English fiction, though not, as yet, extensively; he had begun his life-long study of English and Scottish song; and through the agency of his mother and Betty Davidson he had been brought into intimate contact with the world of Scottish folk-lore. He had learned to read French with some ease, and to find his way through the pages of a Latin school text. And all this despite the fact that the hard conditions of life at Mount Oliphant made anything approximating regular and long-continued periods of study absolutely impossible. Had Jeffrey taken the pains to examine the chronicle of these years, he would never have referred to Burns as "the Scottish rustic," and the "unlettered plow-boy" tradition might never have been established. Plow-boy he was, but not unlettered—not even during these years of adolescence.

The second fact to be remembered in estimating the importance of these early years is that at this time Burns first overtasked his strength, and definitely prepared the way for the invalidism that was later to overtake him. The family moved to Mount Oliphant shortly after Burns's seventh birthday. Eleven years were to come and go before the removal to Lochlie. During these years Burns grew into responsibilities which he accepted with the utmost seriousness, and which devolved upon him physical burdens that many mature men would have shrunk from assuming. His spirit never faltered, but his body was unequal to the task. When one undertakes to account for the ultimate collapse, one finds both medical diagnostician and layman uniting in tracing it primarily to the long-continued and excessive physical strain of this period. Gilbert's comment has already been set forth.[66] Physicians of today say that here at Mount Oliphant appeared the first symptoms of that insidious heart trouble which was later to cause Burns's death.[67] And the physical exhaustion rendered him an easy prey to the infection which his naturally robust constitution might otherwise have thrown off.

Finally, it was while Burns was still a young man that he first experienced what he calls the "delicious passion," and first gave expression to the resulting emotions in verse. Hard labor—

love—song: such was to be the rhythm of his mature life. The pattern was already shaping itself during these formative years in the secluded farmhouse of Mount Oliphant.

[1] *Scotland and Scotsmen in the Eighteenth Century, from the MSS. of John Ramsay, Esq., of Ochtertyre.* Edited by Alex. Allerdyce (Edinburgh, 1888, 2v.), II, 554.

[2] Facsimile of the *Glenriddell Manuscripts*, privately printed (Philadelphia, 1914, 2 vols.), I, 27 ff. All quotations from the autobiographical letter will be based on this manuscript, which Burns had made for his friend Robert Riddell, and which he revised with his own hand. Referred to hereafter as *Autobiography.*

[3] Letter of 16 Dec. 1789; *Letters*, I, 376.

[4] C. W., I, 25.

[5] The entire letter, usually referred to as "Gilbert's Narrative," is easily accessible in S. D., IV, 352 ff.

[6] His widow survived him for 36 years, living most of the time with her son Gilbert, but supported in part by an annuity which Robert provided for her when the success of his Edinburgh publication enabled him to do so. An important article in the *Burns Chronicle* for 1900, "Documents bearing on Gilbert's Debt to the Poet," gives all the information available concerning the annuity. An article in the *Chronicle* for 1906, "Burns in Kirkoswald," is interesting because of the information there collected bearing on the early life and character of Burns's mother.

[7] For further information consult *Genealogical Memoirs of the Family of Robert Burns*, by Charles Rogers, Edinburgh, 1877, or Appendix I, vol. I of the Chambers-Wallace *Life and Works of Robert Burns.* A genealogical table showing descendants as well as ancestors appeared in the *Chronicle* for 1921, pp. 120 ff. See also the tables in Scott Douglas, I, xviii f.

[8] See for instance, Angellier, *Robert Burns*, I, 5 ff.

[9] Currie, I, 378.

[10] The seven children of William and Agnes Burnes, with the dates of their births and deaths, were: Robert (January 25, 1759—July 21, 1796); Gilbert (September 28, 1760—April 8, 1827); Agnes (September 30, 1762—October 17, 1834); Anabella (November 14, 1764—March 2, 1832); William (July 30, 1767—July 24, 1790); John (July 10, 1769—October 28, 1785); Isabella (July 27, 1771—December 4, 1858). The first four were born in the cottage at Alloway; the others in the farm house at Mount Oliphant. A reprint of William Burnes's entries in his family Bible may be found in *The Burns Calendar, Kilmarnock*, 1874, *Addenda.*

[11] *Autobiography*, p. 30.

[12] *Ibid.*

[13] Currie, I, 59.

[14] *Ibid.*, 88. The phrase is Murdoch's.

[15] Murdoch's subsequent career was not in all ways fortunate. In 1772 he was well enough thought of to be appointed teacher in the burgh school at Ayr; but in February of 1776 he was dismissed from his post for having spoken with great disrespect of Dr. Dalrymple, minister of the parish church. It is clear that Murdoch then went to London, but just how he lived is uncertain. Apparently he kept a small shop, and earned some money by teaching French. He died on April 20, 1824, shortly after an appeal for funds for his relief had been published in the London press. See William Will's article, "John Murdoch, Tutor of Robert Burns," *Chronicle*, 1929, pp. 60 ff., and "Murdoch Correspondence," *ibid.*, 72 ff.

[16] William Burnes's clay cottage.

[17] Currie, I, 87 ff.

[18] According to Gilbert Burns, *Hannibal* was a loan from Murdoch. It is impossible to identify the book exactly. *Wallace* was William Hamilton's early eighteenth century redaction in English heroic couplets of the Scots poem traditionally ascribed to "Blind Harry." Gilbert states that his brother did not see this book till "some years afterwards."

[19] *Autobiography*, pp. 30 ff.

[20] Obviously true, as Gilbert was less than five years old when he first began attending Murdoch's school.

[21] S. D., IV, 353.

[22] The spelling book was probably Arthur Masson's *English Spelling Book*, third edition, Edinburgh, 1761. The Preface of this work contains the following interesting paragraph:

> Some notice should be taken of several innovations which have been attempted, of late, in English Orthography; such as, in writing Honor, Favor, etc., for Honour, Favour . . . I approve of this method, and could wish Custom would authorise the throwing out as many silent letters in a word as possible. (p. xiv.)

It was perhaps because of this suggestion that Burns formed the habit of omitting the *u* in words of this class, and of using the contracted form *tho'*.

The grammar was the work of a Mrs. Slack, of Newcastle, who under the pseudonym of "A. Fisher" had published a widely used *New Grammar, with English Exercise*. The eighth edition, "improved," appeared in London in 1763.

[23] For an interesting analysis and discussion of the book, now extremely rare, see "Burns's School Reading Book," in Hugh Haliburton's (J. L. Robertson's) *Furth in Field*, London, 1894, 225 ff. For the privilege of actually examining a copy, the present writer is indebted to the Librarian of the Mitchell Library, Glasgow.

[24] Gilbert's Narrative; S. D., IV, 353.

[25] *Ibid.*, p. 354.

[26] *Ibid.*, p. 358.

[27] Thirty years later, despite an astonishing increase in the general level of farm values, the rental of Mount Oliphant was £5 per year less than what William Burnes paid.

[28] *I.e.*, five besides Robert and Gilbert.

[29] Gilbert's Narrative; S. D., IV, 358.

[30] Robert says "Guthrie's and Salmon's."

[31] Gilbert's Narrative; S. D., IV, 354.

[32] *A New Geographical, Historical, and Commercial Grammar*, by William Guthrie. London, 1770.

[33] Gilbert's note would make one think there was but one book, a *Physico and Astro-Theology*. As a matter of fact William Derham, Rector of Upminster, and a fellow of the Royal Society, published his *Physico-Theology* in 1713, and followed it shortly with the *Astro-Theology, or, a Demonstration of the Being and Attributes of God*, London, 1714.

[34] *Astro-Theology*, second edition, London, 1715, p. 5.

[35] *The Wisdom of God Manifested in the Works of the Creation*; London, 1691. The book ran to many editions, and was widely translated.

[36] *Op. cit.* (London, 1827), p. 253.

[37] *A New History of the Holy Bible, from the Beginning of the World to the Establishment of Christianity*, London, 1737; 2v. fol. A second edition, revised and enlarged by the author, appeared in 1742.

[38] There is no definite evidence to this effect. But the 1765–67 Edinburgh reprint in six volumes must be the one he secured, as no other edition appeared during these years. It was probably distributed by Meuros of Kilmarnock, whom Gilbert called the publisher.

[39] S. D., IV, 353.

[40] *Ibid.*, p. 354.

[41] Ibid., p. 355. Gilbert says: "The summer after we had been at Dalrymple school, my father sent Robert to Ayr . . . to his former teacher." Murdoch says: "In 1773 Robert Burns came to board and lodge with me." (Currie I, 90.) Hence the Dalrymple episode, about which Gilbert was slightly uncertain, must have taken place in 1772, when Robert was thirteen years old.

[42] Letter of 21 March, 1787; *Letters*, I, 79.

[43] Letter to Peter Hill, March, 1791; *ibid.*, II, 63.

[44] Currie, I, 90.

[45] *Autobiography*, p. 30.

[46] Quoted, C. W., I, 33 n.

[47] *A Manual of Religious Belief in a Dialogue between Father and Son. Compiled by*

William Burnes . . . and transcribed, with grammatical corrections, by John Murdoch, teacher. Printed in full in C. W., I, 455 ff., and elsewhere.

[48] *Autobiography*, p. 34.

[49] One of the many times when Burns under-rated his command of English; just why, it is hard to tell, though in this particular instance the Scots phrase is quite untranslatable.

[50] *Autobiography*, pp. 33 ff.

[51] S. D., IV, 57.

[52] See Burns's poem "To the Guidwife of Wauchope House," for his versified account of this incident (H. H., II, 104.)

[53] Provost Fergusson, of Doonholm, Ayr, landlord of Mount Oliphant.

[54] "He'll stamp an' threaten, curse an' swear," etc.

[55] *Autobiography*, pp. 33 ff.

[56] This is the only possible inference from the poet's statement, "my seventeenth summer." When Dr. Currie printed the autobiographical letter he changed this, silently, to "nineteenth,"—at Gilbert's suggestion. But the MS. of the original letter is clear, as is the copy made for Glenriddell, and there seems to be no reason for thinking the poet's memory at fault.

[57] *Autobiography*, p. 38.

[58] See an interesting article in the *Burns Chronicle* for 1906, "Burns in Kirkoswald," by James Muir.

[59] The only authority for this is Gilbert's statement in his letter to Mrs. Dunlop. See S. D. IV, 356.

[60] According to Sinclair's *Statistical Account* (X, 496), smuggling had long been almost a recognized industry of Kirkoswald.

[61] *Autobiography*, pp. 38 ff.

[62] *Ibid.*, p. 63 f.

[63] *Op. cit.* I, 46 ff.

[64] *Autobiography*, pp. 39 ff.

[65] See three letters from Burns to William Niven, a fellow student in Rodger's school, *Letters*, I, 1 ff.

[66] See above, p. 47.

[67] See Sir James Crichton-Browne's *Burns from a New Point of View*, London [1926]; and Dr. Harry B. Anderson's "Robert Burns, his Medical Friends, Attendants, and Biographer," in *Annals of Medical History*, March, 1928, 47 ff.

CHAPTER III

LOCHLIE AND IRVINE

WHITSUN of 1777, when the lease on Mount Oliphant expired, saw the nine members of the Burns family once more in the process of moving. Just how they got clear of the obligations incurred at Mount Oliphant is uncertain; the farm gear does not seem to have been attached by the landlord, and the deduction appears warranted that by concerted economy the family managed to leave the place reasonably unburdened by debt. Be that as it may, it must have been with a sense of relief that William Burnes trekked ten miles northeastward to Tarbolton parish, where he had leased the hundred and thirty acre farm of Lochlie at the unduly high annual rental of a pound per acre.

David M'Lure, a merchant of Ayr, was the landlord of the new farm; such complete confidence did he feel in his tenant that, to the ultimate regret of both parties, he failed to draw any written agreement making clear the exact terms of the lease.[1] There appears to have been no misunderstanding, however, concerning the amount of the rental. It seems probable that M'Lure advanced a certain amount of capital to his new tenant. Robert afterwards said, "The nature of the bargain was such as to throw a little ready money in [my father's] hand at the commencement; otherwise the affair would have been impracticable." [2] Some of M'Lure's statements at the time of his subsequent lawsuit bear out the hypothesis that, like Provost Fergusson before him, he had loaned money to Burnes to help him make a new start. In any case the financial arrangements between the two men were involved in an unfortunate uncertainty.

The farm lay two and a half miles northeast of Tarbolton

village, and somewhat more than three miles northwest of Mauchline. Because of the way the roads ran, however, it was as far to Tarbolton as to the larger and more important of the two villages. The farm was approximately four hundred feet above the sea, relatively bare of woodland, and on the whole unattractive in aspect. As one stands in front of the farm house that today occupies the site of William Burnes's last home, one looks southwest over a saucer-like depression surrounded by hills so low as to be utterly unpicturesque, but high enough to cut off all distant views. The land, though obviously fertile under present methods of cultivation, is still inclined to be swampy. In William Burnes's day the soil was undrained and consequently "sour," but was probably better than that of Mount Oliphant.

How much farm stock William Burnes possessed in 1777 is uncertain. Six years later, when the Sheriff "sequestrated" his chattels, he owned six horses, thirteen cows, two calves, three sheep, and a rather numerous assortment of plows, carts, and harrows.[3] On the assumption that the livestock may have doubled during his tenancy of Lochlie, he must have come from Mount Oliphant reasonably well equipped for the new venture.

When one undertakes to follow the Burneses into their new home, and to visualize the conditions of their domestic life, one finds oneself baffled. The house and barn of 1777 have been entirely replaced by more modern buildings. Moreover, there are virtually no records of any sort concerning the first few years at Lochlie. Three letters written by William Burnes have survived the passing of time,[4] but they tell the reader little beyond the fact that Burnes had a strong family affection, was careful in details of farm work, and wrote an admirable hand. There are also three letters dating from this period from Robert to his friend William Niven. One learns little from them, however, except that in the summer of 1780 Burns had "Three acres of pretty good flax" under cultivation, and that by June of 1781 he had "entirely got rid of all connection with the tender sex, I mean by way of courtship."[5] Untoward events, however, must have been few; for neither Robert in his autobiog-

[65]

raphy nor Gilbert in his narrative mentions any serious interruption to the ordinary course of events. Indeed, Robert distinctly says, "For four years we lived comfortably here." [6] For
this reason tradition is probably right in asserting that the years
from 1777 to 1780 were the happiest that the Burnes family as
a whole ever enjoyed.

The seasons must have come and gone without bringing any
notable variations from the usual farm routine. The men and
boys of the family would be busy enough tending the stock and
raising the annual crops of oats, barley, wheat, and flax; the wife
and mother made a little butter and a good deal of cheese, and
did the hundred and one other things that fell to the housewife's
lot. On Sundays the family attended church in Tarbolton, where
the first suggestions of liberalism were just beginning to temper
the sternness of orthodox Calvinism. Dr. Patrick Wodrow, the
"Auld Wodrow" of "The Twa Herds," one of the sixteen children of the renowned Robert Wodrow, author of *The Sufferings
of the Church of Scotland,* was the parish minister. He was
sixty-five years old when the Burnes family moved to Lochlie;
his sermons, though more orthodox than those of Dr. Dalrymple
at Ayr, were nevertheless of a sort to mark him as by intent at
least a liberal. But the parish as a whole was rigidly conservative. Hence it must have been apparent to an observing newcomer that theological trouble was brewing in the neighborhood.
Burns enjoyed watching the storm gather, and expressed himself
vigorously upon debatable matters. His friend, neighbor, and
fellow-poet David Sillar was probably well within the limits of
truth when he afterwards wrote, "I recollect hearing [Burns's]
neighbours observe, he had a great deal to say for himself,
and that they suspected his principles." [7] Which indicates, of
course, that he was becoming known as an opponent of the old
regime.

Despite the unfortunate lack of actual records concerning the
early years at Lochlie, one significant matter is beyond dispute:
it was during these years that Burns's genius for friendship and
his imperious need of human companionship definitely asserted

themselves. Various interpretations may be attached to Gilbert's often-repeated generalization: "His attachment to [the society of women] became very strong, and he was constantly the victim of some fair enslaver." [8] In all probability the statement means no more than that Robert, like any other young man of twenty-two, was not averse to falling mildly in love with the girl who happened to smile at him. There were no "serious" love affairs till after the family had been some time at Lochlie.

Naturally enough, however, Burns enjoyed the recreations which any normal young person finds attractive. During the winter of 1779 a dancing school was organized in the village, and Robert attended it. The autobiographical letter treats the matter thus:

In my seventeenth year,[9] to give my manners a brush, I went to a Country dancing school. My father had an unaccountable antipathy against these meetings, and my going was what to this hour I repent, in absolute defiance of his commands.[10] My father as I said before was the sport of strong passions; from that instance of rebellion he took a kind of dislike to me, which I believe was one cause of that dissipation which marked my future years. I only say dissipation comparative with the strictness and sobriety of Presbyterian country life; for though the will-o'-wisp meteors of thoughtless whim were almost the sole lights of my path, yet early ingrained piety and virtue never failed to point me out the line of innocence.[11]

From this it seems clear that Burns's social instincts were developing, that he already felt distinctly cramped by the drudgery of the farm routine, and that he was independent enough to seek recreation even in the questionable precincts of a dancing school.

But it was the companionship of men rather than of women that Burns seems particularly to have craved at this time, and his situation was such that he was enabled to make friends in a way which had hitherto been denied him. Within a few miles of Lochlie lived several persons whom Burns knew intimately, and some of whom his verses were afterwards to make famous.

[67]

There was David Sillar (1760–1830), for instance, one year younger than Burns, and like him a farmer's son, who lived at Spittleside, a mile out from Tarbolton village. He was something of a poet and fiddler,[12] and a young man of enough education so that he taught the parish school for a month or two during a temporary vacancy. But all this would have been forgotten, along with his own volume of poems written in imitation of Burns's,[13] had he not been the recipient of the two "Epistles to Davie," poems which would have immortalized a man of far slighter native ability than Sillar.

On the not too distant farm of Adamhill lived John Rankine (d. 1810): "Rough, rude, ready-witted Rankine," by no means the most desirable sort of companion for a young man already beginning to strain at the bonds which held him in leash. It was to Rankine that Burns afterwards presented a silver-mounted snuff-box, and to whom he sent his humorous but blackguardly epistle when a first serious offence had brought unwelcome notoriety to himself and Betty Paton.

In Tarbolton village lived John Wilson (d. 1839)—schoolmaster, grocer, apothecary, clerk of the Kirk Session, and, later, hero of "Death and Dr. Hornbook." He amused the village folk by his solemn ways, and he quarrelled with his superior, Dr. Wodrow—a fact which led to his leaving Tarbolton in 1793. He owed Burns no particular debt of gratitude, for the satire in "Dr. Hornbook" was not too genial. But the poem was not written till after Burns left Tarbolton parish; and when the family moved from Lochlie to Mossgiel, in the spring of 1784, Wilson, as Clerk of the Session, signed the "certificate of character" demanded by Church law, in favor of "Agnes Brown, relict of William Burnes, and Robert, Gilbert, Agnes, and Annabella Burnes, her children."[14] Even when the poem was published Wilson took no serious offence, but turned to Burns for advice concerning a possible improvement in his own situation.[15]

Another new acquaintance who became one of Burns's friends, was James Findlay, local Exciseman, and later Burns's official instructor in the technique of the craft; a friendly soul, whose way of life and regular income the young farmer must have observed without displeasure.

Most picturesque of Burns's Tarbolton neighbors, however, and most splenetic, was Alexander Tait, "Saunders Tait" in local idiom, an eccentric bachelor who did a small business as a tailor, but whose chief interest lay in the writing of satiric verses. In his earlier days he had travelled round the countryside cutting and stitching homespun cloth in many a farm house; when years came upon him he settled himself comfortably in a Tarbolton garret, to enjoy the fruits of his thrift, and to castigate whoever provoked his wrath.[16] David Sillar felt his displeasure, expressed in a poem called "Sillar and Tait; or, Tit for Tat," which began with the picturesque couplet

> My pipe wi' wind I maun gae fill 'er,
> And play a tune to Davie Sillar.

Burns too, more than once, was the target of Tait's shafts. Here again on at least one occasion it was a case of tit for tat:

> Now I maun trace his pedigree
> Because he made a sang on me,
> And let the world look and see
> Just wi' my tongue,
> How Rab and Clootie did agree
> When he was young.[17]

What the "sang" was which "Rab" had made, no one now can say. In any case, Saunders was a fickle friend of the Burnes family. When troubles overtook them he wrote many a stanza in derogation not only of the young poet, his rival, but of William Burnes as well.

Such were some of the men with whom Burns was thrown in contact during the early years at Lochlie. Existence in Tarbolton parish, drab as it must have been in some respects, had its bright spots; for Sillar, Rankine, Tait, and Burns formed a quartet that would have added zest and tang to the life of a far larger town. It was in the company of these men, as well as in the more conventional associations of his home, that the boy grew to be a man, and a man of strong natural passions, with a sturdy and independent intellect, a real flair for making verses, and a lovable, picturesque personality. "He wore the only tied hair in the parish," said his friend Sillar, in the letter already quoted. In that one act of independence, almost of defiance, one is inclined to see the mature Burns emerging from the farm lad.

Burns's rapidly developing social instincts found a congenial outlet in November, 1780, through the organization of the Tarbolton Bachelor's Club, sometimes referred to as the Debating Society. The club was not destined to a long life, though the grey stone house where it held its sessions may still be seen by the visitor to Tarbolton. Robert, his brother Gilbert, and five other young men of the vicinity were the original members; Robert was the first President. Whoever cares to, may see the "Rules and Regulations" fully printed by Dr. Currie,[18] and will find them not without interest. In them appears an unusual combination of sentimentalism, decorous formality, and literary aspiration. The young debators took themselves seriously, and enjoyed discussing those ample questions which better known eighteenth century philosophers than they found profitable subjects for speculation. "Whether do we derive more happiness from Love or Friendship?"—"Whether is the savage man or the peasant of a civilized country in the most happy situation?" —such were some of the topics; surprisingly like those which the young Emerson, forty years later, was to debate in his Harvard literary society: "Which is most conducive to individual happiness, a state of celibacy or matrimony? . . . Which is the strongest passion, Love or Ambition?"[19]

Relatively innocuous conviviality was a regular feature of each meeting, and what the contemporary psychology called "amativeness" played its part in the affairs of the club. Each session closed with "A general toast to the mistresses of the club"; furthermore, the rules provided that "every man proper for a member . . must be a professed lover of *one or more* of the female sex." It will be pertinent to recall that phrase when President Robert Burns shall have grown to be some five years older, and shall have become somewhat distracted by his involvements with "one or more of the female sex."

It is also not without significance, in view of Burns's subsequent career, that the tenth and last of the "Rules and Regulations" struck a note of class-consciousness, and announced somewhat defiantly a philosophy of life, both of which were to reappear in the mature work of the poet:

No haughty, self-conceited person, who looks upon himself as superior to the rest of the club, and especially no mean-spirited wordly mortal, whose only will is to heap up money, shall upon any pretence whatever be admitted. In short, the proper person for this society is a cheerful, honest-hearted lad, who, if he has a friend that is true, and a mistress that is kind, and as much wealth as genteelly to make both ends meet—is just as happy as this world can make him.[20]

There is no evidence that Burns himself wrote this paragraph, but it is clear that he approved it; and, indeed, it is hard to believe that any member of the group save Burns could have coined the phrases that might almost have been taken from the poet's writings of five or six years afterwards.

Before the Bachelors' Club was three months old Burns had completed his twenty-second year. Not far from Lochlie there seems to have lived a girl named Alison—or Ellison—Begbie, with whom, probably in the early months of 1781, Burns apparently conducted a decorous but unrewarded epistolary courtship. Unfortunately the entire affair is shrouded in mystery; the originals of the published letters are not known to exist; the texts which have long been before the public are undated. But it seems probable that these printed versions of Burns's drafted copies of letters represent an event of some importance to him, and that the date to which that event is here assigned is the most likely one.

There are five letters in the group, which is doubly interesting because it contains some admirable examples of Burns's early prose.[21] Reading these letters, one gains a vivid impression of the facility with which the young man used the English language.

The letters impress one as being in some ways distinctly more pleasing than Burns's formal attempts in prose of a later date. There is some literary self-consciousness here, some searching for the phrase; there is an occasional touch of bombast:

> The sordid earth-worm may profess love to a woman's person, whilst in reality his affection is centered in her pocket: and the slavish drudge may go a-wooing as he goes to the horse-market. . . . I disdain their dirty, puny ideas.[22]

But on the whole there is little affectation, save perhaps of unnecessary frankness, little apparent dissimulation, and only a tinge—and that in the last letter, after his suit had been rejected—of a sort of flattery which some of Burns's correspondents were to know too well. Occasionally, moreover, the young farmer struck out a phrase which would have done credit to many of the persons whose work covered the pages of his well-thumbed copy of *Letters by the Wits of Queen Anne's Reign*:

> There is one thing, my dear, which I earnestly request of you, and it is this: that you would soon either put an end to my hopes by a peremptory refusal, or cure me of my fears by a generous consent.[23]

It is a moot question whether this shadowy Alison Begbie episode occasioned any poetry. There are no songs that unmistakably refer either to such a girl or to Burns's disappointment; there are several that might be so interpreted. Be this as it may, it is worth remembering that in this, the third of his recorded love-affairs, he did actually proceed to the point of a formal proposal. The first, with Nelly Kilpatrick, his partner in the harvest field, occasioned one song, and little else. The second, with Peggy Thomson, the "charming fillette" who "overset his trigonometry" during his weeks of study at Kirkoswald, stirred his emotions more profoundly, if we may believe his own *ex-post-facto* account. The third brought him to the verge of matrimony. But as yet there were no indications whatsoever of any attempt on Burns's part to gratify his desires in a fashion which later becomes pleasantly easy.

It seems to have been just before Alison Begbie "put an end to [his] hopes by a peremptory refusal" that Burns made up his mind to go to Irvine and enter business as a flax-dresser.[24] Flax growing had been part of the regular farm routine at Lochlie, as there was always a market for the crop; both Robert and Gilbert had sub-leased from their father small parcels of land on which to grow flax for themselves. Once, indeed, a society interested in the development of agriculture awarded to "Robert Burns, Lochlea Farm, Tarbolton Parish," a premium of three pounds for "lintseed saved for sowing." [25] It was only natural for a young man who had thus been engaged in raising flax to covet for himself the profits that accrued through preparing it for the spinners; Irvine was an easy and obvious place to go to learn the trade, for flax-heckling had long been one of the chief industries of the town.

Precisely when Burns left Lochlie is uncertain, but by the middle of the summer of 1781 he was settled in Irvine, busy at the work which was to occupy him till early in 1782. Details of the entire experiment are unfortunately meagre; Irvine traditions—unreliable at best—are contradictory. It is not even absolutely certain where he lived, or where his "shop," as he called it, was situated. But it is well established that Burns formed some sort of engagement or partnership with a man named Peacock, who may have been a relative of the family on Burns's mother's side. It is beyond dispute that he worked hard at his new tasks, and that the confining, unhealthful occupation proved particularly distasteful to the young man accustomed to the vigorous outdoor life of the farm. Before many weeks had passed he found himself suffering from the first of the several nervous breakdowns that were periodically to darken all the rest of his life. Melancholy, unhappy still because Alison Begbie had refused him,[26] he began—for the first time—to grow a-weary of

[73]

the sun, and gave expression to his feelings in "Winter—A Dirge," and "Prayer, under the Pressure of Violent Anguish." [27]

Once at least his father, concerned about his health, came down from Lochlie to visit him,—perhaps when he was making final arrangements for the sale of the cottage at Alloway, which on Martinmas of 1781 passed into the possession of the Shoemakers' Guild of Ayr.[28] The letter [29] which Robert wrote home soon afterwards (December 27, 1781) shows him to have been in a generally unhappy condition. His meal, sent from home, was almost gone; his health was mending only "by very slow degrees;" his nerves were so frayed that he dared neither review the past nor anticipate the future. Only religion gave him any solace; religion, and the thought that he might soon be dead. After all proper allowances have been made for the fact that the letter was written to a religious father, it still is clear that Burns was in decidedly low spirits as the year 1781 drew to a close.

Release from the unhappy flax-dressing experiment came with the New Year. Though Burns's record of the final event is not in all respects intelligible, it is clear enough as regards the main issue: "My partner was a scoundrel of the first water, who made money by the mystery of thieving; and to finish the whole, while we were giving a welcome carousal to the new year, our shop burnt to ashes, and left me, like a true poet, not worth a sixpence." [30] Thus ended Burns's first and only venture into "the business world."

But the months at Irvine had not been spent in absolutely unrelieved gloom. On July 4, 1781, probably though not certainly before he started for Irvine, Burns had been "entered an apprentice" in the St. David Masonic Lodge of Tarbolton, and had paid his fee of twelve shillings six pence. On October first he was back in Tarbolton for a visit, and the minutes of the Lodge for that day show that "Robert Burns in Lochly was passed and raised." [31] Thus began the poet's connection with Freemasonry.

At the same time that he was finding this new and congenial

outlet for his social instincts, Burns was forming what was to prove a long friendship with Richard Brown (1753–1833), afterwards master of a West Indiaman, and a correspondent who was to receive some of the poet's most interesting letters. Brown's influence on Burns was greater than that of any person he had yet known, except his father and—possibly—Murdoch. In his Autobiography Burns devotes more space to him than to any other individual:

I formed a bosom friendship with a young fellow, the first created being I had ever seen, but a hapless son of misfortune. He was the son of a plain mechanic, but a great man in the neighbourhood, taking him under his patronage, gave him a Genteel Education, with a view to bettering his situation in life. The Patron dying, and leaving my friend unprovided for, just as he was ready to launch forth into the world, the poor fellow in despair, went to sea; where, after a variety of good and bad fortune, he was a little before I was acquainted with him, set ashore by an American Privateer, on the wild coast of Connaught, stript of everything. I cannot quit this poor fellow's story, without adding, that he is at this moment, Captain of a large Westindiaman, belonging to the Thames.

This gentleman's mind was fraught with courage, independence and magnanimity, and every noble manly virtue. I loved him, I admired him to a degree of enthusiasm, and I strove to imitate him. I in some measure succeeded. I had the pride before, but he taught it to flow in proper channels. His knowledge of the world was vastly superior to mine; and I was all attention to learn. He was the only man I ever saw, who was a greater fool than myself, when woman was the presiding star; but he spoke of a certain fashionable failing with levity, which hitherto I had regarded with horror. Here his friendship did me a mischief and the consequence was, that soon after I resumed the plough, I wrote the *Welcome*, enclosed.[82]

How much credence one should give to the statement that Brown did Burns "a mischief," is hard to determine. Brown afterwards heatedly denied that his influence could have been in any way responsible for Burns's misconduct. But it is not stretching the probabilities in the slightest to affirm that Brown was precisely the sort of person to set a young poet's imagination on fire, and to make him discontented with the hum-drum existence of a flax-dresser or upland farmer.

More important than this, however, is the fact that Brown at this early time suggested to Burns the propriety of his seriously turning poet. The evidence appears in Burns's letter to Brown written December 30, 1787, and shows that the sailor had the good sense to appreciate the latent poetic ability of his somewhat moody and restless companion:

I have met with few things in life which has given me more pleasure than Fortune's kindness to you, since those days in which we met in the vale of misery; as I can honestly say, that I never met with a man who more truly deserved it, or to whom my heart more truly wish'd it.—I have been much indebted, since that time, to your story and sentiments, for steeling my heart against evils of which I have had a pretty decent share. —My will-o'-wisp fate, you know: do you recollect a sunday we spent in Eglinton Woods? you told me, on my repeating some verses to you, that you wondered I could resist the temptation of sending verses of such merit to a magazine: 'twas actually this that gave me an idea of my own pieces which encouraged me to endeavour at the character of a Poet.[33]

This is a matter of unique interest,—that the first suggestion looking towards "guid black prent" should have come not from the poet's father or schoolmaster, but from the "wild bold generous fellow" commonly accused of having exerted a malign influence on the young poet.

Various traditions concerning Burns's life at Irvine are still current, but among them all there is none that bears indisputable evidence of authenticity. The inquisitive reader may find them recorded—with appropriate reservations—in Chambers-Wallace. It is not necessary to repeat them here, for whether true or false they add nothing to one's understanding of Burns's character. And the main outlines of the Irvine experience are clear enough: he went there in the summer of 1781, worked hard at the flax-dressing trade, disliked it, became ill, despondent, and dissatisfied with his way of life, and was burned out on

January 1, 1782. Soon thereafter—again the exact date is unascertainable—he returned to the farm at Lochlie, and resumed his old place in the family circle.[34] Financially, the flax-dressing venture had proved a complete failure. But Burns's mental horizon had been greatly widened during the months at Irvine; he had also formed at least one significant friendship; and—most important—he had begun to consider himself in "the character of a poet."

Conditions on the farm were anything but satisfactory during the two years immediately following Burns's return. For one thing, the general economic situation was discouraging. The American Revolution had curtailed British over-seas trade, and as a result the Ayrshire weavers found themselves deprived of profitable markets. Food prices were high, crops scanty, and rents out of proportion to the real value of Ayrshire farm land. The smuggling for which the coast of Carrick had long been notorious continued unabated; but though some persons profited by it, this illicit trade brought into Ayrshire none of the fundamental necessities of life, and occupied the attention of many who could better have been employed in some legitimate pursuit. Moreover, the county as a whole had never recovered from the failure of the Douglas Heron & Co. Bank—"that villainous bubble, the Ayrshire Bank," as Burns later called it. Organized in 1769, the bank had been forced into bankruptcy in 1772, and its collapse had brought ruin to scores of Ayrshire families. All in all, the years from 1776 to 1786 were lean years for the southwestern counties of Scotland.

To this general economic distress was added, during the latter part of 1782 and first half of 1783, the sharp pinch of hunger, occasioned by unprecedented weather and consequent crop failures. Sir John Sinclair, who himself experienced the years of famine, left an account so vivid and revealing that parts of it may well be reprinted:

The cold and storminess of summer 1782 excited fears in the minds of the discerning; but none suspected the magnitude of the impending evil. On the 5th of October, when oats and barley were generally green, a frost, armed almost with the rigour of a Greenland climate, desolated, in one night, the hopes of the husbandmen. The grain, frost-bitten, immediately contracted a hoary whiteness, and ripened no more. Potatoes and turnips, dwarfish from the severity of the weather they had experienced, were also much injured by the frost. The produce of the garden was destitute of its usual nourishment. The fields yielded not one third of an ordinary crop. . . . Complete and hopeless ruin stared us in the face . . . If at this critical period the American war had not ceased, if the copious magazines, particularly of pease, provided for the navy, had not been brought to sale—what a direful scene of desolation and horror would have been exhibited in the country! . . .

In the parish of Holywood, in Dumfrieshire, there was a heavy fall of snow on the 2nd of November which covered the corn and lay so long that it could not be cut for several days afterwards.

Even in Ayrshire the snow fell before the corns were cut down; the greatest part were in the fields, and much destroyed by frost . . . This calamity in some districts occasioned a great decrease of population; in others a diminution of births in the succeeding year. It increased the numbers of the poor; impaired the constitutions of multitudes in the lower orders, and entailed on them consumptions and other fatal disorders. Even where no remarkable sickness followed, the hardships and difficulties to which people were reduced by such a calamity made them neglect those rural amusements in which they formerly delighted, and to contract a dull and melancholy look, which continued for several years after.[35]

The family of William Burnes took its share of these general misfortunes, and in addition struggled under the double burden of debt and illness. As early as some time in 1781 David M'Lure, landlord of the Lochlie farm, had commenced an action against his tenant to secure the payment of arrears of rent, or, failing that, to regain possession of the farm.[36] Absence of any written agreement between landlord and tenant complicated the situation; the dispute dragged wearisomely. Details are uncertain, but it seems probable that since 1779 Burnes had made virtually no payments on account of rent. It may also be true, as M'Lure alleged in his petition to the Sheriff of Ayrshire, that by May of 1783 Burnes was preparing to sell everything that he could, pocket the proceeds, and abandon the premises. Such, at any rate, was M'Lure's declaration; what Burnes's reply was one can not say, for the documents appear to have been lost. M'Lure's second petition makes it clear, however, that Burnes claimed to have paid the rent to the autumn of 1782. And, knowing what we do of William Burnes's character, we may be certain that he was not an intentional defaulter.

Whatever the exact situation, there is no dispute as to the outcome. On May 17, 1783, James Gordon, Sheriff's officer, appeared at Lochlie with a warrant, and proceeded at once to inventory and "sequestrate" whatever he could find in the way of farm gear, crops, cattle, "for payment of the current year's rent when due, or at least till sufficient caution is found therefore." [37] And then the town crier went through the parish warning everyone to buy none of the chattels so impounded. In Saunders Tait's picturesque phraseology,

> He sent the drum Tarbolton through
> That no man was to buy frae you;
> At the Kirk door he cry'd it too;
> I heard the yell;
> The vera thing I write 'tis true,
> Ye'll ken yersel.[38]

Small wonder, when such things happened, that Burns acquired a well-rooted dislike of all landlords. As a boy at Mount Oliphant he had sat moodily by while his father read aloud the insolent and threatening letters of the factor who was in charge of Provost Fergusson's estate; here at Lochlie, a grown man, he saw his father's farm stripped of everything valuable, and heard his father's name cried out in warning to one and all. On September 7, 1782, he had written a letter to Thomas Orr, occasionally employed as harvest-hand at Lochlie, in which one sees significant indications of the turn the man's mind was taking. For instance:

[79]

The greater part of men grasp at riches as eagerly as if Poverty were but another word for Damnation & misery, whereas I affirm that the man whose only wish is to become great & rich, whatever he may appear to be, or whatever he may pretend to be, at the bottom he is but a miserable wretch.[39]

Two months later, as if shrinking from the unfriendly criticism of his neighbors, he said to the same friend:

I love to see a man who has a mind superiour to the world and the world's men, a man who, conscious of his own integrity, and at peace with himself, despises the censures and opinions of the unthinking rabble of mankind.[40]

On January 15, 1783, when the landlord was about to sue out the warrant of sequestration, Burns had written to his old teacher Murdoch, and had touched a similar note:

Though indolent, yet so far as an extremely delicate constitution permits,[41] I am not lazy; and in many things, especially in tavern matters, I am a strict eoconomist; not, indeed, for the sake of the money; but one of the principal parts in my composition is a kind of pride of stomach; and I scorn to fear the face of any man living: above everything, I abhor as hell, the idea of sneaking in a corner to avoid a dun—possibly some pitiful, sordid wretch, who in my heart I despise and detest. 'Tis this, and this alone, that endears eoconomy to me.[42]

Such expressions have sometimes been ridiculed as "rhodomontade": unpleasant indications that fustian and bombast came easily to Burns, even so early in his career. But when one visualizes the circumstances under which the family was living when these letters were written, and calls to mind the sensitive pride of the writer, one realizes that Burns was not acting a part; still less was he strutting to his own applause. He was giving imaginatively heightened expression to what ultimately became a sort of fixed idea: a passionate detestation of all sorts of dependence. Independence, liberty, not alone political but economic as well, was indeed a "glorious feast." Once, twice, in early life, he learned from bitter and humiliating personal experience what poverty and debt might mean. Inevitably, the

[80]

experience "got on his nerves," and he became over-strident in protest. But the protest was sincere.

With the poverty of these years, and in part because of it, came illness. For many years before this time William Burnes had been suffering from the inevitable hardships which his lot in life involved. As his sons realized, he had grown old before his day; old, and enfeebled by many years of hard labor. Though a "farmer" and not a "cotter," [43] he was indeed toil-worn; when his health broke it was for no apparent reason save that—as we put it—he had worked himself to death, not figuratively but literally. Early in the summer of 1783 his death seemed imminent. A letter of June 21 from Robert to his cousin James Burness of Montrose contains interesting and significant information concerning the unhappy economic situation ("the present wretched state of this country"), and a few lines of calm and unemotional comment on his father's health: "He has been for some months very poorly in health, & is in his own opinion, & indeed in almost everybody's else, in a dying condition." [44] He lived, however, till the following winter, when "a phthisical consumption . . . after two years' promises, kindly stept in, and snatched him away to 'where the wicked cease from troubling, and where the weary are at rest.' " [45] He died on February 13, 1784.

Thus only was William Burnes spared the humiliation of actually being arrested for debt, and perhaps haled off to jail. Instead of this, his body was borne by his neighbors back to Alloway, and buried in the Kirkyard a third of a mile south of the cottage he had built for his bride. [46] A stern, but at the same time gentle, unselfish, and altogether worthy man, well deserving of the honor and respect of his family, and of the tribute his son Robert paid him in the epitaph he wrote for the tombstone:

> O ye whose cheek the tear of pity stains,
>   Draw near with pious rev'rence, and attend!
> Here lie the loving husband's dear remains,
>   The tender father, and the gen'rous friend;

The pitying heart that felt for human woe,
The dauntless heart that fear'd no human pride,
The friend of man—to vice alone a foe;
For "ev'n his failings lean'd to virtue's side."

At least four months before the death of their father Robert
and Gilbert Burns had leased the farm of Mossgiel, in Mauchline parish, two and one half miles southeast of Lochlie.   The
landlord, Gavin Hamilton, a Mauchline Attorney, who was destined to figure largely in Burns's life, here first appeared within
the circle of the poet's horizon.   He showed a friendly interest
in Burns by giving him a chance to purchase cattle and dairy
utensils at a private sale, and by leasing his farm of one hundred
and twenty acres for ninety pounds per year.[47]

Apparently the only capital the family possessed when the
brothers undertook this new venture was what they had saved
from the Sheriff by filing claims for wages due them as laborers
in the employ of their father.   This, at least, is the tradition;
it is based on a somewhat vague statement by Robert, and a more
specific one by Gilbert.

Robert's remarks are brief and characteristic:

When my father died, his all went among the rapacious hell-hounds
that grovel in the kennel of justice; but we made a shift to scrape a little
money in the family amongst us; with which, to keep us together, my
Brother and I took a neighbouring farm.[48]

Gilbert—accountant for the family—is more specific; what he
says throws interesting light upon the customs of the Burnes
household:

During the whole of the time we lived in the farm of Lochlea with my
father, he allowed my brother and me such wages for our labour as he
gave to other labourers, as a part of which, every article of our clothing
manufactured in the family was regularly accounted for.   When my
father's affairs grew near a crisis, Robert and I took the farm of Mossgiel,
consisting of 118 acres, at the rent of £90 per annum (the farm on which
I live at present), from Mr. Gavin Hamilton, as an asylum for the
family in case of the worst.   It was stocked by the property and individual

savings of the whole family, and was a joint concern among us. Every member of the family was allowed ordinary wages for the labour he performed on the farm. My brother's allowance and mine was £7 per annum each.[49] And during the whole time this family concern lasted, which was four years, as well as during the preceding period at Lochlea, his expenses never in any one year exceeded his slender income. As I was intrusted with the keeping of the family accounts, it is not possible that there can be any fallacy in this statement in my brother's favour. His temperance and frugality were everything that could be wished.[50]

The remainder of the Mossgiel chronicle belongs in a later chapter. It was before the death of William Burnes, however, that the two eldest sons had made the necessary preparations for moving away from what by this time had come to be a scene of misery and general unhappiness. When one reviews the incidents of the concluding months at Lochlie, one wonders that Burns's spirits sank no lower than they did. His father was dead; the crops and stock had been sold by the Sheriff; the sons were forced to enter claims against a bankrupt estate in order to save a pittance with which to make another beginning. It should be remembered, however, that the poet himself was under no financial obligation to any one. However sharp the pinch may have been, he had lived scrupulously within his income, and was in a position to start his own first experiment in farming without being in any man's debt.

There may be no causal connection between the death of Burns's father and the poet's first departure, of which there was to be any positive evidence, from the propriety which had hitherto marked his relations with women. It is a fact, however, that the two events took place at about the same time. The girl was Elizabeth Paton, employed by Burns's mother as house servant or dairy maid. Her home was at Largieside, a mile across the fields from Lochlie, where the inquisitive visitor can still discover the grass-grown foundations of the old farm-house.[51] The poet's niece Isabella Begg later described her—from hearsay —as

[83]

an exceedingly handsome figure, but very plain looking; so active, honest and independent a creature, that she had become a great favourite with her mistress, who, when her situation became known, was most anxious that Burns should have married her, but both my aunts and uncle Gilbert opposed it. The girl herself acknowledged he had broken no promise to her. They thought the faults of her character would soon have disgusted him. She was rude and uncultivated to a great degree; a strong masculine understanding, with a thorough (tho' unwomanly) contempt for every sort of refinement. . . . My mother says she does not believe that ever woman loved man with a more heartfelt devotion than that poor creature did him.[52]

Once again the rest of the story belongs in a subsequent chapter, for "Dear-bought Bess" was not born till May 22, 1785. Lochlie, however, witnessed the beginning of an acquaintance which, not long after William Burnes's death, took the form of a *liaison*.[53]

This affair with Betty Paton is the last of the incidents that figure prominently in Burns's life during the Lochlie period. In a way it may be said to signalize almost symbolically the conclusion of the first large chapter in his history, or the beginning of the second. Till the winter of 1783–4 he had been in spirit as well as in fact his father's son—subjecting himself to his advice and correction, eating at his table, plowing his fields, and receiving his money as wages. He had not always submitted unquestioningly, and once he had left home to set up a business of his own. The experiment, however, had failed, and he had resumed his old place on the farm. But with the death of his father he became over-night his own man—the recognized head of the family group, but destined to go his own way and live his own life, for better or worse. And the first action of the man, when his father's restraining influence was removed, was in sharp defiance of the moral code in which his father believed, and to which he himself had hitherto adhered. In this respect the man who left Lochlie in the spring of 1784 was radically different from the boy who had journeyed thither with his father in May of 1777.

But the Burns of the later years at Lochlie was in two important characteristics very like the younger Burns of Mount Oliphant. He read as eagerly as ever; he wrote with even more enthusiasm and success than he had done before.

No one can be specific as to the exact dates of Burns's reading; his own statements are not always in agreement. It is clear, however, that by the end of the Lochlie period he had become at least superficially acquainted with Shenstone, Mackenzie, Thomson, Sterne, "Ossian," Richardson, Locke, Hume, and Robertson; that he had read widely in English and Scottish song collections, though by no means as exhaustively as he was to do later; and—most important of all—that he knew his Ramsay and Fergusson from cover to cover. When one remembers that this was in addition to the considerable amount of reading he had done at Mount Oliphant, one realizes that by his twenty-fifth birthday he had made himself a rather well educated young man, especially as regards the sentimental and Deistic writers of his own century. That he had energy enough to carry his literary studies so far, in the face of poverty, ill-health, and domestic unhappiness, is tribute enough to his force of character. In fact, it must be evident that the Burneses as a family were "reading people," though it seems the part of wisdom to be somewhat sceptical concerning the old tradition that "country neighbours who happened to enter their family-room (the kitchen) at the dinner hour were surprised to find them all —father, brothers, and sisters—sitting each with a book in one hand and a spoon in the other." [54] Be this as it may, Burns grew to manhood in an atmosphere well calculated to foster his own natural inclinations towards good reading.

The writing which Burns accomplished at Lochlie and Irvine is of two sorts: prose and verse. The not inconsiderable amount of prose takes the form of letters, and the opening sections of the *First Commonplace Book*. One need read only a few scattered paragraphs of the letters to realize that by 1781 or 1782 Burns had taught himself to write well in the somewhat rigid "epistolary" style of the late eighteenth century, although in such a letter as that of June 21, 1783, to his cousin James Burness, the unpleasant formalism usually associated with that style is reduced to a minimum. In the best of these letters the observing student may see abundant evidence of literary talent: the vocabulary is extensive, the phrasing fresh, vigorous, and in general that of a man entirely at ease when he takes up his pen. Were these early letters of no other significance, they would still be valuable as making it clear that Burns was one of the fortunate persons who seem to have been born to write well.

In the *First Commonplace Book*, to use the title commonly accorded the "Observations, Hints, Songs, Scraps of Poetry, etc., by Robt. Burness," [55] one sees the poet consciously striving after literary effects, and at times posing a little before his own mirror. He began it in the spring of 1783; the introductory paragraph suggests that he expected the booklet to be read by other eyes than his own, a fact which does not seem to have been true of the early letters:

As [the author] was but little indebted to scholastic education, and bred at a plough-tail, his performances must be strongly tinctured with his unpolished, rustic way of life; but as I believe, they are really his own, it may be some entertainment to a curious observer of human-nature to see how a Ploughman thinks, and feels, under the pressure of Love, Ambition, Anxiety, Grief, with the like cares and passions, which, however diversified by the Modes, and Manners of life, operate pretty much alike I believe, in all the Species.[56]

What follows is a curious mixture of original poetry, somewhat self-conscious criticism of himself and his verses, amateurish philosophizing, and not uninteresting "observations" on life and literature. Many of the entries are dated. It thus becomes possible to use these jottings as critical annotations on the story of Burns's life; some of the paragraphs take on added meaning when read in connection with the appropriate events in the family history. For instance, under date of March 1784, one month after his father's death, and at the very time the bankrupt family was being turned out of Lochlie, appears the "Penitential

Thought, in the Hour of Remorse, Intended for a Tragedy."
In any other setting than the proper one, the blank verse fragment seems inconsequential enough; read in the light of what
was happening in the early months of 1784, the lines become
significant if not poetical:

> All devil as I am, a damned wretch;
> A hardened, stubborn, unrepenting villain:
> Still my heart melts at human wretchedness;
> And with sincere, though unavailing sighs
> I view the helpless children of distress.
> With tears indignant I behold th' Oppressor
> Rejoicing in the honest man's destruction
> Whose unsubmitting heart was all his crime.
> Even you, ye hapless crew, I pity you,
> Ye, whom the seeming good think sin to pity;
> Ye, poor, despis'd abandon'd vagabonds,
> Whom Vice as usual, has turn'd o'er to ruin.
> O! but for kind, though ill requited friends
> I had been driven forth like you forlorn
> The most detested, worthless wretch among ye. . . .[57]

Immediately thereafter appears a paragraph which is obviously the germ of the "Address to the Unco Guid":

Let any of the strictest character for regularity of conduct among us,
examine impartially how many of his virtues are owing to constitution
& education; how many vices he has never been guilty of, not from
any care or vigilance, but from want of opportunity, or some accidental
circumstance intervening; how many of the weakness's of mankind
he has escaped because he was out of the line of such temptation; and,
what often, if not always, weighs more than all the rest; how much he is
indebted to the world's good opinion because the world does not know
all: I say any man who can thus think, will scan the failings, nay the faults
& crimes, of mankind around him, with a brother's eye.[58]

Obviously, both the poem which ultimately gave enduring expression to these ideas, and this prose first draft, gain greatly

in significance when read against the background of the actual circumstances which occasioned them.

Or again, under date of April, 1784, appears a brief entry which stands as a sort of prefatory note to the lines known as "Winter: A Dirge," and is of value as throwing light on the poet's psychological make-up:

> There is scarcely any earthly object gives me more—I don't know if I should call it pleasure, but something which exalts me, something which enraptures me—than to walk in the sheltered side of a wood or high plantation, in a cloudy, winter day, and hear a stormy wind howling among the trees & raving o'er the plain.[59]

Slightly more than a year later, in August of 1785, he wrote as follows:

> However I am pleased with the works of our Scotch Poets, particularly the excellent Ramsay, and the still more excellent Ferguson (sic), yet I am hurt to see other places of Scotland, their towns, rivers, woods, haughs, etc., immortalized in such celebrated performances, whilst my dear native country, the ancient Baileries of Carrick, Kyle, & Cunningham, famous both in ancient & modern times for a gallant and warlike race of inhabitants; a country where civil, & particularly religious Liberty have ever found their first support, & their last asylum; a country, the birthplace of many famous Philosophers, Soldiers, & Statesmen, and the scene of many important events recorded in Scottish History, particularly a great many of the actions of the GLORIOUS WALLACE, the SAVIOUR of his country; yet, we have never had one Scotch Poet of any eminence, to make the fertile banks of Irvine, the romantic woodlands & sequestered scenes on Aire (sic), and the heathy mountainous source, & winding sweep of Doon, emulate Tay, Forth, Ettrick, Tweed, &c. This is a complaint I would gladly remedy, but Alas! I am far unequal to the task, both in native genius & education.
>
> Obscure I am, & obscure I must be; though no young Poet, nor Young Soldier's heart ever beat more fondly for fame than mine.[60]

It is good evidence of the nervous sincerity of this entry that the long introductory sentence never comes to a legitimate grammatical close—a circumstance most unusual in Burns's writings.

And the concluding sentence, concerning the poet's desire for fame, when read in connection with the observations that precede it, is of more value to the student interested in reconstructing Burns's personality than many a page of mere biographical chronicle.

Another significant entry is that of September, 1785, in which Burns comments on Scottish song and music. Here it becomes evident that the poet's concern over these matters was not—as has sometimes been supposed—a late and more or less accidental development, due in considerable measure to the suggestions made by James Johnson, editor of the *Scots Musical Museum*. On the contrary, his interest in them was clearly developed at this time, a year before the publication of his first volume had forced him into the rôle of "Scotia's bard." The entry as a whole is full of interest, but too long to be quoted entire; the nub of it appears in the statement that "it might be possible for a Scotch Poet, with a nice, judicious ear, to set compositions to many of our most favorite airs": which, of course, is exactly what Burns was to do five years later, when Johnson and Thomson offered to Burns the media for the publication of such "compositions." [61]

Space forbids a more detailed examination of the *Commonplace Book*. Enough has been said, however, to show the importance of the booklet to any one seriously interested in Burns's life, and to demonstrate his continuing interest in the writing of prose.

But it is the poems written during this period of Burns's life that are of chief concern to the student. Inevitably the years at Lochlie saw relatively little verse composed, and none at all published. The physical burden under which Burns labored was excessive. The farm labor was arduous,—so arduous, indeed, as seriously to impair the young man's health. Furthermore, the unrest occasioned by poverty was not conducive to literary pursuits.

Nevertheless during these years Burns wrote approximately a score of poems that have been preserved, and—*a priori*—not a

[89]

few that must have been lost. Apart from any questions of literary merit, these poems are worthy of study as Burns's juvenilia; one or two, moreover, will be found to possess distinguishing poetic excellence as well as historical significance.[62]

The group as a whole makes it clear that Burns's early work was pronouncedly imitative. Though Dr. Otto Ritter's careful studies [63] record as significant literary parallels far too many examples of what most scholars would call only coincidences of idea or form, they are nevertheless indispensable to any person seriously interested in tracing Burns to his sources. They show Burns's debt, during these early years, to many minor song writers, both Scottish and English: to Mrs. Cockburn and Lady Wardlaw, among the better known writers of vernacular lyrics; to a group of eighteenth century English poets: Young, Gay, Thomson, Beattie, Pope, and Macpherson; and to Ramsay and Fergusson. The English influence came first through school books and early reading. Not till after Burns had made a beginning at poetry, and had become discouraged, did he fall under the influence of his immediate predecessors in the vernacular. "Rhyme," he afterwards wrote when describing his way of life at this time, "except some religious pieces, which are in print, I had given up; but meeting with Ferguson's Scotch Poems, I strung anew my wildly-sounding, rustic lyre, with emulating vigour." [64]

Even a superficial study of these poems establishes another fact of interest: as early as 1780 Burns was more than casually attentive to Scottish music, and had already formed the habit of using a tune as the starting point for a lyric. There is a tradition—as usual, somewhat hard to trace to its source—that before 1781 Burns, possibly in emulation of David Sillar, had begun a not wholly unsuccessful attempt to play the violin. Later in life he made the often-repeated statement that the first step in writing a song was to become thoroughly familiar with the tune to which it was to be sung. Apparently he was doing the same thing, more or less by instinct, at the very beginning of his poetic career.

[90]

In a similar way the language of these poems is indicative of what was to be Burns's future practise. Running one's eye down the pages of the early poems, one sees a good deal that is pure English; indeed, noticeably more of the early work is in English than in Scots. But there is enough in the vernacular to show Burns's growing interest in the dialect, and to give an indication of the ease with which he could use it. There is also a considerable amount of verse written in what is neither English nor "braid Scots," but a curious mingling of both; a sort of dialectical hybrid in which now one and now the other element predominates. In other words, except for the fact that proportionately more English appears in the early poems than in the mature work, the situation as regards language is the same in these juvenilia that it was to be in the poems of later years.

Far more interesting than the fact that these Lochlie and Irvine productions shadow forth Burns's later practise in several respects, is the fact that they show him to have been at the very outset of his career a facile—almost a brilliant—rimester and metrist. Looking at the eighteen poems printed by Chambers-Wallace as probably composed during this period, one discovers that they are cast in seventeen different stanza forms or rime schemes, some of which are elaborate enough to have tested the powers of an older hand than Burns's. The young poet who thus played about among the metrical patterns handed down to him by his predecessors was skilfull in shaping his words to fit a given tune, adept in using internal rimes to relieve a somewhat conventional verse form, obviously delighted by words "in tuneful order," and full of a boyish exuberance such as that which prompted him to run the rime *mien-seen-green* through all the fourteen stanzas of "The Lass of Cessnock Banks." Juvenile some of these experiments may have been; they are the apprentice's sketches, however, of one who was to attain full mastership in his craft, and that at no late date.

Furthermore, two of these early productions make it clear that Burns was already on the verge of becoming a poet of great and original genius. Turn to "Poor Mailie's Elegy" and "Mary

[91]

Morison," and no further evidence on this score will be needed.[65]
The young man who composed "Mary Morison" had done far
more than master the somewhat conventional phraseology of the
Scottish love song. Conventional enough the beginning and
end of the lyric may be; the second stanza, however, shows a
surer touch:

> Yestreen, when to the trembling string
>   The dance gaed thro' the lighted ha',
> To thee my fancy took its wing;
>   I sat, but neither heard nor saw.
>   Tho' this was fair, and that was braw,
> And yon the toast of a' the town,
>   I sigh'd and said amang them a':—
> Ye are na Mary Morison!

And the author of "Poor Mailie's Elegy" had done more than
read Robert Sempill's "Habbie Simpson" and Fergusson's "On
the Death of Scotch Music." He had caught the very essence
of an old and characteristic element in the vernacular tradition; he
had retouched his borrowings to fit his own imaginative experiences. The result is a poem in which the combination of sympathy, humor, pathos, and sheer artistry announces very definitely the arrival of "the real Burns."

On the whole, then, the years at Lochlie, though they closed
in bitterness occasioned by the bankruptcy and death of William
Burnes, brought much to Burns besides disappointment and disaster. They brought him new experiences and new friendships,
a constantly widening horizon, and an ever-growing sense of his
own powers. They were years of increasing pride and of developing ambition, albeit of hard physical labor and depressing ill-
health. And—still more significant—it was at the close of these
seven years that he found himself without the steadying influence
of his father's presence and example; that he first allowed his
passions to drive him beyond the bounds of propriety; and that
he first wrote poetry of distinction. The astonishing chronicle
of the ensuing two years at Mossgiel was to be merely the devel-

opment of a theme that was thus announced in all its essentials
during the tenancy of Lochlie.

[1] Thus Gilbert Burns (S. D., IV, 359). See also documents in the suit of M'Lure vs.
William Burnes, *Chronicle*, 1910, pp. 149 ff.

[2] *Autobiography*, p. 35.

[3] See *Chronicle*, 1910, pp. 149 ff., for the Sheriff's inventory. Burnes may possibly
have sold some of his stock in anticipation of the sequestration.

[4] Two may be found in S. D., IV, 363 f. The third is reproduced in facsimile in
Charles Rogers's *Book of Robert Burns* (Edinburgh, 1890, 3 v.), II, 153.

[5] *Letters*, I, 1 ff.

[6] *Autobiography*, p. 35.

[7] Letter of Sillar to Robert Aiken, first published in *Poems of Robert Burns*, Edinburgh, 1811 (Printed for the Trustees of the Late James Morrison, 2 vols.), II, 257.

[8] Gilbert's Narrative; S. D., IV, 359.

[9] This expression, strictly interpreted, would place the episode in 1775, when the family
was still at Mount Oliphant. Hence biographers have heretofore treated the affair as belonging to that period. But a recently published letter from James M'Candlish to Burns,
dated 13 February, 1779, says, "You say you are attending a dancing school this winter,"
and thus shows clearly that Burns's memory must have been at fault. *Complete Writings
of Robert Burns* (Boston, 1927, 10 vols.), VII, 23.

[10] Here is a good example of Dr. Currie's editorial practise. He altered the harsh phrase
"in absolute defiance of his commands" to "in opposition to his wishes." Burns, however,
not only used the phrase in the original of his letter to Dr. Moore, but repeated it in the
copy he made for Robert Riddell of Glenriddell.

[11] *Autobiography*, p. 36. Just as Gilbert Burns tried to temper the warmth of his
brother's statements concerning Jacobitism, so he attempted to soften the statements in
the preceding passage: "I wonder how Robert could attribute to our father the lasting
resentment of his going to a dancing school against his will, of which he was incapable.
I believe the truth was that he, about this time, began to see the dangerous impetuosity of
my brother's passions, as well as his not being amenable to counsel, which often irritated
my father; and which he would naturally think a dancing school was not likely to correct. But he was proud of Robert's genius, which he bestowed more expence in cul-
tivating than on the rest of the family. . . . He had indeed that dislike of dancing
schools which Robert mentions; but so far overcame it during Robert's first month of
attendance, that he allowed all the rest of the family that were fit for it to accompany him
during the second month. Robert excelled in dancing, and was for some time distractedly
fond of it." (Currie, I, 79.)

[12] It may have been because of Sillar's example that Burns himself about 1780 made
some effort to learn the fiddle. See "David Sillar," by H. Makinson; *Chronicle*, 1915,
pp. 70 ff.

[13] *Poems, Chiefly in the Scottish Dialect*, by David Sillar, Kilmarnock, 1789. The
volume was printed on the same press and from the same type as Burns's first edition,
and is exactly comparable in its typography.

[14] David Lowe, *Burns's Passionate Pilgrimage*, p. 187, Glasgow, 1904. The two
youngest children were not mentioned in the certificate.

[15] See some interesting letters, *Letters*, II, 42 f.

[16] Lowe's *Passionate Pilgrimage*, *passim*, gives the best account of Tait and his ways
that is readily available, and also reprints characteristic fragments of his verses. A copy
of the very rare *Poems and Songs by Alexander Tait* [Paisley], 1790, is in the Mitchell
Library, Glasgow. See appendix to this volume for Tait's songs on Burns and his family.

[17] See Appendix, p. 499.

[18] Currie, I, 363 ff.

[19] *Journals of Ralph Waldo Emerson* (Boston, 1910, 10 vols.), I, 39 f.

[20] Currie, I, 367.

[21] The only published letters of Burns's ante-dating these to Ellison Begbie are those
written to William Niven in 1780. See *Letters*, I, 1 ff.

[22] *Letters*, I, 7.

[23] *Ibid.*, p. 10.

[24] The only definite connection between the Begbie affair and Burns's removal to Irvine is found in one sentence of his last letter to Ellison: "I expect to remove in a few days a little further off"—which probably refers to the contemplated removal from Lochlie. (*Letters*, I, 10.)

[25] The entry appears in the *Glasgow Mercury* for January 16–23, 1783 (Vol. VI, No. 264, p. 25).

[26] Burns later wrote, concerning his state of mind at this time, "To crown all, a belle fille whom I adored, and who had pledged her soul to me in the fields of matrimony, jilted me with peculiar circumstances of mortification. The finishing evil, that brought up the rear of this infernal file, was my hypochondriac complaint being irritated to such a degree that for three months I was in a diseased state of body and mind, scarcely to be envied by the hopeless wretches who have just got their sentence, 'Depart from me, ye cursed!'" (*Autobiography*, p. 41.) There is no reason for believing that Ellison Begbie ever promised to marry him; but the passage as a whole represents Burns's state of mind not inaccurately.

[27] The exact dates of composition of these two poems are undeterminable, as is the case with much of Burns's early work. That they belong to the later part of the sojourn at Irvine, however, is reasonably certain.

[28] See M'Bain, *Burns' Cottage*, pp. 43 ff., for a detailed account of the sale. Burnes received £160 sterling for his leasehold and property rights. He had previously sold two acres to other purchasers.

[29] See *Letters*, I, 4.

[30] *Autobiography*, p. 41. It is possible that the "partner" was not Peacock, with whom Burns is said soon to have quarrelled, but another flax-dresser whose shop was in the High Street.

[31] A facsimile of the minute book, showing both entries, is published in the *Chronicle* for 1929, p. 139. The accompanying article, "Burns and Freemasonry in Ayrshire," by R. T. Halliday, gives all the verifiable details concerning Burns's connection with Ayrshire lodges, and corrects certain current mis-statements. Two recent accounts of Burns's Masonic affiliations and activities are William Harvey's *Robert Burns as a Freemason*, Dundee, 1921, and Dudley Wright's *Robert Burns and his Masonic Circle*, London, 1929. Neither book is entirely reliable.

[32] *Autobiography*, pp. 41 ff. The poem referred to is "A Poet's Welcome to his Love-begotten Daughter."

[33] *Letters*, I, 151. When the Kilmarnock volume was published, Burns sent Brown an inscribed copy, which still survives.

[34] "It might be supposed from his own narrative that he immediately deserted the business and Irvine together; but his sister reports that he did not return to Lochlea till the ensuing March." Chambers, I, 62.

[35] *Analysis of the Statistical Account of Scotland*, Edinburgh, 1825. Part II, Appendix No. III, "On the Famines," pp. 40 ff.

[36] All the documents that have been brought to light are printed in the *Chronicle* for 1910, pp. 149 ff.

[37] *Ibid.*

[38] See Appendix, p. 499.

[39] *Letters*, I, 11.

[40] *Ibid.*, p. 12.

[41] Such a casual reference to his health is significant in view of his subsequent early breakdown.

[42] *Letters*, I, 13 f.

[43] *I.e.*, he leased a farm himself; he was not, like the cotter in Burns's poem, a hired laborer.

[44] *Letters*, I, 15.

[45] *Autobiography*, p. 35.

[46] As every visitor to Alloway knows, William Burnes's grave is directly in front of the ruined church which his son immortalized in "Tam o' Shanter."

[47] See letter of 18 October, 1783; *Letters*, I, 17.

[48] *Autobiography*, p. 43.

[49] The usual wage for a farm hand at the time. In addition to the money, the laborer received lodging and food.

[50] Gilbert's Narrative; S. D., IV, 360 f.

[51] I am indebted to Mr. J. C. Ewing for pointing this out to me.

[52] Quoted, C. W., I, 119.

[53] I am indebted to Mr. J. C. Ewing for the information concerning the date of the child's birth. He quoted to me a letter signed by Elizabeth Paton in which she said: "On May 22 I gave birth to a daughter of whom Robert Burns is the father." I have not myself seen the letter. The child was baptized on May 24, 1785, on which date the Tarbolton Parish Register records the fact that "Robert Burns and Elizabeth Paton had their daughter Elizabeth baptized." (C. W., I, 396, n.)

[54] C. W., I, 58.

[55] The best easily available reprint is in S. D., IV, 51 ff. The original is a stitched MS. booklet of twenty-two folio leaves.

[56] S. D., IV, 53.

[57] Ibid., p. 58. The four lines beginning "Ev'n you, ye hapless crew," furnish part, at least, of the motif of "The Jolly Beggars."

[58] Ibid., p. 59.

[59] Ibid., p. 61.

[60] Ibid., p. 91.

[61] Ibid., p. 93.

[62] The following poems were almost certainly composed at Lochlie or Irvine: The Tarbolton Lasses; "Ah, Woe is me"; Montgomerie's Peggy; The Ploughman's Life; The Lass of Cessnock Banks; Winter—A Dirge; A Prayer under the Pressure of Violent Anguish; "My Father was a Farmer"; The Death and Dying Words of Poor Mailie; Poor Mailie's Elegy; John Barleycorn; Mary Morison; Bonie Peggy Alison; The Rigs o' Barley; "Now Westlin' Winds"; My Nanie O; The Ploughman's Life; and The Ronalds of the Bennals. A few others may belong in this group.

[63] The most important is Quellenstudien zu Robert Burns, 1773–1791; Berlin, 1901. See also Robert Burns' Beziehungen zur Litteratur, by Heinrich Molenaar, Erlangen, 1899, and Robert Burns. Studien zu seiner dichterischen Entwicklung, by Max Meyerfeld, Berlin, 1899.

[64] Autobiography, p. 43.

[65] It is only fair to say that neither of the two poems can be assigned with absolute certainty to this period; but the weight of the evidence is in favor of the belief that they were composed before the family left Lochlie.

CHAPTER IV

MOSSGIEL

1

LIFE ON THE FARM

SPRING of 1784 could not have been far advanced when Robert and Gilbert Burns moved the family from Lochlie, out of which they had been driven by their father's bankruptcy, to the new home at Mossgiel. The journey was not a long one. A short two miles down the highway in a southeasterly direction brought them to the farm which the two men had leased "as an asylum." A little more than a mile beyond it lay Mauchline village; four miles to the west was Tarbolton. The farm was in Mauchline parish,—a fact which had necessitated the issuing of a "certificate of character" by the Tarbolton Kirk Session, in order that the new-comers might be properly accepted by the spiritual authorities of the parish into which they were moving.

The lease on the property had been executed the preceding autumn, and was somewhat more favorable to the tenants than had been the agreement between M'Lure and William Burnes concerning Lochlie. One hundred and eighteen acres of relatively bare upland, for which the brothers were to pay an annual rental of ninety pounds, a small house—which Gavin Hamilton had built as a country home for himself—containing the customary two rooms downstairs and a loft or garret above; and the necessary barn and byre—such was Mossgiel farm.

As in the case of both Mount Oliphant and Lochlie the earth was poor—a thick clay, from which much of the fertile top-soil had long since been removed by the combination of heavy rain-

[96]

storms and poor methods of agriculture. Lying a little more than six hundred feet above the sea, on the height of land between the valleys of the Irvine and the Ayr rivers, and unenclosed by either forests or high hills, the site was one from which Wordsworth later looked out over a not unpleasing scene:

> "There!" said a Stripling, pointing with meet pride
> Towards a low roof with green trees half concealed,
> "Is Mossgiel farm, and that's the very field
> Where Burns plowed up the daisy." Far and wide
> A plain below stretched seaward, while, descried
> Above sea-clouds, the peaks of Arran rose;
> And, by that simple notice, the repose
> Of earth, sky, sea, and air was vivified.[1]

It is a pleasant enough prospect today, as one stands in front of the well cared for grey stucco farm house that has replaced Burns's simpler one, and looks off towards the south. Virtually all the southern half of Ayrshire lies before one. In the foreground the gently rolling countryside slopes down towards the river Ayr, the course of which can just be traced through the center of the picture, and rises again, beyond, to a height considerably greater than that of Mossgiel. To the left, or east, the hills attain almost to the dignity of mountains, though there are no sharp peaks or deep-cut valleys. It is a quiet, friendly landscape, composed for the most part of tilled fields and pastures where cattle graze in the soft warmth of an Ayrshire summer. If the day is clear, there will be a glint of light in the southwest, where the waters of the Firth of Clyde reflect the afternoon sunshine; and still farther to the west the rugged outlines of the mountain peaks of Arran will form a somewhat sterner background for the picture. All this is much as it was when Burns knew it; for even the railroads and smoothly surfaced motor highways have altered none of the major features of the countryside.

The family found itself somewhat crowded in the new quarters. Robert and Gilbert, relinquishing the relative comfort

[97]

of the lower floor to their mother, sisters, and younger brothers, slept in the garret. Here three small apartments had been finished off, one as a storage closet and two as bedrooms. The two brothers seem to have occupied the middle chamber. Under the single window, a skylight in the sloping roof, stood Robert's desk, a table with one drawer.[2] Two plowmen and a boy— "Wee Davoc"—before long were added to the establishment; at the time Burns wrote the poetic inventory of his possessions (1786), all the labor which might have been performed by female servants fell to the lot of his mother and sisters. Financial responsibility rested upon Robert and Gilbert, who had leased the property from Gavin Hamilton, who in turn held it from the Earl of Loudon, the proprietor, and chief land-owner of the district. Nevertheless, as Gilbert pointed out, the new venture was a "joint concern" of the whole family, all of whose savings went into it, and each of whom drew regular wages for the labor performed. The elder boys were allowed seven pounds per year; the others received smaller sums.

That Burns, in common with the rest of his family, intended to give diligent attention to farm work, is indisputable. As yet no serious thought of escape from the inherited and almost inevitable mode of life seems to have occurred to him. "I entered on this farm," he later wrote, "with a full resolution: 'come, go to, I will be wise!' I read farming books, I calculated crops; I attended markets; and in short, in spite of the devil, the world, and the flesh, I believe I should have been a wise man; but the first year, from unfortunately buying in bad seed, the second, from a late harvest, we lost half of both our crops. This overset all my wisdom, and I returned like the dog to his vomit, and the sow that is washed, to her wallowing in the mire."[3]

It is obvious enough, in view of what happened later, that other circumstances than bad seed and a late harvest were responsible for diverting Burns from his farmer's life. It is worth remembering, however, that at the outset his intentions were clear and praiseworthy.

For aid in stocking the farm the two brothers had turned to

the landlord, Gavin Hamilton. As early as October 18, 1783, Burns had written him a letter which is of interest not only as showing the customs than in vogue, but also as indicating Robert's unwillingness to trust his own judgment in matters agricultural:

SIR—

As you were pleased to give us the offer of a private bargain of your cows you intend for sale, my brother & I this day took a look of them and a friend with us on whose judgement we could something depend, to enable us to form an estimate— If you are still intending to let us have them in that way, please appoint a day that we may wait on you and either agree amongst ourselves or else fix on men to whom we may refer it, tho' I hope we will not need any reference.

Whatever of your dairy utensils you intend to dispose of we will probably purchase.[4]

In other words, even before the death of his father Robert had taken prompt measures for the welfare of the family, but at the same time had been unwilling to trust himself in concerns where till that time his father's opinion would have been decisive. That the same conditions prevailed after the removal to Mossgiel, and that Burns felt the absence of his father's voice from the family councils, seems certain. None the less it was Robert who was the head of the family, and to whom the rest looked as leader. That Gilbert "took charge of everything," [5] or that Robert was the sort of farmer whom the genial imagination of Allan Cunningham has pictured, is highly improbable.

Life on the farm, so far as the fundamental problem of gaining a living was concerned, was much what it had been at Lochlie. There were the same crops of oats, barley, wheat, and rye to be raised; the same dairy work to be performed by mother and sisters. This much we know. But records are few as to what actually happened from week to week in the new home. The late spring and summer of 1784 found Burns suffering from a severe physical breakdown—one of the recurring manifestations of the endocarditis which had already fastened itself firmly upon him, and which was to cause his death twelve years later.

[99]

An entry in the *Commonplace Book* under date of August, 1784, shows that the trouble had been of some duration:

"A prayer, when fainting fits, & other alarming symptoms of a Pleurisy or some other dangerous disorder, which indeed still threaten me, first put Nature on the alarm." [6]

It was at this time that Burns's medical friends gave him unsound advice—as indeed they were to continue to do till he was safely beyond their reach. Instead of the rest which might have restored the normal strength of his heart, he was ordered to take cold baths, and was allowed to continue with the full burden of the farm work on his shoulders. His natural bodily vigor brought him safely through this first attack; and the depression of spirits, the "hypochondria," which with Burns was one of the inevitable by-products of illness, this too gave place to his more normal zest for living. But each attack left its mark on his constitution, and brought the ultimate collapse rapidly nearer.

During this period Burns was finding his Masonic affiliations increasingly pleasurable. St. David Lodge, Tarbolton, claimed him as a member, and even after his removal to Mauchline parish he attended the meetings of the Tarbolton Lodge. From July, 1784, till he went up to Edinburgh in November of 1786, he served as Depute-Master.

But the most astonishing feature of the early months at Mossgiel was the rapid development of Burns's literary ambition and power. Various entries in the *Commonplace Book* [7] show him to have been thinking seriously about the art which he was practising with constantly increasing pleasure and effectiveness, and show also that the hopes to which he ultimately gave expression in "The Vision" were already shaping themselves in his mind. A statement by Gilbert should be quoted in this connection:

Among the earliest of his poems was the *Epistle to Davie*. Robert often composed without any regular plan. When any thing made a strong impression on his mind, so as to rouse it to poetic exertion, he would give way to the impulse, and embody the thought in rhyme. If he hit on two or three stanzas to please him, he would then think of proper introductory, connecting, and concluding stanzas; hence the middle of a poem was often first produced. It was, I think, in summer, 1784, when in the interval of harder labour, he and I were working in the garden (kail-yard), that he repeated to me the principal part of this epistle. I believe the first idea of Robert's becoming an author was started on this occasion. I was much pleased with the epistle, and said to him I was of opinion it would bear being printed, and that it would be well received by people of taste. . . . Robert seemed very well pleased with my criticism, and we talked of sending it to some magazine, but as this plan afforded no opportunity of knowing how it would take, the idea was dropped.[8]

Publication does not seem to have been definitely in Burns's mind as he was writing his earlier poems. He rimed "for fun," as he himself put it; his verses circulated among his friends in manuscript; they brought him local renown, and made him talked about. Not unnaturally he enjoyed this publicity, even when it was of a somewhat unsavory sort:

> What tho' they ca' me fornicator,
> An' tease my name in kintra clatter?
> The mair they talk, I'm kend the better;
> E'en let them clash.[9]

Yet despite his understandable pride at finding himself an object of local wonder, it was the sheer creative instinct in Burns that produced the work on which his early reputation was founded. Rarely did he indulge in *ad hoc* composition. Fame as a poet of Ayrshire he coveted; but there was in him none of the journalist's instinct to rush into print. Not till the early months of 1786 did Burns allow his interest in poetry and other concerns to distract him from his primary task of earning a living from the soil. He was first and foremost a farmer, studying agricultural books, attending fairs, and always laboring to the limit of his strength. The results, however, were discouraging. One year, as he pointed out, the seed was bad; another brought early frosts; each time the harvest was scanty. The same ill-luck that had made the closing years at Mount Oliphant unhappy, and had brought the Lochlie establishment to bankruptcy, was still attending William Burnes's eldest son. But the thrift and industry to which the family had long since become habituated carried them through somehow, till the success of Robert's Edinburgh volume enabled him to mitigate part of the financial distress.

In the autumn of 1785 occurred the death of John Burns, youngest of the four sons. All details are lacking; an entry in the Mauchline Parish Register merely records the fact: "Died, John Burns, Mossgiel; buried Nov. 1st 1785." To this is appended the statement that a second quality mort-cloth was used at the funeral.[10] No reference to this break in the family circle appears in any of the poet's letters.. But the fact of John's death at this time seems well established; it is, indeed, almost the only thing we know about the lad.

There are virtually no further records concerning the actual week-by-week existence of the Burns family at Mossgiel. Nevertheless this period of the poet's life was made memorable in three ways, each of which demands somewhat extensive treatment. First of all, it was during these months that he became acquainted with an interesting group of men living in Mauchline; second, it was at this time that he became seriously involved with "one or more of the female sex," to quote again from the rules of the Tarbolton Bachelors' Club; and finally, it was at this time that he published the 1786 Kilmarnock edition of his poems. When these three matters have been reviewed, the account of Burns's life at Mossgiel will be complete.

2

MAUCHLINE: THE TOWN AND ITS INHABITANTS

The village of Mauchline, in which the life of the parish was brought to a focus, and in which Burns found diversion and relief from farm work, was carefully described by the Reverend

MOSSGIEL

William Auld—"Daddy Auld"—for Sir John Sinclair's *Statistical Account*. He estimated the population of the village itself, in the year 1791, at one thousand persons; nearly as many more lived within the borders of the parish, but outside the village. Many of Auld's flock earned their livelihoods in the nearby stone quarries, or in the coalpit and iron mine at Killoch. But the majority were farmers, either actually engaged, like Burns, in tilling the soil, or living contentedly on the savings of by-gone years. They were, in general

a sober, industrious people, charitably disposed, careful and even punctual in attending the church on Sundays, and on sacramental occasions; and their practise in the main is agreeable to their profession. . . . The inhabitants . . . are . . . addicted to exercise and temperance, two great sources of long life and good health.[11]

By 1791, however, a somewhat new and unaccustomed prosperity had cast a tinge of worldliness over Auld's domain, and the Dominie, though uncomplaining, must have had misgivings:

The manner of living and dress is much altered from what it was about 50 years ago. At that period, and for some time after, there were only two or three families in this parish who made use of tea daily; now it is done by at least one half of the parish, and almost the whole use it occasionally. At that period, good twopenny strong ale and home-spirits were in vogue; but now even people in the middling and lower stations of life deal much in foreign spirits, rum-punch, and wine. . . . As to dress, about 50 years ago there were few females who wore scarlet or silks. But now nothing is more common than silk caps and silk cloaks, and women in a middling station are as fine as ladies of quality were formerly.[12]

The village was situated at the intersection of two important highways: the Ayr-Edinburgh and Dumfries-Kilmarnock post-roads. Travelers from distant parts of Scotland stopped at The Whitefoord Arms for a glass of ale or a night's lodging, while groups of wastrels or vagabonds could find refuge under Poosie Nansie's hospitable roof. And thirteen different horse

[103]

or cattle fairs each year, besides an annual race day, gave evidence of Mauchline's importance, at the close of the eighteenth century, as a center of a considerable portion of Ayrshire.

Fortunately for the person who wishes to visualize Burns's actual environment, the town of today is not unrecognizably different from that of a century and a half ago. It is a quiet, friendly little village, where the one constable leaves his post in the Cross to guide the visitor's motor car to a safe parking place in front of James Armour's old house in the Cowgate, "so that one o' thae busses winna tak a wheel aff ye while ye're lookin' about."

The old church in which Burns listened to Daddy Auld has disappeared, taken down in 1827 after six hundred and thirty years of service; but the present building, completed in 1829, was erected on the same spot in the center of the churchyard, which is itself the center of the entire village. To walk around this burying-ground, looking at the well-marked graves, and at the one- and two-storeyed red sandstone houses that crowd close in to the iron picket fence, is to find oneself suddenly transported to the very heart of Burns's world. There in the northwest corner rests Dr. Auld himself, his grave within a few feet of the house where lived Gavin Hamilton, whom Auld prosecuted for his scandalous disregard of ecclesiastical law. South of the church, but not far from its friendly shelter, "Holy Willie" sleeps under a somewhat battered stone, and nearer, perhaps, than he would have chosen to the grave of "Racer Jess." Gavin Hamilton's grave occupies the most prominent place in the churchyard—a square plot, neatly enclosed, just south of the main entrance to the church itself, where no worshipper could pass without seeing it. And northeast of the church lie the Armours, and Jean's four daughters who died in infancy.

Southeast of the churchyard, and distant from it by only the narrow width of Loudon street, stands Poosie Nansie's—Agnes Gibson's—old hostelry of questionable repute, in 1786 a haven for social outcasts who foregathered there to "Drink their orra

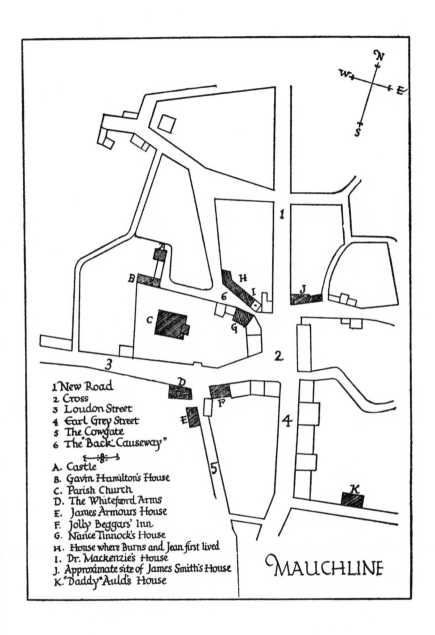

1 New Road
2 Cross
3 Loudon Street
4 Earl Grey Street
5 The Cowgate
6 The "Back" Causeway

A. Castle
B. Gavin Hamilton's House
C. Parish Church
D. The Whiteford Arms
E. James Armour's House
F. Jolly Beggars' Inn
G. Nance Tinnock's House
H. House where Burns and Jean first lived
I. Dr. Mackenzie's House
J. Approximate site of James Smith's House
K. "Daddy" Auld's House

MAUCHLINE

duddies." It is still a public house, and still owned by a Gibson. Fifteen feet to the west is Johnnie Dow's "Whitefoord Arms," in Burns's day the most pretentious of the village ale-houses, but now occupied by the Mauchline Co-operative society as a general store. Between the two is the Cowgate, up which Burns walked on his way to James Armour's home. Today it is a crooked little alley running a few rods to the southeast; in Burns's time, however, it was the chief approach to the town from the south.

At the northeast corner of the burying ground, and so close to it that there is only the narrowest of foot-paths between the iron fence and the rear of the building, stands Nanse Tinnock's home. In Burns's day it too was an ale house, conveniently provided with a rear door that opened from the second storey directly into the church yard for the benefit of "yillcaup commentators." It is an Old Ladies' Home today, but externally, at least, much the same as when Burns was living. Twenty feet from Nanse's front entrance, across Castle Street, formerly the Back Causeway and the chief thoroughfare to the north, is the house where Burns rented a room for Jean, in February, 1788, and where her second twins were born on March 3. Dr. John Mackenzie's home is next door; Smith's shop was only a few rods away. Across New Street, and around a corner, one can still discover the building in which John Richmond lodged. Indeed, it makes little difference which one of the streets that branch uncertainly out from the center of town one chooses to follow. Everywhere one finds signs of the old days, and encounters names that sound strangely familiar.[18]

In or near this little village Burns lived for three years. Here he came in contact with several men who played important rôles in his life, and who must certainly be factored into the equation by anyone attempting to understand Burns's world from 1784 to 1787.

Certainly the most prominent of these persons was William Auld (1709–1791), minister of the Parish Kirk, the "Daddy Auld" of "The Kirk's Alarm," and "Father Auld" of Burns's prefatory note to "Holy Willie's Prayer." He was a sturdy upholder of the old order, uncontaminated by the moral gospel of the Moderates, zealous in preaching, diligent in spiritual supervision, and so popular with the people of his parish that the membership of the Mauchline Kirk grew from 850 in 1771 to 1400 in 1786.[14] He was seventy-five years old when Burns moved into his parish, and for forty-two years had been minister of the established church. As presiding officer of the Kirk Session he bore the obligation of reprimanding offenders; and though there is no official record that Burns ever appeared in public before him because of the Betty Paton affair, still, if we are to believe the evidence of the "Epistle to John Rankine," it must have been Auld, as chief of the "Poacher Court," who mulcted the poet of his "gowd guinea" for that offense. Certainly it was Auld who later reprimanded Burns and Jean Armour for their misconduct.

Burns respected Auld; probably he feared him. He omitted him from the list of ministers satirized in "The Holy Fair;" when he mentioned him at all, it was without any trace of rancour. And though Auld was not remiss in reprimanding his errant parishioner, it is probable that he both understood and in a sense admired the brilliant young farmer, poet, and sinner, who was to make his parish known to the entire world.[15]

Auld's first lieutenant in parish administration was William Fisher (1737–1809), who in 1772 had become an elder of Mauchline Kirk and member of the Kirk Session. In the note which Burns later prefixed to "Holy Willie's Prayer" the poet characterized him as "a rather oldish bachelor elder in the parish of Mauchline, and much and justly famed for that polemical chattering which ends in tippling orthodoxy, and for that spiritualized bawdry which refines to liquorish devotion." He appears to have been something of a canting hypocrite, and possibly a knave; certain it is that in 1790 Auld rebuked him, officially, for intoxication; he was accused—unofficially, and probably erroneously—of stealing from the poor-box entrusted to his care; he finally froze to death beside the road one stormy February night in 1809. But had he been ten times the rascal that his worst enemies represented, he would still be remembered with gratitude by all readers of Burns, for it was he who was the hero of "Holy Willie's Prayer"—as caustic and mordant a piece of satire as ever was penned in the British Isles. When men like Fisher represented the temporal power of orthodox Calvinism, it was small wonder that rebels against the establishment were easy to find; or that a rebel like Burns, embittered by personal humiliation and by the treatment of his friend Hamilton, should have broken forth in derisive mockery.

Of an entirely different stamp from Auld and Fisher was Gavin Hamilton (1751–1805), Burns's landlord, patron, and friend. He had lived in Mauchline village since his birth in 1751. When Burns first met him he was following his father's example by serving as a "writer," or attorney; he was also collector of the civil poor fund, and was known as "the poor man's friend." His house, which still stands virtually unaltered, was near the center of the village, adjacent both to an ancient rectangular tower, popularly known as Mauchline Castle, and to the northwest corner of the churchyard.[16]

Some time before Burns moved to Mauchline parish, Hamilton had leased the farm of Mossgiel from the Earl of Loudon (patron of the parish church, and chief landowner in the district), hoping, apparently, to use it as a place of escape from the somewhat congested summer life of Mauchline. His plans miscarried, however, and he was glad to turn the farm over to Robert and Gilbert Burns on the terms that have already been stated.

One hardly need record the fact that Hamilton's uniformly helpful friendliness to Burns extended far beyond the usual courtesies which a generous landlord might show to his tenant. Burns's "Dedication to G—— H——," in the Kilmarnock volume, is ample evidence of the sympathy that existed between the two men. Moreover, the poem assigns a clear reason for Hamilton's disfavor in orthodox circles: he was one of the moderates who paid scant attention to the niceties of dogma—

As Master, Landlord, Husband, Father,
He does na fail his part in either.
But then, nae thanks to him for a' that;
Nae godly symptom can ye ca' that;
It's naething but a milder feature
Of our poor, sinfu' corrupt nature:

. . . .

That he's the poor man's friend in need,
The Gentleman in word and deed,
It's no through terror of D-mn-t-n;
It's just a carnal inclination,
And Och! that's nae r-g-n-r-t--n! [17]

In addition to being thus doctrinally unsound, Hamilton was an occasional transgressor against some of the minor regulations of the Church. From August, 1784, till July, 1785, he was involved in a dispute with the Kirk Session, which had censured him for misconduct. At once he appealed from the Session to the Presbytery of Ayr; when that court found in Hamilton's favor, the Session in turn carried the matter to the Synod of Glasgow and Ayr, which upheld the Presbytery. The questions at issue were in a sense trivial. When Hamilton was furnished with a written statement of the charges brought against him he found only these four specifications:

1. Unnecessary absence from Church two Sabbaths in Decr. and three Sabbaths in Jany. together.
2. Setting out on a journey to Carrick on the third Sabbath of Jany.
3. Habitual, if not total, neglect of family worship.
4. Abusive letter to the Session, dated 13 Novr 1784. [18]

It is apparent, however, that in undertaking to bring Hamilton to justice Auld and his colleagues felt that they were prosecuting one in whom the very spirit of ecclesiastical rebellion was incarnate; and that Hamilton, in resisting them, was equally conscious of the fact that he was opposing not the Mauchline Kirk Session, but an antiquated and tyrannical system of Church administration. That he won his case, and was declared free from all blame, speaks well for the fairness of the higher ecclesiastical courts.

Burns watched the progress of the case with keen interest; when it finally came to an end, he delighted in ridiculing Hamilton's discomfited opponents. And when the Kilmarnock volume appeared, Hamilton took forty copies for distribution among his friends—the most practical sort of evidence concerning his admiration for his poetic tenant.

One of the clerks in Hamilton's office was John Richmond (1765–1846).[19] With him Burns became more personally intimate than with Hamilton, whose social status was distinctly above that of the poet. Only six years younger than Burns, Richmond was the convivial soul in whose company Burns is traditionally believed to have been when he saw the assemblage of beggars in Poosie Nansie's. Like Burns, he was disciplined by the Mauchline Kirk Session for fornication—a fact which entitled him to function as clerk of the "Court of Equity" over which Burns represented himself as presiding. He left Mauchline in 1785 and went to Edinburgh, where at the close of 1786 he was to share with Burns his room in Baxter's Close, Lawnmarket. Still later he returned to Mauchline, married the Janet Surgeoner who had figured with him in the Session records, and lived as a relatively busy and decorous lawyer till 1846.

Burns considered Richmond his most intimate personal friend in Mauchline. In a letter of 17 February, 1786, written after Richmond had gone to Edinburgh, Burns said: "I am extremely happy with Smith; he is the only friend I have now in Mauchline."[20] When he was in trouble with the Armours, in was in Richmond that he confided;[21] when a brother of Jean Armour, on September 3, 1786, brought Burns news of the birth of Jean's twins, it was to Richmond that he first sent the news: "Wish me luck, dear Richmond! Armour has just brought me a fine boy and girl at one throw. God bless the little dears!"[22]

There is a tradition that Richmond and Burns fell out during the latter part of Burns's Edinburgh visit. If certain of the Laing Manuscripts in the University of Edinburgh Library, signed by Joseph Train, actually trace back to gossip communicated by Richmond to an unidentified "Mr. Grierson," who passed it on to Train, Richmond was neither friendly nor veracious in what he said about the poet. But the Laing MSS. should probably be disregarded entirely, or thought of only as examples of Train's misdirected ingenuity. And Richmond had best be remembered as Burns's most congenial personal friend of the first year at Mossgiel.

When Burns wrote to Richmond that he was "extremely happy with Smith," he was referring to James Smith (1765–?), linen draper in Mauchline, who had a shop nearly opposite to Nanse Tinnock's Inn. Burns's associations with Smith seem to have been almost as intimate as those with Richmond. Smith had the honor of being addressed by Burns in not the least successful of his poetic epistles,[23] from the phraseology of which it is clear that the two men were on terms of unreserved intimacy. When the trouble with Jean was distracting him, it was through Smith that Burns sent word to Jean that he would meet her, "So help me Heaven in my hour of need."[24] It was to Smith that Burns, in a confidential moment, wrote the sentence which even his most consistent apologists find it hard to read without regret:

I am an old hawk at the sport, and wrote her such a cool, deliberate, prudent reply, as brought my bird from her aerial towerings, pop down at my foot, like Corporal Trim's hat.[25]

When Burns and Jean acknowledged themselves to be married, in the spring of 1788, it was in a letter to Smith that Burns made the first reference to the fact:

There is, you must know, a certain clean-limbed, handsome, bewitching young hussy of your acquaintance, to whom I have lately and privately given a matrimonial title to my corpus. . . . I intend to present Mrs. Burns with a printed shawl, an article of which I daresay you have variety: 'tis my first present to her since I have *irrevocably* called her mine, and I have a kind of whimsical wish to get the said

[112]

first present from an old and much-valued friend of hers and mine, a trusty Trojan, on whose friendship I count myself possessed of a life-rent lease.[26]

Like Richmond, Smith left Mauchline soon after his friendship with Burns had begun, under censure of the Kirk Session. For an undetermined period he lived at Linlithgow, where he was in business; he then emigrated to Jamaica, where he died— no one knows just when. But as in the case of Richmond, his later years are of scant interest to the student of Burns. The important fact is that Smith, Richmond, and Burns formed a happy triumvirate in village revelry, till offenses against the decorum of Mauchline society sent two of the three into other parts of the kingdom.

It was also at Mauchline that Burns became really acquainted with the first of the many physicians who were to figure more or less prominently in his life,[27] Dr. John Mackenzie (?1759– 1837). He was exactly Burns's age, an enthusiastic Mason, and one of Gavin Hamilton's intimate friends. A letter from his pen, published as an appendix to Josiah Walker's biography in the Morison Edition of Burns's poems,[28] indicates that Mackenzie first saw Burns when he had been called to Lochlie to attend the poet's dying father.

When Burns suffered a serious physical breakdown in the summer of 1784, it was Mackenzie who attended him. Still later, when the Kilmarnock volume had been published, Mackenzie helped his friend by introducing him to Professor Dugald Stewart,[29] Sir John Whitefoord, and Henry Erskine, and by showing Dr. Hugh Blair some parts, at least, of the poet's work. In a letter of 1 December, 1786, Burns referred to Mackenzie as his "very warm and worthy friend;" and though only a few communications seem to have passed between the two men after Burns left Mauchline, it is certain that the phrase indicates truthfully the nature of their relationship.[30] Like Burns, Mackenzie was an ardent Mason. He wrote pamphlets on controversial subjects, under the signature "Common Sense," and was a keen observer of contemporary life. More important, however, is

[113]

the fact that he was a friend of the entire Burns family, and did perhaps as much as anyone to make the poet's subsequent entry into Edinburgh easy and successful.

But the man who fairly earned the title of Burns's first and most influential patron was Robert Aiken (1739–1807), a resident not of Mauchline but of Ayr. He was twenty years older than the poet, a distinguished lawyer, and the Surveyor of Taxes for Ayrshire to whom on February 22, 1786, Burns sent his poetic "Inventory" of his possessions. He acted as Gavin Hamilton's attorney when the dispute with the Mauchline Kirk Session reached the Presbytery. As a result he figures in "Holy Willie's Prayer" as "that glib-tongued Aiken" who had brought discredit to both minister and elder, and also as "Orator Bob" in "The Kirk's Alarm." He enjoyed exercising his very considerable elocutionary powers, and according to the poet's own statement, "read [him] into fame."

When the Kilmarnock Edition was published, Aiken himself disposed of 145 copies—nearly a quarter of the entire edition. Within a few weeks of the appearance of the volume he was influential in starting the movement which ultimately gave Burns his position in the Excise. When the poet went up to Edinburgh, it was with two of Aiken's friends, Creech and Smellie, that he arranged for the publication of the 1787 edition—a fact which Burns communicated to Aiken in a letter headed "Dear patron of my Virgin Muse." The only suggestion of a rift in the friendship between the two men came at the time of the trouble with the Armours, when, according to Burns, "old Mr. Armour prevailed with [Aiken] to mutilate that unlucky paper." [31] In other words, so Burns at least believed, it was Aiken who destroyed whatever written document Burns had given Jean. But if the incident caused Burns some pain at first, he quickly recovered his poise; and Aiken's subsequent devotion to his interests left no doubt that among those friends who were not of the poet's own social class, he was one of the staunchest. When Burns dedicated the "Cotter's Saturday Night" to him, he was anticipating the extent of his indebtedness to Aiken.

[114]

Several other friends whom Burns made at this period of his life lived, like Aiken, not in Mauchline but in nearby towns. There was, for instance, the Reverend John M'Math (d. 1825), assistant to Dr. Wodrow in the Parish Kirk at Tarbolton. Somewhat more liberal than his superior in the charge, and untainted with any suggestion of the ecclesiastical hypocrisy which Burns particularly disliked, he was the sort of preacher who could request a manuscript copy of "Holy Willie's Prayer"—and have his request granted. There is no evidence that Burns and M'Math ever met after Burns went up to Edinburgh; indeed, they do not appear at any time to have been on terms of personal intimacy. But it is worth noting that the young farmer's circle of acquaintances included a clergyman of M'Math's standing and general disposition, and that Burns knew him well enough to address one of his poetical epistles to him.[32]

In Kilmarnock lived two persons who must be included in this brief survey of Burns's friends—John Goldie (1717–1809?) and Robert Muir (1758–1788). The former was a wine merchant who had abandoned the ranks of orthodoxy, and had signalized his defection by publishing *Essays on Various Subjects, Moral and Divine*[33]—a work so widely read, and so telling in its attack upon theological bigotry, that it was popularly called "Goldie's Bible." When to this first work he added, six years later, *The Gospel Recovered*, he found himself hailed as the chief opponent not only of the more conservative branches of the Presbyterian Church, but of the entire group of literalistic interpreters of the Scriptures. There is still current the tradition that Goldie called on Burns at Mossgiel, heard him read some of his poems, and arranged for him to meet various Kilmarnock folk who might aid him in publishing his work. Actual evidence, however, is lacking; it seems more probable that Burns's acquaintance with Goldie began in 1785 after the publication of *The Gospel Recovered*, to which the poet referred in the subtitle of the "Epistle to John Goldie." In any case the vigorous stanzas of this poem show that Burns admired Goldie for his attack upon "sour bigotry;" they do not indicate any special

[115]

degree of personal friendship. Incidentally, it is notable that this poem, dated August, 1785, was among the earliest of Burns's satires on orthodox Calvinism. It was mild, in comparison with some which were to follow; nevertheless the touch was there: the instinct to single out the weakest spot in his opponent's armor, the telling personal allusion which adds point to the more general satire, the vigorous phrase, and the brilliantly successful metre.

Robert Muir was an acquaintance of a different character, though like Goldie a wine merchant by vocation. Born one year before Burns, he died of tuberculosis on April 22, 1788, but had made such an impression on Burns that shortly after his death the poet wrote thus about him to Mrs. Dunlop:

> Muir, thy weaknesses were the aberrations of Human-nature, but thy heart glowed with everything generous, manly, & noble; and if ever emanation from the All-Good Being animated a human form, it was thine! [34]

Turning through the extant letters from Burns to Muir, one discovers that between March and September of 1786 their friendship grew so rapidly that by the latter date Burns was addressing Muir as "My friend, my brother." Muir subscribed for seventy-two copies of the Kilmarnock edition; he was later to take forty of the first Edinburgh. He was one of the first to whom Burns reported the birth of Jean's twins; the first published reference to the proposed Edinburgh visit is found in a letter to Muir; when Burns had begun to settle himself into the life of the capital, it was to Muir that he wrote of his experiences. Similarly, while on the Highland tour in the summer of 1787, Burns sent one of his pleasant journal-letters to his friend at home. Finally, when Muir was far gone with consumption— indeed, less than two months before his death—Burns wrote to him in a vein of cheerful seriousness concerning the future:

> Now that I hope to settle with some credit and comfort at home, there was not any friendship or friendly correspondence that promised me more pleasure than yours— I hope I will not be disappointed.— I

trust the Spring will renew your shattered frame and make your friends happy.— You and I have often agreed that life is no great blessing on the whole.— The close of life indeed, to a reasoning eye, is

> Dark as was Chaos, ere the infant sun
> Was roll'd together, or had try'd his beams
> Athwart the gloom profound—

But an honest man has nothing to fear.— If we lie down in the grave, the whole man a piece of broke machinery, to moulder with the clods of the valley—be it so; at least there is an end of pain, care, woes and wants: if that part of us called Mind, does survive the apparent destruction of the man . . . a man, conscious of having acted an honest part among his fellow-creatures; even granting that he may have been the sport, at times, of passion and instincts; he goes to a great unknown Being who could have no other end in giving him existence but to make him happy; who gave him those passions and instincts, and well knows their force.[35]

Taken all in all, it makes a pleasant story, this friendship between the young farmer and the wine merchant of the nearby town, especially as one sees the business man helping his friend make a little money through the sale of his poems, and the poet pausing in his labors to write encouragingly to the dying merchant.

Such were some of the men whom Burns knew while he lived at Mossgiel. They came from no one social group, but represented, in a sense, a cross-section of Scottish town life—the clergy, both orthodox and liberal, the lawyers and physicians, the independent merchants and store keepers, the clerks. With all of them Burns had something in common; all of them respected him; many of them loved him. His genius for friendship showed perhaps to best advantage during the months when he was in intimate contact with these men, sharing their recreations, observing their "fauts and follies," but also delighting in their stalwart virtues, turning to them for aid and counsel when he was in trouble, and in the end immortalizing them by the magic touch of his pen.

[117]

3

THREE LOVERS OF BURNS

And then there were the lasses. Burns had believed himself
to be in love before the Mossgiel period opened; no serious results, however, had attended any of the early affairs. But during his brief tenancy of this farm he found himself deeply involved with three young women of the neighborhood. These
three incidents make so important a chapter in Burns's history that
it will be well to consider each one separately.

Elizabeth Paton

As has already been pointed out, Elizabeth Paton was a servant
in the household of William Burnes. Within a few months
after his death (13 February, 1784) her love for Robert, who
was no longer under the restraining influence of his father, led
her to give herself to him on terms which involved no promise
of marriage, but which ultimately involved her in trouble all
too common among her class in eighteenth century Scotland.
When the family moved to Mossgiel, in the spring of 1784, she
returned to her home at Largieside, where Burns continued to
visit her. In the autumn her difficulty became a matter of local
gossip. John Rankine, whose company Burns had enjoyed
during the later years at Lochlie, seems to have twitted Burns
over the situation. The result was, first, a negligible pair of
stanzas, "To John Rankine in Reply to an Announcement," [36]
and, second, and much more significant, the "Epistle to John
Rankine." [37] Burns rarely wrote with more *verve* than when
composing the thirteen stanzas of this clever but blackguardly
epistle. Never again was he to be so successful in this vein.
But the importance of the poem, for the student, is its statement,
if one accepts the epistle at its face value, that Burns and Elizabeth Paton were disciplined by the church authorities for their
misdeeds. There is no indication in the extant records of Mauch-

[118]

line parish that either of the two came under official censure at this time; nevertheless Burns is unequivocal in saying that he had been before the "Poacher Court," and had been fined a guinea.[38]

Whether or not Burns actually had to "thole the blethers" of the Kirk Session, or whether his indignation against the poacher court was as yet unfounded on personal experience, is hard to determine. But by the time the Epistle was written—the late autumn of 1784—he was being pointed out as a sinner, and he had made the discovery that certain of his pious critics were no better than they should be; all of which, in view of the satirical powers that were just beginning to be aroused in him, might have given some of the "lads in black" occasion for thought!

But by the middle of November, the bravado which had expressed itself in the "Epistle to John Rankine" had all filtered out. In a letter to his old harvest-field companion Thomas Orr, Burns lets one see something of his real state of mind:

> I am at present so cursedly taken in with an affair of gallantry that I am very glad Peggy is off my hand as I am at present embarrassed enough without her.—I don't chuse to enter into particulars in writing but never was a poor rakish rascal in a more pitiful taking.[39]

There is little of the hardened sinner in these sentences; on the contrary, Burns was anything but happy as he looked forward to the birth of his first child. This event, as has already been pointed out, took place on May 22, 1785; two days later the child was baptized, and was admitted by Burns to be his daughter. Not long afterwards Burns wrote "A Poet's Welcome to his Love-begotten Daughter," the wistful sincerity of which is in sharp contrast with the broad humor of the "Epistle to Rankine." The poem is good evidence of the strength of Burns's parental affections. He loved his children, however much they may at times have complicated his situation; he never expressed this love more convincingly than when thus acknowledging his first-born.[40]

Such is the story of Burns's relations to Elizabeth Paton. The incident signalized Burns's departure from the mode of life in which he had been nurtured; and when once he had lived through the emotional perturbation occasioned by the affair, and had found that life continued to move in its regular channels, despite what some of his neighbors may have said of him —why, from that time forth it became easier for him to offend. His own words fit the case better than any one else's:

> I waive the quantum o' the sin,
> The hazard of concealing;
> But, och! it hardens a' within
> And petrifies the feeling.[41]

For Burns, the experience with Elizabeth Paton marked the beginning of the hardening process.

Jean Armour

It is obvious that the entire account of Jean Armour (1765–1834) and Robert Burns should not be compressed into any one chapter of this chronicle. From 1785 till the end of the story his entire life was enwrapped with hers. But the beginning of their eleven or twelve years of intimacy lies in the Mossgiel period; moreover, the events of the first two years of their acquaintanceship were in a sense the most important elements in Burns's life at Mossgiel.

The young woman who was to become Burns's wife was one of the eleven children of James Armour, a master mason and contractor, and one of Mauchline's respected citizens. According to the parish register, she was born on February 25, 1765; [42] her early years were all spent under her father's roof in Mauchline village. Naturally enough there is no real evidence as to when she and Burns first saw one another. The well-known tradition which makes a dance held at the close of April, 1784, the occasion of their first meeting, may possibly be founded on fact. Both Burns and Jean were fond of such affairs; she was a handsome girl of nineteen years, whom the poet could not have overlooked in any company; he was the sort of man whom all women, of whatever station in life, were sure to observe. In any case the two must have become acquainted not long after the poet's family moved into the Mossgiel farmhouse, for it was rapidly becoming habitual for Burns to seek the company of the lasses, and Jean was one of the "Belles of Mauchline."

It is also purely a matter of conjecture as to how fast their friendship developed. During the autumn of 1784 Burns was worried by his responsibility for Betty Paton's unhappy condition; the birth of her daughter, in May of 1785, could hardly have failed to serve as something of an anchor for Burns's affections. But it did not take him long to be "aff wi' the auld love;" the summer of 1785 must have seen him more and more constantly in the company of Jean, and before the close of the year their intimacy had taken a form which made discovery and disgrace inevitable.

When the situation became clear, in the late winter of 1785–6, Burns's first impulse was to marry Jean. A letter to Gavin Hamilton,[43] and the introductory sentences of the letter to Arnot,[44] indicate that he would have taken this step, had the attitude of Jean and her family been different. By June, to be sure, he had changed his mind; [45] but until Jean "rejected" him and her family turned against him, he was willing and eager to make her his wife.

Indeed, he may already have done so, though possibly without realizing it. It is beyond dispute that Burns gave Jean some sort of written document intended to render her offense less heinous in the eyes of her parents. This may actually have been an acknowledgement of private marriage; it may have been merely a promise of marriage. If the former, if Burns and Jean had actually accepted one another as man and wife, even in the strictest privacy, and without the presence of witnesses, then they were legally though irregularly married, *per verba de presenti*. If the latter, then too, in all probability, they were man and wife; for a promise to marry, sealed by anticipatory consummation, constitutes in Scottish law a true and valid marriage.[46]   It is clear enough in this case that the consummation took place, certainly before and, *a priori*, after the paper was drawn up.   The probability, then, seems overwhelming that this fact, in conjunction with whatever acknowledgment or promise Burns gave Jean, did indeed make them man and wife.[47]

Whether or not Burns and Jean at this time thought themselves to be married, is a moot question, hardly to be answered today when the all-important document is no longer in existence.   But this at least is clear: Jean had in her possession a paper which seemed in some very real way to mitigate the gravity of her offense.   With it in her hands she told her parents of her condition, only to be met by such anger as compelled her to surrender the precious document to her father.   Shortly thereafter James Armour, unwilling to have his daughter bound in any way to a penniless farmer already burdened with one illegitimate child and in disfavor with the orthodox because of his "principles," "prevailed with [Mr. Aiken of Ayr] to mutilate that unlucky paper," as Burns himself put it.[48]   He believed that by so doing he had annulled the contract—whatever its nature—between Burns and his daughter, and had assured her status as a single woman.   That he had not, that the destruction of the paper had in law no effect upon the married state of the two principals, is a matter of only theoretical interest.   At least from the time of James Armour's act both Burns and Jean believed themselves to be single persons, and comported themselves accordingly.

When Armour thus chose for his daughter the disgrace of unmarried motherhood in preference to any alliance with Burns, Jean herself was living at Paisley, with Andrew Purdie, her uncle.   Possibly she had fled from her father's anger; possibly her mother had sent her away with the hope of avoiding the gossip and scandal that must inevitably result if she remained at home.   The mischief had already been done, however. News of her plight soon reached the Kirk Session, which, as in duty bound, took cognizance of the unhappy situation.   The minutes concerning the matter are of interest not merely in connection with Burns and Jean, but also as first-hand evidence of the methods by which the church maintained its authority:

April 2, 1786. The Session being informed that Jean Armour, an unmarried woman, is said to be with child, and that she has gone off from the place of late, to reside elsewhere, the Session think it their duty to enquire . . . But appoint James Lamie and William Fisher to speak to the parents.

April 9, 1786. James Lamie reports that he spoke to Mary Smith, mother to Jean Armour, who told him that she did not suspect her daughter to be with child, that she was gone to Paisley to see her friends, and would return soon.

June 18, 1786. Jean Armour, called, compeared not, but sent a letter directed to the minister, the tenor whereof follows:—"I am heartily sorry that I have given and must give your Session trouble on my account. I acknowledge that I am with child, and Robert Burns in Mossgiel is the father. I am, with great respect, your most humble servant,

JEAN ARMOUR.

Machlin, 13 June 1786." [49]

Thus Jean admitted her fault, and waited docilely for the public reproof which church law and custom made inevitable. She had come home from Paisley only nine days before the Session received her letter—come home to find Burns planning to exile himself to Jamaica, and possibly to discover that he was in love with another woman, whom he had promised to marry. But she made no claim upon him as her husband; on the contrary, she admitted herself, by implication at least, to be unmarried.

Burns, meantime, seems to have been more perturbed than Jean. He appeared before the Session on June 25, and acknowledged his responsibility in the matter. He realized that he might be legally married to Jean, despite the mutilation of the "unlucky paper." He considered himself ill-treated by the Armours; he was piqued by their refusal of him as a son-in-law; he felt that Jean had "deserted" him. Moreover, he seems to have heard that Jean, during her stay in Paisley, had

[123]

become acquainted with a young man named Robert Wilson; he may even have believed that she was planning to marry him. A letter to David Brice of Glasgow, one of Burns's intimate friends, tells so much concerning his state of mind that the larger part must be quoted entire. The letter is dated from Mossgiel, 12 June, 1786:

DEAR BRICE:

. . . Poor ill-advised, ungrateful, Armour came home on friday last.—You have heard all the particulars of that affair; and a black affair it is.—What she thinks of her conduct now, I don't know; one thing I know, she has made me compleatly miserable.—Never man lov'd, or rather ador'd, a woman more than I did her; and, to confess a truth between you and me, I do still love her to distraction after all, tho' I won't tell her so, tho' I see her, which I don't want to do.—My poor, dear, unfortunate Jean! How happy have I been in her arms!— It is not the losing her that makes me so unhappy; but for *her* sake I feel most severely.—I foresee that she is in the road to, I am afraid, *eternal* ruin; and those who made so much noise, and showed so much grief, at the thought of her being *my wife*, may, some day, see her connected in such a manner as may give them more real cause of vexation.—I am sure I do not wish it: may Almighty God forgive her ingratitude and perjury to me, as I from my very soul forgive her! and may His grace be with her, and bless her in all her future life!—I can have no nearer idea of the place of eternal punishment than what I have felt in my own breast on her account.—I have tryed often to forget her: I have run into all kinds of dissipation and riot, Mason-meetings, drinking matches, and other mischief, to drive her out of my head, but all in vain: and now for a grand cure: the Ship is on her way home that is to take me out to Jamaica; and then, farewell dear old Scotland, and farewell dear, ungrateful Jean! for never, never, will I see you more.[50]

A curious letter—containing no suggestion of self-reproach, but blaming the girl as if she alone had been responsible for the unhappy turn of events.

All the facts concerning Burns's proposed trip to Jamaica, referred to in the letter to Brice, will probably never be known. Even the reasons that prompted him to plan the voyage are not clear. Possibly he wished to establish himself overseas in such a position that he could marry and support a family. Possibly he looked to Jamaica as a haven of refuge from James Armour's wrath and the noise of wagging tongues in Mauchline. The most specific information he himself seems to have vouchsafed is contained in a letter to James Smith, written on August 14, 1786. In it he explains that he is not sailing to Savannah-la-Mar in the brig *Nancy*, as he had proposed to do, but that on the first of September he will take ship directly to Port Antonio, where Charles Douglas's estate was located.[51] Apparently Burns was planning to act as bookkeeper for this gentleman, whom he terms "my master," at a salary of £30 per year. There is no evidence that he seriously considered indenting himself to pay for the passage, although his own statement to this effect[52] has been given wide currency.

Between the time of the letter to Brice concerning Jean, June 12, and that to Smith about Jamaica, August 14, Burns suffered the humiliation of three public penitential appearances in the Kirk. On July 9 he wrote thus to Richmond:

> I have waited on Armour since her return home; not, by——, from any the least view of reconciliation, but merely to ask for her health; and—to you I will confess it, from a foolish hankering fondness—very ill-plac'd indeed.—The Mother forbade me the house; nor did Jean show that penitence that might have been expected.—However the Priest, I am informed, will give me a Certificate as a single man, if I comply with the rules of the Church, which for that very reason I intend to do.—
>
> I am just going to put on Sackcloth & ashes this day.—I am indulged so far as to appear in my own seat. *Peccavi, Pater; miser[er]e mei.*[53]

That Burns was allowed to stand in his own pew, and not in the public "place of repentance," is of some interest. It is also worth recounting that Jean's family wished him to stand beside her, but Dr. Auld forbade it. A letter to Brice, written July 17, records this feature of the penitential exercise:

I have already appeared publickly in Church, and was indulged in the liberty of standing in my own seat.—I do this to get a certificate as a bachelor, which Mr. Auld has promised me.—I am now fixed to go for the West Indies in October.—Jean and her friends insisted much that she should stand along with me in the kirk, but the minister would not allow it, which bred a great t[rouble, I as]sure you, and I am blamed as the cause of it, tho' I am su[re] I am innocent; but I am very well pleased, for [all] that, not to have had her company.[54]

On August 6 Burns and Jean, in company with three other similar offenders, made the third and last of their public appearances, listened to Auld's formal rebuke, and were "absolved from the scandal," so far as ecclesiastical law was concerned. The minister's words were succinct and to the point, though, as it later developed, not efficacious enough to turn the two young sinners from their evil ways:

You appear there to be rebuked, and at the same time making profession of repentence for the sin of fornication.

The frequency of this sin is just matter of lamentation among Christians, and affords just ground of deep humiliation to the guilty persons themselves.

We call you to reflect seriously in contrition of heart on all the instances of your sin and guilt, in their numbers, high aggravation, and unhappy consequences, and say, having done foolishly, we'll do so no more.

Beware of returning to your sin as some of you have done, like the dog to his vomit, or like the sow that is washed to her wallowing in the mire. [55]

Thus Burns and Jean felt the displeasure of the Kirk, and paid the penalty exacted by its ordinances.

The civil law, however, was still to be reckoned with. James Armour had no desire to accept Burns as a son-in-law; neither did he propose to see the man who had brought disgrace upon his family slip quietly away to Jamaica, leaving the expected child unprovided for. Consequently, knowing that Burns was about to publish a volume of poems from which he might derive some profit, Armour took the steps necessary to obtain security in a capital sum for the child's support. He persuaded Jean, against her will, to sign a complaint, with the result that a warrant was soon issued against Burns. He, however, had anticipated this legal action by executing a deed of trust to his brother Gilbert, conveying to him all his property, including "the profits that may arise from the Publication of my Poems presently in the Press," and also giving to him, as trustee for Burns's daughter Elizabeth Paton, "the Copyright of said Poems:" all this in order that Gilbert might make good his agreement to "aliment clothe and educate my [natural daughter Elizabeth Paton] in a suitable manner as if she was his own." [56]

Having thus put his property beyond the reach of James Armour, Burns virtually went into hiding to escape service of the warrant—probably the useful writ *in meditatione fugae*. A despairing letter to Richmond, written from Old Rome Foord on July 30, 1786, tells much of the poet's state of mind, as well as of his plans:

My Dr Richmond,

My hour is now come—You and I will never meet in Britain more.— I have orders within three weeks at farthest to repair aboard the *Nancy*, Capn. Smith, from Clyde, to Jamaica, and to call at Antigua.—This, except to our friend Smith, whom God long preserve, is a secret about Mauchlin.[57]—Would you believe it? Armour has got a warrant to throw me in jail till I find security for an enormous sum.—This they keep an entire secret, but I got it by a channel they little dream of; [58] and I am wandering from one friend's house to another, and like a true son of the gospel, "have no where to lay my head."—I know you will pour an execration on her head, but spare the poor ill-advised girl for my sake; tho' may all the Furies that rend the injured enraged Lover's bosom, await the old harridan, her Mother, until her latest hour! May Hell string the arm of Death to throw the fatal dart, and all the winds of warring elements rouse the infernal flames to welcome her approach! For Heaven's sake burn this letter, and never show it to a living creature. —I write it in a moment of rage, reflecting on my miserable situation— exiled, abandoned, forlorn. I can write no more—let me hear from you by the return of Connel—I will write you ere I go.[59]

[127]

The day after this letter was written, Burns's first book, *Poems, Chiefly in the Scottish Dialect,* was published. The story of this memorable volume is to be told later on; it is enough for the present to record the fact that as fame came to Burns, fame and a reasonable amount of money, James Armour's wrath became less violent. Writing to Richmond, on the first of September, Burns said:

I am under little apprehension now about Armour.—The warrant is still in existence, but some of the first Gentlemen in the county have offered to befriend me; and besides, Jean will not take any step against me, without letting me know, as nothing but the most violent menaces could have forced her to sign the petition. . . . She would gladly now embrace that offer she once rejected, but it shall never more be in her power.[60]

Consequently the poet returned to the farm at Mossgiel to live his accustomed life till the time should be ripe for emigration to the West Indies. Here he was found on Sunday evening, September 3, by a brother of Jean's, who had come out from the village to tell him that his sister had just given birth to twins. The Mauchline parish Register contains the following entry:

Burns, Robert, Tenant in Mossgiel, and Jean Armour had twin children, Born 3d., and Baptized 5th Sept.; called Robert and Jean.[61]

Thus ended the opening chapter in the history of Robert Burns and Jean Armour. That at first he loved her sincerely, and later continued to love her, despite what he considered her illtreatment of him, is obvious. Such melancholy verses as "The Lament," "Despondency," "To Ruin," and "Song, Composed in Spring," all of them written at this time, evidence the fact that his depression over his "rejection" was deep-seated. That he had been willing to marry her, indeed, that he believed he had taken some steps towards marrying her by giving her the "unlucky paper," is equally certain. Nevertheless any one who reads the record carefully will see that during the summer of 1786 Burns looked forward with eagerness to receiving his certificate of bachelorhood, and that by the time he had received absolution from the Church he had abandoned all thought of marrying Jean. He wished only to leave the country, and to have his status as a single man unquestioned. Hence the preparations for Jamaica, and the docile submission to church discipline. At the same time he was in no sense a happy man, even after the publication of the Kilmarnock edition had brought him fame and money. As late as October he wrote thus to his friend Robert Aiken:

I have for some time been pining under secret wretchedness, from causes which you pretty well know—the pang of disappointment, the sting of pride, with some wandering stabs of remorse, which never fail to settle on my vitals like vultures, when attention is not called away by the calls of society, or the vagaries of the Muse. Even in the hour of social mirth, my gaiety is the madness of an intoxicated criminal under the hands of the executioner.[62]

The reason for this perturbation is hard to discover until one remembers that the months from April to October of 1786 were the months when Burns was harassed not only by the results of his intimacy with Jean, but also by the fact that he had at this very time promised to marry another girl, Mary Campbell, the "Highland Mary" of song and legend. The story of Burns and Mary Campbell is the third of the three major episodes in the love-life of the young poet.

Mary Campbell

So much has been written concerning Burns and Mary Campbell (?–1786) that it may appear a work of supererogation to do more than re-tell the story, as it is to be found in such a standard biography as that, say, of Chambers-Wallace. But even in the chronicle of these conservative and dependable scholars there is much unverifiable gossip and tradition interwoven with a small amount of ascertainable fact. The result is an account of such a nature as to leave the reader constantly bewildered, and

[129]

uncertain, when he comes to the end of the tale, as to whether any element of it can be unquestioningly believed. Hence it seems desirable, even at the risk of some repetition, to set forth at this point what can fairly be called the orthodox and dependable evidence in the case, then to reconstruct the story of the two persons, as best one may, on the basis of these facts, and finally to present one not unimportant piece of relatively new evidence, of which all except the most recent of Burns's biographers have been ignorant.

The most trustworthy anchor to windward on which the student of Burns and Highland Mary can rely is this: early in the nineteenth century, long before the mythmakers had begun their work with Burns, Greenock tradition unhesitatingly identified the grave in which a girl named Mary Campbell had been buried, and, furthermore, knew her to have been the Highland Mary of Burns's lyrics. For proof one need only cite a minute of the Greenock Burns Club:

> 23d Feb. 1803. It was unanimously decided to request permission from Mr. M'Pherson to allow the Club to add a tablet to the memory of Mary Campbell on his lairs.[63]

Who Peter M'Pherson was, and how related to the young woman buried in his plot, or "lair," is of little moment.[64] It is enough to point out that in 1803 the Greenock Burns Club felt no uncertainty concerning the various matters involved in their request. The woman buried in M'Pherson's lair was Mary Campbell, and Mary Campbell, as the subsequently erected monument made clear, was "Highland Mary."

It should be particularly borne in mind that this action of the Greenock Club was taken long before the biographers had made capital out of the Highland Mary episode. By 1803 only Heron's and Currie's lives of Burns had been published; Heron did not mention the incident at all; Currie treated it briefly and cryptically. The information which lay behind the request of the Greenock Burns Club did not trace back to any biographer; it rested upon what must have been common knowledge in

Greenock; and common knowledge, when it is well established within seven years of the death of one of the two principals in such a story, is weighty authority.

A second substantial fact which emerges from the haze of conjecture is a Bible in two volumes, published at Edinburgh in 1782 by Alex Kincaid, and now preserved in the poet's monument at Ayr. On the end-papers are inscriptions—the most important elements of which, the proper names, have unfortunately been rendered virtually illegible—which suggest, but do not prove, that Burns once gave the Bible to some one whose first name began with "M", and that he was eager to convince that person of the sanctity of promises.[65] "Thou shalt not forswear thyself," he had written, "but shalt perform unto the Lord thine oath"—and more to the same effect upon the other fly-leaf. These Biblical quotations escaped the mutilation which overtook the proper names, and still remain to prove that Burns held the pen which traced them.

To connect this Bible with Mary Campbell, buried in the Old West Kirkyard at Greenock, is not an easy task. The Bible first attracted general notice in 1840, when it came to light in the town of Caledon, fifty miles east of Toronto, Canada. Here it was in the possession of a William Anderson, believed to have been a nephew of Mary Campbell. Shortly after its discovery, the Bible was returned to Scotland, and deposited in the Ayr monument.[66]

At least two pieces of evidence antedating the discovery at Caledon serve to connect the Bible with Burns and Mary. On page 81 of the first (1828) edition of Lockhart's *Life of Burns* one reads of "the accidental discovery of a Bible, presented by Burns to Mary Campbell, in the possession of her still surviving sister at Ardrossan." There then follows an accurate copy of the inscriptions still legible in the Bible.

One apparently hitherto unnoted piece of evidence antedates Lockhart. Among the entries in the Bills of Mortality included in the *Gentleman's Magazine* for October, 1827, appears the following:

Scotland, Sept. 27, at Greenock, aged 85, the mother of Burns's "Highland Mary." Among the little stores of the deceased, there was nothing to be found as mementoes of the gifted bard, but the Bible which he gave to his beloved Mary on that day when they met by the banks of Ayr. . . . It has written on the first leaf in Burns's handwriting . . . "Thou shalt not forswear thyself, but perform unto the Lord thine oaths." It is to be regretted that two letters which he wrote after her death to the afflicted mother have been destroyed; the old woman said she could never read them without tears.[67]

Such a paragraph, in such a place, seems good evidence concerning the problem under discussion. Taken in connection with the minute of the Greenock Burns Club, it goes far towards proving that Mary Campbell, or "Highland Mary," died in Greenock; was buried in the Old West Kirkyard; and left with her family, as souvenir of her friendship with Burns, a Bible inscribed as is the Bible now in the Ayr monument. Indeed, that this Ayr Bible is the one actually given by Burns to Highland Mary, seems as well established as any matter of the sort can be.

A third piece of what may be called external evidence, is found in a letter from George Thomson to Burns, written in November, 1792. After commenting on some of the songs Burns had sent for publication in the *Select Scotish Airs*, Thomson added a post-script;

P. S. Your verses upon "Highland Mary" are just come to hand: they breathe the genuine spirit of poetry and, like the music, will last for ever. Such verses, united to such an air, with the delicate harmony of Pleyel superadded, might form a treat worthy of being presented to Apollo himself. I have heard the sad story of your Mary: you always seem inspired when you write of her.[68]

It is probable that Burns and Thomson never met; it is beyond dispute that they were never intimate personal acquaintances. None the less Thomson had heard the story of Mary Campbell —obviously from the lips of some mutual acquaintance. There is nothing in Thomson's letter to indicate the nature of the "sad story;" his remark, however, effectively disposes of the suggestion that the Highland Lassie never existed at all, but was a creature of Burns's brain: "an ideal of womanhood to which his thought ascended from the mire of this world . . . as Dante's to his Beatrice of dream." [69]

So far as actual evidence is concerned, this is virtually all that has been brought forward, outside of the writings of Burns himself, as basis for the story of the poet and his Highland love. There is, of course, a vast amount of futile and unsubstantiated gossip—how much, only one who has investigated the matter can even conjecture. But piece by piece it proves to be of no significance; hence the entire mass had best be disregarded.

Turning to Burns's own work, one finds nine documents, of varying degrees of interest and importance, which may reasonably be interpreted as referring to the Highland Mary episode. Arranged in chronological order, in so far as this order can be determined, they are these:

1. A song, "My Highland Lassie." [70] The song was first published in 1788, in vol. II of the *Museum*; it was probably written in the spring of 1786.

All that the song tells the reader is that when Burns was looking to the Indies he had apparently promised to marry a Highland Lassie. Burns's note on this insignificant composition, however, is of great importance in the case; for when read in connection with the lyric it dates Burns's parting from "Highland Mary" as having taken place on the second Sunday of May, 1786:

The Highland Lassie, O. This was a composition of mine in very early life, before I was known at all in the world.[71] My Highland lassie was a warm-hearted, charming young creature as ever blessed a man with generous love. After a pretty long tract of the most ardent reciprocal attachment, we met by appointment, on the second Sunday of May, in a sequestered spot by the banks of Ayr, where we spent the day in taking fare[w]el, before she should embark for the West Highlands to arrange matters among her friends for our projected change of life. At the close of Autumn following she crossed the sea to meet me at

Greenock, where she had scarce landed when she was seized with a malignant fever, which hurried my dear girl to the grave in a few days, before I could even hear of her illness.[72]

This indefinite and somewhat equivocal note first appeared in Cromek's *Reliques*, in a section transcribed—"the most part, at least," said Cromek—from the interleaved copy of the *Musical Museum* which Burns had prepared some time before 1794 for his friend Robert Riddell of Glenriddell. For exactly one hundred years it was accepted as perhaps the most significant point of departure for all discussions concerning Highland Mary. Then, with the publication of James C. Dick's *Notes on Scottish Song by Robert Burns*,[73] the world of scholarship was aghast to learn that no such entry was to be found in the interleaved *Museum*, the original of which Dick had succeeded in discovering, or ever had been there. That Cromek had forged it was the easy conclusion.

Fortunately for everyone concerned, however, Mr. Davidson Cook and Professor J. De L. Ferguson have recently rehabilitated Cromek's reputation,[74] and it is again possible to accept the note as Burns's, not Cromek's.

Reduced to their lowest terms, then, the song and accompanying note tell of Burns's love for a Highland girl, of their intent to marry, of their parting on the second Sunday of May in the year when he was planning a trip to the West Indies, and of her death the following autumn. In other words, these two documents give a reasonably complete outline of the entire episode.

2. A song, "Will ye go to the Indies, my Mary."[75] This song was first published by Currie (1800), though it had been sent to Thomson in a letter dated October 26, 1792. The following comment by Burns accompanied the text:

In my very early years, when I was thinking of going to the West Indies, I took the following farewell of a dear girl. . . . You must know that all my earlier love-songs were the breathings of ardent Passion, & tho' it might have been easy in aftertimes to give them a polish, yet that polish, to me, whose they were, & who perhaps alone cared

[134]

for them, would have defaced the legend of the heart, which was so faithfully inscribed on them.[76]

The only new element here is the proper name Mary. All the rest was either stated or implied in the "Highland Lassie" items.

3. A letter to John Arnot, written April, 1786.[77] The letter exists today only in the form of a transcript which Burns made for Robert Riddell about 1792. The significance of the letter lies in Burns's statement that in April, 1786, after losing Jean, he was looking for "another wife."

4. A letter to David Brice, 12 June, 1786.[78] The letter states that Burns is still in love with Jean Armour, though greatly desirous of forgetting her. In a moment of confidence he pleads guilty to "dissipation and riot . . . and other mischief," all undertaken for the purpose of driving Jean from his thoughts. What the "other mischief" may have been, he seems never to have told.

5. A letter to Robert Aiken, *ca.* 8 October, 1786.[79] Here Burns refers to "the consequences of my follies, which may perhaps make it impracticable for me to stay at home." He then continues in this astonishing vein:

> Besides, I have been for some time pining under secret wretchedness, from causes which you pretty well know—the pang of disappointment, the sting of pride, with some wandering stabs of remorse, which never fail to settle on my vitals like vultures, when attention is not called away by the calls of society or the vagaries of the Muse. Even in the hour of social mirth my gaiety is the madness of an intoxicated criminal under the hands of the executioner.

One wishes one knew what Aiken pretty well knew—why Burns, after the trouble with the Armours had blown over, after the publication of the Kilmarnock volume had made him at least locally famous, and after he had done penance and—probably —received his certificate of bachelorhood—why after all this he still felt like "an intoxicated criminal under the hand of the

executioner." One wonders, too, why Burns says the consequences of his follies *may* make it impracticable for him to stay
at home; Why the futurity, suggested by the word *may?*
What was Burns awaiting that might conceivably drive him from
Scotland, as the Armour affair had almost done?

5. A letter to Mrs. Dunlop, 7 July, 1789.[80] In it appears
a single sentence which may possibly be significant in this connection: "Yours . . . has given me more pain than any letter,
one excepted, that I ever received."

Nothing could be less definite than that, or harder to use as
evidence in any argument. Yet as one reads the letter one remembers that Burns's sister Mrs. Begg later told how, one
afternoon in the autumn of 1786, when the family was gathered
in the Mossgiel farmhouse, "a letter for [Robert] was handed
in. He went to the window to open and read it, and she was
struck by the look of agony which was the consequence. He
went out without uttering a word." [81]

If the letter referred to by Mrs. Begg told of Mary Campbell's death, and if it was the "one excepted" which Burns still
had in mind when he received Mrs. Dunlop's, it is clear that
the memory of his sorrow was still present in the summer of
1789.

7. A letter to Mrs. Dunlop,[82] 8 November, 1789, enclosing
a copy of "Thou lingering Star," and commenting on it. Accompanying the text was this brief statement:

> You ask me to send you some Poetry. . . . I shall send you a Song
> I made the other day, of which your opinion, (*sic*) as I am too much in-
> terested in the subject of it, to be a Critic in the composition.

This poem, commonly called "To Mary in Heaven," though
Burns himself never used this title, lies at the heart and center
of all conjecture concerning "Highland Mary." Had it and
its companion piece, "Highland Mary," not been written, it is
a fair guess that there would have been no problem, and Mary
Campbell would have been only one of a score of girls whose
names are more or less closely associated with that of Burns.

[136]

What the poem says is clear enough: that Burns loved a Mary, from whom he parted by the banks of the Ayr; that she died; that he can not forget her, but groans with anguish when he thinks of her. When read in connection with the poet's own guarded comment in the letter to Mrs. Dunlop, the verses seem to warrant Scott Douglas's remark:

> When we find Burns, after eighteen months' experience of loving wedlock with his own Jean, suddenly appealing to the shade of Mary in these words:—
>
> > Seest thou thy lover lowly laid?
> > Hear'st thou the groans that rend his breast?
>
> we feel constrained to say, "If this is not the language of remorse, what is it?" [83]

One might add, what occasion had Burns to feel *remorse* at all?

8. A letter to Mrs. Dunlop, dated 13 December, 1789, [84] in which appears the following significant passage:

> . . . If there is another life, it must be only for the just, the benevolent, the amiable, & the humane; what a flattering idea, then, is a World to come! Would to God I as firmly believed it, as I ardently wish it! There I shall meet an aged Parent, now at rest from the many buffetings of an evil world against which he so long & bravely struggled . . . There should I, with speechless agony of rapture, again recognise my lost, my ever dear MARY! whose bosom was fraught with Truth, Honor, Constancy, & Love—
>
> > My Mary, dear, departed Shade!
> > Where is thy place of heavenly rest?
> > Seest thou thy Lover lowly laid?
> > Hear'st thou the groans that rend his breast!
>
> . . . Your goodness will excuse this distracted scrawl which the Writer dare scarcely read, and which he would throw into the fire, were he able to write any thing better or indeed any thing at all.

Here we find Burns referring, not in verse but in prose, to a Mary whom he loved, and who had died: "my ever dear Mary."

For three years since her death he had scrupulously kept all direct allusions to her out of his correspondence; then, in a sudden outburst, he let the name appear, accompanied by such expressions as only love and remorse could well provoke.

9. A letter to George Thomson, 14 November, 1792.[85] Here appears the text of the song "Highland Mary" ("Ye banks and braes and streams") which had been written not long before the date of the letter, but was not published till 1799, in vol. II of the *Select Scotish Airs*.

The song is the only one in which Burns actually uses the phrase "Highland Mary." Like "Thou lingering Star" it is unequivocal in saying that Burns loved a Mary; that they parted "wi' mony a vow;" that she died; and that her memory still lives in his heart.

In the accompanying letter Burns is even more noncommittal than usual:

> The Subject of the Song is one of the most interesting passages of my youthful days; and I own that I should be much flattered to see the verses set to an Air which would insure celebrity.—Perhaps, after all, 'tis the still glowing prejudice of my heart, that throws a borrowed lustre over the merits of the Composition.

With this vague reference, the list of Burns's own allusions to Highland Mary comes to an end.

Reviewing the evidence thus presented by Greenock tradition, the Bible, Thomson's letter, and Burns's letters and poems, the reader will find himself assenting to something like the following as a statement of fact: In the spring of 1786, when Burns had been "rejected" by Jean Armour and her family, when he believed himself to be a single man, and when he was planning to go to the West Indies, he pledged himself to marry a Mary Campbell. How she came to be near Mauchline at the time is uncertain; what her family connections may have been is equally undetermined. That Burns knew her, loved her, and promised to marry her, is all one can say with assurance. Between April and October of 1786 he wrote two songs commemorating this promise, and three letters in which one is inclined to see veiled references to the situation in which he found himself. During the month of October Mary Campbell, who had gone to Greenock to prepare for her wedding, died of a "malignant fever," and was buried in the Old West Kirkyard. Shortly thereafter Burns changed his mind about Jamaica, and went to Edinburgh instead. From October of 1786 to July of 1789 Burns never referred to the incident in any way in either prose or verse, but maintained an absolute and unbroken silence, so far as extant records go, on everything connected with Mary Campbell. This silence he broke, with a veiled allusion, in July of 1789; four months later the love which he still felt for Mary Campbell, and the bitter remorse occasioned by her death, found expression in "Thou Lingering Star." Immediately afterwards, in a letter to Mrs. Dunlop, he made unequivocal confession of his undying love for Mary. Then again for three years he remained silent, till in 1792 he wrote "Highland Mary" and sent the verses to Thomson. Never again did he refer to the incident in any way. So much seems clear.

The heart of the whole problem, however, is the nature of Mary Campbell's relations to Burns. Concerning this matter, Scottish tradition is well established: Mary Campbell lives today as a beautiful ideal of womanly purity and nobility. Henley, to be sure, cast doubt on the accuracy of the portrait which biographers of half a century had been painting, and found himself roundly abused for his pains.[86] Mrs. Carswell states that Mary Campbell was the mother of a child of Burns's, but gives no supporting evidence.[87] But the old interpretation is still virtually the only one to be found in Burns literature, and seems as definitely a part of the general tradition as any item in that curiously built up fabric of fact and imagination. Angellier, free from Scottish national prejudice, phrased this interpretation so well that his words may fairly stand as the best expression of the currently accepted theory:

Ce fut le plus pur, le plus durable et de beaucoup le plus élevé de ses amours. Au-dessus de tous les autres, dont quelques-uns furent plus ardents, il se dresse avec la blancheur d'un lis. . . . C'est [l'amour pour Mary] qui conduisit Burns dans la sphère la plus élevée où il atteignit, lui qui inspira ses plus hauts efforts de spiritualité. La douce fille des Hautes-Terres aux yeux azurés fut sa Béatrice et lui fit signe du bord du ciel.[88]

Or, as Allan Bayne has put it more recently,

Highland Mary for ever remains as the inspirer of Burns at his best, and so is linked to him eternally; and whoever seeks to defile this ideal maiden deserves the reprobation of all pure-minded men and women.[89]

In other words the accepted, and acceptable, theory concerning Burns and Mary Campbell represents their love, which Burns called "the most ardent reciprocal attachment,"[90] as untainted by anything earthly, as on an entirely different plane from that which Burns felt for other women whom he loved, and as of so spiritual a nature that had it not been blighted by Mary's early death, it might well have led Burns to heights which he never attained.

Before subscribing to this theory, one should realize that it leaves certain obvious and pertinent queries unanswered. First, how can one reconcile Burns's continuing love for Jean, even after his rejection by her and her family, with the fact (which this hypothesis makes it necessary to admit) that at precisely the same time he was loving Mary Campbell in this pure, noble, and altogether spiritual fashion?[91]

This problem long ago presented itself to Burns's biographers, some of whom tried to solve the riddle by placing the Highland Mary episode much earlier in the poet's life. Attempts thus to dodge the issue were of little avail, however; the two affairs were going on concurrently, and must be so treated.

Second, a satisfactory explanation for Burns's sudden change of mind concerning Jamaica is hard to find, if one accepts the traditional interpretation of the Highland Mary affair. Early in October, 1786, he was planning to emigrate;[92] on October 30 he was still of the same mind.[93] But by the fifteenth of No-

[140]

vember the Edinburgh visit had been decided upon, and the date virtually settled.[94] Dr. Blacklock's famous letter to Lawrie has long been discounted as a material reason for Burns's sudden change of plan; it is hardly probable that the review of the Kilmarnock volume, which appeared early in November in the *Edinburgh Magazine,* could have overthrown the well-matured project. There had been no recent change in Burns's relations to the Armours. What had happened to make possible the sudden modification of his whole program?

Third, what did Burns mean when, in the letter to Aiken already quoted, he said "the consequence of my follies . . . *may* make it impracticable for me to stay at home?" As he wrote, he seems to have had in mind the possibility that some future development might drive him into exile, as the Armour affair nearly had done. What was this something which was worrying him?

Fourth, what adequate reason can be given for Burns's astonishing reticence concerning the whole episode? It has been suggested that this was due to his growing love for Jean, whom he later married. But Burns was never over considerate of Jean's feelings. One remembers that five or six years later he brought Anne Park's daughter into his home, and that Jean reared the baby more or less unconcernedly along with her own. No, there seems to have been some unique cause operating to seal Burns's lips concerning himself and Mary Campbell.

Fifth, if Burns's silence is hard to explain, even more difficult is it to account for the fact that after Mary's death her family adopted an attitude of persistent hostility towards Burns. It is only fair to say that the evidence on this point is not as substantial as one might wish; nevertheless it carries some weight, and may fairly be allowed to stand till rebutted. Wallace sums it up, with proper conservatism, thus:

> Mary's parents and other near relatives, who afterwards settled in Greenock, shrank for many years from all acknowledgement of Burns as her lover. Her father is believed to have burned the poet's letters to her, and to have forbidden his name to be mentioned.[95]

Apparently the father, at least, felt towards Burns as one might feel towards a man who had brought disgrace upon one's family.

Sixth, Currie's vague treatment of the episode, in his *Life of Burns*, is hard to account for. He said that it would be "improper to reveal" the details of the affair, and passed on to other matters.[96] In some respects Currie was none too tender of Burns's reputation; in this one instance, however, he intimated that he knew more than he told, and that there were cogent reasons for not telling what he knew. Such actions are hard to explain if Burns's relations to Mary Campbell were what most people believe them to have been.

Finally, one may well ask whether it is probable, *a priori*, that the Burns who in 1784 had made Betty Paton his mistress, and had acknowledged the child she bore him, and who in 1785 and 1786 found himself in a similar relationship to Jean Armour, and who during the next few years treated May Cameron and Jennie Clow and Anne Park in the same manner,—whether it is probable that this man was metamorphosed, for the period of a few months, into the ideal lover of an Ayrshire Beatrice? On the contrary, the more one thinks about it, the more out of character seems the portrait of Burns which the "Mariolaters" have painted.

But if this venerable and orthodox hypothesis is to be rejected, something must be found by way of a substitute. And when in November of 1920 the remains of Mary Campbell were exhumed from their resting place in the Greenock Old West Kirkyard, and re-interred in the Greenock Cemetery, one hitherto virtually over-looked piece of evidence came to light, on the basis of which a new hypothesis may be constructed. Archibald Macphail, a member of the Greenock Burns Club, described the entire proceedings for the Greenock *Telegraph*,[97] and recorded, without comment, the fact that "at the foot of the grave the bottom of an infant's coffin was found. This, while sodden, was quite sound." If the child whose body lay thus at the feet of Mary Campbell was her child, the whole situation becomes crystal clear.

Let it be admitted that the "if" at the beginning of the last sentence can hardly be removed from the equation. The evidence is inconclusive. The burial records of the Old West Kirk seem to be lost; there may have been other interments in that grave. But this at least can be said with assurance: the coffin thus brought to light was in all probability that of a child whose mother was buried in the same grave; and since Mary Campbell was buried in this grave she may well have been the mother, and Burns, who at the time of her death was her betrothed lover, may have been the father; in all probability he must have been the father. In that case we find ourselves confronting the fact that Mary Campbell may have been Burns's mistress, and have died in childbirth, or have suffered a miscarriage and died shortly thereafter of typhus fever, which tradition says was the cause of her death.

Assuming, for the sake of the argument, that this hypothesis is correct, one finds a story something like this shaping itself. During the early months of 1786, when Burns had involved himself with Jean Armour to such an extent that the relationship became notorious, he was also on terms of intimacy with Mary Campbell. He gave the "unlucky paper" to Jean, but it was destroyed, apparently about the middle of April. Burns thus found himself, so he and the Armours thought, and so the church authorities later decided, a single man. Chagrined by the attitude of the Armours, but relieved of one obligation by their action, he decided to marry Mary Campbell, whose claim upon him had by this time become as strong as Jean's. About the middle of May, Mary disappeared from Mauchline, where she probably had been living, taking with her Burns's promise of marriage and the inscribed Bible. Burns busied himself with the preparation of his Kilmarnock volume, and also with the preliminaries of the Jamaica trip. Then James Armour, apprehensive lest Burns leave the country without providing for Jean's expected child, sued out a warrant for him. Burns thereupon became virtually a fugitive from justice, torn by a conflict of emotions which can easily be imagined. With two luckless

[143]

young women on his hands at once, and the father of one loosing "the pack of the law" at his heels, his gayety may well have become "the madness of an intoxicated criminal under the hands of the executioner." The birth of Jean's twins on September 3 complicated the situation still further, for Burns's parental affections were of the strongest. So he delayed his departure for the Indies, eager to remain in Scotland if he could, but fearful of what the future might hold in store; for it was quite possible that Mary Campbell's father might take the same attitude which James Armour had taken. Then suddenly, towards the end of October, with no warning, came a letter telling of Mary's death in child-birth. For the only time in his career, so far as we know, Burns's lawless love of a woman had cost her her life, and the life of her child. In a certain sense, however, the death of Mary Campbell made Burns's problem a simpler one, no matter how bitter may have been his remorse. The Armour situation he by this time felt competent to handle; and so, sealing his lips concerning Mary, at the end of the month following her death he went to Edinburgh instead of to Jamaica.

Something like that *may* have been the story of Burns and Mary Campbell. At once the question arises, does this hypothetical account fit better into the pattern of known facts than the equally hypothetical account which has come to be generally accepted? Does it clear up any of the uncertainties which the traditional hypothesis leaves one to puzzle over? If it does, it may fairly be accepted as the true account of the relationship.

Returning, then, to the seven unsolved problems listed in the preceding pages, one finds that the first two disappear entirely when one exchanges the accepted hypothesis for that of this chapter. Instead of having to picture the Burns who made Jean Armour his mistress, as being at the same time the ideal lover of an ideal maiden, one need only regretfully accept the fact that he was carrying on two illicit love affairs at the same time. Then the "other mischief" to which he alluded in his letter to Brice is easy of interpretation: it refers only to his *liaison* with Mary Campbell; the "most ardent reciprocal attachment,"

[144]

which according to Burns was the tie that bound him to Mary, becomes exactly what one might have expected it to be, Burns being Burns.

The second and third problems—the reason for Burns's sudden change of mind concerning Jamaica, and his statement that "the consequences of [his] follies may make it impracticable for [him] to remain at home"—these too cease to be in any way puzzling. He knew, as he wrote, that Mary was to bear his child; he could not be sure, however, whether her parents would accept him as a son-in-law, or would proceed against him as Armour had done. Hence the uncertainty, the delay, the perturbation. Hence, too, the sudden change of plan, and the decision not to leave Scotland, when fate relieved him of the obligation of supporting Mary Campbell and her child.

Equally simple is the solution for the fourth and fifth of the difficulties—Burns's reticence concerning Mary, and the unforgiving attitude of her family towards him. So obvious are both of these developments, as aftermaths of Mary's death in child-birth, that no comment is necessary. Neither is there need for explaining Currie's reticence, and his statement that it would be "improper to reveal" the details of the episode.

Finally, if one accepts the hypothesis which this chapter has presented, one is no longer perplexed by a Dr. Jekyll-Mr. Hyde conception of Burns; his character is no longer inconsistent with itself. The pattern of the year 1786 takes on a new harmony, and Burns's career as a whole becomes suddenly more intelligible.

With the death of Mary Campbell the story of Burns's life at Mossgiel comes to a close, except for the single and important matter of the Kilmarnock volume, which demands a chapter by itself. The two years and a half during which he lived with his brothers and sisters on Gavin Hamilton's farm had been years of hard labor at uncongenial but necessary tasks; of love, which cast the deepest shadows over Burns's life, but which also tinged these shadows with an unfading radiance; and of poetry so notable in its brilliance that everything Burns had written before this time becomes insignificant. They were years in which Burns made friends whose esteem and affection he was never to lose, and in which his daring assertion of his own personality brought him into sharp conflict with established authority. Finally, it was during the last months of this period that the village rimester won renown as a poet, and saw fame come to him in such measure as he had not dared dream of a year and a half before.

[1] *Poetical Works of William Wordsworth*, Cambridge edition, p. 719.

[2] See William Jolly, *Robert Burns at Mossgiel*; Paisley, 1881; *passim*.

[3] *Autobiography*, p. 43 f.

[4] *Letters*, I, 17.

[5] C. W., I, 113.

[6] S. D., IV, 71.

[7] See the passages printed in S. D., IV, 53 ff., concerning the opportunity for a poet of Ayrshire, the nature of Scottish song and music, the possibility of setting words to old tunes, the best method of writing songs, and similar matters. See also Chapter III, pp. 85 ff., above.

[8] Currie, III, 378 ff. From a letter to Dr. Currie, 2 April, 1798.

[9] "A Poet's Welcome," H. H., II, 37.

[10] "Mauchline and its Neighbourhood", by "E. R."; *Chronicle*, 1893, pp. 53 ff.

[11] *Op. cit.*, II, 109 ff.

[12] *Ibid.*

[13] William Jolly's *Robert Burns at Mossgiel*, Paisley, 1881, contains much information concerning Mauchline village.

[14] Edgar, II, 378.

[15] Interesting information concerning Auld will be found in Edgar, II, 377 ff.

[16] Concerning the old tower, often spoken of as a priory, Mr. G. W. Shirley writes to me thus: "The building has puzzled antiquaries. There was no priory at Mauchline, but the land was owned, before the Reformation, by Melrose Abbey. It may have been erected by the Abbey as a grange. There are certainly ecclesiastical windows in it, but they are suspected as being products of a pseudo-mediaeval revival in the 18th century. It was known in documents as The Place of Mauchline."

[17] McNaught's facsimile of 1786 edition (Kilmarnock, 1909, D. Brown & Co.), p. 187.

[18] *Robert Burns and the Ayrshire Moderates* [by John Gairdner], privately printed, Edinburgh, 1883, pp. 36 ff. All the more important documents relating to the famous case may be found in this booklet.

[19] There is an interesting article (anon.) on "John Richmond, Mauchline Friend of Burns," in the *Chronicle*, 1925, pp. 55 ff.

[20] *Letters*, I, 22.

[21] See three letters, *Letters*, I, 32, 35, and 40. The last, an extremely important one unpublished till 1908, is dated 1 September, 1786, and throws much light on Burns's situation at the time.

[22] *Letters*, I, 41.

[23] "Epistle to James Smith," H. H., I, 59.

[24] Letter of 1 Aug. ? 1786; *Letters*, I, 35.

[25] Letter of 30 June, 1787; *ibid.*, p. 98.

[26] Letter of 28 April, 1788; *ibid.*, p. 218.

[27] See William Findlay's *Robert Burns and the Medical Profession*, Paisley, 1898.

[28] Edinburgh, 1811; II, 261.

[29] Stewart later recorded his impressions of Burns in a letter to Dr. Currie. See Currie, I, 133 ff.

MOSSGIEL

[30] Later in life Mackenzie practised at Irvine, where he presided at the inaugural dinner of the Irvine Burns Club.

[31] Letter to Gavin Hamilton, 15 April, 1786; *Letters*, I, 24.

[32] "To the Rev. John M'Math," H. H., II, 76. After 1791, when he resigned his charge, M'Math's life was an unhappy one. (See C. W., I, 193, n.)

[33] Glasgow, 1779.

[34] *Letters*, I, 373.

[35] Letter of 7 March, 1788; *Letters*, I, 207.

[36] H. H., II, 70.

[37] *Ibid.*, I, 176.

[38] See also "The Fornicator," stanza 2:

"Before the congregation wide
I pass'd the muster fairly,
My handsome Betty by my side,
We got our ditty rarely."

—*Merry Muses*, 1827 reprint, p. 13.

The song is by Burns.

[39] Letter of 11 Nov., 1784, *Letters*, I, 20. Peggy was probably the Peggy Thomson of Kirkoswald.

[40] The poem was not published till four or five years after Burns's death. The subsequent history of the child is not uninteresting. She was baptized on May 24, 1785, and was brought up at first by her own mother, and later by Burns's mother and brother Gilbert. When she became twenty-one years old she received two hundred pounds from the sum that had been raised for the support of the poet's family—good indication of the affection which Scotland had come to feel for all the poet's kin. She married a John Bishop, and died on January 8, 1817.

[41] "Epistle to a Young Friend," stanza 6; H. H., I, 140.

[42] Burns himself, in his Family Bible, gave the date of Jean's birth as February 27, 1767. The parish register is correct.

[43] 15 April, 1786; *Letters*, I, 24.

[44] *Ibid.*, p. 26. A sentence in a letter to Richmond, 17 Feb., 1786, "I have some very important news with respect to myself, not the most agreeable", is probably to be understood as a reference to Jean's condition. If so, it is Burns's first allusion to the affair.

[45] See the letter to Smith, *Letters*, I, 35, and note concerning the probable date.

[46] "In the case of a promise of marriage followed by a *copula*; if the promise hath been declared by a written marriage contract in the usual style, the subsequent *copula* must doubtless be considered as the perfection or consummation of the prior contract; . . . and, indeed, though the promise *de futuro* should be barely verbal, the canonists, and upon their authority both our judges and writers, are agreed that a *copula* subsequent to such promise constitutes marriage, from a presumption or fiction that the consent *de presenti*, which is essential to marriage, was at that moment mutually given by the parties, in consequence of the anterior promise." John Erskine: *An Institute of the Law of Scotland* (1871, 2 vols.), I, 139.

[47] The account of Burns's marriage given by Mrs. Carswell, *The Life of Robert Burns*, *passim*, can not be supported by real evidence. Concerning Scottish marriages, see "The Gretna Green Marriages," by David C. Herries; *Transactions of the Dumfriesshire and Galloway Natural History and Antiquarian Society*, 22 October, 1926.

[48] Letter to Hamilton, 15 April, 1786; *Letters*, I, 24.

[49] *Chronicle*, 1893, p. 56.

[50] *Letters*, I, 30.

[51] *Ibid.*, p. 37.

[52] See *Autobiography*, p. 46. Burns's record of events at this period of his life is confused, vague, and inaccurate—perhaps intentionally so.

[53] *Letters*, I, 32 f.

[54] *Ibid.*, p. 33.

[55] Edgar, II, 402, n.

[56] *Letters*, I, 33 f. The document was executed on July 22, 1786. See "Documents bearing on Gilbert's Debt to the Poet," by D. M'Naught, *Chronicle*, 1900, 77 ff. Gilbert

carried out his part of the agreement with scrupulous care. His accounts show that part of the interest due Burns's estate on the £200 loan was regularly charged off as expense relating to the daughter Elizabeth.

[57] On the reason for the change to a later date, see letter to Smith of August 14, *Letters*, I, 37.

[58] Perhaps Jean herself; perhaps Aiken, Armour's lawyer, but Burns's friend.

[59] *Letters*, I, 35.

[60] *Ibid.*, p. 40.

[61] C. W., I, 396, n. Robert lived until 1857; Jean died at the age of fourteen months. See letter to Richmond, *Letters*, I, 132.

[62] *Letters*, I, 46 f.

[63] C. W., I, 432, n.

[64] He was, perhaps, the husband of a cousin of Mary Campbell's mother. The records show that he bought the lair on October 12, 1786.

[65] Facsimiles of the inscriptions are easily accessible in S. D., I, 298 f.

[66] See the account in C. W., I, 475 ff.

[67] *Op. cit.*, p. 382.

[68] C. W., III, 367. The original of this letter is lost.

[69] H. H., IV, 287.

[70] *Ibid.*, III, 10.

[71] Burns several times uses such phrases to indicate the time before the Kilmarnock volume had brought him fame.

[72] Cromek's *Reliques* (1808), p. 237.

[73] London, 1908.

[74] See an article in the *Chronicle* for 1922, where Mr. Cook shows that many of the notes branded by Dick as spurious were actually Burns's own notes, though taken from a source or sources other than the *Museum* interleaves. Ferguson's article, "In Defense of R. H. Cromek," *Philological Quarterly*, July, 1930, makes it clear that in the *Reliques*, at least, Cromek did "a substantially honest and straightforward piece of work."

[75] H. H., IV, 15.

[76] *Letters*, II, 127.

[77] *Ibid.*, I, 26.

[78] *Ibid.*, p. 30 f.

[79] *Ibid.*, p. 46. No editor since Currie has seen the MS. of this letter.

[80] *Ibid.*, p. 343.

[81] C. W., I, 431.

[82] *Letters*, I, 367.

[83] S. D., I, 299.

[84] *Letters*, I, 372.

[85] *Ibid.*, II, 132.

[86] See *Henley and Burns*, edited by J. D. Ross, Stirling, 1901.

[87] See *The Life of Robert Burns*, by Catherine Carswell (New York, 1931), pp. 178 ff., and elsewhere.

[88] A. Angellier, *Robert Burns*, I, 161.

[89] *Chronicle*, 1906, p. 108.

[90] See note to "My Highland Lassie, O," above, p. 133.

[91] On June 12, 1786, Burns wrote Brice: "Never man lov'd, or rather ador'd, a woman more than I did [Jean]: and to confess a truth between you and me, I do still love her to distraction after all." *Letters*, I, 30.

[92] See letter to Aiken, *Letters*, I, 46 ff.

[93] See "To Major Logan," H. H., II, 99, stanza 12.

[94] See letter to Mrs. Dunlop, *Letters*, I, 49 ff.

[95] C. W., I, 431.

[96] Currie, I, 125.

[97] Issue of January 4, 1921. The article was reprinted, in an altered form, in the *Chronicle*, 1922, pp. 78 ff.

CHAPTER V

THE KILMARNOCK VOLUME

1

THE MAKING OF THE BOOK

IT is impossible to tell precisely when Burns decided to publish a volume of poems. Throughout 1785 his pen had been steadily busy; and though much that he wrote during this year was definitely not intended for the public eye, as witness the many significant omissions from the Kilmarnock volume, it is unthinkable that he should have composed such an astonishing body of verse without at least considering the most obvious method of winning the fame which he coveted.

To be sure, Scottish poems were not by any means as popular in 1785 as they were to become after Burns's success had inspired his imitative rivals to follow his example. The vernacular Muse was definitely in retirement. Even the success of Ramsay, and the somewhat limited popularity of Fergusson, had not served to re-establish the Lowland dialect as a literary vehicle. Scots had once been the language of poetry; from the time of the Reformation to the date of the Kilmarnock volume, however, it had been more or less in eclipse. Hence when Burns finally made up his mind to follow the example of Fergusson and give to the world a collection of Scottish poems he was undertaking a distinctly unusual proceeding, and not by any means merely following the example of his contemporaries.

Nevertheless he had already won a gratifying though purely local success by allowing his verses to circulate in manuscript; he had for some time been seriously considering the problems involved in his ambitious design of making himself known as a Scottish poet; he thought well of his own work.[1]   Consequently when one reads, in the "Epistle to James Smith,"

> This while my notion's taen a sklent
> To try my fate in guid, black prent,

one may fairly infer that for some time previous to the date of this poem the general notion of publication had been germinating in his mind.

Be this as it may, the last six months of 1785 and the first three of 1786 saw him piling up manuscript at a rate which is little short of miraculous.   Then the affair with Jean Armour, which broke about his ears in April of 1786, sent him looking for ready money with which to pay his passage to the West Indies.   On April 3 he wrote Aiken that his "Proposals for Publishing" were just going to the press;[2] on April 17 the subscription blanks were actually ready for distribution.[3]

The document which thus announced Burns's intention to the world was brief:

> Proposals for Publishing by subscription,
> Scottish Poems, by Robert Burns.
>
> The work to be elegantly printed, in one volume, octavo.   Price, stitched, three shillings.   As the author has not the most distant mercenary view in publishing, as soon as so many subscribers appear as will defray the necessary expense, the work will be sent to the press.[4]

There then follows a brief quotation from Ramsay, and the necessary "We, the undersubscribers, engage to take the above-mentioned work on the conditions specified."

Two minor matters are perhaps worthy of comment in this connection.   First, Burns's original plan was to publish only poems in the vernacular; there is no suggestion that any English verse was to be included.   Second, the energetic disclaimer of any desire to make money, though characteristic of Burns, who hated the thought of even indirectly asking for financial aid, was entirely out of accord with the facts.   He was looking to

[150]

his poems to provide him with sorely needed funds; he was energetic in supplying his friends with "Proposals," that they in their turn might add their friends' names to the lists of subscribers.

For example, the letters written at this time show that John Ballantine, a banker at Ayr, received one of the blanks; apparently, however, he made no special use of it. M'Whinnie, an Ayr attorney, secured twenty subscriptions; John Kennedy, of Dumfries House, near Cumnock, Ayrshire, factor to the Earl of Dumfries, was responsible for as many more, as was John Logan of Knockshinnock. But it was "Orator Bob" Aiken, with his one hundred and forty-five subscriptions, Robert Muir of Kilmarnock with his seventy, Smith, Burns's Mauchline friend, with forty-one, Gavin Hamilton with forty, and the poet's brother Gilbert with seventy, who were most successful in promoting the sale of the proposed volume.[5]

The printer to whom Burns entrusted his manuscript was John Wilson of Kilmarnock. He was a man of Burns's age, who may possibly have been more willing to risk such a venture than an older and better known publisher might have been. How Burns got in touch with him, even the exact location of his shop, must apparently remain matters of conjecture. But the poet had many Kilmarnock friends who could have introduced the young writer to his printer, and Wilson must have known that Burns's local reputation would ensure the sale of at least enough copies to pay his bill, which ultimately amounted to £35–17–0.[6]

When the actual work of printing began on July 13, Burns himself was hardly in a position to give undivided attention to his new responsibilities as an author. How and when he read the proofs, indeed how he managed to see the job to its close at all, is hard to imagine. These were the weeks when he was doing penance for his affair with Jean, planning for his trip to Jamaica, and "wandering from one friend's house to another," as he put it, to escape service of the warrant which Armour had sworn out against him. But he succeeded somehow, despite the perturbation which such a letter as that to Richmond of July 30 makes apparent; and on July 31 the edition of six hundred and twelve copies was ready for distribution.

The book sold far beyond the list of three hundred and fifty persons who had subscribed for it in advance. By August 28 Wilson had left on hand only thirteen copies; the author himself seems to have taken but three. On October 6, Burns, who had assumed entire charge of distributing the copies and collecting for them,[7] settled the account with Wilson in full, and at the same time

made him the offer of a second edition, on the hazard of being paid out of *the first and readiest,* which he declines. By his account, the paper of a thousand copies would cost about twenty seven pounds, and the printing about fifteen or sixteen: he offers to agree to this for the printing, if I will advance for the paper; but this, you know, is out of my power; so farewell hopes of a second edition till I grow richer! an epocha which, I think, will arrive at the payment of the British national debt.[8]

Apparently Wilson felt that Burns's friends had already given all that could be expected in the way of financial support; Burns himself was unwilling to risk the twenty pounds that he said he made from the publication, and that he needed to finance his Jamaica trip.[9] This being the case, and neither author nor publisher having much faith in the marketability of a second printing, the two men brought their relations to a close, each having done more to make the other known to the world than he could well have dreamed.

The popularity of the book was immediate, and extended well beyond the localities in which Burns was personally known. Robert Heron, Burns's first biographer, is a poor authority to quote in any connection; but as regards this one matter he may be allowed to testify:

Old and young, high and low, grave and gay, learned or ignorant, all were alike delighted, agitated, transported. I was at that time resident in Galloway, contiguous to Ayrshire; and I can well remember, how that even plough-boys and maid-servants would have gladly bestowed the wages which they earned the most hardly, and which they wanted to purchase necessary clothing, if they might but procure the works of Burns. . . . On a Saturday evening I opened the volume, by accident, while I was undressing to go to bed. I closed it not, till a late hour on the rising Sunday morn, after I had read over every syllable it contained.[10]

But other readers besides Burns's own friends, and un-named plowboys and maid-servants, enjoyed the book, and told the author so. John M'Adam of Craigen-Gillan, for instance, received from Burns a poetical epistle of seven stanzas, written "in answer to an obliging letter he sent in the commencement of my poetic career."[11] However much Burns may have felt, and expressed, an unrelenting class-consciousness, it is certain that actually he enjoyed the praises of the "great folk":

> Now deil-may-care about their jaw,
> The senseless, gawky million;
> I'll cock my nose aboon them a':
> I'm roos'd by Craigen-Gillan.

Sir William Cunninghame of Robertland, Mrs. Alexander Stewart of Stair, to whom Burns twice sent manuscript parcels of songs,[12] both seem to have praised the work, and to have admitted the author to their circles of friends. The Reverend George Lawrie, minister of Loudon parish, not only enjoyed it himself, but sent a copy to Dr. Thomas Blacklock, in Edinburgh; and the blind poet whom Dr. Johnson had met and praised, and whom Benjamin Franklin had befriended, expressed his approbation in a letter which ultimately found its way to Burns. Inasmuch as this letter contained the first appreciation of Burns's work which came from outside his own immediate world, it is of enough interest to be reprinted:

Edin., Sep. 4th, 1786.

REVEREND AND DEAR SIR—

I ought to have acknowledged your favor long ago, not only as a testimony of your kind remembrance, but as it gave me an opportunity of sharing one of the finest, and, perhaps, one of the most genuine entertainments, of which the human mind is susceptible. A number of avocations retarded my progress in reading the poems; at last, however, I have finished that pleasing perusal. Many instances have I seen of nature's force and beneficence, exerted under numerous and formidable disadvantages; but none equal to that, with which you have been kind enough to present me. There is a pathos and delicacy in his serious poems; a vein of wit and humour in those of a more festive turn, which cannot be too much admired, nor too warmly approved; and I think I shall never open the book without feeling my astonishment renewed and increased. It was my wish to have expressed my approbation in verse; but whether from declining life or a temporary depression of spirits, it is at present out of my power to accomplish that agreeable intention.

Mr. Stewart, professor of morals in this university, had formerly read me three of the poems, and I had desired him to get my name inserted among the subscribers: but whether this was done or not I never could learn. I have little intercourse with Dr. Blair, but will take care to have the poems communicated to him by the intervention of some mutual friend. It has been told me by a gentleman, to whom I showed the performances, and who sought a copy with diligence and ardour, that the whole impression is already exhausted. It were therefore much to be wished, for the sake of the young man, that a second edition, more numerous than the former, could immediately be printed; as it appears certain that its intrinsic merit, and the exertion of the author's friends, might give it a more universal circulation than any thing of the kind which has been published within my memory.

T. Blacklock.[13]

Some time after receiving this letter Lawrie sent it to Gavin Hamilton, and Hamilton gave it to Burns,[14] whose pleasure at being thus recognized ultimately found expression in the well-known paragraphs of the autobiographical letter to Dr. Moore.

Whether through Blacklock's efforts, or through those of some other well-wisher, the volume reached the office of *The Edinburgh Magazine*, edited by James Sibbald.[15] The October number of this journal, published on November 3, was advertised as containing "ample extracts from the poems of R. Burns, a ploughman in Ayrshire." The accompanying article, the first published review of the Kilmarnock edition, shows Sibbald—or whoever wrote the review for him—to have been a perspica-

cious critic, though distinctly in bondage to the "polite" standards of the day. Quite appropriately he called Burns "a striking
example of native genius bursting through the obscurity of
poverty and the obstructions of a laborious life." Then, to show
that he was not unfamiliar with more "elegant" poetry than
Burns's, he added,

> To those who admire the creations of untutored fancy, and are blind
> to many faults for the sake of numberless beauties, his poems will yield
> singular gratification. His observations on human character are acute
> and sagacious, and his descriptions are lively and just. Of rustic pleas-
> antry he has a rich fund, and some of his softer scenes are touched with
> inimitable delicacy. . . . The character Horace gives to Osellus is
> particularly applicable to him—
>
> *Rusticus abnormis sapiens, crassaque Minerva.*[16]

Five weeks later Henry Mackenzie, then editing the short-
lived *Lounger*, published a review that praised Burns both enthusiastically and intelligently, but that confirmed the reader
in the impression that the poet was a "Heaven-taught ploughman":

> Though I am very far from meaning to compare our rustic bard to
> Shakespeare, yet whoever will read his lighter and more humorous poems
> . . . will perceive with what uncommon penetration and sagacity this
> Heaven-taught ploughman, from his humble and unlettered station, has
> looked upon men and manners.[17]

With these two reviews originated the "unlettered plow-
boy" tradition—a tradition that Burns himself was careful to
foster,[18] and that was to persist long after the facts had become
known which should have made clear the inaccuracy of any such
characterization of Burns. Plowboy he was, in a sense, though
anything rather than unlettered.

To a limited extent the volume was read outside of Scotland.
The Monthly Review (London), for example, carried in its
number for December, 1786, a nine-page review, of a generally

favorable nature. In February of 1787 *The English Review* (London) printed an article, possibly the work of Dr. John Moore, which showed that the writer had given the book careful attention, and had found it commendable. A few sentences from the concluding paragraph deserve reprinting:

> The stanza of Mr. Burns is generally ill-chosen, and his provincial dialect confines his beauties to one half of the island. But he possesses the genuine characteristics of the poet: a vigorous mind, a lively fancy, a surprizing knowledge of human nature, and an expression rich, various, and abundant . . . His situation, however, is critical. He seems to possess too great a facility of composition, and is too easily satisfied with his own productions. Fame may be procured by novelty, but it must be supported by merit. We have thrown out these hints to our young and ingenious author because we discern faults in him which, if not corrected, like the fly in the apothecary's ointment, may give an unfortunate tincture and colour to his future compositions.[19]

But despite the fact that the Kilmarnock volume was thus noticed in London, its circulation was largely confined to Ayrshire. Not till the 1787 Edinburgh edition was off the press did Burns make any real impression on English readers.

The unpretentious three-shilling paper-covered volume which called forth these comments contained two hundred and thirty-five pages of verse, an unnecessarily apologetic Preface, and a reasonably well-prepared Glossary of five pages. It is needless, after the lapse of a century and a half, to indulge in any superlatives of praise; but it is perhaps fair to say that the literary historian will search the annals of English poetry long and hard before finding many other first volumes which so unmistakably announce the advent of a great and original genius.

Furthermore, the person who wishes to form any estimate of what Burns had actually accomplished, poetically, by the summer of 1786, should remember one fact which has never been adequately stressed: the poems which he had already written, but which he omitted from the published collection,[20] seem today to have been at least as notable, when considered as a group, as those which he included. Hence before attempting any comment on the published work, it will be well to examine some of the omissions from the volume.

2
OMISSIONS FROM THE VOLUME

To begin with the least significant of these unpublished items, there were in Burns's desk at least four religious pieces,[21] products of his early attempts at versifying, which he quite properly excluded. They might have seemed somewhat stilted and unpoetical; and, being entirely English, were out of keeping with the original plan of the book.

Two poems which it is perhaps not unfair to group together as autobiographical were excluded for obvious reasons: "A Poet's Welcome" and "The Court of Equity." The former, one of Burns's most wistful and appealing lyrics, was too intimately personal; the latter too broad. Neither was published till after Burns's death. Similarly "Adam Armour's Prayer," though relatively innocuous, was definitely not the sort of poem to print.

There were also eight poetic epistles which Burns might have published, but which he omitted for reasons which it is not hard to discover. The "Reply to an Announcement by John Rankine," and the stanzas to Gavin Hamilton recommending a boy ("I hold it, Sir, my bounden duty") were too slight to be of interest to anyone save the person addressed. The third "Epistle to Lapraik," the "Epistle to John Kennedy," "The Inventory," and the second "Epistle to Davie," were also destitute of any general appeal.

Two of the rejected epistles, however, that to his Kilmarnock friend John Goldie, and the one to the Reverend John M'Math, assistant minister at Tarbolton, would have brought delight to many a reader. In them Burns took up the cudgels in behalf of theological liberalism, and showed such enthusiasm in his attacks on "sour bigotry" that had the two poems appeared beside "The Holy Fair" he might well have expected the "Blackcoats and reverend wigs" to take whatever unfavorable notice they could of the intrepid author. But, not wishing to involve his friend M'Math in ecclesiastical dispute, Burns quite properly kept his name out of all discussion by suppressing the poems. For the omission of the letter to Goldie there were other reasons. Goldie, far more energetically controversial than Burns himself, was already known as the foremost opponent of the old regime; he must have been delighted with Burns's epistle. Had it been printed, it would have been "good publicity," if nothing more. But Burns let it lie in the desk drawer, apparently because he did not wish to risk a direct challenge to the orthodox establishment. It was one thing to express oneself in confidence to a friend; it was quite another matter for a young poet who had twice been liable to Church discipline, who even as he was correcting his proofs was in terror of the Sheriff, and whose sole chance for happiness seemed to depend upon the sale of the volume he was preparing—it was quite another matter for this young upstart to publish these confidences. So Burns "played safe."

When one has found this explanation for the omission of the "Epistle to John Goldie," one has also said virtually all that need be said concerning Burns's careful exclusion of six of his most powerful satires: "Death and Dr. Hornbook," "The Twa Herds," and "Holy Willie's Prayer," all composed during 1785, and the "Address of Beelzebub," "The Ordination," and the "Address to the Unco Guid," which were probably written not long before the volume went to press. One of the six, the "Address of Beelzebub," is a bitter piece of social and political satire ridiculing the noble leader of a movement, then on foot, to prevent emigration from certain poverty-stricken districts of the Highlands. There was a sting, a lash, in the couplets which Pope or Juvenal might have admired; Burns rarely wrote more feelingly or more eloquently:

> They, an' be damn'd! what right hae they
> To meat or sleep or light o' day,
> Far less to riches, pow'r, or freedom,
> But what your lordship likes to gie them?

[158]

But hear, my lord! Glengary, hear!
Your hand's owre light on them, I fear;
Your factors, grieves, trustees, and bailies,
I canna say but they do gaylies;
They lay aside a' tender mercies,
An' tirl the hullions to the birses.
Yet while they're only poind and herriet,
They'll keep their stubborn Highland spirit.
But smash them! crash them a' to spails,
An rot the dyvors i' the jails!
The young dogs, swinge them to the labour;
Let wark an' hunger mak them sober!
The hizzies, if they're oughtlins fawsont,
Let them in Drury Lane be lesson'd! [22]

And so on for many couplets. Such mordant irony was of a sort that any reader could appreciate; to publish the poem, however, would have been to challenge powers with which Burns dared not risk a conflict.

Of a different sort was "Death and Dr. Hornbook." John Wilson, clerk of the Kirk Session at Tarbolton, the man who had signed the certificate of character which William Burnes's widow took with her when she moved from Tarbolton to Mauchline parish, was an inoffensive but somewhat pompous schoolmaster-grocer-apothecary, who was also building up a small practice as an amateur medical practitioner. Burns's not too good-natured lampoon was perhaps pardonable so long as it was circulated in manuscript only; had it been published, however, it would have constituted an unnecessary offense to a neighbor who was, at worst, harmlessly amusing.[23]

It is more difficult to account for Burns's failure to print the "Address to the Unco Guid." If the poem was written before July of 1786, and it may have been, for the thesis of the poem and some of the very phraseology had appeared some time before in an entry in the *Commonplace Book*, it is surprising that Burns did not publish it. There is nothing personal about it, except as it is Burns's *apologia* for his own errors. It is free from anything which could be termed religious or ecclesiastical satire. It is a plea, as eloquent as can well be conceived, for "Poor Frailty." The fact that Burns did not publish it till the 1787 Edinburgh edition, may well mean that it was not written till after his experience in doing penance for the Armour affair, and hence not till after the Kilmarnock volume was in the press.

There can be no uncertainty, however, over the reason for the omission of "The Twa Herds," "The Ordination," and "Holy Willie's Prayer." The first is a superbly readable account of a dispute between Russell of Kilmarnock and Moodie of Riccarton over a matter of their parish boundaries. When these two,

> The twa best herds in a' the wast
> That e'er gae gospel horn a blast

came to "a bitter black outcast," the opportunity for satire was one which Burns could not pass by. The poem circulated among his friends; "with a certain side of both clergy and laity," Burns wrote later, "it met with a roar of applause." [24]   To print it, however, with its sarcastic allusions to half a dozen prominent Auld Light ministers, and its praise of as many more of Burns's friends among the liberal clergy, would have been to compromise his friends, and needlessly to exasperate his—and their— opponents.

For the same reason Burns allowed "The Ordination," written in ironical celebration of the selection of a staunch conservative for the second parish in Kilmarnock, to remain unpublished till the Edinburgh edition of 1787.

The stanzas which the world knows as "Holy Willie's Prayer" Burns himself never printed. Not till 1799 could a publisher be found bold enough to allow this grim and trenchant piece of irony to find its way to the general reader. Again, superlatives are needless; yet one can hardly resist saying that this poem alone would have admitted Burns to the fellowship of

Swift and Aristophanes. Indeed, one is hard put to it to find anywhere in literature another hundred lines of satiric verse which can rank with it. Here is the merciless pillorying of a specific individual, and of an individual as well known in his community as was Euripides in the Athens that delighted in *The Frogs.* Here is the devastating attack upon the general system of belief which that individual represented; here is the artistic restraint which kept the portrait of William Fisher from becoming a mere caricature, and hence from losing its significance as satire. Here is the brilliant phrase, the flawless rhythm, and —burning through every line—the *saeva indignatio* which only genius can impart to the printed page.

In addition to the religious pieces, poetic epistles, and satires, which Burns thus withheld from publication, there were also some forty lyrics, besides the songs in "The Jolly Beggars," which were ready to his hand when he was supplying John Wilson with copy. Four of the forty were used as stop-gaps at the close of the book, being tucked in, apparently, to fill up space, along with the trivial epitaphs and epigrams. Five more of these songs written before July, 1786, were afterwards included in the 1787 Edinburgh edition, but three-fourths of this very considerable group remained unpublished till Johnson and Thomson began turning to Burns for copy. One may fairly ask why the poet should have treated these lyrics in this somewhat contemptuous fashion. Why did he send to the printer such lugubrious failures as "To Ruin" and "Man Was Made to Mourn," and withhold "Mary Morison" and "Green Grow the Rashes?"

Not because he himself was not interested in Scottish song. For two years at least, as the entries in the *Commonplace Book* show, he had been thinking seriously about this phase of Scottish national culture. He had read extensively in the published collections, though not, of course, as widely as he was to do later. He had already developed his own song-writing technique: a scrap of an old lyric, a tune, an occasion which demanded a new set of stanzas, or a mood or experience which called for commemoration—and the song took shape in his mind. Further-more, he enjoyed this particular sort of poetic composition; he appreciated and at times meticulously criticized his own produc-tions; he was already more than a mere learner in the art which by 1793 he had mastered. Certainly he did not omit the songs from the published volume because he personally felt them to be insignificant.

No, the reason for Burns's failure to publish more of his songs in the 1786 volume must be sought not in any opinion he himself had formed concerning them, but in the literary taste of the audience he was addressing. Apparently he felt that, having advertised a volume of Scottish poems, he must live up to his contract, and not risk offending his audience by working off on them verse of a sort with which Lowland folk were more or less familiar, and which the bulk of his readers would hardly have considered worth three shillings.

So again, as in the case of the omitted satires and epistles, one sees Burns acutely conscious of his audience, unwilling to chal-lenge established authority by too drastic criticism of popular dogmas or prominent ministers, and loath to offend the gen-erality of his readers by giving them mere songs when they had asked for poems.

Finally, there remains "The Jolly Beggars," "that puissant and splendid production," to quote Arnold's happy phrase, which seems to have been written during 1785 or the early part of 1786, and which would have added distinction to any col-lection of poetry. This expression of one of Burns's moods, this picture of one phase of Scottish life, this outspoken de-nunciation of things as they were, Burns excluded from his volume.

The actual history of the poem is still wrapped in doubt. Not till 1799 was it published in complete form;[25] even yet there is little in the way of actual evidence as to when it was written, or what, precisely, was the occasion which gave it birth. The only surviving statement by Burns himself is disappointingly vague. Writing to George Thomson, in September of 1793, he said:

THE KILMARNOCK VOLUME

I have forgot the Cantata you allude to, as I kept no copy, & indeed
did not know that it was in existence; however, I remember that none
of the songs pleased myself, except the last—something about

> Courts for cowards were erected,
> Churches built to please the priest.[26]

Such an astonishing remark, that Burns had "forgot the
Cantata," can be interpreted in only one of two ways. By 1793,
when the Excise Board had been examining his conduct, either
he had come to feel that it would be the part of wisdom not to
remember his youthful follies, or else the absorbing events of
the preceding six years had actually driven from his mind all
but the most vague recollections of this unrivalled product of
his lavishly creative imagination. The second alternative
seems less probable than the first.

In either case, however, it is clear that Burns had the poem
definitely in mind when he was preparing the 1787 Edinburgh
edition, and planned to publish it in that volume. As Professor
Ferguson has recently put it,

> Some notes by Hugh Blair, now in the Esty collection, show that
> Burns had intended to include the glorious *Jolly Beggars* in his Edin-
> burgh edition, but Blair condemned both that poem and another, now
> lost, entitled *The Prophet and God's Complaint*, and Burns omitted
> them.[27]

There is no indication that Burns ever again contemplated publishing the poem.

For the origin of "The Jolly Beggars," one is forced to trust
to tradition that traces back directly to Burns's intimate friend,
John Richmond. Richmond once told Robert Chambers, and
Chambers gave the story to the world, how Burns, Smith, and
Richmond, one night during the poet's residence at Mossgiel,

> dropped accidentally, at a late hour, into the humble hostlery of . . .
> Poosie Nansie. . . . After witnessing much jollity amongst a com-
> pany who by day appeared abroad as miserable beggars, the three young
> men came away, Burns professing to have been greatly amused by the
> scene, but particularly with the gleesome behaviour of an old maimed

soldier.   In the course of a few days he recited a part of the poem to Richmond, who informed me that, to the best of his recollection, it contained, in its original form, songs by a sweep and a sailor, which did not afterwards appear.[28]

It is a plausible story; something of the sort may have taken place.   But no gossip by Richmond, no possible discovery of an actual date for Burns's visit to Poosie Nansie's hostelry, can ever explain or account for the finished product.

Criticism hesitates and falters before the task of commenting on the poem, even in the possibly incomplete form in which it exists.[29]   But some things must be said.

To begin with the less impressive merits of the work, one notes the absence of the poetic diction, which, borrowed from eighteenth century England, Burns allowed to mar many of his more elaborate works.   Only once does a false note of this kind intrude:

> The caird prevail'd—th' unblushing fair
> In his embraces sunk;
> Partly wi' love o'ercome sae sair,
> An' partly she was drunk.

And even here the objectionable phrase, "th' unblushing fair," though out of harmony with the simplicity and directness of Burns's vigorous diction, is so inoffensive as to cause only the slightest interruption in the movement of the poem as a whole; it may, indeed, be a humorous imitation of the prevailing poetic diction.

Again, omitting for the time being all consideration of the content of the poem, one discovers a richness of metrical form, a plentitude of appropriate and perfectly executed rhythmical patterns, which would have ranked Burns, had he never written anything else, among the masters of English prosody.   For example, the eight songs, or "airs," are cast in eight different stanza forms, which range all the way from the conventional *a-b-a-b* iambic quatrain of the first bard's song, to the rushing anapaestic couplets of "I once was a maid," or to the challenging

[164]

trochees of "See the smoking bowl before us." There is a lavishness in Burns's prosody which is all but concealed by the ease with which he handles the different patterns, and which bears testimony not alone to his thorough knowledge of his English and Scottish predecessors, but also to his well-nigh perfect control of his pen. The songs in "The Jolly Beggars" lack the wistful pathos which has popularized many of the songs which Burns wrote during his later years. There is more skillful use of artfully chosen vowel sounds, of "tone color," in some of the later songs; there is far more poignant pathos. But for sheer technical virtuosity the songs of this "forgotten" cantata will stand comparison with anything Burns ever wrote.

Nor was this technical skill unaccompanied by other and greater, though perhaps more obvious, merits. To say that the narratives woven into the poem move with swift precision, or that the touches of characterization are as sure and revealing as the brief descriptive passages in which Burns set the stage and framed the picture, or that the concluding lyric sounds as grimly defiant a note as may be found in the literature of Revolutionary Europe—to say this is to say what every reader of the poem has felt for himself. It may not be out of place, however, to point out that save in the concluding lyric of "The Jolly Beggars" Burns stepped completely out of his own character, and, dramatist that he was *in posse* if not *in esse,* saw the world accurately through the eyes of characters whom he himself had created. Never again was he to give such sure indication of his genius as in this "puissant production," which he wrote and suppressed!

Such, then, were some of the poems which Burns might have included in his first volume, but which, out of deference to public opinion and regard for his neighbors and for his own reputation and future prospects, he withheld from publication: some insignificant religious poems; a group of rimed epistles; half a dozen satires; a large number of songs; and "The Jolly Beggars." They would have made a notable collection, these unpublished works; at least as notable as that which John Wilson printed!

[165]

3

THE PUBLISHED POEMS

When one opens the Kilmarnock volume one finds forty-four poems; nine are insignificant epitaphs or epigrams, and four others distinctly trivial songs. Omitting these thirteen, which Burns inserted at the end of the book, one has thirty-one items to reckon with; it is these thirty-one poems that made Burns known to the world. To enumerate the varieties of work here represented is to realize how many-sided was the genius which thus found its first public expression.

Once again to begin with the least significant features, there were half a dozen poems, reminiscent of Burns's periods of physical and mental depression,[30] which are of interest chiefly because they show Burns to have been well acquainted with those English poets in the imitation of whom he was least happy.

There also were two poems which it is not unfair to think of as inspired by Burns's interest in Scottish and British politics: "The Author's Earnest Cry and Prayer" and "A Dream." In each Burns appears as more than a superficial observer of a phase of the nation's life concerning which the majority of his friends and neighbors felt little concern. Though by no means as vigorous as the suppressed "Address of Beelzebub," they were timely, and in places at least, brilliant, examples of that rare sort of political satire which remains readable after the conditions which occasioned it have ceased to exist.

The same thing is true, *mutatis mutandis*, of the best of the poetic epistles, of which there were nine specimens in the volume.[31] There was nothing in these examples of Burns's mastery of an old literary form which his first readers would not have considered thoroughly enjoyable; there is little which the reader of today does not find worth while, despite the lapse of a century and a half.

Two themes in particular run through this group of poems: Burns's delight in writing verse, and his uneasiness in the "neck-halter" of what he considered an inequable, although—so far

[166]

as he was concerned—endurable, distribution of "this warld's gear." The epistles to Smith, Lapraik, and Simpson, are perhaps the most valuable of all poetic sources of information concerning the delight which Burns found in writing verse. His ambitions, his materials, even his methods of composition, are all touched upon. The stanzas in which he sets forth his ideas on these matters are not those that the world knows best, to be sure; but they are simple, direct, vigorous, and informing. Two from the epistle to Simpson may well stand as illustrations of the way in which Burns handled this theme:

> Yet when a tale comes i' my head,
> Or lassies gie my heart a screed—
> As whiles they're like to be my dead,
> (O sad disease!)
> I kittle up my rustic reed;
> It gies me ease.

Or again, with a lilting charm which even the pardonable exaggeration of the last lines can not conceal:

> We'll sing auld Coila's plains an' fells,
> Her moors red-brown wi' heather bells,
> Her banks an' braes, her dens an' dells,
> Whare glorious Wallace
> Aft bure the gree, as story tells,
> Frae Southron billies.

The first of the two poems addressed to Lapraik contains a group of stanzas in which Burns's literary ambition and his ever-present class-consciousness are interestingly interwoven:

> I am nae Poet, in a sense,
> But just a Rhymer like, by chance,
> An' hae to Learning nae pretence;
> Yet, what the matter?˙
> When'er my Muse does on me glance,
> I jingle at her.

[167]

Your Critic-folk may cock their nose,
And say, "How can you e'er propose,
You, wha ken hardly verse frae prose,
    To mak a sang?"
But by your leaves, my learned foes,
    Ye're maybe wrang.

What's a' your jargon o' your schools,
Your Latin names for horns an' stools;
If honest Nature made you fools
    What sairs your Grammar?
Ye'd better ta'en up spades and shools,
    Or knappin-hammers.

A set o' dull, conceited Hashes
Confuse their brains in Colledge classes!
They gang in Stirks, and come out Asses,
    Plain truth to speak;
An' syne they think to climb Parnassus
    By dint o' Greek!

Gie me ae spark o' Nature's fire,
That's a' the learning I desire;
Then, tho I drudge thro' dub an' mire
    At pleugh or cart,
My Muse, tho hamely in attire,
    May touch the heart.

A considerable part, at least, of Burns's undying appeal is explained in those last two lines.

Concerning the second of the two themes that appear in these epistles, this at least is clear: the bitterness which tinctures every line of the suppressed "Address of Beelzebub" is hardly suggested in the published works. One finds discontent here, and some murmurings of the rebellious spirit which flamed out in "A Fig for those by Law Protected." But either Burns was definitely keeping himself in check as he wrote these letters to his friends, or else the violence which marked some of his protests against things as they are was not so much a part of his general attitude towards life as the result of some specific irritation. The tone of the passages in which Burns allows his discontent to appear is on the whole surprisingly genial. He was definitely "in opposition," and had been for some time before 1786. With the squire, the landlord, the aristocrat, he had little in common. But he was willing to accept what fate had sent him, and to find what happiness he could in his lot:

> A man may hae an honest heart,
>   Tho' Poortith hourly stare him;
> A man may tak a neebor's part,
>   Yet hae nae cash to spare him.[32]

Or again, with a touch of hopefulness, even,

> But, Davie lad, ne'er fash your head,
>   Tho' we hae little gear;
> We're fit to win our daily bread,
>   As lang's we're hale and fier.
>   "Mair spier na, nor fear na";
>   Auld age ne'er mind a feg;
> The last o't, the warst o't,
>   Is only but to beg.[33]

It was a rebel, surely enough, who wrote the nine epistles; but a rebel who had himself well under control, and who allowed just enough of the spirit of protest to appear in his pages to win the favor of his fellows in "poortith cauld," but not enough to bring down upon himself the disfavor of established authority.

To include the "Address to the Deil" in this group of epistles may seem somewhat odd; yet surely the poem belongs here and nowhere else. Beyond dispute, it is one of Burns's half dozen masterpieces. Other poets had had their say concerning this "Prince . . . that led the embattled Seraphim to war," but no one had ever treated him with such genial, though not contemptuous, intimacy; nor had any one save Burns succeeded in so humanizing his personality, while at the same time allowing him to retain his obviously supernatural powers and character.

The poem is good proof, moreover, of how close Burns was to the old Scottish world of primitive superstition and pagan folk-lore. The devil of Burns's poem is far more than the incarnation of evil against whom Calvinistic divines warned their auditors. He is this, to be sure; but he is also the spirit who lights his ghostly lantern in the depths of the swamp, or haunts the river fords in time of freshet, to lure unwary travelers to their death. He is the less malign, mischief-loving sprite who frightens the wanderer on the moor, charms the cream in the churn, and casts his spell upon "dawtet, twal-pint Hawkie." This many-sided personality Burns admitted almost to the rôle of a friend. It must have caused men like Russell and Auld no small amount of concern to see him treated with such friendly geniality, and in particular to hear the unholy suggestion that even this Prince of Evil, if only he would mend his ways, might have a chance of salvation!

In the many poems dealing with Scottish manners and customs,[34] Ayrshire folk found themselves pictured with a truthfulness which left the critic little chance for objection, and yet with an art which raised the commonplaces of everyday life to a high level of significance. There is inequality here, to be sure; "Scotch Drink" is a relatively trivial piece of Bacchanalianism; "Hallowe'en" is distinctly overloaded with details which too frequently, even for Burns's first readers, required elucidation in foot-notes. "To a Daisy" is a weak imitation of its prototype, "To a Mouse;" and the lines to the louse, clever though they are, add but little to the volume's enduring merit. Even "The Twa Dogs," with its brilliant picturing of the state of mind of the "poor folk" for whom Burns was writing, and its uncannily accurate exposition of what may be called "dog psychology," even this falls short of the high level attained by the best of the group. And the two poems on Mailie are so lacking in what the contemporary world calls "human interest" that to enjoy them to the full one must be familiar with the tradition which established the mock-elegy as a legitimate type of vernacular literature.

There remain, however, after these exclusions have been

made, four poems on which Burns might well have staked his reputation: "The Cotter's Saturday Night," "The Auld Farmer's Salutation to his Mare," "The Holy Fair," and "To a Mouse." Something must be said concerning each of these.

The primary appeal of "The Cotter's Saturday Night" was distinctly local. It was a poem written by a man who had grown up on an Ayrshire farm, and who was writing for persons situated as he had been. The Cotter is not Tennyson's Old Farmer; he is not one of Whittier's New Englanders; he resembles Wordsworth's Michael in only one respect, love of his family. And though this motif, like the patriotic theme which widens the horizon of the poem in the concluding stanzas, is all but universal in its appeal, the entire *mise-en-scène* is such as to make it virtually impossible for any save one of Burns's own countrymen to appreciate the full significance of the poem.

Yet Burns has suffered much through a sort of criticism in which the critic's patriotism has blinded him to considerations that would have been patent enough to an outsider. Hence it may not be inappropriate to attempt, at least, to restore the balance by considering "The Cotter's Saturday Night" not as a vignette of Ayrshire farm life, nor even as a glowing expression of a Scotsman's devotion to his native land, but as a work of art.

When one approaches the poem from this detached or objective point of view, one realizes that it is an astonishingly uneven piece of work. The unity of tone, of mood, and of diction, which marked the "Address to the Deil," for instance, have here entirely disappeared. The best of Burns and virtually the worst of Burns lie side by side in unseemly incongruity. Several illustrations of this fact could be cited; one will suffice:

> The parents partial eye their hopeful years;
> Anticipation forward points the view;
> The Mother, wi' her needle an' her sheers,
> Gars auld claes look amaist as weel's the new.

Here is not merely a sudden and disconcerting change from English to Scots, but also a bewildering transition from the elaborate idiom of the worst of English neo-classicists to the simple diction of Burns's own household. The fundamental defect in the first two lines is not primarily linguistic. It is clear that Burns could write English as easily as Scots. But unfortunately when he wrote English he was inclined to imitate those English poets with whose work he had grown familiar early in life, but whose genius was as different from his as Strawberry Hill and Twickenham were from Mossgiel farm. The Burns who wrote

> Anticipation forward points the view

was in bondage to a literary tradition utterly foreign to Scottish vernacular poetry as well as to his own genius. And the simple truthfulness and homely beauty of

> The Mother, wi' her needle an' her sheers,
> Gars auld claes look amaist as weel's the new,

are in unpleasant juxtaposition to the stiff solemnity for which Pope and his followers were responsible. Burns speaking his own mind, or recording what he had seen, was straightforward, vigorous, poetic; Burns borrowing from "the wits of Queen Anne's reign" was weak and inept. There is far too much of this borrowing in "The Cotter's Saturday Night."

Again, the Spenserian stanza which Burns chose for the poem was a form in which he moved uneasily. Many poets have found it a difficult stanza; in Burns's hands it proved a cumbersome tool, and drove him to such banalities, for his concluding Alexandrines, as

> To help her parents dear, if they in hardship be,

or the different but equally unfortunate

> Beneath the milk-white thorn that scents the evening gale.

However skillful Burns may usually have been as a metrist, this particular stanza, with its slow movement and languorous cadences, was hard for him to handle.

It is probably true, also, that even the most enthusiastically patriotic Scot will admit the tone of the moralizing passages to be unfortunately inflated and bombastic. The passage opening with the line

O happy love! where love like this is found!

and the stanza beginning

Compar'd with this, how poor Religion's pride

show Burns in one of his least pleasing veins. He was not a convincing preacher. Had he omitted these sections entirely, he would have improved the total effect of the poem. They jar unpleasantly on the ear, however true some of the ideas they set forth may be.

In short, "The Cotter's Saturday Night" lacks the unity and simplicity which Burns instinctively imparted to his best productions. Here is no perfect whole, built up of fittingly selected details, but an incongruous mingling of discordant elements.

But when one has admitted these criticisms of the poem as valid, one should also realize that this Ayrshire idyll has virtues which in the judgment of many readers far outweigh its defects, and that these virtues seem destined to keep it perennially fresh and readable. Once again to state the obvious, the central theme of the poem, the simple dignity of an honest laborer's home life, makes its unfailing appeal wherever manual labor is performed. Moreover, in developing this theme Burns anticipated by fifteen years what Wordsworth was later to say in the *Preface* concerning the value of accurate observation and simple, natural diction. Here is the poet writing with his eye on the object, and part of the time, at least, using the "language of conversation among the lower and middle classes"—to quote Wordsworth's most extreme statement of his theory. The accuracy of the poet's vision every reader can illustrate for himself; it is noteworthy that the passages which best exemplify this phase of Burns's skill are also the passages in which the diction is simplest and most natural.

It is true that even the best of "The Cotter's Saturday Night,"

[173]

THE LIFE OF ROBERT BURNS

is not poetry of the highest order. But it is poetry which does not lose its charm with the passing of time, and which brings happiness and good cheer to a worldwide audience of simple folk. "The Auld Farmer's Salutation to his Mare" is unmarred by any of the unfortunate elements which one detects in the poem just discussed; and though it does not touch upon either of the two themes that give "The Cotter's Saturday Night" its widest appeal, love of home and love of father-land, it has the artistic beauty of a perfect piece of *genre* painting, which the longer poem lacks. Nor indeed is it without a universal audience; for despite the definitely Scottish flavor imparted by the broad and consistently maintained dialect, its fundamental theme is the sympathy that exists the world over between man and the beasts that labor for him. There is virtually none of this in Wordsworth, who knew farm life only from the outside; there is little in Crabbe or Cowper, whose descriptions of rural England one inevitably thinks of in connection with Burns's. Burns alone of the greater English poets touched this note; he alone had the genius to realize that the affection which the farmer feels for his "auld trusty servan'" is both universal and poetic. And the close of the poem, homely as it is in diction, leaves one not far from the pathos of "John Anderson my Jo." It is only a short step from

> We've worn to crazy years thegither;
> We'll toyte about wi' ane anither;
> Wi' tentie care I'll flit thy tether
>   To some hain'd rig,
> Where ye may nobly rax your leather
>   Wi' sma' fatigue,

to the beauty of

> John Anderson my Jo, John,
> We clamb the hill thegither;
> And monie a cantie day, John,
> We had wi' ane anither;
> Now we maun totter down, John,

And hand in hand we'll go,
And sleep thegither at the foot,
John Anderson, my Jo!

"The Holy Fair," though by no means as caustic as "Holy Willie's Prayer," is in some ways more effective than the suppressed poem because it is uniformly good natured. There is no personal animus here; only keen observation and faithful representation, accompanied by devastating though never bitter laughter. The person who reads the poem today learns much concerning one phase of Scottish life a century and a half ago; he discovers, too, how satire originally occasioned by a definite set of local conditions, may remain perennially readable and enjoyable if it is directed not merely against those conditions, but also against a fundamental characteristic of human nature. The hypocrisy of the "unco guid" has always been irritating to their ungodly neighbors, and has provoked them to either curses or mockery. The mood of "Holy Willie's Prayer" is the mood of a man angered to the point of blasphemy. The mood of "The Holy Fair" is the mood of a man who sees "through the shows of things into the things themselves," as Carlyle would put it, and laughs at what he sees. The laughter is the more destructive because it is untinged by ill-nature.

Interestingly enough, the poem shows Burns following the examples of Chaucer and Shakespeare by making use of a specific prose "source." It is a commonplace, of course, that he often turned to Ramsay, Fergusson, and to many of the eighteenth century neo-classicists, for suggestions for his own work. But "The Holy Fair" is unique in that it is based not merely on Fergusson's "Leith Races," which it follows as regards externals, but also on a document published in 1759 under the title of *A Letter from a Blacksmith to the Ministers and Elders of the Church of Scotland.*[35] It is a pungent piece of prose, indicative of one way in which the spirit of protest was finding expression. A few sentences will show that the unknown author had a genuine journalistic talent, and also that Burns at times followed his source rather closely:

[175]

In Scotland they run from kirk to kirk, and flock to see a Sacrament, and make the same use of it that the papists do of their pilgrimages and processions—that is, indulge themselves in drunkenness, folly, and idleness. . . . At the time of the administration of the Lord's Supper, upon the Thursday, Saturday and Monday, we have preaching in the fields near the church. Allow me, then, to describe it as it really is: at first you find a great number of men and women lying upon the grass; here they are sleeping and snoring, some with their faces towards heaven, others with their faces turned downwards, or covered with their bonnets; there you find a knot of young fellows and girls making assignations to go home together in the evening, or to meet in some alehouse; in another place you see a pious circle sitting around an ale-barrel, many of which stand ready upon carts for the refreshment of the saints. . . . In this sacred assembly there is an odd mixture of religion, sleep, drinking, courtship, and a confusion of sexes, ages and characters. When you get a little nearer the speaker, so as to be within reach of the sound, tho' not of the sense of the words, for that can only reach a small circle . . . you will find some weeping and others laughing, some pressing to get nearer the tent or tub in which the parson is sweating, bawling, jumping, and beating the desk; others fainting with the stifling heat, or wrestling to extricate themselves from the crowd; one seems very devout and serious, and the next moment is scolding or cursing his neighbours for squeezing or treading on him; in an instant after, his countenance is composed to the religious gloom, and he is groaning, sighing, and weeping for his sins: in a word, there is such an absurd mixture of the serious and comick, that were we convened for any other purpose than that of worshipping the God and Governor of Nature, the scene would exceed all power of farce.[86]

It should be remembered that scenes like this which the unknown pamphleteer found so worthy of note were to be observed annually in many of the larger Scottish parishes. The Sacrament of the Lord's Supper, the central, the climactic episode of the church year, was as a rule celebrated only once in a twelve-month. To be avoidably absent from it was almost equivalent to apostasy; to be temporarily debarred from it by church authority, was to be made a conspicuous example of evil living, and might end in excommunication. Several contiguous parishes often united to hold one joint service, so that each group might have the chance to hear all of the coöperating ministers. Because of the crowds that attended, it was impossible for the entire service to take place in any church building. Hence the preaching parts of the exercises were held in a field near the kirk, and if possible also near a public house where refreshment could be had. Inevitably "The Occasion," as it was popularly called, became a sort of degenerated secular fair, with alcohol, religious enthusiasm, and simple licentiousness each playing its part in stirring the emotions of the audience.

Of course it was through no desire on the part of the ministers that the "tent preaching"—to use another of the popular designations—developed into what Burns and his innominate predecessor knew it to be. The persons in charge of the annual services did what they could to maintain them on a high level of decorum. But all the laws of mob psychology were against them, and it is probably no exaggeration to say that by 1785 many of the annual "Occasions" were little better than scandalous.

Naturally enough, the orthodox ministers were most active— and most vociferous—in maintaining the old institution. Hence as Burns observed, and inevitably participated in, the affair from year to year, he came to think of it not merely as an event where Fun, Superstition, Hypocrisy, and genuine religious enthusiasm, were curiously intermingled in the audience, but also as an opportunity which the different ministers were glad to seize upon as giving them a chance to display their oratorical powers and persuasive abilities. When finally he burst forth in laughter, his shafts were directed in part at the congregation, and in part at the preachers, whom he knew well, and whose personal peculiarities he hit off with the deftness of a trained cartoonist. The result is a flawless piece of personal and social satire.

This very fact of its flawlessness differentiates "The Holy Fair" sharply from much that Burns wrote. It was his misfortune to compose under such pressure that of necessity he sent many a poem to his publishers in a condition which he himself knew to be unfinished and imperfect. "The Holy Fair," however, shows none of the blemishes that might have marred so long a poem. The mood of good-natured banter, with the undertone of more serious satire, is maintained from beginning to end. Even the language is surprisingly and effectively consistent. Not once does Burns exchange the vernacular for English. There are no indications that the exigencies or rime or rhythm ever forced him to say aught save what he wished to say. Furthermore, his use of the ninth line "tag" or "tail" is little less than brilliant. Each of the twenty-seven stanzas concludes with a short phrase that rounds out the sense of the whole stanza; each of these twenty-seven tags differs from every other, but each ends with the same word, "day." There is no simple repetition, as of a refrain; in each stanza the thought is incomplete till the short ninth line has made its contribution to the whole. As a result, what was in effect a highly artificial and difficult verse-form seems to the reader most simple, natural, and inevitable, the only form in which "The Holy Fair" could possibly have been cast.

Here too is a swiftly moving narrative, rendered picturesque by specific detail and concrete image; here is sure characterization which humanizes every episode in that narrative, and which clearly differentiates the various personages from one another. Here is diction which appears as simple and natural as the everyday speech of the cottage fireside, but which proves, on closer examination, to be as difficult to praise as it is to imitate. Here is the occasional phrase, like "yill-caup commentators," which bewilders the reader by its brilliant appropriateness. Here are playful banter, mordant irony, broad comedy, and subtle sarcasm, all blended into a tissue of uniform color and tone. Here too is the recklessly skillful juxtaposition of incongruities which only a great comedian could have made effective. And here is the combination of power and ease of which great art alone can boast, and which the world has long admired and wondered at, whether it be exemplified in the vibrationless pulsings of a great engine, or in the moving simplicity of a line of verse.

Yet however highly one may praise "The Holy Fair," it is doubtful whether the poem belongs in the same class with "To a

Mouse," which, in its way, is as superbly inimitable as *Hamlet* or "The Rime of the Ancient Mariner." Like them, it bears the marks of stark genius. To read it understandingly is to realize the truth of Emerson's utterance, "I ask not for the great, the remote, the romantic; what is doing in Italy or Arabia; what is Greek Art or Provençal minstrelsy; I embrace the common, I explore and sit at the feet of the familiar, the low." By the sheer power of his sympathetic and creative imagination, Burns has touched "the familiar, the low," and transformed it not into an object of sensuous beauty, but into something far more notable—a perennially beautiful symbol of human life.

There is no need to use many words in commenting upon a poem which has passed into the literature of the entire world. But it is perhaps worth pointing out that here, in eight short stanzas, one sees Burns's uncannily accurate poetic vision supplying him with the materials out of which to construct his poem; one sees his artist's imagination culling the important from the unimportant details, and then, by what mysterious process can never be explained, raising everything to a high level of poetic significance; one see, too, his skill in transmitting to his reader the results of this imaginative re-working of the products of his observation. As has often been suggested, great art shows three qualities in proper proportion: observation, imagination, and sense of form, or technique. If any one of the three predominates to the detriment of either of the others, the resulting poem is sure to be lacking in balance, in harmony. There is no such disproportion in "To a Mouse." On the contrary, each of the three qualities makes its contribution to what Emerson termed "the perfect whole."

The meticulous critic will perhaps object that once in the poem Burns's literary sense played him false. The two lines

> I'm truly sorry Man's dominion
> Has broken Nature's social union,

fail to ring true. They smell of the lamp, and witness Burns's reading in the "classics" of eighteenth century England. But

there are no other flaws in the picture, and this is small enough
to be unobserved save by the seeker after defects. To offset
it one has a plenitude of riches. Indeed, to quote any single
phrase, or stanza even, and say "Here is Burns at his best," is
to omit much that another reader might find equally memorable.
But one may well point to the expression

> At me, thy poor earth-born companion
> An' fellow mortal

as an example of Burns's ability to tell the truth in language
which is beyond praise for its simple effectiveness. There is
nothing maudlin in the phrase, nor is there any blinking of the
facts. Seeking some bond between himself and the mouse,
Burns instinctively hits upon the one tie which unites the farmer
at his plough and the "poor beastie" among the stubble: both
are earth-born, and born to die. In that act of veracious yet
imaginative synthesis one phase of Burns's genius shows at its
clearest.

Or again, take the sentence

> That wee bit heap o' leaves an stibble
> Has cost thee monie a weary nibble.

Here in the first line Burns presents with simplicity and accuracy
what he sees as he looks at the nest he has crushed. In the second he lets his imagination play over these crude materials, with
the result that the little vignette is not a still-life pastel, but a
picture endowed with life and motion. Out of its context, the
word "nibble" is perhaps as unpoetic as any that one could well
imagine; in its context, however, it is the one word necessary
to give perfection to the couplet. And only a great artist could
have found and used that word.

Finally, consider the concluding two stanzas, where Burns
deftly but surely shifts the emphasis from the mouse to himself.
Here there is none of the sentimentalism and conventional
moralizing that at times mar the products of Burns's more serious moods. The poignancy of the stanzas is the greater because

of the restraint with which they are composed, and because the intensity of feeling is not allowed to break forth into ineffective heroics. On the contrary, Burns has both his emotions and his technique well under control. Gradually, almost imperceptibly, the minor chords become more pronounced; the shadows of a November twilight deepen over the field where the poet stands. By the time the last word has burned its image into the mind of the reader, the tragedy of the mouse has become the tragedy of Burns himself, and of all heart-broken folk who review the past with regret, or await the future with misgiving:

> But, Mousie, thou art no thy lane
> In proving foresight may be vain;
> The best-laid schemes o' Mice an' Men
> Gang aft agley,
> An lea'e us nought but grief an' pain
> For promis'd joy.
>
> Still, thou art blest, compar'd wi' me!
> The present only toucheth thee;
> But, och, I backward cast my e'e
> On prospects drear;
> An' forward, tho' I canna see,
> I guess, an' fear!

There is nothing else in the Kilmarnock volume quite so notable as "To a Mouse."

When one considers this first volume as a whole, one discovers certain conclusions shaping themselves in one's mind. First of all, it is of no little importance to the literary historian that here one finds the simple language and homely, every-day material, which one associates with Cowper and Wordsworth. *The Task* had appeared one year before Burns's first publication; *The Lyrical Ballads* were still over twelve years in the future. Burns's work was fully as important a harbinger of what is popularly called "The Romantic Movement" as *The Task,* and not much less significant than the unpretentious book-

let which contained "Tintern Abbey." There was none of the
conscious literary reformer in Burns, as there was in Wordsworth.
Indeed, Burns's many imitations of the very poets whose theory
and practise Wordsworth was later to decry, show him to have
been unquestioning in his allegiance to the old school, so far as
English verse was concerned. But at the same time his instincts
were on the other side. When he trusted these instincts, and
forgot his studies in the "Classics," the result was poetry which
Wordsworth was later to read with delight, but which Pope
would probably have ridiculed.

Here, too, is the culmination of the Scottish vernacular tradition, the finest expression of the national instinct for poetry which
had borne good fruit in the work of the old "Makars," and,
more recently, had encouraged Ramsay and Fergusson in their
attempts to re-establish a native Scottish literature. Even Dunbar is insignificant in comparison to Burns, and Ramsay and
Fergusson are of interest largely because Burns did with superb
success what they had attempted with only mediocre results.
Save for Burns, they would be forgotten; as, save for Burns,
Scottish poetry would be lacking in any single figure of unquestioned and enduring distinction. But Burns could not have been
what he was, had the examples of these men not been before him
as he wrote.

Historical values, however, are relative values. Forgetting
the fact that Burns's first publication is entitled to a considerable
section in the history of English romanticism, and to an even
larger part in any account of Scottish vernacular literature, and
considering it only as a volume of poetry, one still finds much
to say. It was very definitely a book written by a farmer, but
by a farmer whose contacts with the soil had neither deadened
his perceptions nor blinded him to the importance of the world
which lay beyond the boundaries of Ayrshire. There is a sturdy
provincialism in these poems, as there is in many of Kipling's;
and it is a provincialism which strengthens the book as a whole,
and never weakens it.

It was a volume, moreover, written by a rebel against orthodox

[182]

ecclesiastical authority, and against the established order of things in general. Tyranny, whether of Kirk or landlord, Burns hated; he had suffered under both, and knew their sting. Better than most of his neighbors, for his horizon was far wider than theirs, Burns realized that liberty—economic, religious, political—was indeed a "glorious feast." Nevertheless he did not allow himself to become embittered by the situation in which he found himself. Only when Authority and Hypocrisy joined hands did he cease to temper his ridicule with good nature.

Clearly enough, too, this farmer and rebel was also a poet. His eye was alert for those manifestations of Nature's power with which he came most intimately in contact, and which he could most readily weave into a setting for the human drama that was his primary concern. To the query why Burns, who grew up within sight of the ocean and hills, paid but scanty attention to these grander aspects of Nature, the answer seems easy. They were too large, too impressive, to be used as framework for anything; moreover, the Nature which he knew and wove into his poetry was that of farmyard and cornfield, of burn and tree embowered glen, the Nature which every tiller of the soil knows best. His poet's instinct was usually sure enough to keep him from the pitfall of an artificial enthusiasm for matters which were, in effect, extraneous to his world. But the worlds that lay around him he saw with clarity, both the world of Nature and that of Humanity.

To be sure, Burns's reaction to this world was by no means as profound as Wordsworth's, for instance. Occasionally, as in the last stanza of "To a Mouse," one notes in Burns a suggestion of that sort of imaginative synthesis which glorifies Wordsworth's best work. His utterances on such matters as religion, democracy, and what has recently come to be called internationalism, are in harmony with the truest ideals of today. In all these he was far ahead of his age. Usually, however, Burns was content to tell what he had seen, without reflecting on the significance of the phenomenon. For this very reason, perhaps, the generality of readers find him more easy of approach than the Sage of Rydal. It is easier to see than to think; it is easier to show men what is worth looking at than to instruct them in the meaning of life. Burns offered his readers the simpler of the two alternatives. As they turned his pages they found that his materials had been selected with the imaginative insight of a sure artist, albeit that artist was not in any large way a thinker.

Obviously, too, this poet was a master of his craft. The more one reads the best of Burns, the more one admires his technique. The ease with which he moved in many elaborate verse patterns, adapting form to content with unerring skill; the sureness with which he selected the right word, the perfect phrase; the deftness with which he wove vowels and consonants into musical cadences and patterns—these elements of Burns's technique are sometimes overlooked, so apparently artless is the finished product. But the art is there, and in rich measure.

Finally, the Kilmarnock volume was the work of a warm-hearted, sympathetic human being, who "could love and could hate;" who lived in full enjoyment of the Nature that lay around him, as well as of the human companionship which he coveted; who made no parade of his accomplishments and never denied his failings; who hated hypocrisy above everything; who believed in the simpler human virtues—honesty, friendliness, generosity, kindness to humble men and women, and to the animals who labor for them; and who, through the exposition of this simple philosophy, and through the sympathetic picturing of his own environment, did indeed touch the heart of the entire world.

[1] "I weighed my productions as impartially as in my power; I thought they had merit . . . To know myself had been all along my constant study. I weighed myself alone. I balanced myself with others. I watched every means of information how much ground I occupied as a man and as a poet." *Autobiography*, p. 45.

[2] *Letters*, I, 23.

[3] About one hundred of the Proposals seem to have been printed. In a letter to M'Whinnie, Burns says, "I have no less than eight dozen, which is a great deal more than I shall ever need." *Letters*, I, 25.

[4] Transcribed from the unique copy in the Burns Museum, Alloway.

[5] Statistics compiled from Burns's letters and from the summary of Burns's accounts with Wilson, his printer. See C. W., I, 468 ff.

[6] C. W., I, 468 ff.

[7] See letter to John Logan, 10 August, 1786; *Letters*, I, 37.

[8] Letter to Aiken, 8 Oct., 1786; *ibid.*, p. 46.

THE KILMARNOCK VOLUME

[9] *Autobiography*, p. 46.

[10] Robert Heron, *A Memoir of the Life of the late Robert Burns*, Edinburgh, 1797, p. 17.

[11] H. H., II, 87.

[12] The so-called *Stair MSS* and *Afton MSS.*

[13] C. W., I, 417.

[14] In the margin of p. 46 of the Glenriddell copy of the *Autobiography*, opposite the phrase "A letter from Dr. Blacklock to a friend of mine," Burns has written: "B. to Lawrie. L. to G. Hamn."

[15] See an article (anon.) "About James Sibbald," *Chronicle*, 1923, pp. 91 ff., and also an article (anon.) "Burns's *Poems*: Reviews of the First Edition," *Chronicle*, 1927, pp. 89 ff.

[16] Quoted, C. W., I, 444. See also a commendatory letter from Allan Ramsay of Dumbartonshire, published 13 November, 1786, in the *Edinburgh Evening Courant*, and reprinted in the *Chronicle*, 1930, 30 ff.

[17] *Early Reviews of Robert Burns*, ed. John D. Ross; Glasgow, 1900, p. 6.

[18] See *Letters*, Introduction, p. xxxiii.

[19] Quoted in *Chronicle*, 1927, pp. 91 ff.

[20] A letter to John Ballantine, ? April, 1786 (*Letters*, I, 24), shows that Burns consulted both Ballantine and Aiken concerning possible omissions.

[21] "Stanzas written in the Prospect of Death;" "Paraphrase of the First Psalm;" "Prayer under the Pressure of Violent Anguish;" "The Nineteenth Psalm Versified."

[22] H. H., II, 154.

[23] Lockhart's statement that the satire actually drove Wilson out of Tarbolton is false, like many other "facts" for which this biographer and his confidential advisor Allan Cunningham were responsible. It is interesting to note that Wilson in September of 1790 sought Burns's advice concerning giving up his school and moving to Edinburgh, to seek work as an engrossing clerk. See Burns's letter advising against such a step, *Letters*, II, 42.

[24] *Autobiography*, p. 44.

[25] Stewart and Meikle, Glasgow. See H. H., II, 279 ff.

[26] *Letters*, II, 198 ff.

[27] *Ibid.*, I, xxxv. See also, by the same author, "Burns and Hugh Blair," *Mod. Lang. Notes*, November, 1930, pp. 400 ff.

[28] Chambers, I, 181.

[29] For instance, something may be missing before the first Bard's song; this character, who speaks for Burns himself, is never properly introduced. All the others are.

[30] "The Lament," "Despondency," "To Ruin," "Man was Made to Mourn," "Winter," and "A Prayer in the Prospect of Death."

[31] "Epistle to James Smith," "Epistle to Davie," "Epistle to a Young Friend," "A Dedication to Gavin Hamilton," "Epistle to J. Lapraik," "Epistle to the Same," "To William Simpson," "Epistle to J. Rankine," and the "Address to the Deil."

[32] "Epistle to a Young Friend," stanza 4; H. H., I, 140.

[33] "Epistle to Davie," stanza 2; *ibid.*, p. 118.

[34] "The Twa Dogs," "The Holy Fair," "Hallowe'en," "The Cotter's Saturday Night," "The Death of Poor Mailie," "Poor Mailie's Elegy," "The Auld Farmer's Salutation to his Mare," "To a Mouse," "To a Daisy," "To a Louse," "Scotch Drink."

[35] First edition, London, 1759; second, London, 1791.

[36] *Op. cit.* (1791), pp. 11 ff.

CHAPTER VI

EDINBURGH: THE FIRST WINTER

1

"AULD REEKIE"

IT was on Monday morning the twenty-seventh of November, 1786, that Burns mounted a horse borrowed from his friend George Reid of Barquharie and rode out of Mauchline towards Edinburgh. The decision to try his fortune in the capital had been reached at least two weeks before, for on the fifteenth of November he had referred to the journey, in a letter to Mrs. Dunlop, in terms which indicate that his mind was made up.[1] No one cause can be assigned for the adventurous step; many valid reasons might be adduced, but a few will suffice. Burns was eager for fame, and hoped to bring out an Edinburgh edition of his poems; his friends encouraged him in the project; he was already interested in a possible Excise appointment, and the offices of the Excise Board were in Edinburgh. If worst came to worst he could sail for the West Indies from Leith, in the *Roselle*, which was advertised to leave towards the close of December. Consequently, like many another young poet bred in the country, he turned his back upon the farm, and upon "Auld Coila's woods and fells," and sought the highroad that led him towards the city.

His route took him, for the first day's journey, to the farm of Covington Mains, near the village of Biggar, in Lanarkshire, where a hospitable Mr. Prentice acted as host at supper. Apparently he spent the night at the neighboring farmhouse of James Stoddart.[2] The next day he rode on, and by the end of the afternoon found himself climbing the hill towards the western end of the High Street, near which, in Baxter's Close, Lawnmarket, lived his old friend John Richmond, in a room rented from a Mrs. Carfrae. Here Burns unpacked his saddle-bags, arranged with laudable promptness for the return of the "pownie" to its owner, and settled comfortably down to share Richmond's bed, and to await what the future might have in store for him.

The particular building in which the two friends lodged has not survived the passing of time, but in many respects the Old Town of today is not unrecognizably different from the city which Burns was to find so enthralling. Lady Stair's house, in Lady Stair's Close, which Burns looked out upon from the single window of Richmond's room, is still in existence, a picturesque relic of a period long antedating the close of the eighteenth century. Castle Rock, surmounted by its age-old fortress, still keeps guard over the towering tenement houses, or "lands," eight stories high, of the city that had grown up in its protecting shadow. To stand at the main entrance-port of the Castle and to look off towards the east is to see spread out beneath one a panorama as fascinating to the modern visitor as it must have been to Burns. Directly in front, and extending towards the east, stretches the mile-long highway known as "the backbone of Edinburgh." The western end, that nearest the Castle, is still called the Lawnmarket, though the tradesmen's shops responsible for its name have long since disappeared. The central part is the High Street, frequented by advocates, clergymen, and University professors; the lower, or eastern end, is the Canongate, where more humble folk have their dwellings. Up and down this crowded street presses a throng of hurrying humanity very like that which Burns saw hemmed in between the almost over-hanging walls of the grey stone buildings. Shops and stalls and booths and public houses still cluster close beside the roadway; peddlar's carts, laden with fish or coals, still creak slowly over the pavement, while the vendors scan the windows for possible purchasers; the same low-lying pall of

[187]

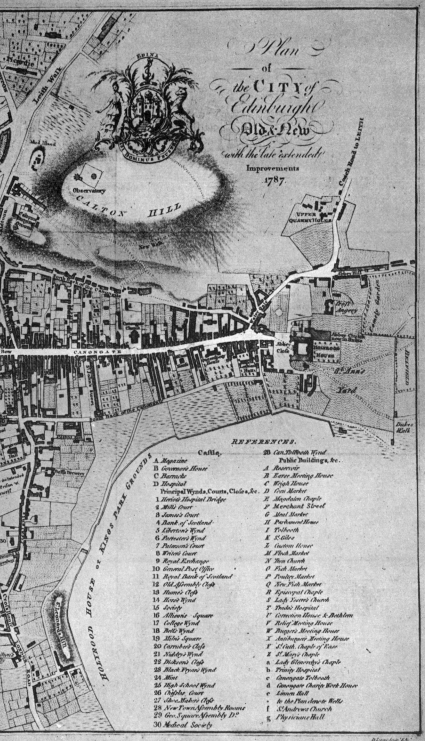

Plan
of
the CITY of
Edinburgh
Old & New
with the late extended
Improvements
1787

EDINA

SI DOMINUS FRUSTRA

Observatory
CALTON HILL

Leith Walk

Mud Island

Coach Road to LEITH

UPPER QUARRY HOLES

Physic Garden

CANONGATE

Abbey
Close

HOLYROOD
HOUSE

St Anne's
Yard

Dukes
Walk

HOLYROOD HOUSE or KINGS PARK GROUNDS

REFERENCES.

Castle.
A Magazine
B Governor's House
C Barracks
D Hospital

Principal Wynds, Courts, Closes, &c.
1 Heriot's Hospital Bridge
2 Mills Court
3 James's Court
4 Bank of Scotland
5 Liberton's Wynd
6 Forrester's Wynd
7 Paterson's Court
8 Writer's Court
9 Royal Exchange
10 General Post Office
11 Royal Bank of Scotland
12 Old Assembly Close
13 Hume's Close
14 Horse Wynd
15 Society
16 Alison's Square
17 College Wynd
18 Bell's Wynd
19 Milns Square
20 Carrubers Close
21 Niddry's Wynd
22 Dickson's Close
23 Black Fryars Wynd
24 Mint
25 High School Wynd
26 Chalmers Court
27 Shoe Makers Close
28 New Town Assembly Rooms
29 Geo. Square Assembly Do.
30 Medical Society

28 Can. Tolbooth Wynd

Public Buildings, &c.
A Reservoir
B Extee Meeting House
C Weigh House
D Corn Market
E Magdalen Chaple
F Merchant Street
G Meal Market
H Parliament House
I Tolbooth
K St Giles
L Custom House
M Flesh Market
N Tron Church
O Fish Market
P Poultry Market
Q New Fish Market
R Episcopal Chaple
S Lady Yester's Church
T Trades Hospital
U Correction House & Bethlem
V Relief Meeting House
W Bugers Meeting House
X Antiburgers Meeting House
Y St Cuth. Chaple of Ease
Z St Mary's Chaple
a Lady Glenorchy's Chaple
b Trinity Hospital
c Canongate Tolbooth
d Canongate Charity Work House
e Linnen Hall
* to the Plan denote Wells
f St Andrews Church
g Physicians Hall

smoke rises heavily from a thousand chimneys. St. Giles's Cathedral still lifts its ornate cupola above the surrounding roofs, and John Knox's house, unchanged in any fundamental respect during three and a half centuries, forms yet another link with an age which even to Burns must have seemed long gone by.

At the lower end of the Canongate, marking the eastern limit of the "royal mile," stands Holyrood Palace, only a little less gloomy today, in its Gothic propriety, than it was in 1786—unoccupied now, as then, except during the sessions of the Assembly or occasional visits of royalty. Beyond it, at the southern or right hand side of the picture, and over a confused mass of chimney pots, tile roofs, and church belfries, looms the rocky crag known as Arthur's Seat, famed in song and ballad, and as picturesque today, in its bluff isolation, as when Burns first looked upon it. North of Holyrood, and thus on the left side of the panorama, and beyond the ravine which in 1772 had been spanned by the North Bridge, rises Calton Hill, where witches had been burned in the good old days. And still further to the north, over the roofs of the New Town which even in 1786 was rapidly coming into existence, the waters of the Firth of Forth glisten under an occasional burst of sunshine. Thus in picturesque location, general environment, and not a few architectural details, the Old Town of 1931 bears a very definite resemblance to the Edinburgh of 1786.

In many respects Burns's Edinburgh was surprisingly more "modern" than the city with which his father had become familiar while working as a gardener in "The Meadows" thirty years before. To turn through such a volume as the *Fugitive Pieces* [3] of William Creech, is to realize how rapid had been the changes that came over the city between 1763 and 1783. Some of the matters recorded by Creech seem trivial, as, for instance, the fact that "In 1763 there was no such thing known as an umbrella; but an eminent surgeon"—Burns's friend "Lang Sandy" Wood—"who had occasion to walk a great deal in the course of his business, used one about the year 1780; and in 1783 umbrellas were much used, and continue to be so." [4]

[188]

Most of Creech's comments, however, are genuinely significant. It is clear that manufacture and commerce were increasing rapidly, that the accumulation of money was becoming more easy, and that as Edinburgh grew wealthy it became less concerned about some of the old-time loyalties. For example:

> In 1763 it was fashionable to go to church, and people were interested about religion. Sunday was strictly observed by all ranks as a day of devotion; and it was disgraceful to be seen on the streets during the time of public worship. Families attended church, with their children and servants; and family worship was frequent. . . .
>
> In 1783 attendance on church was greatly neglected, and particularly by the men. Sunday was by many made a day of relaxation; and young people were allowed to stroll about at all hours. Families thought it ungenteel to take their domestics to church with them. The streets were far from being void of people in the time of public worship; and, in the evenings, were frequently loose and riotous; particularly owing to bands of apprentice boys and young lads.[5]

Or again, concerning more serious matters:

> In no respect were the manners of 1763 and 1783 more remarkable than in the decency, dignity, and delicacy of the one period, compared with the looseness, dissipation, and licentiousness of the other. Many people ceased to blush at what would formerly have been reckoned a crime . . .
>
> In 1763 the fines collected by the kirk treasurer for bastard children amounted to £154; and, upon an average of ten succeeding years, they were £190.
>
> In 1783 the fines for bastard children amounted to £600, and have since greatly increased . . .
>
> In 1763 there were five or six brothels, or houses of bad fame, and a very few of the lowest and most ignorant order of females sculked about the streets at night. A person might have gone from the Castle to Holyrood House (the then length of the city), at any hour in the night, without being accosted by a single street-walker. Street-robbery and pocket-picking were unknown.
>
> In 1783 the number of brothels had increased twenty-fold, and the women of the town more than a hundred-fold. Every quarter of the

city and the suburbs was infested with multitudes of females abandoned to vice. . . . Street-robbers, pick-pockets, and thieves, had much increased.[6]

In this iniquitous city the visitor of 1787 could have found ready-to-hand various diversions which Creech considered almost as malevolent as the acknowledged vices of the town. Golf lured young men away from the Church on a Sabbath morning; horse-racing and gambling robbed them of their savings; cockfighting brutalized them; dancing [7] and theatre-going, popular with both men and women, sowed the seeds of many sorts of misfortune. And then there were the clubs, which met in taverns where men sought freedom from the close imprisonment of their lodgings in the "lands," or relaxation after the day's work. Creech did not object to this phase of Edinburgh life, though some of the clubs were deserving of censure. Even a guarded description of the observances and ritual of certain of these assemblages is impossible; the bawdry of the *Merry Muses* will suggest the general tone. When Burns was introduced by Smellie to the Crochallan Fencibles, for example, he found himself in an atmosphere of "sculduddery" which it is hard to believe that otherwise respectable business and professional men could have enjoyed. But enjoy it they did, not infrequently to their own—or someone else's—hurt. All in all, then, the Edinburgh which Burns knew was a city in which a country poet might well have come to disaster, no matter what experiences he had previously undergone.

If the manners of the city were in these respects open to reproach, it is also true that the intellectual life of the capital was at a relatively low ebb during Burns's sojourn. David Hume had been dead for slightly more than ten years when Burns first saw the city; Lord Kames for more than four. Principal Robertson was still living, to be sure, and Adam Smith, but both men were in ill health; and though both appear on Burns's subscription list—Smith for four copies—they had virtually withdrawn from society.[8]

EDINBURGH: THE FIRST WINTER

There were no persons in the Edinburgh of 1787 to fill the places of these men. Adam Ferguson and Hugh Blair were both men of distinction, to be sure; Mackenzie, "Man of Feeling," was enjoying a considerable local—and temporary—reputation; Henry Erskine, Dean of the Faculty of Advocates, was a brilliant and popular barrister; Dr. Blacklock a thoroughly respectable minor poet. But the glory of the years from 1750 to 1770 had departed; the new age of Scott and Jeffrey had not yet arrived. Meanwhile Edinburgh society held its Assemblies, dined, and danced, and drank; kept up a brave show of life within the old city, and turned with eager curiosity to the Ayrshire poet who was to furnish diversion of a new sort.

Though at first blush it might seem that Burns had gone up to this Scottish Babylon alone and unheralded, yet actually this was far from being the case. His most intimate personal friend, Richmond, was living in Edinburgh, and was eager to welcome him. He had already met Professor Dugald Stewart, and knew that he could count on his aid with the "literati," as they were styled. His friend James Dalrymple of Orangefield had provided him with some sort of introduction to the Earl of Glencairn,[9] who was to do far more towards making Burns's visit a success than the poet could have dared to hope. Thus in each of the three groups of Edinburgh society with which Burns was to come in contact—the nobility, the literary or professional class, and the clerks, artisans, and students—Burns was certain of at least one friend.

Then too, his Masonic affiliations gave him access to a sort of social intercourse in which he always found keen pleasure. The record is not entirely above suspicion,[10] but it seems probable that within ten days of his arrival in Edinburgh Burns had been introduced to the influential members of the Canongate Kilwinning Lodge. Furthermore, the journalists were kindly disposed towards him. The October, November, and December numbers of the *Edinburgh Magazine* carried extracts from the Kilmarnock volume; on December 9 Henry Mackenzie's laudatory review appeared in *The Lounger*.

[191]

On the whole, then, the stage was admirably set for Burns's entrance, and he was well prepared to take advantage of any opportunity that might present itself. His fame as a "heaven-taught plowman" had preceded him; he was in the full vigor of physical maturity; in intellectual power he was at least equal to any of the persons whom he was to meet in Edinburgh; he was a brilliant conversationalist, in an age when conversation was esteemed as an art; he had a veritable genius for friendship. It would be hard, in all the annals of English literature, to find a more auspicious set of circumstances attending the first appearance of a country poet on the unfamiliar stage of a great city than those with which fortune and his own ability had presented Burns.

He made the most of his one chance. Since the year 1773, when Dr. Johnson had condescended to allow Edinburgh a fleeting glimpse of his greatness, there had been no such visitor to the city; no one to whom the city had so promptly and so willingly yielded itself captive. Dinners, assemblies, social gatherings of all sorts, kept Burns busy, and brought him in touch with interesting and appreciative people. Rimesters eager to attract his notice and share his fame addressed their poetic epistles to him through the columns of Edinburgh newspapers; he himself was prompt in publishing the "Address to Edinburgh" and "Address to a Haggis" in the *Caledonian Mercury*. He took his part in Edinburgh club life—both the decorous and the disreputable. The exclusive Caledonian Hunt was prompt with its welcome, and generous with its subscription. The Crochallan Fencibles, whose sessions gave Burns an opportunity to display his skill at a type of versification which Mrs. Dunlop condemned, seem to have enrolled him formally as a member; certainly they delighted when he joined them at Daniel Douglas's tavern in the Anchor Close. The Canongate Kilwinning Lodge, the most influential Masonic group in Edinburgh, affiliated him on February 1, 1787. An excerpt from the records makes this fact indisputable:

[192]

EDINBURGH: THE FIRST WINTER

1st February 1787. . . . The R. W. Master having observed that Brother Burns was at present in the Lodge, who is well known as a great poetic writer, and for a late publication of his works, which have been universally commended, submitted that he should be assumed a member of this Lodge, which was unanimously agreed to, and he was assumed accordingly.[11]

There is no evidence that Burns was recognized as "poet laureate" of this Lodge till long after his death. Not till 1815 does any direct reference to the "laureateship" appear in the records. But Burns enjoyed his association with the Kilwinning Masons, and found in the group some of Edinburgh's leading citizens.

Impelled by his genuine respect for Robert Fergusson's poetic accomplishment, and by the realization that his act would bring him a valuable sort of notoriety, Burns had not been long in Edinburgh before he announced his desire to erect a stone over Fergusson's unmarked grave in the Canongate parish cemetery. On the sixth of February, 1787, he wrote to the "Bailies of the Canongate," who transferred his request to the proper persons, the Managers of the Kirk and Kirkyard Funds of Canongate, asking the necessary permission. The following minute was the result:

Thereupon the said Managers, in consideration of the laudable and disinterested motion of Mr. Burns, and the propriety of his request, did, and hereby do, unanimously, grant power and liberty to the said Robert Burns, to erect a headstone at the grave of the said Robert Fergusson, and to keep up and preserve the same to his memory in all time coming.[12]

Having received this authorization, the poet commissioned Robert Burn to erect the stone, for which he prepared an appropriate inscription.[13] Four years later he paid the bill, sending the money from Dumfries to his friend Peter Hill, and commenting thus on the affair:

I send you by the bearer, Mr. Clarke, a particular friend of mine . . . £5, 10s. per acct. I owe to Mr. Robt. Burn, Architect, for erecting the stone over poor Ferguson.—He was two years in erecting it, after I commissioned him for it; & I have been two years paying him, after he sent me his account; so he & I are quits.—He had the hardiesse to ask me interest on the sum; but considering that the money was due by one Poet, for putting a tomb-stone over another, he may, with grateful surprise, thank Heaven that ever he saw a farthing of it.[14]

Teas, dinners, "Mason meetings," and tombstones were all of minor importance, however, when compared to the two major accomplishments of Burns's first winter in Edinburgh: the enlargement of his circle of friends, and the publication of the 1787 edition of his poems. To tell something concerning the persons who made this winter a happy one, so that the reader can understand how many people of widely differing outlooks and positions came within the bounds of Burns's steadily expanding horizon, and then to recount the various steps in the publication of the 1787 volume, will be to indicate the chief interests of the period from November of 1786 to May of 1787.

2

NEW FRIENDSHIPS

In the group of persons who welcomed Burns to Edinburgh there is no one entitled to precede James Cunningham, fourteenth Earl of Glencairn (1749–1791). Only ten years older than the poet, and akin to him in his attitude towards politics and religion, Glencairn expressed his admiration for Burns in such fashion that the poet unhesitatingly called him "the Patron from whom all my fame & good fortune took its rise." [15]

The paths of these two men seem first to have crossed in June of 1785, when Glencairn, patron of Kilmarnock parish, presented the Reverend William Mackinley, a staunch conservative, to the vacant ministry, and occasioned Burns's satire "The Ordination." The choice of an Auld Licht for the pulpit was no indication of Glencairn's own attitude toward the religious controversy then raging, but merely an appropriate acquiescence in the desires of a majority of the parishioners.[16]

[194]

When Burns went up to Edinburgh he at once sought out Glencairn, and found himself welcome. "I have adopted Lord Glencairn as my titular Protector," he afterwards wrote.[17] Immediately the Earl invited him to his home and introduced him to his friends. When the subscription lists for the 1787 edition were opened, Glencairn and his mother put their names down for twenty-four copies. Furthermore, as Burns said in an early letter to Gavin Hamilton, "Through my Lord's influence it is inserted in the records of the Caledonian Hunt, that they universally, one & all, subscribe for the 2d edition."[18] (This, it should be remembered, took place within ten days of Burns's first arrival in Edinburgh.) Hence it came about that the the list of subscribers printed at the front of the volume is headed "The Caledonian Hunt—100 copies;" in return for which very considerable assistance Burns dedicated the work to the "Noblemen and Gentlemen" of that benevolently inclined association.

When the book was ready to appear, Burns asked Glencairn's permission to publish in an Edinburgh newspaper his "Verses Intended to be Written below a Noble Earl's Picture,"—which would have been the best sort of advertising. Glencairn, however, withheld his permission, and the poem was not printed until 1834. When Burns was leaving Edinburgh, he wrote a somewhat inflated letter to the Earl, thanking him "for all that patronage, that benevolence, and that friendship with which you have honored me."[19] In January of 1788 he was again the petitioner, asking the Earl's aid in securing an Excise appointment; this time, apparently, his request was granted. These things are matters of record and of common knowledge. But there are no entries in the *Commonplace Book*, no letters, to show the full extent of Glencairn's friendship for Burns, or the amount of assistance which he gave him. These are largely matters of inference. It is clear that Burns was not overstating his debt when, shortly after the Earl's death on January 30, 1791, he wrote thus to Alexander Dalziel:

[195]

God knows what I have suffered, at the loss of my best Friend, my
first my dearest Patron & Benefactor; the man to whom I owe all that
I am & have! I am gone into mourning for him; & with more sincerity of grief than I fear some will, who by Nature's ties ought to feel
on the occasion (*sic*).[20]

To put the entire matter succinctly, one might say that Glencairn's friendship meant as much for Burns in Edinburgh as
had Gavin Hamilton's and Bob Aiken's during the years at
Mossgiel. Of a distinctly different sort was the relationship between
Burns and George Alexander, Fourth Duke of Gordon (1745–
1827) and Jane Maxwell (d. 1812), his Duchess. The Duchess
was "a beauty," given to exhibiting her skill as a dancer, and
proud of being free from the drag of convention. Eccentric
but brilliant and vivacious, she was the acknowledged leader of
Edinburgh society, and the sort of woman concerning whom a
staid barrister could write in February of 1786:

The good town is uncommonly crowded and splendid at present.
The example of dissipation set by Her Grace the Duchess of Gordon
is far from showing vice [in] her own image. It is really astonishing
to think what effect a single person will have on public manners, when
supported by high rank and great address. She is never absent from
a public place, and the later the hour, so much the better. It is often
four o'clock in the morning before she goes to bed, and she never requires more than five hours' sleep. Dancing, cards, and company occupy her whole time.[21]

This vivacious creature "took notice" of Burns, and by so
doing certified him as socially eligible. Let Andrew Dalzel,
Professor of Greek in the University of Edinburgh, tell the
story in a letter dated January 25, 1787:

We have got a poet in town just now, whom everybody is taking notice
of—a ploughman from Ayrshire—a man of unquestionable genius, who
has produced admirable verses, mostly in the Scottish dialect, though some
nearly are in English. . . . He runs, however, the risk of being spoiled
by the excessive attention paid him just now by persons of all ranks.

[196]

Those who know him best, say he has too much good sense to allow himself to be spoiled. Everybody is fond of showing him everything here that the place furnishes. I saw him at an assembly t'other night. The Duchess of Gordon and other ladies of rank took notice of him there. He behaves wonderfully well; very independent in his sentiments, and has none of the *mauvaise honte* about him, though he is not forward.[22]

As early as December, 1786, Mrs. Cockburn, whose fame as a poetess had already been established by her "Flowers of the Forest," had written thus concerning the welcome which Burns was receiving from Edinburgh society:

The town is at present agog with the ploughman poet, who receives adulation with native dignity, and is the very figure of his profession, strong and coarse, but has a most enthusiastic heart of love. He has seen Duchess Gordon and all the gay world. . . . The man will be spoiled, if he can spoil; but he keeps his simple manners, and is quite sober. No doubt he will be at the Hunters' Ball tomorrow, which has made all women and milliners mad.[23]

Burns's acquaintance with the Duke and Duchess of Gordon was sufficiently intimate that in September of 1787, when he was making the most exten⁻ive of his tours through the Highlands, he called at Gordon Castle, and was cordially received. The Duke was something of an amateur versifier himself, and Burns afterwards included a specimen of his work in Johnson's *Museum*. In praising his Lordship's skill in such matters Burns made one of his trenchant remarks about song-writing:

The mob of mankind, that many-headed beast, would laugh at so serious speech about an old song; but, as Job says, "O that mine adversary had written a book!" Those who think that composing a Scotch song is a trifling business, let them try.[24]

But it was to the Duchess, rather than to the Duke, that Burns was indebted during the first weeks of his Edinburgh visit. She smiled on him, and thereby assured his social success. Henry Erskine (1746–1817), the brilliant Dean of the Faculty of Advocates, was as cordial as Gordon and Glencairn. The second son of the Earl of Buchan, and connected by marriage with the Earl of Glencairn, Erskine was at the height of his power and reputation when Burns first knew him.   Less than two years before he had won a verdict of £21,580 in favor of Forbes of Ferintosh, whose hereditary right to distill and sell whiskey free of Excise tax had been abrogated by the Distilleries Act of 1785, and whose suit against the government Erskine had carried to this highly successful conclusion.   For many years Dean of the Faculty of Advocates, he was generally considered the most brilliant of Scottish barristers, and is still remembered —with gratitude—as the man who, on the occasion of Dr. Johnson's visit to Edinburgh, had pressed a shilling into Boswell's hand—"For the sight of your bear!"

Burns met Erskine before he had been many days in the city, for on December 7 he wrote to Gavin Hamilton that

> My Lord Glencairn & the Dean of Faculty, Mr. H. Erskine, have taken me under their wing; and by all probability I shall soon be the tenth Worthy, and the eighth Wise Man of the world.[25]

Precisely what Erskine did to make Burns's stay in Edinburgh a success does not appear in the written record; conjecture, however, is neither difficult nor unsafe.   He allowed it to be known that he was Burns's friend, and that he approved of both the man and his poetry.   This approval, bestowed early and ungrudgingly, did much to make Burns's path easy.

There was a certain element of the spectacular in Burns's intimacy with men like Erskine and Glencairn.   The friendship of Alexander Cunningham (d. 1812), an attorney and future Writer to the Signet, brought Burns no such immediate notoriety, but developed into a companionship that endured till Burns's death.   But because most of the records certifying to this friendship fall in the later years of Burns's life, the entire story had best be postponed to the Dumfries chapter.

Very different from Cunningham was Henry Mackenzie (1745–1831), author of *The Man of Feeling* and *The Man of*

[198]

the World, editor of *The Lounger,* and the acknowledged leader among Edinburgh's professional men of letters. Burns's admiration for Mackenzie antedated the Edinburgh experience by at least four years. In a letter to Murdoch, written 15 January, 1783, he had expressed a high opinion of *The Man of Feeling,* "a book I prize next to the Bible." [26] Burns's estimate of the man and his work may have been somewhat more flattering than that of most of his contemporaries. Nevertheless Mackenzie's position in 1786 was calculated to inspire any rural rimester with awe. Consequently when Mackenzie's eulogistic review appeared in *The Lounger,* only eleven days after Burns had reached Edinburgh, the young poet must have felt that Fortune was indeed smiling on him.

There is no evidence that the two men remained on intimate terms after Burns left Edinburgh. But it was worth much to the poet to have had Mackenzie's approbation at a time when his entire future seemed to depend on the reception of his 1787 volume.[27]

Dugald Stewart (1753–1828), Professor of Philosophy in the University of Edinburgh, was a person whom only a man of genuine worth could possibly have won as a friend. He had first met Burns on October 23, 1786, when Dr. John Mackenzie, at Stewart's request, had brought Burns to Stewart's country house, Catrine Bank, near Mauchline, to dine.[28] The two men, though not far apart in years,—Stewart had been born in 1753—were representatives of widely separated social strata. One was the son of a University Professor, who had followed his father's way of life, and who came to Ayrshire only as a "summer visitor;" his world was the world of books and libraries. The other was the son of an unsuccessful farmer, who was himself a farmer in a small way, and who was under a cloud because of his conduct. But each appreciated the worth of the other, and between the two there sprang up a genuine friendship.

When Stewart returned to Edinburgh at the opening of the University term, he took a copy of Burns's Kilmarnock edition to Henry Mackenzie, and thus brought about the *Lounger* review. When Burns followed him to Edinburgh, Stewart made him welcome at his home, and introduced him to his colleagues on the faculty. Burns later sought Stewart's critical advice concerning his poems, and gave heed to his opinions.[29] Indeed, of all his new friends, Stewart was the man whom Burns seems to have rated most highly, so far as innate worth was concerned. In the second *Commonplace Book*, which was not intended for publication, Burns thus characterized him:

> The most perfect character I ever saw is Mr. Stuart (*sic*). An exalted judge of the human heart, and of composition. One of the very first public speakers; and equally capable of generosity as humanity. His principal discriminating feature is; from a mixture of benevolence, strength of mind, and manly dignity, he not only at heart values, but in his deportment and address bears himself to all the Actors, high and low, in the drama of Life, simply as they merit in playing their parts. Wealth, honors, and all that is extraneous of the man, have no more influence with him than they will have at the Last Day. His wit, in the hour of social hilarity, proceeds almost to good-natured waggishness; and in telling a story he particularly excells.[30]

Stewart, on his part, left a signficant record of his impressions of Burns in the form of a letter to Dr. Currie, incorporated in that editor's *Life and Works of Robert Burns*. Concerning his first meeting with the poet, at Catrine Bank, Stewart wrote:

> His manners were then, as they continued ever afterwards, simple, manly, and independent; strongly expressive of conscious genius and worth; but without anything that indicated forwardness, arrogance, or vanity. He took his share in conversation, but not more than belonged to him. . . . Nothing, perhaps, was more remarkable among his various attainments, than the fluency, and precision, and originality of his language, when he spoke in company; more particularly as he aimed at purity in his turn of expression, and avoided more successfully than most Scotchmen the peculiarities of Scottish phraseology.

Good evidence, this, concerning that disputed question, Burns's command of English! Of the first winter in Edinburgh, Stewart said:

EDINBURGH: THE FIRST WINTER

He came to Edinburgh early in the winter following, and remained there for several months. By whose advice he took this step, I am unable to say. Perhaps it was suggested only by his own curiosity to see a little more of the world; but I confess I dreaded the consequences from the first. . . . The attentions he received during his stay in town from all ranks and descriptions of persons, were such as would have turned any head but his own. I cannot say that I could perceive any unfavourable effect which they left on his mind. He retained the same simplicity of manners and appearance which had struck me so forcibly when I first saw him in the country; nor did he seem to feel any additional self-importance to the number and rank of his new acquaintances. His dress was perfectly suited to his station, plain and unpretending, with a sufficient attention to neatness. If I recollect right, he always wore boots; and, when on more than usual ceremony, buck-skin breeches.

The variety of his engagements, while in Edinburgh, prevented me from seeing him so often as I could have wished. In the course of the spring he called on me once or twice, at my request, early in the morning, and walked with me to Braid Hills in the neighbourhood of the town, where he charmed me still more by his private conversation than he had ever done in company. He was passionately fond of the beauties of nature; and I recollect once he told me, when I was admiring a distant prospect in one of our morning walks, that the sight of so many smoking cottages gave a pleasure to his mind, which none could understand who had not witnessed, like himself, the happiness and the worth which they contained. . . .

I should have mentioned before, that notwithstanding various reports I had heard . . . of Burns's predeliction for convivial and not very select society, I should have concluded in favour of his habits of sobriety, from all of him that ever fell under my own observation. . . .

In the course of [the summer of 1787] I was led by curiosity to attend for an hour or two a Mason-Lodge in Mauchline, where Burns presided. He had occasion to make some short unpremeditated compliments to different individuals from whom he had no reason to expect a visit, and everything he said was happily conceived, and forcibly as well as fluently expressed. . . . His manner of speaking in public had evidently the marks of some practice in extempore elocution.[31]

This is interesting and valuable testimony, not merely as to Burns's conduct in Edinburgh, but as to the general impression

[201]

the "ploughboy poet" made upon the Professor of Philosophy who was glad to count him among his friends.

Stewart's predecessor in the chair of Moral Philosophy had been Adam Ferguson (1723–1816), who had retired from active teaching in 1785. In 1787 he was still prominent in the life of the capital, however, and not infrequently opened his home in the Sciennes to gatherings of literary folk. At one of these assemblages took place the only recorded meeting between Burns and Walter Scott. The latter's account of the incident, though well known, is important enough to bear reprinting in part. Writing to Lockhart in 1827, Sir Walter said:

As for Burns, I may truly say, *Virgilium vidi tantum.* . . . I saw him one day at the late venerable Professor Ferguson's, where there were several gentlemen of literary reputation, among whom I remember the celebrated Dr. Dugald Stewart. Of course we youngsters sate silent, looked, and listened. The only thing I remember which was remarkable in Burns' manner was the effect produced upon him by a print of Bunbury's, representing a soldier lying dead on the snow, his dog sitting in misery on the one side, on the other his widow, with a child in her arms. These lines were written beneath:

> Cold on Canadian hills or Minden's plain
> Perhaps that parent wept her soldier slain;
> Bent o'er her babe, her eye dissolved in dew;
> The big drops, mingling with the milk he drew,
> Gave the sad presage of his future years,
> The child of misery baptized in tears.

Burns seemed much affected by the print, or rather, the ideas which it suggested to his mind. He actually shed tears. He asked whose the lines were, and it chanced that nobody but myself remembered that they occur in a half-forgotten poem of Langhorne's, called by the unpromising title of "The Justice of the Peace." I whispered my information to a young friend present, who mentioned it to Burns, who rewarded me with a look and a word, which, though of mere civility, I then received, and still recollect, with very great pleasure.

His person was strong and robust; his manners rustic, not clownish; a sort of dignified plainness and simplicity, which received part of its ef-

fect perhaps from one's knowledge of his extraordinary talents . . .
There was a strong expression of sense and shrewdness in all his line-
aments; the eye alone, I think, indicated the poetical character and temperament. It was large, and of a dark cast, and glowed (I say literally
glowed) when he spoke with feeling or interest. I never saw such
another eye in a human head, though I have seen the most distinguished
men in my time.[32]

Had Professor Ferguson done nothing but furnish this occasion for bringing Burns and Scott together, he would have justified his existence.

Still another University man whom Burns knew was Dr.
Hugh Blair (1718–1800). Forty-one years older than the
poet, Blair had begun preaching in 1741. In 1758 he was installed as minister of the High Church, Edinburgh, and thus
found himself occupying the most prominent pulpit of the
Church of Scotland. The following year, when Burns was born,
he began a series of lectures in the University. Here he had
such success that in 1762 a special chair was created for him,
and to his duties as minister he added those of Professor of
Rhetoric and Belles Lettres.

By this time he had become one of Edinburgh's best known
public figures. He was pompous and vain, rather too scrupulous
concerning his dress, obviously self-satisfied, and somewhat lacking in a sense of humor.[33] But he was an able preacher, and a
University teacher who introduced young men to a field of study
which of recent years had been neglected. His canons of taste,
naturally enough, had been formed from the study of the classics and of eighteenth century English poets. As a result he
was so inclined to formalism that Dr. Blacklock doubted whether
Blair would appreciate Burns's Scottish poems. "His taste is
too highly polished," Blacklock had written, "and his genius
too regular in its emotions to make allowances for the sallies
of a more impetuous ardour."[34] Blacklock, however, was wrong
in his estimate of his contemporary. Though Blair advised
Burns to suppress "The Jolly Beggars,"[35] he approved of "John
Barleycorn" and "Death and Dr. Hornbook," and may have

[203]

suggested to Burns one emendation which greatly improved "The Holy Fair." The Kilmarnock edition had read:

> [Moodie] speels the holy door
> Wi' tidings o' s-lv-t-n.

The 1787 Edinburgh changed the last word:

> Wi' tidings o' d-mn-t-n.

It is clear that Blair objected to "salvation," and said in his notes on the poem, that "the Author may easily contrive some other Rhyme in place of the word Salv-n." [36] If he actually proposed the word which Burns adopted, as is commonly alleged, he was not utterly in bondage to an age of decorum, nor totally destitute of humor.

Burns and Blair were never intimate companions, yet each felt a genuine interest in the other. Burns realized that the older man had treated him with friendly courtesy; Blair respected and admired Burns. When Burns was about to leave Edinburgh he sent Blair a copy of Beugo's engraving of himself, accompanied by this letter:

REVEREND AND MUCH RESPECTED SIR:

I leave Edinburgh tomorrow morning, but could not go without troubling you with half a line, sincerely to thank you for the kindness, patronage, and friendship, you have shewn me. I often felt the embarrassment of my singular situation: drawn forth from the veriest shades of life to the glare of remark; and honored by the notice of those illustrious names of my country whose works, while they are applauded to the end of time, will ever instruct and mend the heart. However the meteor-like novelty of my appearance in the world might attract notice, and honor me with the acquaintance of the permanent lights of genius and literature, those who are truly benefactors of the immortal nature of man, I knew very well that my utmost merit was far unequal to the task of preserving that character when once the novelty was over; I have made up my mind that abuse, or almost even neglect, will not surprise me in my quarters. . . .[37]

Blair's reply, written immediately after receiving Burns's letter, is too long to be quoted in full, and the sections in which Blair complacently rehearsed his own services to literature and advised Burns concerning his future are relatively beside the point. One paragraph, however, is of interest in connection with the gossip, later set on foot, to the effect that Burns's Edinburgh months were months of dissipation:

> Your situation, as you say, was indeed very singular; and in being brought out all at once from the shades of deepest privacy to so great a share of public notice and observation, you had to stand a severe trial. I am happy that you stood it so well; and, as far as I have known or heard, though in the midst of many temptations, without reproach to your character or behaviour.[38]

If an attorney were summoning witnesses to testify to his client's sobriety and general worth, he could find many less credible persons than the senior minister of the High Church and Professor of Rhetoric and Belles Lettres.

Among Burns's new friends one finds still another member of the University faculty, the Reverend William Greenfield (d. 1827). When Burns first reached the city, Greenfield was Professor of Rhetoric and minister of St. Andrew's church. Three months later he became Blair's associate in the pulpit of the High Church, where his learning and eloquence found ample opportunity for expression. By 1796 he had risen to such a commanding position that the University of Edinburgh conferred the Doctorate of Divinity on him; in the same year he was elected Moderator of the General Assembly. Towards the close of 1798, however, he found himself involved in such difficulties that he suddenly fled to England, where, deprived of all academic honors, and excommunicated by the church, he lived under an assumed name till 1827.[39]

The details of Greenfield's fall have been mercifully concealed by his contemporaries. It is enough to record that on March 1, 1798, in his capacity of Moderator of the General Assembly, he signed a "Warning to the Churches."[40] In December of the same year the records of the Presbytery of Edinburgh state that

A letter from Dr. Greenfield was laid before the Presbytery, by which he resigned into the hands of the Presbytery his office as one of the ministers of the High Church, and his character as a minister of the Gospel. The Presbytery accepted Dr. Greenfield's resignation of the said office, and in consequence of certain flagrant reports concerning his conduct, which his desertion of his charge, and his quitting his country, seemed to preclude the Presbytery from considering groundless, they unanimously deposed him from the office of the holy ministry, and laid him under a sentence of excommunication.[41]

But in the winter of 1787 he was at the height of his power; there could hardly have been anyone in Edinburgh whom a young poet would more eagerly have sought as a friend.

Greenfield welcomed Burns with hearty sincerity. Before even the month of December had passed Burns was writing thus to him, confiding in him his expectations for the future:

Never did Saul's armour sit so heavy on David when going to encounter Goliah, as does the encumbering robe of public notice with which the friendship and patronage of some "names dear to fame" have invested me.—I do not say this in the ridiculous idea of seeming self-abasement, and affected modesty.—I have long studied myself, and I think I know pretty exactly what ground I occupy, both as a Man & a Poet; and however the world, or a friend, may sometimes differ from me in that particular, I stand for it, in silent resolve, with all the tenaciousness of Property. I am willing to believe that my abilities deserved a better fate than the veriest shades of life; but to be dragged forth, with all my imperfections on my head, to the full glare of learned and polite observation, is what, I am afraid, I shall have bitter reason to repent.—

I mention this to you, once for all, merely, in the Confessor style, to disburthen my conscience, and that—"When proud Fortune's ebbing tide recedes,"—you may bear me witness, when my bubble of fame was at the highest, I stood, unintoxicated, with the inebriating cup in my hand, looking forward, with rueful resolve, to the hastening time when the stroke of envious Calumny, with all the eagerness of vengeful triumph, should dash it to the ground.[42]

[206]

Burns had the highest opinion of Greenfield as a man; as a preacher, he preferred him to Blair himself. In particular, he delighted in the fact that Greenfield was unencumbered by Blair's solemn and at times amusing dignity. The second *Commonplace Book* contains an appreciative estimate of him:

Mr. Greenfield is of a superiour order. The bleedings of humanity, the generous resolve, a manly disregard of the paltry subjects of vanity, virgin modesty, the truest taste, and a very sound judgement, characterize him. His being the first Speaker I ever heard is perhaps half owing to industry. He certainly possesses no small share of poetic abilities; he is a steady, most disinterested friend, without the last affectation of seeming so; and as a companion, his good sense, his joyous hilarity, his sweetness of manners and modesty, are most engagingly charming.[43]

Greenfield did little that contributed directly to the success of Burns's Edinburgh volume, but he did much to add to the poet's happiness during his months in the city. Like Blair, he realized the genius of the man, and, in addition, he delighted in the charm of Burns's personality.

It was Burns's poetry that first brought him to the notice of Dr. Thomas Blacklock, (1721–1791), the blind scholar and versifier whom both Johnson and Benjamin Franklin had befriended. Blacklock had been born in 1721, and before he was a year old had the misfortune to lose his eyesight as the result of small-pox. His natural talents for scholarship, poetry, and music, were not extinguished by this misfortune, however, and he made himself into a man of broad culture and very considerable intellectual power. For a few years he served as minister of Kirckudbright parish church. But his blindness proved a serious handicap in this work, and after 1765 he lived in Edinburgh, supporting himself by writing, tutoring, and furnishing lodgings to University students. He had published a volume of poems in 1746; though there is no touch of the vernacular in this early work, nor in what he did afterwards, he came to be recognized as a "Scottish" poet. Till approximately 1785 he continued to produce a considerable amount of conventional but not hopelessly uninspired verse.[44]

When the Kilmarnock edition of Burns's poems appeared, Blacklock was both prompt and enthusiastic in his praise. His letter to Lawrie showed Burns that he might hope for success outside his own immediate circle, and doubtless encouraged him in his resolution to visit Edinburgh. Why Burns delayed paying his respects to Blacklock when first he reached Edinburgh is uncertain; probably his engagements with persons more actively prominent in society kept him busy. But the fact is that after Burns had been two weeks in the city Blacklock wrote again to Lawrie making certain suggestions concerning a second edition of Burns's poems, and adding:

By the by, I hear that Mr. Burns is, and has been some time, in Edinburgh. These news I am sorry to have heard at second hand; they would have come much more welcome from the bard's own mouth. I have, however, written Mr. Mackenzie, the Man of Feeling, to beg the favour that he would bring us together.[45]

Towards the end of the month Burns received a letter from Lawrie telling him of Blacklock's wishes. Shortly thereafter he presented himself to his blind admirer, in whom he found, as he put it later, "what I would have expected in our friend, a clear head and an excellent heart."[46]

There are few records showing precisely how Blacklock's friendship for Burns found expression, though we know that once at least he gave a breakfast in honor of the poet. It is equally certain that the two men kept in touch with one another long after Burns had permanently withdrawn from Edinburgh. In November of 1788, for instance, Burns wrote to enquire after Blacklock's health, and said,

Can I be indifferent to the fate of a Man, to whom I owe so much? a Man whom I not only esteem but venerate?[47]

A little less than a year later the two men exchanged rimed epistles,[48] from the tone of which it appears that Burns was still on intimate terms with the older man, and that each had a well-rooted respect for the other. On the first of September, 1790, Blacklock sent a second riming letter to Burns, asking him to help his friend Anderson to launch a projected periodical, *The*

Bee.[49] Blacklock had given Burns several songs and a few tunes, all his own compositions, for the *Musical Museum;* it seemed only fair that Burns should reciprocate in kind. But nothing came of Blacklock's request, for Burns was busy about other matters, and within a year the older man was dead.

It is perhaps not to be wondered at that Blacklock, who all his life was interested in young men with literary or scholarly ambitions, should have been attracted to Burns when the Kilmarnock volume appeared, nor that he should have extended the conventional courtesies to him when he visited Edinburgh. But that there should have grown up between the two men a mutual esteem which terminated only with Blacklock's death, is another—perhaps unnecessary—piece of evidence concerning what one may call the many-sidedness of Burns's personality.

But of course Burns's most intimate Edinburgh acquaintances, the persons with whom he associated on terms of unquestioned social equality, were neither members of the nobility nor University professors. They were somewhat less dignified and less decorous folk; men in whose company Burns could unbend, and could live in the happy freedom that had marked his relations to Smith and Richmond.

One of this group of companions was William Smellie (1740–1795). Long before the poet had seen the roofs of Edinburgh —for Smellie was nineteen years older than Burns—he had won a considerable reputation as printer, publisher, editor, and translator. But he was uncouth, and had a touch of the blackguard about him. He was the founder of the somewhat disreputable Crochallan Fencibles, and seems to have deserved the title which Burns applied to him, "Veteran in Genius, Wit, and B-dry." [50] Possibly the most picturesque of Burns's Edinburgh acquaintances, the poet characterized him thus:

Crochallan came:
The old cock'd hat, the brown surtout the same;
His grisly beard just bristling in its might,
('Twas four long nights and days to shaving-night);

His uncomb'd, hoary locks, wild-staring, thatch'd
A head for thought profound and clear unmatch'd;
Yet, tho' his caustic wit was biting rude,
His heart was warm, benevolent, and good.[51]

It was Smellie who printed the 1787 volume, and in whose disorderly shop Burns corrected his proofs. After Burns left Edinburgh he had but few direct contacts with his old printer. But he never forgot him, nor ceased to speak of him in terms of mingled admiration and amusement. It is to be regretted that the many letters which Burns wrote to Smellie between 1788 and 1795 were burned as "totally unfit for publication."

Closely associated with Burns and Smellie in the publication of the 1787 volume was Peter Hill (1754–1837), who, like Cunningham, remained in touch with the poet almost to the time of his death. In 1787 he was one of the clerks in Creech's publishing office; in this capacity he came in intimate contact with Burns, and did much to assist him in bringing out the Edinburgh volume. In 1788 he opened a book-shop of his own, and ultimately became well enough known as a business man to be elected treasurer of the city of Edinburgh.

When Burns left Edinburgh he kept in close touch with Hill. He ordered books from him, both for his own personal collection and for the Monkland Friendly Society. The two men exchanged occasional gifts, Burns sending parcels of cheese or smoked salmon to the dining table at which he had been often a guest, and Hill reciprocating with a book or two for Burns's shelves. The last letter that Hill was to receive from Burns shows clearly enough the nature of their friendship:

MY DEAR HILL:

By the chaise, the driver of which brings you this, I send your *annual* Kipper:—but on the express condition that you do not, like a fool as you were last year, put yourself to five-times the value in expence of a return.—

I have just time to beg that you will make my best compliments to my fair friend, Mrs. Hill; Cameron, my kinsman; & Ramsay, my yoke-fellow in the L—d! God be with you all!—In a week, or ten days, thou shalt hear *at large* from—

Thine—

R. BURNS.[52]

There were to be no more letters, however, for Burns was a broken man when he wrote so hopefully to his old friend, and six months later he was dead.

Still another congenial personal friend, during the first winter in Edinburgh, was Robert Ainslie (1766–1838), a young law student. Burns and Ainslie had met in the early days of the Edinburgh visit, apparently at a Masonic affair, and at once had become intimate. Ainslie, seven years younger than Burns, was clever, "full of fun," and blessed with a boundless supply of good nature. Though he later developed into a straight-laced barrister and Kirk elder, given to writing religious book-lets, in 1787 he must have been quite the ideal "young man about town." In Burns's letters to him there is a note of play-fulness which appears but rarely in the poet's other correspon-dence. "I have not had one hearty mouthful of laughter since that merry-melancholy moment we parted," [53] Burns wrote, after having spent the first two and a half weeks of his Border Tour in Ainslie's company. And again, two months later,

There is one thing for which I set great store by you as a friend, and it is this—that I have not a friend upon earth, besides yourself, to whom I can talk nonsense without forfeiting some degree of his esteem. Now, to one like me, who never cares for speaking anything else but nonsense, such a friend as you is an invaluable treasure. I was never a rogue, but have been a fool all my life; and, in spite of all my endeavours, I see now plainly that I never shall be wise. Now it rejoices my heart to have met with such a fellow as you, who, though you are not just such a hopeless fool as I, yet I trust you will never listen so much to the temptations of the devil, as to grow so very wise that you will in the least disrespect an honest fellow because he is a fool. In short, I have set you down as the staff of my old age, when the whole list of my friends will, after a decent share of pity, have forgot me.[54]

[211]

Shortly thereafter, when Ainslie found himself embarrassed by the birth of an illegitimate son, Burns wrote:

Call your boy what you think proper, only interject Burns.—What do you [say] to a scripture name; for instance—

Zimri Burns Ainslie,

or

Achitophel, etc. etc.—

look [in] your bible for these two heroes.—If you do this, I will repay the Compliment.[55]

There was a serious side to this friendship, however. Late in the autumn of 1787, when Burns was suffering from one of his periodic attacks of hypochondria, he wrote thus:

You will think it romantic when I tell you, that I find the idea of your friendship almost necessary to my existence. You assume a proper length of face in my bitter hours of blue-devilism, and you laugh fully up to my highest wishes at my good things. I don't know, upon the whole, if you are one of the first fellows in God's world, but you are so to me. I tell you this now in the conviction that some inequalities in my temper and manner may perhaps sometimes make you suspect that I am not so warmly as I ought to be, Your friend.[56]

Ainslie was the sort of person whom one could trust in circumstances where tact, friendship, and taciturnity were required. Burns could confide in him when Jean was a second time in disgrace, or send a message by him to Clarinda, or utilize him as errand boy in an even more perplexing situation. In May of 1787 May Cameron, an Edinburgh servant girl, wrote to Burns saying that she was in trouble:

I beg, for God sake, you will write and let me know how I am to do. You can write to any person you can trust to get me a place to stay till such time as you come to town yourself.[57]

Burns, who was at Dumfries when the letter reached him, at once forwarded it to Ainslie, with these instructions:

[212]

Please call . . . for the wench and give her ten or twelve shillings . . . and advise her out to some country [friends] . . . Call immediately, or at least as soon as it is dark, for God sake, lest the poor soul be starving.—Ask her for a letter I wrote her just now, by way of token.—it is unsigned.[58]

Apparently Ainslie discharged the commission, but not to the complete satisfaction of the girl, for she afterwards had served on Burns the writ *in meditatione fugae.*

This, however, was but a minor incident in the history of Burns's relations to his young companion. Ainslie added to Burns's Edinburgh life just that touch of lightness, of geniality, of good cheer, that Burns especially craved. "My dearest friend," he called him; the epithet seems to have been well chosen.

As Ainslie was Burns's travelling companion on the Border Tour, so William Nicol (1744–1797) had the privilege of accompanying Burns on his second and most extensive trip through the Highlands. He was fifteen years older than the poet, and a somewhat pedantic and ill-natured schoolmaster. But he was blest with a fondness for convivial relaxation after his day's work in the Edinburgh High School; he was a radical in politics and religion; he admired Burns and his work wholeheartedly. He was also sufficiently adept at brewing "a peck o' maut" to have occasioned the most rollicking of Burns's relatively few bacchanalian lyrics. Mrs. Dunlop did not approve of him; but Burns loved him and named one of his sons for him.

No one knows just when or where the two men first became acquainted. Nicol, though successful as a teacher, was no favorite in Edinburgh society, and Burns's letters recording the celebrities whom he met during the first winter contain no reference to "Kind, honest-hearted Willie." But on June 1, when Burns was making his Border Tour, he wrote to Nicol from Carlisle; perhaps because he was in England and wished to make his "Scottish prejudice" more than usually obvious, he couched the rather long letter in "braid Scots." Incidentally, this vigorous and amusing *tour de force* is the only considerable example of

[213]

vernacular prose which Burns left behind him.[59] When a few
months later Burns and Nicol were touring the Highlands together, Nicol proved an impatient travelling companion. He
hurried Burns away from Castle Gordon, for instance, because
he felt offended at the poet's being shown more honor than was
accorded to him. But the men remained on most friendly terms,
and when Burns was farming at Ellisland, Nicol loaned him
his bay mare, Peg Nicholson, to use or to sell.[60] The horse died,
as horses will, and Burns announced the fact to Nicol in one of
his most amusing letters:

That d-mned mare of yours is dead. . . . I fed her up and had her
in fine order for Dumfries fair; when four or five days before the fair,
she was seized with an unaccountable disorder in the sinews, or somewhere in the bones of the neck; with a weakness or total want of power
in her fillets; and, in short, the whole vertebrae of her spine seemed to be
diseased and unhinged; and in eight and forty hours, in spite of the two
best farriers in the country, she died and be d-mned to her.[61]

The most interesting of Burns's few letters to Nicol concerned
a more serious matter than the demise of Peg Nicholson. During the winter of 1793, when Burns was in difficulties with the
Excise Board, and was accused of refusing to rise when the orches-
tra in the Dumfries theatre played "God Save the King," Nicol
took him to task for his conduct:

DEAR CHRISTLESS BOBBIE:

What is become of thee? Has the Devil flown off with thee, as the
gled does with a bird? If he should do so there is little matter, if the
reports concerning thy *imprudence* are true. What concerns it thee
whether the lousy Dumfriesian fiddlers play "Ca ira" or "God save the
King"? Suppose you *had* an aversion to the King, you could not, as a
gentleman, wish God to use him worse than He has done. . . .[62]

and much more of the same sort.

Burns's reply was another *tour de force* of irony and good-
natured banter:

[214]

EDINBURGH: THE FIRST WINTER

O Thou, wisest among the Wise, meridian blaze of Prudence, full moon of Discretion, & Chief of many Counsellors!—How infinitely is thy puddle-headed, rattle-headed, wrong-headed, round-headed slave indebted to thy supereminent goodness, that from the luminous path of thy own right-lined rectitude, thou lookest benignly down on an erring wretch, of whom the zig-zag wanderings defy all the powers of Calculation, from the simple copulation of Units up to the hidden mysteries of Fluxions! . . .[63]

and so on for a full page of first-rate fooling.

When one remembers Burns's situation in the winter of 1793, and recalls the hardships against which he was struggling, one gives thanks for such persons as Ainslie and Nicol, for it was they who best responded to the large measure of pure fun in Burns's nature. Even during the relatively untroubled months of the first winter in Edinburgh, Burns must have found their companionship a welcome relief after the more formal sessions with Blair and Dugald Stewart.

It was also during the winter of 1787 that Burns first found himself in association with Dr. John Moore (1729–1802). Moore was known to the late eighteenth century for a variety of reasons. He had travelled much, and had won some distinction as a surgeon. His *View of Society and Manners in France* (1779) had become popular long before the Revolution focussed the attention of the world on that storm-center of European politics. His first and best novel, *Zeluco* (1786), was a distinct favorite at the time of its publication, and gave Byron some suggestions for the character of Childe Harold. His *Journal During a Residence in France* (1793) was an accurate and readable account of the early stages of the Revolution. By the time it was published Moore's position was such that Burns always addressed him with the greatest deference, and considered him one of the major figures in contemporary English literature. But today he is remembered as the recipient of Burns's autobiographical letter, and as the father of Lieutenant General Sir John Moore, who died at the head of his troops at Corunna.

[215]

It was Mrs. Frances Dunlop who brought about the friendship between the two men—a friendship that found expression entirely through the medium of letters, for they never saw one another personally. Late in 1786 she sent Moore, who was then living in London, a copy of the Kilmarnock edition.[64] On December 30, 1786, she wrote Burns enclosing Moore's letter of acknowledgement, in which he praised Burns's work enthusiastically. On January 17, 1787, Burns followed Mrs. Dunlop's suggestion and himself wrote to Moore, alluding to "extracts of letters" which Mrs. Dunlop had sent him, but concealing the fact that Moore's entire letter lay open before him. In this first item in the correspondence Burns was too modest and too "literary;" none the less the letter is interesting as showing that Burns was not dazzled by his Edinburgh reception:

Your criticisms, Sir, I receive with reverence; only I am sorry they mostly came too late: a peccant passage or two that I would certainly have altered were gone to the Press. . . .

I know very well, the novelty of my character has by far the greatest share in the learned and polite notice I have lately got; and in a language where Pope and Churchill have raised the laugh, and Shenstone and Gray drawn the tear; where Thomson and Beattie have painted the landskip, and Littleton and Collins described the heart; I am not vain enough to hope for distinguished Poetic fame.[65]

Moore's reply,[66] patronizing in tone but obviously sincere in its praise of Burns's work, must have brought joy to the young poet's heart. A month later Burns wrote again, and once more alluded to the fact that his present reputation was out of proportion to his merits as a poet:

I scorn the affectation of seeming modesty to cover self-conceit. That I have some merit I do not deny; but I see with frequent wringings of heart, that the novelty of my character, and the honest national prejudice of my countrymen, have borne me to a height altogether untenable to my abilities.[67]

Moore did not permit Burns's letters to lie long unanswered, but returned a characteristic message almost by the next mail:

[216]

EDINBURGH: THE FIRST WINTER

Your letter of the 15th gave me a great deal of pleasure. It is not surprising that you improve in correctness and taste, considering where you have been for some time past. And I dare swear there is no danger of your admitting any polish which might weaken the vigour of your native powers.[68]

Throughout Moore's letters one finds just such strange but understandable combinations of what—*ex post facto*—seems crass stupidity, with what is obviously good sense. For Moore to suggest that association with Edinburgh's "literati" could possibly "improve" Burns, and at the same time to express the perfectly rational hope that he would not allow the example of these polite folk to weaken his native vigor—this was just what one learns to expect from Moore. In the same letter Moore urged Burns to write less in Scots, told him he was sending him a copy of his *View of Society* "as a small mark of [his] esteem," and reported that his youngest son was translating "Hallowe'en" into Latin verse!

When Burns acknowledged the gift of Moore's book he again showed how completely in the dark he was as to the relative merits of his own and his correspondent's work:

I shall return to my rural shades, in all likelihood never more to quit them. I have formed many intimacies and friendships here, but I am afraid they are all of too tender a construction to bear carriage a hundred and fifty miles. To the rich, the great, the fashionable, the polite, I have no equivalent to offer; and I am afraid my meteor appearance will by no means entitle me to a settled correspondence with any of you, who are the permanent lights of genius and literature.[69]

Moore's next letter is the most interesting he ever wrote to Burns. In it one sees again his intuitive good sense, and also his failure to comprehend the fact that Burns was, in effect, *sui generis*:

Some of the poems you have added in this last edition are very beautiful, particularly the "Winter Night," the "Address to Edinburgh," "Green grow the Rashes," and the two songs immediately following: the latter of which is exquisite. By the way, I imagine you have a peculiar talent for such compositions, which you ought to indulge . . .

[217]

It is evident that you already possess a great variety of expression and command of the English language; you ought, therefore, to deal more sparingly, for the future, in the provincial dialect—why should you, by using *that*, limit the number of your admirers to those who understand the Scottish, when you can extend it to all persons of taste who understand the English language? In my opinion you should plan some larger work than any you have as yet attempted . . . The Greek and Roman stories you can read in some abridgment, and soon become a master of the most brilliant facts, which must highly delight a poetic mind. You *should* also, and very soon *may*, become master of the heathen mythology, to which there are everlasting allusions in all the poets, and which in itself is charmingly fanciful. What will require to be studied with more attention is modern history: that is, the history of France and Great Britain, from the beginning of Henry the Seventh's reign. I know very well you have a mind capable of attaining knowledge by a shorter process than is commonly used, and I am certain you are capable of making a better use of it, when attained, than is generally done.[70]

It would be hard to find a more curious assortment of judgments both accurate and inaccurate than Moore managed to pack into that single paragraph.

When Burns next wrote to his self-appointed literary advisor it was to send him the famous "Autobiographical Letter," dated August 2, 1787. Comment on the significance of this document is unnecessary, as every one knows that it is the starting point for all biographical studies of the poet.

It is interesting to note, moreover, that not only did Burns feel moved thus to take Moore into his confidence, but that he kept Moore informed as to the subsequent course of his life. Early in 1789 he wrote what might fairly be called a postcript to the autobiography, bringing his story "down to date." Here one finds a summary of Burns's dealings with Creech, the record of his marriage to Jean, and his most definite statement concerning the loan to Gilbert. This last section is important enough to be reprinted in full:

On my last return from Edinburgh it cost me about £180 to save [my family] from ruin. Not that I have lost so much: I only interposed between my brother and his impending fate by the loan of so much. I give myself no airs on this, for it was mere selfishness on my part: I was conscious that the wrong scale of the balance was pretty heavily charged, and I thought that throwing a little filial piety and fraternal affection into the scale in my favor might help to smooth matters at the *grand reckoning.*[71]

It is unnecessary to follow the two men through all their correspondence. Burns was over-awed by Moore's reputation, and felt that praise from him was indeed praise from Caesar. He was nevertheless wise enough to welcome Moore's applause and to disregard his advice. He did not abandon the Scottish vernacular, nor worry himself over "heathen mythology," nor give up the verse forms in which he moved with most ease. He followed his own instinct in these matters, and his instinct was a surer guide than Moore's somewhat conventional taste. But Moore's interest and approbation meant much to the young poet, and the autobiography is good evidence of how completely Burns admitted his unseen friend to his confidence.

Women played but a small part in Burns's life during his first winter in Edinburgh. There was the Duchess of Gordon, to be sure, with probably half a score of her followers, eager to exhibit Burns at teas and assemblies. There were May Cameron and probably Jennie Clow, each of whom bore a child whom Burns admitted to be his. By only one person, however, does Burns's heart seem to have been touched.

The girl was Margaret Chalmers (1763?–1843). Apparently Burns met her at Dr. Blacklock's, early in the winter. The daughter of an Ayrshire farmer, she was connected by marriage with Gavin Hamilton's family, and was both handsome and accomplished. Interested in literature, and possessed of some skill in writing, she had endeared herself to Dr. Blacklock by her ability and willingness to sing Scottish songs and ballads. Burns too enjoyed her skill as a ballad-monger, and before long he was in love with her. It is virtually certain that she was the woman he had in mind when he wrote to Gavin Hamilton, on January 7, 1787, that he had "almost persuaded" the daughter of an East

Lothian farmer to marry him. His third Highland tour, which he made in October, 1787, was undertaken largely that he might see Peggy Chalmers at Harvieston, where he spent ten happy days in her company. But his suit was in vain, for she became engaged to Lewis Hay, an Edinburgh banker, whom she married in December of 1788. Before this event terminated the correspondence between the two, Burns had himself married Jean; and, indeed, by the first of January 1788 he was writing to Peggy only as an "ever dear friend." In this rôle she added much to his happiness by allowing him to treat her as a confidante, and by furnishing him with the sort of sympathetic understanding which he craved. Had she been willing to marry him, the tale of the next few years might have been radically different.

Such were some of the persons with whom Burns found himself thrown in contact during his first Edinburgh winter. As had been true at Lochlie and Mauchline, they came from no one group, but represented widely differing social classes and intellectual points of view. The nobility, the men of letters, the clergy, the University faculty, the lawyers, the teachers, the tradesmen—they were all listed among Burns's friends. It was a far cry from the Duchess of Gordon to a servant girl like May Cameron, or from Professor Dugald Stewart to John Richmond. But one thing they all had in common: their admiration for the man who came among them heralded as a "heaven-taught ploughman;" who proved to be inferior to no one in sheer native ability, and superior to every one as regards that mysterious something called "personality;" who saw clearly enough that Fate would return him to the obscure world from which he had come; and who never allowed himself to be "spoiled" by adulation or embittered by criticism.

3

THE 1787 EDITION

Happy as Burns was in the manifold pleasures and activities that Edinburgh offered him, he never forgot that he had come to the city on a poet's mission.   He wished to publish another edition of his poems.   Despite the distractions of an unfamiliar way of life, he went promptly about this important matter almost as soon as he was comfortably settled in Richmond's lodgings.

Burns's first move, made perhaps at the suggestion of the Earl of Glencairn, was to select William Creech (1745–1815) as his literary agent.   As Edinburgh's leading publisher, closely connected with the great London house of Cadell, Creech occupied a unique position.   He was a not unskillful though somewhat wooden writer, as his *Fugitive Pieces* testify, and a critic whose judgment was accepted by many persons.   He was, moreover, thoroughly conservative and a model of propriety, as became the Secretary of the Edinburgh Chamber of Commerce, the publisher who had brought out the works of Beattie, Campbell, and Mackenzie, and the man who in his younger days had been tutor to an Earl's son.

When Burns first met Creech, early in December, 1786, Creech was living in Craig's Close, near the High Street, where the "literati" foregathered of a morning to discuss matters of common interest.   His shop, or office, was immediately below the flat where Allan Ramsay had opened the first circulating library.   But Creech himself paid little attention to the details of business; his clerks and managers, Peter Hill for instance, did that for him.   As one of these trusted employés later put it:

Being so much occupied with literary people, he seldom handled his own money.   His clerk balanced the cash every night, and carried on *that* to next day.   He had a *levée* in his house till twelve every day, attended by literary men and printers.   Between twelve and one he came to the shop, where the same flow of company lasted till four, and then he left us, and we saw no more of him till next day.   He was a very good-natured man, and was never known to prosecute any one for a debt.[72]

He might have added that Creech was never known to hurry about paying a debt which he himself owed, and that he was notoriously economical when providing refreshments for his friends.

It did not take the two men long to reach an understanding. On December 13 Burns wrote John Ballantine, "I am nearly agreed with Creech to print my book." [73] On the next day Creech advertised the book as "in the press, to be published for the sole benefit of the author." [74] By this time subscription bills had already been distributed. The Earl of Glencairn, so Burns informed Aiken in a letter of December 16,

sent a parcel of subscription bills to the Marquiss of Graham with down-right orders to get them filled up with all the first Scottish names about Court.—He has likewise wrote to the Duke of Montague and is about to write to the Duke of Portland for their Graces' interest in behalf of the Scotch Bard's Subscription.[75]

It is worth remembering that Creech was not technically the publisher of the new book, but acted as Burns's "agent," as the poet expressly stated in the letter just quoted.[76] All financial responsibility rested on Burns. Smellie, the printer, and Scot, the bookbinder, looked to him for their money, not to Creech. So Creech cannily protected himself against loss in case of unexpected shortage of sales, and at the same time gained the credit of adding another "notable" to his list of authors. None the less it would have been hard for Burns to find any one better able to care for his literary venture than the "little, upright, pert, tart, tripping wight" [77] who was both a member of Edinburgh society and a publisher, and who always affected black silk breeches and generously powdered hair.

One gathers that the first half of the type-setting proceeded with gratifying speed, for in a letter to John Ballantine, dated 14 January, 1787, Burns said, "I have this day corrected my 152d page." [78] Not till March 22, however, was the proof-reading finished. On that day Burns wrote to Mrs. Dunlop, and added this postcript:

I have today corrected the last proof sheet of my poems, and have now only the Glossary and subscribers names to print.—Printing this last is much against my will, but some of my friends whom I do not chuse to thwart will have it so.—I have both a second and a third Edition going on as the second was begun with too small a number of copies.— The whole I have printed is three thousand.—Would the profits of that afford it, with rapture I would take your hint of a military life, as the most congenial to my feelings and situation of any other, but "What is wanting cannot be numbered." [79]

This paragraph, unpublished till 1898, is of interest to the biographer because it shows that Burns had at least considered purchasing an officer's commission, and to the bibliographer because it gives the clue to the facts underlying the existence of the two forms of the 1787 edition, the so-called "skinking" and "stinking" variants. The "Address to a Haggis," as Burns wrote it, contained the line

Auld Scotland wants nae *skinking* ware—

which makes good sense. But, as Burns makes clear in this letter to Mrs. Dunlop, there were not enough copies of the edition printed to fill the large number of orders received. So after the type had been distributed it was all re-set, and in this second form the line accidentally appeared thus:

Auld Scotland wants nae *stinking* ware.

In addition to this proof-reader's blunder, there were many other minor differences between the two forms, some apparently due to Burns himself, and some to the carelessness of Smellie's workmen. No public mention was made of these facts, however, and the book was finally given to the world on April 21, 1787, without any reference to the fact that it was appearing in two forms. The price to subscribers was five shillings; to other persons, six.

One of the interesting problems connected with the 1787 edition is the precise nature of the agreement between Burns and Creech. Unfortunately there is much uncertainty on the matter, for few of the papers relating to that agreement seem to have survived. One thing, however, is certain. Shortly before the book was ready for distribution, and when the large number of subscriptions guaranteed its success, Creech purchased the copyright. He thus put himself in a position to issue new editions, should he care to, solely for his own profit. The "Memorandum of Agreement" drawn up between Burns and Creech is of enough interest to be reproduced in full:

17 APRIL, 1787. MEMORANDUM OF AGREEMENT . . .

By advice of friends, Mr. Burns having resolved to dispose of the property of his *Poems*, and having consulted with Mr. Henry M'Kenzie upon the subject, Mr. Creech met with Mr. Burns at Mr. M'Kenzie's house upon Tuesday, the 17th April 1787, in the evening, and they three having retired and conversed upon the subject, Mr. Burns and Mr. Creech referred the sum, to be named by Mr. M'Kenzie, as being well acquainted with matters of this kind, when Mr. M'Kenzie said he thought Mr. Burns should have a hundred guineas for the property of his *Poems*.

Mr. Creech said that he agreed to the proposal, but as Scotland was now amply supplied with the very numerous edition now printed, he could write to Mr. Caddell of London, to know if he would take a share of the Book, but at any rate Mr. Burns should have the money named by Mr. M'Kenzie, which Mr. Burns most cordially agreed to, and to make over the property upon these terms, whenever Mr. Creech required him.

Upon Monday, the 23rd of April 1787, Mr. Creech informed Mr. Burns that he had remained in Town, expecting Mr. Caddell's answer, for three days, as to his taking a share of the property of the *Poems*; but that he had received no answer; yet he would, as formerly proposed and agreed to, take the whole matter upon himself, that Mr. Burns might be at no uncertainty in the matter.

Upon this both parties considered the transaction as finished.

EDINBURGH, Oct. 23, 1787.

On demand I promise to pay Mr. Robert Burns, or Order, One Hundred Guineas, value received.

WILLIAM CREECH.

Received the contents—May 30, 1788.   ROBERTS BURNS.[80]

When thus disposing of his copyright Burns overlooked the fact that he had already sold to his brother Gilbert all rights to approximately two-thirds of the poems, and that in so far as the poems which had been published at Kilmarnock were concerned, he had no title to convey to Creech. "I hereby dispone and convey to him in trust for behoof of my said natural daughter the Copyright of said Poems," Burns had written, in the Trust Deed executed on July 22, 1786, and properly recorded. By April 17, 1787, he had forgotten this entirely, and sold the poems all over again to Creech.

Creech thus purchased, or thought that he purchased, the "property" of the poems, in April of 1787. He did not, however, pay a penny at this time. Not till the 23rd of the following October did he even sign a note for the amount specified; and not till May 30, 1788, and then only after persistent pressure from Burns, did he finally pay the hundred guineas.

In addition to this investment, Creech had a considerable interest in the immediate financial success of the 1787 edition. He subscribed for five hundred copies, at the regular price of five shillings, which he was at liberty to re-sell to non-subscribers for six shillings. He thus stood to make a clear profit of £25. Furthermore, it is probable that he received some commission for acting as Burns's "agent;" that is, for distributing copies to subscribers, and collecting the money due.[81] In any case he handled the funds paid in by subscribers, except such small sums as may have been sent direct to Burns.

After the book was published Creech was dilatory in settling accounts with the author. As late as September 28, 1787, one finds Burns writing to Patrick Miller that

I am determined not to leave Edinr. till I wind up my matters with Mr. Creech, which I am afraid will be a tedious business.[82]

In January of 1788, though Burns by this time had Creech's note for the hundred guineas, he was still awaiting payment, and in no happy mood. When rumors of Creech's possible insolvency had begun to drift around, he wrote to Margaret Chalmers:

[225]

I have broke measures with [Creech], and last week I wrote him a frosty, keen letter. He replied in forms of chastisement, and promised me upon his honor that I should have the account on Monday; but this is Tuesday, and yet I have not heard a word from him. God have mercy on me! a poor, d-mned, incautious, duped, unfortunate fool! [83]

Towards the middle of March one of his letters to Clarinda was concerned largely with this same problem:

That arch-rascal Creech has not done my business yesternight, which has put off my leaving town till Monday morning. Tomorrow at eleven I meet with him for the last time; just the hour I should have met far more agreable company.

You will tell me this evening whether you cannot make our hour of meeting to-morrow one o'clock. I have just now written Creech such a letter, that the very goose-feather in my hand shrunk back from the line, and seemed to say, "I exceedingly fear and quake." I am forming ideal schemes of vengeance. O for a little of my will on him! [84]

Two weeks later, when Burns had finally left Edinburgh, Creech was still procrastinating. But the letter which Burns wrote him was not at all in the tone suggested by his remarks to Clarinda:

As I am seriously set in for my farming operations, I shall need that sum your kindness procured me for my Copy-right.—I have sent the line to Mr. John Sommerville, a particular friend of mine, who will call on you; but as I do not need the sum, at least I can make a shift without it till then, any time between [now] and the first of May, as it may suit your convenience to pay it, will do for me.[85]

By May 25 disquieting rumors concerning Creech's solvency were definitely in the air. Hence Burns turned to his friend James Johnson, publisher of the *Museum*, for help:

I am really uneasy about that money which Mr. Creech owes me pr Note in your hand, and I want it much at present as I am engaging in business pretty deeply both for myself & my brother. A hundred guineas can be but a trifling affair to him, and 'tis a matter of most serious importance to me.[86]

Five days later, as the receipted note shows, Creech paid the entire amount, but without interest.

Beyond a doubt Creech had before this time turned over to Burns considerable sums of money, though just how large they were, and when the payments were made, it is now impossible to tell. Then in February of 1789, when Burns was again in Edinburgh, Creech made some further payment in final settlement. Currie, who was in a position to see documents that have now disappeared, gave this as his summary of the matter:

> It is true there was a difference between our high-souled poet and Mr. Creech, and some of Burns's friends have a notion that Mr. Creech did not use him liberally. For my own part, I have found the correspondence among Burns's papers, and I can see no proof of any ill-usage.[87]

Burns himself admitted as much, in a letter to Dr. Moore:

> I was at Edinr. lately, and settled finally with Mr. Creech; and I must retract some illnatured surmises in my last letter, and own that at last, he has been amicable and fair with me.[88]

Clearly, however, there had been a good deal of delay, for the book had appeared twenty-three months before the date of this letter.

The account of this dispute between Burns and Creech brings up the more interesting matter of Burns's profits from the publication. Here again no one can make any authoritative statement. Robert Heron, who had no reason for mis-stating the facts, said in his *Memoir of the Life of the Late Robert Burns* (the earliest biography to be published):

> Mr. Creech has obligingly informed me that the whole sum paid to the poet for the copyright, and for the subscription copies of the book, amounted to nearly £1100. Out of this sum, indeed, the expenses of printing the edition for the subscribers, were to be deducted.[89]

The reader who is mathematically inclined may compute for himself what Burns's gross receipts might have been. Two thousand eight hundred and seventy-six copies were subscribed for in advance, as shown by the lists prefixed to the published volume; at the bottom of page xlvi, where the long roll of names came to an end, Burns noted that "Some subscriptions have not yet come to hand, and perhaps some have been mislaid." Assuming that three thousand copies were printed, as Burns told Mrs. Dunlop, and were actually sold to subscribers at the five-shilling rate, and that Burns collected all the money due him, one discovers that the receipts from this source would have been only £750. Adding to this the amount received for the copyright, one has a total of £855. In addition, there may have been some one or two hundred copies printed and sold for Burns's account to non-subscribers at the six-shilling rate, which might have brought the total to as high as £950. Even granting all this, one still finds Creech's figure of £1100 rather too large for acceptance. And, unfortunately, no one knows what Burns paid Creech by way of commission, nor Smellie for printing, nor Scot for binding the book. So when all is said and done one must trust Burns's incidental remarks as the only reliable source of information. It was to his two confidential friends Mrs. Dunlop and Dr. Moore that he wrote most explicitly on this matter. To Moore he said:

I believe I shall in whole, £100 copyright included, clear about £400 some little odds; and even part of this depends upon what the gentleman has yet to settle with me. I give you this information . . . but I give it to yourself only; for I am still much in the gentleman's mercy. Perhaps I injure the man in the idea I am sometimes tempted to have of him: God forbid I should.[90]

To Mrs. Dunlop Burns was more specific, and less complaining:

By Mr. Creech, who has at last settled amicably & fully as fairly as could have been expected, with me, I clear about 440 or 450 £.—[91]

That is as precise as any one can be concerning Burns's profits.[92] A comparison of the Edinburgh with the Kilmarnock edition reveals certain interesting facts. First of all, instead of being delivered "stitched," in a blue paper cover, the new work was substantially bound in boards. The Preface of 1786 was omitted, and in its place stood the Dedication to the Caledonian Hunt. Pages ix to xlvi contained the names of subscribers. The original glossary of five pages was expanded to one of twenty-four—a much more useful linguistic tool for the non-Scottish reader. In the Kilmarnock edition the old Scottish gerund or gerundive forms in *-an* or *-in* had been used; in the 1787, these were replaced by the modern forms in *-ing*. Finally, in place of two hundred and thirty-five pages of poetry, there were now three hundred and forty-three, each of virtually the same size as a page of the Kilmarnock volume. There were thus slightly more than a hundred pages of hitherto uncollected and for the most part unpublished verse in the Edinburgh edition; enough, in fact, to warrant the general impression that it was much more than a reprint with a few additions.

When one scrutinizes the poetical contents of the two editions, one discovers that they are identical to page 54—page for page, line for line, except as regards minor textual changes which need not be recorded here. Then, immediately after "The Holy Fair," Burns inserted four poems, "Death and Dr. Hornbook," "The Brigs of Ayr," "The Ordination," and "The Calf," the first and third of which had certainly been written before the Kilmarnock volume appeared, but had been excluded from it. Again, after "The Vision," which in its 1787 form contained a number of new stanzas, Burns inserted the "Address to the Unco Guid" and "Tam Samson's Elegy," both of which may have been written between the dates of the two publications. Five hitherto unpublished religious poems which must have delighted Mrs. Dunlop, the political ballad "When Guilford Good our Pilot Stood," which in its original form had been composed long before, but withheld from the printer, and five unpublished songs, were also included. Finally, two poems composed specially for the new work, the "Address to a Haggis" and the "Address to Edinburgh," complete the list of additions. Three insignificant epitaphs that had been used as "filler" in the Kilmarnock volume were quite properly cancelled.[93]

Nearly all of this uncollected poetry had been written before even the Kilmarnock edition had appeared. Between July of 1786, when the first work was published, and December, when the second went to press, Burns had had scanty leisure for poetry. He had been distracted by the Armour difficulty, and harrowed by the tragic conclusion of his intimacy with Mary Campbell. For some weeks he had been busy with arrangements for the trip to Jamaica. When the necessity for that flight had passed, he had almost at once become involved in preparations for the winter at Edinburgh. When he reached the capital he was allowed little opportunity for writing of any sort.

Hence one turns the pages of the 1787 volume in vain if one is seeking evidence of any strengthening of Burns's poetic powers, or of interest in new and hitherto unattempted forms of verse. "The Brigs of Ayr," the most pretentious of the poems written too late for the Kilmarnock volume, is a less readable example of the old *débat* than "The Twa Dogs." The "Address to Edinburgh" is not Burns at his worst, but it would be hard to find many more convincing illustrations of his least effective writing. In one song, "Green Grow the Rashes, O," Burns gave clear indication of a lyric genius that had not even been foreshadowed by the Kilmarnock volume; the "Address to the Unco Guid" was a superb example of personal apologetics. But these two are the only notable pieces that appear in the hundred-odd pages of "new" material. The conclusion is inevitable that Burns the poet was as well represented by the 1786 as by the 1787 volume.

But the 1787 volume attracted far more attention from the reviewers than had its predecessor. Though most of the published comments were favorable, there was almost at once an undertone of a quite different sort. To some persons Burns appeared as a foe to all propriety and decorum, and even as a sacrilegious upstart whose writings were subversive of both morality and Christian faith. For example, "A Friend to Virtue" lost no time in publishing a parody of Burns's "To a Daisy," introduced by the following statement:

On reading Burns's poems, and some other productions in his defence, my feelings have been so shocked, that I should think it criminal not to contribute with the virtuous few who have already appeared on the side of injur'd truth.—It is certainly a very agreeable article of licentious faith, that although led astray by fierce passions and wild pleasures, "Yet the light that led us astray is light from heaven."—Burns's vision, page 140.—Such articles, together with the contaminating spirit that runs through this work, are calculated to do more injury to religion, and virtue, than all the atheistical, deistical, and heretical books that have been written this last century.[94]

In one important respect this 1787 volume did for Burns what the Kilmarnock had not accomplished: it made him known to a large and influential reading public, and extended his fame far beyond the limits of Scotland. It was published in London, by Cadell and Davies, at the same time as in Edinburgh; pirated editions appeared in Dublin and Belfast before the year was out; Philadelphia saw a similar reprint in 1788, and New York in 1789. The man who had ridden into Edinburgh on that November afternoon of 1786 was unknown outside a few parishes; by the first of May, 1787, he was well on his way to becoming a personage of more than national importance.

As soon as the book was published, Burns began saying farewell to his Edinburgh friends. To some he sent proof copies of Beugo's engraving of the Nasmyth portrait, which had served as frontispiece to the volume; to a few of his most intimate associates he presented copies of the book itself. He had no thought that his day as a poet had ended; indeed, even as he was packing his saddle bags he was promising to write songs a-plenty for James Johnson and his *Scots Musical Museum*. But he realized that Edinburgh had nothing more to offer him. He had enjoyed his day in society; he had brought out his book. On both counts his success had been beyond all his hopes. And so, swiftly, before the reaction should set in, he said farewell to

[231]

THE LIFE OF ROBERT BURNS

"Auld Reekie," and on Saturday, the fifth of May, once again on horseback, rode south to the Border Marches in search of rest and relaxation.

[1] *Letters*, I, 49.

[2] See letter to George Reid, 29 Nov., 1786; *ibid.*, p. 53.

[3] *Edinburgh Fugitive Pieces*, by William Creech, Edinburgh, 1815. See especially the "Letters containing a comparative view of Edinburgh in 1763, 1783, and 1793."

[4] *Op. cit.*, p. 91.

[5] *Ibid.*, p. 100.

[6] *Ibid.*, pp. 101 ff.

[7] The Edinburgh Assembly Room, where the most impressive social events were held, was one of the two largest in Britain.

[8] It is interesting to note that Adam Smith proposed to aid Burns by making him a "Salt Officer" in the Customs Service, at a salary of £30 per year.

[9] "I have found a worthy, warm friend in Mr. Dalrymple of Orangefield, who introduced me to Lord Glencairn." Letter to John Ballantine, 13 December, 1786; *Letters*, I, 56 f.

[10] See James Marshall's *A Winter with Robert Burns*; Edinburgh, 1846. Unfortunately Marshall accepted as authentic virtually all bits of gossip that he ran across.

[11] C. W., II, 45.

[12] *Ibid.*, p. 58.

[13] *Ibid.*, p. 59.

[14] Letter of 5 Feb., 1792; *Letters*, II, 109.

[15] Letter to Dr. Moore, 28 Feb., 1791; *ibid.*, p. 57.

[16] The poem was excluded from the 1786 volume, but included in the 1787.

[17] Letter to Lady Elizabeth Cunningham, 22 Jan., 1789; *Letters*, I, 289.

[18] Letter of 7 Dec., 1786; *ibid.*, p. 55.

[19] Letter of 4 May, 1787; *ibid.*, p. 89.

[20] Letter of 10 March, 1791; *ibid.*, II, 61.

[21] Quoted, C. W., II, 72.

[22] *Ibid.*, p. 79.

[23] *The Songstresses of Scotland*, by Sarah Tytler and J. L. Watson, London, 1871, 2 vols.; I, 180. The "Hunters' Ball" was the ball given by the Caledonian Hunt.

[24] Letter of 6 Nov., 1787; *Letters*, I, 136.

[25] *Ibid.*, p. 55.

[26] *Ibid.*, p. 13.

[27] See *The Anecdotes and Egotisms of Henry Mackenzie*, edited by H. W. Thompson, Oxford, 1927, pp. 150–152, for Mackenzie's impressions of Burns.

[28] See Stewart's letter to Currie, Currie, I, 133 ff.

[29] See a letter dated 20 Jan., 1789; *Letters*, I, 288.

[30] C. W., II, 87.

[31] Currie, I, 133 ff.

[32] *Memoirs of the Life of Sir Walter Scott, Bart.*, by J. G. Lockhart (Boston, 1873, 6v.), I, 166 ff.

[33] For example, he could not understand the venereal slang of the "Epistle to John Rankine." See "Burns and Hugh Blair," by J. DeL. Ferguson, *Mod. Lang. Notes*, November, 1930, pp. 440 ff.

[34] C. W., I, 449.

[35] See Ferguson, "Burns and Hugh Blair," *Mod. Lang. Notes*, Nov., 1930, pp. 400 ff.

[36] *Ibid.*

[37] Letter of 3 May, 1787; *Letters*, I, 88.

[38] Letter of 4 May, 1787; C. W., II, 97.

[39] After 1809 he contributed to the *Quarterly Review*, using the name Richardson.

[40] *Scots Magazine*, LX, 212.

[41] *Ibid.*, 863.

[42] Letter of December, 1786; *Letters*, I, 59.

[43] C. W., II, 86.

[44] An attractive collected edition was published shortly after his death: *Poems by the late Reverend Dr. Thomas Blacklock*; Edinburgh, 1793. The "Life" is by Mackenzie, the "Man of Feeling."

[45] Letter of 11 December, 1786; C. W., II, 42.

[46] Letter to Lawrie, 5 Feb., 1787; *Letters*, I, 70.

[47] *Ibid.*, p. 274.

[48] C. W., III, 112 and 113.

[49] *Ibid.*, p. 201.

[50] Letter to Peter Hill, 2 Feb., 1790; *Letters*, II, 6.

[51] H. H., II, 236.

[52] Letter of 29 January, 1796; *Letters*, II, 314.

[53] Letter of 29 May, 1787; *ibid.*, I, 92.

[54] Letter of 23 July, 1787; *ibid.*, p. 102.

[55] Letter of 23 August, 1787; *ibid.*, p. 119.

[56] Letter of 23 Nov., 1787; *ibid.*, p. 140.

[57] C. W., II, 121.

[58] *Letters*, I, 226.

[59] *Ibid.*, p. 94.

[60] The horse was named after an insane woman, Margaret Nicholson, who in August of 1786 had tried to stab George III.

[61] Letter of 9 Feb., 1790; *Letters*, II, 8. See "Elegy on Willie Nicol's Mare," H. H., II, 223.

[62] C. W., III, 394.

[63] *Letters*, II, 150.

[64] It is possible that Moore wrote the review which appeared in *The English Review*, London, in February, 1787.

[65] Letter of January, 1787; *Letters*, I, 69.

[66] C. W., II, 40.

[67] Letter of 15 Feb., 1787; *Letters*, I, 76.

[68] Letter of 28 Feb., 1787; C. W., II, 57.

[69] Letter of 23 April, 1787; *Letters*, I, 85.

[70] Letter of 23 May, 1787; C. W., II, 94.

[71] Letter of 4 Jan., 1789; *Letters*, I, 284.

[72] Quoted, C. W., II, 266, n.

[73] *Letters*, I, 56 f.

[74] C. W., II, 22.

[75] *Letters*, I, 58. Neither Portland nor Montague appears in the list of subscribers.

[76] "Mr. Creech . . . is my agent, forsooth." C. W., II, 22.

[77] "On William Creech"; H. H., II, 235.

[78] *Letters*, I, 66.

[79] *Ibid.*, pp. 80 ff.

[80] C. W., II, 92. The original of this agreement may be seen in the Burns Museum, Alloway.

[81] Creech's advertisement when the volume was ready contained the following statement: "As the book is published for the sole benefit of the author, it is requested that subscribers will send for their copies; and none will be delivered without money." C. W., II, 90.

[82] *Letters*, I, 126.

[83] Letter of 22 Jan., 1788; *ibid.*, p. 172.

[84] Letter of 19 March, 1788; *ibid.*, p. 211.

[85] Letter of 31 March, 1788; *ibid.*, p. 214.

[86] Letter of 25 May, 1788; *ibid.*, p. 222.

[87] Letter of 30 Dec., 1797, to Cadell and Davies; C. W., III, 28.

[88] Letter of 23 March, 1789; *Letters*, I, 314. See also a letter to Jean, 20 Feb., 1789 (*Letters*, I, 308).

THE LIFE OF ROBERT BURNS

[89] *Op. cit.*, Edinburgh, 1797; p. 31.
[90] Letter of 4 Jan., 1789; *Letters*, I, 284.
[91] Letter of 25 March, 1789; *ibid.*, p. 316.
[92] A quite valueless pamphlet, *William Creech, Robert Burns'* (*sic*) *Best Friend*, by J. C. Carrick (Dalkeith, 1903), throws no light on the problem.
[93] "Epitaph on a Henpecked Country Squire;" "Epigram on said Occasion;" "One Queen Artemisa."
[94] British Museum chap-book, 1787; n.p.

CHAPTER VII

VACATION TOURS: AN INTERLUDE

Four times between April and November of 1787 Burns enjoyed the luxury of a vacation tour. He had always been interested in what lay beyond the horizon, but until the profits from the Edinburgh volume began to come in, he had had neither leisure nor funds for adventuring. At Mount Oliphant and Lochlie he had been bound to the soil, in fact if not in name; the months at Irvine had done something to widen his horizon, but they had been devoted, for the most part, to labor even more irksome than that of the farm. When he moved to Mossgiel, as responsible head of the family group, he had even scantier opportunity for roving. In fact, during all Burns's early years his traveling had been done entirely through the medium of books. But the insatiable curiosity and interest in things outside his own world that had compelled him to spend his boyhood days in reading, made it inevitable, when at last the occasion presented itself, that he should seize it greedily, and should invest part of his little capital in an endeavor to see more of the Scotland whose poet he aspired to be. Hence he decided to postpone his "return to the plow," as he called it, till after he had gratified in some measure his instinct for physical and intellectual adventure.

The same innate sense of the importance of what he was doing and thinking that prompted him to keep his *Commonplace Books*, and to preserve careful copies of many letters, was responsible for the Journals which make it easy to follow Burns on the most important of the four journeys, the first and third. For the first of these holiday tours Burns selected the Border Marches south and west of Edinburgh, and chose his intimate friend Bob Ainslie as traveling companion. The two men left Edinburgh on Satur-

[235]

day, May 5, on horseback, Burns riding no borrowed "pownie," as he had done six months before, but bestriding his own recently purchased mare "Jenny Geddes."

The route which the travelers had marked out for themselves led them first of all to Berrywell, Ainslie's home, near the village of Duns, southeast of Edinburgh. Here on Sunday they went to church, and Burns had the pleasure of realizing that he was being stared at and whispered about. His fame had preceded him into the provinces, and he found the applause of country folk as welcome as the more formal approbation of the Edinburgh gentry.

Monday, May seventh, brought the two friends to Coldstream, where they crossed the Tweed and set foot on English soil. Nearly half a century afterwards Ainslie remembered that as soon as Burns found himself in England he "uncovered, [knelt] down with uplifted hands, and apparently rapt in a fit of enthusiasm . . . prayed for and blessed Scotland most solemnly, by pronouncing aloud, in tones of the deepest devotion, the two concluding stanzas of the 'Cotter's Saturday Night.' "[1]

It is an interesting picture, if one is interested in Burns as romantic biographers have tried to represent him. The poet's Journal, however, contains no evidence of any such hysterical outburst, but shows him acting like a normal man:

Monday [May 7]—Coldstream—went over to England—Cornhill —glorious river Tweed—clear and majestic—fine bridge. Dine at Coldstream with Mr. Ainslie and Mr. Foreman. Beat Mr. F. in a dispute about Voltaire. . . . Sleep at Coldstream.[2]

Ainslie's picture of Burns on his knees in an ecstasy of patriotic fervor is probably apocryphal. He merely crossed the river into England, dined with a friend, discussed French philosophy, slept comfortably, and on Tuesday, May 8, recrossed the river and was again in Scotland.

Next on the route was the historic abbey town of Jedburgh, where Queen Mary had lodged in 1566, and where Prince Charlie had spent a day during his audacious march into England. Two or three days passed pleasantly enough here, for Burns's associates were interesting and at times amusing. Here too on the tenth of May Burns was "waited on by the magistrates, and presented with the freedom of the burgh," though there seems to be no corroborating record in the town archives.[3]

From Jedburgh the travelers rode slowly up the valley of the Tweed, visiting Melrose, Selkirk, and Ettrick. The Journal is too detailed for effective quotation, but a letter to Creech, written at Selkirk on May 13, gives a succinct summary, and indicates that the vacation jaunt was bringing its fair share of discomforts:

MY HONORED FRIEND:

The inclosed ["Willie's Awa"], I have just wrote, nearly extempore, in a solitary Inn in Selkirk, after a miserable wet day's riding.—I have been over most of East Lothian, Berwick, Roxburgh, & Selkirk Shires; and next week I begin a tour through the north of England.—Yesterday, I dined with Lady Hariot, sister to my noble patron,—Quem Deus conservet!—I would write till I would tire you as much with dull Prose as I dare say by this time you are with wretched Verse; but I am jaded to death.[4]

From Selkirk, Burns and Ainslie doubled back, after some exploration of local scenes celebrated in song and ballad, to Duns, and on to Berwick and Eyemouth, on the coast of the North Sea. At Eyemouth, on Saturday, May 19, Burns's Masonic brethren of St. Abb Lodge welcomed him with gratifying enthusiasm. The Lodge records show that

At a general encampment held this day the following Brethren were made Royal Arch Masons—namely, Robert Burns . . . and Robert Ainslie. . . . Robert Ainslie paid one guinea admission dues; but on account of R. Burns's remarkable poetical genius, the encampment unanimously agreed to admit him gratis, and considered themselves honoured by having a man of such shining abilities for one of their companions.[5]

The next day saw the travelers following the coast north and west towards Dunbar. "Past through the most glorious corn country I ever saw," wrote the farmer-poet, "till I reached Dunbar, a neat little town." [6] But no allusion to Cromwell's visit to the same country in 1650 escaped him; nor, indeed, is there evidence in the Journal that Burns was in any way interested in the larger historic associations of the country through which he was passing, though he had a keen eye for scenes celebrated in Scottish song and ballad.

By the 24th of May Burns was at Berrywell and Duns for the third time, and though Ainslie returned to his studies in Edinburgh, his pretty sister Rachel did what she could to keep the poet in good humor. None the less Burns missed his friend, and within a few days sent him a letter that made no pretence of concealing his loneliness:

Here am I, a woeful wight on the banks of Tyne.—Old Mr. Thos. Hood has been persuaded to join our Partie, and Mr. Kerr & he do very well, but alas! I dare not talk nonsense lest I lose all the little dignity I have among the sober sons of wisdom & discretion.[7]

On Sunday, May 27, Burns again crossed the Tweed and a second time entered England. By the 29th he had ridden as far south as Newcastle; by the 31st he had crossed the island to Carlisle. Here he met a

strange enough romantic adventure, in falling in with a girl and her married sister—the girl, after some overtures of gallantry on my side, sees me a little cut with the bottle, and offers to take me in for a Gretna Green affair. I, not being quite such a gull as she imagines, make an appointment with her, by way of *vive la bagatelle*, to hold a conference on it when we reach town. I meet her in town and give her a brush of caressing and a bottle of cyder; but finding herself *un peu trompée* in her man, she sheers off.[8]

From Carlisle Burns returned to Scotland by way of Dumfries, where on June 4, he received the freedom of the Burgh.[9] Here too he found May Cameron's appeal for help awaiting him. And six miles up the river Nith was Patrick Miller's estate of Dalswinton, where a farm was for rent, and where Burns spent a day looking at the vacant property.

VACATION TOURS: AN INTERLUDE

On the ninth of June, after an absence of slightly more than half a year, he walked unannounced into the farmhouse at Mossgiel, greeted the members of his family, and went back down the road to Mauchline village, to see Jean. A letter to his old friend James Smith says much concerning his state of mind at the time:

> I slept at John Dow's, and called for my daughter; Mr. Hamilton and family; your mother, sister, and brother; . . . all, all well. I date this from Mauchline, where I arrived on Friday even last. If any thing had been wanting to disgust me completely at Armour's family, their mean, servile compliance would have done it. Give me a spirit like my favorite hero, Milton's Satan.[10]

It had been a leisurely tour, this first vacation jaunt. There was little plan or order about it, except that when Burns left Edinburgh he knew in general that he was going south and west, and ultimately would reach his home in Mauchline. To map the travelers' progress from day to day is to realize that they journeyed as the spirit moved them—doubling on their tracks, returning later to visit places they could more easily have seen before, and in general letting each day suffice for itself. The Journal shows clearly that Burns's interest in human nature was unflagging, that he enjoyed good dinners and evenings of talk over the port, and that places celebrated in Scottish song or ballad had a strong fascination for him. He does not seem to have been historically-minded, however, nor to have felt more than a casual interest in "scenery."

Burns had left Mossgiel virtually unknown, and had returned a national hero. He had gone away poor, and had returned the possessor of what must have seemed incredible riches. He had gone away, in part at least, to escape from the entanglements which Jean Armour and he had woven around one another, and from the anger of her father. He returned to find Jean as alluring as ever, and her parents complaisant. "On my éclatant return to Mauchline, I was made very welcome to visit my girl," he afterwards wrote Mrs. Dunlop; "[and] the usual consequences began to betray her." [11]   In other words, though Burns had gone up to Edinburgh to find a larger stage for his activities, and to break loose from some of the clogs that bound him to Mauchline, as soon as he returned for a brief visit he took a step destined again to attach him to the world in which he had grown up, and to the woman whom less than a year before he had sworn "by Hell" he would never marry.

As Burns walked the familiar streets of Mauchline, and listened to the praises of friends who gathered in the taverns to talk with him, the old perplexity as to the future returned to disquiet him. What to do? Where to live? How to live? Once again he thought of Jamaica as a port of refuge. "I cannot settle to my mind," he wrote Smith;

> Farming, the only thing of which I know anything, and heaven above knows but little do I understand of that, I cannot, dare not risk on farms as they are. If I do not fix, I will go for Jamaica. Should I stay in an unsettled state at home, I would only dissipate my little fortune, and ruin what I intend shall compensate my little ones for the stigma I have brought on their names. [12]

At the same time that he was thus writing to Smith, he was confiding in Nicol concerning the secret of another source of unhappiness. "I never," he wrote,

> thought Mankind very capable of anything generous; but the stateliness of the Patricians in Edinr, and the servility of my plebeian brethren, who perhaps formerly eyed me askance, since I returned home, have nearly put me out of conceit altogether with my species. [13]

In other words, it was a restless and discontented poet who had come back to Mauchline. He had enjoyed his months in Edinburgh, but had never considered settling down there. He would have been unhappy in such an environment. He was, however, more aware than ever of the pettiness of life in the village that he called home. The Edinburgh gentry had already begun to forget him, and his friends in Mauchline had begun to treat him as if he were a member of the gentry. Jean was almost too willing, and no longer even distantly concerned about marriage. Already three illegitimate children claimed his support; May Cameron, in Edinburgh, was soon to add another to his charge. And he had by no means forgotten Mary Campbell, dead for love of him.

Restless, unhappy, Burns sought solace in action. Within two weeks of his return to Mauchline he had saddled Jenny Geddes and was off again, alone this time, bound for Glasgow and the West Highlands.

This second vacation tour is a perplexing affair. If Burns kept a Journal, it does not seem to have survived. The letters written at the time, though addressed to three of his most intimate friends—Ainslie, Richmond, and Smith—are vague as to material facts. Nevertheless the one to Ainslie, though only a fragment, does furnish a specific place and date:

ARROCHAR, June 25, 1787.

My DEAR FRIEND & BROTHER ARCH,

I write this on my tour through a country where savage streams tumble over savage mountains, thinly overspread with savage flocks, which starvingly support as savage inhabitants. My last stage was Inverary—tomorrow night's stage, Dumbarton. I ought sooner to have answered your kind letter, but you know I am a man of many sins.[14]

Obviously, Burns was on his way home when he wrote. On June 29 he was made a Burgess of Dumbarton, though he never seems to have referred to the fact in writing.[15]

Three days later he sent a long letter to James Smith, recounting in pleasant vein some of the amusing incidents of the trip, and inserting one paragraph concerning more serious matters:

I have yet fixed on nothing with respect to the serious business of life. I am, just as usual, a rhyming, mason-making, raking, aimless, idle fellow. However, I shall somewhere have a farm soon. I was going to say, a wife too; but that must never be my blessed lot. I am but a younger son of the house of Parnassus, and, like other younger sons of great families, I may intrigue, if I choose to run all risks, but must not marry.[16]

A fragment of a letter in the Gribbel Collection, Philadelphia,

[241]

shows him to have been back at Mosgiel on July 2. Five days later he wrote to Richmond, and referred to an amusing incident which he had recounted at length in the letter to Smith:

> I have lately been rambling over by Dumbarton and Inverary, and running a drunken race on the side of Loch Lomond with a wild Highlandman; his horse, which had never known the ornaments of iron or leather, zigzagged across before my old spavin'd hunter, whose name is Jenny Geddes, and down came the Highlandman, horse and all, and down came Jenny and my Bardship; so I have got such a skinful of bruises and wounds, that I shall be at least four weeks before I dare venture on my journey to Edinburgh.[17]

Only one other brief allusion to this trip need be quoted. The first paragraph of the autobiographical letter to Dr. Moore, dated Mauchline, 2 August, 1787, reads thus:

> For some months past I have been rambling over the country, partly on account of some little business I have to settle in various places.[18]

Such a statement suggests that one of Burns's reasons for making the trip to the west was to collect money due him for copies of his poems. It also leaves the reader with a feeling that other than financial considerations operated to send him on this hurried journey into the heart of Argyllshire. Inevitably one asks whether the trip may not have had something to do with the "Highland Mary" episode. For eight months the body of Mary Campbell had rested in the Old West Kirk burying ground at Greenock. Her family—by vague tradition—is supposed to have come from Argyllshire. There is no actual record that Burns visited Greenock on this journey; but his sister long afterwards told Dr. Chambers that "he went first to Glasgow, from which he sent home a present to his mother and three sisters; namely, a quantity of *mode silk.*" [19] If he actually went to Glasgow, a trip down the Clyde to Greenock, where lay the body of the woman he had promised to marry, would have seemed inevitable. If he made such a visit to Mary Campbell's grave, he might well have been in a mood to write Smith that he could never marry. But one can make no definite assertions, and should be wary of conclusions based on tradition, gossip, or mere possibility. All that can be truthfully said is this: between the middle of June and the first of July, 1787, Burns journeyed from Mauchline into the Argyllshire Highlands; one of the reasons for the tour may have been his desire to visit Mary Campbell's grave, and to talk to members of her family.

Home again at Mossgiel, Burns spent the month of July in relative idleness. He was nursing the bruises received when Jenny Geddes had fallen with him; he was writing letters, for there was business connected with the Edinburgh volume to be attended to, and there were friends in Edinburgh who were interested in his welfare. For Dr. Moore, in London, Burns composed a long autobiographical letter in which he reviewed his entire life up to this time. And always there was Jean.

But idleness of this sort ill suited Burns's temperament. He was concerned over Creech's delay in settling accounts; he wished to make a trip through the Central Highlands with Nicol. Consequently the first week of August saw him again in the saddle, bound for Edinburgh.

When he reached the city he once more went to Richmond's lodging in the Lawnmarket, but moved, in a day or two, to Nicol's home in Buccleuch Square, where he could live in greater comfort.

Social diversions played but a small part in Burns's life during this visit to Edinburgh. There were more important concerns than teas and dinners: Creech, dilatory as ever, must be forced to pay what was still due on the 1787 edition; May Cameron was demanding security for the support of her expected child; not till August 15 was Burns discharged from the menace of the writ she had sued out against him. James Johnson, busy arranging the material for the second volume of his *Musical Museum*, was eager for Burns's advice and assistance. These matters took time and energy. But by the 25th of August Burns and Nicol were ready to leave the city on what was to prove the most extensive of Burns's holiday expeditions.

[243]

The two men rode in a chaise. "Nicol thinks it more comfortable than horseback," Burns told Ainslie, "to which I say, Amen; so Jenny Geddes goes back to Ayrshire." The trip lasted twenty-two days, and covered some six hundred miles of the central Highland district. As in the case of the Border Tour, Burns kept a Journal, which has recently been published in facsimile.[20] Thus for the first time it becomes possible to read what Burns himself actually wrote while on the trip. Hitherto all reprints of the Journal have included certain intrusive material, inserted apparently by Lockhart or Allan Cunningham, at places where the poet's own observations were not what these arch-emendors thought they should have been. Concerning Bannockburn, for instance, Burns wrote thus:

> Come on to Bannockburn—shown the old house where James 3d was murdered—the field of Bannockburn—the hole where glorious Bruce set his standard—Come to Stirling.[21]

This laconic comment was not sufficient for Lockhart, who was assisted by Cunningham in the preparation of his *Life*. Turning to page 156 of the first (1828) edition of that widely-read biography, one finds this statement:

> At Bannockburn he writes as follows: "Here no Scot can pass uninterested. I fancy to myself that I see my gallant countrymen coming over the hill, and down upon the plunderers of their country, the murderers of their fathers, noble revenge and just hate glowing in every vein, striding more and more eagerly as they approach the oppressive, insulting, blood-thirsty foe. I see them meet in glorious triumphant congratulation on the victorious field, exulting in their heroic royal leader, and rescued liberty and independence."

None of this is in the manuscript, or ever was. It is in Honest Allan's best and most florid vein, and is almost certainly from either his pen or his associate's, Lockhart. Hence the student who wishes to read Burns's account of his trip at first hand must disregard all versions of the Journal except the facsimile. Here he will find the poet's narrative ample enough to make possible the reconstruction of the entire tour.[22]

[244]

VACATION TOURS: AN INTERLUDE

The two travelers left Edinburgh on Saturday, August 25, and drove west to Linlithgow. Here Burns's interest in history and architecture prompted him to comment on the "tolerably fine, but melancholy ruin," of the old royal Palace; his associations with the Presbyterian Church evoked the following:

> What a poor, pimping business is a Presbytyrean place of worship, dirty, narrow, and squalid, stuck in a corner of old Popish grandeur such as Linlithgow, and, much more, Melrose! ceremony & show, if judiciously thrown in, absolutely necessary for the bulk of mankind, both in religious and civil matters.[23]

It is apparent that Burns began the Journal with the intention of making his entries somewhat detailed, and of recording his sensations as well as his acts. But after a few days he grew distinctly laconic. As a result, the greater part of the record concerns only Burns's actual whereabouts, with occasional comments on the persons he met and the appearance of the countryside.

From Linlithgow Burns and Nicol continued west to Falkirk, and thence north to Stirling. On Monday, August 27, they were in Harvieston, where Gavin Hamilton's relations made them welcome, and where Burns might have seen Margaret Chalmers, had she not been temporarily absent in Edinburgh. Charlotte Hamilton was there, however, and made one of the group that conducted Burns to various points of local interest.[24]

The visit to Harvieston was brief, and on Tuesday, August 28, the two friends drove north through the Ochil Hills to Crief, and the next day to Taymouth, at the northern end of Loch Tay. From here their route led them east, down the river Tay to Dunkeld, and past the remains of a "Druid Temple" which Burns thought of enough interest to warrant a few lines of description:

> Come down Tay to Dunkeld . . . Druid's Temple—3 circles of stones—the outermost sunk—the 2d has 13 stones remaining—the innermost has 8—two large detached ones like a gate, to the south-east—say prayers in it.[25]

[245]

A graceful lyric, "The Birks of Aberfeldy," records Burns's impressions of the Falls of Moness, near Aberfeldy; but he did not linger in this picturesque neighborhood, nor use it as subject matter for much poetry.

Friday the 31st of August saw Burns driving through the pass of Killiecrankie, where any Jacobitically inclined Scotsman could have found abundant food for thought. The Journal records the fact that he visited "the gallant Lord Dundee's stone." But no further comment, either in prose or verse, was evoked by the shade of Claverhouse; it was left for Wordsworth to write the sonnet some years later. Towards the close of this day Burns reached Blair, the seat of the Duke of Athole.

Partly because Josiah Walker, whom Burns had met at Edinburgh, was tutor in the Duke's household, Burns was made welcome at Blair Castle for two happy days. Supper the first night, a more formal dinner the next, with gracious entertainment between, made this one of the memorable incidents of the entire journey.

Walker afterwards commented at length on the conduct of his friend; and though one detects a certain patronizing air in the paragraph, the record as a whole is much to Burns's credit:

My curiosity was great to see how he would conduct himself in company so different from what he had been accustomed to. His manner was unembarrassed, plain, and firm. He appeared to have complete reliance on his own native good sense for directing his behaviour. He seemed at once to perceive and to appreciate what was due to the company and to himself, and never to forget a proper respect for the separate species of dignity belonging to each. He did not arrogate conversation, but, when led into it, he spoke with ease, propriety, and manliness. He tried to exert his abilities, because he knew it was ability alone that gave him a title to be there. The Duke's fine young family attracted much of his admiration; he drank their healths as *honest men and bonnie lasses,* an idea which was much applauded by the company, and with which he has very felicitously closed his poem ["The Humble Petition of Bruar Water"].[26]

[246]

The Journal makes no allusion to the fact, but it was at this place that Burns met Robert Graham of Fintry, who was afterwards to be of notable service to him in connection with the Excise.[27]

On Sunday, September 2, Burns left Blair and drove still further north, through a wild and desolate country, towards Inverness. "Snow on the hills 17 feet deep," says the Journal; "no corn from Loch Gairie to Dalwhinnie." [28] Just before reaching Inverness, the most northwesterly point of the journey, on Tuesday, September 4, the travelers came to

Castle Cawdor—where Macbeth murdered King Duncan—Saw the bed in which King Duncan was stabbed.[29]

On Thursday, September 6, Burns crossed Culloden Muir, and though the Journal contains this laconic phrase, "reflections on the field of battle," the poet's Jacobitism did not burst out in any lyric protest.

From Culloden, Burns and Nicol followed the southern shore of the Firth of Moray, passing through Kildrummie, Nairn, Brodie, Forres, and Elgin, till on Friday, September 7, they reached Castle Gordon, at Fochabers. Here the Duke and Duchess of Gordon made Burns as welcome as they had done in their town house in Edinburgh during the preceding winter.

The Duke makes me happier than ever great man did—noble, princely, yet mild, condescending and affable, gay and kind—The Duchess charming, witty, kind, and sensible—God bless them.[30]

It was here, according to an often-repeated statement which traces back to Currie, who said he had his information from a resident of Fochabers, that Nicol, affronted at not having been included in the invitation to the Castle, refused to sleep in the inn at Fochabers, and insisted on driving ahead to Cullen for the night. Burns makes no reference to any such circumstance in the Journal, but in a letter to James Hoy alludes to "that unlucky predicament which . . . tore me away from Castle Gordon," [31] and blames Nicol for the incident.

Burns's interest in farm life made him at times an observant traveler. He remembered the rich corn fields of the south, and was depressed by the backward condition of agriculture in the Highlands:

The country is sadly poor & unimproven, the houses, crops, horses, cattle, etc., all in unison—cart-wheels with low, coarse, unshod, clumsy work: an axle-tree which had been made with other design than to be a resting shaft between the wheels.[32]

From Cullen the road led a little south of east through Banff to Peterhead, on the coast of the North Sea. Here the two men turned south, skirting the shore, passed through Ellon, and on to Aberdeen, which they reached on the evening of Sunday, September 9. It is interesting to note that here Burns met Andrew Shirrefs, a minor poet who was soon to publish a volume in unsuccessful emulation of Burns, and Bishop Skinner, son of the author of "Tullochgorum."

This was the first time that Burns had visited the part of Scotland where once his father's family had been established, and it was characteristic of him that he looked up various cousins. The Journal records one pleasant family reunion:

Near Stonehaven the coast a good deal romantic—meet my relations—Robert Burnes, writer in Stonehaven, one of those who love fun, a gill, a punning joke, and have not a bad heart—his wife a sweet hospitable body, without any affectation of what is called town-breeding.[33]

Two letters,[34] but not the Journal, show that Burns also met another cousin, James Burness, of Montrose, to whom he had written ahead from Inverness, and with whom he maintained a correspondence, off and on, during his entire life.

At Montrose, on Thursday, September 13, Burns took ship to sail "along that wild rocky coast, and see the caverns, particularly the Geary Pot."[35] So far as extant records show, this was one of the two times that Burns was actually on the ocean, although he had lived most of his life within sight of it.[36]

VACATION TOURS: AN INTERLUDE

The voyage was only a morning's sail, however, for at noon the travelers landed at Arbroath, whence they drove southwest to Dundee for the night. Perth was the next stopping place, and then Kinross, where the poet indulged in "Reflections in a fit of the colic." The final entry thus announces the end of the tour:

Sunday [September 16] come through a cold barren country to Queensferry—dine—cross the Ferry—and come to Edinburgh.[37]

Three days later Burns sent nine copies of the Edinburgh edition to his cousin James Burness at Montrose, to be transmitted "as marked on the blank leaves"—good evidence that he had not forgotten his business affairs as he traveled. Nor had he forgotten the family at Mossgiel, for the day after reaching Edinburgh he wrote at some length to his brother Gilbert, recounting the events of the trip, and in particular telling of the pleasant meeting with the Burness cousins:

I arrived here safe yesterday evening after a tour of 22 days, and travelling near 600 miles; windings included.—My farthest stretch was, about 10 miles beyond Inverness . . . I returned by the coast: Nairn, Forres, and so on to Aberdeen, thence to Stonehive where James Burness from Montrose met me by appointment.—I spent two days among our relations, and found our aunts, Jean and Isbal, still alive, and hale old women; John Caird, though born the same year with our father, walks as vigourously as I can; they have had several letters from his son in New York.—William Brand is likewise a stout old fellow: but farther particulars I delay till I see you. . . . The rest of my stages are not worth rehearsing—[wa]rm as I was from Ossian's country where I had seen his very grave, what cared I for fisher-towns and fertile Carses? . . . My duty, and many Compliments from the North, to my Mother; and my brotherly Compliments to the rest.—I have been trying for a birth for William, but am not likely to be successful.[38]

Clearly enough, Burns had not been "spoiled" by his city experiences. He was still the friendly, companionable, person of 1785, devoted to his family, eager to do his part in promoting the interests of all the group, and absolutely without a thought

[249]

THE LIFE OF ROBERT BURNS

that his success as a poet would change in any material way the destined orbit of his life.

Back in Edinburgh on the 16th of September, Burns again called on Creech in a vain attempt to collect his money, wrote a letter or two to Patrick Miller concerning the farm near Dumfries that he had inspected, spent some time with Johnson and the *Museum*, and, as he had done in Mauchline three months before, tried perplexedly to solve the riddle of the future. Whether he should risk everything on another farming venture, or—perhaps—try for a gauger's commission in the Excise, he could not be sure. But if he were happily married, one part at least of his problem would be solved. He knew well enough by this time that Jean was again to bear his child, but he had not the slightest intention of marrying her. He loved Margaret Chalmers; if she would have him—why, Jean could be taken care of as he had cared for May Cameron. Money would do much. Accordingly he decided to pay another visit to the friends at Harvieston, where Peggy Chalmers was living.

The record of this fourth tour is none too clear, for again Burns kept no Journal, and wrote but few letters while on the trip. But he had as traveling companion Dr. James M. Adair, whom he had met through his friend Lawrie of Loudon. When Currie was preparing his life of Burns, Adair sent him an account of the tour. Though the story is obviously inaccurate as regards dates, it may be accepted as substantially correct in other respects.

The two men left Edinburgh early in October, 1788, hurried west through Linlithgow to Stirling, and on to Harvieston in Clackmannanshire. Once again Gavin Hamilton's relatives made Burns and his friend welcome. For eight or ten days the young men were guests of the family, and rode out on

excursions to visit various parts of the surrounding scenery, inferior to none in Scotland in beauty, sublimity, and romantic interest; particularly Castle Campbell, the ancient seat of the family of Argyle; and the famous cataract of the Devon, called the *Caldron Linn;* and the *Rumbling Bridge,* a single broad arch, thrown by the Devil, if tradition is to be believed, across the river.[89]

Burns was happy. In what proved to be his farewell letter to Margaret Chalmers, written a year later, he referred thus to the richness of this experience:

> When I think I have met with you, and have lived more of real life with you in eight days than I can do with almost anybody I meet with in eight years—when I think on the improbability of meeting you in this world again—I could sit down and cry like a child! [40]

Nothing came of Burns's plan so far as he and Margaret Chalmers were concerned. Adair, however, was more fortunate, and on November 16, 1789, was married to Peggy's intimate friend Charlotte Hamilton, to whom Burns on this occasion had introduced him. "Thus was I indebted to Burns," he wrote solemnly, "for a connection from which I have derived, and expect further to derive, much happiness." [41]

In the intervals between riding about with the young people of Harvieston, Burns found time to visit John Ramsay of Ochtertyre, in the parish of Kincardine, and also Sir William Murray, of another Ochtertyre, in Strathern. Sir William understood the sensitive nature of his guest, and was tactful enough to make Burns feel completely at home. In a letter to Nicol Burns wrote:

> I find myself very comfortable here, neither oppressed by ceremony nor mortified by neglect. [42]

In the same vein he reported to William Cruikshank:

> I have nothing, my dear Sir, to write you, but that I feel myself exceedingly comfortably situated in this good family; just notice enough to make me easy but not to embarrass me. [43]

While the guest of Ramsay, Burns received some good advice concerning his future. That he should write a play was uppermost in Ramsay's mind, and after that, some Scottish "Georgics." "But to have executed either of these plans," said Ramsay in a letter to Currie, "steadiness and abstraction from company were

[251]

wanting, not talents." [44]   More interesting is Ramsay's report of Burns's comment on his Edinburgh critics:

I asked him whether the Edinburgh Literati had mended his poems by their criticisms.   "Sir," said he, "these gentlemen remind me of some spinsters in my country, who spin their thread so fine, that it is neither fit for weft nor woof."   He said he had not changed a word except one, to please Dr. Blair.[45]

Apparently Blair's change of "salvation" to " damnation," in "The Holy Fair," was a stroke of genius which Burns could not forget.

The remainder of the tour was interesting, but devoid of any great significance.   The two young men met a sturdy and unrelenting Jacobite in the person of Mrs. Bruce of Clackmannan, who "knighted" both of them with the very sword her illustrious ancestor Robert Bruce had carried.   In reverent mood they knelt beside the grave of Bruce himself at Dunfermline, and in a different spirit they visited the Abbey Church—once Catholic, but then Presbyterian.   Adair's record is brief:

At Dunfermline we visited the ruined abbey, and the abbey-church, now consecrated to Presbyterian worship.   Here I mounted the *cutty-stool*, or stool of repentance, assuming the character of a penitent for fornication; while Burns from the pulpit addressed to me a ludicrous reproof and exhortation, parodied from that which had been delivered to himself in Ayrshire, where he had, as he assured me, once been one of seven who mounted the *seat of shame* together.[46]

On the twentieth of October Burns returned to Edinburgh, the victim of "a miserable cold, for which the medical gentlemen have ordered me into close confinement, 'under pain of Death,' —the severest of penalties." [47]   With this, Burns's vacation experiences came to an end.   He was back once more in the city, with an eventful winter ahead of him.

Whoever reads the Journals of Burns's expeditions, and the letters written by the way, will discover that as regards recording his sensations or commenting on scenery, he was not a good traveler. In an age given to lengthy, sentimental, and pseudo-scientific chronicling of voyages and tours, Burns was laconic almost to the point of taciturnity. His comments are ample enough to show that he was a keen observer of men and women, interested—as always—in unusual or humorous displays of human nature. But when he undertook to please his hosts by writing poetry about their favorite "prospects," the results were flat and insipid. Adair commented on Burns's failure in this respect:

> I am surprised that none of these scenes should have called forth an exertion of Burns's Muse. But I doubt if he had much taste for the picturesque. I well remember that the ladies at Harvieston, who accompanied us on this jaunt, expressed their disappointment at his not expressing in more glowing and fervid language his impressions of the Caldron Linn scene, certainly highly sublime, and somewhat horrible.[48]

Apparently Burns had expected to follow his trade as poet while journeying through Scotland. On the long Highland tour he carried with him Dr. John Geddes's copy of the 1787 Edinburgh edition, conveniently provided with blank leaves bound in at both ends.[49] But he was wise enough not to indulge in *ad hoc* versification, except when circumstances made it absolutely necessary for him to leave a poetic souvenir on his host's library table.

This failure to coin the Highland Tours into poetry might have been confidently foretold by any one who had read Burns's earlier work understandingly. He was interested in human nature, not in scenery. Furthermore, the men and women who live in his pages were not persons with whom he had only a casual acquaintance. A "bonie lass," to be sure, might provoke a song at first sight. But in general Burns wrote best about persons whom he knew intimately, whose lives he had shared, whose virtues and weaknesses he knew almost as well as he knew his own. Pleasant though the experiences of these journeys were on the whole, they were not of the sort that Burns could easily transmute into poetry.

[253]

But Burns had profited by his vacation experiences. He had seen much of Scotland; he had used his leisure to give serious consideration to his position in society and his future means of livelihood; he had become more and more interested in Johnson's *Musical Museum,* and in the fascinating task of composing Scottish songs; he had made new friends, some of whom, as it proved, were to become his staunch supporters. He returned to Edinburgh fully determined to wind up affairs with Creech as rapidly as possible, and then to settle once and for all the disturbing question of how to earn a living. Accordingly he unpacked his belongings at No. 2 (now No. 30) St. James's Square, where William Cruikshank, Classical Master in the Edinburgh High School, had generously offered him a room.

[1] Quoted, C. W., II, 104; from *Chambers's Edinburgh Journal,* April 28, 1832.
[2] Photostat of manuscript of Journal, lent to me by Professor J. DeL. Ferguson.
[3] *Ibid.*
[4] *Letters,* I, 90.
[5] C. W., II, 114.
[6] Photostat of Journal.
[7] Letter of 29 May, 1787; *Letters,* I, 92.
[8] C. W., II, 118. This entry is no longer in the manuscript, which terminates with the record of May 28.
[9] See "Burns and his Dumfries Burgess Ticket," by G. W. Shirley; *Chronicle,* 1924, 90 ff.
[10] Letter of 11 June, 1787; *Letters,* I, 95.
[11] *Ibid.,* p. 233. The letter is dated 10 August, 1788, but is postmarked July 17.
[12] Letter of 11 June, 1787; *ibid.,* p. 95.
[13] Letter of 18 June, 1787; *ibid.,* p. 96.
[14] *Ibid.,* p. 98.
[15] See "Robert Burns a Burgess of Dumbarton," by J. M. Menzies; *Chronicle,* 1927, 82 ff.
[16] Letter of 30 June, 1787; *Letters,* I, 98.
[17] Letter of 7 July, 1787; *ibid.,* p. 100.
[18] *Ibid.,* p. 104.
[19] Chambers, II, 99.
[20] *Journal of a Tour in the Highlands* [edited] by J. C. Ewing. London, 1927.
[21] Facsimile, p. 6.
[22] It is worth pointing out that even the editor of the Facsimile, Mr. J. C. Ewing, has been loath to abandon the traditional version. In his Introduction (p. 7), he writes: "[The Journal] appears . . . to have been transcribed and extended by the Poet at some date subsequent to 1789. This extended 'Journal' came into the hands of John Gibson Lockhart who, in his 'Life' of Burns printed 'some fragments of his journal recently discovered and now in my hands.' It was afterwards published more fully—for some unknown reason not *in extenso*—by Allan Cunningham, in his edition of Burns's 'Works.' The present location of these 'fragments' being unknown to the present writer, the typographical version of the 'Journal' which accompanies the facsimile has been compiled from the Bixby manuscript and the Lockhart-Cunningham text."
[23] Facsimile, p. 2.
[24] See a letter to Gavin Hamilton, 28 August, 1787; *Letters,* I, 121.
[25] Facsimile, p. 8.

[26] Currie, I, 179.

[27] See letter to Josiah Walker, 5 Sept., 1787; *Letters*, I, 123.

[28] Facsimile, p. 15.

[29] *Ibid.*, p. 14. Not in Burns's handwriting; apparently inked over his faded script by Dr. Currie.

[30] *Ibid.*, p. 21. Also in Currie's hand.

[31] *Letters*, I, 131.

[32] Facsimile, p. 22.

[33] Facsimile, p. 16. This entry is not now in the MS., which has been mutilated, but appears in the editor's transcript.

[34] *Letters*, I, 123 and 124.

[35] Facsimile, p. 16. Last four words only in MS.

[36] Burns had "gone for a sail" at Eyemouth, while on his Border Tour with Ainslie.

[37] Facsimile, p. 29. Currie's hand.

[38] Letters, I, 124. Caird and Brand, the two old men referred to, were brothers-in-law of the poet's father.

[39] Adair's narrative; Currie, I, 169 f.

[40] Letter of 16 Sept., 1788; *Letters*, I, 256.

[41] Currie, I, 169.

[42] Letter of 8 Oct., 1787; *Letters*, I, 128.

[43] Letter of 8 Oct., 1787; *ibid.*, p. 129.

[44] C. W., II, 194.

[45] *Ibid.*

[46] Currie, I, 171. When Burns listened to Auld's words of reproof, there were five sinners in the group, including himself and Jean. See *Chronicle*, 1893, p. 56.

[47] Letter to Patrick Miller, 20 Oct., 1787; *Letters*, I, 130.

[48] Currie, I, 170. As examples of verse composed by the way, see "The Humble Petition of Bruar Water," "Verses Written near Loch Ness," and "On Castle Gordon."

[49] See the facsimile, *The Geddes Burns*, privately printed by the Bibliophile Society; Boston, 1908. In the preface to this volume the name of the owner is erroneously given as Alexander Geddes.

CHAPTER VIII

EDINBURGH: THE SECOND WINTER

1

"AULD REEKIE" AGAIN

Iт was in no happy mood that Burns began his second winter in Edinburgh. The letters he wrote at this time are those of a man depressed and restless. For one thing, he was sick. The hard cold that had sent him to bed on his return from Harvieston was followed by an attack of "hypochondria"—"bitter blue-devilism" he called it in a letter to Ainslie—which threw him into a state of body and mind quite different from that in which he had come up to the city eleven months before. Then too, the "great folk" who had made much of him during the preceding winter either were not in Edinburgh or were paying little attention to him. Peter Hill, Creech's assistant, had not forgotten him, nor had Smellie, his old printer, nor Bob Ainslie, who lived not far from Cruikshank's home. But society was no longer interested in the plowman poet. To make matters still worse, Creech was proving an adept at delay. Burns did succeed, on the 23rd of October, in securing Creech's signature to a promissory note for the hundred guineas due for the copyright, but could not persuade him to make any payments in cash. Finally, the large problem of Burns's future way of life was still unsolved. All in all, one can hardly blame him for thinking back somewhat wistfully to the care-free existence of a year before.

On one matter, however, Burns seems to have had no doubts. He should not, perhaps could not, return to the farm at Mossgiel, and sink his life in that of the family group. He had no

[256]

desire to marry Jean Armour, nor to live in the same village with her father. There was trouble brewing again; the old writ might be re-issued. But Burns had no thought of shirking his responsibilities to his family. He would turn over to Gilbert, who was a relatively capable farmer, half the profits of the Edinburgh volume. This would give Gilbert more working capital than he could possibly secure in any other way, would enable him to support his mother and sisters, and would permit Burns himself to leave Mauchline without being unfair to his relatives.[1]

Whenever Burns considered his future prospects, two alternatives presented themselves. There was the Excise, which he had already thought of as a means of keeping body and soul together. His friends had offered to help him to a gauger's commission; Robert Graham of Fintry, whom he had met at Athole House, might be of assistance. Then there was the obvious possibility of leasing a farm—Patrick Miller's, for example—some distance from Mauchline, and continuing the mode of life to which he had become habituated. The decision was not an easy one to make.

Meanwhile, existence in Edinburgh was not unendurable. Even though Creech would do nothing but promise, there were evenings of happy relaxation in the homes of friends like Ainslie and Peter Hill. Moreover, public honors were still coming to the poet. In the second week of November Burns journeyed fifteen miles west to the Royal Burgh of Linlithgow, where he was made and created Burgess and Guild Brother of the said Burgh, having given his oath of fidelity according to the form used thereanent.[2]

Occasionally there were social events that brought back shadowy memories of the preceding winter; for example, a tea on December 4, at the home of John Nimmo, Excise officer, whose sister then and there introduced Burns to an attractive Mrs. M'Lehose. And in James Johnson's engraver's shop, not far from St. James's Square, the poet could spend as many hours as he pleased discussing Scottish song with the enthusiastic publisher of the *Museum,* or with Stephen Clarke, organist of the Episcopal Chapel.

Indeed, this matter of song-writing was proving even more fascinating than Burns had expected it to be. Janet Cruikshank, the twelve year old daughter of his landlord, could help him by picking out the tunes on her harpsichord; when once the melody was firmly in his mind, the words somehow came by themselves. So before the second winter in Edinburgh had fairly begun, Burns was happily at work on *The Scots Musical Museum.*

2

BURNS AND *THE SCOTS MUSICAL MUSEUM*

As has already been pointed out, Burns's interest in Scottish song was anything but a development of his last years. The first *Commonplace Book* shows that as early as 1784 he had been seriously considering this neglected phase of Scottish culture—neglected, that is, by persons who professed to be interested in "literature." He had already conceived the plan of fitting new words to old and popular Scottish tunes; even before the Kilmarnock volume was off the press he had written more than forty songs. That he published so few of them was due not to lack of interest on his part, but to a feeling—probably well founded—that his prospective readers would not consider them "poetry." So Burns let most of his songs lie neglected in his writing-desk.

During his first winter in Edinburgh, however, he had met James Johnson (d. 1811), an engraver, and in a small way a publisher of music, and a member of the Crochallan Fencibles. Johnson, a man of little education or talent, had formed the ambitious design of collecting all available Scottish songs, having simple accompaniments written for them, and then publishing both words and music under the happily chosen title of *The Scots Musical Museum.* Realizing that with Burns's help he might produce a work which would outclass all existing collections of the sort, he approached Burns for aid. With char-

[258]

acteristic generosity, and with an enthusiasm founded on his own interest in the very material that Johnson was proposing to publish, Burns fell in with the scheme, and began active collaboration.

The first volume of the *Museum* was well on towards completion before Burns became involved in the project. It appeared towards the close of May, 1787, and contained only two songs by Burns himself,[3] though a few others may have been "collected" by him. Not long before the volume was published, Burns had left Edinburgh for his Border tour. As he was about to "march" he sent Johnson a letter that indicated his pleasure at being engaged in so congenial a task:

> I have sent you a Song never before known, for your collection; the air by McGibbon, but I know not the Author of the words, as I got it from Dr. Blacklock.
>
> Farewel, my dear Sir! I wished to have seen you, but I have been dreadfully throng as I march tomorrow.—Had my acquaintance wt. you been a little older, I would have asked the favor of your correspondence; as I have met wt. few people whose company & conversation gave me so much pleasure, because I have met wt. few whose sentiments are so congenial to my own.[4]

After the spring or summer of 1787 Burns was the actual though unacknowledged literary editor of the *Museum*, as Stephen Clarke was the musical editor. How Burns interested other persons in the undertaking, and how his own enthusiasm rose as the work proceeded, appear from a letter to the Reverend John Skinner, author of the rollicking Scottish song "Tullochgorum":

> I regret, and while I live I shall regret, that when I was in the north, I had not the pleasure of paying a younger brother's dutiful respect to the author of the best Scotch song ever Scotland saw—"Tullochgorum's my delight!" The world may think slightingly of the craft of song-making, if they please, but, as Job says—"O that mine adversary had written a book!"—let them try. There is a certain something in the old Scotch songs, a wild happiness of thought and expression, which peculiarly marks

[259]

them, not only from English songs, but also from the modern efforts of song-wrights, in our native manner and language . . .

There is a work going on in Edinburgh, just now, which claims your best assistance. An engraver in this town has set about collecting and publishing all the Scotch songs, with the music, that can be found. Songs in the English language, if by Scotchmen, are admitted, but the music must all be Scotch. Drs. Beattie and Blacklock are lending a hand, and the first musician in town presides over that department. I have been absolutely crazed about it, collecting old stanzas, and every information remaining respecting their origins, authors, &c. &c. This last is but a very fragment-business; but at the end of his second number—the first is already published—a small account will be given of the authors, particularly to preserve those of latter times. Your three songs . . . go in this second number . . . If you would be so kind to this undertaking as send any songs, of your own or others, that you would think proper to publish, your name will be inserted among the other authors—"Nill ye, will ye." [5]

As time passed, Burns's friendship for Johnson became well established. In May of 1788 it was Johnson who acted as the poet's collection-agent in the dispute with Creech, and who succeeded in securing the hundred guineas that Creech owed for the copyright. In the autumn of the same year, despite the fact that Burns was more than busy with his new farm of Ellisland, he was as active as ever in Johnson's behalf. For example, on November 15, 1788, he wrote thus:

I have sent you two more Songs.—If you have got any tunes, or any thing to correct, please send them by return of the Carrier . . .

I can easily see, my dear Friend, that you will very probably have four Volumes.—Perhaps you may not find your account, *lucratively*, in this business; but you are a Patriot for the Music of your Country; and I am certain, Posterity will look on themselves as highly indebted to your Public spirit.—Be not in a hurry; let us go on correctly; and your name shall be immortal . . .

I am preparing a flaming Preface for your third Volume. [6]

Burns was modest, withal, in his editorial capacity. Not only did he accept no compensation of any sort from Johnson, but he was willing to defer to his publisher's judgment in disputed matters:

My trunk was unaccountably delayed in Edinr. & did not reach me till about ten days ago, so I had not much time of your music.—I have sent you a list that I approve of, but I beg & insist that you will never allow my opinion to overrule yours.[7]

When Johnson's energy flagged, Burns virtually took entire charge of the work. Thus in October of 1793 one finds him saying:

Why did you not send me those tunes & verses that Clarke & you can not make out?—Let me have them as soon as possible, that, while he is at hand, I may settle the matter with him.—He & I have been very busy providing & laying out materials for your fifth volume.—I have got about a dozen by me.—If you can conveniently, let me have half a dozen copies of your fourth volume; I want no more.—As soon as the Bound copy of all the volumes is ready, take the trouble of forwarding it.[8]

Even as late as September of 1795 Burns wrote Johnson at great length, sending careful instructions as to where to find texts for volume V, which was already overdue. He added, "I will overhaul Ritson, in my next; & I have, besides, ten or a dozen songs to send you." [9]

Within seven weeks of his death Burns was still urging Johnson to make speed with Volume V:

How are you, my dear Friend? & how comes on yr. fifth volume?—You may probably think that for some time past I have neglected you & your work; but, Alas, the hand of pain, & sorrow, & care has these many months lain heavy on me!—Personal & domestic affliction have almost entirely banished that alacrity & life with which I used to woo the rural Muse of Scotia.—In the meantime, let us finish what we have so well begun.—The gentleman, Mr. Lewars, a particular friend of mine, will bring out any proofs (if they are ready) or any message you may have. . . .

Many a merry meeting this Publication has given us, & possibly it may give us more, though, alas! I fear it.—This protracting, slow, consuming illness which hangs over me, will, I doubt much, my ever dear friend, arrest my sun before he has well reached his middle carreer, &

will turn over the Poet to far other & more important concerns than studying the brilliancy of Wit or the pathos of Sentiment. . . . Let me hear from you as soon as convenient. Your Work is a great one; & though, now that it is near finished, I see if we were to begin again, two or three things that might be mended, yet I will venture to prophesy, that to future ages your Publication will be the textbook & standard of Scotish Song & Music.

I am ashamed to ask another favor of you because you have been so very good already, but my wife has a very particular friend of hers, a young lady who sings well, to whom she wishes to present The Scots Musical Museum. If you have a spare copy, will you be so obliging as to send it by the very first Fly, as I am anxious to have it soon. Yours ever.[10]

After that, Johnson was to have no further letters from the man who had made the *Museum* notable.

Burns's connection with the *Museum* is not hard to summarize. Virtually all the poetry that he wrote between the spring of 1787 and the autumn of 1792 went into it. All told, he sent Johnson over two hundred songs, set to the tunes which he himself considered most appropriate. Many of these songs were absolutely and entirely his own creation; others were adaptations of old and ineffective lyrics; still others were mosaics of fragments lifted from many different sources. But in virtually every case the text furnished Johnson was Burns's; even his most obvious borrowings were re-shaped by his genius, and, as Henley and Henderson put it, "stamped with his image and lettered with his superscription." [11]

Furthermore, Burns arranged the index "cyphers" or key-letters, indicating the authorship of as many of the songs as he thought it proper to ascribe to an author; he wrote the Prefaces for volumes II, III, and IV; he scrutinized everything that went into these three volumes with the care of a trained editor. Without his aid the work would never have been finished. As it was, however, the *Museum* became at once, and still remains, the standard collection of Scottish songs and music.[12]

The debt, however, was not all on one side. Without the

spur of Johnson's initial enthusiasm, and the opportunity for publication afforded by the *Museum*, Burns's lyric accomplishment could not have been as astonishing as it was. Hence any estimate of Burns as a writer of songs must take into account the fact that it was Johnson who opened the gates through which Burns poured the lyric flood at which the world still wonders.

One other matter concerning Burns's connection with the *Museum* should be recorded here. Some time before autumn of 1792 Burns's friend Robert Riddell of Glenriddell came into possession of an interleaved copy of the four volumes of the *Museum* which had already been published. Whether Burns gave it to him, or he procured it for himself, is uncertain. In any case, it was in this copy that Burns inscribed the explanatory notes which have been invaluable aids for all future editors, which formed the basis for Cromek's *Reliques*, and which are now available, in an accurate transcript, in J. C. Dick's *Notes on Scottish Song by Robert Burns*. Whoever will take the trouble to read Dick's work, will discover that Burns's enthusiasm for Scottish song found expression in scholarly investigation as well as in lyrical composition.[18]

3

CLARINDA

If it was *The Scots Musical Museum* that thus spurred Burns to poetic activity during the second winter in Edinburgh, it was an interesting young woman named M'Lehose who provided him with his most intense and disturbing emotional experience. The general outlines of the episode are clear enough; details, after a century and a half, inevitably remain obscure. Even the chronology of the many letters that passed between the two persons is not always easy to determine. More important still, the inner significance of the episode is open to question. It has been called a piece of philandering; it has been dignified into a tragedy; it has been dismissed as an ironic comedy. But concerning the major facts there is no dispute: the woman sought

Burns's acquaintance; she loved him; she would gladly have married him, except for the fact that she was already the wife of James M'Lehose, who had deserted her, and from whom she could see no way of freeing herself. And Burns loved her "beyond anyone in all the circle of creation." The story that builds itself around these two persons forms the most interesting incident in Burns's second winter in Edinburgh.

Nancy Craig (1759–1841), as she was called by her friends, had been born only three months later than Burns. She was the daughter of a highly esteemed Glasgow surgeon. By the time she was fifteen she was known as a beauty. At the age of seventeen she married James M'Lehose, an attorney of her native city, and a man of whom her parents did not wholly "approve." Slightly more than four years later they separated. In the summer of 1782 she took lodgings in Edinburgh, where through the generosity of a kinsman, Lord Craig, and with the aid of small annuities from the Glasgow Faculty of Procurators and the Glasgow Faculty of Physicians, she was able to maintain herself and her children in frugal decency.[14] She was a good Calvinist, and regular in attendance on the services of the Tolbooth Church, where the Reverend John Kemp was minister.

Naturally interested in letters, she was eager to write well herself, and tried her hand—with some small degree of success —at both prose and verse. This afforded her one avenue of escape from the monotony and unhappiness of her life; another was opened to her by her children, whom she cared for with unremitting devotion; still a third by religion, to which she turned, in a somewhat effusive but not insincere manner, when the weight of sorrow or the pressure of human emotions became unendurable. That she was a sentimentalist is obvious in every page she ever wrote. Her state of mind, her psychology, is as clear as crystal. She might well have written,

Nondum amabam, et amare amabam,

for her matrimonial experiences had awakened none of the deeper emotional responses of which she was capable. When in the

[264]

autumn of 1787 Burns returned to Edinburgh after his vacation tours, Mrs. M'Lehose, though she had never met the poet, seems to have grasped the fact that here was a man who might bring into her life that which she most coveted—the privilege of loving and being loved. Straightway she set about the relatively simple task of arranging a meeting between Burns and herself.

It was on December 4, 1787, at a "tea party" in the house of John Nimmo, an Excise officer, that she first had the chance to speak to Burns. She had asked her friend Miss Nimmo [15] to arrange the affair; when the introduction had been accomplished, she at once invited Burns to call upon her, and appointed Thursday, December 6, as the day.

When Thursday came, Burns found it impossible to keep the appointment; instead of presenting himself at Mrs. M'Lehose's lodgings in the Potterrow he sent a note asking to postpone the tea-drinking till Saturday evening, and enclosed a poetic "bagatelle" for his new-found friend's perusal. Saturday brought another disappointment. Returning to St. James's Square late Friday night, Burns injured his knee so severely by "an unlucky fall from a coach" that it did not need the command of his friend Dr. Sandy Wood to confine him to his room, and to forbid him to put his foot to the ground. Again Burns sent a letter of apology and explanation, to which Mrs. M'Lehose promptly replied. Thus, through an accident chargeable to "a drunken coachman" the voluminous Sylvander-Clarinda correspondence had its inception.

To record all the incidents covered by this series of long and rapidly exchanged letters would be unprofitable. Certain matters, however, are interesting and significant enough to be set forth in some detail.

For example, though it was the woman who made the first move, the man was not slow in response. In the letter of December 8, the second that he had written, Burns said,

I can say with truth, Madam, that I never met with a person in my life whom I more anxiously wished to meet again than yourself.— . . . I know not how to account for it—I am strangely taken with some people; nor am I often mistaken. You are a stranger to me; but I am an odd being: some yet unnamed feelings; things, not principles, but better than whims, carry me farther than boasted reason ever did a Philosopher. Farewell! every happiness be yours! [16]

Nancy replied the same evening, enclosing some of her own verses, and opening the door to almost any sort of letter in return:

These "nameless feelings" I perfectly comprehend, tho' the pen of a Locke could not define them. Perhaps *instinct* comes nearer their description than either "Principles or Whims." Think ye they have any connection with that "heavenly light which leads astray"? One thing I know, that they have a powerful effect upon me, and are delightful when under the check of *reason* and *religion*. . . . Pardon any little freedoms I take with you . . . Keep up your heart, you will soon get well, and we shall *meet*. Farewell. God bless you.[17]

Four days later Burns wrote:

I stretch a point indeed, my dearest Madam, when I answer your card on the rack of my present agony. Your friendship, Madam! By heavens, I was never proud before! Your lines, I maintain it, are poetry, and good poetry; mine were indeed partly fiction, and partly a friendship which, had I been so blest as to have met with you *in time*, might have led me—God of love only knows where.[18]

The word which thus appeared for the first time caused a flutter of pleasant uneasiness in Nancy's heart. In her reply she said,

When I meet you, I must chide you for writing in your romantic style. Do you remember that she whom you address is a married woman?

And then, with winsome naïvete,

My chief design in writing you today was to beg you would not write me often, lest the exertion should hurt you. Meantime, if my scrawls can amuse you in your confinement, you shall have them occasionally. . . . Be patient. Take care of yourself. My best wishes attend you.[19]

Burns's answer was that of a man well versed in feminine psychology. After solemnly assuring her that he would not for the world make love to her, he did it in every line of a long letter, but ended on a note which he knew would be unexceptionable:

> With the most sacred respect and heart-felt esteem, My dear Madam, Your humble servant.[20]

Thus the story began.

At Christmas the two friends again exchanged poems, and began using the names Sylvander and Clarinda. On December 28 Burns ventured a little further than he yet had dared—

> I do love you if possible still better for having so fine a taste and turn for Poesy.—I have again gone wrong in my usual unguarded way, but you may erase the word, and put esteem, respect, or any other tame Dutch expression you please in its place.[21]

And so on, with guarded impetuosity.

Frightened, Clarinda turned to her Bible:

> Religion, the only refuge of the unfortunate, has been my balm in every woe. O! could I make her appear to you as she has done to me! . . . I entreat you not to mention our corresponding to one on earth. Though I've conscious innocence, my situation is a delicate one.[22]

Three days later, without waiting for a reply, she wrote again:

> My heart was formed for love, and I desire to devote it to Him who is the source of love! Yes: we shall surely meet in an "unknown state of being," where there will be full scope for every kind, heartfelt affection—love without alloy, and without end.[23]

All this, be it remembered, after only one meeting, and that at a "tea party."

One may learn something of Burns's state of mind at this time from a sentence in a letter to his old friend Richard Brown, whose vessel was in port at Irvine:

> Almighty Love still "reigns and revels" in my bosom; and I am at this moment ready to hang myself for a young Edinr. widow.[24]

[267]

The second personal interview took place on January 4. Burns's knee was so far recovered that by the aid of a sedan chair he visited Clarinda at her lodgings. Here, like Othello, he plied his suit by telling the story of his life, and gave Clarinda a copy of his autobiographical letter to Dr. Moore. Three days later she wrote at great length, and advised him never to marry. Naturally enough; for if she could not have him, she did not wish any one else to. At the same time she was sufficiently mistress of her emotions to recollect her pocket book, and the drain which the correspondence was putting upon it:

I have paid the porter, and you may do so when you write. I'm sure they sometimes have made us pay double.[25]

During the rest of January the two lovers—for such by this time they admittedly were—met at Clarinda's home at least six times. On one of these occasions Burns told Clarinda of Jean's "situation." Clarinda, commenting on the news in later letters, somewhat cold-heartedly said: "I love you for your continued fondness, even after enjoyment"; "I wish a certain affair happily over." [26]

There was, however, nothing cold-hearted about Clarinda's regard for Sylvander. She walked in St. James's Square in the hope that even though she could not see him—she did not know precisely which was his room—he could at least see her. And when Saturday evening, January 12, brought Burns to her lodgings, she allowed herself such freedom in her demonstrations of affection that by Sunday night her conscience was troubling her:

I will not deny it, Sylvander, last night was one of the most exquisite I ever experienced. Few such fall to the lot of mortals! Few, extremely few, are formed to relish such refined enjoyment. That it should be so, vindicates the wisdom of Heaven. But though our enjoyment did not lead beyond the limits of virtue, yet today's reflections have not been altogether unmixed with regret.[27]

[268]

The interview of Wednesday evening, January 23, brought still more uneasiness in its train. Early the next morning Clarinda began an elaborate allegorical letter expressive of her feelings. The emotional strain proved too great, however, and after twenty lines concerning "the bar of Reason," "Religion, clad in a robe of light," "the Bower of Peace," and "the Temple of Hymen," she slipped back into her natural idiom:

> Sylvander, to drop my metaphor, I am neither well nor happy today: my heart reproaches me for last night. If you wish Clarinda to regain her peace, determine against everything but what the strictest delicacy warrants.
>
> I do not blame you, but myself. I must not see you on Saturday, unless I find I can depend on myself acting otherwise.[28]

The next day she again sought consolation in religion:

> You and I are capable of that ardency of love for which the wide creation cannot afford an adequate object. Let us seek to repose it in the bosom of our God.[29]

Clarinda's religious enthusiasm did not limit itself to concern over her own soul; she was eager that Burns should be undeviating in his adherence to the cardinal points of Calvinistic faith. She wrote long pages concerning such matters; she paraphrased Mr. Kemp's sermons; she urged Burns to listen to one of them ("You'll easily get a seat"); but sooner or later she always came back to what was still nearer her heart, her love for the man she could not marry.

By the sixth of February Clarinda was telling Burns that she hoped some time to have her freedom: "Your friend may yet live to surmount the wintry blasts of life and revive to taste a spring time of happiness."[30] In return, Burns assured her that he was hers "for life."

By the thirteenth people had begun to talk; worse still, some one who considered himself privileged to advise Clarinda, possibly Mr. Kemp, possibly Lord Craig, had written her a letter of reproof, which she sent to Burns. Whereupon Burns wrote four letters in rapid succession; two on the thirteenth, two on the fourteenth. "How shall I comfort you," he asks, "who am the cause of the injury? Can I wish that I had never seen you? That we had never met? No; I never will!" [31]

Having thus put the question he was afterwards to phrase in his most poignant quatrain,

> Had we never lov'd sae kindly,
> Had we never lov'd sae blindly,
> Never met, or never parted,
> We had ne'er been broken hearted,

Burns proceeded to the ultimate avowal which Clarinda feared but for which she had been waiting:

I esteem you, I love you as a friend; I admire you, I love you, as a woman beyond anyone in all the circle of creation. [32]

Four days after penning this confession and apology Burns rode out of Edinburgh; by late afternoon he was in the Black Bull Inn, Glasgow. There were matters to be attended to in the west. In Glasgow he bought cocoa for his landlord Cruikshank, and spent an evening with his friend Richard Brown, whose vessel was in port again, and with his young brother William. The return to Mauchline was leisurely. At Paisley he looked in on Alexander Pattison, a merchant; at Kilmarnock he wrote to Clarinda and called on Robert Muir, the wine-merchant who had helped him with the 1786 edition, and who was now far gone with tuberculosis; at Dunlop House, Stewarton, where Mrs. Dunlop made him welcome and gave him much advice, he spent two pleasant days. On the morning of Saturday, February 23, he reached Willie's Mill, Tarbolton, where Jean was in seclusion, awaiting her second confinement. Mentally, Burns compared her to Clarinda, whose letter he knew would be waiting for him at Mauchline post office, and whose gift of two shirts for little Robert he would soon be unpacking from his saddle-bags. On the afternoon of the same day he reached Mauchline, found Clarinda's letter, and wrote briefly in reply. He had seen Jean, was "disgusted" with her,

[270]

could not "endure her." He was going to Dumfries to inspect Mr. Miller's farm; if that proved unattractive, why, "The Excise must be my lot." [33]

Before the middle of March Burns was again in Edinburgh.[34] Clarinda was no longer much concerned about Mr. Kemp's disapproval; during Burns's absence she had found comfort in Bob Ainslie, who had called often, and with whom she had felt free to discuss her love for Burns. By the time the poet himself was again at her home in the Potterrow she had come to "feel a sensation so delightful, so serene, as makes me almost hope that Heaven approves our union." [35]

Whether or not Burns told Clarinda of all that had happened during his absence is uncertain.[36] But the two met at least four times more in Clarinda's lodgings, and even ventured to walk the streets of Edinburgh side by side. Thursday evening, March 20th, they spent together; Burns's letter of the 21st, the last Clarinda was to receive before the poet's marriage, contained his final protestation of undying love:

Will you open, with satisfaction and delight, a letter from a man who loves you, who has loved you, and who will love you to death, through death, and for ever?[37]

Saturday, March 22nd, found them again together. A pair of wine glasses, and the verses beginning "Fair Empress of the Poet's Soul," seem to have been the poet's parting gifts on this occasion, for on Monday, March 24, he left Edinburgh to return to his old way of living, and, as he probably knew, to marry the woman who was already the mother of four of his children.

News of Burns's wedding reached Clarinda before long. Angry, chagrined, disappointed beyond words, she kept her counsel till nearly a year had elapsed. Then, in a letter which is lost, she upbraided Burns, called him a villain, and with characteristic naïveté asked him why he had not called on her during one of his hurried trips to Edinburgh! Burns's defense of his conduct forms one of the most revealing letters of the entire series:

[271]

MADAM:

The letter you wrote me to Heron's carried its own answer in its bosom: you forbade me to write you, unless I was willing to plead guilty to a certain Indictment you were pleased to bring against me.—As I am convinced of my own innocence, and, though conscious of high imprudence & egregious folly, can lay my hand on my breast and attest the rectitude of my heart; you will pardon me, Madam, if I do not carry my complaisance so far as humbly to acquiesce in the name of, Villain, merely out of compliment to YOUR opinion; much as I esteem your judgment and warmly as I regard your worth.—I have already told you, and I again aver it, that at the Period of time alluded to, I was not under the smallest moral tie to Mrs. B———; nor did I, nor could I then know, all the powerful circumstances that omnipotent Necessity was busy laying in wait for me.—When you call over the scenes that have passed between us, you will survey the conduct of an honest man, struggling successfully with temptations the most powerful that ever beset humanity, and preserving untainted honor in situations where the austerest Virtue would have forgiven a fall—Situations that I will dare to say, not a single individual of all his kind, even with half his sensibility and passion, could have encountered without ruin; and I leave you to guess, Madam, how such a man is likely to digest an accusation of perfidious treachery! [38]

In other words, said Burns, instead of upbraiding me for marrying Jean, you should thank me for having protected you against the impetuosity of your own passions. This probably comes pretty close to the truth of the whole matter.

Ten months later one finds the correspondence renewed, and Burns still defending himself against Clarinda's accusations. Still later, in July of 1791, he wrote:

I have recd. both your last letters, Madam, & ought & would have answered the first long ago.—But on what subject shall I write you? How can you expect a Correspondent should write you, when you declare that you mean to preserve his letters with a view, sooner or later, to expose them on the pillory of derision & the rack of criticism? This is gagging me compleatly as to speaking the sentiments of my bosom. [39]

To this Clarinda replied at once:

You surely mistake me, Sir! "Expose your letters to criticism!" Nothing could be further from my intention: read my letters and you will find nothing to justify such an idea.   But I suppose they are burned, so you can't have recourse to them.   In an impassioned hour I once talked of publishing them, but a little cool reflection showed me its impropriety. . . .   I am pleased with your reception of the Poem, and no less so with your beautiful stanzas in consequence.   The last I think particularly elegant. . . .   It has procured me a short visit from the Muse, who has been a stranger since the "Golden Dream" of '88.[40]

In November of the same year she wrote to tell him of the destitution of a girl named Jenny Clow, who had a claim on Burns's generosity.   Thus the correspondence with Clarinda began anew, and before long Burns was writing in the vein of 1788: "My dearest Nancy;" "My ever-dearest of women;" "My ever dearest Nancy."   On December 6, 1791, Burns was again in Edinburgh, and saw Clarinda, for the last time, as it proved. On the twenty-first of December he sent her three songs in her honor; one of them was "Ae Fond Kiss."

A month later Mrs. M'Lehose sailed for Jamaica to join her husband.   Before leaving she wrote one final letter, as she thought, to the man whom she loved:

Agitated, hurried to death, I sit down to write a few lines to you, my ever-dear, dear friend!   We are ordered aboard on Saturday, to sail on Sunday.   And now, my dearest Sir, I have a few things to say to you, as the last advice of her who could have lived or died with you!   I am happy to know of your applying so steadily to the business you have engaged in; but, oh remember, this life is a short, passing scene!   Seek God's favour, keep His commandments, be solicitous to prepare for a happy eternity!   There, I trust, we will meet, in perfect and never-ending bliss. . . .   Farewell.   I will ever, ever remain, your leal friend, A.M.[41]

With that farewell the story virtually came to a close, though there was a brief renewal of the correspondence on Clarinda's precipitate return from Jamaica, where she found her husband living with a negro mistress.

It is clear, however, that Clarinda's love for Burns persisted during the years that were to come.   Her private Journal, in which she made entries almost to the day of her death, contains this significant memorandum, dated December 6, 1831—just forty years after her final interview with the poet:

> This day I can never forget. Parted with Burns, in the year 1791, never more to meet in this world. Oh, may we meet in Heaven! [42]

Such, in brief, was the tale of Sylvander and Clarinda. It was more than a bit of philandering on his part; on hers, it came close to tragedy, for she loved him much. And he loved her; loved her, so it seems, as he never loved any other woman, unless possibly it were Mary Campbell. Sentimentalism and artificiality mar the letters in which this story unfolds itself, as every reader knows. But beneath the veneer of affectation one still feels the pulsings of a genuine passion. That Burns held himself in check, and saved Clarinda from the disaster which she invited, is to his credit. It is also to his credit that when he fully realized the hopelessness of his love, he went back to Mauchline and married the girl whose claim on him was infinitely greater than he had allowed Clarinda's to become.

4

THE EXCISE APPOINTMENT

No matter what was Burns's state of mind or of health during this winter in Edinburgh, he never forgot his business affairs. By March 20, 1788, he had extracted something approximating a final statement from Creech, and part of the money still due him. He had also moved steadily towards a solution of his still unsolved major problem, his future means of livelihood. On the one hand there was the Excise possibility; on the other, Miller's farm in Dumfriesshire. The story of how Burns both secured his gauger's appointment and leased his farm, and then returned to Jean, will conclude the account of his second winter in Edinburgh.

Burns's first definite allusion to a possible Excise appointment appears in a letter to Robert Aiken, probably written early in October, 1786:

I have been feeling all the various rotations and movements within, respecting the Excise. . . . Should you, my friends, my benefactors, be successful in your applications for me, perhaps it may not be in my power in that way to reap the fruit of your friendly efforts.[43]

From this it is clear that Aiken was busying himself on Burns's behalf; who the other persons were, referred to as "my friends and benefactors," is uncertain; *a priori*, John Ballantine may have been one of them. But the point is of litle significance; it is enough to remember that as early as the autumn of 1786 Burns had the Excise definitely in mind, and that his friends were trying to help him towards a position. The fact that he was still worried over the Jean Armour and Mary Campbell entanglements, and uncertain whether he could remain in Scotland, is unimportant in this connection.

The next allusion to Burns's interest in the Excise appears in a letter of December 6, 1786, from Sir John Whitefoord, an Ayrshire laird to whom Burns had written immediately after his first arrival in Edinburgh: "I have been told you wish to be made a gauger."[44] After this casual remark nothing of significance appears in the record for a year. Burns had the Excise constantly in mind as a possibility; not till January of 1788 did he start active measures. Then he took the matter up with two most influential personages, Robert Graham of Fintry and the Earl of Glencairn. To Glencairn he wrote:

MY LORD,

I know your Lordship will disapprove of my ideas in a request I am going to make to you, but I have weighed seriously my situation, my hopes and turn of mind, and am fully fixed to my scheme if I can possibly effectuate it.—I wish to get into the Excise; I am told that your Lordship's interest will easily procure me the grant from the Commissioners; and your Lordship's Patronage and Goodness which have already rescued me from obscurity, wretchedness and exile, embolden me to ask that interest.[45]

Soon after writing this letter Burns found himself in some sort of official relation to the Excise Board; just what, seems past discovery. It has been said [46] that through the efforts of his friend and physician, "Lang Sandy" Wood, who at the time was caring for his injured knee, he was enrolled as an "expectant." This would have been the natural procedure. There is no definite information covering the point, however, and tradition is notoriously unreliable. And only two years later Burns wrote to his friend Bob Ainslie in such a fashion as to make the accepted statement seem unfounded:

I don't know if I have informed you that I am now appointed to an Excise Division, in the middle of which my house & farm lie.—In this I was extremely lucky.—*Without ever having been an Expectant,* as they call their Journeymen Excisemen, I was directly planted down to all intents & purposes an officer of Excise, there to flourish and bring forth fruits—worthy of repentance.[47]

But despite this uncertainty as to precisely how Burns entered the service, the following letter to Robert Graham of Fintry makes it clear that the Excise Board received some sort of application from him, and acted favorably upon it. It also shows that Burns did not hesitate to solicit aid from the man whom he had met for the first time only a few months before at Blair Castle:

Sir:

When I had the honor of being introduced to you at Athole-house, I did not think of putting that acquaintance so soon to the test.—When Lear, in Shakespeare, asks old Kent why he wished to be in his service, he answers: "Because you have that in your face which I could like to call Master;" for some such similar reason, Sir, do I now solicit your Patronage.—You know, I dare say, of an application I lately made to your Board, to be admitted an Officer of Excise.—I have, according to form, been examined by a Supervisor, and today I give in his Certificate with a request for an Order for instructions.—In this affair, if I succeed, I am afraid I shall but too much need a patronizing Friend.—. . .

I had intended to have closed my late meteorous appearance on the stage of Life, in the country Farmer; but after discharging some filial and fraternal claims, I find I could only fight for existence in that miserable manner. . . .

I know, Sir, that to need your goodness is to have a claim on it; may I therefore beg your Patronage to forward me in this affair till I be appointed to a Division; where, by the help of rigid Economy, I shall try to support that Independance so dear to my soul, but which has too often been so distant from my situation.[48]

No farming for him, but only the Excise: thus at least he felt when writing to a member of the Board, for Graham might well have hesitated to recommend a candidate who proposed to serve as both farmer and gauger.

Not long afterwards the wind was in a different quarter, and we find Burns telling Clarinda that

I have almost given up the excise idea.—I have been just now to wait upon a great Person. . . . I have been question'd like a child about my matters, and blamed and schooled for my Inscription on Stirling window.—. . . Come, curse me Jacob![49]

Three weeks later Burns had again changed his mind. The information appears in a letter to Peggy Chalmers, whom he could not forget despite Clarinda's charms:

Tomorrow, my dear Madam, I leave Edinburgh . . . I have altered all my plans of future life. A farm that I could live in, I could not find; and indeed, after the necessary support my brother and the rest of the family required, I could not venture on farming in that style suitable to my feelings. You will condemn me for the next step I have taken: I have entered into the Excise. I stay in the West about three weeks, and then return to Edinburgh for six weeks' instructions; afterwards, for I get employ instantly, I go où il plait à Dieu—et mon Roi. . . . I got this without any hanging on, or mortifying solicitation; it is immediate bread, and though poor in comparison of the last eighteen months of my existence, 'tis luxury in comparison of all my preceding life: besides, the commissioners are some of them my acquaintances, and all of them my firm friends.[50]

A month later, on March 17, Burns again mentioned the Excise in a letter to Clarinda:

My Excise affair is just concluded, and I have got my order for instructions: so far good. Wednesday night I am engaged to sup among some of the principals of the Excise, so can only make a call for you that evening; but next day, I stay to dine with one of the Commissioners, so cannot go till Friday morning.[51]

This was the situation when the second winter in Edinburgh came to an end with Burns's departure from the city on March 24, 1788. He had taken the necessary preliminary steps; he had been accepted as a candidate; the order for his instructions was about to be issued. With the powerful aid of Glencairn and Fintry he had in two months' time brought matters to this satisfactory conclusion. Thus, whatever might happen to his farming venture, he had insured some sort of livelihood for himself and the woman whom he was soon to marry.

5

THE RETURN TO THE FARM

The story of what led up to Burns's leasing Ellisland can be told in relatively few words. As early as December, 1786, when he had been only two weeks in Edinburgh, he wrote to John Ballantine, recording the first meeting between himself and the man who was to be his Ellisland landlord:

An unknown hand left ten guineas for the Ayrshire Bard in Mr. Sibbald's hand, which I got. I since have discovered my generous unknown friend to be Patrick Miller, Esq., brother to the Justice Clerk; and drank a glass of claret with him by invitation at his own house yesternight.[52]

A month later to the same friend he said:

I am still "dark as was Chaos" in respect to Futurity.—My generous friend, Mr. Peter Miller . . . has been talking with me about the lease of some farm or other in an estate called Dasswinton which he has lately bought near Dumfries.—Some life-rented, embittering Recollections whisper me that I will be happier anywhere than in my old neighborhood, but Mr. Miller is no Judge of land; and though I dare say he means to favour me, yet he may give me, in his opinion, an advantageous bargain that may ruin me.[53]

[278]

Thus when the Ellisland suggestion was first made to Burns he foresaw—without realizing it—exactly the result which time brought about: an "advantageous bargain" that would have ruined him had he not been able to escape from it.

The winter of 1787 passed with nothing definite accomplished. Not till the Border Tour brought Burns into Dumfriesshire does he seem to have done anything further in the matter. Then he wrote Nicol to this effect:

> I have been with Mr. Miller at Dalswinton, and am to meet him again in August. From my view of the lands, and his reception of my Bardship, my hopes in that business are rather mended; but still they are but slender.[54]

Here matters rested till the end of September, when Burns was in Edinburgh between the long tour of the Highlands and the visit to Harvieston with Dr. Adair. At this time he wrote to Miller himself:

> I am informed you do not come to town for a month still, and within that time I shall certainly wait on you, as by this time I suppose you will have settled your scheme with respect to your farms. . . . Should I unfortunately miss you at Dalswinton, perhaps your Factor will be able to inform me of your intentions with respect to the Elesland (*sic*) farm.[55]

On October 20, the day of his return from the trip with Adair, he again wrote to Miller:

> In two or three days, if I get better, and if I hear at your lodgings that you are still at Dalswinton, I will take a ride to Dumfries directly.— From something in your last, I would wish to explain my idea of being your Tenant.—I want to be a farmer in a small farm, about a plough-gang,[56] in a pleasant country, under the auspices of a good landlord.— I have no foolish notion of being a Tenant on easier terms than another. . . . These are my views & wishes; and in whatever way you think best to lay out your farms, I shall be happy to rent one of them.[57]

Once again things came more or less to a standstill. Within six weeks Burns was confined to his room by a seriously injured knee; what energy he had after this accident, was devoted to the Clarinda correspondence, to Johnson's *Museum*, and to the Excise possibility. And indeed, as has just been pointed out, when he was petitioning the Earl of Glencairn and Robert Graham for aid in this last matter, he represented himself as having given up all thought of being a farmer. In doing so he may have been thoroughly sincere; at all events it was as late as February 23, 1788 that he said to Clarinda:

I set off tomorrow for Dumfriesshire.—'Tis merely out of Compliment to Mr. Miller, for I know the Excise must be my lot.[58]

Ten days later he had again changed his mind, and wrote in a different vein to Clarinda:

I am thinking my farming scheme will yet hold. A worthy, intelligent farmer, my father's friend and my own, has been with me on the spot: he thinks the bargain practicable. I am myself, on a more serious review of the lands, much better pleased with them. I won't mention this in writing to anybody but you and Mr. Ainslie. Don't accuse me of being fickle: I have the two plans of life before me, and I wish to adopt the one most likely to procure me independance.[59]

The "worthy intelligent farmer" was John Tennant of Glenconner, to whom Burns had appealed for aid.[60] Here again, as in the case of the Mossgiel farm stock, Burns was unwilling to trust his own judgment in matters agricultural, and turned for advice to one of his father's friends, rather than to a member of his own generation.

After this inspection by Tennant things moved rapidly. Late in February or early in March Burns wrote Ainslie:

I am just returned from Mr. Miller's farm. My old friend whom I took with me was highly pleased with the bargain, and advised me to accept of it. . . . I shall in all probability turn farmer.[61]

A few days later he had made up his mind, as appears from a letter to Robert Muir:

[280]

EDINBURGH: THE SECOND WINTER

I took old Glenconner with me to Mr. Millar's farm, and he was so pleased with it that I have wrote an offer to Mr. Millar, which, if he accepts, I shall sit down a plain farmer, the happiest of lives when a Man can live by it.[62]

When arrangements had been completed it was good, kindly, sympathetic Peggy Chalmers who first learned of the fact:

I know, my ever dear friend, that you will be pleased with the news when I tell you I have at last taken a lease of a farm. Yesternight I compleated a bargain with Mr. Miller, of Dalswinton, for the farm of Ellisland, on the banks of the Nith, between five and six miles above Dumfries. I begin at Whitsunday to build a house, drive lime, &c.; and heaven be my help! for it will take a strong effort to bring my mind into the routine of business.[63]

With this announcement, the problem of what Burns should do for a living had been solved. He had qualified for both of the two modes of life that seemed open to him, and even while bargaining for the farm had arranged matters so that in case of emergency he would have his Excise commission to fall back upon. But it is clear that the farm was his first choice.

Before turning to the last matter with which this chapter is concerned, Burns's marriage to Jean, it will be worth while to comment briefly on a statement which Allan Cunningham makes in his *Life of Burns*, and which has been repeated so often as to become part of the Burns tradition. In the first (1834) edition of Cunningham's *Life and Works of Burns*, one reads that

Burns was assisted in the choice of the farm, and the terms on which it was taken, by one or two Ayrshire friends: there were other farms to let of a superior kind on the estate, and these were pointed out by my father, a steward to the proprietor—a Lothian farmer of skill and experience—but the fine romantic look of Ellisland induced Burns to shut his eyes on the low-lying and fertile Foregirth; upon which my father said, "Mr. Burns, you have made a poet's—not a farmer's choice."[64]

A pleasant enough remark, in Honest Allan's most recognizable vein. There is no shred of evidence, however, that Burns was influenced by the "fine romantic look" of the property. All that we know goes to show that Burns leased Ellisland because it was the only farm which Miller offered to him,[65] and because an experienced farmer, Tennant of Glenconner, advised him to close the bargain. His failure at Ellisland was not due to letting sentiment get the better of good judgment in farming matters.

6

JEAN ARMOUR AGAIN

While Burns had thus been spending a busy winter writing songs, making love to Clarinda, assuring himself of his Excise commission, and leasing a farm, Jean had again been suffering for her misdeeds. When Robert had returned to Mauchline in June of 1787, after his Border Tour, he discovered that her parents had entirely forgotten their wrath of the year before. Where once they had forbidden him the house, they now made him welcome not only to their house, but to Jean. Marriage with this man whom Edinburgh had delighted to honor might not be so bad a fate for Jean after all, they seem to have felt. The easiest way to ensure her marriage to Burns would be to let Nature take its course; the poet had offered to marry her a year before when she had been in trouble; naturally, they must have thought, he would do so again.

Burns, however, had no such plan in mind, and Jean was happy enough to have him once more to herself. She made no conditions and expected no promises. So when Burns left her in the autumn and returned to Edinburgh she was again bound to him by the strongest of ties, but had no "unlucky paper" as evidence of his intentions.

There is no indication as to how Burns and Jean kept in touch with one another during the autumn and early winter of 1787, but it is beyond doubt that they devised some effective and secret means of communication. No suggestion of marriage seems to have been made by either of them. Consequently when for the second time Jean's parents discovered their daughter's situation, they learned to their chagrin that the man for whom they had virtually set a trap had indeed taken the bait but eluded the snare.

Thereupon James Armour's wrath flamed up again, and Jean took refuge in Tarbolton, where Burns had arranged with William Muir and his wife to give her shelter. Here Burns found her, on February 23, 1788, as he was riding back to Mossgiel from Dunlop House.

It must have been an interesting interview. Obviously there was little time to waste, and so—still without discussing marriage—the two young people made their plans for the immediate future. Jean would return to Mauchline, despite her father's anger and the prattle of village gossip, as soon as Robert could provide a room for her; she would do anything that Robert might ask, as she always had done. And Robert would ride on to Mauchline, make his peace with her parents, and let Jean know when to follow him.

He kept his word, though the keeping of it must have cost him dear in both pride and money. He had his interview with the Armours, and persuaded at least one of them to relent; he rented a room for Jean in Archibald Muckle's house in the Back Causeway, just across the street from Nance Tinnock's, and next door to Dr. John Mackenzie's home; he furnished it, at least with a bed. Having done this he told Ainslie all about it in a letter written about the first of March, for Ainslie endorsed it "March 3, 1788," which must have been the date he received it. The printable and relevant parts of the letter are these:

I have been through sore tribulation, and under much buffeting of the Wicked One since, I came to this country. Jean I found banished like a martyr—forlorn, destitute, and friendless; all for the good old cause: I have reconciled her to her fate: I have reconciled her to her mother: I have taken her a room: I have taken her to my arms: I have given her a mahogany bed: I have given her a guinea . . . But—as I always am on every occasion—I have been prudent and cautious to an astounding degree; I swore her, privately and solemnly, never to attempt any claim on me as a husband, even though anybody should persuade her she had such a claim, which she has not, neither during my life, nor after my death. She did all this like a good girl.[66]

Such was Burns's state of mind on March first. On the third of March Jean's mother and Burns's own physician Dr. John Mackenzie attended her when she gave birth to twin daughters.[67]

In none of his letters does Burns make any allusion to this event. Three years afterwards, however, he made this entry in his family Bible:

March 3, 1788, were born to them twins again, two daughters, who died within a few days of their birth.

The Burial Register of Mauchline contains two laconic entries, which bring the brief stories of these unnamed children to a somewhat pathetic close:

Jean Armour's child unbaptized, buried March 10.
Jean Armours' child unbaptized,   March 22.[68]

Thus again death had intervened to lighten Burns's cares, and again his silence on the entire incident may be taken as an indication that he felt the burden of grief more keenly than has sometimes been recognized.

A week or ten days after the birth of the twins Burns returned to Edinburgh to conclude his settlement with Creech, in so far as he could do so, to arrange finally for the Excise instructions, and to say farewell to Clarinda. On March 24, 1788, he left Edinburgh; on the twenty-sixth he was again in Glasgow, writing to his friend Brown a letter which despite its confused condition makes clear the fact that he was in no happy state of mind as he said farewell to the woman whom he could not marry, and returned to her whom only four weeks before he had forced to swear never to claim him as a husband:

I am monstrously to blame, my dear Sir, in not writing you, and sending you the Directory.—I have been getting my tack extended, as I have taken a farm; and I have been racking shop accounts with Mr. Creech; which, both together, with watching, fatigue, and a load of Care almost too heavy for my shoulders, have in some degree actually fever'd me.—I really forgot the directory yesterday, which vexed me:

THE BACK CAUSEWAY, MAUCHLINE

"Jean's Room" was on the second floor
of the house in the left foreground.

From an unpublished pen and ink drawing by Adrian de Friston

but I was convulsed with rage a good part of the day. . . . I am
vexed about the Directory; but, my dear Sir, forgive me: these eight
days, I have been positively crazed. . . . I am ever, my dearest Friend,
yours. . . .[69]

By the time of this letter to Brown, Burns had certainly decided to marry Jean. He had leased the farm of Ellisland; he
needed a wife to assist in the housekeeping. Peggy Chalmers
had refused him; Clarinda was an impossibility. Jean had suffered for him; he had experienced some qualms of conscience
on her account. She loved him; of that there had never been
any doubt. And he—well, to Mrs. Dunlop he wrote:

I found a once much-loved and still much lov'd Female, literally &
truly cast out to the mercy of the naked elements, but as I enabled her
to *purchase* a shelter; and there is no sporting with a fellow-creature's
happiness or misery.[70]

In his second *Commonplace Book*, intended for his own eye
alone, he was more candid:

Wedlock, the circumstance that buckles me hardest to Care, if Virtue
and Religion were to be anything with me but mere names, was what
in a few seasons I must have resolved on; in the present case it was
unavoidably necessary. Humanity, Generosity, honest vanity of character, Justice to my own happiness for after-life, so far as it could depend,
which it surely will a great deal, on internal peace, all these joined their
warmest suffrages, their most powerful solicitations, with a rooted Attachment, to urge the step I have taken. Nor have I any reason on
her part to rue it. I can fancy *how*, but have never seen *where*, I could
have made it better. Come then, let me return to my favourite Motto,
that glorious passage in Young—

> On *Reason* build *Resolve*,
> That column of true majesty in man.[71]

Various traditions have long been afloat as to when, where,
and by whom Burns and Jean were actually married, and Mauchline residents still point out the very room in Gavin Hamilton's
house where the ceremony took place. No records seem to have

survived, however, nor did any person save a clergyman have the right actually to solemnize a marriage. But at some time near the end of March Burns and Jean admitted themselves to be married persons, and thus satisfied all the requirements of Scottish civil law. The probability is that there were no witnesses, but the marriage was valid none the less.

What is possibly an allusion to the fact of this private marriage appears in a letter of April 7 to Peggy Chalmers:

I am going on a good deal progressive in mon grand bût, the sober science of life. I have lately made some sacrifices for which were I viva voce with you to paint the situation and recount the circumstances, you would applaud me.[72]

Not till April 28, however, when he wrote to his old friend James Smith, did he make any definite allusion to the changed relationship:

To let you a little into the secrets of my pericranium, there is, you must know, a certain clean-limbed, handsome, bewitching young hussy of your acquaintance, to whom I have lately and privately given a matrimonial title to my corpus.[73]

Under this phrase, "lately and privately," Burns concealed the exact facts of his marriage from even his intimate friend Smith; the research of a century and a half has not been able to dispell the cloud of uncertainty which he cast over his actions. He almost certainly was not married on March 24; he may have been on April 7; on April 28 he was, and had been for some time; his marriage, moreover, had been "private," in both the ordinary meaning of the term, and in the meaning recognized by Scottish law. More than that it is impossible to say, except to repeat that if all the facts had been presented to a Scottish court Burns would probably have been held to be a married man ever since the spring of 1786, and to add that even the private marriage in the spring of 1788 was insufficient to satisfy the Church, which had given no ecclesiastical sanction to this act. Consequently the final episode in the curious tale of Burns's marriage is still to be recounted. But from the spring of 1788 Jean Armour was legally his wife, and the one living child, of the four that she had borne to him, was no longer under the stigma of illegitimacy.[74]

To think back over the many incidents and experiences that crowded themselves into Burns's life between November 29, 1786, when he first saw the gray roofs of Edinburgh, and March 24, 1788, when he returned to Mauchline to marry Jean, is to realize that these sixteen months divided themselves sharply but naturally into three distinct periods. The first extended from November 29, 1786 to May 5, 1787, when Burns left the city with Bob Ainslie for the Border Tour. The second embraced the months from May 5 to October 20, when Burns completed the fourth of his vacation journeys. The third extended from October 20 to March 24, when he left Edinburgh with the lease of Ellisland in his pocket.

The first was a period enriched by new friendships, and made notable by the publication of the 1787 volume. The second was an interval of relaxation: of travel, on what must have seemed to Burns a large scale; of happy association with old friends in Ayrshire; and of renewed intimacy with Jean Armour. The third brought him under the spell of Clarinda, saw him working enthusiastically for Johnson's *Museum*, arranging for both the Excise commission and his return to farming, and—at the very close—returning to Jean.

No additional comment seems necessary concerning the second and third of these episodes. But the first may well be reverted to again, for it was in many ways the most important of the three, and the one in which Burns stood in most danger of being "spoiled," to use a homely but pertinent adjective.

Fortunately he escaped this fate. The testimony is unanimous and conclusive that he not only kept himself clear of the relatively innocuous stain of alcoholism, but—what was more important—that his native dignity was unruffled by flattery and admiration. Moreover, his consciousness of his own powers saved him from the pitfall of a fawning subservience or false modesty. He did not refuse the patronage of "great folk;" indeed, at times he sought it, eagerly and openly. But he preserved his own intellectual integrity, and remained his own man throughout the entire experience. Just as he accepted little advice concerning methods of "improving" his poems, so he refused to permit any one else to shape the future course of his life for him.[75]

Neither did he allow himself to be deluded into thinking that the dazzling popularity which came to him during his first winter in Edinburgh would continue indefinitely. He was gratified by his sudden rise to fame; he was undismayed by the certainty that Edinburgh would soon have had enough of him, and that he must return to the obscurity from which he had emerged. References to the inevitable eclipse are plentiful in the letters written early in 1787; perhaps a single paragraph addressed to the Reverend George Lawrie will best show Burns's state of mind and general clarity of vision on this point:

You are dazzled with news-paper accounts & distant reports, but in reality I have no great temptation to be intoxicated with the cup of Prosperity.—Novelty may attract the attention of mankind a while; to it I owe my present eclat: but I see the time not distant far when the popular tide which has borne me to a height of which I am perhaps unworthy shall recede with silent celerity and leave me a barren waste of sand, to descend at my leisure to my former station.—I do not say this in the affectation of modesty; I see the consequence is unavoidable, and am prepared for it.—I had been at a good deal of pains to form a just, impartial estimate of my intellectual Powers before I came here; I have not added, since I came to Edr, anything to the account; and I trust, I shall take every atom of it back to my shades, the coverts of my unnoticed, early years.[76]

All in all, then, the Edinburgh months made no fundamental change in Burns's personality or way of life. He enjoyed the splendor of Edinburgh, and delighted in the varied life which the city opened to him. But he had grown to full manhood before he borrowed George Reid's "pownie" for his memorable November ride. One looks in vain for any signs of perplexity as he stepped to the center of the largest stage on which he was ever to appear. He surveyed his audience without embarrassment; indeed, it was the audience, rather than the actor, that felt bewildered. Edinburgh widened Burns's horizon, enriched his life in many ways, and made him known to the world as he had never been before. It made no alteration in his soul-stuff, however. He was the same man in the spring of 1788 that he had been in the autumn of 1786, and his life went on much as it would have done had "Auld Reekie" never had the honor of welcoming him.

[1] The sum loaned to Gilbert seems to have been £200. Compound interest was to be paid at five per-cent per year. Out of this interest Gilbert was to deduct two items: five pounds per year as an "annuity to my mother allowed by my brother to be paid her out of the interest of his money in my hands," and the cost of supporting Elizabeth Paton, Burns's daughter, which amounted to between seven and eight pounds per year. Thus Gilbert actually saw the principal of his debt slowly lessening, till by the date of Robert's death it amounted to only £182–16–3. Just when the loan was made is not clear. On May 27, 1788, Burns wrote to James Johnson that he was "engaging in business pretty deeply both for myself and my brother," which indicates that he was at least planning to lend money to Gilbert. He had referred to "filial and fraternal claims" in a letter to Graham of Fintry dated January, 1788. Gilbert's "bill," or note, was not drawn till 21 December, 1792, as is made clear by Gilbert's carefully kept account books. The money had undoubtedly been advanced some time before this date.

As to the total amount of Gilbert's debt, there is some uncertainty. One hundred and eighty pounds is the sum commonly stated; Gilbert says two hundred. Syme and Nicol were in the habit of saying that this should have been three hundred. The probabilities are that two hundred pounds was the sum definitely advanced by Burns at the time and on the conditions noted above. It is also certain that from time to time he had sent money to the Mossgiel household. The manuscript of his Border Tour Journal, for example, contains Burns's memoranda of the numbers of two five-pound bank notes which had been sent by the post to Gilbert. He also writes to John Ballantine (January, 1788), directing him to pay over to Gilbert the money which Ballantine had collected from sales of the Edinburgh Edition in Ayr. (*Letters*, I, 158.) But there is no reason for thinking that Gilbert was a hundred pounds in error in his reckoning. See *Chronicle*, 1900, 77 ff.

[2] C. W., II, 206. The Burgess ticket is dated November 16.

[3] "Green Grow the Rashes," and "Young Peggy Blooms our Bonniest Lass."

[4] Letter of 4 May, 1787; *Letters*, I, 89.

[5] Letter of 25 October, 1787; *ibid.*, p. 133.

[6] *Ibid.*, p. 275.

[7] Letter of 24 April, 1789; ibid., p. 325.

[8] Letter of [Oct., 1793]; *ibid.*, II, 212.

[9] *Ibid.*, p. 312.

[10] Letter of 1 June, 1796; *ibid.*, p. 322.

[11] H. H., III, 295.

[12] Vol. I appeared in May, 1787; Burns had little to do with it. Vol. II (March, 1788), Vol. III (Feb., 1790), and Vol. IV (Aug., 1792) were practically Burns's work, either as author or editor. Vol. V was not published till December, 1796, five months after Burns's death. He had prepared much of the text, however. Vol. VI, which Johnson brought out without any aid from Burns, was not published till June, 1803. For further details see J. C. Dick's *The Songs of Robert Burns;* London, 1903, pp. xxxvi ff.

THE LIFE OF ROBERT BURNS

[13] Dick's assertions concerning the accuracy of Cromek's editorial work should be corrected by reference to Davidson Cook's article "Annotations of Scottish Songs by Burns," *Chronicle*, 1922, and J. DeL. Ferguson's "In Defense of R. H. Cromek," *Philological Quarterly*, July, 1930.

[14] Four children had been born to her; one had certainly died by 1782, and probably two.

[15] Probably the sister of the host, not the daughter. Clarinda later said, "Was I a man, *old as she is*, I should have chosen her before most women that I know." C. W., II, 219. (Italics mine.)

[16] *Letters*, I, 143.

[17] C. W., II, 219.

[18] Letter of 12 Dec., 1787; *Letters*, I, 145.

[19] Letter of 16 Dec., 1787; C. W., II, 220.

[20] Letter of 20 Dec., 1787; *Letters*, I, 146.

[21] *Ibid.*, p. 148.

[22] Letter of 28 Dec., 1787; C. W., II, 230.

[23] Letter of 1 Jan., 1788; *ibid.*, p. 231.

[24] Letter of 30 Dec., 1787; *Letters*, I, 151.

[25] Letter of 7 Jan., 1788; C. W., II, 241.

[26] *Ibid.*, pp. 246 and 311.

[27] Letter of 13 Jan., 1788; *ibid.*, p. 250.

[28] *Ibid.*, p. 271.

[29] *Ibid.*, p. 272.

[30] *Ibid.*, p. 281.

[31] *Letters*, I, 186.

[32] *Ibid.*, p. 187.

[33] *Ibid.*, p. 194.

[34] The exact date seems past discovering. A letter to Margaret Chalmers, dated March 14, shows that he had reached the city at least as early as the thirteenth.

[35] Letter of ? 18 March, 1788; *Chronicle*, 1929, p. 13.

[36] Jean's second twins had been born on March 3; one had been buried on the tenth.

[37] *Letters*, I, 209. The date of the letter is conjectural; it may have been written on March 14.

[38] Letter of March 9, 1789; *ibid.*, p. 312.

[39] Letter of July, 1791; *ibid.*, II, 82.

[40] Letter of 2 August, 1791; C. W., III, 273.

[41] Letter of 25 Jan., 1792; *ibid.*, p. 307. Original in Burns Museum, Alloway. The phrase "your leal friend" is printed "your real friend"; Clarinda's handwriting, however, is clear and unmistakable in the manuscript.

[42] *The Book of Robert Burns*, II, 63.

[43] *Letters*, I, 46.

[44] C. W., II, 16.

[45] *Letters*, I, 178.

[46] See C. W., II, 268, for example. The tradition may trace back to Allan Cunningham. See his *Life of Robert Burns* (London, 1834), I, 198.

[47] Letter of 1 Nov., 1789; *Letters*, I, 363. (Italics mine.)

[48] *Ibid.*, p. 157. The letter is undated, but must have been written late in January of 1788.

[49] Letter of 27 Jan., 1788; *ibid.*, p. 175. The inscription was occasioned by the neglected condition of the old castle and Parliament hall. The concluding four lines were of a sort that any would-be placeman might well regret:

> The injured Stuart line is gone,
> A race outlandish fills the throne;
> An idiot race, to honor lost;
> Who know them best, despise them most.

[50] Letter of 17 Feb., 1788; *ibid.*, p. 192. As a matter of fact, Burns did not take his instructions in Edinburgh, but in Ayrshire; he did not "get employ instantly," but waited till the early autumn of 1789.

[51] *Ibid.*, p. 210.
[52] Letter of 13 Dec., 1786; *ibid.*, p. 56.
[53] Letter of 14 Jan., 1787; *ibid.*, p. 66.
[54] Letter of 18 June, 1787; *ibid.*, p. 96.
[55] Letter of 28 Sept., 1787; *ibid.*, p. 126.
[56] About the size that one "plough-gang" (two men and four horses) could cultivate.
[57] *Letters*, I, 130.
[58] *Ibid.*, p. 194.
[59] Letter of 2 March, 1788; *ibid.*, p. 197.
[60] See letter of 7 Feb., 1788; *ibid.*, p. 182.
[61] *Ibid.*, p. 199. Ainslie received the letter 3 March, 1788.
[62] Letter of 7 March, 1788; *ibid.*, p. 207.
[63] Letter of 14 March, 1788; *ibid.*, p. 208.
[64] *Op. cit.*, I, 210.
[65] Gilbert Burns said: "I never understood that Mr. Miller gave my brother the choice of any farm but Ellisland." C. W., II, 320, n.
[66] *Letters*, I, 199.
[67] The statement concerning Mackenzie rests upon a poem by Saunders Tait. See Appendix, "Burns's Hen Clockin."
[68] Edgar, II, 403.
[69] Letter of 26 March, 1788; *Letters*, I, 211. The MS. bears the date March 20, which is obviously an error. Burns had not left Edinburgh on March 20.
[70] Letter of 13 June, 1788; *ibid.*, p. 226.
[71] C. W., II, 345.
[72] *Letters*, I, 216.
[73] *Ibid.*, p. 218.
[74] A letter from Burns to Richard Brown, dated 7 March, 1788 (the date is probably an error), reads thus:

"I found Jean—with her cargo very well laid in; but unfortunately moor'd, almost at the mercy of wind and tide: I have towed her into a convenient harbour where she may lie snug till she unload; and have taken the command myself—not ostensibly, but for a time, in secret." (*Letters*, I, 206.)

The phrase "taken the command" might be interpreted as meaning that Burns had already married Jean; more probably it signifies only that he had assumed the direction of her affairs by renting a room for her, and seeing that she had proper attention. The phrasing of the letter suggests that it was written before the birth of the twins; if so, the date must be wrong.
[75] "I have the advice of some very judicious friends among the Literati here, but with them I sometimes find it necessary to claim the privilege of thinking for myself." (Letter to Mrs. Dunlop, 22 March, 1787; *Letters*, I, 80.)
[76] Letter of 5 Feb., 1787; *Letters*, I, 70.

CHAPTER IX

ELLISLAND

1

THE FARM

Six miles northwest of the Burgh of Dumfries, and approximately forty-five miles southeast of Mauchline, lay Burns's new farm of Ellisland, pleasantly situated on the west bank of the river Nith.[1] The Dumfries-Glasgow post road, which ran east of the river, and a less important highway half a mile back from the river on the west side, allowed the poet, on rare days when work was not too pressing, to keep in touch with the life of the town where he was to spend his last five years. The farm, however, was not in Dumfries parish but in Dunscore, which Burns's new minister, the Reverend Joseph Kirkpatrick, described for Sinclair's *Statistical Account*. The parish was an oddly shaped piece of rolling lowland, twelve miles long, and four miles broad at the widest point. So narrow was it at the center, however ("only a few yards" wide), that in appearance it resembled the hour-glass by which the good dominie might have timed his sermons.

To the ministerial chronicler the parish as a whole did not appear a promising field. The soil was poor, the number of baptisms was not increasing, there were only seventy-two plows, fevers and rheumatisms were general, the schools were badly taught ("the encouragement being so inconsiderable, the parish cannot be supposed to have well qualified teachers"), and the most notable object in the entire vicinity, a large yew tree that grew in the corner of the burying ground, had just been blown down.[2]

Perhaps Kirkpatrick did the parish scant justice. At any rate, Burns's friend Robert Riddell suggested as much in certain *Addenda to the Statistical Account*:

> I need only observe that the present minister of Dunscore had the finest field for statistical investigation—in singular tenures, fine views, improvements which have had a rapid progress, and many miscellaneous articles. How he has executed it, let the reader judge. I think it the worst account yet printed, except the account of the parish of Terregles. Much more may be said of Dunscore, but the ignorance and stupidity of the minister is such, and so great a Mule he is, that no good can be done with him.[3]

Be all this as it may, the farm which Burns had leased from Patrick Miller, proprietor of Dalswinton, lay at the eastern end of the parish; twelve miles away, at the western extremity, was Craigenputtock, where, forty years later, Carlyle was to write his review of Lockhart's *Life of Burns*, and to wrestle with the "Queer piece on clothes" that ultimately became *Sartor Resartus*. To gain an impression of Burns's new home in its environment of hill and valley one should tramp a mile or two west from the farm itself, climb to the top of a hill which rises to the height of a few hundred feet, and then look out over the country where Burns rode his two hundred miles a week as a gauger. To the southeast, in the center of the picture, is Ellisland itself. The farm buildings that Burns erected have given place to more modern ones, though the present house and byre may be, in part at least, the original structures. The landscape of gently rolling pastures, woodland, and tilled fields is much the same as when Burns knew it. Patrick Miller's mansion of Dalswinton, Robert Riddell's homestead of Friar's Carse, and the ancient keep known as the Isle, though somewhat obscured by the thick growth of trees, are not hard to identify. The river Nith winds its way past Ellisland, past the ruins of Lincluden Abbey, or

[295]

College, and on through Dumfries to the Solway, which, on a cloudless day, shows blue in the middle distance, with the hills of Cumberland rising beyond it.

To the west and north the outlook is more rugged, for here the hills are distinctly higher, and the valleys between are deep and sharply outlined. If a friendly Dumfriesian shows one precisely where to look, one may see Dunscore Kirk not far from the center of this picture. It is not the same edifice in which Burns listened to Mr. Kirkpatrick's orthodox sermons,[4] for that was torn down in 1823, but the very one which Carlyle pointed out to Emerson while the two men talked together in front of Craigenputtock farm-house. On the whole, it is a pleasant section of Dumfriesshire, this Ellisland neighborhood; good to look upon, especially when the sun is shining, and rich in memories of Burns and Carlyle, of Covenanting folk who held their conventicles in its shadowy glens a century before Burns saw it, and many of whom today rest beneath "Old Mortality's" tomb-stones in the church-yards of the district, and of Wallace and Bruce, who still earlier had followed their Southron foes up and down these peaceful valleys.

Ellisland itself, some hundred and seventy acres, was in a sadly run-down condition when Burns took it over, and is none too alluring today. The soil is far from the best. The buildings, to be sure, are substantial structures of stone overcast with lime, and are conveniently grouped around three sides of a square, with the house next to the river, the barn to the north, and the byre to the south of the open yard. But they are small and ill-lighted; even on dry days the yard, which is open towards the west, is pitted with mud-holes; and when a North Atlantic rain-storm sweeps over the near-by hills, the immediate environment becomes almost a morass. A century and a half ago the entire farm was unfertilized, unfenced, and undrained. Its value as a source of income lay far in the future; a fact which Burns, the tenant, discovered to his cost, and which Patrick Miller, the owner, ultimately admitted. A decade and a half after Burns's death Miller wrote thus concerning Ellisland:

When I purchased this estate about five and twenty years ago, I had not seen it.   It was in the most miserable state of exhaustion, and all the tenants in poverty. . . .   When I went to view my purchase, I was so much disgusted for eight or ten days that I then meant never to return to this county.[5]

Miller's arrangement with Burns seemed to be a generous one.   He gave his tenant three hundred pounds with which to build a farmhouse and fence the fields; the rental was fifty pounds annually for three years, and thereafter seventy pounds during the seventy-six year term.

The lease—printed in full in the Appendix to this volume— allowed Burns to take possession on Whitsunday, which in 1788 fell on May 25.   As early as March 31, 1788, however, anticipating the fact that he would need local advice and assistance, Burns had written from Mauchline to an unidentified resident of Nithsdale asking his aid:

SIR:

I have at last fairly signed my tack with Mr. Miller, and must commence operations at Whitsunday.—I am an entire Stranger in your Country; and Heaven knows shall need advice enough: will you be so very good as take a poor devil of a sojourning Rhymster under your care? . . .

I shall be at Brownhill for anything I know on thursday night; will you be able to spare me an hour or two on friday?   I want two men servants for the summer; if you know of any, please bespeak me them, or direct me to them.—I would like one of them a married man, as I can give him a house, and perhaps for this summer, a cow's grass; but I won't make a custom of that any more than this season.[6]

Whitsun came and went, however, without finding Burns at Ellisland.   Affairs connected with the Excise, and with the family at Mossgiel, kept him busy till the second week of June. Then it was to Mrs. Dunlop that he sent the first letter from the new home:

This is the second day, my honored Friend, that I have been on my farm.—A solitary Inmate of an old, smoky *"Spence"*; far from every

Object I love or by whom I am belov'd, nor any acquaintance older than yesterday except Jenny Geddes the old mare I ride on.[7]

The fact that Burns came thus alone to Ellisland, and not with his wife and son Robert, was due to the lack of any suitable habitation. Burns himself was forced to live a mile down the river from his farm, near the tower of the Isle. Here the outgoing tenants, David Cullie and his wife, gave Burns shelter in what seems to have been little better than a hut—smoky, ill-lighted, and open to every draught of wind that blew down the valley of the Nith. To Margaret Chalmers he wrote:

This hovel that I shelter in, while occasionally here, is pervious to every blast that blows, and every shower that falls; and I am only preserved from being chilled to death by being suffocated with smoke.[8]

The lines "To Hugh Parker" describe the poet's lodgings in a half dozen picturesque couplets:

Here, ambush'd by the chimla cheek,
Hid in an atmosphere of reek,
I hear a wheel thrum i' the neuk,
I hear it—for in vain I leuk:
The red peat gleams, a fiery kernel,
Enhuskéd by a fog infernal.
Here, for my wonted rhyming raptures,
I sit and count my sins by chapters;
For life and spunk like ither Christians,
I'm dwindled down to mere existence;
Wi' nae converse but Gallowa' bodies,
Wi' nae kend face but Jenny Geddes.[9]

Burns's problem was complicated by the necessity of spending a considerable amount of time with his family at Mossgiel. On July 18 he wrote to Peter Hill, from Mauchline:

You injured me, my dear Sir, in your construction of the cause of my silence.—From Ellisland in Nithsdale to Mauchline in Kyle is forty & five miles; there, a house a-building, & farm enclosures & improvements to tend; here, a new—not so much indeed a *new* as a *young* wife—

ELLISLAND

Good God, Sir, could my dearest Brother expect a regular correspondence from me![10]

A few days later he told Alexander Cunningham that he was "eight or ten days at Mauchline and [Ellisland] alternately,"[11] and on the second of August he wrote again to Mrs. Dunlop:

> . . . I would write to you from Nithsdale, & give you my direction there, but I have scarce any opportunity of calling at a Post Office once in a fortnight.—I am six miles from Dumfries; am scarcely ever in it myself; and as yet, have little acquaintance in the neighbourhood.—Besides, I am now very busy on my farm, building a dwelling-house; as at present I am almost an Evangelical man in Nithsdale, for I have scarce "Where to lay my head."[12]

To remedy this situation, and to provide a home to which Jean might come, was Burns's first task. Allan Cunningham knew how such an affair should have been conducted, and put into circulation a pleasant legend:

> During the progress of the work, Burns was often to be found walking among the men, urging them on, and eyeing with an anxious look the tedious process of uniting lime and stone. On laying the foundation he took off his hat, and asked a blessing on the home which was to shelter his household gods. I inquired of the man who told me this, if Burns did not put forth his hand and help him in the progress of the work? "Aye, that he did, mony a time. If he saw us like to be beat wi' a big stane he would cry, 'Bide a wee,' and come rinning. We soon found out when he put to his hand—he beat a' I ever met for a dour lift." When the walls rose as high as the window-heads, he sent a note into Dumfries ordering wood for the interior lintels. Twenty carpenters flocked round the messenger, all eager to look at the Poet's handwriting. In such touches the admiration of the country is well expressed.[13]

The sober truth is that Burns turned the building of his house over to a contractor, and devoted his energies to farming. And not for many months was he a familiar enough figure in Dumfries to make the arrival of a letter in his hand a matter of any significance whatsoever.

The house-building proved slow. Autumn saw virtually

[299]

nothing accomplished; at New Year's Burns was still homeless, and despairing. On January 22, 1789, he wrote to Morrison, a Mauchline carpenter who was making furniture for him:

> Necessity oblidges me to go into my new house, even before it be plaistered.—I will inhabit the one end untill the other is finished.—About three weeks more, I think, will at farthest be my time beyond which I cannot stay in this present house.—If ever you wished to deserve the blessing of him that was ready to perish; if ever you were in a situation that a little kindness would have rescued you from many evils; if ever you hope to find rest in future states of untryed being; get these matters of mine ready! My servant will be out in the beginning of next week for the Clock.[14]

Shortly thereafter Burns wrote two letters to Thomas Boyd, his mason, which show the situation vividly enough to warrant their being reprinted in full:

> I see at last, dear Sir, some signs of your executing my house within the current year.—I am oblidged to set out for Edinr tomorrow se'ennight so I beg you will set as many hands to work as possible during this week.—I am distressed with the want of my house in a most provoking manner.—It loses me two hours' work of my servants every day, besides other inconveniences. In G-d's sake let me but within the shell of it![15]

Three Sundays after this first appeal Burns said:

> I arrived from Edinr yesternight and was a good deal surprised at finding my house still lying like Babylon in the prophecies of Isiah. I beg, dear Sir, for humanity's sake, that you will send me out your hands tomorrow.[16]

Even these two requests failed to complete the house, which seemed to lie under a curse. As late as April 15, more than ten months after he had begun to till the Ellisland acres, Burns was still dating letters from the Isle.[17] If he could have been continuously at Ellisland, instead of being forced to ride to Mauchline every week or ten days, progress would have been more rapid. Things being as they were, however, the delay was

BILL FROM MATTHEW MORISON, MAUCHLINE

From the original in the collection of Mr. Oliver R. Barrett

doubly irritating; and long before Burns and Jean had actually moved into their first home the poet had begun to make the plans which ultimately led him to abandon the farm altogether.

Nevertheless Burns did not permit the annoying fact of being so long homeless to discourage him. A casual remark in the *Statistical Account* shows him to have been known as an enterprising and progressive farmer:

Cattle and Sheep. The black cattle, in general, are of the Galloway breed; but Mr. Robert Burns, a gentleman well known by his poetical productions, who rents a farm in this parish, is of opinion that the west-country cows give a larger quantity of milk.[18]

As indeed he might be! Even then the Ayrshire strain was one of the best known to dairymen.

Burns was not working his farm single-handed. After Jean joined him, late in 1788, she took charge of the butter and cheese making, and became fairly adept as mistress of the dairy. From the beginning Burns had the assistance of hired servants, though precisely how many, or who they were, seems impossible to determine. In the autumn of 1788, when Burns was gathering his first harvest, he appears to have had three men in his employment. A letter of thanks to Robert Riddell, who had loaned him a boy as an extra hand, makes this fairly clear:

I return you my most grateful thanks for your lad today. Dare I ask him for tomorrow? I dare not ask more: I would not ask even that one, did not staring Necessity compel me. I have not a person I can command but three; your servant makes a fourth, which is all my forces.[19]

Apparently there was no female servant till Jean came down from Mauchline, later in the year.

All in all, then, the picture one has of Burns during the first months at Ellisland is that of an intelligent and energetic farmer, struggling against handicaps that would have discouraged any but the most resolute sort of person, and bending all his energies to bringing the acres he had leased into such condition that they would support him and his family. He was in no sense a poet casually supporting himself by farming; he was first of all a farmer, eager to raise stock and crops and to live in simple happiness on the produce of his acres.

2

FAMILY PROBLEMS

During these early months of Burns's life at Ellisland, Jean Armour and her only living child, Robert, had remained at Mauchline. There was shelter of a sort for the poet himself at the Isle, but none for his small family. So Jean, living perhaps in the rented room in the Back Causeway,[20] but walking out each morning to Mossgiel, busied herself about learning the ways of a farm ("She is regularly & constantly apprentice to my Mother & sisters in their dairy & other rural business," Burns wrote Mrs. Dunlop),[21] and waited till the new home should be completed.

Before she should move from Mauchline to Dunscore parish, however, it was highly desirable for her and her husband to be free from Church censure. Married they were, before the law; but there had as yet been no ecclesiastical sanction or confirmation of the private marriage which had taken place in March or April. When Burns waited on Dr. Auld concerning the matter, the Dominie was skeptical. He may have been uneasy in his mind over the "certificate of bachelorhood" which he had given Burns in the summer of 1786; certainly since that time Burns had been guilty of scandalous conduct both in Mauchline and elsewhere; it behooved Auld, as Moderator of the Kirk Session, to be doubly careful before certifying that his errant young parishioner was free from blame as regards his matrimonial irregularities. So Auld promptly—and properly—demanded proof of the private marriage.

What happened next is not absolutely clear, but apparently Burns invented a pious fiction. He told Auld that he had been "legally fined for an irregular marriage by a Justice of the Peace."[22] Again Auld demanded proof. Now had this "legal" fining "for an irregular marriage" taken place, Burns would have had no difficulty in satisfying Auld's doubts. Moreover, had any Mauchline resident acted as witness to Robert's and Jean's private and irregular marriage, evidence of that marriage would have been easy to secure. But there seems to have been no record of any imposition of a fine, nor any witness to the marriage; for Burns was forced to appeal to his old friend James Smith, in Linlithgow, who had known nothing of Burns's marriage till he had received the poet's letter of April 28 announcing the fact, for aid in helping him out of his predicament. "As soon as this comes to hand," he wrote, "please write me in the way of familiar Epistle that, 'Such things are.' " [23] Or, to phrase the matter baldly, Burns apparently asked Smith to add a substantiating lie to the one he himself had already told Auld.

Whether or not Smith sent the statement that Burns requested, no one can tell. But in some way Burns was able to satisfy Auld, and early in August Robert and Jean made their appearance before the Kirk Session, listened again to Auld's words of reproof, and were married for the third and last time. The entry in the minutes of the Session is as follows:

August 5th, 1778.—Compeared Robert Burns with Jean Armour his alledged Spouse. They both acknowledged their irregular marriage, and their Sorrow for that irregularity, and desiring that the Session will take such steps as may seem to them proper, in order to the solemn confirmation of said marriage.

The Session, taking this affair under their consideration, agree that they both be rebuked for their acknowledged irregularity, and that they be taken solemnly engaged to adhere faithfully to one another as husband and wife all the days of their life.

In regard the Session have a tittle (*sic*) in Law to some fine for behoof of the Poor, they agree to refer to Mr. Burns his own generosity.

The above sentence was accordingly executed, and the Session absolved the said parties from any scandal on this acct.

WILLIAM AULD, modr.   ROBT. BURNS

                                                       JEAN ARMOUR

Mr. Burns gave a guinea note for behoof of the poor.[24]

It is of interest to note that this particular incident seemed to Auld of enough importance to warrant his requiring the two principals to sign their names to the record—a most unusual performance.[25] The first time these two persons had been before him, Auld had adjured them to sin no more. His advice had been disregarded. This time, as he faced the man whom he knew to be the most brilliant, the most untractable, and altogether the most winsomely likeable of all his parishioners, past or present, Auld left nothing undone that would ensure his walking in the way of righteousness. And if Robert and Jean attended the annual Communion Service, held that year on the second Sunday of August, only a few days after their official absolution, Auld must have felt that he had indeed saved two brands from the burning.

Even after Burns and his wife had thus established themselves in the good graces of the Church, there was still no place for Jean at Ellisland. Not till the middle of October did her husband dare to suggest her leaving Mauchline, and then he could offer her only make-shift accommodations. An interesting letter in the Burns cottage Museum at Alloway, unpublished till 1927, throws much light on the situation, and alludes pleasantly to Jean's habit of walking down the Dumfries road to meet her husband as he rode up from Ellisland:

ELLISLAND Tuesday 14th Oct. 1788.

MY DEAREST LOVE,

You need not come on Sunday to meet me on the road, for I am engaged that day to dine with Mr. Logan a[t] Laycht, so it will be in the evening before I arrive at Mauchline.—

You must get ready for Nithsdale as fast as possible, for I have an offer of a house in the very neighbourhood with some furniture in it, all which I shall have the use of for nothing till my own house be got ready; and I am determined to remove you from Ayrshire immediately, as I am a sufferer by not being on my farm myself.—We will want a Maid servant, of consequence: if you can hear of any to hire, ask after them. —The apples are all sold & gone.—I am extremely happy at the idea of your coming to Nithsdale, as it will save us from these cruel separations.

[304]

—The house is one in which a Mr. Newal lived during the summer, who is gone to Dumfries in Winter.—It is a large house, but we will only occupy a room or two of it.—

> I am ever, my dearest Madam,
>> Your faithful husband & humble servt,
>>> ROBT. BURNS.[26]

But something occurred to delay Jean still further, for not till early in December did she join her husband in the house thus made available. That the *ménage* was conducted on the scale suggested by Chambers-Wallace seems altogether unlikely. Largely on the basis of tradition these biographers state that

> In the first week of December [Burns] brought Mrs. Burns to the Banks of the Nith. During the preceding week, two servant-lads and a servant-girl had come from Mauchline, with some cart-loads of the plenishing made by Morison, the Mauchline wright.[27]

Burns's letter to Jean makes it clear that housekeeping in the Newall home was to be most simple; the letter to Morison, dated January 22, 1789,[28] shows that the "matters" which he was preparing for Burns were still unfinished. And the child Robert still remained at Mossgiel, as appears from Gilbert Burns's New Year's greeting to his brother and sister-in-law.[29]

Long before the farmhouse at Ellisland was completed, Burns and his wife were taking a large share in the general family responsibilities. During the first months of 1789 they gave asylum to the children of an Uncle, Robert Burnes, who died on January 3, 1789, and to William Burns, the brother of the poet, who was persistently but unsuccessfully "looking for work." Burns's letter to his cousin, James Burness of Montrose, is interesting evidence concerning the family feeling that bound the members of the group together:

> . . . We have lost poor uncle Robert this winter.—He had long been weak, and with very little alteration in him, he expired Janry 3d.—His Son William, has been with me this winter, & goes in May to bind himself to be a Mason with my fatherinlaw, who is a pretty considerable

Architect in Ayrshire.—His other Son, the eldest, John, comes to me, I expect, in Summer.—They are both remarkable stout young fellows, & promise to do well.—His only daughter, Fanny, has been with me ever since her father's death, and I purpose keeping her in my family till she be quite woman grown, & be fit for better service.—[30]

It seems impossible to determine when the long-awaited farmhouse at Ellisland became habitable, or when Burns and his wife began life together in this their first real home. As has already been pointed out, Burns was living at the Isle as late as April 15. But certainly by the end of spring or beginning of summer he and Jean were established in the farmhouse.

The often-repeated story of the manner of entering the new home, with Bible and salt borne before the master and mistress, is another anecdote which should be written down as pure gossip.[31] The probability is overwhelming that Burns and Jean moved into their partly finished dwelling with no ceremony whatsoever, and with a full share of the discomforts attendant upon such incidents the world over. On June 8, 1789, Burns wrote to Ainslie that he was "condemned to drudgery beyond sufferance," and listed as particular woes

sowing corn with my own hand, a parcel of masons, wrights, plaisterers, &c. to attend to, roaming on business through Ayrshire.[32]

Ultimately, however, the house was made habitable; and there, on the eighteenth of August, 1789, Francis Wallace Burns was born, Mrs. William Burnes having come down from Mossgiel to assist.[33] The poet at once announced the fact to Mrs. Dunlop, in whose honor the child was named:

More luck still! About two hours ago I welcomed home your little Godson.—He is a fine squalling fellow with a pipe that makes the room ring.

Then followed the somewhat laconic afterthought:

His Mother as usual.[34]

[306]

Reading such a sentence, one inevitably finds oneself wondering how large a part Jean was playing in her husband's life. That they were reasonably happy together, seems past a doubt. She "made him a good wife," as the saying goes. The affection expressed in "Of a' the Airts," written during the early months of Burns's marriage, was sincere. Yet except as a homemaker Jean could do little for Burns.

The fact is that Burns without suspecting it was living in very truth a "double life." Burns the tenant farmer, the affectionate member of a family circle, intent upon making "a happy fireside clime," was one person. Burns the poet, the thinker, eagerly seeking to enlarge his intellectual horizon by way of compensation for the cramped and restricted condition of his physical existence—this Burns was an entirely different person. The farmer found happiness with his brothers and sisters, with Richmond and James Smith, with Jean Armour, and with many other young women. But the Burns who lives today turned to other persons for his most satisfying companionships. Before Burns married Jean, she was in no way connected with his inner life. After marriage he felt an affection for her, but an affection which was not in any sense strong enough to bind him firmly to her, and which never seems to have carried over into the realm of the spirit. One can put the matter succinctly by saying that "Holy Willie's Prayer" was written for Burns's real companions, and that Jean Armour could hardly have understood the poem, had she cared to read it.

The slight nature of even the physical charm that Jean held for her husband is evidenced by the affair of Anne Park. Burns met this attractive young niece of the landlady of the Globe Tavern, Dumfries, not long after he had moved to Ellisland. By the summer of 1790 he had forgotten his marriage vows. Cunningham, to make the poet's error seem venial, said that Anne "was accounted beautiful by the customers when wine made them tolerant in matters of taste;" and that Thomson, to whom Burns sent his song "The Gowden Locks of Anna," refused to publish it because he knew the "free character" of the heroine.[35]

For this innuendo concerning Anne's character and reputation Honest Allan had no single shred of evidence. What little is known of her goes to show that she was in no sense a girl of easy virtue, but simply another of the women whom Burns made love to, and who yielded themselves to him because they loved him. Had she been in any way a public character, had such a suggestion even been whispered about her, it is hard to believe that Burns would unhesitatingly have admitted the paternity of her child. He had told Ainslie that he was "vexed" about the affair with May Cameron; no such complaint escaped him concerning Anne Park. Burns's verse in praise of her is frankly physical; he made no pretext of any deep affection for her. But to him she was "my Anna," and no one else's. Hence when her daughter Elizabeth was born on March 31, 1791, Burns at once arranged to have the child cared for by his mother at Mossgiel. Ultimately he brought her to his home in Dumfries, where she grew up as a member of his family.[36]

On the ninth of April, 1791, only nine days after Anne Park's child was born, Jean herself gave birth to another son, named William Nicol Burns. Once more it was Mrs. Dunlop who first heard the news:

On Saturday morning last Mrs. Burns made me a present of a fine boy, rather stouter but not so handsome as your God-son at his time of life was.—Indeed I look on your little Namesake to be my chef d'œuvre in that species of manufacture, as I look on "Tam o' Shanter" to be my standard performance in the Poetical line.[37]

After this incident Jean more or less disappears from the Ellisland records. She tended the dairy, and performed the duties of housewife and mother with devotion and reasonable skill. But her husband continued to find his most stimulating companionships and intellectual interests in a world of which Jean was ignorant.

Further indication of Burns's failure to find happiness in his married life appears in the fact that the summer and autumn of 1789 saw him thinking much of Mary Campbell, and breaking the silence which he had hitherto maintained concerning her. On July 7 he wrote to Mrs. Dunlop a letter that may be reminiscent of the day he received news of Mary Campbell's death; on November 8 he sent her a copy of "Thou Lingering Star;" on December 13 he made his impassioned confession of undying love for "[his] lost, [his] ever-dear Mary." The point need not be stressed, but it seems symptomatic.

In this connection some attention should be paid to the traditional account of the composition of "Thou Lingering Star." Once again Lockhart is responsible for an all-but-universally accepted belief. Quoting M'Diarmid, who purported to be quoting Mrs. Burns herself, Lockhart said:

This celebrated poem was, it is on all hands admitted, composed by Burns in September, 1789, on the anniversary of the day on which he heard of the death of his early love, Mary Campbell. . . . According to [Mrs. Burns] Burns spent that day, though labouring under cold, in the usual work of his harvest, and apparently in excellent spirits. But as the twilight deepened, he appeared to grow "very sad about something, and at length wandered out into the barn-yard, to which his wife, in her anxiety for his health, followed him, entreating him in vain to observe that frost had set in, and to return to the fireside. On being again and again requested to do so, he always promised compliance—but still remained where he was, striding up and down slowly, and contemplating the sky, which was singularly clear and starry. At last Mrs. Burns found him stretched on a mass of straw, with his eyes fixed on a beautiful planet, "that shone like another moon;" and prevailed on him to come in. He immediately on entering the house, called for his desk, and wrote exactly as they now stand, with all the ease of one copying from memory, the sublime and pathetic verses, "Thou lingering star." [88]

Even in Chambers-Wallace one finds the material sections of this story reprinted without question. It is part of the established Burns tradition.

Perhaps all one need say is to suggest that when Lockhart quotes a second person who quotes a third, the cautious reader will beware of believing any part of the resulting statement; and that if Burns wrote a poem to the morning star ("that lovest to greet the rising morn") while lying on a mass of straw in his barnyard during the early evening, he was making himself unnecessarily and inappropriately ridiculous. Finally, if one thinks it probable that so highly finished a lyric as the one under consideration was thus composed and written down with no further revision, he should recall Burns's statement that

the rough material of Fine Writing is certainly the gift of Genius; but I as firmly believe that the workmanship is the united effort of Pains, Attention, & repeated Trial.[39]

The entire story had best be forgotten. *A priori*, there is no more truth in it than in Lockhart's assumption, in the first sentence quoted above, that Mary Campbell died in September.

As if the problems growing out of Burns's marriage, and his relations to Anne Park, had not been sufficient to disturb the even tenor of life at Ellisland, there was still a further complication in the fact that during the first two years on the farm Burns was constantly being called upon to give aid and counsel to his youngest living brother, William. The lad could write a good letter, but could do little else. Robert was steadily on the watch for opportunities for him, and the saddler's trade to which he had been bred was one that furnished employment to men all over the world. But something always happened, and William came back to Robert's fireside for shelter, or begged an overcoat, or borrowed a couple of guineas, with the hope that the next time he would be a success. One of the pleasantest sides of Burns's character appears as one reviews his relations to this well-meaning but unfortunate brother.

The fact that William was something of a problem appears first in the letter that Robert wrote to the family at Mossgiel immediately after the close of his second Highland tour. The lad was then approaching twenty years of age. He had learned his trade, but had not found regular employment. Robert's comment was this:

I have been trying for a birth for William, but am not likely to be successful.[40]

It is possible that by February of 1788 William had a position near Glasgow, for on the eighteenth of that month Burns wrote to Clarinda that William "has come to Glasgow to meet me;" [41] the boy may, however, have ridden up from Mauchline for the visit with Robert. By the end of August, 1788, Burns was enlisting Bob Ainslie's assistance:

> I grasp at your kind offer, & wish you to enquire for a place among the Saddler's shops. If I get him into a first rate shop, I will bind him for a year or two, I almost do not care on what terms.—He is about eighteen; really very clever; & in what work he has seen, not a despicable tradesman; but I will have him a first rate hand if possible.[42]

Nothing seems to have developed in Edinburgh, however, and William was forced to seek shelter with his brother Robert at the Isle. His long visit ended the fifteenth of February, 1789, when he went off to Longtown, where he had work at seven shillings a week. At once he wrote to Robert:

DEAR SIR:

As I am now in a manner only entering the world, I begin this our correspondence with a view of being a gainer by your advice, more than ever you can be by anything I can write you of what I see, or what I hear, in the course of my wanderings. I know not how it happened, but you were more shy of your counsel than I could have wished, the time I stayed with you: whether it was because you thought it would disgust me to have my faults freely told while I was dependent on you, or whether it was because you saw that, by my indolent disposition, your instructions would have no effect, I cannot determine . . . [but I] wish for that advice which you are so able to give. . . .

Please send me . . . two of my coarse shirts, one of my best linen ones, my velveteen vest, and a neckcloth . . .

The great coat you gave me at parting did me singular service the day I came here, and merits my hearty thanks. From what has been said the conclusion is this: that my hearty thanks and my best wishes are all you and my sister must expect from

W. B.[43]

[311]

So Robert gave him advice: to learn taciturnity, for apparently William was garrulous as well as lazy.

At the end of the month Robert wrote a brief letter, but one that tells much concerning his interest in his brother's welfare:

> I have stolen from my corn-sowing, this minute, to write a line to accompany your shirt & hat, for I can no more. . . . If you should not succeed in your tramps, don't be dejected or take any rash step.— Return to us, in that case, and we will court Fortune's better humour. Remember this, I charge you.[44]

By the middle of April William was in trouble:

> MY DEAR WILLIAM:
>
> I am extremely sorry at the misfortune of your legs . . . My house shall be your welcome home; & as I know your prudence (would to God you had *resolution* equal to your *prudence!*) if any where at a distance from friends, you should need money, you know my direction by post.[45]

Two weeks later William was in Newcastle, and reported that he was in love. Robert, now on familiar ground, hastened to give advice:

> Your falling in love is indeed a phenomenon. To a fellow of your turn it cannot be hurtful. I am, you know, a veteran in these campaigns, so let me advise you always to pay your particular assiduities and try for intimacy as soon as you feel the first symptoms of the passion; this is not only best, as making the most of the little entertainment which the sportabilities of distant addresses always gives, but is the best preservative of one's peace. I need not caution you against guilty amours —they are bad everywhere, but in England they are the very devil.[46]

Even love, however, was not a sufficient spur to William's resolution. In midsummer Robert wrote:

> I enclose you the two guinea-notes of the Bank of Scotland, which I hope will serve your need. It is indeed not quite so convenient for me to spare money as it once was, but I know your situation, and, I will say it, in some respects your worth. I have no time to write at present,

[312]

but I beg you will endeavour to pluck up a *little* more of the Man than you used to have. Remember my favorite quotation—

> On Reason build Resolve,
> That column of true majesty in Man.

> What proves the Hero truly great
> Is never, never to despair.

Your mother and sisters beg their compliments. A Dieu je vous commende.[47]

By January of 1790 William was preparing to leave Newcastle for London. Again he asked Robert for advice, this time as to how best to withstand "the temptation to those vices to which young fellows of my station and time of life are so addicted," and expressed the pious hope that "through God's assistance and your instruction" he might "weather the storm."[48] Robert, flattered at being thus linked with Omnipotence in matters with which he, at least, was thoroughly conversant, gave some admirable counsel, and then added this enheartening paragraph:

Write me before you leave Newcastle & as soon as you reach London. —In a word, if ever you be, as perhaps you may be, in a strait for a little ready cash, you know my direction.—I shall not see you beat, while you fight like a Man. Farewell! God bless you![49]

Twice at least after William reached London and found a position, his brother wrote to him. On the seventh of June Robert was "exceedingly happy to hear of [his] welfare," and was about to send him more shirts. On July 16 he told William that John Murdoch, the family tutor of Alloway days, would get in touch with him, and added, "I wish much to hear from you."[50] It is doubtful whether William received this last letter, however, for on July 24 he died. Murdoch had seen him once before his death; on September 14 he wrote Robert at some length concerning the close of William's life. And on October 5 Robert sent a draft in payment of all bills relating to his brother's illness and funeral.[51]

It would be hard to find any incident in Burns's life in which he appears to better advantage than in this of William's attempt to "make a go of it." Affectionate, loyal, generous, never overbearing or dictatorial, and always frank in his counsel, he treated William as he might have treated one of his own sons, had he lived long enough to see him in the years of his young manhood.

3

THE EXCISEMAN

The story of how the newly-married tenant farmer assumed the onerous duties of a gauger, and of the admirable record which he made in the Excise service, is one of the interesting episodes in Burns's life at Ellisland. The account links itself directly with the record of the second winter in Edinburgh, for it was during those months that Burns had assured himself of his appointment. Indeed, when he left Edinburgh, on March 24, 1788, he appears to have thought that his commission was on the point of being delivered. But even for an applicant as well provided with friends as was Burns, the Excise Board's machinery moved slowly. Not till March 31 was the order for his instruction actually issued from the Edinburgh office. The document is interesting evidence of the care with which new appointees were scrutinized before being certified as competent. It is addressed to James Findlay, Excise officer at Tarbolton, whom Burns had known during his residence at Lochlie:

The Commissioners order, that you instruct the bearer, Mr. Robert Burns, in the art of gauging, and practical dry gauging casks and utensils; and that you fit him for surveying victuallers, rectifiers, chandlers, tanners, tawers, maltsters, etc.; and when he has kept books regularly for six weeks at least, and drawn true vouchers and abstracts therefrom (which books, vouchers, and abstracts must be signed by your supervisor and yourself, as well as the said Mr. Robert Burns), and sent to the Commissioners at his expense; and when he is furnished with proper instruments, and well instructed and qualified for an officer (then, and not before, at your perils), you and your supervisor are to certify the same to the Board, expressing particularly therein the date of this letter; and that the above Mr. Robert Burns hath cleared his quarters both for lodging and diet; that he has actually paid each of you for his instructions and examination; and that he has sufficient at the time to purchase a horse for his business.[52]

Prudent folk, these Commissioners of Excise; seeing to it that their servants were clear of debt before allowing them to handle the King's money!

Burns seems to have lived at Mossgiel while undergoing Findlay's instruction. At the close of the six weeks' term he was ready for his commission, which was issued on July 14, 1788. The document—published in full in the Appendix—must have reached him shortly thereafter.

The issuance of a commission, however, did not put an Exciseman to work or entitle him to pay. But Burns was unconcerned; indeed, he had no desire to begin gauging, for he was devoting all his time to improving his run-down farm. Not till September, at the close of his first summer at Ellisland, did he make the preliminary moves towards active employment. By this time Ellisland was promising to be a financial burden, and Burns wished to add an exciseman's salary to the income of a farmer. Accordingly he made a tentative request to be assigned to the district in which his farm was located, and put on the active list. The letter was addressed to Robert Graham of Fintry:

Your Honble Board, sometime ago, gave me my Excise Commission; which I regard as my sheet anchor in life.—My farm . . . does by no means promise to be such a Pennyworth as I was taught to expect.—It is in the last stage of worn-out poverty, and will take some time before it pay the rent . . .
There is one way by which I might be enabled to extricate myself from this embarrassment, a scheme which I hope and am certain is in your power to effectuate.—I live here, Sir, in the very center of a country Excise-Division; the present Officer lately lived on a farm which he

rented in my nearest neighbourhood; and as the gentleman, owing to some legacies, is quite opulent, a removal could do him no manner of injury; and on a month's warning, to give me a little time to look again over my Instructions, I would not be afraid to enter on business.—. . . It would suit me to enter on it, beginning of next Summer; but I shall be in Edinr to wait upon you about the affair, sometime in the ensuing winter.[53]

Exactly what Graham did for Burns one can not tell; but by July of 1789 things had progressed so far in the direction which Burns desired, that the poet felt it incumbent on him to thank Graham in language more inflated than he generally permitted himself to use. Having done so, he added these pertinent remarks:

Mr. Mitchel [the Collector of the Department], did not wait my calling on him, but sent me a kind letter giving me a hint of the business, and on my waiting on him yesterday, he entered with the most friendly ardour into my views and interests. He seems to think . . . that removing the Officer who now does . . . duty in the Division in the middle of which I live, will be productive of at least no disadvantage to the Revenue, and may likewise be done without any detriment to him.— Should the Honorable Board think so, and should they deem it eligible to appoint me to officiate in his present place, I am then at the top of my wishes.[54]

Fourteen lines of pentameter couplets, "To Robert Graham . . . on receiving a Favour, 19th August, 1789," [55] seem to date Burns's receipt of the order assigning him to the district he desired. On August 19 he wrote Mrs. Dunlop that he expected to be put to work "at the commencement of next month," [56] and on October 10, 1789, his name appeared on an official list of all Excise officers, with a notation to the effect that he was on active duty.[57]

One final step remained to be taken before Burns could legally exercise all the powers of his office: he must be formally sworn into the service. This act took place on October 27, as is shown by the minutes of the Justices of Peace Quarter Sessions for Dumfriesshire. Mr. G. W. Shirley has excerpted the following entry from the manuscript journal:

At Dumfries the Twenty-seventh day of October one thousand seven hundred and eighty-nine years.
Quarter Sessions of the Peace. Sedurunt.
George Maxwell of Carruchan, John Welsh, Sheriff substitute, William Lawson of Girthead, Thomas Goldie of Craigmuire and John Bushby of Kempleton, who made choice of the said George Maxwell to be their Praeses.

Mr. Findlater & Mr. Burns qualified	Alexander Findlater Supervisor of Excise & Robert Burns, officer of Excise both in Dumfries Collection qualified themselves, the first as an extraordinary officer of the Customs & the other as an Officer of Excise by taking and swearing the oath of allegeance (*sic*) to His Majesty King George the Second (*sic*) & other oaths appointed by law and subscribing the same with the Assurance. And the Justices adjourn their Quarter Sessioun till the Third Tuesday of November next.[58]

Thus it was that in the autumn of 1789 Burns began drawing King George's pay as an Exciseman. His district, the "Dumfries first Itinerancy," as it was called, was so large that he had to ride two hundred miles a week in order to cover it; his salary was fifty pounds a year, plus an uncertain amount allotted to him out of the fines collected from defaulters whom he reported. It was hard work, and work that brought in only a meagre stipend. But it was better than running into bankruptcy as a farmer; and there was a chance that Burns might prove so good an officer as to earn promotion to a better district.

The varied and exacting nature of the Exciseman's tasks appears from an account given by R. W. Macfadzean, whose long connection with the Excise made it possible for him to write authoritatively on this matter:

In the end of the last century the following were subject to Excise duties: Auctions, bricks and tiles, beer, candles, coaches, cocoa-nuts, coffee, cyder, perry, ver-juice, glass, hops, hides and skins, malt, mead or

Metheglin, paper, pepper, printed calico, silk goods, soap, British spirits, foreign spirits, starch, salt, stone bottles, sweets, tea, tobacco and snuff, wine and wire. The duty upon these articles was, in nearly every case, charged during the manufacture, and the surveillance of the processes entailed upon the officer frequent visits by day and night, on Sunday and Saturday. For example, soap-boilers were surveyed every four hours, candle makers every six hours, and even brick-makers had sometimes to be surveyed twice a day. Each article had several rates of duty. Tanners had to pay fourteen different rates, per lb., per skin, and per dozen skins, according to the kind of hide; and even hare and rabbit skins were not allowed to escape. There were seventy-eight rates of paper duty according to size, kind, and quality; and other similar instances could be given. Of course no single Excise officer had all these manufactures in his station; but he generally had a number of them, and he was never allowed to forget his responsibility with regard to them all. He was expected to detect within the bounds of the district allotted him every article upon which the king's dues had not been paid.[59]

No easy task, this business of being a gauger! On the one side were well-trained superiors, scrutinizing every report and checking every entry; on the other was a populace which was growing increasingly restive under the steadily increasing imposts, and which cherished the belief that to circumvent the Exciseman was legitimate and praise-worthy.

Cunningham and other romantic biographers have put into circulation various stories dealing with Burns's enforcement of the law, and suggesting that he was not above winking at illegal practises if the person guilty of them were in great need, or a woman. One had best be sceptical of all such legendary accounts. What little we know of Burns's actual relations to the Excise shows that he enforced the law to the limit of his ability, and that he early discovered himself handicapped by the fact that offenders whom he reported were well supplied with powerful friends. A letter to John Mitchell, Collector of the Dumfries district, throws much light on both Burns's theory and practise as an Exciseman:

I shall not fail to wait on Captn Riddell tonight.—I wish & pray that the goddess of Justice herself would appear tomorrow among our

Honble. Gentlemen, merely to give them a word in their ear, that, "Mercy to the Thief, is Injustice to the Honest Man."—For my part, I have galloped over my ten parishes these four days, untill this moment that I am just alighted, or rather, that my poor jackass skeleton of a horse has let me down; for the miserable devil has been on his knees half a score of times within the last twenty miles, telling me in his own way, "Behold, am not I thy faithful jade of a horse, on which thou hast ridden these many years!!!" . . .

I find that every Offender has so many Great Men to espouse his cause, that I shall not be surprised if I am committed to the strong Hold of the Law tomorrow for insolence to the dear friends of the Gentlemen of the Country.[60]

Burns did his work well; or, as the official entries in the Board's records show, he "turned out well," despite the fact that he had never been "tried" in the service.[61] In July of 1790 he was promoted to the Dumfries third division, and his salary increased from fifty to seventy pounds a year. In addition to this regular stipend he received a share of the fines exacted from offenders whom he reported, so that his total annual income may have run close to ninety or one hundred pounds. On January 27, 1791, his name was placed on the list of "Persons Recommended for Examiner and Supervisor."[62] That this step had been in contemplation for some time, and that news of Burns's probable promotion had reached his friends, appear from a casual remark in a letter from William Nicol to Ainslie, written six months before. Nicol had heard of Burns's good luck, and was commenting on his probable rise in society:

As to Burns, poor folks like you and I must resign all thoughts of future correspondence with him. To the pride of applauded genius is now superadded the pride of office. He was lately raised to the dignity of an Examiner of Excise, which is a step preparative to attaining that of a Supervisor. Therefore we can expect no less than that his language will became perfectly Horatian: *odi profanum vulgus et arceo.*[63]

In the ordinary course of events, promotion to the offices of Examiner and of Supervisor was by seniority; had Burns lived, he would probably have secured the Examinership in about six years. In the autumn of 1791, however, he confidently expected more rapid advancement. One finds him, for instance, writing to Peter Hill that

> I am now got ranked on the list as a Supervisor; & I have pretty good reason to believe that I shall soon be called out to employ.—The appointment is worth from one to two hundred a year, according to the place of the country in which one is settled.[64]

At the same time Burns was taking steps to secure a better appointment as an officer till his hoped-for promotion should relieve him of the necessity of "gauging." Various persons interested themselves in his behalf; Alexander Findlater, his immediate superior and the Dumfries Supervisor, was most friendly. Finally, in October of 1791, Burns took the matter up directly with Corbet, Supervisor General:

> . . . Mr. F[indlater] tells me that you wish to know from myself, what are my views in desiring to change my Excise Division.—With the wish natural to man, of bettering his present situation, I have turned my thoughts towards the practicability of getting into a Port Division. As I know the General Superrs. are omnipotent in these matters, my honored friend, Mrs. Dunlop of Dunlop, offered me to interest you in my behalf.—She told me that she was well acquainted with Mrs. Corbet's goodness, & that on the score of former intimacy, she thought she could promise some influence with her: and added, with her usual sagacity & knowledge of human nature, that the surest road to the good offices of a man was through the mediation of the woman he loved.—On this footing, Sir, I venture my application; else, not even the known generosity of your character would have emboldened me to address you thus.[65]

Thus by the end of October, 1791, when Burns had been on active duty for little more than two years, he had served creditably enough to have won one promotion, to have hopes of another in the not distant future, and to have the encouragement of Findlater, his Supervisor, in applying for a Port Division while waiting for the Supervisorship. All this while actively engaged in farming his hundred and seventy acres, and—as will appear later—finding time for no inconsiderable amount of poetry. Clearly, he had "turned out well."

[320]

4

TWO ELLISLAND FRIENDSHIPS

The location of Ellisland made it inevitable that Burns should be relatively solitary during his first months on the new farm. Six miles north of Dumfries, and a long half mile east of the nearest main thoroughfare, the home he was building for Jean was distinctly difficult of access. It was not so isolated as Craigenputtock, where Carlyle some years later was to complain about —and enjoy—a "solitude altogether Druidical;" but even today it is not easy to find. In 1788 it was almost as much out of the world as had been Mount Oliphant. As the *Edinburgh Advertiser* put it, "Burns, the Ayrshire Bard, is now enjoying the sweets of retirement at his farm." [66] Fortunately for Burns, however, his nearest neighbor to the north, Robert Riddell of Glenriddell (1755–1794), was a friendly soul who did much to gratify the poet's need of human companionship. And when Riddell was busy about other concerns, there was always Mrs. Dunlop, not to be visited, to be sure, except on rare holidays, but always eager for a letter from her "Dear Burns," and indefatigable in maintaining a correspondence that greatly enriched Burns's three and a half years at Ellisland.

In the spring of 1788 Riddell, a half-pay captain who in 1782 had retired from active service with the Prince of Wales's Light Dragoons, was living at Friar's Carse, half a mile north of Burns's farm, and on the same side of the river Nith. He passed—or posed—as an antiquarian, and ultimately attained to such local renown that shortly before his death the University of Edinburgh created him a Doctor of Laws, and certified that he possessed "uncommon knowledge" in his chosen field. [67] Time, however, has more or less discredited this assertion, and Riddell has joined the large group of persons who are remembered because of their association with Burns.

Riddell's estate had once been the seat of a monastic retreat attached to the powerful Abbey of Melrose. But as early as 1465 it had passed out of the hands of the church, and ultimately found itself in the possession of the eldest branch of the Riddell family, represented in 1788 by Burns's friend and his wife Elizabeth Kennedy Riddell. The amateur antiquary had remodelled the old house in the interests of comfort; but to link himself to the monastic tradition that clung to his acres, he built a "Hermitage," removed a baptismal font from a ruined church at Morton to the entrance hall of Friar's Carse, and constructed an eighteenth century reproduction of a "Druidical circle of stones," or "Druid's Temple," as Burns would have called it, to carry the imagination of a visitor still further into the past.

Riddell was something of a dillettante, who dabbled in music and art, and spent much of his leisure collecting old coins and delving not too deeply into the "antiquities" of his neighborhood. Scottish song was one of the subjects he felt qualified to investigate; and as Burns, in 1788, was in the full flush of his enthusiasm for Johnson's *Museum*, it was but natural that this common interest should draw the two neighbors together.

In fact, Burns had hardly begun work at Ellisland before Riddell made him welcome, and gave him a key to the "Hermitage," where on June 28 Burns composed the earlier version of the lines "Written in Friar's Carse," [68] which may fairly be called the first poetic product of the Ellisland years.

The friendship thus happily begun was made memorable through the preparation of two notable documents: the interleaved copy of the first four volumes of the *Scots Musical Museum*, which has already been described, and the so-called *Glenriddell Manuscripts*. The first allusion to these latter documents appears in a letter, undated, but written probably in May of 1789, in which Burns says:

If my Poems which I have transcribed & mean still to transcribe into your Book were equal to the grateful respect & high esteem I bear for the Gentleman to whom I present them, they would be the finest Poems in the language.[69]

The "book" referred to was in fact two books, blank quartos substantially bound in calf. In one appeared fifty-seven unpublished poems and the autobiographical letter to Dr. Moore, inscribed in part by Burns himself and in part by a clerical amanuensis. In the other the poet himself made copies of twenty-seven letters. The work was not done hurriedly; indeed, it was still unfinished as late as Christmas of 1793, when Burns wrote Mrs. Dunlop:

> I have lately collected, for a friend's perusal, all my letters; I mean, those which I first sketched in a rough draught, & afterwards wrote out fair.—On looking over some old musty papers, which, from time to time, I had parcelled by, as trash that were scarce worth preserving, & which yet at the same time I did not care to destroy, I discovered many of these rude sketches, & have written, & am writing them out, in a bound M.S.S. for my Friend's Library.[70]

Riddell actually had possession of the volume of poetry, which was completed, if one may judge by the date of the manuscript Preface, on April 27, 1791. The volume of prose seems never to have been given to the man for whom it was destined, for before it was finished a regrettable breach between Burns and the Riddell family had occurred, and Riddell himself died on April 21, 1794, without having received the volume intended for his library.

The subsequent history of the manuscripts sounds like a fairy story. When Dr. Currie was preparing his *Life and Works of Burns*, the poet's family sent him all Burns's manuscripts, even to "the sweepings of his desk," as Currie put it, and, *inter alia*, the two Riddell quartos. Dr. Currie's son W. Wallace Currie afterwards came into possession of the volumes; when he in turn died his widow, in 1853, presented them to the Liverpool Athenaeum. There they remained, securely boxed, till 1874, when they were placed in an exhibition case.[71] In July of 1913 the Athenaeum sold them to Quaritch of London for £4500, and Quaritch in turn, in spite of many protests from Scotsmen, sold them to an American dealer from whom they were purchased by Mr. John Gribbel of Philadelphia. Thereupon Mr. Gribbel generously restored them to Scotland, on such terms as make it certain that they will remain in the Scottish National Library, the property of "the people of Scotland for ever." Thus the first literary results of Burns's friendship for Riddell were two unique and invaluable collections of manuscripts.

It is interesting evidence of both Riddell's and Burns's belief in the cultural value of books that the two were associated as leaders in the Monkland Friendly Society. This organization had for its chief object the establishment of a circulating library where the members of the society might find standard works of literature, philosophy, history, and theology. Just when the project was launched is uncertain. In the spring of 1789, however, Burns referred to it in a letter to Peter Hill, Creech's old foreman, who by this time was in business for himself:

> The Library scheme that I mentioned to you is already begun, under the direction of Captn Riddell, & Me! There is another in emulation of it, going on at Closeburn, under the auspices of Mr. Mentieth of Closeburn, which will be on a greater scale than ours; I have likewise secured it for you.—Captain R— gave his infant society a great many of his old books, else I had written you on that subject; but one of these days I shall trouble you with a Commission for "the Monkland friendly Society"—a copy of The Spectator, Mirror, Lounger, Man of Feeling, Man of the world, Guthrie's Geographical grammar, with some religious pieces, will likely be our first order.—[72]

Eleven months later Burns sent an extensive order:

> At a late meeting of the Monkland friendly Society it was resolved to augment their Library by the following books which you are to send us as soon as possible—The Mirror—the Lounger—Man of feeling— Man of the world (these for my own sake I wish to have by the first Carrier) Knox's History of the Reformation—Rae's History of the Rebellion 1715—Any good history of the Rebellion 1745—A Display of the Seccession Act & Testimony by Mr. Gib—Hervey's Meditations—Beveridge's Thoughts—& another copy of Watson's body of Divinity—This last heavy Performance is so much admired by many of our Members, that they will not be content with one Copy, so Captn Riddell our President & Patron agreed with me to give you private instructions not to send Watson, but to say that you could not procure a

[324]

Copy of the book so cheap as the one you sent formerly & therefore you wait farther Orders.[73]

The society, though reorganized after three years, maintained its existence and supported the library until February 2, 1931, when by formal vote it was disbanded, and the books were distributed to appropriate places.[74] For the best summary of its ideals and methods during Burns's lifetime one turns to Sinclair's *Statistical Account*, where appears Burns's own account:

Mr. Riddell got a number of his own tenants, and farming neighbours, to form themselves into a society, for the purpose of having a library among themselves. They entered into a legal engagement, to abide by it for 3 years; with a saving clause or two, in cases of removal to a distance, or of death. Each member, at his entry, paid 5s.; and at each of their meetings, which were held every fourth Saturday, 6d. more. With their entry money, and the credit which they took on the faith of their future funds, they laid in a tolerable stock of books at the commencement. What authors they were to purchase, was always decided by the majority. At every meeting, all the books, under certain fines and forfeitures, by way of penalty, were to be produced; and the members had their choice in rotation. He whose name stood for that night first on the list, had his choice of what volume he pleased in the whole collection. . . .

At the breaking up of this little society, which was formed under Mr. Riddell's patronage, what with benefactions of books from him, and what with their own purchases, they had collected together upwards of 150 volumes. . . . A peasant who can read and enjoy such books, is certainly a much superior being to his neighbour, who, perhaps, stalks beside his team, very little removed, except in shape, from the brutes he drives.[75]

Burns, and not Riddell, was the moving spirit in the concern. As Riddell himself put it,

Mr. Burns was so good as take the whole charge of this small concern. He was treasurer, librarian, and censor to this little society, who will long have a grateful sense of his public spirit and exertions for their improvement and information.[76]

[325]

It is to make clear this point, Burns's public-spirited concern for the general improvement of the community, that his connection with the Monkland Friendly Society has been thus elaborated. However intense may have been his egoism, he was capable of thinking in terms of the entire social group of which he was a member.

The manifold activities of the Ellisland years left Burns relatively little time for poetry. To Johnson he continued to send his lyrics, to be sure, but aside from these there was but little accomplished till Riddell, in the autumn of 1790, put Burns in the way of meeting the antiquary Captain Francis Grose, who persuaded him to write "Tam o' Shanter." Once again it is Gilbert who gives the best account of the incident:

When my father *feued* his little property near Alloway-Kirk, the wall of the church-yard had gone to ruin, and cattle had free liberty of pasturing in it. My father, with two or three neighbours, joined in an application to the town council of Ayr, who were superiors of the adjoining land, for liberty to rebuild it, and raised by subscription a sum for enclosing this ancient cemetery with a wall; hence he came to consider it his burial-place, and we learned that reverence for it, people generally have for the burial-place of their ancestors. My brother was living in Ellisland, when Captain Grose, on his peregrinations through Scotland, staid some time at Carse-house, in the neighbourhood, with Captain Robert Riddell, of Glen-Riddell, a particular friend of my brother's. The Antiquarian and the Poet were "Unco pack and thick thegither." Robert requested of Captain Grose, when he should come to Ayrshire, that he would make a drawing of Alloway-Kirk, as it was the burial-place of his father, and where he himself had a short claim to lay down his bones when they should be no longer serviceable to him; and added, by way of encouragement, that it was the scene of many a good story of witches and apparitions, of which he knew the Captain was very fond. The Captain agreed to the request, provided the poet would furnish a witch-story, to be printed along with it. *Tam o' Shanter* was produced on this occasion, and was first published in *Grose's Antiquities of Scotland.*[77]

Grose's interesting work appeared in two volumes, the first published April 15, 1789, and the second April, 1791. Gilbert's statement as to the place of first publication is slightly inaccurate, for "Tam" was originally given to the world in the *Edinburgh Magazine* for March, 1791, a month before the appearance of the second volume of Grose's work. But the poem was written at Grose's suggestion, and, primarily, for his *Antiquities of Scotland*, where it appears as a footnote to the account of Alloway Kirk, in volume two.

Lockhart is responsible for the statement that Burns wrote "Tam" in a single day:

> The poem was the work of one day; and Mrs. Burns well remembers the circumstances. He spent most of the day on his favourite walk by the river, where, in the afternoon, she joined him with some of her children. "He was busily engaged *crooning to himsell,* and Mrs. Burns, perceiving that her presence was an interruption, loitered behind with her little ones among the broom. Her attention was presently attracted by the strange and wild gesticulations of the bard, who, now at some distance, was a*gonized* with an ungovernable access of joy. He was reciting very loud, and with the tears rolling down his cheeks, those animated verses which he had just conceived." [78]

The story has been often repeated; but coming from Lockhart, who turned to Allan Cunningham for aid, and resting ostensibly on an unpublished journal of Cromek's, it has such a dubious paternity that it should best be forgotten. One remembers that the poet himself later told Mrs. Dunlop that "Tam" had "a finishing polish that I despair of ever excelling." [79] If the phrase means anything, it means that Burns worked hard over the poem, and did not merely toss it off during an afternoon's stroll with his family.[80] In any case the poem is definitely a memorial to Burns's friendship for Riddell. Had the two men not been on intimate terms, Burns and Grose would probably not have met, and the occasion for "Tam" would not have presented itself.

Relations between Burns and Riddell continued on a pleasant basis of mutual esteem till three years after Burns had left Ellisland. Then, early in 1794, occurred an unfortunate episode which broke the friendship between Burns and the entire Riddell family. Before the ultimate reconciliation, Robert Riddell was dead. So at its close the story of the two men was unhappy. But Riddell's friendship meant much to Burns during all the Ellisland years, and as a result of that friendship the world has the interleaved *Museum,* the *Glenriddell Manuscripts,* and "Tam."

Burns's friendship with Mrs. Dunlop had developed before ever he moved to Ellisland and met Glenriddell. It persisted after he had given up farming and was living in Dumfries. But it was during the Ellisland years that this friendship contributed most to Burns's happiness, and that the great majority of the letters evidencing this friendship were written. Hence the interesting story of Burns and Mrs. Dunlop may best be recounted at this point.

"I have been told," wrote Mrs. Dunlop in one of her letters, that "Voltaire read all his manuscripts to an old woman, and printed nothing but what she approved. I wish you would name me to her office." [81] In these two sentences she indicated accurately the nature of her chief function: to serve as a self-appointed critic of all that Burns wrote—generous in praise, and outspoken in criticism. But she did more than this. She scrutinized his personal conduct as well as his poetry; she tried to free him from the burden of poverty; she defended him against his critics; she praised him where praise would help. To say, as does Wallace, that "her almost motherly anxiety concerned itself equally with his character and with his reputation," [82] is to state less than the truth. For it was far more than a motherly anxiety which she felt for the man who from 1786 till the early months of 1795 filled a larger part of her life than any other individual was permitted to occupy.

Frances Anna Wallace Dunlop (1730–1815) had been born in Ayr, on April 16, 1730, a direct descendant of an uncle of Sir William Wallace. In 1748 she had married John Dunlop of Dunlop, twenty-three years older than herself. Thirteen children were born to them, and all but two grew to manhood or womanhood. She was an affectionate mother and grandmother, tireless in her devotion to her family, and blest with a rugged strength which enabled her, even after years had come upon her, to do far more than many women half her age would have dared to undertake.[83] On the fifth of June, 1785, her husband died; for a year thereafter she herself was ill or slowly convalescing. Shortly after the publication of Burns's Kilmarnock volume a copy of the book found its way to her, and straightway a new interest entered her life. As Gilbert Burns later told the story, she

> sent off a person express to Mossgiel, distant fifteen or sixteen miles, with a very obliging letter to my brother, desiring him to send her half a dozen copies of his *Poems*, if he had them to spare, and begging he would do her the pleasure of calling at Dunlop House as soon as convenient.[84]

Thus again a woman had made the first move, and had invited Burns's friendship.

The correspondence which ensued continued till January of 1795, and was resumed again within a few days of Burns's death. At the very beginning Mrs. Dunlop introduced two themes that appear in many of her letters: praise of Burns's work as a whole, and meticulous criticism of details, criticism that took account of both his literary and his personal shortcomings. Her letters were long, sometimes excessively long, even after her eyesight had become so impaired that she had to dictate everything; they were poorly spelled and devoid of all paragraphing.[85] She made many suggestions and asked an indefinite number of questions. Burns did not always take her advice; once or twice—as for instance concerning the authorship of "Auld Lang Syne"—he deceived her; occasionally his neglect in replying to her queries made her suspect that he had not read her letters with care. Then she became outspoken in protest:

> You severely mortified me, nor did I ever in my life feel more degraded in my own eye than by the utter contempt you have shown for those hints which it cost me a great deal to give, and which I now heartily wish I had let alone.[86]

[329]

Not infrequently these hints took the form of protests at what Mrs. Dunlop considered unpardonable offenses against good taste:

Indeed, dr. [dear] Burns, you must forgive me telling you how oft I have felt the mortifying truth that no lady could be justified in acknowledging that your book, spite of the many unspeakable advantages it possesses, had been a mean of recommending its author to her acquaintance or esteem while it contains six stanzas to be found in the Edinburgh edition at pages 26, 39, 97, 256, 283. Nay more, if you abstract the Psalms and Prayers, and insert these [87] in a new corrected version, I will not be able to vindicate to my own heart that intimacy it has been so long my highest ambition and most unwearied endeavour to establish . . . If you are not too angry already, allow me, my Dr. Sir, to add one remark more. There are some words, which, although in themselves perfectly innocent when uttered in the rustic simplicity of a peasant, custom has wholly prescribed in upper life, so that an author should have some very strong temptation before he introduce what it would be an insult to his company for a gentleman to read aloud.[88]

Despite her chagrin over Burns's sins of this sort, Mrs. Dunlop welcomed him enthusiastically when he made his virtually annual visits at Dunlop House, and once, at least, wrote and sent to him a long poem celebrating such an occasion.[89] Like Clarinda, she scribbled verse a good deal, and was eager to have Burns read it and comment on it. "Why don't you tell me their faults," she asked, after having submitted two or three poems to his inspection, "or are they still not worth a criticism from your hand?"[90] Like Clarinda, too, she was concerned about Burns's soul, and urged him to give religion a larger share in his life. Like Clarinda, she thought that he should write to her more often than he did. And like Clarinda she felt hurt when he married, especially as—again like Clarinda—she learned of his act from another than himself:

A circumstance staggers my faith. I am told in a letter that you have been a month married. I am unwilling to believe so important an era of your life has past, and you have considered me as so very little concerned in what concerned you most as never to give me the most distant hint of your wishing such a change or of its accomplishment, while I have had the favour of hearing two or three times of you during that interim.[91]

None the less she remained Burns's devoted friend, and always did what she could to help him along his path. Perhaps the most picturesque of the attempts she made to assist him had to do with the newly established Professorship of Agriculture in the University of Edinburgh. Writing at great length on April 1, 1789, she ultimately came to the main point of the letter:

> I forgot that I meant to bid you read your friend Creech's advertisement in the *Edr. Courant* for proposals about a professor of Agriculture. I would have you give this a little serious attention, since I do not believe there is a man in the kingdom who might so properly blend the theoretical and practical knowledge that plan would seem to require.[92]

Through Mrs. Dunlop and Dr. Moore, Burns's name was actually brought to the attention of W. J. Pulteney, the donor of the endowment, who had reserved to himself the right to select the first incumbent of the chair. But Burns was too wise to attempt the academic life, and nothing came of this somewhat fantastic scheme.

Mrs. Dunlop did not need either Burns's assistance or his permission to defend him publicly and heatedly against charges which some of her letters make quite clear. For example:

> A gentleman told me with a grave face the other day that you certainly were a sad wretch, that your works were immoral and infamous; you lampooned the clergy, and laught at the ridiculous parts of religion, and he was told were a scandalous freeliver in every sense of the word. I said I was certain he must be misinformed, and asked if he knew you. He told me he had been in your company, and knew it was the case. "I beg pardon," said I; "I could not have guessed you had ever seen him, or read his book, by the character you give of either."
>
> Another of the company asked me if I knew you. I said I thought so, and would be exceedingly sorry to be convinced I did not. What did I think of your religion? That it was too exalted and sublime to have any ridiculous parts capable of being laughed at. What of that illiberal mind that could fall foul of so respectable a body of men as the clergy of Scotland? That the Scots Bard was above it; that no man more regarded the pastors of his people when worthy of their calling, but that those

he exposed were wolves in sheep's clothing, the bane of the community, and too black for his ink, low beneath his pen. . . . 'Twas observed I was too warm. I could not acknowledge that was possible in behalf of a character I knew, esteemed, and admired.[93]

The last clause says much concerning Mrs. Dunlop's interest in Burns. She knew him, she esteemed him, she admired him. Had she been only a few years nearer Burns's age, it seems doubtful whether she could have avoided the word which Clarinda feared, but used.

Parenthetically, a letter such as this last must be remembered when one undertakes to find a reason for the slanderous characterizations of Burns which became current immediately after his death. Burns had many critics even before his political liberalism had brought him into conflict with the Tory establishment. If as early as 1788 Mrs. Dunlop found it necessary to defend him against such charges, there is small wonder that after 1796 the accusations were even more bitter.

Burns on his part turned to Mrs. Dunlop as to no one else within the horizon of his life. In periods of depression he sought consolation from her; he welcomed her advice, even if he did not always follow it; he confided secrets to her that he trusted to no one else, as witness his letter concerning Mary Campbell; he named one of his sons Francis Wallace. Without her, his life from 1787 to 1795 would have been far less happy than it was.

Only towards the close of Burns's career did a rift appear between the two friends. Much ink has been spilt in trying to find a cause for the sudden cessation of Mrs. Dunlop's letters, which stopped abruptly after 12 January, 1795. William Wallace's conjecture was that

the explanation of her conduct is to be found in inadvertence, and not in a deliberate design to break off all connection with the poet on account of any moral or political offence he had given her.[94]

But since the publication of Professor J. DeL. Ferguson's article, "New Light on the Burns-Dunlop Estrangement," [95] the answer

[332]

to the unsolved riddle has been clear. In a letter begun on Dec. 20, 1794, first printed in full by Professor Ferguson, Burns alluded to the execution of Louis XVI and Marie Antoinette in the following words:

> What is there in delivering over a perjured Blockhead & an unprincipled Prostitute to the hands of the hangman, that it should arrest . . . attention?

Now as Professor Ferguson puts it,

> When one considers that two of Mrs. Dunlop's daughters had married French royalist refugees, and four of her sons and one grandson were or had been in the Army, we must realize that whatever opinion of the Revolution the lady heard at home must have been of the most uncompromisingly Tory and hostile sort.[96]

Hence naturally enough Mrs. Dunlop took offence at Burns's language and at the violence of his sentiments—and stopped writing to him.

This, then, was the real reason for the breach that separated the two persons after January, 1795. Burns tried, but in vain, to undo what he had done; he suffered for his thoughtless words. Finally, only eleven days before his death, he wrote to say farewell, and incidentally, to summarize his indebtedness to Mrs. Dunlop:

MADAM

> I have written you so often without rec.g any answer, that I would not trouble you again but for the circumstances in which I am.—An illness which has long hung about me in all probability will speedily send me beyond that bourne whence no traveller returns.—Your friendship with which for many years you honored me was a friendship dearest to my soul.—Your conversation & especially your correspondence were at once highly entertaining & instructive.—With what pleasure did I use to break up the seal! The remembrance yet adds one pulse more to my poor palpitating heart! Farewell!!! [97]

This appeal was more than even injured pride could withstand. At once Mrs. Dunlop wrote to Burns, and the day after the poet's death his friend John Lewars sent this word back to Dunlop House:

At the desire of Mrs. Burns I have to acknowledge the receipt of your letter, and at the same time to inform you of the melancholy and much-regretted event of Mr. Burns's death. He expired on the morning of the 21st, after a long and severe illness. Your kind letter gave him great ease and satisfaction, and was the last thing he was capable of perusing or understanding . . .[98]

So the story of Burns and Mrs. Dunlop closed on the old note, and with the poet's last hours came a return of the "ease and satisfaction" which this unique friendship had added to the nine preceding years.

5

INTELLECTUAL INTERESTS

When one attempts to indicate the nature of Burns's intellectual pursuits during his tenancy of Ellisland, one finds much to record. Mention has already been made of his activity for the Monkland Friendly Society, of his friendship with Glenriddell and the resulting two collections of manuscripts, and of his work for Johnson's *Museum*. It might be supposed that for a man engaged in building a house, restoring a reasonable degree of fertility to a worn-out farm, and—after the autumn of 1789 —riding two hundred miles a week on His Majesty's service, for such a person the interests already listed would have sufficed to occupy all his leisure hours and to consume all his spare energy. But Burns's mental appetite was never satisfied. Hence one finds him, during these busy Ellisland years, reading more and more widely, taking part in a heated theological controversy, and giving good evidence of his growing concern in political problems, both local and international. Each of these three matters demands brief treatment.

Hardly had Burns begun life at Ellisland when he turned to his intimate friend Peter Hill for aid in building up his per-

BILL FROM PETER HILL, EDINBURGH

From the original in the collection of Mr. Oliver R. Barrett

sonal library. Hill was just establishing a business of his own; Burns gave him what he could in the way of orders, both for himself and for the Monkland library. On July 18, 1788, he wrote thus:

Your book came safe, and I am going to trouble you with farther commissions. I call it troubling you, because I want only, Books; the cheapest way, the best; so you may have to hunt for them in the evening auctions.—I want Smollett's works, for the sake of his incomparable humor.—I have already Roderick Random and Humphrey Clinker.— Peregrine Pickle, Launcelot Greaves, & Ferdinand Count Fathom I still want; but, as I said, the veriest ordinary copies will serve me.—I am nice only in the appearance of my Poets.—I forget the price of Cowper's Poems, but I believe I must have them.[99]

On April 2, 1789, Burns ordered "A Shakespear" and "an English dictionary—Johnson's, I suppose, is best." [100] A month later a casual remark in a letter to Graham of Fintry shows him to have been extending his reading beyond the field of "polite letters":

By the by the Excise-instructions you mentioned were not in the bundle.—But 'tis no matter; Marshall in his Yorkshire,[101] & particularly that extraordinary man, Smith, in his Wealth of Nations, find my leisure employment enough.[102]

During the close of 1789 and early part of 1790 Burns was much interested in the dramatic performances given at the Dumfries theatre by a company of players under the leadership of George Sutherland.[103] Possibly because of this fact, Burns asked Peter Hill to send him

second-handed or any way cheap copies of Otway's dramatic works, Ben Johnson's, Dryden's, Congreve's, Wycherly's, Vanbrugh's, Cibber's, or any Dramatic works of the more Moderns, Macklin, Garrick, Foote, Colman, or Sheridan's.—A good Copy too of Moliere in French I much want.—Any other good Dramatic Authors in their native language I want them; I mean Comic Authors chiefly, tho' I should wish Racine, Corneille, & Voltaire too.[104]

Whether or not Burns intended to make a study of these playwrights in preparation for his own projected drama, "something in the rural way," [105] one can not tell. But at least he was making ready to utilize his spare hours in adding to his own very considerable knowledge of literature.

On December 5, 1791, Burns paid Hill in full for books that he had recently received—some for his own personal library, and some for the Monkland Society. The list is not long, for Hill had apparently failed on many of his commissions. Hence it may well be reproduced entire, for it presents a significant cross-section of Burns's literary interests at the time. It includes the following items: The English translation (Glasgow, 1761) of Marie Huber's *Letters on the Religion Essential to Man*, which Burns had known for some time, and had given as a Christmas gift to John Tennant of Glenconner as far back as 1786; Fielding's *Joseph Andrews*; four novels by Smollett; the octavo edition of Johnson's dictionary; Shakespeare's, Garrick's and Cibber's dramatic works; Ossian's *Poems*; *The World, The Adventurer*, and *The Idler*; *The Scots Worthies*; Fisher's *Marrow of Modern Divinity*; Price's *On Providence and Prayer*; Blair's *Sermons*; Cole's *On God's Sovereignty*; Smellie's *Philosophy of Natural History*; Isaac Newton's *Letters*; Boyle's *Voyages*; Guthrie's *Geographical Grammar*, which Burns had used as a boy in his father's home; *The Arabian Nights* and *Don Quixote*; a family Bible; the Westminster Confession of Faith; Ainslie's large map of Scotland, mounted on rollers; and Buchan's *Domestic Medicine*. [106]

Here were prose and verse, literature and science, realism and romance, theology both liberal and orthodox, and such standard "family books" as a Bible, a dictionary, a school text or two, and a volume on home medicine. In other words, Burns was buying books for all the members of his household, intending his sons to have the advantages which he had enjoyed, and also laying the foundations of such a personal library as any educated man would wish to possess.

The inclusion in this library of such a subject of controversy as Marie Huber's *Letters*, offensive to the orthodox, and of Fisher's *Marrow of Divinity*, equally obnoxious to the liberally minded, is evidence that Burns was not taking his theology at second hand. He listened to Joseph Kirkpatrick in Dunscore Kirk on Sunday mornings, and found him dull and hopelessly narrow:

> My Parish-priest . . . is in himself one vast constellation of dullness, & from his weekly zenith rays out his contradictory stupidity to the no small edification & enlightening of the heavy & opaque pericraniums of his gaping Admirers.[107]

Nevertheless he read on both sides of the question, and was well armed for any contest that might present itself.

An opportunity to strike a blow for liberalism arose when Dr. William M'Gill, one of the two ministers of Ayr, was accused of heresy. M'Gill had been ordained to the second ministry at Ayr, as colleague to Dr. William Dalrymple, in 1761, only two years after Burns had been born.[108] He had been a friend of the poet's father, had had a share in shaping the beliefs of the entire family, and had won Robert's unqualified approval by his steady if unmilitant setting forth of New Light doctrines. Burns had praised him in "The Twa Herds," and in November of 1787 had assured Mrs. Dunlop that he would take up the cudgels in M'Gill's behalf if he were hounded by his critics:

> I ever could ill endure those surly cubs of "chaos and old night"—those ghostly beasts of prey who foul the hallowed ground of Religion with their nocturnal prowlings; but if the prosecution which I hear the Erebean fanatics are projecting against my learned and truly worthy friend, Dr. M'Gill, goes on, I shall keep no measure with the savages, but fly at them with the faucons of Ridicule, or run them down with the bloodhounds of Satire, as lawful game wherever I start them.[109]

This fuliginous threat was due to rumors that followed hard upon M'Gill's publication of his *Practical Essay on the Death of Jesus Christ* (Edinburgh, 1786), which was found tainted with both Socinianism and Airanism. In November of 1788 Dr. William Peebles, whom Burns had laughed at in "The Holy Fair," denounced both the booklet and its author. M'Gill defended himself; in April of 1789 the case came before the Presbytery of Ayr. Ultimately it reached the General Assembly; but in April, 1790, M'Gill made a qualified recantation, and the case was dropped.

The excitement was at its height in midsummer of 1789; Burns's opportunity had arrived. But the dare-devilism of the letter to Mrs. Dunlop no longer seemed appropriate. Burns was eagerly awaiting orders that would put him on active duty in the Excise; a public challenge to the establishment, even in defense of so popular a character as M'Gill, would have been inopportune. Consequently, though Burns wrote "The Kirk's Alarm" as an expression of his feelings, he cautioned his friends not to let it become public. It was to John Logan, of Knockshinnoch, that he expressed himself most frankly:

I have, as you will see, finished "The Kirk's Alarm"; but now that it is done, and I have laughed once or twice at the conceits in some of the Stanzas, I am determined not to let it get into the Publick; so I send you this copy, the first that I have sent to Ayr-shire except some few of the Stanzas which I wrote off in embrio for Gavin Hamilton, under the express provision and request—that you will only read it to a few *of us*, and do not on any account, give, or permit to be taken, any copy of the Ballad.—If I could be of any service to Dr. M'Gill, I would do it though it should be at a much greater expence than irritating a few bigotted Priests; but as I am afraid, serving him in his present embarras is a task too hard for me, I have enemies enow, God knows, tho' I do not wantonly add to the number.—[110]

It is interesting to note that though a somewhat abbreviated copy of the poem was printed at 1789 as a broadside, "The Ayr-shire Garland, an Excellent New Song: tune, 'The Vicar and Moses' "; the entire poem does not seem to have been published till Allan Cunningham unearthed it for his collected edition.[111] The first two stanzas are in Burns's best satiric vein: brilliant in execution, both personal and general in application, and so phrased as to place before the reader at a glance the fundamental issue around which the controversy was raging:

Orthodox, Orthodox, wha believe in John Knox,
  Let me sound an alarm to your conscience;
There's a heretic blast has been blown i' the wast,
  The "what is not sense must be nonsense,"
Orthodox!   That "what is not sense must be nonsense."

Doctor Mac, Doctor Mac, ye should stretch on a rack,
  To strike evil-doers wi' terror;
To join Faith and Sense, upon any pretense,
  Was heretic, damnable error,
Doctor Mac!   'Twas heretic, damnable error.

That, of course, was just the point at issue: whether common sense could be admitted as an element in the Church's belief.

Burns felt his own insignificance in a contest of such magnitude, and expressed himself picturesquely in a letter of August, 1789:

Whether in the way of my trade I can be of any service to the Revd. Doctor is, I fear, very doubtful.   Ajax's shield consisted, I think, of seven bull hides and a plate of brass, which altogether set Hector's utmost force at defiance.   Alas!   I am not a Hector, and the worthy Doctor's foes are as securely armed as Ajax was.   Ignorance, Superstition, Bigotry, Stupidity, Malevolence, Self-conceit, Envy—all strongly bound in a massy frame of brazen impudence—Good God, Sir! to such a shield, humor is the peck of a sparrow and satire the pop-gun of a school-boy.[112]

During the summer of 1789 the poet dared not discharge his popgun.

Two years later Burns was prompt and vigorous in defence of a man whom he felt to be the victim of an unjustified persecution.   Early in the summer of 1791 James Clarke, schoolmaster of Moffat, found himself attacked, and his position imperilled, on account of allegedly undue severity to some of his pupils. Burns wrote in his behalf to influential persons in Edinburgh, composed at least two letters for Clarke to copy and sign, and followed the matter with eager interest till February of 1792, when Clarke was found guiltless of the charge. Meantime Burns had loaned him money with which to buy the necessities of life—money which was in process of being repaid, little by little, when Burns died. The story is pleasant indication of Burns's loyalty to his friends, and of his willingness to work for one whom he thought to be persecuted by the establishment.

Something of the same spirit appears in Burns's political activities at this time. It was in November of 1788 that he protested against Joseph Kirkpatrick's utterances concerning the House of Stuart. The General Assembly had appointed Wednesday, November 5, the hundredth anniversary of the landing of William of Orange on English soil, as "a day of solemn thanksgiving for that most glorious event—the Revolution."

Burns left two records of his reaction to this centennial celebration, one in a letter to Mrs. Dunlop, not intended for the public eye, and the other an open letter to the editor of the Edinburgh *Evening Courant*. To Mrs. Dunlop he wrote,

I too . . . am just now Revolution-mad, but it is not the tarantula-frenzy of insulting Whiggism, like an ass's colt capering over the generous hound breathing his last; mine is the madness of an enraged Scorpion shut up in a thumb-phial; the indignant groans and bloodshot glances of ruined Right, gagged on the pillory of Derision to gratify the idiot insolence of [usurpation].[118]

The letter to the *Courant* is too long to be quoted entire; parts of it, however, present pertinent evidence concerning Burns's political sentiments at this time:

I went last Wednesday to my parish church, most cordially to join in grateful acknowledgments to the Author of all Good for the consequent blessings of the Glorious Revolution. . . .

Bred and educated in revolution principles, the principles of reason and common sense, it could not be any silly political prejudice that made my heart revolt at the harsh, abusive manner in which the Reverend Gentleman mentioned the House of Stuart . . .

[340]

The Stuarts only contended for prerogatives which they knew their predecessors enjoyed, and which they saw their contemporaries enjoying; but these prerogatives were inimical to the happiness of a nation and the rights of subjects . . .

The Stuarts have been condemned and laughed at for the folly and impracticability of their attempts, in 1715 and 1745. That they failed, I bless my God most fervently; but cannot join in the ridicule against them.—Who does not know that the abilities or defects of leaders and commanders are often hidden until put to the touchstone of exigence; and that there is a caprice of fortune, an omnipotence in particular accidents, and conjunctures of circumstances, which exalt us as heroes, or brand us as madmen, just as they are for us or against us?

Man, Mr. Printer, is a strange, weak, inconsistent being—Who would believe, Sir, that in this our Augustan age of liberality and refinement, while we seem so justly sensible and jealous of our rights and liberties, and animated with such indignation against the very memory of those who would have subverted them, who would suppose that a certain people, under our national protection, should complain, not against a Monarch and a few favourite advisors, but against our whole legislative body, of the very same imposition and oppression, the Romish religion not excepted, and almost in the very same terms as our forefathers did against the family of Stuart! I will not, I can not, enter into the merits of the cause; but I dare say, the American Congress, in 1776, will be allowed to have been as able and enlightened, and a whole Empire will say, as honest, as the English Convention in 1688; and that the fourth of July will be as sacred to their posterity as the fifth of November is to us.[114]

This was a bold utterance—cogent and well phrased. It shows Burns expressing himself in something of the vein of a philosophic historian, looking out on life through a wide-angle lens, and including international developments in the field of his vision. Add to this letter such a poem as that sent to Peter Stuart, Editor of *The London Star*, early in 1790 ("Kind Sir, I've read your paper through"), and one realizes that Burns found time, despite all the discomforts and distractions of Ellisland life, to keep well posted on the affairs of the world.

It was but natural that purely British problems should also

interest him. "The Address of the Scottish Distillers," a vigorous piece of prose,[115] the "Ode to the Departed Regency Bill," [116] and the clever burlesque, "A New Psalm," ("O sing a new song to the Lord"),[117] all of which were published in Peter Stuart's *London Star*, are still readable pieces of political satire, despite the lapse of nearly a century and a half.

This is hardly true of the verse Burns wrote during the Parliamentary election campaign in the spring and summer of 1790, when Peter Miller, the son of Burns's landlord, was a candidate for the Dumfries burghs. The issues were complicated, and, at this distance, appear uninteresting. Instead of supporting Miller, the liberal candidate, Burns preferred Sir James Johnstone, a Tory. The reason for this defection was a purely personal one: the Duke of Queensbury, whom Burns detested, wished a Whig to be elected. Consequently Burns took the opposite side, and wrote election ballads [118] in favor of Johnstone. But the poems can hardly be read understandingly today. They were written to fit a specific and local situation.

When the Bastille fell, in July of Burns's second summer at Ellisland, he was petitioning for assignment to active duty in the Excise. Perhaps on this account he refrained from commenting in writing on the significance of the incident, and from expressing any opinion concerning French developments. But it is clear, from what he later said and did, that his sympathies were with the Revolutionists, and that he followed the development of events in France with the keenest interest.

So despite the heavy drag of farm work and the Excise, Burns maintained a varied and unintermittent intellectual activity during the Ellisland years. He did not write much poetry, except the songs for the *Museum*. But he read widely; he took a share in the unending dispute between the Auld Lichts and the New; he was vividly aware of what was happening in the ever more and more fascinating arena of national and international politics. And regularly he sided with the Liberals.

6

BURNS'S HEALTH

It was at Ellisland that Burns's health first gave him serious concern. Never since the Mount Oliphant days had he for long at a time been free from physical ailments; during those early years he had been sorely over-worked, and his heart had been affected. His recurring attacks of "hypochondria," and the hard colds that sent him to bed "under pain of death,"—these have appeared in the record from time to time. But it was the onerous task of managing the farm and riding two hundred miles a week as a gauger that made the heaviest inroads upon Burns's all too little reserve strength, and made the Ellisland years grievous with physical burdens.

Without attempting to reconstruct a clinical history of Burns's health from the spring of 1788 to the autumn of 1791, when he moved to Dumfries, one may well point out some of the more significant incidents in the record. For example, a letter written on September 23, 1788, to Graham of Fintry, shows under what conditions Burns had been gathering his first harvest:

Though I am scarce able to hold up my head with this fashionable influenza, which is just now the rage hereabouts, yet with half a spark of life, I would thank you for your most generous favor of the 14th, which, owing to my infrequent calls at the post-office in the hurry of harvest, came only to hand yesternight.[119]

Three months later, writing to William Cruikshank, his Edinburgh landlord of the year before, he said,

My knee, I believe, never will be entirely well; and an unlucky fall this winter has made it still worse.[120]

It thus appears that the injury which had confined him to his room in December of 1787, and had been the immediate occasion of the Clarinda correspondence, was still bothering him.

Early in 1789, in a letter to Robert Cleghorn, Burns made

no mention of health, but in a few words said much concerning his general state of mind:

> I must take shame and confusion of face to myself, my dear friend and brother farmer, that I have not written you much sooner.—The truth is, I have been so tossed about between Ayrshire and Nithsdale that, till now I have got my family here, I have had time to think of nothing.[121]

In the autumn of the same year, after the Excise duties had been added to those of the farm, Burns was in a fair way to a nervous breakdown complicated by the heart trouble that had already fastened itself on him. To his brother William he said:

> I would have written you sooner, but I am so hurried and fatigued with my Excise-business, that I can scarcely pluck up resolution to go through the effort of a letter to any body.[122]

About the same time he wrote to Mrs. Dunlop:

> I have somehow got a most violent cold; and in the stupid, disagreeable predicament of a stuffed, aching head, and an unsound, sickly crasis, do I sit down to thank you for yours of the nineteenth of October.[123]

On December 13 he was even more lugubrious:

> Many thanks, dear Madam, for your sheet-full of Rhymes.—Tho' at present I am below the veriest Prose, yet from you every thing pleases.— I am groaning under the miseries of a diseased nervous System; a System of all others the most essential to our happiness—or the most productive of our Misery.—For now near three weeks I have been so ill with a nervous head-ach, that I have been obliged to give up for a time my Excise-books, being scarce able to lift my head, much less to ride once a week over ten muir Parishes.[124]

Then followed the confession of love for Mary Campbell.

At the same time the pinch of poverty was making itself felt, and, as he told Provost Maxwell, he was harassed by trying to make one guinea do the work of three.[125] Thus the year 1789 closed in gloom and illness.

Nor did 1790 at once bring relief. To his brother Gilbert, Burns expressed himself with more than ordinary vigor:

ELLISLAND

Dear Brother,

I mean to take advantage of the Frank, though I have not in my present frame of mind much appetite for exertion in writing.—My nerves are in a damnable State.—I feel that horrid hypochondria pervading every atom of both body & soul.[126]

By the end of January things had brightened a little, however, and Burns could tell Mrs. Dunlop that

My health is greatly better, and I now begin once more to share in satisfaction and enjoyment with the rest of my fellow-creatures.[127]

Regrettably few records of any sort survive from the year 1790. Burns was so busy with the farm and the Excise that he found little time for writing, either poems or letters. Consequently one hardly knows whether this improvement in his health was reasonably lasting. It is fair to assume, however, that had the year been more than normally broken by illness, some account of the misfortune would have found its way into the Dunlop correspondence. Hence one is justified in thinking that physically, at least, the year was reasonably comfortable. Indeed on October 15, writing to Crauford Tait, Burns made this comment on his own condition:

As to myself, a being to whose interest I believe you are still a well-wisher, I am here, breathing at all times, thinking some-times, and rhyming now and then. Every situation has its share of the cares and pains of life, and my situation I am persuaded has a full ordinary allowance of its pleasures and enjoyments.[128]

But in 1791 troubles reappeared. Early in the year he once more told his tale of woe to Mrs. Dunlop:

When I tell you, Madam, that by a fall, not from my horse but with my horse, I have been a cripple some time, & that this is the first day my arm and hand have been able to serve me in writing, you will allow that is too good an apology for my seemingly ungrateful silence.[129]

Then, towards the middle of March, just when the spring plowing demanded his energies, Burns broke his arm.[130] As if this were not enough, the autumn found him laid up as he had been in Edinburgh in 1787:

I was never more unfit for writing.—A poor devil nailed to an elbow chair, writhing in anguish with a bruised leg, laid on a stool before him, is in a fine situation truly for saying bright things.— [181]

By this time Burns was preparing to leave Ellisland, and further discussion of his physical condition belongs in a subsequent chapter. But enough has been said to show that misfortunes came thick upon him during the Ellisland years. His spirit, however, was not broken. He had come to Ellisland eager to enjoy what the future had in store for him; he left it disappointed as regards his farming venture, but otherwise full of hope and zest for living.

7

FAREWELL TO ELLISLAND

Misgivings concerning Ellisland had flashed over Burns's mind almost as soon as the possibility of leasing the farm had been mentioned to him. But he leased the farm, none the less, and in June of 1788 went enthusiastically to work, with no immediate thought save that of living the rest of his days at Ellisland. By the tenth of September, however, when the first harvest had been gathered, he was becoming dubious. To Graham of Fintry he wrote:

My farm, now that I have tried it a little, tho' I think it will in time be a saving bargain, yet does by no means promise to be such a Pennyworth as I was taught to expect. [182]

By the next January he was even less sanguine:

If my farm should not turn out well, which after all it may not, I have my Excise-Commission in reserve. [183]

In July of 1789 the "if" had almost disappeared from the equation:

[346]

I am deliberating whether I had not better give up farming altogether, and go into the Excise wherever I can find employment.—Now that the salary is £50 per ann. the Excise is surely a much superior object to a farm which, without some foreign assistance, must for half a lease be a losing bargain.[184]

By the eleventh of January, 1790, he had definitely made up his mind.   Then it was to his brother Gilbert that he said:

This Farm has undone my enjoyment of myself.—It is a ruinous affair on all hands.—But let it go to hell!   I'll fight it out and be off with it.[135]

The first definite statement concerning means of getting clear of the encumbrance appears in a letter to Graham of Fintry, to whom Burns was constantly turning for aid and advice:

I am going either to give up or subset my farm directly.—I have not liberty to subset, but if my Master will grant it me, I propose giving it just as I have it to myself, to an industrious fellow of a near relation of mine.—Farming this place in which I live, would just be a livelihood to a man who would be the greatest drudge in his own family, so is no object; & living here hinders me from that knowledge in the business of Excise which it is absolutely necessary for me to attain.[136]

The task of actually getting free from the lease was not easy. Tradition—possibly erroneous—has it that by 1791 Burns and his landlord were not on such cordial terms as had formerly prevailed between them.   Even if this was not the case, Burns would never have asked anything in the way of a financial concession from Miller.   But fortunately for the poet a purchaser for the Ellisland acres appeared in the person of John Morin, Laird of Laggin, an adjoining estate, who offered Miller £1900 for the farm.   This made it possible for Miller to accept Burns's renunciation of the lease.   Thus it came about that Burns could write to Peter Hill, in the early autumn of 1791,

I may perhaps see you about Martinmass.—I have sold to My Landlord the lease of my farm, & as I roup off everything then, I have a mind to take a week's excursion to see old acquaintances.—At all events you may reckon on your account about that time.[137]

The "roups" of crops and stock brought Burns a considerable sum of money, though no one can tell exactly how much. But clearly he had no cause to be ashamed of his success as a farmer:

I have nothing new to tell you.—The few friends we have are going on in the old way.—I sold my crop on this day se'ennight past, & sold it very well: a guinea an acre, on an average, above value.[138]

Mrs. Burns, if one may trust the memoranda reported by John M'Diarmid, remembered the details of a subsequent sale at which the remaining farm chattels were disposed of:

The sale was a very good one, and well attended. A cow in her first calf brought 18 gns., and the purchaser never rued his bargain. Two other cows brought good prices.[139]

When these matters had been attended to, there remained only some financial adjustments with the new owner, Morin, concerning the value of the improvements for which Burns had been responsible, and Burns was free from farm life forever.[140]

As one thinks over Burns's entire Ellisland experience, from June, 1788, to November, 1791, one finds certain conclusions shaping themselves in one's mind. First of all, it was a hard life, physically, that Burns lived. Till perhaps the first of May, 1789, he had no home, but found shelter more or less where he could. During much of this time his family was at Mauchline, forty-five miles away. Even had the work at Ellisland not been complicated by the necessity of building a house, enclosing, draining, and fertilizing fields, it would still have been an arduous task to ride back and forth between the old home and the new, with the responsibilities of both on his shoulders. Then too, after September of 1789 he had the Excise duties to perform, as well as those of the farm. The first result of his attempt to bear this double burden was a serious physical breakdown during the latter part of 1789. The less fortunate members of his family looked to him for aid, and he never evaded or even questioned these obligations. So what with ill health, accidents, the increasing pinch of poverty, and the double duties of farmer and gauger, Burns was burdened as he had never been before.

Second, it was probably because of this fact that Burns found scanty opportunity for the sort of friendly intercourse and informal relaxation that had added zest to his earlier years. The location of his home, six miles from the nearest town of importance, was in part responsible for the relatively friendless nature of the Ellisland years. There were some friends, to be sure: Glenriddell, a near neighbor, whom Burns found congenial; a few persons whom he came to know reasonably well as he rode back and forth from Mossgiel; Mrs. Dunlop, who bored him occasionally, but whose sincere devotion to his interests meant much to him. But the difference between life at Ellisland and life at Mossgiel, to say nothing of Edinburgh, must have been unpleasantly apparent to him. As compensation for the lack of intimate friends Burns had the companionship of his wife. But for a full half year she was forced to remain at Mauchline, and even after she joined him, in December of 1788, she added but little to his inner happiness.

Third, the Ellisland period was one in which Burns's intellectual activity never flagged. Despite the pressure of immediate and often uncongenial obligations, he found time to continue his reading, to superintend the affairs of the Monkland library, and to keep persistently at the self-imposed task of making Johnson's *Museum* a success. There are no signs of any mental "slowing down" during these years, nor does Burns's horizon ever seem to have been on the point of contracting. On the contrary his interests were broader in 1791 than they had been in 1787; his world was larger in every way. And the intelligence with which he observed and commented on this world seems the more astonishing when one realizes the arduous nature of his physical life.

Finally, it was at Ellisland that Burns wrote "Tam o'

THE LIFE OF ROBERT BURNS

Shanter," and a score of lyrics which mark him as indisputable master of that difficult *genre*. Here one finds the rollicking fun of "Willie Brew'd a Peck o' Maut," the most care-free and happily abandoned of Burns's relatively few bacchanalian outbursts; here the daring impudence of "I Hae a Wife o' My Ain," and the gentle humor and pensiveness of "Tam Glen." Here is the pathos of "Thou Lingering Star," over-wrought in places, no doubt, but cutting deep with its poignant restraint. Here is the immortal wistfulness of "Auld Lang Syne," an old drinking song newly strung by Burns, and glorified by two stanzas for which he alone was responsible. Here is "Go Fetch to me a Pint of Wine," unexcelled by anything he ever wrote for sheer virtuosity of technique; and here is "John Anderson my Jo," which Burns rescued from absolute disreputability, and touched to undying beauty.

In other words, it was at Ellisland that Burns grew to his full stature as a poet.

---

[1] The farm is now the property of the Ellisland Trustees, and is maintained as a public memorial to the poet. See *Chronicle*, 1929, pp. 20 ff.

[2] *Op. Cit.*, III, 140 ff.

[3] *Addenda*, etc., by Capt. Robert Riddell; ed. Hugh S. Gladstone. Dumfries [1913], pp. 11 ff.

[4] "I have just heard Mr. Kirkpatrick preach a sermon. He is a man famous for his benevolence, and I revere him; but from such ideas of my Creator, good Lord deliver me!" (Burns to Mrs. Dunlop, 21 June, 1789; *Letters*, I, 341.

[5] *General View of the Agriculture, . . . of Dumfriesshire*, by Patrick Miller. Edinburgh, 1812. Quoted, C. W., II, 320.

[6] *Letters*, I, 214.

[7] Letter of 13 June, 1788; *ibid.*, p. 226.

[8] Letter of 16 Sept., 1788; *ibid.*, p. 256.

[9] H. H., II, 116.

[10] *Letters*, I, 235.

[11] Letter of 27 July, 1788; *ibid.*, p. 237.

[12] *Ibid.*, p. 240.

[13] *Life of Burns* (1834), I, 214.

[14] *Letters*, I, 292.

[15] Letter of 8 February, 1789; *ibid.*, p. 306. In Edinburgh Burns had seen Jenny Clow.

[16] Letter of 1 March, 1789; *ibid.*, p. 310.

[17] *Ibid.*, p. 323.

[18] *Op. cit.*, III, 140 ff.

[19] Letter of 16 Sept., 1788; *Letters*, I, 255.

[20] She may have lived at the Mossgiel farmhouse; no one really knows.

[21] Letter of 17 July, 1788; *Letters*, I, 233.

[22] Letter to James Smith, 26 June, 1788; *ibid.*, p. 230.

[23] *Ibid.*

[24] *Chronicle*, 1893, p. 56.

[25] There is some doubt as to whether Jean signed her own name, or Robert signed for her, or whether an unknown third party held the pen.

[26] Facsimile of letter. Newall at this time was factor to Miller, Burns's landlord.

[27] C. W., II, 390.

[28] See above, p. 300.

[29] Letter of 1 Jan., 1789; C. W., III, 16.

[30] Letter of 9 Feb., 1789; Letters, I, 307.

[31] The story was not put into circulation till long after Burns's death.

[32] Letters, I, 339.

[33] Ibid., p. 368.

[34] Ibid., p. 355.

[35] Cunningham, Life and Works of Robert Burns (1834), IV, 337.

[36] It is a curious fact that no one knows what became of Anne Park after the birth of her daughter. She vanishes from the record as completely as if she had never existed, leaving behind her the song, "Yestreen I had a pint of wine," which Burns afterwards called "the best love-song I ever composed," and her child. The daughter, however, lived happily till 1873. On attaining her twenty-first birthday, she received the sum of £200 from the fund raised by admirers of her father's poetry.

[37] Letter of 11 April, 1797; Letters, II, 68.

[38] Life of Robert Burns (1828), p. 184. No such story appears in Hately Waddell's version of M'Diarmid's conversation with Jean.

[39] Letter to ? Henry Erskine, 22 Jan., 1789; Letters, I, 291.

[40] Letter of 17 Sept., 1787; Letters, I, 124.

[41] Ibid., p. 192.

[42] Letter of 23 August, 1788; ibid., p. 249. Apparently Robert was William's guardian.

[43] Letter of 15 Feb., 1789; C. W., III, 42. William was particular about his clothes. See his last letter to Robert, ordering dress shirts; C. W., III, 177.

[44] Letter of 25 March, 1789; Letters, I, 315.

[45] Letter of 15 April, 1789; ibid., p. 323.

[46] Letter of 5 May, 1789; ibid., p. 331.

[47] Letter of 14 August, 1789; ibid., p. 351.

[48] Letter of 24 Jan., 1790; C. W., III, 167.

[49] Letter of 10 February, 1790; Letters, II, 10.

[50] Ibid., II, 21, 31.

[51] See copy of receipt, C. W., III, 229, n., and Murdoch's letter, ibid., 203.

[52] C. W., II, 328.

[53] Letter of 10 Sept., 1788; Letters, I, 252.

[54] Letter of 31 July, 1789; ibid., p. 346.

[55] H. H., II, 127.

[56] Letters, I, 355.

[57] C. W., III, 96.

[58] It is interesting to learn that Findlater was a Customs officer as well as Supervisor in the Excise.

[59] "Burns's Excise Duties and Emoluments," Chronicle, 1898, p. 53.

[60] Letter of ? October, 1790; Letters, II, 38.

[61] The fact that he is reported as "never tried" confirms his statement that he did not serve as an "expectant." See above, chap. VIII, p. 276.

[62] Details from John Sinton's Burns, Excise Officer and Poet; Kilmarnock [1896].

[63] Letter of 13 Aug., 1790; C. W., III, 200.

[64] Letter of ? October, 1791; Letters, II, 95.

[65] Ibid., p. 108. On Corbet's relations to Burns, see an article by J. De L. Ferguson, "Collector William Corbet"; Chronicle, 1931; pp. 65 ff. This letter may not have been written till February of 1792.

[66] Issue of 28 Nov., 1788.

[67] Robert Burns and the Riddell Family, by J. Maxwell Wood; p. 39, Dumfries, 1922.

[68] H. H., I, 258.

[69] Letter to Robert Riddell; Letters, I, 334.

[70] Ibid., II, 223.

[71] See *Some Account of the Glenriddell MSS. of Burns's Poems*, by Henry A. Bright, Liverpool, 1874, or the introductory matter in Mr. John Gribbel's facsimiles of the two volumes, Philadelphia (privately printed), 1914.

[72] Letter of 2 April, 1789; *Letters*, I, 318.

[73] Letter of 2 March, 1790; *ibid.*, II, 15.

[74] The older ones were given to the Trustees of the Ellisland Estate.

[75] *Op. cit.*, III, 599.

[76] *Ibid.*, p. 597.

[77] Currie, III, 384.

[78] Lockhart's *Life of Burns* (1828), p. 200. The quoted sentences Lockhart says are from "A MS. journal by Cromek."

[79] Letter of 11 April, 1791; *Letters*, II, 68.

[80] At least a first draft of the poem seems to have been completed by November of 1790, at which time Mrs. Dunlop commented enthusiastically on a fragmentary copy she had received from an unnamed correspondent. On December 31, however, she criticized the poem severely because of its violation of good taste. It is clear from her letter that by this time Burns had sent her a complete copy.

[81] Letter of 21 May, 1787; *Robert Burns and Mrs. Dunlop*, edited by W. Wallace; I, 36. New York, 1898, 2 vols.

[82] *Ibid.*, I, xiv.

[83] In her sixtieth year she nonchalantly wrote thus to Burns: "Just the day after I wrote you last I got an express telling me [my daughter Susan] was delivered of a dead boy. . . . I had a carriage, but, having also a lame horse, could not use it to fly to my distrest child. I sent to hire, but could find none. I set out on foot to beg from Cunninghame Lienshaw one to Kilmarnock, and so got to Loudoun in time to find the child buried and the disappointed mother in all the agonies of departed hope and bodily weakness. I staid with her till the tenth day was past . . . when the same post brought me your letter and one from John telling me his wife had likewise brought him a son, and begging to see me with all convenient speed. I set off on Thursday night at seven o'clock, came to Glasgow, and even there could hardly find a chaise; got one by twelve, and after spending all night on the road, arrived here next morning, where I found all so well that I might just as well have stayed quietly at home." (Letter of 6 Sept., 1789; *Robert Burns and Mrs. Dunlop*, I, 304.)

[84] *Ibid.*, 1.

[85] In November of 1790 Burns wrote Mrs. Dunlop: "When you prepare [your poetry] for the Press, you have only to spell it right, & place the capital letters properly; as to the punctuation, the Printers do that themselves." (*Letters*, II, 48.)

[86] Letter of 21 May, 1787; *Robert Burns and Mrs. Dunlop*, I, 34.

[87] The objectionable stanzas.

[88] *Ibid.*, II, 159. Letter of 12 July, 1791. Burns at the time was considering the possible omission of his religious pieces from subsequent editions.

[89] *Ibid.*, I, 39.

[90] Letter of 24 Dec., 1788; *ibid.*, p. 187.

[91] Letter of 4 June, 1788; *ibid.*, p. 95.

[92] *Ibid.*, p. 235.

[93] Letter of 5 Nov., 1788; *ibid.*, p. 162.

[94] *Ibid.*, II, 296.

[95] P. M. L. A., Dec., 1929; pp. 1106 ff.

[96] *Ibid.*, p. 1113.

[97] Letter of 10 July, 1796; *Letters*, II, 326.

[98] *Chronicle*, 1918, p. 5. See also Mrs. Dunlop's letter to Gilbert Burns enquiring after his brother's health, written the day of Burns's death. (*Chronicle*, 1904, p. 75.)

[99] *Letters*, I, 235.

[100] *Ibid.*, p. 318.

[101] Between 1787 and 1798 William Marshall published several volumes dealing with the "Rural Economy" of various parts of England; one treated Yorkshire.

[102] Letter of 13 May, 1789; *Letters*, I, 334.

[103] His pass to the Dumfries Theatre may be seen in the Burns House in Dumfries.

[104] Letter of 2 March, 1790; *ibid.*, II, 15.

[105] Letter to Graham of Fintry, 10 Sept., 1788; *ibid.*, I, 252.

[106] C. W., III, 230. The religious works were intended for the Monkland Society. See *Letters*, II, 52.

[107] Letter to Alex. Cunningham, 11 March, 1791; *Letters*, II, 64.

[108] Both M'Gill and Dalrymple are buried in the Ayr Parish Churchyard, on the south bank of the river Ayr, just above the Auld Brig.

[109] Letter of 4 Nov., 1787; *Letters*, I, 135.

[110] Letter of 7 August, 1789; *ibid.*, p. 350.

[111] See H. H., II, 324 ff.; also Cunningham's *Life and Works of Burns*, III, 129.

[112] The recipient of the letter is unknown, but may have been Robert Aiken; *Letters*, I, 349.

[113] Letter of 7 Dec., 1788; *ibid.*, p. 276. The last word, though still legible, has been deleted in the manuscript.

[114] *Ibid.*, 269; 8 Nov. [1788].

[115] Feb., 1789; *ibid.*, p. 303.

[116] April, 1789; H. H., II, 159.

[117] April, 1789; *ibid.*, p. 162.

[118] "Election Ballad for Westerha'" and "The Five Carlins"; *ibid.*, pp. 182 and 177.

[119] *Letters*, I, 259.

[120] Letter of Dec., 1788; *ibid.*, p. 281.

[121] Letter of 23 Jan., 1789; *ibid.*, p. 293.

[122] Letter of 10 Nov., 1789; *ibid.*, p. 368.

[123] Letter of 8 Nov., 1789; *ibid.*, p. 367.

[124] *Ibid.*, p. 372.

[125] Letter of 20 Dec., 1789; *ibid.*, p. 377.

[126] Letter of 11 Jan., 1790; *ibid.*, II, 1.

[127] Letter of 25 Jan., 1790; *ibid.*, p. 4.

[128] *Ibid.*, p. 46.

[129] Letter of 7 Feb., 1791; *ibid.*, p. 55.

[130] See letter to A. F. Tytler, April, 1791; *ibid.*, p. 69.

[131] Letter to Peter Hill, ? October, 1791; *ibid.*, p. 95.

[132] *Letters*, I, 252.

[133] Letter to Lady Elizabeth Cunningham, 22 Jan., 1789; *ibid.*, p. 289.

[134] Letter to Graham of Fintry, 31 July, 1789; *ibid.*, p. 346.

[135] *Ibid.*, II, 1.

[136] Letter of 4 Sept., 1790; *ibid.*, p. 40.

[137] *Ibid.*, p. 95. Ferguson's conjectural date for this letter is October. It was on September 10 that Burns signed the renunciation of the lease for the farm; see *Appendix*, where the entire document is printed.

[138] Letter of 1 Sept., 1791; to Thomas Sloan; *ibid.*, p. 86. This first sale took place before the "sale of the lease" had been legally effected.

[139] *Life and Works of Robert Burns*, by P. Hately Waddell (Glasgow, 1867, 2 vols.); II, Appendix, xxi. There were two sales, one late in August, when Mrs. Burns was in Ayrshire, and a second, early in November, which she witnessed. See letter to Mrs. Dunlop, *Letters*, II, 98.

[140] A caustic "epitaph" on Morin (H. H., II, 253), suggests that there was no love lost between the two men.

CHAPTER X

DUMFRIES

It was Burns's fate to die at a time when, as he himself put it, he had "enemies enow, God knows." His epigrammatic brilliance had alienated not a few persons who might have been his friends, had they not felt the lash of his sarcasm; his political liberalism had offended others; his caustic criticisms of religious orthodoxy had given umbrage to still a third group of his contemporaries. When his pen was no longer to be feared these embittered opponents had their revenge. They magnified his shortcomings, and suppressed facts which would have given the lie to some of their own utterances. The very death-notices in the newspapers implied that he had spent his last years in abject poverty and a close approximation to disgrace. Unfriendly gossip went still further in accusing him of gross moral turpitude.

Influenced by these malicious reports, Burns's first biographers, Heron and Currie, represented him as an alcoholic debauchee, and cut the pattern to which subsequent writers conformed. One after another the chroniclers repeated scraps of unsubstantiated anecdote, until there was woven a veritable tissue of falsehood, representing that Burns's life at Dumfries was rendered sordid by alcoholism and debauchery, and that he was "burned out" long before his death. Carlyle, whose review of Lockhart's life of Burns has probably had more readers than any other single essay on Burns, said without qualification that "he died in the prime of his manhood, miserable and neglected." John Nicol, whose biographical sketch, written for an early edition of the *Encyclopaedia Britannica*, stands virtually unchanged in the last (1929) edition, characterized Burns's life at Dumfries thus:

[354]

DUMFRIES

In the last years of his life . . . Burns became sourer in temper, and plunged more deeply into the dissipations of the lower ranks, among whom he found his only companionship, and sole, though shallow, sympathy.[1]

Henley, in his brilliant but misleading essay, summed up the misrepresentations of a century in this succinct statement:

I propose to deal with the Dumfries period with all possible brevity. The story is a story of decadence.[2]

Any departure from this accepted tradition must run the risk of being ruled out of court as hopelessly uncanonical. Yet when one reads the record of the Dumfries years without bias or prejudice, and especially when one separates what is actually known of Burns during this period from what was first said of him a quarter of a century afterwards, one will discover that Burns lived out his life in a fashion very different from that usually ascribed to him. Not until the last few months was there any real falling off in either the happy enthusiasm with which he accepted what Fate had to offer him, or in the creative genius of what he habitually called his "Muse." It will also be apparent that Burns's early death was due not to chronic alcoholism and debauchery, as has generally been implied, but to endocarditis, which had manifested itself long before, and which his medical advisers had been unable either to diagnose or alleviate.

1

THE TOWN OF DUMFRIES

On Thursday the first of November, 1791, Burns made his farewell call upon the Reverend Joseph Kirkpatrick, minister of Dunscore parish, who had been the poet's spiritual over-lord during the Ellisland years.[3] Early in the next week he moved six miles down the river to the Royal Burgh of which in 1787 he had been made a Freeman.

To a person possessing Burns's interest in Scottish history and legend, Dumfries, the capital town of the Shire, had much to

[355]

offer. Lying on the east bank of the Nith, at approximately the head of tide-water, and commanding the first reliable ford that a traveller from the east came upon as he journeyed westwards, Dumfries had been an important center since before the days of recorded history. Its existence as a Royal Burgh traced back as far as 1186, when William the Lion had conferred this distinction upon it. It was in the chapel of the Minorite Convent, which had once stood near the corner of the present Castle Street and Friar's Vennel, that Robert Bruce in 1305 had slain the Red Comyn, his foremost rival for the Scottish crown. During the ensuing years of bloodshed Dumfries Castle had been the chief fortress in all this vicinity, a vantage point dominating the entire lower valley of the Nith. In 1432 a stone bridge had been built across the river—good indication of the increase of trade and commerce in this part of the Lowlands.[4] Two and a half centuries later the Covenanters had held their conventicles in the glens across the river, or had fled from their homes to hiding places in the hills, pursued by Claverhouse and his dragoons. And in 1746 Prince Charlie, retreating from Preston after his audacious march to Derby, had set up his headquarters in what is today the County Hotel, where the room that he himself used is still preserved unaltered. So once again Burns found himself established where memories of a romantic past were richly abundant.

The lapse of time had not robbed Dumfries of its importance as a center of commerce and industry in southwestern Scotland. It was by far the largest town in which Burns had ever had a fixed abode. In the very year of the poet's arrival Dr. William Burnside, minister of the Second or New Church, made a careful census of Dumfries for Sinclair's *Statistical Account*, and discovered approximately seven thousand persons within the boundaries of the parish. Fifty-six hundred were residents of the town itself, living in the two- or three-storeyed brick and sandstone houses that clustered beside the High Street and its continuation, the Kirkgate, or in the smaller houses farther from the center of the Burgh. Well over a thousand of these residents were actively engaged in trades or business. Among the seven Incorporated Trades, the Shoemakers, with two hundred and thirty-six members of the Guild, were most numerous, though the "Squaremen" (carpenters and joiners) ran them a close second with two hundred and twenty. The Tailors' Guild had eighty-five members; the Hammermen's (workers in metal), seventy; the Weavers', fifty-nine; the Fleshers', or Butchers', thirty-three; the Skinners' and Glovers', twenty-three. Among the unincorporated trades the ecclesiastical enumerator counted seventy-eight persons licensed to sell spirituous liquors—one for every ninety souls in the parish,[5] fifty gardeners, thirty stocking-weavers, thirty lawyers, four apothecaries, three surgeons, and one physician, besides a goodly number of persons earning their livings in miscellaneous useful ways.

Cattle and horse fairs were important features of the town's commercial life, and attracted buyers and sellers from well beyond the limits of Dumfriesshire. Shipping was by no means insignificant. The Nith was navigable to within a few miles of Dumfries, and nearly two hundred small vessels entered and cleared each year, doing a miscellaneous coastwise trade, and importing potatoes, coal, tobacco, and wine. Branches of three Scottish banks were established in the High Street; daily mail coaches to and from Edinburgh, London, and Port Patrick kept Dumfries in close touch with the outside world. All in all, a newcomer might be reasonably sure that his material wants would be well cared for by his industrious fellow townsmen, and that he would not be oppressed by an atmosphere of commercial stagnation.

Nor were his spiritual needs overlooked. If, like Burns, he was a member of the Established Church, he could choose between St. Michael's, which linked the Dumfries of 1791 with that of the days before the Reformation, and the New Church, which had been opened in 1727. If he belonged to one of the several dissenting groups, he could find both Anti-Burgher Seceder and Relief congregations. For persons who admitted no affiliation with Presbyterianism, there were services in Episcopal, Methodist, and—on occasional Sundays—Roman Catholic chapels. One person claiming to be a Quaker found his solitary loyalty recorded by Dr. Burnside.

The cultural and social standards of Dumfries were far above those of most small cities of the period. Many county families of wealth and established position had their winter residences in town, and contributed generously to the civic life of the Burgh. The schools were admirable; even the "two or three boarding schools for the education of young ladies" won Dr. Burnside's approval. The hospital, or "Infirmary," rendered good service to a large number of patients; the Presbytery Library, open since 1720, and the Select Library, established in 1750, ministered to the intellectual needs of the community. One newspaper, the *Weekly Journal*, "circulated public news," and was "useful as a vehicle for advertisements." A well-supported theatre added a definitely metropolitan touch to the life of Dumfries, and gave an opportunity for its residents to enjoy a sort of diversion available in few provincial centers. Several military organizations maintained posts in the town; their officers sponsored a social life which contributed notably to what Dr. Burnside designated as the "Gaierties" of his parish—races, routs, and fortnightly assemblies:

> During our Circuits in Spring and Autumn the Assembly rooms will often exhibit 150 or 200 people as genteel and fashionable as are to be seen in any provincial town whatever.[6]

In one respect, however, Fate was unkind to Burns in sending him to Dumfries. Climatically it was a most unsuitable place for a man with rheumatic tendencies. It was low-lying, humid, oppressive in hot weather, and surrounded by wide reaches of undrained marsh. "Consumptions and rheumatisms are frequent here," said Dr. Burnside; Burns's experience was to coincide with the ministerial observation. But in all other ways the poet was fortunate in his choice of a place in which to spend his last years. For Dumfries was no ordinary "country town;" it was a town where life moved in a fashion definitely suggestive of the cosmopolitanism of Edinburgh.

[358]

In the autumn of 1791 Burns's family consisted of five persons: himself, his wife, and their three living children, all under the age of six—Robert Junior, Francis Wallace, and William Nicol. "Dear-bought Bess," six and a half years old, was living at Mossgiel, under the care of her father's mother and his brother Gilbert; Anne Park's daughter had not yet been brought to the poet's home. He rented from Captain John Hamilton a second floor tenement in what is now Bank Street, where three small rooms and a kitchen must have seemed cramped quarters after the ample spaciousness of Ellisland.[7]

As Mrs. Burns subsequently explained, the family did not come "empty-handed" to Dumfries. The sales of the Ellisland stock and crops had given Burns a considerable amount of ready cash; household furnishings, brought from the farm, must have been more than adequate for the new home. One cow, reserved from the auction, had been driven to town only to be sold because of lack of accessible pasturage.

In the "M'Diarmid Notes" appear some interesting observations by Mrs. Burns concerning the poet's way of life, not necessarily during the first months at Dumfries, but over the five years as a whole:

Burns was not an early riser, excepting when he had anything particular to do in the way of his profession . . . Even tho' he had dined out, he never lay after nine o'clock. The family breakfasted at nine. If he lay long in bed awake he was always reading. At all meals he had a book beside him on the table. He did his work in the forenoon, and was seldom engaged professionally in the evening. Dined at two o'clock, when he dined at home. Was fond of plain things, and hated tarts, pies, and puddings. When at home in the evening, he employed his time in writing and reading, with the children playing about him. Their prattle never disturbed him in the least.[8]

But even though Burns found it pleasant to spend the early morning hours in reading, and to enjoy the new-found freedom from the hard routine of farm drudgery, it is clear that he was not completely happy during the first weeks in the new home. The first letter from Dumfries to his old friend Bob Ainslie, was

couched in a tone even more depressed than that of the early
letters from Ellisland:

> Can you minister to a mind diseased? Can you, amid the horrors
> of penitence, regret, remorse, headache, nausea, and all the rest of the
> d—d hounds of hell that beset a poor wretch who has been guilty of the
> sin of drunkenness—can you speak peace to a troubled soul?
> Miserable perdu that I am, I have tried everything that used to amuse
> me, but in vain: here must I sit, a monument of the vengeance laid up
> in store for the wicked, slowly counting every chick of the clock as it
> slowly, slowly, numbers over these lazy scoundrels of hours, who, d—n
> them! are ranked up before me, every one at his neighbour's backside,
> and every one with a burthen of anguish on his back, to pour on my
> devoted head—and there is none to pity me. My wife scolds me, my
> business torments me, and my sins come staring me in the face, every
> one telling a more bitter tale than his fellow. . . . I have one or two
> good fellows here whom you would be glad to know.[9]

The reference to "my sins" assumes a specific significance when
one recalls that precisely at this time Clarinda reopened her correspondence with Burns, to inform him of the destitution of a
girl named Jenny Clow, and to add:

> In circumstances so distressing, to whom can she so naturally look
> for aid as to the father of her child? [10]

Burns answered the letter at once, asked Mrs. M'Lehose to
send five shillings to the girl, promised to visit her when he was
next in Edinburgh, and added:

> I would have taken my boy from her long ago, but she would never
> consent.[11]

Precisely what was the story lying behind this unqualified admission no one seems to know. In any case, Burns's distress over
the incident was real, and contributed to the depression of the
first weeks at Dumfries.[12]

But it was not in Burns's nature to allow such an affair long
to cloud his happiness. He was glad to be free from farm labor;

TAILOR'S BILL FROM NICHOL RAE, DUMFRIES

From the original in the collection of Mr. Oliver R. Barrett

his family was well; his Excise salary was sufficient to support them in comfortable simplicity; his prospects for promotion in the service were excellent. Furthermore, as he had told Ainslie, there were "good fellows" in Dumfries. Consequently it was with no thought that he was a broken man that Burns began life in his new environment. On the contrary, his zest for living was undimmed, and his eagerness to enjoy what the future had in store was as great as though the Ellisland experiment had not been a failure.

The most interesting features of Burns's life in Dumfries are to be found in the records of his new friendships, of his work in the Excise, and of his literary accomplishment. Each of these topics demands a section by itself. But the reader can hardly see these matters in proper perspective until he has in mind the outline of Burns's actual career in Dumfries, and understands the general nature of his experiences from November of 1791 to December of 1795, when the breakdown of his health put a stop to his participation in the life of the town.

2

DUMFRIES EXPERIENCES

By the time Burns had arranged the furniture in his new home, and familiarized himself with the duties of his new Excise division, he found little more than one month of 1791 remaining to him. He was eager to begin his life in Dumfries unencumbered by entanglements from the past; there were still matters in Edinburgh which needed his attention. Accordingly on November 29 he rode up to the capital, saw Jenny Clow, who would not part with her son but who needed Burns's assistance, called on Clarinda, and discovered that he was still in love with her. Concerning the affair with Jenny Clow no more need be said, for, indeed, no more is known, except that Burns neither denied nor evaded his responsibility. The renewal of the intimacy with Clarinda was more interesting. When Burns returned to Dumfries on December 6 he took with him a "parcel" of Nancy's hair, some of which he made into a braided ring. Six letters from him to her, written during the nine days immediately following their farewell, attested the fact that she was still his "ever-dearest of women." On December 27 he sent her "Ae Fond Kiss," to console her during the tedium of the approaching voyage to Jamaica. Clearly there was still room in Burns's heart for the fair goddess of 1788.

But it was not to be Nancy's fortune to reign unchallenged in that kingdom. Early in 1792, or possibly just at the close of 1791, Burns met Mrs. Walter Riddell, sister-in-law of his former neighbor Robert Riddell of Glenriddell. The friendship that sprang up between the two added much happiness to the remaining years of the poet's life, and went far towards making him forget Clarinda's charms.

The early months of 1792 brought two gratifying indications that Burns had not been forgotten in Edinburgh. At the suggestion of Alexander Cunningham the Royal Archers of Scotland sent Burns an honorary diploma of membership—an unsought and graceful tribute.[13] Immediately thereafter came further evidence of Burns's enduring popularity in the form of a letter from Creech proposing a new edition of his poems.

The summer found Burns concerned over developments in France, and disturbed by the repercussions of these events in Britain. He was reading Burke and Tom Paine, and was siding with the liberals. Though not as close to French affairs as Wordsworth, who was watching the Revolution at short range, Burns needed only to look about him to see liberal clubs suppressed, the Briton's treasured right of free speech abrogated, and even the writ of *habeas corpus* suspended. By November, when he subscribed to Johnston's reform journal, *The Edinburgh Gazetteer*, his mood had become that of a man angered almost past endurance. But it was not politics alone that enlisted Burns's sympathy during the autumn of 1792. On the sixteenth of September he began work for a collection of Scottish songs projected by George Thomson, and thus provided himself with what was to prove his chief intellectual interest during his remaining years. October and November brought him often to the Dumfries theatre, where he was on the free list.[14] George Sutherland, for whom in December of 1789 he had written a versified New Year's Prologue,[15] was still manager of the local stock company; his leading actress was Miss Louisa Fontenelle, a young lady who had made her debut at Covent Garden, and had played the season of 1789–90 in Edinburgh. When her benefit night, November 26, was approaching, Burns composed an "Occasional Address," entitled "The Rights of Woman," which in name at least was reminiscent of Tom Paine's recently published work. The lines are as clever as anything Burns ever wrote in his Popeian manner, and—incidentally—indicate that he was at least considering a Scottish drama. In the letter which accompanied them he doffed his cap with as courtly an obeisance as a country actress could well hope to have accorded her.[16]

Purely domestic matters made November a memorable month. Probably at this time Anne Park's daughter Elizabeth was brought to Burns's home, where she was to grow up as a recognized member of his family. And on the twenty-first of November Elizabeth Riddell Burns was born, and named in honor of the wife of Robert Riddell of Glenriddell. Burns had told Mrs. Dunlop that he wanted no daughters, as he would not be able properly to educate them. None the less he became greatly attached to the little girl, and felt great distress at her obvious lack of robust health.

December brought a slackening of Burns's Excise duties, and leisure for him to ride north to Mossgiel on a visit to his family, and to spend four pleasant days at Dunlop House en route. But the month ended unhappily. Despite the fact that Burns had been busy writing songs for Thomson, he had found time and occasion to give too vigorous expression to his political liberalism. He had enemies who would gladly have seen him discomfitted; by the close of 1792 spies were everywhere. Late in December one of these informers denounced him to the Excise Board as unpatriotic.

With January of 1793 came the inevitable investigation into these charges. Burns was exonerated, but was warned to be more circumspect in the future—a warning which he was inclined to forget. February and March brought more pleasant experiences. In February Creech finally issued the two-volume edition, to which Burns had contributed fifty pages of new material—including "Tam o' Shanter." And early in March he was given an honorary membership in a recently founded quasi-public library. On the fifth day of this month the governing committee of this library

by a great majority resolved to offer to Mr. Robert Burns a share in the library, free of any admission money and the quarterly contributions to this date, out of respect and esteem for his abilities as a literary man; and they directed the secretary to make this known to Mr. Burns as soon as possible, that the application which they understood he was about to make in the ordinary way might be anticipated.[17]

Shortly after receiving this unusual tribute, Burns was chosen a member of the governing committee.

Before Burns had been long at Dumfries the question of schools for his children was giving him concern. The eldest son, Robert, was a promising youngster; his father was eager for him and his brothers to have the best possible education. As William Burnes had done before him, he taught them as he could at home; he employed a tutor for their study of Latin; but he realized the inadequacy of such training. The only hindrance to sending them to the excellent Dumfries schools was the matter of fees, which, for children of others than Burgesses, were high. So in the spring of 1793 Burns took the matter up with the town council, reminding them that he had once been created an honorary burgess, and requesting that "this mark of distinction may extend so far as to put me on the footing of a real Freeman of the Town, in the Schools." [18]

The council at once granted Burns's request, and thus helped him solve this particular problem. Incidentally, the action of the council is good evidence that Burns's political heresies had not brought serious discredit to him, and that his social position in Dumfries was above reproach.

Another incident of the spring of 1793 was the move to a larger house.   Shortly after the birth of the daughter Elizabeth it had become obvious that the tenement in Cawart's Vennel was too crowded for so large a family.   Consequently Burns rented —again from his friend and neighbor Captain Hamilton—a house near the southern end of the Mill Vennel, now Burns Street, to which the family moved at Whitsun.   The new home was reasonably commodious, as the visitor to Dumfries today may discover for himself; though unpretentious without and within, it was the sort of residence which any Dumfriesian of that time would have considered comfortable.   The fact that it was a "detached house" gave it an added air of gentility.[19]   Robert Burns Junior is authority for the statement that a maid-servant was added to the household, to assist his mother in the work which she had heretofore performed unaided.   So all in all Burns's situation, in the spring of 1793, was by no means that of an impoverished poet.   His family was well and comfortably housed; his Excise work left him leisure for the song writing that was dear to him; he was respected and loved by his fellow-townsmen; the economic pressure resulting from war-time conditions had not yet become severe.

The most notable feature of the summer of 1793 was the resurgence of Burns's creative power.   Not since before the appearance of the Kilmarnock volume had there been such a flood of poetry as he poured out at this time for the benefit of Thomson's *Select Scotish Airs*.   In Burns's own phrase, he was "in song" again; as one studies the resulting productions, one realizes that the old genius was still undimmed.

On the last day of September Burns presented four books to the Dumfries library.[20]   On the fly-leaf of one, De Lolme's popular treatise called *The British Constitution*, he wrote:

Mr. Burns presents this book to the Library & begs they will take it as a Creed of British Liberty—untill they find a better.[21]

[365]

Next morning, however, he again secured possession of the volume, and pasted the leaf to the adjoining frontispiece—thus concealing his rash sentence from unfriendly eyes. For some months England had been in a state of war with France. Trials for sedition were becoming all too common at the time; heavy penalties were being inflicted for deeds and words that under normal conditions would have excited no comment. Burns was more cautious than he had been a year before. But the inscription in the volume is still legible, to prove that though the Excise Board's reproof had tamed Burns's exuberance, it had not materially affected his sentiments.

Burns found another cause for worry in the health of his daughter Elizabeth Riddell. He was not the sort of person to make capital out of domestic misfortune, but on December 15 he confided in Mrs. Dunlop concerning this matter:

> These four months a sweet little girl, my youngest child, has been so ill, that every day, a week or less threatened to terminate her existence.[22]

To add to his unhappiness his own health was giving him concern. And late in December—just when, where, or how no one can tell—he offended the entire Riddell family in such a manner as to break the friendship that had become one of his treasured possessions. The story, in so far as it can be reconstructed today, will be told in more detail later. It is mentioned here as one further cause of the unhappiness that clouded the latter part of 1793.

The early part of 1794 brought Burns close to a nervous breakdown. "For these two months," he told Cunningham,

> I have not been able to lift a pen. My constitution and frame were, ab origine, blasted with a deep incurable taint of hypochondria, which poisons my existence.[23]

At the same time he told Peter Hill that he was thinking back to the happy days in Edinburgh, and that "[his] bosom [was aching] with tender recollections."[24]

THE MILL VENNEL, DUMFRIES, 1802

Burns's house stands in the left foreground.

From an unpublished pen and ink drawing by Adrian de Friston,
based on J. Wilson's pencil sketch.

The quarrel with the Riddell family, and especially the estrangement of Mrs. Walter Riddell, were adding a gloom to Burns's life more profound than any mere nervous breakdown could have occasioned. Verbal indiscretions that had offended certain military officers were giving him added cause for uneasiness.[25] Even the work for Thomson was suspended during these unhappy months, and though Burns did send Johnson a generous sheaf of verses for his fifth volume, he wrote but few of the songs at this time.

Early in May an opportunity to leave Dumfries came to Burns in the form of an offer of a position on the London *Morning Chronicle*, a liberal newspaper. But the poet decided not to exchange the assured income of a gauger for the uncertainties of political journalism. The summer found him associating with a small group of Dumfries liberals, and in all probability writing political poetry which he withheld from general circulation and which his family destroyed after his death. Two scraps of verse, however, have survived to indicate both the temper of those hot days, and Burns's readiness at sarcastic repartee. When the poet and his friends were suspected of harboring more radical sentiments than they actually entertained, a loyal rimester addressed them thus:

> Ye Sons of Sedition, give ear to my song:
> Let Syme, Burns, and Maxwell pervade every throng,
> With Craken, the attorney, and Mundell the quack,
> Send Willie, the monger, to hell with a smack.

Burns's reply—an extempore production—was a vigorous quatrain:

> Ye true "Loyal Natives," attend to my song:
> In uproar and riot rejoice the night long!
> From Envy and Hatred your corps is exempt,
> But where is your shield from the darts of contempt?[26]

In June of 1794, Burns felt justified in indulging once more in a brief vacation tour, this time through Galloway, in company with his friend and neighbor John Syme. The poet appears to have kept no Journal, and few letters have survived in which he mentions the trip. But Syme furnished Dr. Currie with a chronicle of the journey, which, though clearly inaccurate in some of its anecdotal details and a year wrong in date, is probably trustworthy as regards the main facts.

About June 22, the two men left Dumfries on horseback, and reached Kenmure by nightfall. Here they spent three days as guests of Gordon, grandson of the Jacobite Earl of Kenmure whose life and titles had been forfeited after the '15. From Kenmure the travellers rode on to Gatehouse, and thence to Kirkcudbright and St. Mary's Isle, where the Earl of Selkirk acted as their host. Here Burns was again in company such as he had enjoyed at Blair Castle and Athole House, on his long Highland tour with Nicol:

We enjoyed a most happy evening at Lord Selkirk's. We had in every sense of the word a feast, in which our minds and our senses were equally gratified. The poet was delighted with his company, and acquitted himself to admiration. . . . Next day we returned to Dumfries, and so ends our peregrination.[27]

It was a short trip, covering little territory, and ending only six days after it had begun. But it is interesting evidence of Burns's continuing love for this sort of adventure, and of the fact that Scottish noblemen were as glad as ever to welcome him to their homes.

Autumn found Burns again writing songs for Thomson, and once again fancying himself in love—on this occasion with Jean Lorimer, the "Chloris" of a few second-rate lyrics. By this time Burns was happier than he had been for some months,—happier, and freer from physical and nervous ailments. Then towards the close of November Mrs. Walter Riddell forgave him and restored him to her good graces; a month later he was appointed Acting Supervisor of Excise, to serve during the illness of Alexander Findlater, his immediate superior. So the year which had begun in gloom and illness came to a distinctly happy end.

During the first three months of 1795 Burns was unusually busy with his Excise duties, for the work of Supervisor was more arduous than that of a gauger. At the same time he was feeling the sharp pinch of financial distress. He was in debt to his landlord, Captain John Hamilton—not because of any financial laxity or indifference, but because in the spring of 1791 he had endorsed a note for a friend named Crombie, and ultimately had been required to pay it.[28] As a result he fell in arrears for his house rent. There followed a period not precisely of estrangement between the two men, who had been warm friends, but of embarrassment on the part of Burns, and of uncertainty on that of Hamilton. In January of 1795 Burns wrote explaining the situation,[29] and saying that a consciousness of his "obscure station in the ranks of life" had kept him from Hamilton's hospitable door.

The probability is that Burns's consciousness of indebtedness, rather than any hesitancy occasioned by his social position, was the actual cause of his aloofness. Memories of the black days at Mount Oliphant and Lochlie were still bitter. To have maintained his financial independence in spite of ill-luck, poor health, and the widespread distress caused by the war, and then to have been overtaken by debt through no fault except generosity to a friend, was galling to the poet's sensitive pride. Fortunately for his self-respect, however, the debt was soon cleared.

During January the situation on the continent, where the chief units of the British army were engaged in the war with France, became so menacing that all but the most confirmed radicals abandoned their revolutionary ideals. Volunteer military organizations sprang up all over the country, called into being by the threat of invasion. Burns followed the general example. On the thirty-first of January, 1795, he joined a group of over sixty of Dumfries's leading citizens in a petition to the War-Office for authority to organize the Royal Dumfries Volunteers.

In this matter of the Volunteers Burns has been the victim of apparently intentional misrepresentation. Allan Cunningham, whose biography of the poet has been almost as influential in establishing the "Burns tradition" as those of Currie and Lockhart, said unqualifiedly that Burns's enrollment in the corps met with "opposition from some of the haughty Tories." [30] The records of the corps, which have been accessible to students in the Ewart Library, Dumfries, since its opening in 1903, show one what the real facts were. Not only was Burns himself one of the organizers of the corps, but till his health broke, at the close of 1795, he was regular in attendance at drills and parades, and for some months served as a member of the committee of five which directed the organization. The Volunteers carried on their roster the names of Dumfries's most respected citizens; membership in the corps was a social distinction. Had Burns been in any sense an unwelcome member, it is inconceivable that he could have had any real share in the activities of such a body.[31] One spirited song, "Does Haughty Gaul Invasion Threat," [32] gave notice to readers far removed from Dumfries that Burns was heartily on the side of King and Country.

The summer saw Burns busy writing lyrics for both Johnson and Thomson; once again he was in song. But early in the autumn misfortunes began to gather around him. His daughter Elizabeth had been taken to Mossgiel in the vain hope that country air would benefit her; during September she died, and so suddenly that Burns was unable to be present at her burial in the Mauchline Churchyard. Then his own health gave way. Throughout December he was a sick man, more seriously ill than he had ever been before. January brought no immediate relief, for a rheumatic fever had fastened itself too firmly upon him to be easily shaken off. From this time to the end of the story, in July of 1796, Burns's existence was clouded by pain and the consciousness of impending disaster.

Such, in brief outline, was Burns's life in Dumfries. Until the final breakdown occurred, he had enjoyed it. He had played an active and honorable part in the life of the town. In

[372]

particular, he had won and retained the friendship of the most intelligent and most representative Dumfriesians; he had made an excellent record in the Excise; he had written much, and much that he wrote takes rank with the best of his earlier work. To say something concerning these three phases of his career in Dumfries, and then to record the incidents of the last six months, will be to complete the chronicle of his life.

3

NEW FRIENDS

Closest to Burns as regards physical proximity, and one of the most helpful of all his Dumfries acquaintances, was John Syme (1755–1831). He was four years older than the poet, had held a commission in the army, and in 1791 had been appointed Distributor of Stamps for Dumfriesshire. He lived across the river in his villa of Ryedale, but his office was on the ground floor of the building in which Burns had his first home. It was but natural that the two men should see one another often. Though from the very nature of the case there was little correspondence between them, it is clear that they soon became warm friends, and were often in one another's company.

By the end of June, 1794, for instance, when Burns made his Galloway tour, Syme was his companion and in a sense his guide. In the same year, when the pot of international politics was boiling furiously, Syme was one of the group that fell into some local disrepute because of liberalism. He was an intelligent observer of foreign affairs, and was discontented with the ultra-conservatism of the government. Like Burns and many another loyal British subject, he winced under the lash of war-time legislation. But he too enrolled in the Dumfries Volunteers, and took an active part in its sessions.

A single sentence in one of Burns's few letters to Syme shows that Syme was interested in poetry as well as in politics, and was in the habit of advising Burns on literary matters:

You know that, among other high dignities, you are my Supreme Court of Critical Judicature, from which there is no appeal.[33]

When the poet's death put an end to all talk about literature and international developments Syme made the arrangements for Burns's funeral. And even before the funeral had taken place he had enlisted the aid of Dr. Maxwell and Alexander Cunningham in raising a fund for Burns's family, and had begun collecting material for the posthumous edition which he knew would be demanded. He assembled much which Dr. Currie could never have discovered, and was in a way as responsible for the success of Currie's *Life and Works of Robert Burns* as the acknowledged editor himself.

In 1829 Syme put on record his impression of Burns's personal charm during the Dumfries years:

The poet's expression varied perpetually, according to the idea that predominated in his mind; and it was beautiful to remark how well the play of his lips indicated the sentiment he was about to utter. His eyes and lips—the first remarkable for fire, and the second for flexibility—formed at all times an index to his mind, and, as sunshine or shade predominated, you might have told, *a priori*, whether the company was to be favoured with a scintillation of wit, or a sentiment of benevolence, or a burst of fiery indignation . . . I cordially concur with what Sir Walter Scott says of the poet's eyes. In his animated moments, and particularly when his anger was roused by instances of tergiversation, meanness, or tyranny, they were *actually like coals of living fire*.[34]

Only once did Syme's acquaintance with Burns result in anything but good to the poet. When Syme was well along in years he recounted to Sir Walter Scott an incident which Scott, accepting the story at its face value, passed on to the public. The story has it that Syme, after a dinner in his own home, rebuked Burns for his fondness for alcohol:

I might have spoken daggers, [said Syme] but I did not mean them. Burns shook to the inmost fibre of his frame, and drew his sword-cane; when I exclaimed: "What! Wilt thou thus, and in mine own house?" The poor fellow was so stung with remorse that he dashed himself down on the floor.[35]

[374]

Thus the "original version" of the anecdote. Others were later set afoot, differing in details from Syme's account, but, like it, representing Burns as having drawn his exciseman's sword-cane upon his friend. The probability is that nothing of the sort ever happened. Syme did not "remember" the incident till long after Burns's death, when the myth-making concerning the poet was in full swing, and when anyone who had ever seen the poet felt at liberty to exercise his ingenuity in setting afloat new pieces of gossip concerning him.

Except in this one instance, however, which may be pardoned in an old man looking back over years long gone by, Syme was as true and loyal a friend as Burns ever had. He did much to make Burns's life in Dumfries happy; after the poet's death he took the lead in the two movements that were to ensure Burns's widow and children against poverty.

Throughout the last ten years of his life, Burns lived in close association with members of the medical profession; after his death it was a Liverpool physician, Dr. James Currie, who edited his collected works, and wrote the first adequate biography. That the poet should know many medical men was inevitable, for he was never in robust health, and turned for advice to the persons best qualified to give it. But even had he been free from all physical discomforts he would still have been found associating with members of the learned professions. His intellectual life was not that of the average Scottish farmer or exciseman. It was the liberal ministers, the lawyers, and—naturally enough—the physicians, whom he found unfailingly congenial. Hence when he moved to Dumfries it was natural for him to seek associates in these same circles.

The physician most closely connected with Burns's last years was Dr. William Maxwell (1760–1834), a Scot who had received his medical education in France, and who had become so enthusiastic over the French Revolution that he joined the Republican army and actually served as one of the guards at the execution of Louis XVI. He was well enough known to have been the subject of a casual remark by Burke in the House of

Commons. But early in 1794, having had his fill of bloodshed, he returned to Scotland and began the practise of his profession at Dumfries. He had experienced no violent anti-Jacobin reaction; on the contrary, he still retained his faith in the fundamental principles which underlay the Revolution, and became a leader in the small group of Dumfries liberals with whom Burns and Syme were associated. He did not join the Volunteer Corps, but took no exceptionable action adverse to the government.[86]

As was true of Burns and Syme, Burns and Maxwell were near neighbors. There are not many written documents testifying to their friendship, for letters did not pass between them. But we know that Maxwell, like Syme, welcomed Burns to his home, and that Burns appreciated the friendly hospitality and good talk which he found there. We know that Maxwell was Burns's physician during the last two years of his life, and that his attention not only to Burns himself but to the entire family was of such a nature that the child born to Mrs. Burns the day of her husband's funeral was named Maxwell. We know that Maxwell joined Syme and Cunningham in their efforts to provide for Burns's family. So one may safely say that though Maxwell's medical skill was no greater than that of the ordinary Scottish physician of the time, his personal affection for Burns, and his whole-hearted devotion to his interests, warrant one in thinking of him as one of the poet's most loyal friends.

Six months before Burns moved to Dumfries, Alexander Findlater (1754–1839) had been appointed Supervisor of the Dumfries Excise district. He thus became the poet's immediate superior in the service, and was in a position to observe his official life, at least, with complete accuracy. As Findlater himself afterwards put it,

My connection with Robert Burns commenced immediately after his admission into the Excise, and continued to the hour of his death. In all that time the superintendance of his behaviour, as an officer of the revenue, was a branch of my especial province, and it may be supposed I would not be an inattentive observer of the *general* conduct of a man and a poet so celebrated by his countrymen.[87]

The relationship between the men was at first purely official. Burns reported to Findlater, and there the matter might have stopped. Indeed, Burns's first letter to Findlater, written from Ellisland, shows that the Supervisor was strict in scrutiny of his subordinate's actions. It is of enough interest to be reproduced, for it gives an illuminating first-hand glimpse into Burns's official life:

DEAR SIR:

I am both much surprised & vexed at that accident of Lorimer's Stock. —The last survey I made prior to Mr. Lorimer's going to Edinr. I was very particular in my inspection & the quantity was certainly in his possession as I stated it.—The surveys I have made during his absence might as well have been marked "key absent" as I never found anybody but the lady, who I know is not mistress of keys, etc. to know anything of it, and one of the times it would have rejoiced all Hell to have seen her so drunk. I have not surveyed there since his return.—I know the gentleman's ways are, like the grace of G——, past all comprehension; but I shall give the house a severe scrutiny tomorrow morning & send you in the naked facts.—

I know, Sir, & regret deeply that this business glances with a malign aspect on my character as an Officer; but as I am really innocent in the affair, & as the gentleman is known to be an illicit Dealer, & particularly as this is the *single* instance of the least shadow of carelessness or impropriety in my conduct as an Officer, I shall be peculiarly unfortunate if my character shall fall a sacrifice to the dark maneouvres of a Smuggler.—

I send you some rhymes I have just finished which tickle my fancy a little.[88]

It would be unprofitable to follow the two friends through the entire period of their acquaintanceship. But two instances of Findlater's regard for the poet and devotion to his interests must be recorded. When Burns's "principles" were being investigated by the Excise Board, Findlater was quick to speak in his behalf. When, after Burns's death, he was being accused of chronic alcoholism, Findlater again came to his defence.

The opportunity to do Burns this service arose in 1815, when Alexander Peterkin reprinted Currie's first edition, on which the British copyright had just expired. To the long introduction prefixed to this reprint, Findlater contributed a letter testifying to Burns's habitual sobriety, and to his general excellence as an officer. Evidence of this sort, coming from one who had known Burns intimately during the last six years of his life, may fairly be considered of greater significance than unsubstantiated gossip.

Findlater, then, should be remembered not only as Burns's superior officer in the Excise, but as a friend who did much to assist him while he lived, and, after his death, to clear his name from charges which ignorance and malice had set on foot.

Just as in Edinburgh Burns had found himself in pleasant contact with members of the University and High School faculties, so in Dumfries he numbered among his associates at least two of the instructors in the Burgh school, James Gray and Thomas White. Gray (d. 1830), an ordained minister, Latin Master and *ipso facto* Rector of the Dumfries Academy from 1794 to 1801, and a fellow-member with Burns in the Volunteer Corps, was in many respects unlike Syme or Findlater; but like them he loved the poet well.

There is virtually nothing in the written records of Burns's life to show that he and Gray were even fellow townsmen; but in 1815, Gray, like Findlater, wrote for Peterkin's reprint of Currie an eloquent letter in defence of the dead poet. This letter makes it clear that Gray knew Burns intimately, and esteemed him as highly as had the University men in Edinburgh. Moreover, Gray was the first person to suggest that if Burns had been as debauched as some of his critics accused him of being, he could hardly have written the amount of poetry which came from his pen during the last years of his life. The following paragraph is perhaps the most pertinent section of this letter:

Not many days passed during [Burns's] stay in Dumfries, in which he did not compose some piece of poetry, or some song, destined to delight the imagination and soften the heart for ages to come.

[378]

It was during the last years of his life that he erected the most lasting monument of his genius, by composing those numberless lyrical effusions that enrich Mr. Thomson's collection; which, for simplicity, pathos, truth to nature, and a fine adaptation to the heart-stirring melodies of our native land, are unrivalled in any language. It came under my own view professionally, that he superintended the education of his children with a degree of care that I have never seen surpassed by any parent in any rank of life whatever. In the bosom of his family he spent many a delightful hour in directing the studies of his eldest son, a boy of uncommon talents. I have frequently found him explaining to this youth, then not more than nine years of age, the English poets, from Shakespeare to Gray, or storing his mind with examples of heroic virtue, as they live in the pages of our more celebrated English historians. I would ask any person of common candour, if employments like these are consistent with habitual drunkenness? [39]

Such comment, made by a man whose position might have warranted his assuming a slightly patronizing attitude towards the poet, is worth even more than that of Findlater, who would possibly have stretched a point in defence of a fellow exciseman. [40]

When Gray's colleague, Thomas White (1758–1825), was buried in St. Michael's Churchyard, Dumfries, not many rods from Burns's grave, the stone erected to his memory recorded the fact that he was "a profound and original mathematician, who taught in the Dumfries Academy forty years, and instructed hundreds who revere his memory." [41] Burns knew him, and enjoyed associating with him; in 1793 he presented to him a copy of his recently published two-volume edition, "as a mark of the most sincere Friendship." [42] It was traditional with White's descendants that Burns was a guest at White's home every Saturday; and though one searches the record in vain for any allusions to this pleasant custom, it is indisputable that White welcomed Burns as a friend and an equal. He did not do much to promote Burns's literary work; his one published comment on Burns was a poem, "A Tribute to the Memory of Burns." But he was one of the leading citizens of Dumfries, a lieutenant in the Volunteer Corps, and was glad to call the poet his friend at a time when according to some biographers Burns was living in disreputable isolation. For this reason, if for no other, White deserves mention in this chronicle.[43]

Once when writing to Peter Hill, Burns listed several acquaintances to whom he wished Hill to present his regards. Among this group was Alexander Cunningham:

> Among our common friends, I must not forget one of the dearest of them, Cunningham.[44]

Though Cunningham (d. 1812) and Burns had met during the poet's months in Edinburgh, not till the Ellisland and Dumfries days are there any letters testifying to their friendship. From this time to the end of the story, however, Cunningham's name appears in the record as often as anyone's.

For example, Cunningham was one of the first persons to whom Burns wrote from the Isle. The letter, containing an account of Burns's marriage, and of the reasons that prompted him to take the step, is not the sort one would send to a casual acquaintance.[45] Cunningham's own love affairs play a part in the correspondence. When he was unexpectedly jilted, Burns sent him a pleasant and amusing letter of condolence. When, three and a half years later, he was married, Burns wrote in his best vein, congratulating him on his good fortune, and making this half-serious analysis of wifely virtues:

> Apropos, how do you like, I mean *really* like, the Married Life?—Ah, my Friend! ·Matrimony is quite a different thing from what your love-sick youths & sighing girls take it to be!—But Marriage, we are told, is appointed by G— & I shall never quarrel with any of *His* Institutions.— I am a Husband of older standing than you, & I shall give you *my* ideas of the Conjugal State—(En passant, you know I am no Latin, is not "Conjugal" derived from "Jugum" a yoke?).—Well then, the scale of Good-wifeship I divide into ten parts—Good-Nature, four; Good-Sense two; Wit, one; Personal Charms, viz. a sweet face, eloquent eyes, fine limbs, graceful carriage (I would add a fine waist too, but that is so soon spoilt you know), all these, one; as for the other·qualities, . . . divide the two remaining degrees among them as you please.[46]

When Burns was being examined by the Excise Board, he eased his mind by writing to Cunningham:

[380]

What are you doing, what hurry have you got on your hands, my dear Cunningham, that I have not heard from you? Are you deeply engaged in the mazes of Law, the mysteries of Love, or in the profound wisdom of modern politics?—Curse on the word which ended the period!

Quere, What is Politics?

Answer, Politics is a science wherewith, by means of nefarious cunning, & hypocritical pretence, we govern civil Polities for the emolument of ourselves & our adherents.

Quere, What is a Minister?

Answer, A Minister is an unprincipled fellow, who by the influence of hereditary, or acquired wealth; by superiour abilities; or by a lucky conjuncture of circumstances, obtains a principal place in the administration of the affairs of government.—

Q. What is a Patriot?

A. An individual exactly of the same description as a Minister, only, out of place.—

I have been interrupted in my Catechism, & am returned at a late hour, just to subscribe my name; to put you in mind that there is a forgotten friend of yours of that name, still in the land of the living, though I can scarcely say, in the place of hope.[47]

So the story went. From the time Burns moved to Ellisland, in the spring of 1788, till the spring of 1794, there are letters in abundance,—genial, friendly, intimate. After that date the actual letters are few, but there was no rift in the friendship. Two weeks before Burns's death he sent Cunningham a detailed account of his health, asked his aid in securing full salary from the Excise Board, and added this sentence indicative of the regard he felt for the Edinburgh attorney:

Mrs. Burns threatens in a week or two to add one more to my Paternal charge, which, if of the right gender, I intend shall be introduced to the world by the respectable designation of Alexr. Cunningham Burns. My last was James Glencairn, so you can have no objection to the company of Nobility.[48]

Cunningham's friendship did much to add happiness to Burns's last years; after the poet's death Cunningham was prompt in associating himself with Syme and Maxwell in launching the two projects which saved the poet's family from poverty. the public subscription for their benefit, and Dr. Currie's collected edition of Burns's works. It is perhaps no overstatement to say that he was one of the few men who best understood and most whole-heartedly admired the poet, and also one of the small group to whom the poet himself owed most during his last years.

This by no means completes the list of Burns's friends at Dumfries. There was John Lewars, for instance, a fellow Exciseman, whom Burns called a "particular friend," and who attended to much of the necessary correspondence at the time of the poet's death, and did for the family those things that only such a friend could have done. There was James Gracie, the banker, who towards the close of Burns's life put his carriage at the poet's disposal,[49] and Samuel Clarke, Jr., Commissary Clerk for the Shire, to whom Burns appealed for aid when an unlucky toast had been ill-received by certain military officers. Gabriel Richardson, the brewer, who later became Provost of Dumfries, was like Collector Mitchell a "friend of the poet, tried and leal." At his home Burns "frequently spent a few hours on Sabbath evenings, . . . besides looking in on week days occasionally."[50] These were all substantial, conservative members of the upper middle class, who not only admitted Burns as a guest in their homes on special occasions, but also welcomed him on the most intimate and familiar terms.

Thanks to these men, there was distinctly more social life for Burns than there had been at Ellisland. Though by comparison with Edinburgh, Dumfries may have seemed somewhat provincial, still Burns was a country-man at heart, used to the ways of simple folk, and happy if they thought him worth knowing. The evenings spent in the Globe Inn, where John and Meg Hyslop were landlord and hostess and where pretty Anne Park had drawn the wine, or in friendly talk with Gray or Richardson at their homes, may well have been as full of satisfaction as the more brilliant ones spent in company of the "great folk" at Edinburgh.

[382]

And then—inevitably—there were women who found Burns's personality fascinating, and who persistently sought his companionship. There was Clarinda, welcoming him to Dumfries with her disturbing letter about Jenny Clow, and before long resuming the correspondence in the vein of "the golden dream of 1788." There was Mrs. Dunlop, solicitous as ever for the poet's welfare, till early in 1795, when his outbursts concerning the French Revolution put an end to her letter writing. Their stories have already been told; it is enough to recall the fact that Burns did not lose touch with them when he moved to Dumfries. Then there was Anne Park, mother of one of Burns's children—or at least, Anne Park may still have been with her aunt at the Globe Inn, though no one seems able to say what became of the poor girl after the birth of her daughter. But in addition to these acquaintances of the earlier days there were three other women who must be mentioned: Jean Lorimer, Jessy Lewars, and Mrs. Walter Riddell.

Jean Lorimer, the "Chloris" of the lyrics sent Thomson, was the eldest daughter of the William Lorimer whose propensity for evading the Revenue laws caused Burns some uneasiness. She had been born at Craigieburn, in 1775. When Burns first moved to Ellisland she was living in her father's home, within two miles of Burns's farm. Here the poet first saw her—a girl of fifteen or sixteen years, known already for the beauty of her face, and the "lint-white" locks of her flaxen hair. She was being courted by one of Burns's friends, a young man named Gillespie; to aid him in his suit (a vain one, as it proved), Burns wrote in praise of Jean the first version of "Craigieburn Wood." Then, apparently, he forgot about the girl till she had had an experience somewhat analogous to Clarinda's. In March of 1793 she made a runaway match with a young tenant farmer from Moffat named Whelpdale. Within a few months her husband was a fugitive and a bankrupt, and Jean had returned to her father's home. Here she saw the poet often, and before long his friendship for her had grown into at least a close approxima-

[383]

tion to love. Writing to Findlater, in September of 1794, Burns said:

I have been among the Angelic World, this forenoon.—Ah!

"had ye but been where I hae been,
"Ye wad hae been sae canty, O!"

But don't be afraid . . . I am in the clouds elsewhere—

"Ah, Chloris, could I now but sit
"As unconcerned as when
"Your infant beauty could beget
"Nor happiness nor pain."—

Let Yesternight—Oh yesternight!

"Kist yestreen—kist yestreen—
"O, as she was kist yestreen,—
"I'll never forget while the hollin grows green
"The bonie sweet Lassie I kist yestreen."—[51]

There then follows the song, "Lassie wi' the Lint-white Locks."

A month later, in a letter to Thomson, Burns told more concerning Chloris. Apropos of the song "Craigieburn Wood" he wrote:

The Lady on whom it was made, is one of the finest women in Scotland; & in fact (entre nous) is in a manner to me what Sterne's Eliza was to him—a Mistress, or Friend, or what you will, in the guileless simplicity of Platonic love.—(Now don't put any of your squinting construction on this, or have any clishmaclaiver about it among our acquaintances.)—I assure you that to my lovely Friend you are indebted for many of your best songs of mine.—Do you think that the sober, gin-horse routine of existence could inspire a man with life, & love, & joy—could fire him with enthusiasm, or melt him with pathos, equal to the genius of your Book?—No, No!!!—Whenever I want to be more than ordinary *in song;* to be in some degree equal to your diviner airs; do you imagine I fast & pray for the celestial emanation?—Tout au contraire! I have a glorious recipe, the very one that for his own use was invented by the Divinity of Healing & Poesy when erst he piped to the flocks of

Admetus.—I put myself in the regimen of admiring a fine woman; & in proportion to the adorability of her charms, in proportion you are delighted with my verses."[52]

An interesting letter—written in Burns's best vein: half banter, half seriousness, and good evidence not alone of the way Burns wrote love songs, but also of the fact that for the time being Chloris was occupying a large part of his affections. By September of 1794 he had given her a copy of the 1793 two-volume edition of his poems, with the six stanzas of "To Chloris" inscribed on a blank leaf; in November of the same year he gave her the first number, or half volume—all that had as yet been published, or was to be published during Burns's lifetime—of Thomson's *Select Scotish Airs*.

But with the coming of 1795, Burns found himself busy about other affairs than song-writing, and Chloris's name appears infrequently in the remaining records. For nearly two years, however, she had added a touch of color and brightness to Burns's world; and though the poetry composed in her honor is but mediocre, one is grateful to her for having brought happiness into a life that was so soon to be wrapped in shadow.[53]

It was the good fortune of Jessy Lewars (1778–1855), to be Burns's nurse and companion during his last illness. She was the sister of his fellow Exciseman, John Lewars. Though only eighteen years old at the time of Burns's death, she befriended both the poet and his wife in a fashion as unique as it was helpful. Inevitably Burns imagined himself in love with her. The verses beginning "Altho' thou maun never be mine"[54] show him once again putting himself "in the regimen of admiring a fine woman," as he had expressed it; incidentally, they evince no slight degree of lyric skill. But there is relatively little verse to record this friendship: a pleasant inscription in a volume of the *Museum* presented to Jessy, an epigram or two, deft and complimentary, and the song already mentioned. Once, however, during the closing weeks of the poet's life, the dying flame burned with all its old-time brilliance. After listening while Jessy played for him on her piano the melody "The Robin Came

[385]

to the Wren's Nest," Burns wrote in her honor the song "O Wert Thou in the Cauld Blast"—a lyric that would have done credit to him at any period of his career. It is not literally Burns's last poetic composition, but it is his last one of distinction. And characteristically it was a product of the same formula that had occasioned the earliest of his boyish attempts, "Handsome Nell": a scrap of an old tune, and a pretty girl. The poetry is far better, now, than that which the boy had written after his harvest-field experience with Nelly Kilpatrick, but the formula is the same.

Long after Jessy Lewars had done what she could to make the dying poet comfortable, and to care for his widow and her new-born son, she entrusted Dr. Chambers with some of her recollections concerning Burns's Dumfries household. Chambers paraphrased her account thus:

As far as circumstances left Burns to his own inclinations, his personal domestic habits were generally simple and temperate. As he was often detained by company from the dinner provided for him by his wife, she sometimes, on a conjecture of his probable absence, would not prepare that meal for him. When he chanced to come home, and find no dinner ready, he was never in the least troubled or irritated, but would address himself with the greatest cheerfulness to any succedaneum that could be readily set before him. They generally had abundance of good Dunlop cheese, sent to them by their Ayrshire friends. The poet would sit down to that wholesome fare, with bread and butter, and his book by his side, and seem to any casual visitor as happy as a courtier at the feast of kings.

He was always anxious that his wife should have a neat and genteel appearance. In consequence, as she alleged, of the duties of nursing, and attending to her infants, she could not help being sometimes a little out of order. Burns disliked this, and not only remonstrated against it in a gentle way, but did the utmost that in him lay to counteract it, by buying for her the best clothes he could afford. Any little novelty in female dress was almost sure to meet with patronage from Burns—all with the aim of keeping up a spirit for neat dressing in his wife. She was, for instance, one of the first persons in Dumfries who appeared in a dress of gingham—a stuff now common, but, at its first introduction, rather costly, and almost exclusively used by persons of superior condition.[55]

[386]

Pleasantly feminine comment, this—with its homely details about arrangements for dinner, and its suggestion of criticism concerning Jean's personal neatness. Only a woman who had been an intimate member of Burns's household could have written thus. And that is precisely what Jessy Lewars was, at a time when both the poet and his wife most needed her friendly ministrations.

But the woman who meant most to Burns during the Dumfries years was Mrs. Walter Riddell (1772–1808). The story of his friendship with her is the story of a companionship broken for a time by an unfortunate incident, but reëstablished shortly before Burns's death, and witnessed by Mrs. Riddell's appreciative character-sketch of the man who had both loved and insulted her.

Maria Woodley, the daughter of William Woodley, had been born in London, on November 4, 1772. In April of 1788 she sailed for the West Indies, where her father was governor of the Leeward Islands. Here, on September 16, 1790, she married Walter Riddell, younger brother of Robert Riddell of Glenriddell. By midsummer of 1791 she was back in London, where her first child was soon to be born. In May of the next year her husband purchased an estate four miles from Dumfries, which he named Woodley Park. Here he and his young wife welcomed Burns as enthusiastically as Robert Riddell had done at Friar's Carse. Mrs. Riddell was young, talented, beautiful; she was interested in things literary; she had a flair for writing verses about equal to Clarinda's in merit; she was at work on a book which she later published under the title *Voyages to the Madeira and Leeward Islands*. She found the poet a friendly critic and a fascinating companion, and not only took him completely into her confidence as literary advisor, but invited him often to Woodley Park, and visited him in his home at Dumfries.

She had probably first met Burns at her brother-in-law's home, Friar's Carse, late in the year 1791, shortly after Burns had seen Clarinda for the last time. The earliest time Mrs. Riddell's name appears in the record, however, is in January of 1792,

[387]

when the poet wrote for her a letter of introduction to his Edinburgh friend, William Smellie.   She wished to consult the eccentric old naturalist with reference to her manuscript.   This is
what Burns said of his new-found friend:

> Mrs. Riddell who takes this letter to town with her, is a Character
> that even in your own way, as a Naturalist & a Philosopher, would be an
> acquisition to your acquaintance.   The Lady, too, is a votary of the
> Muses; and as I think I am somewhat of a judge in my own trade, I
> assure you that her verses, always correct, & often elegant, are very
> much beyond the common run of the Lady Poetesses of the day. . . .
> Lest you should think of a lively West-Indian girl of eighteen, as girls
> of eighteen too often deserve to be thought of, I should take care to re-
> move that prejudice.—To be impartial, however, the Lady has one un-
> lucky failing; a failing which you will easily discover, as she seems rather
> pleased with indulging it; & a failing which you will as easily pardon,
> as it is a sin that very much besets yourself:—where she dislikes, or
> despises, she is apt to make no more a secret of it—than where she
> esteems & respects.[56]

Eight days after receiving this letter of introduction, Mrs.
Riddell joined Burns and a few other persons in a tour of the
lead mines at Wanlockhead, and in a letter recounting the day's
adventures referred to the poet's "interesting remarks and fascinating conversation."   Within a month Burns and Mrs. Riddell were engaged in correspondence.   Burns's first letter opens
with the salutation "My dearest friend," and continues: "Yours
by Mr. Stoddart was the welcomest letter I ever received." [57]
By the early autumn of 1792 the two were on such intimate terms
that Mrs. Riddell was warning Burns against what her brother-
in-law Robert might say about her.   Then, like Clarinda, she
asked Burns to call upon her.   An undated letter of Burns's is
of interest as evidence that once again it was the woman who was
seeking the man's company:

> I will wait on you, my ever-valued Friend, but whether in the morn-
> ing, I am not sure.—Sunday closes a period of our cursed revenue busi-
> ness, & may probably keep me employed with my pen untill Noon.—Fine
> employment for a Poet's pen!

Then, after some sentences concerning his melancholy state of mind, Burns added:

> If my resentment is awaked, it is sure to be where it dare not squeak; & if in LOVE, as, God forgive me! I sometimes am; Impossibility presents an impervious barrier to the proudest daring of Presumption, & poor I, dare much sooner peep into the focus of Hell, than meet the eye of the goddess of my soul! [58]

Clearly enough Burns would have found it easy to adopt with Mrs. Riddell the tone of the letters to Clarinda.

The spring of 1793 saw the two persons often in one another's company. Apparently Mrs. Riddell grew exacting in her demands upon the poet. Like Clarinda, she took him to task for his coldness. Unfortunately her letters to him have not been preserved, but it is easy to read between the lines of his replies. For example:

> I have often told you, my Dear Friend, that you had a spice of Caprice in your composition, & you have as often disavowed it; even perhaps while your opinions were, at the moment, irrefragably proving it.— Could *anything* estrange me from a Friend such as you?—No!—Tomorrow, I shall have the honor of waiting on you.—
>
> Farewell, thou first of Friends, & most accomplished of Women, even with all thy little caprices!!! [59]

Shortly after the receipt of this letter Mrs. Riddell went to London with her husband. In June he sailed for the West Indies; in July his wife returned alone to Woodley Park. At once she sent for Burns, whose company she preferred to that of the officers of the infantry regiment then stationed at Dumfries. Sometimes the poet found his path blocked by military interference:

> I meant to have called on you yesternight, but as I edged up [to] your Box-door, the first object which greeted my view was one of these lobster-coated Puppies, sitting, like another dragon, guarding the Hesperian fruit.—On Sunday I shall have the pleasure and honor of assuring you, in propria persona, how sincerely
>
> I am yours
>
> R B [60]

[389]

So it went for some months, Burns happy in the esteem of a young and beautiful woman, and the woman proud of her hold upon the most brilliant and most companionable man she had ever known.

Then, suddenly, before Walter Riddell had returned from the West Indies, the friendship thus established was all but irreparably shattered. No one today seems able to tell precisely what Burns's offense was, or when the unfortunate affair took place. All one knows is that the morning after having been a guest at a dinner, probably given by Robert Riddell and his wife at Friar's Carse late in December, 1793,[61] Burns wrote thus to his hostess:

MADAM:

I daresay that this is the first epistle you ever received from this nether world. I write you from the regions of Hell, amid the horrors of the damned. The time and manner of my leaving your earth I do not exactly know, as I took my departure in the heat of a fever of intoxication, contracted at your too hospitable mansion.

After half a paragraph of overwrought metaphor, the penitent finally came to the point:

To the men of the company I will make no apology.—Your husband, who insisted on my drinking more than I chose, has no right to blame me; and the other gentlemen were partakers of my guilt. But to you, Madam, I have much to apologize. Your good opinion I valued as one of the greatest acquisitions I had made on earth, and I was truly a beast to forfeit it. There was a Miss I—— too, a woman of fine sense, gentle and unassuming manners—do make, on my part, a miserable, d-mned wretch's best apology to her. A Mrs. G——, a charming woman, did me the honor to be prejudiced in my favor; this makes me hope that I have not outraged her beyond all forgiveness.—To all the other ladies please present my humblest contrition for my conduct, and my petition for their gracious pardon. . . .

Forgive the offenses, and pity the perdition of, Madam,

Your humble Slave.[62]

This letter has traditionally been printed as addressed to Mrs. Walter Riddell, though no definite indication of the addressee survives. The reference to "your husband," however, makes it clear that some one else was the recipient, for Walter Riddell was still in the West Indies.[63] It was probably sent to Maria's sister-in-law.

Despite this apology, the entire Riddell family felt itself insulted, and was unforgiving. Maria, indeed, seems at first to have been somewhat lenient; but she took umbrage at the poet's attitude, and "cut" him on the street. Burns replied by writing the "Monody on a Lady Famed for her Caprice." It was an ungallant set of verses, concluding with the following "Epitaph":

> Here lies, now a prey to insulting neglect,
>   What once was a butterfly, gay in life's beam:
> Want only of wisdom denied her respect;
>   Want only of goodness denied her esteem.[64]

Fortunately for Burns's reputation, there is much doubt as to whether the equally regrettable "Epistle from Esopus to Maria" is actually his work.[65] If he wrote it, and permitted it to circulate in Dumfries, the only apology one can make for him is to recall the fact that the winter of 1794, when this unfortunate quarrel was going on, was a time of illness accompanied by a severe nervous breakdown. Even so, however, the poet should have remained silent. But it was not in his nature to be charitable towards a woman who was refusing to forgive him. He went out of his way to tell Clarinda something of the story, and to entrust her with a copy of the "Monody," and of the even more ill-natured "Lines Pinned to Mrs. Riddell's Coach."[66]

Meantime Walter Riddell, who had returned from abroad in late March or April, 1794, found himself unable to complete the payments for his Woodley Park estate. Accordingly it was offered for sale, and was repurchased by the previous owner, Goldie. The Riddells remained in the neighborhood of Dumfries, however, and by November of 1794 both Burns and Mrs. Riddell found the bitterness waning. A sentimental trio of stanzas which the poet sent her, "Canst Thou Leave me Thus, my Katy,"[67] elicited an equally sentimental reply, "Stay, my

Willie, yet Believe me." [68] In March of 1795, she made Burns
a present of a book, accompanied by another poetic expression of
regret and regard. By August the breach between the two was
completely closed, for Burns was "perusing with great pleasure
[her] elegiac verses," pronouncing them "brilliant," and "scolding" her for making such a despotic use of her power over men.

In the autumn of 1795, after the death of Burns's daughter
Elizabeth Riddell (named in honor of Mrs. Robert Riddell),
the poet again apologized for not having replied to all of Maria's
letters:

> A severe domestic misfortune has put all literary business out of my
> head for some time past.—Now I begin to resume my wonted studies.—
> I am much correspondence in your debt: I shall pay it soon.[69]

But Mrs. Riddell was not destined to receive many more communications from Burns. By December of 1795 his health was
giving way; after that date the few months of life that were left
to him were shadowed by the illness which sent him to his grave.
Apparently Mrs. Riddell was ignorant of his serious condition,
for in June of 1796 she invited him to attend the Assembly to
be held in honor of the King's birthday. Burns's letter, the last
he ever wrote to her, speaks eloquently concerning his physical
and mental condition:

> I am in such miserable health as to be utterly incapable of shewing my
> loyalty in any way.—Rackt as I am with rheumatisms, I meet every face
> with a greeting like that of Balak to Balaam—"Come, curse me Jacob;
> & come, defy me Israel!". . .
>
> I may perhaps see you on Saturday, but I will not be at the Ball.—
> Why should I?—"Man delights not me, nor woman neither!" Can
> you supply me with the Song, "Let us all be unhappy together?" Do, if
> you can, & oblige le pauvre miserable.[70]

A month later, when Burns was making a final attempt to regain his health at Brow, Mrs. Riddell, who at the time was living not far away, invited him to dine with her, and sent her carriage to bring him to her lodgings. Not long afterwards she
wrote thus to a friend:

I was struck with his appearance on entering the room. The stamp of death was imprinted on his features. He seemed already touching the brink of eternity. His first salutation was: "Well, Madam, have you any commands for the other world?" I replied, that it seemed a doubtful case which of us should be there soonest, and that I hoped he would yet live to write my epitaph. He looked in my face with an air of great kindness, and expressed his concern at seeing me look so ill. . . . He shewed great concern about the care of his literary fame, and particularly the publication of his posthumous works. He said he was well aware that his death would occasion some noise, and that every scrap of his writing would be revived against him to the injury of his future reputation: that letters and verses written with unguarded and improper freedom, and which he earnestly wished to have buried in oblivion, would be handed about by idle vanity or malevolence, when no dread of his resentment would restrain them, or prevent the censures of shrill-tongued malice. . . .

He lamented that he had written many epigrams on persons against whom he entertained no enmity, and whose characters he should be sorry to wound. . . . I had seldom seen his mind greater or more collected. There was frequently a considerable degree of vivacity in his sallies, and they would probably have had a greater share, had not the concern and dejection I could not disguise damped the spirit of pleasantry he seemed not unwilling to indulge.

We parted about sunset on the evening of that day (the 5th of July, 1796): the next day I saw him again, and we parted to meet no more! [71]

Though Mrs. Riddell may have displayed a little malice towards Burns immediately after the unfortunate dinner, she showed only the most considerate regard for him during his last months and after his death. Indeed, so far as extant records go, she never committed to paper anything in derogation of the man whose companionship she had sought, whatever she may have said to her friends in moments of understandable chagrin. On the contrary, hardly was Burns in his grave when she wrote a generous and sympathetic character sketch of him for the Dumfries *Weekly Journal*, and thus won the distinction of being the first person to publish a memoir of the poet. Based on intimate personal acquaintance, this sketch may well be considered the most reliable source of accurate, first-hand information concerning Burns's character and demeanor during his last five years.[72]

With this friendly tribute Mrs. Riddell bade farewell to Burns. Like Clarinda and Mrs. Dunlop she had sought his acquaintance; like them she had fallen under the spell of his personality; like them, too, she had been estranged by actions which later she forgave. And as one reads between the lines one finds the conclusion inescapable that she too, like Clarinda, loved the poet well.

Such, then, were the companionships that enriched Burns's life at Dumfries. As had been true in Mauchline and Edinburgh, his friends were drawn from no one social group or class; many sort of persons found him interesting and stimulating. They sought his companionship, and to each he gave generously of himself—too generously, at times; for there was alcohol a-plenty, and the sessions at the Globe Inn, or in the homes of Lorimer or Findlater, sometimes lasted too long. But not till death was almost upon him did this zest for living, this joy in sharing his life with others, show any diminution. He loved men and women, and found his chief happiness in associating with them, as he had done throughout all the years of his mature life.

4

THE DUMFRIES EXCISEMAN

The sober business of life during Burns's residence at Dumfries, was, of course, the Excise. Enough has already been said concerning his relations to the service to show that by the autumn of 1791, after two years of active duty, he had a thoroughly commendable record to his credit. Furthermore, he was satisfied with his prospects. "The Excise . . . is the business for me.—I find no difficulty in being an honest man in it," he wrote to Cleghorn just before leaving Ellisland.[73] He had been transferred from the arduous "Dumfries first itinerancy," where he had to ride two hundred miles a week, to the "Dumfries third division," a district that lay entirely within the town, and which annually brought in some twenty pounds more than his first assignment. Early in 1791 he had been recommended for promotion to an "Examiner and Supervisorship." Furthermore, he had won the friendship and respect of his superiors in the service. Findlater, the Dumfries Supervisor, was one of his intimate friends; Mitchell, the Collector, had already "entered with the most friendly ardour into [his] views and interests." [74] William Corbet, one of the two general Supervisors for Scotland, had become interested in Burns through Mrs. Dunlop, [75] and was in a position to be of assistance to him. And Robert Graham of Fintry, member of the all-powerful Excise Board, was Burns's firm friend, always ready to do what he could to further his interests. So when the poet moved to Dumfries he was as well fortified with influential allies as a member of the service could hope to be. Clearly he had no grounds for complaint, so far as his decision to give up farming and live entirely on his Excise salary was concerned.

So it was as a gauger in the town of Dumfries that Burns began the last period of his life: "surveying" stocks of taxable articles, collecting the revenues due the government, reporting defaulters and delinquents, and occasionally seizing a small quantity of smuggled tea, silk, or spirits.

Lockhart, indeed, represents Burns as having at this time figured prominently in the dramatic capture of a smuggling vessel, the brig *Rosamond*. The story has become so generally current that some attention must be paid to it. The material parts of Lockhart's account are these:

On the 27th of February [1792] a suspicious-looking brig was discovered in the Solway Frith, and Burns was one of the party whom the Superintendent conducted to watch her motions. She got into shallow water the day afterwards, and the officers were enabled to discover that her crew were numerous, armed, and not likely to yield without a struggle. Lewars, a brother Exciseman, an intimate friend of our poet, was accordingly sent to Dumfries for a guard of dragoons; the superintendent, Mr. Crawford, proceeded himself on a similar errand to

Ecclefechan, and Burns was left with some men under his orders, to watch the brig and prevent landing or escape. From the private journal of one of the excisemen (now in my hands) it appears that Burns manifested considerable impatience while thus occupied, being left for many hours in a wet salt-marsh, with a force which he knew to be inadequate for the purpose it was meant to fulfil. One of his comrades hearing him abuse his friend Lewars in particular, for being slow about his journey, the man answered that he also wished the devil had him for his pains, and that Burns in the meantime would do well to indite a song upon the sluggard: Burns said nothing; but after taking a few strides by himself among the reeds and shingle, rejoined his party, and chanted to them the well-known ditty "The Deil's run awa wi' the Exciseman." Lewars arrived shortly afterwards with his dragoons; and Burns, putting himself at their head, waded, sword in hand, to the brig, and was the first to board her. The crew lost heart and submitted, though their numbers were greater than those of the assailing force. The vessel was condemned, and, with all her arms and stores, sold by auction next day at Dumfries: upon which occasion, Burns, whose behaviour had been highly commended, thought fit to purchase four carronades by way of trophy.[76]

No more picturesque legend was ever invented by the ingenious brain of a romantic biographer. One has but to visualize the scene to realize its utter impossibility: a smuggling brig "in shallow water" attacked by a squadron of cavalrymen with Burns at their head; boarded, captured, condemned, sold as a prize—and all within twenty-four hours. The whole thing would do full justice to Gilbert and Sullivan.

If the stark impossibility of the affair is not at once apparent to the reader, he should recall the fact that no mention of any such incident has ever been found in the carefully scrutinized records of the Excise Board, and that Burns himself made no allusion to it in any of his correspondence, but said explicitly that he composed the song "The Deil's Awa" "at one of [Mr. Mitchell's] Excise Court dinners." [77]

Once put into circulation, however, the fiction grew. Joseph Train, an antiquary with imaginative propensities, represented himself as having seen the private diary of Superintendent Crawford, and as having found there an account of the seizure and sale of the vessel, the brig *Rosamond*, by Burns himself; and a document written by Lewars detailing the circumstance of Burns having purchased the four carronades and despatched them as a present to the French Assembly.[78]

Again all substantiating records have mysteriously disappeared. Inasmuch as both Lockhart and Train have long since been convicted of serious deviations from the truth, one may fairly conclude that this is but another instance of the facility with which one lie will breed another, and that the brig *Rosamond* affair should be absolutely deleted from any account of Burns's life.

But even though Burns never won the praises of his superiors by wading out to a smuggling vessel and capturing her, he did the routine work of his office in commendable fashion. In 1792 one finds him writing thus to Corbet, who had given him an appointment to the Dumfries first, or Port, division, the best assignment a gauger could hold in the Dumfries territory:

When I was honored with your most obliging letter, I said to myself —"A simple letter of thanks will be a very poor return for so much kindness; I shall likewise send the gentleman a cargo of my best & newest rhymes."—However, my new Division holds me so very busy, & several things in it being rather new to me, my time has hitherto been totally engrossed . . . At last, by way of compromise, I return you by this my most grateful thanks for all the generous friendship & disinterested patronage, for which, now & formerly, I have the honor to be indebted to you; and as to the Rhymes, another edition, in two volumes, of my Poems being in the Press, I shall beg leave to present a copy to Mrs. Corbet, as my first, & I will venture to add, most effectual mediator with you on my behalf.[79]

Thus in the early autumn of 1792 Burns was still happily successful in his official relationships.

Shortly thereafter, however, as political feeling grew more and more tense, Burns's radical opinions and utterances involved him in difficulty. In December of 1792 he was denounced to the Excise Board as unpatriotic; as a regular part of the routine in such cases, an inquiry into his conduct and principles was ordered. As soon as Burns learned of this he wrote, somewhat hectically, to his friend and patron Robert Graham of Fintry, a member of the Board:

SIR:

I have been surprised, confounded & distracted by Mr. Mitchel, the Collector, telling me just now, that he has received an order from your Honble. Board to enquire into my political conduct, & blaming me as a person disaffected to Government. Sir, you are a Husband—& a father—you know what you would feel, to see the much-loved wife of your bosom, & your helpless, prattling little ones, turned adrift into the world, degraded & disgraced from a situation in which they had been respectable & respected, & left almost without the necessary support of a miserable existence.—Alas, Sir! must I think that such, soon, will be my lot! And from the damned, dark insinuations of hellish, ground-less Envy too! . . . To your patronage, as a man of some genius, you have allowed me a claim; & your esteem, as an honest Man, I know is my due: to these, Sir, permit me to appeal; & by these may I adjure you to save me from that misery which threatens to overwhelm me, & which, with my latest breath I will say it, I have not deserved.— [80]

Possibly Burns was unduly perturbed. Graham sent him a summary of the charges lying against him, and apparently gave him to understand that there was no occasion for alarm. So at once Burns wrote to Mrs. Dunlop:

The political blast that threatened my welfare is overblown.—I have corresponded with Commissr Graham, for the Board had made me the subject of their animadversions; & now I have the pleasure of informing you that all is set to rights in that quarter.—Now as to these inquisitorial informers, Spies, Persecutors, &c., may the d-vil and his angels be let loose to—but hold! I was praying most fervently in my last sheet, and I must not so soon fall a-cursing in this. [81]

The same day Burns acknowledged Graham's kind offices in the matter, and took up at some length "the charges which malice and misrepresentation have brought against me." The nature of these charges appears clearly from Burns's denials:

It has been said, it seems, that I not only belong to, but head a dis-affected party in this place.—I know of no party in this place, Republican

[398]

or Reform, except an old party of Borough-Reform; with which I never had anything to do.—

. . . I was in the playhouse one night, when Ça Ira was called for.— I was in the middle of the Pit, & from the Pit the clamour arose.—One or two individuals with whom I occasionally associate were of the party, but I neither knew of the Plot, nor joined in the Plot; nor ever opened my lips to hiss, or huzza, that, or any other Political tune whatever—. . .

I never uttered any invectives against the king.—His private worth, it is altogether impossible that such a man as I, can appreciate; and in his Public capacity, I always revered, & ever will, with the soundest loyalty, revere, the monarch of Great Britain, as, to speak in Masonic, the sacred KEYSTONE OF OUR ROYAL ARCH CONSTITUTION.

As to REFORM PRINCIPLES, I look upon the British Constitution, as settled at the Revolution, to be the most glorious Constitution on earth, or that perhaps the wit of man can frame; at the same time I think . . . that we have a good deal deviated from the original principles of that Constitution; particularly, that an alarming System of Corruption has pervaded the connection between the Executive Power and the House of Commons.—This is the Truth, the Whole truth, of my Reform opinions; opinions which, before I was aware of the complection of these innovating times, I too unguardedly (now I see it) sported with: but henceforth, I seal up my lips . . .

Of Johnston, the publisher of the Edinr Gazetteer, I know nothing . . . If you think that I act improperly in allowing his Paper to come addressed to me, I shall immediately countermand it.—I never, so judge me, God! wrote a line of prose for the Gazetteer in my life.—. . .

As to France, I was her enthusiastic votary in the beginning of the business.—When she came to show her old avidity for conquest, in annexing Savoy, &c. to her dominions & invading the rights of Holland, I altered my sentiments.—A tippling Ballad which I made on the Prince of Brunswick's breaking up his camp, & sung one convivial evening, I shall likewise send you, sealed up, as it is not every body's reading.— This last is not worth your perusal; but lest Mrs. FAME should, as she has already done, use, & even abuse, her old priviledge of lying, you shall be the master of everything, le pour et le contre, of my political writings & conduct.[82]

After this full statement concerning his political heresies, Burns suggested that he be given the Supervisorship of the

[399]

Galloway district, in place of the present officer who "is and has been for some time very ill." He felt certain that he was again in good standing with the Board, and could look forward to the rapid promotion of which he had all along been hopeful.

But the storm was not yet past. What happened subsequently appears from a letter of Burns's to John Erskine of Mar, grandson of the Jacobite earl whose titles had been forfeited for his share in the " '15." Erskine had heard that Burns had actually lost his position on account of his political utterances, and had written to Glenriddell enquiring whether this report were true. If it were, he proposed to raise a fund for the poet's benefit. Glenriddell, who was still on good terms with Burns, showed him Erskine's letter. Thereupon Burns addressed Erskine himself:

. . . My much-esteemed friend, Mr. Riddell of Glenriddell, has just read me a paragraph of a letter he had from you.—Accept, Sir, of the silent throb of gratitude; for words would but mock the emotions of my soul.—

You have been misinformed, as to my final dismission from the Excise: I am still in the service.—Indeed, but for the exertions of a gentleman who must be known to you, Mr. Graham of Fintry, a gentleman who has ever been my warm & generous friend, I had, without so much as a hearing, or the smallest previous intimation, been turned adrift, with my helpless family, to all the horrors of Want.—Had I had any other resource, probably I might have saved them the trouble of a dismissal; but the little money I gained by my Publication, is almost every guinea embarked, to save from ruin an only brother; who, though one of the worthiest, is by no means one of the most fortunate of men.—

In my defence to their accusations, I said, that whatever might be my sentiments of Republics, ancient or modern, as to Britain, I abjured the idea.—. . . But that, where I must declare my sentiments, I would say that there existed a system of corruption between the Executive Power & the Representative part of the Legislature, which boded no good to our glorious Constitution; & which every patriotic Briton must wish to see amended.—Some such Sentiments as these I stated in a letter to my generous Patron, Mr. Graham, which he laid before the Board at large, where it seems my last remark gave great offence; & one of our

Supervisors general, a Mr. Corbet, was instructed to enquire, on the spot, into my conduct, & to document me—"that *my* business was to *act*, not to think; & that whatever might be Men or Measures, it was for me to be silent & obedient." [83]

When Corbet came down from Glasgow to hold the investigation, Findlater, the Dumfries Supervisor, testified that Burns was "exact, vigilant, and sober; that, in fact he was one of the best officers in the district." [84]   The Examiner, moreover, found him guiltless of any disloyalty.   Hence no indication appears on the records of the Excise Board that Burns was even reprimanded for his conduct.   But beyond a doubt Corbet gave him some friendly advice.

For certainly Burns's actions had been well calculated to draw the fire of the official establishment, especially in the nervous year 1792.   He had always been inclined to recklessness in conversation, and must have said many things which it was easy for malice or ignorance to distort.   He had written verses showing a questionable sympathy with the American Revolutionists; he had been an "enthusiastic votary" of France in 1789; he had written Jacobite songs a-plenty, and though that was a dead cause politically, still even a poetical espousal of the Stuarts was ill-calculated to please a Hanoverian administration.   While living at Ellisland he had taken an active part in the Parliamentary election, and had not hesitated to make sport of powerful local politicians.   He had ridiculed the national government in verses like the "Ode to the Departed Regency Bill" and the "Stanzas of Psalmody;" more recently he had written the song, "Here's a Health to Them that's Awa," with its full-throated praise of the buff and blue.   Beyond a doubt he had composed other pieces of liberal verse that have not been preserved.   All in all, then, Burns the Exciseman had been playing with fire ever since he first had gone on active duty in the autumn of 1789.   That he was merely advised, in a friendly way, to be more reticent in the future, was due to the fact that his superiors knew him to be a good officer, despite his political heterodoxy, and were glad to shield him from official disapproval. [85]

Early in 1793, Burns used his knowledge of Excise matters as basis for a suggestion to the Provost and Town Council of Dumfries. Part of the Burgh revenue came from an impost popularly known as the "twa pennies on ale," a tax levied on ale brewed within the town, but not on that which was imported.[86] Burns proposed that the Council rectify this situation, and thus add materially to the corporate income. Provost David Staig, to whom Burns's letter was addressed,[87] brought the matter before the Council, and ultimately the plan was put into effect—good indication of Burns's knowledge of the details of Excise matters, and of his interest in the civic welfare.

War-time conditions, which cut off importations, and thus reduced the incidental income of the Excise officers, worked a hardship upon Burns. By January of 1794 he apparently was afraid that the Board might order a general reduction in the stated salaries paid the gaugers; to forestall this he proposed—again to Graham of Fintry—a plan for effecting what he was pleased to call "an economy of the public monies":

. . . What I have long digested, & am going to propose, is the reduction of one of our Dumfries Divisions.—Not only in these unlucky times, but even in the highest flush of business, my Division, though by far the heaviest, was mere trifling.—The others were still less.—I would plan the reduction as thus.—Let the second Division be annihilated, & be divided among the others.—. . .

I assure you, Sir, that, by my plan, the Duties will be equally well charged, & thus an Officer's appointment saved to the Public.[88]

This was not the first instance in which Burns, who would have considered his own dismissal, on any grounds, an act of pure tyranny, had suggested that an officer be discharged in order that his own prospects might be bettered. He was alert for any opportunity to improve his own situation and to add to his income. If he had been accused of selfishness in such matters, his defence would probably have been the relatively valid one of economic necessity. He could not tolerate the thought of running into debt; to live within his income had always been one of his cardinal principles. As the increasing cost of living made his salary less and less adequate for the support of his growing family, he quite frankly proposed for his relief such measures as seemed practicable.

In December of 1794, Burns's ability as an Exciseman was recognized by his appointment as acting supervisor in place of Findlater, who was ill.[89] In contrast to the easy work demanded of a gauger, the new duties kept Burns constantly busy. Certain leaves of the official diary which he was required to keep have been reproduced in facsimile.[90] "Here one can still read the record of the actual time spent on government business. For instance, on December 24, 1794, he was on duty from eight o'clock in the morning till eight at night; . . . on January 18 (?), from seven in the morning till four in the afternoon; on February 19, from seven in the morning till six in the evening; on February 23, from five in the morning till seven at night. No eight-hour day here; nor was the work of a kind that could be performed by an unintelligent man. On the contrary, it demanded a considerable amount of skill not only in dealing with persons, but also in keeping a somewhat elaborate set of books, which had to make clear every transaction, and were regularly scrutinized for even the slightest irregularity."[91]

It was in this way that Burns had a taste of what would have been in store for him had the desired promotion been forthcoming. Findlater, however, resumed his work early in April, and the poet went back to his gauging.

Almost at once word came to him that he was again in danger of censure from the Board, though not because of politics. The incident was a minor one; but despite this fact Burns's letter of explanation is an important document, because it affords incontrovertible proof that the poet's position was in no sense a sinecure, and that he was subject to most rigid scrutiny. The letter is addressed to John Edgar, Excise Office, Edinburgh:

I understand that I am to incur censure by the Wine-Account of this District not being sent in.—Allow me to state the following circumstances to you, which, if they do not apologise for, will at least extenuate my part of the offence.—

The General Letter was put into my hands sometime about the beginning of this month; as I was then in charge of the District, Mr. Find-later being indisposed.—I immediately, as far as in my power, made a survey of the Wine-Stocks; & where I could not personally survey, I wrote the officer of the Division. In a few days more, & previous to Collection-week, Mr. Findlater resumed charge; & as in the course of Collection he would have both the Officers by him, & the Old Books among his hands, it very naturally occurred to me the Wine-acct business would rest with him.—At the close of that week, I got a note from the Collector that the Account making up was thrown on my hands.—I immediately set about it; but one Officer's books, James Graham of Sanquhar, not being at hand I wrote him to send me them by first post. Mr. Graham has not thought proper to pay the least attention to my request, & today I have sent an express for his Stock-book.—

This, Sir, is a plain state of Facts; & if I must still be thought censureable, I hope it will be considered, that this Officiating Job being my first, I cannot be supposed to be completely master of all the etiquette of the business.—

If my supposed neglect is to be laid before the Honourable BOARD, I beg you will have the goodness to accompany the complaint with this letter.[92]

Apparently Burns's explanation was considered adequate, for the Board took no action in the matter.

Only one further detail concerning Burns and the Excise remains to be set forth. Not long after the beginning of 1796 he found it impossible to perform even the relatively easy duties of the Dumfries first division. There is nothing to show precisely when he went on sick-leave, but certainly by the end of April he was entirely incapacitated. In that month he wrote Thomson:

Almost ever since I wrote you last [in February], I have only known Existence by the pressure of the heavy hand of Sickness; & have counted time by the repercussions of PAIN! [93]

A rule of the Board provided that when an Exciseman was thus temporarily off duty, his normal salary should be continued, but the increment of fifteen pounds, which had been voted some time before, should be stopped. Naturally enough

[404]

Burns was concerned over the prospect, and planned to petition the Board for full pay. He made the situation clear in a letter to Alexander Cunningham, written two weeks before his death:

> The Medical folks tell me that my last & only chance is bathing & country quarters & riding.—The deuce of the matter is this; when an Excise-man is off duty, his salary is reduced to 35£ instead of 50£.— What way, in the name of thrift, shall I maintain myself & keep a horse in Country-quarters—with a wife & five children at home, on 35£? I mention this, because I had intended to beg your utmost interest & all the friends you can muster, to move our Commissrs of Excise to grant me the full salary.—I dare say you know them all personally.—If they do not grant it me, I must lay my account with an exit truly en poëte, if I die not of disease, I must perish with hunger.[94]

A brief note in amplification of the foregoing was posted five days afterwards:

> As to me, my plan is to address the Board by petition, & then if any friend has thrown in a word 'tis a great deal in my favor.[95]

There is some uncertainty as to what action the Board took, if any. In a letter to the Glasgow *Courier*, March, 1834, Findlater said:

> Commissioner Graham, regretting, I have no doubt, his inability to comply with the poet's wishes as to the full salary, sent him a private donation of £5, which, I believe, nearly or totally compensated the loss.[96]

Currie's statement, as emended for his second and subsequent editions, was that

> His full emoluments were . . . continued to him by the kindness of Mr. Stobbie, a young expectant in the Excise, who performed the duties of his office without fee or reward.[97]

That is probably what actually took place. In any case this is clear: to the end of his life Burns held the affection and respect of his companions in the Excise, of both his fellow gaugers and his superior officers; they wished him well, and did what they could to relieve his mind of the inevitable worry which ill-health brought with it.

[405]

All in all, it is a pleasant picture that clings to one's memory as one thinks over these concluding scenes. One remembers John Lewars, busy over the small matters that only an intimate friend could have attended to; and Stobbie, still an expectant, walking the poet's rounds and filling out the reports for him to sign; and Findlater, testifying to his subordinate's worth as an officer; and loyal Graham of Fintry, always ready to lend his powerful assistance in times of emergency.

Burns had gone into the Excise in 1788 for only one reason: to support himself and his family. He knew well enough that it was an occupation which involved hard and uncongenial labor, and that the Exciseman, if not actually a disreputable character, was a person in general disrepute throughout Scotland. He made an excellent record in the service; he kept his self respect; he lost none of his old friends; he made many new ones; he supported his family in comfortable independence. All of which seems somewhat hard to fit into what Henley called a "story of decadence."

In a certain sense, "the whole story of Burns's connection with the Excise may be read in an entry of three words, which appears in the Board's alphabetical register of officers. Here appear scraps of information concerning the various employees, most interesting of which are the 'characters,' or official ratings of the different officers: 'indifferent'; 'indifferent, drinks'; 'a sober, weak man'; 'can do, but drinks'; 'could once do, drinks'; 'a drucken creature'; 'a sober, weak, officer'; 'a weak man, but sober'. Burns is characterized thus: 'Never tried; a poet. Turns out well'." [98] The last three words sum it all up, and leave little more to be said.

5

LITERARY WORK

The reader of Henley's essay is sure to gather the impression that Burns was "burned out," so far as creative ability was concerned, long before he ceased writing, and that the last years of his life were barren of significant poetry.[99]   Yet as a matter of fact, Burns accomplished an astonishing amount of literary work at Dumfries, and this in spite of the handicaps imposed by crowded living quarters, the duties of the Excise, financial difficulties, domestic misfortune, concern over civic affairs, and illness.   He sent Creech approximately fifty pages of unpublished material for the 1793 two-volume edition of his poems; he wrote many lyrics for Johnson's *Museum*, and continued to act as the real editor of that collection; he worked indefatigably for George Thomson and his *Select Scotish Airs*, furnishing him at least sixty songs, and with extensive, pertinent, and scholarly comments on Scottish song and music.   He made a careful study of all available song-collections, including not only such obvious works as Ramsay's, Herd's, Pinkerton's, and Ritson's, but going so far afield in his reading that modern scholars have been constantly baffled in their attempts to follow him.[100]   And during the early part of the Dumfries period he busied himself in completing for Glenriddell the volume of letters which was still in Burns's possession when Glenriddell died, and in annotating Glenriddell's four interleaved volumes of the *Museum*.   Burns's connection with the various Glenriddell MSS, and with the *Scots Musical Museum*, has already been set forth, and need not again be reviewed.   The other matters here mentioned, however, the 1793 volume, and Burns's work for George Thomson, have been referred to only incidentally, and demand more extensive treatment.

The 1793 Edition

The 1793 Edinburgh, in two volumes, was the third and last edition of Burns's poems with which he himself was directly concerned.   The first, the Kilmarnock of 1786, he had published and distributed himself, without the assistance of even a literary agent.   The second, the Edinburgh of 1787, had been brought out with the aid of Creech; Burns, however, had assumed all financial responsibility.   Both of these earlier editions had been published by subscription.   As has already

[407]

been pointed out, the success of the Edinburgh volume had been pronounced. Consequently in July of 1790, Creech, who owned the copyright, actually advertised a new edition as forthcoming, but did nothing further in the matter. A year later he wrote to Burns asking his aid in such a venture, and Burns, glad to have an opportunity to make Creech wait as he himself had once been forced to wait, made no reply to the letter.[101] Creech was not perturbed; he had recently been elected a Bailie of Edinburgh, and was enjoying his civic honors; business affairs were of secondary importance.

In September of 1791, however, Davies, junior partner in the London firm of Cadell and Davies, with which Creech's relations were close, took up the matter with Creech:

Mr. Cadell says he believes he wrote you about the new edition of Burns's *Poems;* but in case he has not, he bids me tell you, Sir, that he recommends 1000 to be printed in 2 vols. crown 8vo, on a fine wove paper, and that it be finished in two or three months, in time for his sale.[102]

Such a recommendation, indicative of an English interest in Burns, should have stirred Creech to action. He thought the matter over, however, for some time, and in April of 1792, seven months after receiving Davies's letter, wrote to Burns, asking what new material he could furnish. Burns's reply was interesting and characteristic:

SIR:

I this moment have yours . . . I suppose, at a gross guess that I could add of new materials to your two volumes, about fifty pages.—I would also correct & retrench a good deal.—These said fifty pages you know are as much mine as the thumb-stall I have just now drawn on my finger which I unfortunately gashed in mending my pen. A few Books which I very much want, are all the recompense I crave, together with as many copies of this new edition of my own works as Friendship or Gratitude shall prompt me to *present* . . .

If the thing were possible that I could receive the Proof-Sheets by our Dumfries Fly, which runs three times a week, I would earnestly wish to correct them myself.[103]

[408]

When offering Creech these fifty pages of poetry—and "Tam o' Shanter" proved to be among the lot—Burns asked no return in money, but simply a few books for his own library, and copies of the new edition to present to his friends. Apparently he felt that it would be useless to drive a bargain with the man who had been so dilatory in settling for the 1787 edition. Creech might pay "in kind," out of his book-seller's stock; actual cash he would hesitate to relinquish. So Burns waived the matter of financial return, collected his MSS, sent them to A. F. Tytler of Edinburgh for criticism, and then gave them to Creech.

With astonishing promptness Creech got the edition under way. On June 3, 1792, only four weeks after Burns had written him, he in turn wrote to Cadell:

I enclose a sheet of Burns's *Poems*, now going on, that you may have the plate in readiness. There will be fifty pages of additional poems to this edition.[104]

Having made so good a beginning, however, Creech allowed matters to drag, and not till February 16, 1793, was the new work announced in the Edinburgh *Courant*. On Monday, the 18th, it was actually published, under the title *"Poems, Chiefly in the Scottish Dialect.* The Second Edition greatly enlarged with New Poems. By Robert Burns."

Ten days later Burns wrote to Creech, saying nothing about the books he wished for his own library, and asking for only twenty copies of the new edition, to give to "a few Great Folk whom I respect and a few Little Folk whom I love." How many Creech allowed him is uncertain; enough, however, so that Burns could send presentation volumes to several of his friends, including the Earl of Glencairn, younger brother of his Edinburgh patron; Patrick Miller, landlord of the Ellisland farm; Glenriddell; and Mrs. Graham of Fintry.

There is little reason for commenting in detail on this publication. Apparently Burns did not himself revise all the proofs, for one finds him thanking A. F. Tytler "for taking the trouble of correcting the press work."[105] This fact may account for the

[409]

unduly large number of typographical blunders. Furthermore, Tytler seems to have thought that because Burns asked his advice concerning various poems, he was at liberty to make not a few unauthorized changes in the poet's text. So in some minor respects the two volumes are distinctly inferior to what they would have been had Creech sent Burns the proof-sheets "by the Dumfries Fly."

But of course Tytler was not responsible for the fact that among the new material in the volumes there was but one poem of genuine distinction, "Tam o' Shanter." Here, for the only time in his life, Burns had tried his hand at a sustained narrative, and had achieved a notable success. But "Tam" had actually been published two years before, and must have been widely known by the spring of 1793. So all in all, this two-volume edition contained little that added in any way to Burns's reputation as a poet. But that there was a demand for such an edition, and that the demand came in the first instance from England, is good evidence of the extent to which Burns's poetical reputation had spread.

George Thomson and the Select Scotish Airs

Though the two-volume Edinburgh edition was not published till after Burns had been some fifteen months at Dumfries, it represented, on the whole, work done some time before. To see at first hand the poetic products of the Dumfries years, one turns to the fifth volume of Johnson's *Museum*, and to George Thomson's collection of songs.[106] Only when one has examined this latter work, and has studied the voluminous correspondence which passed between poet and publisher, can one realize the astonishing creative activity that Burns maintained almost to the day of his death.[107]

George Thomson (1757–1851), whose recent biographer inaccurately called him "The Friend of Burns,"[108] had been born on March 4, 1757, at Limekilns, Dunfermline. The son of a schoolmaster, he had received a good education, and had read law for a time. But when Burns knew him he was supporting himself by serving as Clerk to the Board of Trustees for the Encouragement of Manufactures in Scotland. He was something of a musician, and, in an amateurish way, knew a good deal about Scottish song. During the summer of 1792 he interested Andrew Erskine in a plan for collecting and publishing all available native Scottish song-tunes, together with appropriate and respectable words. This last consideration gave him some uneasiness, for many of Scotland's best-known tunes were wedded to hopelessly broad verses. But in September of 1792 he persuaded Burns's friend Alexander Cunningham to give him a letter of introduction to the poet. This he despatched to Burns, accompanied by a full account of his project, and a request for Burns's aid. The material parts of his own letter were these:

For some years past I have, with a friend or two, employed many leisure hours in collating and collecting the most favourite of our national melodies, for publication. We have engaged Pleyel, the most agreeable composer living, to put accompaniments to these, and also to compose an instrumental prelude and conclusion to each air . . . To render this work perfect, we are desirous to have the poetry improved wherever it seems unworthy of the music. . . . Some charming melodies are united to mere nonsense and doggerel, while others are accommodated with rhymes so loose and indelicate as cannot be sung in decent company. To remove this reproach would be an easy task to the author of "The Cotter's Saturday Night." . . .

We shall esteem your poetical assistance a particular favour, besides paying any reasonable price you shall please to demand for it . . . Tell me frankly, then, whether you will devote your leisure to writing twenty or twenty-five songs, suitable to the particular melodies which I am prepared to send you. A few Songs exceptionable only in some of their verses, I will likewise submit to your consideration; leaving it to you either to mend these or make new Songs in their stead.[109]

This, then, was Thomson's original request: that Burns would write, for pay, twenty or twenty-five songs, and emend a few others.

[411]

Burns's reply was immediate and enthusiastic:

I have just this moment got your letter.—As the request you make to me will positively add to my enjoyments in complying with it, I shall enter into your undertaking with all the small portion of abilities I have, strained to their utmost exertion by the impulse of Enthusiasm. . . . Will you let me have a list of your airs, with the first line of the verses you intend for them . . . I say, the first line of the verses, because if they are verses that have appeared in any of our Collections of songs, I know them & can have recourse to them. Apropos, if you are for *English* verses, there is, on my part, an end of the matter.—. . .

As to remuneration, you may think my Songs either *above*, or *below* price; for they shall absolutely be the one or the other.—In the honest enthusiasm with which I embark in your undertaking, to talk of money, wages, fee, hire, &c., would be downright Sodomy of Soul!—A proof of each of the Songs that I compose or amend, I shall receive as a favor . . . I have some particular reasons for wishing my interference to be known as little as possible.[110]

Critics have sometimes wondered why Burns, who was committed to Johnson in a similar undertaking, the *Scots Musical Museum*, should thus eagerly have pledged himself to Thomson. The answer is not far to seek. Johnson had already begun to lose interest in his venture; without Burns's aid, it would have been dead long before. Moreover the *Museum*, though an admirable collection, was not in any sense a first-rate piece of book-making. It was crudely engraved; the printing and paper were unattractive. Thomson, who at first seemed to have abundant funds at his command, proposed to issue his work in the best possible form, with musical accompaniments by a famous composer. He offered Burns an opportunity to participate in what promised to be a work of distinction; the poet's professional pride prompted him to accept the offer.

Burns felt, moreover, that in thus undertaking to rewrite old songs, or to furnish new words for popular Scottish tunes, he would be doing a genuine service to the nation whose Bard he aspired to be. Hence the refusal even to consider monetary reward. He had never been averse to taking money for the

[412]

poems that he composed and published. "The profits of the labours of a Man of genius are, I hope, at least as honorable as any other profits whatever," he had written to Patrick Carfrae.[111] But the songs of Scotland were in a different category from "The Cotter's Saturday Night." What Burns might be able to accomplish in this field, could not be paid for in any coin. And Burns knew that he could accomplish much. One notes the assurance with which he said "if they are verses that have appeared in *any* of our collections of songs, I know them"!

Reviewing the early letters that passed between the two collaborators, one finds two not uninteresting facts at once apparent. The first is that Burns was extremely modest concerning his share in the work. As had been the case with the *Museum*, he had no thought of playing the literary dictator. In this mood he wrote:

> Don't let it enter your head that you are under any necessity of taking my verses.—. . . Tho' you should reject one half of what I give you, I shall be pleased with your adopting t'other half; & shall continue to serve you with the same assiduity.—[112]

In the second place, it is obvious that Burns was a student of Scottish music as well as of Scottish folk poetry—a consideration which had much to do with his success as a writer of lyrics actually intended to be sung. Throughout the correspondence one sees evidence of the care with which he scrutinized his various compositions, to make sure that the verses would actually "fit" the tunes. A sentence such as this, apropos of "O saw ye Bonie Lesley," is characteristic:

> Every seventh line ends with three syllables, in place of the two in the other lines, but you will see in the sixth bar of the second part, the place where these three syllables will always recur, that the four semi-quavers usually sung as one syllable will with the greatest propriety divide into two—thus [two bars of music].[113]

Still more pertinent evidence of Burns's interest in music may be seen in the Ewart Library, Dumfries. Among the many

Burns items in this collection are two volumes of the *Musical Museum* which had been in the poet's home, and which his son Robert gave to friends from whom they ultimately came to the library. On page 201 of volume II the song "And I'll Kiss Thee Yet" is printed. Over the sixth note in the melody, a "quaver," Burns himself has written the word "crotchet." An identical correction appears on page 202, vol. II, over the tenth note of the melody of "Rattlin' Roarin' Willie." Had Burns not been alert to the significance of these minutiae, he would never have detected such slight misprints, or taken the pains to correct them.[114]

Thomson soon discovered that he had found an invaluable assistant. None the less he took his editorial responsibilities seriously, and did not hesitate to criticize Burns's taste:

I am highly pleased with your humorous and amorous rhapsody on "Bonie Lesley:" it is a thousand times better than "The Collier's Lassie." "The deil he could na scaithe thee," &c., is an eccentric and happy thought. Do you not think, however, that the names of such old heroes as Alexander sound rather queer unless in pompous or more burlesque verse? Instead of the line "And never made anither," I would humbly suggest "And ne'er made sic anither;" and I would fain have you substitute some other line for "Return to Caledonie" in the last verse, because I think this alteration of the orthography and of the sound of Caledonia disfigures the word and renders it Hudibrastic . . .

You perceive, my dear Sir, I avail myself of the liberty which you condescend to allow me, by speaking freely what I think . . . The wren will often see what has been overlooked by the eagle.[115]

By the end of January, 1793, Thomson realized that with Burns's aid he could publish a far larger collection than he had at first contemplated:

The number of songs which I had originally in view was limited; but I now resolve to include every Scotch air and song worth singing leaving none behind but mere gleanings, to which the publishers of *omnegatherum* are welcome.[116]

Burns was in no way appalled by this change of plan, but seemed pleased at the enlargement of his field of work. To

ensure the completeness of Thomson's collection Burns authorized him to reprint anything of his that had appeared in the
Museum, assuring him that Johnson had no copyright on this
material.[117]   And obviously he was happy in his new work:

You cannot imagine how much this business of composing for your
publication has added to my enjoyments.—What with my early attachments to ballads, Johnson's Museum, your book, &c.   Ballad-making is
now as compleatly my hobby-horse, as ever Fortification was Uncle
Toby's; so I'll e'en canter it away till I come to the limit of my race
(God grant that I may take the right side of the winning-post!) & then
chearfully looking back on the honest folks with whom I have been
happy, I shall say, or sing, "Sae merry as we a' hae been." [118]

This is precisely what Burns was to do for Thomson: to keep
steadily at work till he came to the limit of his race; furnishing
new texts or revising old ones, suggesting sources of interesting
material, and commenting, in penetrating and scholarly fashion,
upon both the words and the music that were to be published.

Early in the summer of 1793 Thomson's first number, or
half-volume, containing twenty-five songs, was published.   He
sent Burns a copy, and added:

I cannot express to you how much I am obliged to you for the exquisite new songs you are sending me; but thanks, my friend, are a poor
return for what you have done.   As I shall be benefited by the publication, you must suffer me to enclose a small mark of my gratitude, and
to repeat it afterwards when I find it convenient.   Do not return it,
for, by Heaven! if you do, our correspondence is at an end.[119]

Burns accepted—under protest—the five pound note which
Thomson enclosed, but warned him never again to commit such
an offence.   After this exchange of courtesies the two friends—
for though they had not met face to face they were now on intimate terms—went on as before, collecting, editing, criticising
and approving of one another's work.

By the end of August, "Peter Pindar," [120] a rimester who was
providing Thomson with English verses, had proved so dilatory
that Thomson turned to Burns for help:

[415]

I stand pledged to furnish English verses along with every Scottish song, and I must fulfil what I have promised; but I certainly have got into a scrape if you do not stand my friend. A couple of stanzas to each air will do as well as half a dozen; and to an imagination so infinitely fruitful as yours this will not be a Herculean labour.[121]

Forgetting his explicit stipulation, made some time before, that he should not be asked for English verses, Burns accepted this new obligation without demur:

You may readily trust, my dear Sir, that any exertion in my power, is heartily at your service.—But one thing I must hint to you, the very name of Peter Pindar is of great Service to your Publication; so, get a verse from him now & then, though I have no objection, as well as I can, to bear the burden of the business.[122]

Without realizing that he was doing so, Burns expressed in this last phrase his whole connection with Thomson's *Select Airs:* so long as he lived, he bore the burden of the business, as he had done for the *Scots Musical Museum.* With no thought of money, or even of fame, for himself, he wrote song after song, turned them over to his friend without even keeping a MS copy for himself, and went on writing more.

It is unnecessary to follow Burns and Thomson through all the correspondence of four years, for the nature of their relationship has already been made clear. It will be worth while, however, to indicate briefly at what times during the Dumfries years Burns was most active in Thomson's behalf, and also to recall some few of the better known songs written for the *Select Airs.*

Concerning the first of these two matters one can speak with assurance, for the number of letters which Burns sent to Thomson is a fair index of his activity. During the last three months of 1792, immediately after receiving Thomson's first appeal for aid, the poet wrote often, and gave Thomson a considerable amount of material. With the coming of the New Year, and the flurry in the Excise over Burns's loyalty, the correspondence inevitably slackened. But from June to October of 1793 the poet was again uninterruptedly at work. There was a certain stimulus, no doubt, in the fact that the first number of the collection had just been published; but aside from this it is clear that the summer of 1793 was with Burns a period of astonishing creative activity, comparable, indeed, to the months at Mossgiel when he was piling up the MSS that went into the Kilmarnock volume.

The close of 1793 and early months of 1794 saw Burns suffering from a nervous breakdown, and harried by the quarrel with the Riddell family. For some months there were no letters to Thomson. But by September these troubles had passed, and though Burns did not write as often as he had done a year before, he sent long letters filled with pertinent comments on Scottish song, and containing many texts of his own composition.

Early in 1795, when Burns was serving as acting supervisor in place of Findlater, there was again a falling off in the number of letters. Apparently the new Excise responsibilities left little time for poetry. But by the time summer had come Burns was again back in harness, as enthusiastic as ever.

Autumn of 1795 brought with it the death of Burns's daughter Elizabeth, a recurrence of the old hypochondria, and a serious attack of the rheumatic fever that had long afflicted him. Nevertheless he was in no mood to abandon the enterprise. No better evidence could be adduced concerning Burns's unflagging enthusiasm, despite hardships all but unendurable, than the following letter, written to Thomson so late as February, 1796:

Many thanks, my dear Sir, for your handsome, elegant prese[nt to] Mrs. B——— [123] & for my remaining vol. of P. Pindar. Peter [is] a delightful fellow, & a first favorite of mine.—Now to business. How are you paid by your Subscribers here? I gave you in the names of Robt Riddell of Glenriddell, & his brother, Walter Riddell of Woodleypark . . . I also supplied another Subscriber, Mr. Sharpe of Hoddam, with the second set of Sonatas (my own copy) so charge him accordingly. —Mr. Gordon of Kenmure, who subscribes for the Songs only, unknown to me at the time, in a money transaction where I was concerned, paid the 10/6 to my account; so there I am your debitor.—

[417]

I am much pleased with your ideas of publishing a Collection of our songs in Octavo with etchings.—I am extremely willing to lend every assistance in my power.—The twenty-five Irish airs . . . I shall chearfully undertake the task of finding verses for.[124]

So instead of writing only some twenty or twenty-five Scottish songs, as he had originally agreed to do, Burns was by this time furnishing English words as well as Scottish, for as many tunes as Thomson should send him, and undertaking, in addition, to compose verses for a volume of Irish airs that he had suggested to Thomson as early as 1793.

Burns was not destined to accomplish much in this last field, however. By April he realized that his race was nearly run:

Alas! my dear Thomson, I fear it will be some time e'er I tune my lyre again! "By Babel streams," &c.—Almost ever since I wrote you last, I have only known Existence by the pressure of the heavy hand of Sickness; & have counted time by the repercussions of PAIN! Rheumatism, Cold, & Fever have formed, to me, a terrible Trinity in Unity, which makes me close my eyes in misery, & open them without hope.[125]

None the less Burns still kept at work. As late as July 4, 1796, he wrote Thomson from Brow:

I recd. your songs: but my health being so precarious nay dangerously situated, that as a last effort I am here at a sea-bathing quarters. Besides my inveterate rheumatism, my appetite is quite gone, & I am so emaciated as to be scarce able to support myself on my own legs.—Alas! is this a time for me to woo the Muses? However, I am still anxiously willing to serve your work; & if possible, shall try:—I would not like to see another employed, unless you could lay your hand upon a poet whose productions would be equal to the rest.—You will see my alterations & remarks on the margin of each song.—. . . My address is still Dumfries. Farewel! & God bless you! [126]

Thus within seventeen days of his death Burns was not only "still anxiously willing to serve," but was revising the MS that Thomson was still sending him, and commenting, as only he could do, upon the various songs and tunes.

Eight days later he wrote again, asking for five pounds with which to pay a local tradesman, and adding:

[418]

I do not ask all this gratuitously; for upon returning health, I hereby promise & engage to furnish you with five pounds' worth of the neatest song-genius you have seen.—I tried my hand on Rothiemurche this morning.—The measure is so difficult, that it is impossible to infuse much genius into the lines—they are on the other side. Forgive me! [127]

He had already sent Thomson approximately sixty songs and invaluable suggestions and comments; he knew that he was dying; yet he felt that he should apologize for not being able to do more!

When one examines this astonishing amount of lyric verse, one discovers that it contains not a few of Burns's most notable productions. Here, for example, is "Highland Mary," written in the autumn of 1792, with its somewhat rhetorical but nevertheless moving reminiscence of Mary Campbell. Here too is "Duncan Gray," composed only a month later, but showing in its whimsical humor an entirely different side of Burns's personality. And here is "Scots Wha Hae," perhaps the most thrilling and defiant of all the battle-songs of the nation.

This last song has had an interesting history. In Syme's account of the Galloway tour on which he accompanied Burns, there appears the following paragraph:

I told you that in the midst of the storm on the wilds of Kenmure, Burns was rapt in meditation. What do you think he was about? He was charging the English army, along with Bruce, at Bannockburn. He was engaged in the same manner on our ride home from St. Mary's Isle, and I did not disturb him. Next day he produced me the following address of Bruce to his troops, and gave me a copy for Dalzell.[128]

It is a pleasant anecdote, especially the statement, "I did not disturb him," which caught Carlyle's attention. But unfortunately Burns's own account of the genesis of the poem differs materially from Syme's. Writing to Thomson, in the autumn of 1793, Burns said:

There is a tradition, which I have met with in many places of Scotland, that [the old air "Hey tuttie taitie"] was Robert Bruce's March at the battle of Bannock-burn.—This thought, in my yesternight's evening walk, warmed me to a pitch of enthusiasm on the theme of Liberty &

Independance, which I threw into a kind of Scots Ode, fitted to the Air, that one might suppose to be the gallant ROYAL SCOT's address to his heroic followers on that eventful morning.[129]

Chambers-Wallace remark, "There is a discrepancy here which cannot be altogether cleared up."[130] The difficulty will disappear if one will remember that Burns's comments on his songs, in his many letters to Thomson, are usually reliable, and that Syme was certainly doing his best, when he wrote Currie, to make his own relations to Burns seem uniquely important. There is no more reason for believing that "Scots Wha Hae" was composed in the midst of a storm on the "wilds of Kenmore" than there is for believing that "Tam" was written during an afternoon stroll with Jean and young Robert. Syme was setting the fashion for future writers by inventing an anecdote which might only possibly have been true. Moreover, it is virtually certain that Burns's Galloway tour was not made till nearly a year after the song had been sent to Thomson.

In any case, however, Burns sent the song to Thomson in August, 1793, set to the tune "Hey Tuttie Taitie," and accompanied by this further statement:

I shewed the air to Urbani, who was highly pleased with it, & begged me to make soft verses for it; but I had no idea of giving myself any trouble on the subject, till the accidental recollection of that glorious struggle for Freedom, associated with the glowing ideas of some other struggles of the same nature, *not quite so ancient*, roused my rhyming Mania.[131]

So once again France and Scotland had become allies. Burns veiled his enthusiasm for the revolution of 1789 behind his admiration of the Bruce; and though ostensibly denouncing the English tyrant of 1314, he was in fact protesting against the reactionary spirit represented not only by the crowned heads of the continent, but by the very British government whose pay he was receiving.

When the song reached Thomson he was both laudatory and critical. He praised the poem, but objected to the tune as in-

MANUSCRIPT OF AULD LANG SYNE

From the original in the collection of Mr. Oliver R. Barrett

sipid, suggested the air "Lewie Gordon" as more appropriate, and showed how, by adding two syllables to the last line of each stanza, Burns could make the ode fit the tune Thomson preferred.

Burns accepted Thomson's suggestion, and furnished him with a revised text, weaker in every stanza than the original. When the second volume of Thomson's collection appeared in 1799, the poem was included, in this emended form. But the merit of the original was too apparent to permit of its being permanently rejected. Consequently in his third volume Thomson reprinted the song in its first form, and set to the tune for which Burns had written it. So in the end Burns's instinctive preferences were respected, and the world knows "Scots Wha Hae" as the poet intended it to be known.

Still another of the songs sent to Thomson in the autumn of 1793 is "Auld Lang Syne." This, however, had been written some time before, and should not be used as evidence of Burns's literary activity at Dumfries.[132] But "Contented wi' Little" was a product of November, 1794—a genial expression of a mood into which Burns must frequently have fallen, but which should not in any sense be thought of as his philosophy of life.

Two months later, with the nonchalance of unconscious genius, Burns wrote for Thomson "A Man's a Man for A' That." The accompanying comments are, in a way, as interesting as the poem itself:

A great critic, Aikin on songs, says that love & wine are the exclusive themes for song-writing.—The following is on neither subject, & consequently is no Song; but will be allowed, I think, to be two or three pretty good *prose* thoughts, inverted into rhyme. . . . I do not give you the foregoing song for your book, but merely by way of *vive la bagatelle*; for the piece is not really Poetry.[133]

One hardly knows how to interpret such indifference. It may be true, as Professor John Macunn suggested in his *Ethics of Citizenship*, that Burns had been reading *The Rights of Man*, and knew that he was borrowing both ideas and phraseology from Tom Paine's impassioned prose. There are striking verbal similarities between Burns's poem and certain passages in Paine; *a priori*, Burns would not have allowed such a document as *The Rights of Man* to remain long unread. If Burns realized his debt to Paine, then both the phrase "prose thoughts inverted into rhyme," and the modest disclaimer, would be entirely intelligible.

Or it may be that the poet, remembering how his enthusiastic liberalism of 1792 had brought him to the unfavorable notice of the authorities, chose intentionally to belittle what he knew would be interpreted as an unqualified criticism of the existing social order.

But one need feel no concern over Burns's disparaging remarks, for the song is absolutely unaffected by them. It is, without doubt, too rhetorical; there is bombast in some of the lines. But to criticize it on this score, and not to admit its enduring merits, is to speak ill-advisedly. Flawless in its metrics, brilliant in phrasing, and glowing with fiery intensity, the poem takes its place among the half dozen of Burns's most notable lyrics. Less anarchistic than "The Jolly Beggars," which represented the embittered mood of 1786, unmarred by personal animosity or prejudice, these five stanzas may fairly be considered the best expression of Burns's social and political philosophy at the close of his life. The old rebellion against things as they are is still unquelled, though less outspoken than it once had been; the personal pride, the contempt for "yon birkie ca'd a Lord," have been tempered by the passing of time, but not extinguished. Especially in the first two stanzas Burns is still thinking as a humble Scot, harassed by poverty, though proud of his ability to rise superior to it. But the third and fourth show him extending the scope of his vision, and including in his synthesis the entire European social system, with its oppressive and burdensome aristocracy. And in the concluding stanza, where Burns again widens his horizon till it embraces all humanity, the "Ayrshire Bard" speaks as a veritable citizen of the world.

Incidentally, it may not be uninteresting to note that there are only two hundred and sixty-three words, all told, in the poem, and that two hundred and forty of this total are monosyllables. It is easy to read, this last of Burns's great lyrics; its very simplicity is one cause of its widespread appeal. Where one person comprehends and enjoys Shelley's elaborately allegorical criticism of the world as he knew it, a hundred understand and delight in "A Man's a Man for A' That."

As one reviews this story of Burns's relations to Thomson, one sees him unflagging in his attention to Thomson's interests; one sees him acquiescing generously in every petition for aid; one sees him busy over Thomson's affairs when he was too ill to rise from his chair without assistance; one sees him, within nine days of his death, composing verses for a tune Thomson wished to publish, and actually begging Thomson's pardon for not being able to do more. It would be difficult to find many such records in English literature.

Thomson, on his part, hardly treated Burns with fairness. He disregarded Burns's instructions about the settings of the songs, he apparently rewrote his end of the correspondence when he published it, and he certainly mutilated the manuscripts of Burns's letters, in order that his relations to Burns might appear in the best possible light—which certainly does not entitle him to be thought of as wholeheartedly a friend of Burns.[134]

Two minor matters relating to Burns's literary work at Dumfries must be mentioned. The first is his connection with the journalistic press. From time to time, as has appeared in this chronicle, Burns sent poems and brief pieces of prose to London newspapers, particularly to Peter Stuart's *Star*. In the spring of 1789 he had been invited to join the *Star* as a regular contributor;[135] the request was probably repeated a year later. Each time Burns declined. In the spring of 1794 the proprietors of the London *Morning Chronicle* made the poet the offer of a regular salary, conditioned, apparently, upon his moving to London. The exact details are uncertain; the offer was tempting enough so that Burns considered accepting it. He decided, however, not to exchange his assured position in the

Excise for the uncertainties of London journalism. His letter, explaining his reasons for declining, was addressed to Patrick Miller, through whom the invitation had been extended:

> Your offer is indeed truly generous, & most sincerely do I thank you for it; but in my present situation, I find that I dare not accept it.—You well know my Political sentiments; & were I an insular individual, unconnected with a wife & a family of children, with the most fervid enthusiasm would I have volunteered my services: I then could & would have despised all consequences that might have ensued.—My prospect in the Excise is something; at least, it is, encumbered as I am with the welfare, the very existence, of near half-a-score of helpless individuals, what I dare not sport with.—
>
> In the meantime, they are most welcome to my Ode; only, let them insert it as a thing they have met with by accident, & unknown to me. . . . I will now & then send [Mr. Perry, the Editor] any bagatelle that I may write.—. . . Should these be worth his while, to these Mr. Perry shall be welcome; & all my reward shall be, his treating me with his Paper.[136]

Here again Burns was offering to write what he could to aid a friend, and asking no compensation in money. The whole incident is significant as showing the poet's continuing interest in literary work, the extent to which his reputation had spread, and his willingness to enlarge the scope of his activity even while he was carrying a heavy load for both Johnson and Thomson.

The second of these minor considerations is Burns's connection with a collection of more or less unprintable songs known as *The Merry Muses of Caledonia*. Throughout the poet's letters to his intimate friends there are casual remarks showing his familiarity with this sort of verse. An occasional bit of rhyme, of which only a line or two can today be printed, attests his own skill in composing such *facetiae*. The opening pages of his second *Commonplace Book* record his intention there to preserve "Poems and fragments that must never see the light." [137] In the course of time he got together, for his own entertainment and that of his friends, a number of such things; he wrote some amusing ones himself. The collection thus formed he allowed

[424]

to circulate in MS, with the result that his responsibility for it became somewhat widely known. Andrew Erskine, for example, wrote to him in January, 1793, reminding him of his promise to let him see his "unpublished productions, *religious and amorous.*" [138] In December of the same year Burns wrote to John M'Murdo:

> I think I once mentioned something of a collection of Scots songs I have for some years been making: I send you a perusal of what I have got together. I could not conveniently spare them above five or six days, and five or six glances of them will probably more than suffice you. A very few of them are my own. When you are tired of them, please leave them with Mr. Clint, of the King's Arms. There is not another copy of the collection in the world; and I should be sorry that any unfortunate negligence should deprive me of what has cost me a good deal of pains.[139]

It is beyond dispute, then, that Burns made a collection of "Cloaciniads," some of which he merely wrote down, and some of which he composed himself, and that he allowed his friends to share its beauties with him.

As certain is it that Burns never intended these scraps of merry drollery to be published, or to be in any formal way associated with his name. Especially towards the close of his life he was worried lest, as Mrs. Riddell guardedly put it, "many indifferent poetical pieces . . . would now, with all their imperfections on their head, be thrust upon the world."

Precisely what Burns foresaw as an unfortunate possibility did actually take place. About 1800 *The Merry Muses of Caledonia* was printed in Scotland, not credited to Burns on the title page, but so generally ascribed to him by common gossip that various reprints have boldly claimed his authorship for the entire collection. The student interested in determining Burns's exact relation to this publication will consult Dr. Hans Hecht's article, "Robert Burns und die Merry Muses." [140] But the material facts, and the only facts of importance except to the specialist, are those here set forth. Like most of his contemporaries, Burns enjoyed Rabelaisian humor. But he never intended his own private collection of it to be published, or to be thought of as forming any part of his literary work.

6

THE END OF THE STORY

By January of 1796 Burns's work was done. During the six months of life that remained to him he was an invalid, sinking steadily to his death. The story of these six months adds nothing to the record of Burns's literary accomplishment, and might profitably be condensed into a few sentences, were it not for the fact that certain prevalent opinions concerning Burns's financial and social position at the close of his life, and the reasons for his early breakdown and death, must be examined in some detail. No other course would be fair to his memory.

For some time before his death Burns had been worried about money matters. The general economic situation was discouraging; his own family expenses were increasing; once again he was trying to make three guineas do the work of five. Towards the close of 1795, he had been obliged to write to his friend Collector Mitchell, asking the return of a guinea, or—possibly, for there is no way of being entirely certain—begging the loan of "one-pound-one." The letter was a pleasant little *jeu-d'esprit* in verse, done in Burns's best manner; but reading between the lines one realizes that only necessity could have forced him to write it.[141]

Soon afterwards Burns wrote to James Clarke, the Moffat schoolmaster whom he had befriended and to whom he had advanced money, asking the repayment of that loan. Clarke's reply indicates that Burns had represented himself as being in hard straits:

Your letter makes me very unhappy; the more so as I had heard very flattering accounts of your situation some months ago. A note [for one guinea] is enclosed; and if such partial payments will be acceptable, this shall soon be followed by more.[142]

[426]

Clarke wrote thus in the winter of 1796. From this time to the end of his life Burns was more and more concerned about finances, till during the last few weeks of his life his distress became acute. The cause of this alarm, as all the world knows, was the fact that early in July a Dumfries merchant named Williamson, from whom Burns had purchased his Volunteer's uniform, took steps to collect the £7-6s which Burns owed him. The poet by this time knew himself to be dying; he remembered how his father's last weeks had been spent in terror of debtor's prison; in his weakened condition he imagined himself in the same predicament. Without stopping to consider that there must have been at least a score of persons in Dumfries who would gladly have assisted him in any financial difficulty, he wrote a pathetically distracted letter to his cousin James Burness of Montrose:

My DEAREST COUSIN,

When you offered me money-assistance little did I think I should want it so soon.—A rascal of a Haberdasher to whom I owe a considerable bill taking it into his head that I am dying, has commenced a process against me, & will infallibly put my emaciated body into jail.—Will you be so good as to accomodate me, & that by return of post, with ten pound. —O, James! did you know the pride of my heart, you would feel doubly for me! Alas! I am not used to beg! [143]

On the same day he wrote to Thomson, on whom not long before he had laid an injunction never to send him money:

After all my boasted independance, curst necessity compels me to implore you for five pounds.—A cruel scoundrel of a Haberdasher to whom I owe an account, taking it into his head that I am dying, has commenced a process, & will infallibly put me into jail.—Do, for God's sake, send me that sum, & that by return of post.—Forgive me this earnestness, but the horrors of a jail have made me half distracted. [144]

Each of these persons at once sent Burns the sums requested, though the money did not reach him till after he had virtually lost consciousness. [145]

It would be an exaggeration to say that financial worry hastened Burns's death. But it is certain that his last days were

[427]

rendered unhappy by petty debts which loomed unnnecessarily large before him. When he died, he owed probably thirty or forty pounds—part to Captain Hamilton for current house rent, part to Williamson for his uniform, and the rest in petty amounts to local tradesmen. To offset these debts there were due to him from his brother Gilbert approximately two hundred pounds, and a few small sums from friends to whom he had made occasional advances.

Such were the real facts. Yet many a reader of Burns believes that he lived his last years in penury and died in bankruptcy—an idea as wide of the truth as any of the exaggerated reports set on foot after his death. Inevitably there were times when Burns was without ready cash for current expenses, and was forced to borrow. But he was never in danger of bankruptcy—not in the hard days at Lochlie when he limited his expenses to the seven pounds a year paid him by his father, nor in the Ellisland years when he saw the profits from the Edinburgh volume gradually eaten up by his farm, nor yet in Dumfries. He was no spendthrift or wastrel. The worst one can truthfully say of him is that he was unfortunate in some of his financial dealings and imprudent in some of his generosities. But throughout his entire life he lived scrupulously within his income, and supported himself and his family in honorable independence.

As regards social position, Burns was far happier in Dumfries than has been sometimes believed. Much has been made of an anecdote, recounted first by Lockhart, implying that Burns's last years were saddened by social ostracism visited on him because of his personal misconduct:

[Mr. McCulloch] . . . was seldom more grieved, than when riding into Dumfries one fine summer's evening . . . to attend a county-ball, he saw Burns walking alone, on the shady side of the principal street of the town, while the opposite side was gay with successive groups of gentlemen and ladies, all drawn together for the festivities of the night, not one of whom appeared willing to recognize him. The horseman dismounted and joined Burns, who, on his proposing to him to cross the street, said, "Nay, nay, my young friend—that's all over now." [146]

Saturday Noon

My Dear Sir,

my hours of bathing
have interfered so unluckily a to have
put it out of my power to wait on
you. — In the mean time, as the
tides are over I anxiously wish to return to
town, as I have not heard any news of
Mrs Burns these two days. — Dare I
be so bold as to borrow your Gig?
I have a horse at command, but it
threatens to rain, & getting wet is
perdition. — any time about three in
the afternoon, will suit me exactly. —

gratefully & sincerely
R. Burns

LETTER TO JOHN CLARK WRITTEN AT BROW, 16 JULY 1796,
FIVE DAYS BEFORE BURNS'S DEATH

From the original in the collection of Mr. Oliver R. Barrett

What actual evidence there is confirms one in the *a priori* opinion that here, as in many other places, Lockhart was merely drawing upon his imagination.   The letters written during the summer and autumn of 1794, when the incident is supposed to have taken place, are sparkling with Burns's customary zest for living; at the close of the year he was appointed Acting Supervisor in the Excise.   In the spring of 1795 he was busy helping Patrick Heron of Kerroughtree in his Parliamentary campaign; at the same time he was active in the organization of the Dumfries Volunteers.   Had he sunk so low in the esteem of his fellow citizens as Lockhart implied, he must perforce have played a very different rôle in the life of the town.   No, the old tradition that Burns spent his last months cut off, by his own misconduct, from the company of respectable Dumfriesians, is utterly false.   He had political and personal enemies who might conceivably have been glad to see him suffer as he is supposed to have done.   But Dumfries as a whole, and the best part of it in particular, was cordial and friendly.

When one turns to a consideration of Burns's health during his last six months, one is justified in saying that his last illness had its beginning as far back as December, 1795.   Never was he to be really free from the rheumatic fever that during December and January brought him "to the borders of the grave." [147]   During February, Burns was in a more normal condition.   By April, however, he was again seriously ill, and though his spirits revived a little with the coming of warm weather, there was no real improvement in his condition.   In May, he wrote Thomson:

I have great hopes that the genial influence of t[he a]pproaching summer will set me to rights, but as yet I cannot boast of returning health.   I have now reason to believe that my complaint is a flying gout:—a damnable business! [148]

On July 3, Burns began a final attempt to check the disease that was killing him.   Acting on the explicit advice of his physician

[429]

he left Dumfries and went to Brow, twenty-four miles away, on the Solway Firth, where he hoped to find relief in sea-bathing and the quiet of country life. Four days later he wrote to Alexander Cunningham, suggesting that he speak a good word for him to the Excise Board, and telling more about his health:

Alas! my friend, I fear the voice of the Bard will soon be heard among you no more! For these eight or ten months I have been ailing, sometimes bedfast & sometimes not; but these last three months I have been tortured with an excruciating rheumatism, which has reduced me to nearly the last stage.—You actually would not know [me] if you saw me.—Pale, emaciated, & so feeble as occasionally to need help from my chair—my spirits fled! fled!—but I can no more on the subject—only the Medical folks tell me that my last & only chance is bathing & country quarters & riding.[149]

Brow had nothing of real value to offer Burns. The spring water which had given the place a local reputation was innocuous at best; the sea bathing did him more harm than good. He was anxious about Jean, who was again awaiting the birth of a child; he was steadily growing more feeble. Hence he returned to Dumfries, probably on Monday, the 18th of July. He had enjoyed a farewell visit with Maria Riddell; he had written half a dozen letters and one or two songs; he understood perfectly well that the end was at hand. When he reached Dumfries, in the gig of his friend John Clark of Locherwoods, he wrote at once to his father-in-law at Mauchline:

MY DEAR SIR:

Do, for Heaven's sake, send Mrs. Armour here immediately. My wife is hourly expecting to be put to bed. Good God! What a situation for her to be in, poor girl, without a friend! I returned from sea-bathing quarters today, and my medical friends would almost persuade me that I am better; but I think and feel that my strength is so gone that the disorder will prove fatal to me.[150]

Apparently it was the last document of any sort that Burns was to write, this letter imploring aid for Jean; for three days later, on Thursday, the twenty-first of July, he died.

It was a brief span of life—not quite thirty-seven and a half years. Inevitably one finds oneself wondering what causes contributed to its early termination. And at once certain traditional explanations present themselves. For example, the world at large has long held the opinion that Burns was a confirmed alcoholic, especially during the Dumfries years, and that in effect he drank himself into an early grave.

There is a certain justification for this impression. Though Burns's bacchanalian verse does not bulk large in quantity, it was obviously written with no mere feigned enthusiasm. His letters too contain ample evidence of his fondness for a bottle of port. To Mrs. Dunlop he made candid confession of his sins:

> Occasional hard drinking is the devil to me.—Against this I have again & again bent my resolution, & have greatly succeeded.—Taverns, I have totally abandoned: it is the private parties in the family way, among the hard drinking gentlemen of this country, that does me the mischief—but even this, I have more than half given over.[151]

Burns's first influential biographer, Dr. Currie, a physician who decried the use of alcohol in any form or degree as a beverage, represented him as far more an "occasional hard drinker," and stated categorically that he was "perpetually stimulated by alcohol." Later biographers followed Currie's lead, till the tradition of alcoholism was firmly established.

Actual evidence, however, contradicts this impression. The testimony of Findlater and Gray has already been set forth; many more character witnesses as credible might be summoned if necessary.[152] When one has discarded unsubstantiated gossip set on foot thirty years after Burns's death, one will discover that the persons who knew him best during what have been called his "evil days" were unanimous in testifying to his habitual sobriety.

And, indeed, one hardly requires the words of these friends of the poet to controvert the old misconception. One should remember the amount of literary work Burns accomplished at Dumfries, the excellent record he made in the Excise, and the success with which he cared for his family on an income that never, apparently, exceeded £90 per year. It is impossible to reconcile the alcoholic debauchee theory with these admitted facts.

In this connection some attention must be paid to the widely circulated story of an unfortunate carousal at the Globe Inn, and the resulting fatal illness. Perhaps the most succinct version, and certainly the one that has about it the most convincing air of authenticity, is that of Dr. Chambers:

> Early in the month of January, when his health was in the course of improvement, Burns tarried to a late hour at a jovial party in the Globe Tavern. Before returning home, he unluckily remained for some time in the open air, and, overpowered by the effects of the liquor he had drunk, fell asleep. In these circumstances, and in the peculiar condition to which a severe medicine had reduced his constitution, a fatal chill penetrated to his bones; he reached home with the seeds of a rheumatic fever already in possession of his weakened frame. In this little accident, and not in the pressure of poverty or disrepute, or wounded feelings or a broken heart, truly lay the determining cause of the sadly shortened days of our great national poet.[153]

The incident might conceivably have taken place. But Burns's statements in letters to his friends indicate that he was confined to his room during nearly all of January; and even had he wandered to the Globe Inn—less than a quarter of a mile from his home—on some winter night, it is altogether improbable that he would have been so reckless as to drink himself into insensibility, or that his friends would have allowed him to fall asleep in the snow on the way home. Furthermore, when one examines the various accounts of the story, one discovers that Currie, who first told it, said merely that "he dined at a tavern, and returned home about three o'clock in a very cold morning, benumbed and intoxicated," [154] and that subsequent accounts disagree as to what happened, or when. When once Currie had started the story, however, in its vague and not too incriminating form, other biographers seized upon it, and embroidered it to suit their fancy. The more one examines the legend, the more difficulty one finds in fitting it into the known facts of Burns's last year. So even though there are persons in Dumfries today who will point out the precise spot where Burns fell asleep in the snow, the conservative student will brand the entire story as fiction, and disregard it.

Another current explanation for Burns's early death is to be found in the charge that his health was shattered by venereal infection. Dr. Currie stated without qualification, but without giving any authority for his accusation, that "from October, 1795, to the January following, an accidental complaint confined [Burns] to the house."[155] The tradition of venereal infection thus set on foot may be found, in one form or another, in many biographies of the poet, and must at least be considered.

Absolutely to prove or disprove Currie's charge is impossible; but there is not a little evidence tending to show that he was mistaken. For example, the records of the Dumfries Volunteers show that Burns was active in the affairs of the corps till well into November, 1795. Josiah Walker, who was to publish his *Life of Burns* in 1811, visited the poet in this same month. The two men tramped together along the banks of the Nith, and passed the evenings with mutual friends at the Globe Inn. Walker's account makes it clear that at this time Burns was not in any sense a sick man. Far more important is the fact that no trace of any such infection ever marred the ruddy health of Jean Armour Burns. And the poet himself, who was absolutely frank in admitting his errors, makes no statement that could possibly be distorted into even a suggestion that his breakdown was in any way occasioned or accompanied by venereal disease. He says explicitly that he was ill with rheumatic fever.

One should remember that Currie was inaccurate and unreliable; he was not above juggling facts to fit the case he was trying to make. In this particular instance he was endeavoring to picture Burns as a victim of alcoholism, and to show the horrors of any sort of indulgence. In his mind, moreover, the use of alcohol led directly to the further misfortunes of which he was accusing Burns: "He who suffers the pollution of inebriation, how shall he escape other pollution?" [156]

The probability is that Currie seized upon some chance remark—it should be remembered that he himself saw Burns only once, and then for but a brief time—realized that it fitted well into his anti-alcohol propaganda, and passed it on to the world as a fact. The conservative reader will enter a verdict of "Not proven" opposite this charge.

One should not be satisfied, however, with the mere negation of these two time-honored accusations. And fortunately it is now possible to advance a rational and reasoned explanation for Burns's early death. Within the past few years two physicians of distinction, independently of one another, have collected all of Burns's allusions to his health, as they appear in his letters, and the remarks pertaining to the same subject made about him by others. On the basis of this material they have constructed fairly complete clinical histories of his "case," and have given their diagnoses. Sir James Crichton-Browne, of Dumfries, in his *Burns from a New Point of View*,[157] states his opinion thus:

Burns died of endocarditis, a disease of the substance and lining membrane of the heart . . . At Mount Oliphant, from his thirteenth to his fifteenth year, the heart trouble was well declared . . . At Mossgiel in 1784 there was an exacerbation of the disease . . . It is characteristic of the mild types of this insidious form of heart disease from which Burns suffered, that its victims, until it is far advanced, are able to go about and take an active share in affairs, as if there was nothing the matter with them. But they are visited at different intervals during its course of twenty or thirty years by feverish attacks, significant often of another milestone on the downward journey, in which, with a quickened pulse, they become weak and qualmish, and are highly strung, nervous, and easily agitated. It is attacks of this kind that are occasionally tabulated in [Burns's] correspondence.[158]

Sir James then examines in detail Burns's records of his various illnesses, and concludes thus:

It will not, I think, be disputed that Burns died of rheumatic endocarditis.[159]

[434]

The second physician to analyze Burns's health record was Dr. Harry B. Anderson of Toronto. He summarizes his conclusions thus:

The case was an ordinary one of rheumatism with heart complications, shortness of breath, faintness, weakness, rapid, irregular pulse (auricular fibrillation), and towards the end, fever, parched tongue, and delirium, presumably due to a bacteriological endocarditis which developed as a terminal infection.[160]

The situation, then, seems to be something like this: To controvert the old and widely disseminated charges of alcoholism and venereal infection one has, first, the testimony of several persons who knew him intimately, and who flatly denied the truth of one slander; one has, second, the evidence of an astonishing amount of literary work successfully carried on under adverse conditions, and at the very time he was supposed to have been tottering into a drunkard's grave; one has, finally, the opinion of physicians of today, who find in the clinical record no sign of alcoholism or venereal disease, but every characteristic symptom of a rheumatic endocarditis, which manifested itself early in life, reappeared with increasing virulence from time to time, became acute early in 1796, and occasioned his death in July of that year.

To accept this answer to the question "What caused Burns's early death," is not to deny that from time to time Burns drank with characteristic recklessness, or that he was unchaste in his relations to women. He liked whiskey, and used it too generously—his own, and that of his friends. But he was never a drunkard, and he did not throw away his health in brothels. The physical disaster that overtook him in 1796 had announced itself long before, and was due to causes that would have brought about an early collapse even if he had been as confirmed a foe to alcohol as Dr. Currie. Had the medical science of 1785 been as far advanced as that of a century and a half later, it is at least conceivable that many years might have been added to Burns's life. But he would have been hopelessly unhappy under

[435]

the sort of regimen which would today be prescribed for a person suffering from endocarditis. Moreover, the imperative necessity of earning a living would have made it impossible for him to accept any routine of well-ordered quiet and rest. It is regrettable that the heavy farm labors of Mount Oliphant and Lochlie fell upon him at just the time he should have been free from undue physical burdens, for when once his heart had been as seriously overtaxed as it was during these years, some sort of premature collapse became inevitable. It is still more unfortunate that at Ellisland he was forced to be both farmer and gauger. But, conditions being what they were, the wonder is that the end did not come sooner, and that Burns was able to live out his brief span of life in such joyous enthusiasm.

Except for the last six months, the years at Dumfries were years of happy and varied activity: of friendly intercourse with men and women who loved Burns and welcomed him to their homes; of creditable and at times arduous labor in the Excise; of intelligent concern in international developments as well as in local matters; of unremitting attention to the interests of the two friends who were collecting and publishing the songs of Scotland. As evidence that Burns's poetic genius was undimmed, one has the scores of lyrics composed at Dumfries—a superb group, glorified by "A Red, Red Rose," "Ae Fond Kiss," "Ye Banks and Braes o' Bonie Doon," and "Scots Wha Hae." And if one seeks proof that Burns's spirit was still unconquered, one should recall the fact that on July 12, only nine days before his death, he was writing one last song for Thomson, and asking pardon for not being able to do more. This was the mood in which Burns waited for the wheel to come full circle.

7

AFTERWARDS

Burns's funeral, arranged by Syme, and conducted in military manner by the Dumfries Volunteers, the Cinque Port Cavalry, and the Angusshire Fencibles, took place on Monday, July

[436]

25.[161] He was buried in the northeast corner of St. Michael's churchyard, approximately a quarter of a mile from his home. Almost as his body was being lowered into the grave his wife gave birth to a son, whom she named Maxwell, in honor of the friend who for two years had been the family physician. For nearly twenty years the poet's body lay in this grave, under a simple and unmarked stone provided by Mrs. Burns. On September 12, 1815, however, it was transferred to the Mausoleum that had been erected by public subscription in the southeast corner of the same churchyard. Here it rests today; beside it lies the body of Jean Armour Burns, who survived her husband till March 26, 1834.

Even before the day of Burns's funeral a public subscription for the relief of his family had been set on foot by his friends.[162] The sum thus realized ultimately amounted to approximately twelve hundred pounds. To this was added at least as much more, derived from the profits of Dr. Currie's *Life and Works of Robert Burns*. To the end of her life Mrs. Burns occupied the house in the Mill Vennel, enjoying the comfortable independence which these sums, well-invested, made possible. Three of her sons grew to manhood: Robert Junior, James Glencairn, and William Nicol.[163] Both Elizabeth Paton's daughter, "Dear-bought Bess," and Anne Park's daughter, also named Elizabeth, were recognized as Burns's children; each received, from the subscription fund, the sum of two hundred pounds as dowry. Thus Burns's family was saved from the poverty which he had dreaded, and Scotland—perhaps a little tardily —gave what proof she could of her affectionate regard for her greatest son.

[1] *Op. cit.*, IV, 441.
[2] H. H., IV, 334.
[3] See letter to Kirkpatrick, 22 Oct., 1791; *Letters*, II, 97.
[4] The westernmost arch of the present "Old Bridge" is probably part of the original structure; the rest is more recent. (G. W. S.)
[5] At least twenty more were annually fined for selling without licenses.
[6] Manuscript notes, now in Ewart Public Library, Dumfries. Parts of these notes were published in the *Statistical Account*. (G. W. S.)
[7] The street is commonly said to have been called The Wee Vennel in Burns's day. No such name seems to have been known to Dumfriesians, who referred to the street as

either The Stinking Vennel, because of the open sewer in the middle of the roadway, or Cawart's Vennel. (G. W. S.)

[8] Waddell, II, Appendix, xxii.

[9] *Letters*, II, 99. The date of the letter is uncertain; it may be November, 1791, as is here assumed. It may be later.

[10] C. W., III, 300.

[11] Letter of 23 November, 1791; *Letters*, II, 100.

[12] Since the publication of Ferguson's edition of Burns's *Letters*, the complete text of letter No. 295 has come to light. This makes it clear that on Jan. 6, 1789, Burns was planning to go to Edinburgh, see Jenny Clow, "settle that matter with her, and free her hand of the process." Apparently she too, like May Cameron, had served him with a writ.

[13] The diploma is dated 10 April, 1792. Cunningham suggested that Burns write a poem on archery; Burns declined.

[14] The performances were distinctly meritorious.

[15] H. H., II, 146.

[16] *Letters*, II, 132.

[17] C. W., IV, 54.

[18] Letter of March, 1793; *Letters*, II, 154.

[19] The house is now the property of the Dumfries Industrial School; the second floor is maintained as a Burns Museum. The somewhat squalid surroundings, painfully apparent to the visitor today, were not in evidence in 1793, but are one of the unfortunate results of the growth of manufacturing in Dumfries. However, a move is on foot to purchase and remove the nearby tenements.

[20] Smollett's *Humphrey Clinker*, Mackenzie's *Julia de Roubigné*, Knox's *History of the Reformation*, and John De Lolme's *The British Constitution*.

[21] *Letters*, II, 211.

[22] *Ibid.*, p. 223.

[23] Letter of 25 Feb., 1794; *ibid.*, p. 234.

[24] *Ibid.*, p. 231.

[25] See letter to Clarke; *ibid.*, p. 249.

[26] C. W., IV, 133.

[27] Syme's Account; C. W., IV, 20. Burns's letter to McCulloch (*Letters*, II, 245), makes it clear that the year was 1794, and not 1793, as Syme said.

[28] See letters to James Gracie, April, 1791, and David Sillar, June, 1791; *Letters*, II, 72, 82.

[29] See letters of 29 and 31 January; *ibid.*, pp. 285, 286.

[30] *The Life and Works of Robert Burns* (1834), I, 319.

[31] See W. Will, "Robert Burns as a Volunteer;" *Chronicle*, 1920, 5 ff.

[32] H. H., III, 195; first published in the *Edinburgh Courant*, 4 May, 1795.

[33] Letter of May, 1795; *Letters*, II, 299.

[34] C. W., IV, 218.

[35] *Ibid.*, p. 219. Note.

[36] William Will, in his article "Burns as a Volunteer" (*Chronicle*, 1920, pp. 5 ff.), states that Dr. Maxwell was a member of the corps. This is an error, for his name does not appear on any of the rolls.

[37] Peterkin's reprint (1815) of Currie; I, xciii.

[38] Letter of June, 1791; *Letters*, II, 81. Lorimer was father of "Chloris." See below, pp. xxx ff.

[39] *Op. cit.*, I, lxxxv.

[40] In 1801 Gray left Dumfries to accept the Latin Mastership in the Edinburgh High School. Here he remained till 1822. Shortly thereafter he became a chaplain in the service of the East India Company. He died in India in 1830.

[41] *Memorials of St. Michael's*, by William M'Dowall, Edinburgh, 1876; p. 265.

[42] *Letters*, II, 159.

[43] Concerning White, see William M'Diarmid's *Sketches from Nature* (London, 1830), pp. 305 ff.

[44] Letter of March, 1791; *Letters*, II, 62.

[45] Letter of 27 July, 1788; *ibid.*, I, 237.

[46] Letter of 10 Sept., 1792; *ibid.*, II, 118.

[47] Letter of 20 Feb., 1793; *ibid.*, p. 149.

[48] Letter of 7 July, 1796; *ibid.*, p. 325. The child, born the day of Burns's funeral, was named Maxwell. Mrs. Burns was probably unaware of her husband's intentions in the matter. James Glencairn had been born Aug. 12, 1794.

[49] See Burns's letter, 13 July, 1796; *ibid.*, p. 329.

[50] John McIlraith, *Life of Sir John Richardson;* London, 1868; p. 3.

[51] *Letters,* II, 260. The lines to Chloris are by Sir Charles Sedley. Burns probably found them in the *Tea-Table Miscellany.*

[52] Letter of 19 Oct., 1794; *ibid.*, p. 264.

[53] Chloris's subsequent history was most unhappy. Her husband, Whelpdale, was a thorough reprobate, who abandoned her with even less compunction than M'Lehose had shown for Clarinda. The details of her later life are available in James Adams's *Burns's Chloris: a Reminiscence;* Glasgow, 1901.

[54] Written in May, 1796; H. H., III, 237.

[55] Chambers, IV, 125 f.

[56] Letter of 22 Jan., 1792; *Letters,* II, 106. Mrs. Riddell's book was published towards the close of the year.

[57] *Letters,* II, 110.

[58] *Ibid.*, p. 216.

[59] Letter of April, 1793; *ibid.*, p. 163.

[60] Letter of ? November, 1793; *ibid.*, p. 215.

[61] A letter dated 12 January, 1794, from Burns to (probably) Mrs. Walter Riddell, makes it clear that the breach had already taken place. (*Letters,* II, 229.)

[62] *Letters,* II, 226. The letter is undated.

[63] Information concerning Mrs. Riddell and her husband from "Maria Riddell, the Friend of Burns," by Hugh Gladstone, *Transactions,* Dumfriesshire and Galloway Natural History and Antiquarian Society, 1914–1915, pp. 16 ff. The article adds much to our knowledge of Mrs. Riddell's life. Proof of Walter's absence is to be found in his wife's letters to Smellie, printed in Robert Ker's *Memoirs of William Smellie* (Edinburgh, 1811), II, 360–388.

[64] H. H., II, 271.

[65] See "Robert Burns and Maria Riddell," by J. DeL. Ferguson; *Mod. Philol.*, November, 1930; pp. 169 ff.

[66] See letter of 25 June, 1794; *Letters,* II, 247.

[67] C. W., IV, 172.

[68] *Ibid.*, p. 175.

[69] *Letters,* II, 314.

[70] Letter of ? 1 June, 1796; *ibid.*, p. 323.

[71] Chambers, IV, 202.

[72] Maria Riddell's character sketch was originally published in an August number of the Dumfries *Weekly Journal* for 1796. In the years that have followed it has been many times reprinted, with greater or less degrees of accuracy. It is impossible now to determine precisely what the original version was, for there seems to be no copy of that particular number of the Dumfries *Journal* in existence. But it is clear, as Mr. J. C. Ewing pointed out to me, that Mrs. Riddell revised her article for Currie's 1801 edition of his life of Burns, and that she wished the text which she herself sent to the publishers of this edition to be considered the authentic text. Hence the version which appears in Currie's second and subsequent editions is the one which may fairly be called authentic.

[73] Letter of ? October, 1791; *Letters,* II, 93.

[74] Letter to Graham of Fintry, 31 July, 1789; *ibid.*, I, 346.

[75] See an important article by J. DeL. Ferguson: "Collector William Corbet," *Chronicle,* 1931, p. 65.

[76] Lockhart's *Life of Burns* (1828), pp. 218 f.

[77] Letter to J. Leven; ? March, 1792; *Letters,* II, 112.

[78] C. W., III, 317.

[79] Letter of Sept., 1792; *Letters,* II, 123. See letter to Marie Riddell, *Letters,* II, 110, concerning this appointment. The salary was seventy pounds a year; the "perquisites" fifteen or twenty more.

[80] Letter of 31 December, 1792; *ibid.*, p. 139.

[81] Letter of 5 Jan., 1793; *ibid.*, p. 141.

[82] Letter of 5 Jan., 1793; *ibid.*, p. 143.

[83] Letter of 13 April, 1793; *ibid.*, p. 169.

[84] John Sinton: *Burns, Excise Officer and Poet;* Kilmarnock [1896], p. 28.

[85] It is interesting to note that even after this experience, Burns in June of 1794 composed and sent to Mrs. Dunlop the "Ode for General Washington's Birthday" (*Letters,* II, 246).

[86] The incident has usually been treated as of August, 1795. But in his letter concerning the use of the Dumfries schools (March, 1793), Burns referred to the "twa pennies," and to his having collected some ten pounds from this source in a few weeks. Hence Professor J. DeL. Ferguson's assumption, in the *Letters,* followed by the present writer, that 1793 is the correct date.

[87] *Letters,* II, 147 and 154.

[88] Letter of 7 Jan., 1794; *ibid.*, p. 228.

[89] See letter to Mrs. Dunlop, 29 Dec., 1794; *ibid.*, p. 280.

[90] See Sinton, *Robert Burns, Excise Officer and Poet,* pp. 35 and 37.

[91] F. B. Snyder: "Burns's Last Years;" *Studies in Philol.,* Oct., 1929; p. 463.

[92] Letter of 25 April, 1795; *Letters,* II, 295.

[93] *Ibid.*, p. 319.

[94] Letter of 7 July, 1796; *ibid.*, p. 325.

[95] *Ibid.*, p. 327.

[96] Quoted, C. W., IV, 264, n.

[97] Currie, I, 229.

[98] F. B. Snyder: "Burns's Last Years;" *Studies in Philol.,* Oct., 1929; p. 463.

[99] For example, "We can see for ourselves that the Burns of the Kilmarnock volume and the good things in the *Museum* had ceased to be some time before the end." H. H., IV, 336.

[100] For pertinent evidence on this last point, see Davidson Cook's "Burns's *Old Bacchanal* Found at Last"; *The Bookman* (London), January, 1925.

[101] See Burns's letter to Peter Hill; *Letters,* II, 95. The date of the letter is uncertain.

[102] Quoted, C. W., III, 260, n.

[103] Letter of 16 April, 1792; *Letters,* II, 113.

[104] Quoted, C. W., III, 325, n.

[105] Letter of 6 Dec., 1792; *Letters,* II, 138.

[106] *A Select Collection of Original Scotish Airs;* London [1793–1818], 5 vols.

[107] It is of course true that a few of the lyrics sent to Thomson had been composed before the Dumfries period. But the great majority were written at Dumfries, and specifically for Thomson's work.

[108] J. Cuthbert Hadden: *George Thomson, the Friend of Burns.* London, 1898.

[109] Letter of Sept., 1792; C. W., III, 330.

[110] Letters of 16 Sept., 1792; *Letters,* II, 122. The last sentence was probably added because the fourth volume of the *Museum* had just come out, with a preface, by Burns, promising a fifth volume. Burns did not wish Johnson to think that he was abandoning him in order to take up with Thomson.

[111] Letter of 27 April, 1789; *Letters,* I, 326.

[112] Letter of 26 Oct., 1792; *ibid.*, II, 126.

[113] Letter of 8 Nov., 1792; *ibid.*, p. 129.

[114] I am indebted to Mr. G. W. Shirley for this interesting piece of evidence.

[115] Letter of Nov., 1792; C. W., III, 366.

[116] Letter of 20 Jan., 1793; *ibid.*, p. 390.

[117] Letter of 7 April, 1793; *Letters,* II, 166.

[118] *Ibid.*

[119] Letter of 1 July, 1793; C. W., III, 431.

[120] His real name was John Wolcott (1738–1819).

[121] Letter of 20 August, 1793; C. W., IV, 28.

[122] Letter of August, 1793; *Letters,* II, 191.

[123] A shawl.

[124] Letter of Feb., 1796; *ibid.*, II, 317.

[125] Letter of April, 1796; *ibid.*, p. 319.

[126] *Ibid.*, p. 324.

[127] Letter of 12 July, 1796; *ibid.*, p. 328. The song, "Fairest maid on Devon banks," was Burns's last poem.

[128] C. W., IV, 20.

[129] Letter of 30 August, 1793; *Letters*, II, 194.

[130] *Op. cit.*, IV, 38.

[131] *Letters*, II, 194.

[132] He had sent a copy to Mrs. Dunlop on Dec. 7, 1788, though without admitting the authorship. *Letters*, I, 276.

[133] Letter of January, 1795; *ibid.*, II, 283.

[134] For the sake of completeness, the following information concerning the dates of Thomson's different numbers is inserted:
The first set or number was published in May of 1793; the second, completing the first volume, in 1798. The third and fourth both appeared in 1799. Volume III was published as a unit in 1801; volume IV in 1805; and volume V, containing thirty songs instead of fifty, and a version of "The Jolly Beggars," not until 1818. See J. C. Dick: *The Songs of Robert Burns*, London, 1903, p. xxxvii.

[135] See Burns's letter to Stuart; *Letters*, I, 333.

[136] Letter of May, 1794; *ibid.*, II, 239. The "Ode" was "Scots wha hae."

[137] C. W., II, 84.

[138] *Ibid.*, III, 392.

[139] Letter of December, 1793; *Letters*, II, 222.

[140] Herrig's *Archiv*, CXXIX, 363 ff.

[141] For text, see H. H., II, 137.

[142] Letter of 18 Feb., 1796; C. W., IV, 262. On June 26 Burns again asked Clarke for money.

[143] Letter of 12 July, 1796; *Letters*, II, 327.

[144] *Ibid.*, p. 328.

[145] See Chambers, IV, 222.

[146] Lockhart, *Life of Burns* (1828), p. 212.

[147] Letter to Cleghorn; January, 1796; *Letters*, II, 315.

[148] *Ibid.*, p. 320.

[149] Letter of 7 July, 1796; *ibid.*, p. 325.

[150] *Ibid.*, p. 330.

[151] Letter of 31 December, 1792; *Letters*, II, 140.

[152] See F. B. Snyder: "Burns's Last Years"; *Studies in Philol.*; Oct., 1929.

[153] Chambers, IV, 183.

[154] Currie, I, 219.

[155] *Ibid.*

[156] *Ibid.*

[157] Hodder and Stoughton; London; [1926].

[158] *Op. cit.*, pp. 62 f.

[159] *Ibid.*, p. 85.

[160] "Robert Burns, his medical friends, attendants, and biographer;" in *Annals of Medical History*, X (March, 1928), 47 ff.

[161] Allan Cunningham's well known account of the ceremonies is a work of the imagination, worthy of no credence whatever.

[162] The Edinburgh *Courant* for July 28, 1796, contains notices of a projected edition of Burns's poetry, signed by Cunningham and Syme, and of a subscription, signed by Patrick Miller, Dr. Maxwell, Syme, James Fergusson, and Cunningham.

[163] Francis Wallace died 9 July, 1803; Maxwell, 23 November, 1799. James Glencairn, 18 November, 1865; William Nicol, 21 February, 1872.

[441]

CHAPTER XI

THE MAN AND THE POET

SUCH were the chief facts of Burns's life. Despite a few uncertainties, the story as a whole is clear and easy to comprehend. The boy at Alloway and Mount Oliphant was more intellectually alert than most Ayrshire lads of his age; he was more given to reading and to writing letters. But except for these interests, which only his father and schoolmaster recognized, he was in no apparent way an unusual youngster. Lochlie saw him enjoying the friendship of neighboring young men, taking to himself more and more of the farm responsibility, raising stock, harvesting the crops, delighting in his rapidly developing skill as a poet, and for the most part suppressing the restiveness which a hard and confining way of life engendered in him. But this restiveness was becoming an ever larger element in Burns's psychology, and by the time the death of his father threw the management of the family affairs into his hands, the steady-going farm lad had developed into an embittered rebel. When the strict moral code in which he had been nurtured acted as a check to his natural desires, he broke the code and gratified those desires. When the Kirk Session reprimanded his friends for petty infractions of church discipline, he replied with "Holy Willie's Prayer." When the state put the strength of the law at the disposal of the laird, to assist him in maintaining the economic *status quo*, Burns wrote "The Address of Beelzebub." Finally, smarting under censure for his own misdeeds, and fully conscious that half of his fault consisted in having been found out, he gave the ultimate expression to the spirit of protest in "The Jolly Beggars." No more defiant

[442]

blast ever blew from the trumpet of a rebel than the last song of this cantata.

Fortunately for Burns, this restiveness was in part alleviated by the publication of his first volume. Then came Edinburgh, and popularity which gratified but never bewildered him. He understood the ephemeral nature of his success, and even before the 1787 volume was off the press he had begun making plans for the inevitable return to the farm, and for the Excise.

When at last, with money in his pocket, he left Edinburgh, it was to go unostentatiously back to Mossgiel, where he turned over nearly one half of his profits to the less fortunate members of his family, and once more put himself under a heavy debt to the woman whom ultimately he was to marry. Ellisland saw him again holding the plow, and again finding it impossible to wrest even an inadequate living from the stubborn soil. There was still joy to be had in poetry, however; and when the move to Dumfries brought with it release from farm life, it was this undying happiness in song-writing that kept Burns's spirit buoyant; this, and his genius for friendship, which neither unfamiliar ways of life nor illness could bedim.

But there was tragedy in Burns's later years. In denying him the "life of literary leisure with a decent competence" which was "the summit of [his] wishes," Fate prevented him from ever doing full justice to his poetic endowment. The consciousness of this fact engendered unhappiness, melancholia, a sense of repression, at times almost of futility. None the less Burns possessed capacities which enabled him to find reasonable satisfaction in that which was allotted to him. And when he saw the end approaching he had the gratifying realization that fame had come to him in rich measure, even though he had never given complete expression to his creative genius.

All this will seem patent enough to anyone who cares to read the record. Equally clear is it that the Burns who lived this sort of existence was superbly courageous, and blessed with an enthusiasm for life which not even recurring attacks of depressing illness could wholly overshadow. Further comment on

[443]

these personal traits is unnecessary. It will be worth while, however, to pry a little more deeply into the fascinating problem of Burns's personality, and then to point out one or two of the less obvious characteristics of his poetry, before bringing this chronicle to a close.

1

BURNS THE MAN

When Maria Riddell wrote her character sketch of Burns, she did not hesitate to ascribe to him what she called an "irresistible power of attraction." Possibly she came as close to the heart of the matter as one could expect to come in a single phrase. To call Burns's personality "magnetic," would be merely to use a hackneyed adjective for the elusive quality which Mrs. Riddell knew to be the most obvious of his personal attributes. "An irresistible power of attraction": to phrase the matter thus was to state what every friend of the poet had found true. Wherever he went, he became the center of the group; all talk ceased when he entered a room. His own conversation was more brilliant than that of any of his associates. Without regard for social tradition, men of all ranks sought his company. Plowmen and inn-keepers found him congenial; university professors were glad to have him in their homes; lairds and lords welcomed him not as a peasant phenomenon but as a friend. Women were "swept off their feet," as the Duchess of Gordon put it, by the fascination of his personality. They loved him, sometimes more than they knew. They offered themselves to him without condition or reserve, for there was no one else quite like him. Scott saw him once; and though Sir Walter was a mere boy at the time, he never forgot the experience. One recalls the expression he used in writing to his son-in-law a quarter of a century afterwards: "His eye glowed; yes, I say literally glowed." What was true of Burns's eye was true of his entire personality; it was glowing, irresistible.

Testimony concerning this central fact of Burns's personality comes from his friends; his own letters and poems offer little evidence on this score. But one need not go beyond Burns's own work for information with which to round out this picture of the man. Reviewing that work in its entirety, one sees Burns's sense of humor written as large as any single quality. He was a man whom Chaucer or Cervantes or Dickens would have found companionable; Mark Twain would have delighted in his ability to see the incongruities and inconsistencies in human character, and in the genius which enabled him to clothe truth in the garb of fun. Like Clemens, Burns was humorist and moralist at the same time; his sense of humor saved him from taking his preacher's function too seriously; his consciousness of the significance of human life prevented him from degenerating into a mere entertainer. There was a range in his humor which one finds but rarely among the English poets. His laughter was by turns playful, witty, tenderly human, uproariously indecent, or ironically bitter. His moods were as changeable as the skies of his native Ayrshire, but even in the hours of blackest depression his ability to laugh at what Fate might offer him saved him from the misanthropy which could easily have been his lot.

Almost as obvious as Burns's humor was his pride. When one has said this one should add that this pride was not so much personal as social, for Burns the individual was modest, and not inclined to over-rate either himself or his performances. But Burns the representative of Scotland's laboring folk was a different person. His haughty independence, his strong sense of the worth of the people whose spokesman he aspired to be, his contempt for rank or wealth unaccompanied by personal merit, —these are some of the elements which went to the making of that pride. And all these are obvious in his poetry.

Then too there was an aggressive sensitiveness about Burns which is almost as apparent today as it must have been during his lifetime. He carried a chip on his shoulder. It is significant that this trait was well established as early as the Lochlie years. Dr. John Mackenzie, who first saw Burns in 1783, when he had been called to minister to the poet's dying father, afterwards wrote thus of his experience:

Gilbert, in the first interview I had with him at Lochlea, was frank, modest, well informed, and communicative. The poet seemed distant, suspicious, and without any wish to interest or please. He kept himself very silent in a dark corner of the room: And before he took any part in the conversation, I frequently detected him scrutinizing me during my conversation with his father and brother.[1]

This acute sensitiveness, which, especially in Burns's young manhood, was not unaccompanied by suspicion, contributed to both Burns's happiness and his unhappiness. He enjoyed life intensely, when it was to his liking; he delighted in the affection and applause of his friends. At the same time he winced under criticism, and was quick to take offense where he thought an injury had been done him. And when his anger had been roused, he was prompt and devastating in retaliation, though ready and generous in forgiveness. The numerous personal satires are evidence of Burns's fondness for sarcastic repartee, and also suggest the reason why his victims were not over charitable to him after his death.

Contrasting interestingly with this sensitiveness was Burns's recklessness. He was more concerned over public opinion than has generally been recognized; he scrutinized his poetry carefully before printing the Kilmarnock volume, and excluded much merely to avoid unnecessary offence to established authority. Except in this one respect, however, he was not given to caution —not even after the welfare of his family was dependent upon his discretion in word and deed. He was the most outspoken critic of orthodox Presbyterianism that Scotland produced during his lifetime. His criticism, moreover, was neither tempered by vague generalization nor veiled in allegory; it was direct, personal, mordant. He was a sturdy champion of political liberalism; and even when the anti-Jacobin reaction had made liberalism almost synonymous with treason, he clung to his faith and refused to be silenced. Burns enjoyed playing with fire, nor seemed much concerned if at times he himself was scorched. His passionate desire for freedom, for liberty to think and act and write and speak as he chose, never waned. And in undertaking to gratify that desire he acted with a recklessness which at times seems bewildering.

This same unwillingness to subject himself to restraint appears as one examines Burns's more intimately personal conduct. He was never the drunken rake that some persons still believe him to have been; he did not throw away his health in taverns or brothels. But it is no exaggeration to say that between 1784 and 1788 Burns successfully played the rôle of a village Don Juan. Even after his marriage, in the spring of 1788, he was not completely under control. For feminine virtue as such he had no more regard than for the consequences, to himself, of his licentiousness. At least fourteen children, of whom only five were certainly born in wedlock, put the matter beyond dispute. To run through the list of his known mistresses, and to realize that, *a priori*, there must have been others who escaped public disgrace, is to see this side of Burns at a glance. Elizabeth Paton, Jean Armour, May Cameron, Jennie Clow, Anne Park, and probably Mary Campbell,—these are the women whose names actually appear in the record. Though Burns married one, and supported the children of two others, there is no apologizing for or explaining away such a record. To plead that Burns was penitent and remorseful when he brought sorrow to anyone who had loved him, or that he was frank in confession, or to urge that times were different, does not alter the harsh fact that for some years he was as recklessly promiscuous in his sexual relations as though the "moral law" he professed to respect had been non-existent.

One fact, however, can fairly be urged in extenuation: wherever one traces Burns's footsteps one finds women seeking his company. The chances are that the luckless girls who were the mothers of his children had sought his companionship, and had offered themselves to him without reserve.

As one thinks over this phase of Burns's character, however, one pleasant consideration becomes apparent: his affectionate nature is as obvious as his recklessness. He loved his children without stopping to consider their exact legal status, and cared for them as well as he could, though at times he found it not hard to forget their mothers. Even Jennie Clow's son might have been brought up as an admitted member of the poet's family circle, like the daughters of Elizabeth Paton and Anne Park, had his mother been willing to part with him. Following the example set by his father before him, Burns wished his children to have a better chance in life than he had enjoyed. He was concerned over their education, and never begrudged the time necessary for tutoring them. "I have a genius for paternity," he once admitted to a friend. He might have added that as a concomitant of this talent he was endowed with a parental affection strong enough almost to justify the misdeeds that caused it to function.

Burns's loyalty to other members of his family is as obvious as his love for his children. Only once, and that in his younger days, does he seem seriously to have thought of leaving the family circle and striking out for himself. The failure of this single experiment, the Irvine flax-dressing fiasco, sent him promptly back to his father's roof, not so much for shelter as because he realized that he belonged there. The death of his father left him as head of the family group, and all his plans were made with their welfare in mind. The projected trip to Jamaica was not of his own seeking; it was forced on him by circumstances. When in the autumn of 1786 he rode up to Edinburgh, it was not to begin an entirely independent life of his own, but to make the money with which to ensure the happiness of the entire household. When he gave Gilbert nearly half the profits of the Edinburgh edition, he seems to have had no thought that the loan would ever be repaid. The capital was Gilbert's to use in his farm work; the interest was to be applied towards the support of Burns's mother and his daughter Elizabeth Paton. Not until July of 1796, when Burns was dying, and was himself hard pressed for money, is there anything to suggest that he might ask Gilbert to take up his note.[2] When his brother William was futilely trying to make a fair start in life, Robert gave him shelter and money and clothing as well as advice. He offered asylum to unfortunate relatives, and never lost touch with his cousins in the north. In other words, he was consistently loyal to the members of his family; they were his people, and, as a matter of course, he loved them and did what lay in his power to make them happy.

It was in part because of this warmly affectionate nature, and the frankness with which he discussed his own emotional life, that Burns appears to have been unduly sentimental. No matter how often he might remind himself and his correspondents of his favorite quotation,

> On reason build resolve,
> That column of true majesty in man,

it was not Burns's intellect but his emotions that controlled his actions. There were deep wells of sentiment in his nature, and a sympathy, or compassion, that embraced all of Burns's

> . . . earth-born companions,
> And fellow mortals.

He found it difficult, however, to give expression to that sentiment without allowing it to appear as a somewhat effervescent sentimentalism. Occasionally he held himself in check; "To a Mouse" and the central quatrain of "Ae Fond Kiss" are notable for their restraint. But as a rule Burns wore his heart on his sleeve.

If one seeks an explanation for Burns's life-long habit of sentimentalizing, one finds two contributing causes. First of all, he was that sort of person. He thought much about his own emotional experiences, and was restless till he had recorded those experiences in prose or verse. One need not read beyond the pages of the first *Commonplace Book* for proof of this. Furthermore, Burns lived at a time when a fog of sentimentalism, or "sensibility," as the eighteenth century called it, was in the air, and when the literature with which he came in contact was saturated with it. Thomson, Sterne, Mackenzie, Richardson—these were his tutors, who added the force of their examples to his own natural inclination; these, and the earlier Scottish song-writers, who on this score of sentimentalism were as persistent offenders as Burns himself. Small wonder that the austerity and reserve of the greatest personalities and greatest poetry are not to be found in Burns.

Inevitably a person of Burns's emotional make-up was bound to be concerned about religion, and to adopt for himself a faith in which sentimentalism should be apparent. It is a mistake to think of Burns as either irreligious or non-religious. He was bred in a deeply religious environment, with which he was fundamentally in accord, and with which he remained in accord. He was caustic in his criticism of certain Old Light clergymen, and equally trenchant in his ridicule of the Calvinist's dogmas of Original Sin and Election. But no one can read Burns's letters without realizing that to him religion was a matter of profound significance. Only when Religion joined hands with Hypocrisy, or assumed the shape of an intolerant and irrational dogmatism, did he become satirical.

Indeed, were one to estimate Burns by his letters to Mrs. Dunlop and Clarinda, one might judge him to have been more concerned over religion than over any other single factor in human life. But one should remember that when he wrote to either of these two friends, he was eager to please and cautious not to offend. He knew that both women were greatly worried about the state of his soul. Hence he was inclined to be too zealous in his protestations of piety.

One need make no such reservation about Burns's letters to Aiken and Cunningham. In them he spoke with complete frankness; what he says is worth examining. After the birth of Jean's first twins, and before the death of Mary Campbell, when Burns was distractedly trying to find some means of escape from the net which he had woven around himself, he wrote thus to Aiken:

THE MAN AND THE POET

You may perhaps think it an extravagant fancy, but it is a sentiment, which strikes home to my very soul: though sceptical in some points of our current belief, yet, I think, I have every evidence for the reality of a life beyond the stinted bourne of our present existence; if so, then, how should I, in the presence of that tremendous Being, the Author of existence, how should I meet the reproaches of those who stand to me in the dear relation of children, whom I deserted in the smiling innocency of helpless infancy? O thou great unknown Power!—Thou almighty God! who hast lighted up reason in my breast, and blessed me with immortality!—I have frequently wandered from that order and regularity necessary for the perfection of Thy works, yet Thou hast never left me nor forsaken me! [3]

Belief in God and in the immortality of the soul: these were the two cardinal points in Burns's religious faith; in this simple faith he found genuine comfort and satisfaction. A letter to Cunningham contains the clearest statement Burns ever made on this point:

There are two great pillars that bear us up, amid the wreck of misfortune and misery. The one is composed of the different modifications of a certain noble, stubborn something in man, known by the names of courage, fortitude, magnanimity. The other is made up of those feelings and sentiments which, however the sceptic may deny them or the enthusiast disfigure them, are yet, I am convinced, original and component parts of the human soul; those *senses of the mind,* if I may be allowed the expression, which connect us with, and link us to, those awful obscure realities—an all-powerful and equally beneficent God, and a world to come, beyond death and the grave. The first gives the nerve of combat, while a ray of hope beams on the field: the last pours the balm of comfort into the wound which time can never cure.

I do not remember, my dear Cunningham, that you and I ever talked on the subject of religion at all. I know some who laugh at it, as the trick of the crafty few to lead the undiscerning many; or at most as an uncertain obscurity, which mankind can never know anything of, and with which they are fools if they give themselves much to do. Nor would I quarrel with a man for his irreligion, any more than I would for his want of musical ear. I would regret that he was shut out from what, to me and to others, were such superlative sources of enjoyment . . .

These are no ideal pleasures, they are real delights; and I ask, what of

[451]

the delights among the sons of men are superior, not to say equal, to them? [4]

In these paragraphs a single phrase, "senses of the mind," gives a clear indication of the dualism in Burns's religion. His theology was anything but the austere Calvinism which even his father had been unable to accept; it was a mild Deism, in part emotional, in part rationalistic. The God in whom he believed was not the God whom Auld worshipped; he was the "Unknown Power" of Pope and Shaftesbury. Burns had sentimentalized the God in whom his parents had taught him to believe, and he had also endowed him with common sense—an attribute which the Calvinist never associated with Deity.

To give full credence to the second element in his theology, the doctrine of immortality, Burns at times found difficult. He was sceptic as well as sentimentalist, and realized the tenuity of the arguments supporting this belief. But for the most part he was content to follow the rest of mankind, and trust that the universal instinct for immortality would not prove fallacious. In framing for himself a religious creed of this nature, Burns was once more both following his own natural bent, and conforming to one of the general tendencies of eighteenth century British thought.

When thinking of Burns as a sentimentalist, however, one should not forget that he was also a man of unusual intellectual power. He was alert, observant, inquisitive—always eager to widen the horizon of his own experience. His life-long habit of reading is evidence in point; his comments on his reading, appearing as casual remarks and allusions in his letters, attest his habit of thinking as he read. His thorough familiarity with the Bible and with the literature of polemical divinity is not astonishing, in view of the time and place in which Burns grew to manhood. Doubtless there were other farmers in Ayrshire as well informed on these matters as was he. But he did not limit his study to matters theological or scriptural. The very poetry which justifies one in calling him a sentimentalist is also evidence of the extent and thoroughness of his literary studies.

[452]

Scottish literature since the Reformation he knew intimately, both his own immediate predecessors in the field of what may be called legitimate vernacular poetry, and the unknown authors of Scottish song and ballad. Indeed, in this fascinating world of Scottish song, Burns was certainly the best informed man of his day. He knew eighteenth century English literature almost as well as Scottish. He was steeped in Pope and Thomson and their contemporaries; unconscious echoes of their work, and conscious imitations of it, appear on scores of his pages. He was reasonably well-read in eighteenth century philosophy; he knew enough about the economic and political history of Great Britain to comment intelligently upon the developments of the preceding century and a half. He was keenly alive to the trend of contemporary thought in Europe and America, as well as to world-wide political developments. The eagerness with which he read London and Edinburgh newspapers, and the promptness with which he complained when they failed to reach him, are symptomatic. He read a great deal, he thought a great deal; in his reaction to facts he was shrewd and clear-headed.

To the casual reader Burns may seem to have been a surprisingly unintelligent farmer. Neither he nor his brother nor his father was ever really successful in this rôle. Mount Oliphant was abandoned because it was running the family into debt; Lochlie brought actual bankruptcy and a sheriff's sale; Mossgiel was saved to Gilbert Burns only by the advance of Robert's capital; Ellisland proved a ruinous bargain. It might seem strange that in this all-important concern of earning a living from the soil the men of the Burns family should have been such consistent failures.

The fact is, however, that Burns's lack of success in this respect was due to underlying economic conditions, and not to absence of agricultural skill. One remembers that Burns won a prize for his lint seed, that he was one of the first to introduce Ayrshire cattle into Dumfriesshire, and that the sale of his crops at Ellisland brought him a guinea an acre above the average for farm crops in that neighborhood. Burns was zealous in his

[453]

study of agricultural text-books, prompt to take advantage of new methods, and successful in raising both stock and crops. That he could not live in comfort on these products of his industry was due to the widespread overcapitalization of farm values. Had Burns been fortunate enough to own his land, he would have been both successful and happy as a farmer. Always forced to pay unduly high rentals for only moderately productive soil, he had the same experience as countless other tenant farmers of the time: to pay the landlord meant to starve the family; to feed the family meant to run in debt to the landlord. Burns preferred the second alternative, and failed as a farmer. The failure, however, was forced upon him by circumstances he could not control.

Indeed, it is beyond dispute that throughout his entire life Burns displayed those qualities which justify one in calling him a good business man. Henley's characterization of him as a "faun of genius" is as wide of the mark as Allan Cunningham's picture of a visionary poet dreaming away his time by the banks of the Nith. The field of his business activities was not large, but in that field he was shrewd, clear-headed, industrious, happy, and, except as regards farming, successful. To the time of his final illness he lived scrupulously within his means; he supported his large family on an income that never exceeded one hundred pounds a year; he gave generously to friends who were in need; he educated his children; he lived in a manner which made it possible for him not only to accept the hospitality of his many friends, but also to return their courtesies in appropriate fashion. All this he did despite the handicap of persistent ill-health, and the unrelenting pressure of arduous daily obligations. Poet he was, in very truth; but he was also a steady-going man of affairs, richly endowed with the homely virtue of common sense.

Yet when one has thus tagged Burns with certain appropriate adjectives, one realizes that one has told only part of the truth concerning him. There is a perplexing quality, or combination of qualities, about him, which is still baffling, even after the

[454]

lapse of a century and a half. It must have been far more bewildering to his contemporaries, no one of whom seems actually to have understood him. Ainslie knew him only superficially; Nicol and Smith no better; his own wife hardly at all. She loved him, in her way; she gave him her body; she cared for him as well as she could while he lived, and spoke well of him after his death. But she never really understood him. Perhaps Daddy Auld and Dugald Stewart and Maria Riddell came as near to comprehending Burns as any of his acquaintances, but even they could hardly have realized what manner of man he was.

He is somewhat more understandable today than he was during his lifetime, for today we realize that Burns combined two personalities in one: he was a Scottish farmer and gauger, and he was a genius as well. Fate had put him into a situation where his life might have been absolutely simple, disturbed only by the relatively easy problem of earning a living. But Fate had also endowed him with abilities beyond those of any British poet of his generation, and with an intense and consuming ambition. Inevitably there arose a conflict, the age-old struggle between inward talent and outward environment, to use the language of *Sartor*. And because Burns found it impossible to reconcile the two, and thus to put a stop to the conflict that was harassing him, he was melancholy, unhappy, restless.

A good deal might be written concerning Burns's ambition. One sees evidences of it wherever one turns: in the early pages of the first *Commonplace Book*, in his letters, in his fondness for circulating his verses in manuscript, in his eagerness to publish, to write for Johnson, for Thomson, for London newspapers. But his was the creative ambition of the artist, not the acquisitive ambition of the man who seeks much for himself. For Robert Burns, farmer and exciseman, he asked but little: money enough to ensure a modest independence; the opportunity to educate his children; friends; the respect of his fellows. But for the Burns who aspired to be "Scotia's Bard" he coveted unlimited

fame and honor, and, above all, the opportunity to give full expression to his poetic genius.

One should remember, in this connection, that Burns was
never satisfied with the mere act of publishing, nor content with
"getting his name in the papers." He had a fine critical sense,
he disliked slovenly work, he sought leisure to revise what he
had written, to give it the touch he knew he could impart. But
for all this he had little time. The Kilmarnock edition was
brought out at top speed, and when Burns was all but distracted
by the developments of the spring and summer of 1786. The
visit to Edinburgh gave him an opportunity to issue a second
edition, but again he was forced to work hurriedly, lest the opportune moment for publication should pass. When he wrote
for Johnson and Thomson there was no such pressure upon him,
for neither editor was inclined to haste. But even so the demands which other obligations made upon Burns's time and
energy compelled him to write as rapidly as if publication had
been imminent. Consequently one sees him sending off song
after song without even retaining a copy for himself, forced to
be content with results which he knew were far from perfect.

But of course he was not really satisfied. He was well aware
that only occasionally had he done full justice to himself, and
that there were within him many unrealized possibilities. The
consciousness of this fact prompted him to use his failing strength
in pathetic attempts to revise what he had previously written,
and to add still more to his total output. Only two months before his death he wrote Thomson:

> I have no copies of the songs I have sent you, & I have taken a fancy
> to review them all, & possibly may mend some of them; so, when you
> have compleat leisure, I will thank you for either the Originals, or
> copies.—I had rather be the author of five well-written songs than of
> ten otherwise.—My verses to "Cauld kail" I will suppress; as also those
> to "Laddie lie near me."—They are neither worthy of my name, nor
> of your book.[5]

It is indicative of the seriousness with which Burns took his
poetic function that in his letters he habitually capitalized the

word *Poet*. The realization that he had never done full justice to his poetic endowment made his life unhappy. Indeed, as one remembers the recurrent attacks of hypochondria which clouded Burns's mature years, the low spirits, the "blue devilism," one wonders whether this consciousness of failure was not one of the chief causes of these unhappy moods. There was a physical condition, of course, behind the months of melancholia. But there was also the haunting and ever-present spectre of incompleteness, which nothing could exorcise.

Moreover, it was in part at least the fear that he might "cease to be" before he had given full expression to his powers, that made Burns dread the approach of death. He was naturally concerned over what the future held in store for his family; poverty for them he dreaded even more than for himself. Almost as appalling, however, was the consideration that he might leave undone what he knew he was qualified to accomplish. His last letter to Thomson, written only two weeks before he died, is eloquently revealing:

> I am still anxiously willing to serve your work . . . You will see my alterations & remarks on the margin of each song.[6]

One might perhaps ask why Burns was not satisfied with his Edinburgh success, which had been unqualified, phenomenal. A smaller man, a less clear-sighted man, would have been thoroughly happy, and would have spent the rest of his life in complacent and stupid retrospection. Not so Burns. At the height of his Edinburgh renown he understood perfectly well that he was a nine-days wonder, and would inevitably return to a position of comparative obscurity. A few Scottish towns might bestow honorary Burgesships upon him; a few English reviews might praise him. But the glory would be short lived. Moreover, he could never have been satisfied with even long-continued applause unless it had been accompanied with the realization that he had done all that lay in him to do. That happy realization he never enjoyed.

Looked at from one point of view, the story of Burns's entire life is a story of continued and baffling disappointments. He wished to be successful and contented as a farmer; he was unsuccessful and restive. He wished to be happy with Jean, to find full satisfaction in the home which he had created; this too was denied him, for the friendships that meant most to him were formed outside that home. He wished liberty to speak and write as he pleased concerning political developments in England and on the continent; he was told to obey and not to think. He wished to live in simple but unquestioned economic independence; and though he all but succeeded in this ambition, his last weeks were clouded by the consciousness of debt and fear of imprisonment. Above all he wished to write to the very limit of his ability; but better than anyone else he understood the inadequacy of the actual performance, when judged by the high standards of what he might have accomplished. Hence in large measure arose the dissatisfaction which made him unhappy.

It would be unfair, however, to close this brief analysis of Burns's character on any such minor chord. Far better to forget the disappointments and the weaknesses, and to recall once more the courage that kept him unhesitatingly at work to the very end of his life; the fundamental sincerity that justified Carlyle in ranking him with the "heroes"; the light-heartedness, the joy in living, which made him a welcome guest wherever he went; the stark genius which enabled him to write "The Jolly Beggars," and half a score of the world's greatest songs.

There is an old tradition that Burns, as he lay dying, turned to his wife and said, "Don't be afraid; I'll be more thought of after a hundred years than I am now." One may be pardoned for not examining too critically the evidence for the authenticity of this remark. It is pleasant to think, as one of his sons believed, that he actually spoke the words, and that his last hours were spent not in regret over his failure to do more, but in the gratifying consciousness of a unique and enduring accomplishment.

2

BURNS THE POET

Historically, Burns's poetry is easy to characterize. It shows evidence of his debt to three widely separated schools of poetry, and of the thoroughness with which he had absorbed what each school had to offer. First of all, he was a child of eighteenth century England. He knew the writers of that century; he had studied them, and not merely read them casually. He was also a direct descendant of Fergusson and Ramsay and the Sempills of Beltrees. These men, too, he knew; and as the world has long realized, he drew lavishly upon them for verse forms, for suggestions for poems, and not infrequently for actual phraseology. And then there were the many writers of Scottish songs, the forgotten rimesters whose attempts to give expression to the emotional life of the common people were hardly considered "poetry," but whose work constituted an important and living element in Scottish culture. Burns's acquaintance with this field was as intimate as with the work of his immediate Scottish predecessors. To each of these three groups or schools Burns owed much; his poetry could not have been what it was had any one of these influences been absent.

Literary influences, however, are of interest primarily to the specialist. The general reader may wish to omit all consideration of antecedents, and to concern himself only with such pertinent questions as will aid him in making his own evaluations of Burns's poetry *qua* poetry. When undertaking such a task, one will do well to disregard the poems which are obvious failures, and to pay but scant attention to those of uncertain merit. To be sure, there is in Burns a smaller proportion of downright ineffective work than in, say, Coleridge or Wordsworth. But no one can turn the pages of a collected edition without realizing that Burns, in common with most poets, wrote too much, and that his real worth can most readily be apprehended through an examination of, roughly, one fifth of his published verse.

Perhaps the best way to arrive at some reasoned understanding

[459]

of the nature and merit of this best of Burns's poetry will be to ask three relatively simple questions concerning the poet who wrote it. First, it is pertinent to enquire where Burns found the raw material which he transformed into the finished artistic product; or, more formally, where did he direct his poetic vision? Second, what can be said of his imaginative re-working of this material? And third, what of his technique, or power of expression?

Vision

To phrase a complicated matter simply, a poet, looking out upon the universe around him, might well consider that universe as the product of three factors. There is the world of Man, the world of Nature, and the world of the Supernatural —all curiously intermingled, and each contributing its own peculiar element to the resulting whole. One poet looks steadily at the world of Man; *quidquid agunt homines* interests him; Nature and the Supernatural he passes by with only a casual glance. Another draws his inspiration not so much from his fellow-men as from the world of hill and stream and starlight, and daffodils beside a mountain lake. A third directs his vision still elsewhere. His consciousness of man's insignificance in the face of the majesty of Nature sets him brooding upon the mystery behind it all; God, and the measureless forces that underlie creation, seem more important than anything else in man's experience. Even man's fantastic attempts to give expression to his consciousness of a supernatural world in the myths and legends of folk lore may appear more significant than the records of actual human existence. It will rarely be the case that a poet will look steadily at any one of these three factors, to the complete exclusion of the other two. But one at least he will probably neglect, and one he will find of intense and compelling interest.

It is clear that the Supernatural held but little attraction for Burns. There are "Hallowe'en" and "Tam o' Shanter"; but the first is a relatively unsuccessful attempt to record in verse popular customs which Burns considered little more than children's games; and "Tam," glorious though it be in its way, is unique among Burns's poems. It is his finest ghost story. Even in "Tam," moreover, it is the human and natural elements, not the supernatural, which constitute the enduring fabric of the poem. And though Burns wrote much concerning religion, he wrote but little religious poetry. So one may fairly exclude the Supernatural as a primary source of Burns's poetic inspiration.

Equally clear is it that Burns turned often to Nature for the crude materials of his poetry. He was keenly sensitive to certain manifestations of Nature's power, and somewhat blind to others. The mountains and the sea he never really appreciated, though he lived most of his life virtually within sight of both. They were no part of the day by day experience of a Lowland farmer. Hence Burns, in company with his fellow toilers, paid little attention to them. On the other hand, he was a keen and alert observer of the less impressive but—to the farmer—more important natural phenomena. He knew the flowers and shrubs that grew beside the road; he understood the animals that lived on every farm: the old mare, the ewe and her lamb, the shepherd dog, even the mouse in the field—they were his friends, and worthy of being treated in his verse. He was familiar with the streams and burns that beautify an Ayrshire landscape. He knew also the flooded rivers that swept away bridges and made horseback travel precarious; rain-storm and hail-blast that brought destruction to crops awaiting the harvesters were part of his actual experience. All these belonged to his world; he pictured them with vividness and astonishing accuracy.

Rarely, however, does one find a poem in which Nature, even of the sort that Burns knew best, seems to have been the poet's primary concern. Burns was not given to "view hunting." He treated Nature in his verse as he experienced it in his life: he made it the setting, the background, for the human drama. The world of Nature played a large part in the lives of Burns and his neighbors; it plays a large part in his poetry. But it functions only incidentally in this poetry. For to Burns men and women were far more important and more interesting than anything else in the universe; his poetic vision was focused on them, and not on the surrounding hillsides and meadows.

To say that Burns's primary concern was with men and women is more accurate than to say that he was interested in Man. He could not possibly have written an "Essay on Man." He knew his friends and neighbors, however, rather better than they knew themselves; he was interested in their manifold affairs; it was of them, and of people like them all over the world, that he delighted to sing.

As one thinks over the poems in which Burns pictured the men and women whom he knew, one realizes that certain human relationships, or activities, or aspirations, made an unusually strong appeal to his sympathies. There is no inclusive cross-section of Scottish life pictured in these poems; not a few types are missing—types that Chaucer, for example, would have included in a portrait gallery. But even so there is enough and to spare; and some of the relationships that Burns found significant in southern Scotland are equally significant on the opposite side of the globe.

When one enumerates the human types that Burns was most fond of picturing, one finds it inevitable to begin with the farmer. There is little ostensibly bucolic poetry in Burns; except in "The Cotter's Saturday Night" he never undertook to describe in detail the life that he knew best. But by the time one has read the Kilmarnock volume one has learned much concerning the way of life of this farmer—his manner of speech, his regard for the beasts that toil for him, his attitude towards the laird to whom he pays his rent, his fondness for relaxation when the day's work is done, his family affection, his religious faith. They are primarily local in their appeal, these pictures of Ayrshire farm life; yet because the labor of the farmer is the most fundamental of all human occupations, Burns's portraits of his friends and

[462]

neighbors are of interest wherever seed is sown or harvest garnered.

No other single type appears quite as often in Burns as does the farmer. But there are certain human aspirations, or tendencies, which Burns pictured with such vigor and enthusiasm that one hardly knows where to turn to find them more ably set forth. For Man seeking liberty—political, economic, or religious—Burns felt an intense sympathy. Enough has been said in this volume to make clear Burns's kinship with the spirit of rebellion that swept over Occidental civilization during the latter part of the eighteenth century. Especially during the Mossgiel years, and again after 1793, when France and England were at war, Burns's passionate love of liberty found trenchant expression in printed poems as well as in daily conversation.

In estimating the part that this sympathy played in Burns's emotional life, one should remember that when Burns laid himself open to attack by pleading the cause of those whom he considered unjustly oppressed, he was not speaking as a philosophical observer of human events, safely removed from the affairs about which he was generalizing. He was speaking as one who had suffered, and who would continue to suffer till the wrongs should be righted. The laws under which he lived, and which gave stability to an economic system that had sent his father into a bankrupt's grave, were framed by men in whose selection he had no voice; better than some of the colonists who had used the phrase in 1776, he knew what taxation without representation might mean. Small wonder that his sympathies were with these American colonists, and, later, with the French Revolutionists. He knew, too, what religious intolerance might entail in the way of suffering. He had seen his friends prosecuted for heresy and persecuted by an organization as relentless as it was efficient. He had himself winced under the lash of the Church.

It was inevitable that in the large group of poems dealings with man seeking liberty, both the occasion and immediate appeal should again be local. But in this phase of his thinking

[463]

Burns showed himself to be far more than an Ayrshire farmer; he was a man of international sympathies, sensitive to new ideals which were destined to affect the entire human race.

Man wresting his living from the soil, and man seeking liberty —these were two characters in the human drama with whom Burns was always concerned. A third was man the hypocrite. Once again the genesis of the poems was local, specific, personal. Holy Willie and Black Russell were living human beings, walking the streets of Mauchline and Kilmarnock. It was these actual persons, and not mere personifications of religious guile, whom Burns pictured. He wasted none of his scorn in vapid generalizations; he was only slightly concerned with Hypocrisy, but he hated hypocrites. Consequently he aimed each shaft at some definite and easily recognizable target. Rarely did a shaft miss the mark.

It is a commonplace that satire usually ceases to be of interest when the immediate occasion for it has passed. As soon as a poem has to be "explained" in footnotes it is dead, except to the scholar—as witness such a masterful piece of political verse as "Absalom and Achitophel." Burns was wise enough to avoid over-loading his satires with localisms, even though they were concerned with local personalities. He focused his vision not upon the incidental details peculiar to one specific situation, but upon certain fundamental human traits. Hence "The Holy Fair" and "Holy Willie's Prayer" are still as readable as the best of Juvenal, or as Chaucer's satiric portraits of hypocritical ecclesiastics. There is humor in Burns's satire, even good natured humor; there is also the *saeva indignatio* which witnesses the poet's scorn for the individuals whom he was picturing. And there is a broadly human quality about this satire which lifts it above the level of local or even national interests, and makes it appeal wherever Burns's language can be understood or translations procured.

Again, Burns's poetic vision was never long diverted from Man the Lover. It is a mistake to assume, as some persons have done, that there was an actual "affair" behind each of

Burns's love songs. Gifted as he was in the theory and practice of love-making, he was not capable of the multifarious emotional variations which would have been necessary had there been a personal experience underlying each lyric. Indeed, not a few of these lyrics are written from the point of view of a girl —good indication of the fallacy of the popular belief. But it is undeniable that Burns's nature made it easy for him to fall in love, and that not infrequently the fire which glows in the best songs is but a pale reflection of a vivid and moving emotional experience. This, however, is a relatively insignificant consideration. Far more important is the fact that Burns understood both the tragedy and the sublimity of human love, and built his noblest poems around these themes.

Finally, wherever Burns's vision may at times have been directed, it was sure sooner or later to come to rest upon himself. His was the instinct of the true lyric poet, who finds his own emotional experiences of compelling interest, and is never satisfied till he has recorded these experiences in verse. "Look in thy heart, thou fool and write," might well have been blazoned above Burns's desk. Even in "The Jolly Beggars," where for a time he steps off the stage and abandons it, as a dramatist should, to the characters whom he has created, even here he appears in his own person at the close of the cantata, and "The Bard's Song" is Burns speaking his mind without regard for dramatic proprieties. Intensely self-conscious, ill at ease when repressed or hampered in his utterances, but happy when allowed to express himself in his own way, Burns found a large proportion of his poetic material in the life of that man whom he knew most intimately.

It was towards men and women, then, and incidentally towards the forms of Nature with which Burns and his friends were most familiar, that the poet's vision was chiefly directed. The Supernatural held but little interest for him; Nature he saw as the background for the pageant of human life. In reproducing in verse the elements of this pageant which most unfailingly caught his attention, he chose material which had

[465]

an immediate local interest, and—more important—with which he himself was familiar. He never went to the library for a subject. Some of this poetry is too provincial to win the full approbation of other than Scottish readers. But the best of it is poetry which all the world knows and enjoys, because it is written about those elemental human activities and attributes which are as widespread as the race of men and women.

Imagination

It is relatively easy thus to point out the objects on which Burns's vision was most often focused. But to throw any light upon the operations of that baffling something which we call his imagination, is indeed hard. One can identify the different elements which went into a completed work of art, and still remain relatively unenlightened as to how these different elements became fused into a single whole. One can follow Coleridge in his devious intellectual wanderings, by the aid of that admirable guide book *The Road to Xanadu,* and still "The Ancient Mariner" will appear an altogether mysterious entity. Similarly, one can see Burns gathering a handful of facts from his observations of life—watching the people who walked the streets of Mauchline, or sitting on the edge of the crowd and delighting in the spectacle presented by the Holy Fair. One knows well enough from what sources Burns drew his material. But precisely how he transformed this raw material into the finished artistic product, who can tell? What goes on in the crucible of a poet's mind?

But despite the obvious impossibility of ever saying anything which shall really explain the workings of Burns's imagination, a few observations will do a little towards clarifying the problem. For example, one can read Burns from cover to cover without finding any suggestion that his imagination had about it the visionary quality so prominent in the work of a poet like Shelley. He wrote no verses to the skylark, which soars out of sight of human eyes. He remained in close touch with the soil of common experience, seeing life as his friends saw it, and finding it always fascinating, though at times somewhat bewildering. And never did he seek an escape from life through the imaginative creation of a dream world.

Again, it is clear that Burns's was not in any profound sense a reflective imagination, as was Wordsworth's, or Walt Whitman's. He was not given to thinking things over, or to attempting a synthesis of human experience. The brooding note rarely appears in his poetry; one finds few indications of "recollection in tranquillity," for Burns was neither tranquil nor reflective in temperament. Phenomena that would have induced in Wordsworth the mood of "impassioned contemplation," left Burns relatively unmoved. He saw clearly, he took a keen delight in the varied spectacle unrolled before his eyes. Occasionally he treated some natural object as symbolic of human experience; but for the most part he was content to see, to enjoy, and to reproduce in his verse such elements of this spectacle as had given him most pleasure.

In this process of reproducing human life, Burns's imagination operated as instantaneously as the high-speed lens of a camera, but with a selective power which the camera does not possess. Given the proper impulse, the current of feeling began at once to flow, and the expression followed hard upon the incident which it celebrated, as the electric light glows the instant the proper contacts have been made. It is no uncommon thing to read in Burns's letters that such and such an occurrence happened but recently, and "today I send you the enclosed poem." Before this poem was ready for publication it might need revision; but the primary act of composition was reasonably sure to be the immediate result of some specific stimulus.

When one considers the selective power of Burns's imagination, one realizes that in this respect he was akin to the great artists. He could make the necessary exclusions so important to a masterpiece. Intuitively he knew what to reject, what to keep in the half light of the background, and what to bring out in full color in the center of his canvas. Other eighteenth

[467]

century poets had written of Scottish life and manners; many
more were to follow Burns's example and publish volumes in
imitation of his. But all of them except Burns are virtually
forgotten. He alone had the power of singling out those
elements of Scottish life most certain to prove significant to his
readers; he alone had the artist's selective imagination.

This selective process was inevitably accompanied by an ideal-
ization of the object thus singled out. There was nothing novel
or unique in this; ever since lyric poets first began to write they
have been prone to idealize the subjects of their verse—provided they have had the genius to do so. But in Burns's case
the imaginative glorification of the ordinary is especially notable.
Mary Campbell was perhaps an illiterate Highland servant girl;
in Burns's lyrics, however, she appears as an ideal of all that is
fair and lovely in womanhood. William Fisher, "Holy
Willie," was in sober truth little more than a village busy-body,
who fell into some of the errors for which he rebuked Mauchline townsfolk. But to Burns he appeared as the very incarnation of ecclesiastical tyranny and hypocrisy; Burns made his
name a by-word for all time. What is thus obvious of Fisher
and Highland Mary was also true of virtually everything upon
which Burns looked. Idealized by his imagination, even the
humblest object glowed with beauty and significance, and furnished him with fitting material for poetic treatment.

Power of Expression

It is not enough, however, for the poet to see clearly, and
then imaginatively to rework the material which he has collected. He must in addition have the gift of song—the power
to combine words in such patterns that other people, reading
what he has written, shall see what he has seen, and feel—in
some measure at least—what he has felt. What can one say
concerning this element in Burns's poetic equipment, this matter of technique, or power of expression?

One observation suggests itself instantly: Burns's metrical
skill was almost uncanny. Blank verse, the ten-syllabled coup-

let, and the sonnet, he rarely attempted; the Spenserian stanza he used with little success. But in the many forms which had come down to him through Fergusson and Ramsay, and in the countless varieties of song-patterns which his work for Johnson and Thomson required him to use, in all these he moved with consummate ease. Some of these verse-forms were as simple as an English quatrain well can be; others were bafflingly elaborate. But it made little difference to Burns what the metrical pattern might be; he was the assured master of virtually everything that he attempted.

The exigencies of an elaborate rime-scheme never perplexed him. So large and flexible was his vocabulary, and so sure his skill in selecting words, that he became actually playful in his versifying. Internal rimes, double and even triple rimes, lend their touches of whimsical effectiveness to his verses, and never are they used merely to display his metrical virtuosity. In different mood, when playfulness would have been inappropriate, Burns could be grimly laconic, and could round off a stanza with the sharp crack of a single monosyllable.

Particularly notable was his success with various types of *rimes couées*. In the exacting verse-form of "The Holy Fair" each of the twenty-seven nine-line stanzas concludes with a four-syllabled line ending in the word *day*. Burns varies this "tail line" from stanza to stanza, and always makes it appear not as something tacked on by way of refrain, but as the logical, the inevitable, development of the thought. And there are many other poems in which Burns used this same difficult stanza with the nonchalance and the success of genius.

He had, moreover, unusual skill and good taste in selecting a verse-form appropriate to the thought he wished to express. Granted that for many of his lyrics the form was virtually dictated by the tune to which he was fitting words, the fact remains that for the rest of his work he had no such guide, and that never did he compose a Scots poem which is ineffective because of incongruity between the metre and the idea or mood. Indeed, test Burns as one will, on this score the verdict is always

[469]

the same: he was one of the relatively few unquestioned masters of English metrics.

Then too, Burns possessed an uncanny skill in coining memorable phrases, in fitting words together in what seem "inevitable" combinations. To read any of his better known poems is to see first hand evidence of this fact; or to study Burns's lyric, "A Red, Red Rose," in connection with the old songs which went to its making, is to realize how sure was his instinct in this respect. There is hardly an idea or an image in Burns's stanzas which was not suggested by one of the earlier songs. But the old songs were crudely expressed, childish, inept. Burns took a phrase here, an adjective there, an entire line somewhere else, rearranged the material thus selected in a new and harmonious pattern, and the result is one of the world's perfect lyrics. The electric magnet is not more unerring in selecting iron from a pile of trash than was Burns in culling the inevitable phrase or haunting cadence from the thousands of mediocre possibilities.

Concerning Burns's mastery of tone color, not so much need or can be said. He was not so subtle an artist as Tennyson or Coleridge, nor so skilled in selecting precisely the correct combination of vowel and consonant sounds to express or create a desired mood. Wordsworth, in "The Solitary Reaper," showed a more notable command of verbal harmonies than Burns ever displayed. Yet if one will examine such a song as "Go Fetch to Me a Pint of Wine," one will discover no mean amount of this particular sort of technical skill. Burns was interested in sounds; in musical sounds; in musical sounds blended into harmonious word patterns. It was no accident that sixty years before Poe wrote "To One in Paradise" Burns had discovered the sonorous and melancholy effectiveness of "no more."

Of Burns's narrative skill we have but few examples; these few, nevertheless, show that he understood the difficult art of telling a story in verse. He was not a narrative genius like Chaucer or Tennyson or William Morris; had his talent been akin to theirs he would of necessity have left more than "Tam o' Shanter," and the incidental narratives in "The Holy Fair,"

"The Jolly Beggars," and a few other poems, as evidence of the fact. But in "Tam," his one long narrative, Burns displayed a command of the rimed short story that would have done credit to many a more practised hand. The narrative is swift, brilliant, dramatic; it moves from an entirely human and plausible introduction to an absolutely unbelievable and supernatural conclusion. Yet so skillfully is the tale told, and so deft the transition from the world of fact to the world of impossibility, that the reader unwittingly adopts Coleridge's formula, and practises that "momentary suspension of disbelief" which enables him to accept "Tam" almost as he accepts "The Ancient Mariner."

It is in part Burns's skillfully drawn descriptions that humanize "Tam" and make it believable. Only a few strokes of the brush suffice to paint the ale house and the ruined Kirk, and to picture such a midnight thunderstorm as is hard to equal in English verse. This descriptive power, displayed at its best in "Tam," appears almost as effectively in a score of other places. One finds but few poems in which Burns seems to have been consciously setting up his easel and endeavoring in any formal way to depict what he saw before him. There are many passages, however, which bear good witness to his life-long love of Nature, and to the skill with which he could reproduce whatever had particularly caught his attention: storms and running water, or the smaller details of farmyard and roadside.

Burns was equally adept in hitting off the essential characteristics of the men and women whose portraits he from time to time included in his poems. The eulogies, such as the "Dedication to Gavin Hamilton," are somewhat ineffective. Burns wrote them in too reverential a mood. As a result they appear stilted, formal, conventional. But the satires suffer from no such blemishes. The incidental character sketches in "The Holy Fair," or the full length study of Holy Willie, and many of the dramatic lyrics, show Burns's genius for portraiture at its best. He had the skill of the born cartoonist, who avoids the gross exaggeration which would render his caricature ineffective, and instinctively singles out the two or three features of his subject most certain to be recognized—and laughed at—by the crowd.

To re-read some of these passages in which Burns described his neighbors and their world, is to realize again how close he was to the ordinary run of humanity. One might almost say that he wrote as anyone would have written, only better. One finds in his descriptions of Nature none of the lush and exotic sensuousness of Keats, none of the etherealness of Shelley, none of the mysticism of Wordsworth. Similarly in his sketches of men and women one misses the subtleties of analysis which distinguish the work of such portrait painters as Browning and Edwin Arlington Robinson. Burns merely pictured the world as it appeared to him and his friends, but pictured it more accurately, more sympathetically, more vividly, and more honestly than any of his friends could possibly have done.

It is this quality of intellectual honesty, this unflinching candor, which most certainly lifts Burns's work above that of his many imitators. He was magnificently courageous, and always eager to tell what he thought to be the truth concerning life. He accepted it for what it was, and discovered that other people had seen indistinctly what he saw clearly, and had been unable or unwilling to admit the facts which he never concealed. "Sincerity," Carlyle called it, this truth-telling propensity of Burns's. "Honesty" or "candor" would have done as well. It is one of the surest marks of Burns's greatness, and is in no way vitiated by his habit of idealizing individual objects or persons.

But it was not in the few narratives, nor in the more numerous poems which may loosely be called descriptive, that Burns best demonstrated his right to the name he never tired of applying to himself. The bards were essentially singing folk, and "Scotia's Bard" was at heart a lyric poet. It was no accident that his first poem was a song, or that with another song he ended his career. He had the lyric instinct, and, coupled with it, a superb lyric technique. Though many of Burns's songs fall short of the standards he set up for himself, there are but few which one rejects as absolutely unworthy, and there are many which defy all criticism. Perfect in their simplicity, hauntingly beautiful in cadence and rhythm, and glowing with emotional intensity, these best of Burns's songs must be included in any collection of the world's greatest lyrics. To read them, is to see first-hand evidence of Burns's poetic genius; to hear them well sung, to the tunes for which they were written, is to realize why they form a unique group in English literature. There is nothing else quite like them. There are many superb lyrics which were never intended to be set to music, and which lose in effectiveness when forcibly wedded to melodies. There are admirable songs which would soon be forgotten if divorced from the tunes that keep them alive. But Burns was poet and musician too; his best songs are poems; not a few of his noblest poems are songs.

Beyond a doubt it is the love songs that have won the widest and most deserved popularity. They are frank and unequivocating, glorifying the happiness which love engenders, and admitting unhesitatingly that from misplaced or misguided love there arises the most poignant woe. The group as a whole is as many-sided as life itself. Here one finds the ribald enthusiasm of "I Hae a Wife o' my Ain," the bantering playfulness of "Tam Glen," the quiet serenity of "John Anderson," the wistful pathos of "Ye Banks and Braes," the stark tragedy of "Ae Fond Kiss," and a dozen other variations upon this central theme. "Simple, sensuous, and impassioned," these lyrics have touched the hearts of men and women for a hundred and fifty years, and bid fair to be read as long as human love endures.

As one looks at Burns in the perspective of this century and a half, it is no village rimester or poet of a few parishes whom one sees. Had he been this, he would long ago have been forgotten, as his many imitators have deservedly been forgotten. Picken, Sillar, Macaulay, Turnbull, Morrison, Tait, Mylne, Learmont, Janet Little—these are by no means all the persons who between 1788 and 1791 followed Burns's example and published their poems, "chiefly in the Scottish dialect." Today only antiquarians and bibliographers know their names, while Burns is read wherever the English tongue is spoken or understood. Already he seems one of the giants of English literature.

If one asks how it came that Burns escaped the oblivion which so swiftly overtook his contemporaries, one finds the answer in the fact that he alone bore the marks of great and original genius, of a genius that immortalizes itself. He saw life accurately, and understood both its facts and its values. Other persons rarely deceived him; he never deceived himself. Moreover, Burns was not content to write of the superficialities of the life which he observed. He dug down beneath the surface, and drove his shaft so deep that he touched the very core of universal human experience. His themes need no footnotes: the beauty of nature, the sympathy between man and the brute beasts, the dreams and longings and aspirations of humble men and women, the passionate joy and poignant tragedy of human love, the age-old miracles of birth and death. These themes are not Scottish; they are not British; they are the inalienable property of human beings the world around. Wherever roses bloom red or stars shine clear on winter nights these are the very stuff of human life.

And Burns never made the mistake of spurring his imagination beyond its power. He understood his limitations, and the nature of the subjects with which he was qualified to deal. But he also understood how to cull out significant from trivial material, and could see enduring poetic values in the commonest of incidents and situations. In his hands, the dialect of a few counties rose to a beauty and dignity it had never before attained. His art—at its best—was of that supreme sort which conceals itself in its own perfection. When he spoke, it was with no suggestion of apology or hesitation. That which was in him, he uttered; clearly, simply, unequivocally, and not infrequently with such prophetic fervor or haunting beauty that verses which he tossed carelessly aside passed overnight into the literary

[474]

treasure-house of the race, and seem as well assured of immortality as any English poetry written since Milton.

If it be true, as Joseph Conrad once put it, that the chief aim of the literary artist is to make his readers see, then Burns may be said to have attained that goal. But Burns does more than make us see; he makes us feel, he makes us think, he makes us enjoy living. To but few poets is it ever given to do more.

[1] *Poems by Robert Burns;* Edinburgh, 1811; II, 262.
[2] See letter to James Burness, 12 July, 1796; *Letters,* II, 327: "I have been thinking over & over my brother's affairs & I fear I must cut him up; but on this I will correspond at another time, particularly as I shall [need] your advice."
[3] Letter of 8 Oct., 1786; *ibid.,* I, 46.
[4] Letter of 25 Feb., 1794; *ibid.,* II, 235.
[5] Letter of May, 1796; *ibid.,* p. 320.
[6] Letter of 4 July, 1796; *ibid.,* p. 324. Thomson did not preserve these final instructions.

APPENDIX

A. BIBLIOGRAPHICAL NOTES

1. *General Bibliographies*

THERE is no inclusive general bibliography of Burns. The best substitutes for such a work are:

[GIBSON, JAMES], *The Bibliography of Robert Burns.* Kilmarnock, James M'Kie, 1881.

ANGUS, W. CRAIBE, *The Printed Works of Robert Burns. A Bibliography in Outline.* Glasgow, 1899.

Three recent studies will assist the person who wishes to amplify these works and bring them more nearly down to date:

EWING, J. C., "A Selected List of Editions of the Works of Robert Burns, and of Books upon his Life and Writings." Reprinted from *The Library World.* London, 1899.

The Craibe Angus Burnsiana. Privately printed. 1902.

"A Bibliography of Robert Burns, 1759–1796." *Publications of the Edinburgh Bibliographical Society*, IX, 57 ff. 1909.

Invaluable to the student of Burns's songs, or of British song literature, is:

DICK, JAMES C., "Bibliography." In *The Songs of Robert Burns*, xxv ff. (London, 1903).

A most useful bibliography of works dealing with Scottish life and manners will be found in:

ANGELLIER, AUGUSTE, *Robert Burns*, II, 416 ff. Paris, 1893. 2 vols.

[477]

APPENDIX

2. *The most important Biographies, Biographical Studies, and Editions*

From among the hundreds of such documents, three products of the forty years immediately following Burns's death stand out as of unusual importance: the lives by Currie (1800), Lockhart (1828), and Allan Cunningham (1834). It was the work of these three men that established the "Burns tradition," and it was to the work of these three men that virtually every other critic and biographer turned for his material. Of the three, Lockhart was probably the least influential. Hence the person who reads any life of Burns written before 1850 may be reasonably sure that he is reading a diluted form of either Currie or Cunningham.

In 1851–52 Robert Chambers, after many years of study, published his *Life and Works of Robert Burns*, a document which at once superseded all earlier biographies and editions. Chambers had gone behind the returns as set forth by Currie and Cunningham, and had examined for himself the primary sources of information. Consequently the biographers and critics of the second half of the nineteenth century owed as much to him as their predecessors had owed to Currie and Cunningham.

The following highly selective list undertakes to introduce the student to the most interesting documents in this section of the Burns bibliography, and to make some pertinent comments on each item.

[RIDDELL, MARIA], (MRS. WALTER RIDDELL), "Memoir Concerning Burns." In the *Dumfries Journal*, August, 1796. Many times reprinted—by Currie, Chambers, etc.

This is the first character study of Burns to be published. It is dated August 7, 1796, and thus must have been written during the fortnight immediately following his death. Mrs. Riddell had known the poet intimately during the last five years of his life; her memoir may fairly be considered the most authentic contemporary source of information concerning his character and demeanor during this period.

APPENDIX

No copy of the *Dumfries Journal* containing the original article is known to this writer; Currie's reprint in his 1800 edition (I, 247 ff), probably represents with reasonable accuracy what was there printed. Shortly afterwards, however, Mrs. Riddell revised her article for Currie's second (1801) edition, and requested the publishers, Cadell and Davies, to cancel the original form and substitute the new one. This was done; hence the text that appears in Currie's second and subsequent editions may be considered that which she wished the world to know.

HERON, ROBERT, "Original Memoirs of the Late Robert Burns." In *The Monthly Magazine and British Register*. London, January to June, 1797. Republished as *A Memoir of the Life of the Late Robert Burns*. Edinburgh, 1797. Reprinted, with a few verbal changes, in Robert Chambers's *Biographical Dictionary of Eminent Scotsmen*, I, 440 ff. Glasgow, 1832–1835. 4 vols.

Because this is the earliest formal biography of Burns, it possesses an interest quite out of proportion to its merit. Heron, a professional man of letters whose last years were spent in Newgate Prison, gathered up such information concerning Burns's life as was current in Dumfries, and added a few pages dealing with his personal reputation and the vogue of his poems. He seems to have taken great delight in blackening the poet's character, and by so doing furnished the starting point for the tradition of alcoholism and debauchery.

[CURRIE, JAMES], *The Works of Robert Burns, with an Account of his Life*. London, 1800. 4 vols. A second edition, somewhat revised, appeared in 1801; a third in 1802; a fourth in 1803. The eighth edition was published in 1820. In addition to these eight in twenty years, all published by Cadell and Davies, several pirated reprints of the four volumes appeared in Ireland, Scotland, and the United States. There were also scores of cheap editions and biographies based directly upon Currie.

Dr. James Currie, a Liverpool physician, did not know Burns intimately; indeed, he saw him only once, and then for but a brief time during a visit to Dumfries in 1792. But he was an appreciative reader of Burns's verse, and when the poet died he assisted materially in the public subscription for the benefit of his family.

The same friends—Syme, Maxwell, and Cunningham—who were responsible for this subscription, also undertook the collection of material for a complete edition of Burns's verse and prose. Various persons were considered as possible editors and biographers, among them being Mrs. Walter Riddell, Professor Dugald Stewart, and Syme himself. When Dr. Currie, whose only writing had been for medical journals, was first proposed, he demurred strongly. It is clear, however, from the tone of the correspondence that passed at the time, that he really wished to undertake the task, and was gratified, when, in the autumn of 1796, he was selected.

Early in 1797 Syme sent Currie the material which Burns's friends had been gathering. As Currie afterwards put it, he

viewed the huge and shapeless mass with astonishment! Instead of finding, as I expected, a selection of [Burns's] papers, with such annotations as might clear up any obscurities, . . . I received the complete sweepings of his drawers and of his desk (as it appeared to me), even to the copy-book on which his little boy had been practising his writing. No one had given these papers a perusal, or even an inspection: the sheep were not separated from the goats; and—what has, perhaps, not happened before since the beginning of the world,—the manuscripts of a man of genius, unarranged by himself, and unexamined by his family or friends, were sent, with all their sins on their heads, to meet the eye of an entire stranger! [1]

For three years Dr. Currie labored at the task thus imposed upon him, assisted only casually by Syme and Gilbert Burns. In the autumn of 1800 the four volumes appeared, in an edition of 2000 copies, priced at £1/11/6 per set.

Currie had done his work without fee or compensation of any sort, actuated solely by his respect for Burns's memory, and his desire to assist in raising money for the benefit of his family. In this generous ambition he was eminently successful, for the

Trust Fund received the entire profits from the sale of the first edition, which amounted to approximately twelve hundred pounds.

Currie undertook, moreover, to tell the story of Burns's life in such a way as to bring out the best of the poet's characteristics, and to conceal the worst. Here he failed; for instead of picturing Burns as he was, Currie—a persistent and unrelenting foe to alcohol as a beverage—represented him as a confirmed alcoholic, and hinted that out of charity to Burns's memory he was concealing even worse things that he might have revealed:

> Perpetually stimulated by alcohol in one or other of its various forms . . . in his moments of thought he reflected with the deepest regret on his fatal progress, clearly foreseeing the goal towards which he was hastening, without the strength of mind necessary to stop, or even to slacken, his course. His temper became more irritable and gloomy; he fled from himself into society, often of the lowest kind. And in such company, that part of the convivial scene, in which wine increases sensibility and excites benevolence, was hurried over, to reach the succeeding part, over which uncontroled passion generally presided. He who suffers the pollution of inebriation, how shall he escape other pollution? But let us refrain from the mention of errors over which delicacy and humanity draw the veil.[2]

Thus the tradition, originated by Heron, that Burns drank himself into an early grave, was given broadcast to the world.

Concerning Currie's reliability as editor and biographer, this is perhaps all that need be said: his editorial conscience was that of the days before accuracy had come to be considered a scholarly *sine qua non.* He made not a few errors through sheer inadvertence and carelessness. Furthermore, he was quite candid in announcing his purpose of avoiding controversial subjects. In the dedication to Captain Graham Moore, R. N., Currie wrote:

> All topics are omitted in the writings, and avoided in the life of Burns, that have a tendency to awake the animosity of party.[3]

To this desire to publish a book free from all offense of a political nature, Currie added a natural but regrettable instinct that

APPENDIX

prompted him to soften Burns's language whenever it might have shocked the "delicate" sensibilities of his readers. Hence he was not above garbling or re-arranging Burns's texts in order to secure what he thought would be unexceptionable results.

Yet however harsh one may feel inclined to be in criticism of such editorial technique, one should not forget that Currie was but ill-prepared for the task which Fate assigned him; that his methods were in no way out of keeping with the general literary tradition of his day; and that he did give to the world an edition and biography of Burns which carried the poet's fame into all parts of the English speaking world.

IRVING, DAVID, *The Lives of the Scottish Poets*. Edinburgh, 1804. 2 vols. (The life of Burns appears in vol. II, 443 ff.)

Irving based his work on Currie, and beyond correcting one or two errors that had appeared in Currie's first edition, added virtually nothing of his own. His introductory paragraph, a sort of anticipatory summary of the entire essay, branded Burns as a "bad lot," and gave added weight to the tradition of alcoholism and debauchery. Fortunately for Burns, however, Irving's work was not widely popular.

CROMEK, R. H., *Reliques of Robert Burns*. London, 1808.

Though in no sense a biography, this work is probably more important to the student of Burns than any other single document published between Currie (1800) and Chambers (1851). Here one finds eighty of Burns's letters, many of which had been hitherto unavailable; the "Strictures on Scottish Songs and Ballads" of which Cromek transcribed "the chief part" from Robert Riddell's interleaved set of the first four volumes of the *Scots Musical Museum*; and a considerable amount of uncollected and in part unpublished poetry. The "Strictures on Scottish Songs" have a unique value, for though some are the work of Riddell and not of Burns, the great majority are the poet's own comments on the lyrics he had collected, revised, or written himself, for the *Musical Museum*.

[482]

APPENDIX

When J. C. Dick's *Notes on Scottish Song by Robert Burns* was published in 1908, Cromek's reputation as an editor—already none too good—was seriously besmirched, for it appeared that he had forged many of the most interesting "Strictures." Now, however (1932), one is entirely warranted in accepting these dubious notes as "genuine Burns," and in agreeing with Professor Ferguson's dictum that here at least Cromek did "a substantially honest and straightforward piece of work." [4]

[JEFFREY, FRANCIS], Review of Cromek's *Reliques*. In *Edinburgh Review*, XIII, 249 ff. January, 1809.

The article pays little attention to the book under discussion, but concerns itself chiefly with Burns's character and accomplishments. It is clear that Jeffrey had read Burns with intelligent appreciation; nevertheless he was over-much concerned with "the lowness of [Burns's] origin," and the harmful effect his humble birth and inadequate education had exercised upon his poetry. "The most lamentable trait of vulgarity," which Jeffrey detected in much that Burns had written, he ascribed, in common with his lack of chivalry, to this peasant ancestry and bringing-up.

The review accepted and passed on without question the "unlettered plough-boy" tradition, and gave still wider currency than it had yet received to the idea that Burns was a confirmed alcoholic. On the whole, however, it is a complimentary article, and—having the authority of the *Edinburgh Review* behind it—did much to establish Burns in "the rank of a great and original genius." Furthermore, it was the first notable piece of critical writing occasioned by Burns's poetry.

[SCOTT, WALTER], Review of Cromek's *Reliques*. In *The Quarterly Review*, I, 19 ff. February, 1809.

Scott's inveterate Toryism, and perhaps a slight tinge of professional jealousy, prevented him from writing as penetrating a comment on Burns as one wishes one might have had from his pen. Except for the fact that he was in bondage to the chivalric

[483]

tradition, Scott was probably better equipped to understand Burns's character and work than any other man of his generation. As it was, however, he adopted a distinctly patronizing attitude towards his predecessor, and like Jeffrey harped on the sad results of Burns's plebeian origin.

In two respects, however, Scott's review was a notable contribution to Burns literature: here for the first time appeared unqualified praise of "The Jolly Beggars," which Scott felt had been unjustifiably excluded from the pages of Currie and Cromek; and here was the earliest intelligent exposition of Burns's method of song-writing. Scott knew the national songs of Scotland as well, perhaps, as Burns had known them; he did not esteem them so highly; indeed, he regretted that Burns's interest in song-writing had been allowed to divert him from more important projects. But he understood Burns's lyrical technique:

> With all these disadvantages, the Scottish songs and tunes preserved for Burns that inexpressible charm which they have ever afforded to his countrymen. He entered into the idea of collecting their fragments with all the zeal of an enthusiast; and few, whether serious or humorous, past (*sic*) through his hands without receiving some of those magic touches, which, without greatly altering the song, restored its original spirit, or gave it more than it had ever possessed. So dexterously are these touches combined with the ancient structure that the *riffaciamento*, in many instances, could scarcely have been detected, without the avowal of the Bard himself. Neither would it be easy to mark his share in the individual ditties. Some he appears entirely to have re-written; to others he added supplementary stanzas; in some he retained only the leading lines and the chorus; and others he merely arranged and ornamented.[5]

This is sound criticism—accurate, and well phrased. And that Scott was not wholly out of sympathy with Burns is evident from the fact that he could quote the quatrain beginning "Had we never lov'd sae kindly," and remark that it "contains the essence of a thousand love-tales." [6]

APPENDIX

[WALKER, JOSIAH], *Poems by Robert Burns, with an Account of his Life.* Edinburgh, 1811. 2 vols.

Carefully disclaiming to present more than "the most interesting part" of Burns's poetry, this edition marks a great advance over Currie's because it includes "The Jolly Beggars," "Holy Willie's Prayer," "The Kirk's Alarm," "The Twa Herds," and twelve other songs or poems which Currie had omitted. Here also are to be found seven previously unpublished letters from Burns to Richard Brown, and two highly interesting and important letters, from Davie Sillar and Dr. John Mackenzie, setting forth in some detail their recollections of Burns.

The "Account of the Life and Character of Robert Burns" is the work of Josiah Walker, who was secretary and tutor in the household of the Duke of Athole at the time Burns made his visit to Blair Castle in 1787, and who visited Burns at Dumfries in 1795. In general, Walker depended upon Currie for the facts of Burns's life. He corrected a few minor misstatements; added his own somewhat patronizing comments on Burns's character; and apologized rather unnecessarily for misdeeds some of which, at least, the poet never committed. It is worth remembering, however, that in so far as he could, Walker confined himself to recounting the ascertainable facts of Burns's life; he did not embroider his narrative with unsubstantiated gossip or fictitious anecdote.

PETERKIN, ALEXANDER, *The Life and Works of Robert Burns, as Originally Edited by James Currie, M. D.* Edinburgh, 1815. 4 vols.

The British copyright on Currie's first (1800) edition expired at the close of 1814; during the following year Alexander Peterkin, a Scottish attorney with journalistic proclivities, reprinted it, entire. His chief personal contribution was a long preface (98 pages) in which he undertook to disprove many of the assertions that had been made concerning Burns's character and habits, and to set before the public a more accurate portrait of him than had yet appeared. After reviewing all the important biographies of Burns, and the more significant critical essays, Peterkin published letters from Gilbert Burns, James Gray, Alexander Findlater, and George Thomson, all of which bore out his contention that Burns had been shabbily treated by the writers of the preceding two decades. But having done what he could in this way to rehabilitate Burns's reputation, Peterkin made the mistake of reprinting Currie's life, and thus, in effect, gave added currency to the misrepresentations which he had hoped to correct. Peterkin's work is notable, however, as the first attempt on a large scale to free Burns from the weight of charges which time has since shown to be largely exaggerated.

PAUL, HAMILTON, *The Poems & Songs of Robert Burns, with a Life of the Author.* Air (*sic*), 1819.

The significance of this edition lies in the fact that Paul, one of the most liberal of the New Light clergy, made his life of Burns the occasion for a spirited defence of the poet against the charge of impiety or hostility to established religion. Without condoning Burns's admitted offenses against the "moral law," Paul praised the ecclesiastical satires, and represented Burns as a friend of true religion:

> Thus, we think, we have demonstrated that Burns has contributed his share towards accomplishing the abolition of tent preaching and stools of repentance—proving the disastrous consequences of popular elections and leading the liberal mind to a rational view of the nature of prayer, pointing out the danger of mistaking the operations of party spirit for the exercise of zeal in the cause of truth, and in short checking that flood of fanaticism with which the land is in danger of being deluged, by those who darken counsel by words without knowledge.[7]

Paul's defence of Burns reached a climax in his remarks on "Holy Willie's Prayer:"

> This is not only the prayer of Holy Willie, but it is merely the metrical version of every prayer that is offered up by those who call themselves

the pure reformed Church of Scotland. . . . The terrible view of the Deity exhibited in that able production is precisely the same view which is given of him, in different words, by many devout preachers at present. . . . The gloomy forbidding representation which they give of the Supreme Being has a tendency to produce insanity and lead to suicide.[8]

For such remarks, Paul found himself sharply criticized by persons whose stubborn orthodoxy both Burns and his defender had offended. The fact that he could make them, however, and still retain his position as a minister, is indicative of a wholesome change in the general temper of Scottish Presbyterianism.

CURRIE, JAMES, and BURNS, GILBERT, *The Works of Robert Burns . . . The Eighth Edition . . . To which are now Added some Further Particulars of the Author's Life.* London, 1820. 4 vols.

Cadell and Davies, authorized publishers of Currie's various editions, paid Gilbert Burns £250 for preparing this eighth edition of their astonishingly popular work. They expected him to furnish a considerable amount of new biographical matter, as well as some hitherto unpublished poems or letters. It was their hope that a completely new version of Currie would be forthcoming, which would at once supersede all existing editions and biographies. So sanguine were they, that they promised Gilbert a second £250 when the sales of the edition should warrant a second printing.

At the same time that they were making plans for an entirely new work, the publishers warned Gilbert that he must not cast any aspersions on the general accuracy of Currie's portrait of his brother. As a result Gilbert, by nature somewhat timid, found his hands tied, and was unable to do more than contribute a few unimportant letters, a slight amount of trivial information concerning Burns's family since the poet's death, an appendix on the thread-bare subject of the peasantry in Scotland, and five pages concerning "my brother's habits." Here he might have been expected to strike a real blow in defence of his brother.

APPENDIX

But nothing of the sort did he dare attempt, and the general impression that Burns was a confirmed alcoholic remained unshaken by Gilbert's timid denials. The edition proved a drug on the market, and Gilbert never received his second check.

CUNNINGHAM, ALLAN, "Robert Burns and Lord Byron." In *The London Magazine*, August, 1824. Reprinted entire in David Hogg's *Life of Allan Cunningham*, 237 ff. Dumfries, 1875.

This article is included in the bibliography for only one reason: it is the first of Allan Cunningham's large contributions to the Burns legend, and, like his later work, is absolutely untrustworthy. As William Scott Douglas put it, "Literary impudence never went beyond this." [9] But so plausibly did Cunningham write, that for half a century he was accepted as a thoroughly reliable witness in all matters pertaining to Burns.

LOCKHART, JOHN G., *Life of Robert Burns*. Edinburgh, 1828. (Vol. XXIII of *Constable's Miscellany*.)

The three most influential of Burns's early biographers were Currie, Lockhart, and Cunningham. Between them, they cut the pattern to which virtually every other writer has more or less consciously adhered. Of the three, Currie was the most honest, and Cunningham the most untrustworthy. But in a certain way Lockhart was even more misleading than Cunningham. "Honest Allan's" fabrications were of a sort that one suspects even as one reads them; Lockhart, with his pretence of absolute accuracy, was harder to detect in the act of falsifying the record. But his biography is as unreliable as anything that Cunningham ever published about Burns.

This work, dedicated to James Hogg and Allan Cunningham, "in testimony of admiration and esteem," was at once accepted as the authoritative pronouncement concerning Burns; ultimately it ran into many editions. The best that one can say of it today, however, is that it occasioned Carlyle's review. It is inexcusably inaccurate from beginning to end, at times demonstrably mendacious, and should never be trusted in any respect or detail.

[CARLYLE, THOMAS], Review of Lockhart's *Life of Robert Burns.* In *Edinburgh Review*, XLVIII, 267 ff. December, 1828.

Carlyle accepted without question the tradition of alcoholism, poverty, and disgrace. Except in this one respect, however, his portrait study of Burns is not open to serious criticism, and his comment on Burns's poetry is sound and sympathetic. All in all, if one were forced to limit one's reading about Burns to a single essay, one would do well to choose Carlyle's.

CUNNINGHAM, ALLAN, *The Works of Robert Burns, with his Life.* London, 1834. 8 vols.

By the time Cunningham brought out this widely read and often reprinted edition, he had attained a position of some distinction as editor and critic, and was thought to be peculiarly well fitted to act as Burns's biographer. He could write a readable page of either verse or prose; he was an indefatigable workman; although he was spending his mature years in London, he had a Scotsman's understanding of the part of the world where both he and Burns had been born; he had already been certified by Lockhart as a competent authority on all Burns matters.

This biography certainly pictures Burns more or less as he actually was, but is absolutely unreliable as regards specific facts. Anything that Cunningham says may be true; nothing that he says should be believed without corroborating testimony.

HOGG, JAMES, and MOTHERWELL, WILLIAM, *The Works of Robert Burns.* Glasgow, 1838–1841. 5 vols.

The inquisitive student will find pleasure in turning the pages of Hogg's "Life of Burns," included in this edition (V, 1 ff.), and will discover it to be a most astonishing document—perhaps the worst life of Burns written before the twentieth century.

CHAMBERS, ROBERT, *The Life and Works of Robert Burns.* Edinburgh, 1851–52. 4 vols.

Dr. Robert Chambers, Scottish author and publisher, and one of the two founders of the firm of W. & R. Chambers, was the first person after Currie to make an independent and exhaustive study of the sources of information concerning Burns:

> I have . . . entered upon a minute examination of all the materials which exist for a biography of the poet, and collected new and authentic particulars from all available sources, including the memory of his youngest sister, Mrs. Begg, who still survives.[10]

The result of Chambers's research was a work which marked a great advance over everything that had previously appeared, and which remained the standard life and edition for nearly half a century.

Chambers wished Burns to tell the story of his own life, in so far as this was possible. Hence, instead of writing a formal biography, he adopted the plan of printing Burns's verse and prose in its proper chronological order, and of adding such comments of his own, in the form of connecting links, notes, and explanatory passages, as seemed necessary to produce a well rounded account of the poet's career. Mrs. Isabella Burns Begg gave Chambers the benefit of her recollections of Robert's life; other persons who had known him, or who had access to printed records, added what they could. Chambers adopted a properly critical attitude towards this new material, for he realized the uncertainty of the human memory when dealing with incidents half a century in the past. He undertook to discriminate between ascertained fact and mere possibility. Consequently, though the reader may at times be annoyed by the underlying plan of the book, and may wish that the biographical narrative were not so persistently interrupted by the texts of Burns's own works, he may be sure that he is not being intentionally misled. Occasionally, to be sure, Chamber's respect for Burns's memory, or his desire not to offend living persons, led him to conceal part of what he knew. His offenses on this score are slight, however, and it is probably no exaggeration to say that his four volumes constitute the most important work on Burns published during the three quarters of a century immediately following the poet's death.

[DOUGLAS, WILLIAM SCOTT], *The Works of Robert Burns.* Edinburgh, 1877–1879. 6 vols.

The editor's purpose is clearly stated in his preface to vol. I:

It cannot . . . be alleged that any exhaustive effort has, as yet, been made to collect the whole of [Burns's] poems and correspondence, and present these in the most attractive shape;—shewing the author's text with critical exactness, unabridged and untampered with, and recording the numerous and interesting variations in his manuscripts and several authorized editions. To supply that desideratum is the chief aim of the present publication.[11]

When Scott Douglas began work upon this distinguished edition of Burns, he had the advantage of Chambers's painstaking foundation-work; he was thoroughly familiar with the vast amount of Burns literature; he was in possession of several unpublished Burns manuscripts; he could discriminate between what had been proved and what had not. He limited his project to the preparation of a variorum edition of Burns's writings, and did all that he could to make that edition thoroughly reliable. The results justified the labor. The first three volumes contain the texts of Burns's poems, with variant readings culled from manuscripts and printed sources. The last three volumes contain Burns's prose. Each text, whether of prose or verse, is accompanied by such critical annotations as Scott Douglas thought necessary to its intelligent reading; in these notes one discovers not a little biographical information previously·unavailable, and still significant. Throughout the entire six volumes there are numerous facsimiles, maps, and other appropriate illustra-

APPENDIX

tions. In lieu of formal biographical essay there is a "Summary of [Burns's] Career and Genius." (I, 1 ff.) The various appendixes are rich in material pertinent to various phases of the general problem of Burns's life and work.

Though subsequent investigations have brought to light many facts unknown to Scott Douglas, nothing has been done which makes it possible for the student to disregard his work as editor and annotator.

The work as a whole has been several times republished; the original edition is the most desirable, however, because many of the maps and other illustrations were omitted from the later reprints.

ANGELLIER, AUGUSTE. . *Robert Burns. La Vie. Les Oeuvres.* Paris, 1893. 2 vols.

Angellier's work marked a new departure in the study of Burns. For his first volume, *La Vie*, the author made a searching examination of everything that could contribute to his understanding of Burns and his world, and pictured Burns in his *milieu*, against the proper background of social and political and religious life. His second volume, *Les Oeuvres*, was planned on the same generous lines, and is an acute and sympathetic study of Burns's poetry in its relations to English and Scottish literature, and to the development of eighteenth century European thought.

Were it not that much has been discovered since Angellier wrote, and that Angellier himself was rather too prone to accept as fact what time has shown to be mere gossip, there would have been little need for amplifying or supplementing Angellier's biography.

The critical bibliography (II, 406 ff.) will be of the greatest assistance to the student interested in Scottish life and manners.

WALLACE, WILLIAM, *The Life and Works of Robert Burns.* Edited by Robert Chambers, revised by William Wallace. Edinburgh, 1896. 4 vols.

This edition, commonly referred to as Chambers-Wallace, is a revised form of Chamber's 1851–52 *Life and Works.* Wal-

[492]

lace's remarks, in the Preface to vol. I, make clear his purpose and general attitude:

> During his life-time, Dr. Chambers accumulated much biographical and other material which, for reasons that the lapse of time has deprived of force, he was unable fully to utilise. The last forty years have also witnessed an extraordinary production of literature relating to the life and works of Burns; as a consequence, several poems and letters of the Poet have been discovered and published . . . Under these circumstances, it has become desirable to issue a new and revised edition of Dr. Chambers's work, without departing in any important degree from its original plan. . . . An effort has been made to remove the difficulties that stand in the way of the English reader of Burns, by copious explanatory notes and a full marginal glossary of Scots words.[12]

The extent of Wallace's revision was far greater than this modest announcement would have led one to expect. Actually, he re-wrote the four volumes, retaining Chambers's arrangement, and sometimes much of his phraseology, but always adding copiously from his own store of information. The new footnotes alone, for example, contain enough fresh material to justify the entire edition. So admirable is Wallace's work in most respects, that one wishes he had been more candid in his treatment of Highland Mary, and—above all—that he had refrained from introducing long quotations into his narrative without giving any indication of their sources.

HENLEY, W. E., and HENDERSON, T. F., *The Poetry of Robert Burns.* Edinburgh, [1896–1897]. 4 vols. (The Centenary Burns.)

The great merit of the Centenary Burns is that it presents the best text of Burns's poetry, a text based on a meticulous examination of all available documents. The bibliographical information concerning each of Burns's publications gives in succinct form the important facts about these volumes; further and more detailed information appears in the notes to each poem. Here too one finds—and for the first time—definitive proof of the way Burns dealt with the old songs he retouched for Johnson and Thomson. Other editors and critics had stated the general facts; Henley and Henderson collected the evidence, and made it possible for the student to follow Burns into his workshop.

Henley's biographical essay (IV, 233 ff.) is brilliant, informative, but in certain respects misleading. Apparently suspecting the truth concerning Highland Mary, but without the evidence furnished by the exhumation of her body, Henley quite properly ridiculed the "Mariolaters" who had set her up as a beautiful ideal of spotless womanhood. He was also well within bounds in pointing out the extent of Burns's debt to earlier Scottish vernacular poetry. It is to be regretted, however, that he persistently magnified Burns's moral failings, and was so blind as to call the Dumfries years a period of "decadence."

The student who wishes to see how Henley's treatment of Burns was received by Scottish reviewers will consult an interesting booklet, *Henley and Burns, or, The Critic Censured,* edited by John D. Ross; Stirling, 1901.

WALLACE, WILLIAM, *Robert Burns and Mrs. Dunlop.* London, 1898. Also New York, 1898. 2 vols.

In this work appear the texts of the nearly two hundred extant letters that passed between Burns and Mrs. Dunlop. Ninety-seven, all previously unpublished, are her work; seventy-six, of which approximately one half were previously unpublished, are the work of the poet. The importance of such a collection need not be stressed; it is an invaluable supplement to the material published by Chambers-Wallace, and is the only place in which Mrs. Dunlop's letters are available.

HECHT, HANS, *Robert Burns. Leben und Wirken des schottischen Volksdichters.* Heidelberg, 1919.

Without doubt this may be called the best brief life of Burns that has yet appeared—accurate, reliable, and free from the time-honored mass of gossip and anecdote. It is regrettable that the volume has not been translated into English, for it is just the sort of biography that the general reader should have readily available.

[494]

APPENDIX

BUCHAN, JOHN, *The Complete Writings of Robert Burns* . . . With an Introduction by John Buchan. London and Boston, 1929. 10 vols.

This widely advertised edition of Burns's prose and verse ("The Large-paper Edition") is almost without value to the student. There are, to be sure, four negligible and hitherto unpublished poems, certain letters which had appeared only in the *Chronicle,* and one interesting and unpublished letter from James M'Candlish to Burns. But the work as a whole makes no contribution to the literature of Burns.

CARSWELL, CATHERINE, *The Life of Robert Burns.* London, 1930. Also New York, 1931.

The author of this most recent biography has made herself master of virtually everything that is known concerning Burns. She writes vividly and entertainingly. It is therefore doubly unfortunate that in telling the story of Burns's life she has woven together fact and fiction in a most baffling manner. Instead of rejecting the unsubstantiated and discredited gossip of a century and a half, Mrs. Carswell has gathered much of it into her narrative, has scrupulously neglected to give her authorities for statements that even the amateur reader will realize demand documentation, and, when two or more possible interpretations have presented themselves in explanation of a single fact, she has silently eliminated all except the one that most appeals to her, and has recounted this one as if it were the only possibility. It is no overstatement to say that this life of Burns is essentially as unreliable as anything Allan Cunningham ever wrote.

FERGUSON, J. DE LANCEY, *The Letters of Robert Burns.* Oxford, 1931. 2 vols.

Here one has what may fairly be called the definitive edition of Burns's prose, edited as such a work should be. Professor Ferguson has traced the originals of some five hundred and forty-five of the seven hundred and fifteen known Burns letters or prose documents, and has given to his readers a faithful transcript of

[495]

what Burns himself actually wrote, instead of what some early nineteenth century editor thought he should have written. The editorial matter is ample but never obtrusive. To say that these two volumes do for Burns's prose what the Centenary did for his poetry is to state only the most obvious reason for calling them the most notable contribution to Burns scholarship since the Centenary appeared. With the Henley-Henderson text of the poems, and the Ferguson text of the letters, the student has at his disposal virtually all of Burns's literary output, in the form in which he wrote it. And to the student of Burns's life his letters are at least as important as his poems.

3. *Source Material for Scottish Ecclesiastical and Economic History*

From among the vast number of documents dealing with these phases of Scottish life, a few stand out as of notable importance:

SPOTTISWOODE, JOHN, *The History of the Church of Scotland*. London, 1665.

This is probably the most valuable of the early histories dealing with the Church of Scotland before the Restoration.

WODROW, ROBERT, *The History of the Sufferings of the Church of Scotland*. Edinburgh, 1721–22. 2 vols.

These two large folios are at once a monument to the zeal and learning of "the great Dr. Wodrow," and the best source of information concerning the condition of the Church between 1660 and 1688.

[CHAMBERLAYNE, EDWARD], *Magnae Britanniae Notitia; or, The Present State of Great Britain*. London, 1755.

An invaluable work of reference, containing the sort of information one looks for today in *Whitaker's Almanac*. The 1755 edition was the 38th of the English section and the 17th of the Scottish.

APPENDIX

SALMON, THOMAS, *A New Geographical and Historical Grammar.* Edinburgh, 1749. Several later editions.

A useful compendium of information, much like Chamberlayne's *Notitia,* but more extensive in scope.

SINCLAIR, SIR JOHN, *The Statistical Account of Scotland.* Edinburgh, 1791–1799. 21 vols.

An early reviewer of the first volume of *The Statistical Account* said:

that no Publication of equal information or curiosity has appeared in Great Britain since Doomsday Book; and that from the ample and authentic facts which it records, it must be resorted to by every future Statesman, Philosopher, and Divine, as the best basis that ever has yet appeared for political speculation.

There was little exaggeration in this statement.

Sinclair had the distinction of editing what is in effect a carefully compiled census of Scotland as it was in the year 1790. His method was this: to each Parish Minister of the Church of Scotland he sent what he called "a variety of Queries, for the purpose of elucidating the Natural History and Political State" of that minister's own parish. From the returns to this questionnaire he intended to compile "a general Statistical View of North Britain." The clergymen did their work so well, however, that Sinclair soon abandoned his original plan, and printed the various accounts as separate articles, all except a few of the earliest ones being in the words of the ministers themselves. Nine hundred and thirty-eight parishes were thus described in the first twenty volumes; the final volume contained interesting addenda and well-prepared indices.

Among so many separate articles there must of necessity be great unevenness of merit. Some of the accounts are vividly written and packed with significant information. Others, inevitably, are somewhat superficial. But the average of excellence is extremely high, and the work as a whole a *sine qua non* to the study of Scotland during the latter half of the eighteenth century. Incidentally, the account of Ayr parish was written by Burns's friend William Dalrymple, and that of Mauchline by Daddy Auld himself.

SINCLAIR, SIR JOHN, *Analysis of The Statistical Account.* Edinburgh, 1825. Two parts.

The title of the work describes it accurately. It is the work of Sinclair himself, who in vol. I of the *Statistical Account* had announced his intention of publishing an epitome and analysis, but who for over a quarter of a century had been prevented from completing this useful part of his task. The Appendices contain a small amount of new material.

*　　*　　*

Three works of value to the student unable to consult the original sources mentioned above are:

EDGAR, ANDREW, *Old Church Life in Scotland.* Paisley, 1885; Second Series, Paisley, 1886.

ALLARDYCE, ALEXANDER [Editor], *Scotland and Scotsmen in the Eighteenth Century.* From the MSS. of John Ramsay, Esq., of Ochtertyre. Edinburgh, 1888. 2 vols.

GRAHAM, HENRY GRAY, *The Social Life of Scotland in the Eighteenth Century.* London, 1909.

For other works on Scottish life, history, scenery, etc., consult Angellier's bibliography mentioned above.

B. POEMS BY SAUNDERS TAIT

From *Poems and Songs,* by Alexander Tait. [? Paisley], 1790.

A copy of this extremely rare volume is in the Mitchell Library, Glasgow; no other is known to the present writer. Tait was a staunch conservative in religion; to him the New Lights were almost as offensive as the Roman Catholics. His volume of poetry is a strange compound of ballads dealing with Scottish history, songs on Paisley lads and lasses, and satires on persons who had offended him. Among these were William Burnes and his son Robert. Tait paid his respects to these two neighbors in the following three poems:

B-rns in his Infancy

Now I maun trace his pedigree
Because he made a sang on me,
And let the world look and see,
    Just wi' my tongue,
How Rab and Clootie did agree,
    When he was young.

Now Rab he's thriving like a plant,
Auld Symie ca's him his young saint,
And 's learn'd him vastly weel to chant,
    And mak fine rhyme,
Tells him wi' jilts he'll let him rant,
    In a wee time.

Now he's come to the age o' ten,
And has begun to chase a hen
Out through the kitchen, but and ben,
    He toddles at her;
The thing grows weary 't as ye'll ken,
    Gies her a blatter.

Now he is fifteen years and mair,
There's not his match in anywhere,
No, not in Clydesdale nor Ayrshire,
    He beats our Lairds;
His grandfather 's gi'en him plenty lear,
    To play his cards.

B-rns in Lochly

To Lochly ye came like a clerk,
And on your back was scarce a sark,
The dogs did at your buttocks bark,
    But now ye're braw,

Ye poucht the rent ye was so stark,
    Made payment sma'.

Man! I'm no speakin' out o' spite,
Else Patie wad upo' me flyte,
M'L-re ye scarcely left a mite
    To fill his horn,
You and the Lawyers gi'ed him a skyte,
    Sold a' his corn.

He sent the drum Tarbolton through
That no man was to buy frae you,
At the kirk door he cry'd it too,
    I heard the yell,
The vera thing I write 'tis true,
    Ye'll ken yersel.

M'L-re he put you in a farm,
And coft you coals your arse to warm,
And meal and maut—Ye did get barm,
    And then it wrought,
For his destruction and his harm,
    It is my thought.

He likewise did the mailing stock,
And built you barns, the doors did lock,
His ain gun ye did at him cock,
    And never spar'd,
Wi't owre his head came a clean knock
    Maist kill'd the Laird.

Auld Nick he did himsel disguise,
This is his servant's loudest cries,
M'L-re's downfall is B-rn's rise,
    Give ear to me,
Ye Lairds and Gentry, he surpriz'd,
    Sic tricks to see.

M'L-re's estate has ta'en the fever,
And heal again it will be never;

APPENDIX

The vagabonds they ca' you clever,
　　You're sic a sprite,
To rive frae him baith ga' and liver,
　　And baith the feet.

B-RNS'S HEN
CLOCKIN IN MAUCHLINE

Ye whunstane hearted Mauchline wretches!
Wha wallop aye in deep debauches,
Wi' me ye hae got merry catches,
　　Tis truth I'm saying,
I have a chicken in my hatches,
　　To me she's layin'.

I catch'd her in a green kail yard,
I neither neb nor feathers spar'd,
But a' my strength on her I war'd,
　　To mak her clock,
Now she's fa'en till't, he this out rair'd,
　　Come help, gude fouk!

The wives they up their coats did kilt,
And through the streets so clean did stilt,
Some at the door fell wi' a pelt,
　　Maist broke their leg,
To see the Hen, poor wanton jilt!
　　Lay her fourth egg.

The wives they sat them down to rest,
And view'd poor Chuckie in her nest,
To see how Robin had her drest,
　　For sic a breeze,
She's now a ship amang the rest,
　　On foamin seas.

The wives they let the anchors fall,
And at the cables they did haul,

APPENDIX

And mounted up the sails so tall,
    Then gave a swear,
The anchor grip, it held so baul,
    She wadna steer.

Then Robin he fell on his knees
And pray'd to Clootie for a breeze,
That to his mind wou'd give great ease,
    And settle strife,
That she might skip the roarin' seas,
    And save her life.

But Robin's prayers had na strength,
M'Kenzie then he cam at length,
And pull'd the ship out by main strength,
    With skill o' notion,
And then she trimly swims at length
    Upon the ocean.

Now she is sailing in the Downs,
Calls at the ports of finest towns,
To buy bed hangings, and galleons,
    Away she goes;
So trimly, as she sails the rounds,
    Mang the Chinose.

She's got some packs o' human leather,
Wi' lugs, wi' een, wi' tongue to blether,
And a fine cap and peacock feather,
    And wi't she's douse,
With a grand besom, made o' heather,
    To sweep her house.

Now she returns so tight and clever
As fast as woodcock, snipe, or pliver,
M'Kenzie he does her deliver
    In Mauchline town;
I'm sure twa came out through the river,
    A double round.

M'Kenzie gets a double dram,
Wi' a good slice o' bacon ham;
The wives sit down, drink aff ram tam,
    The soldier's joy!
B-rns is the clever vale de cham,
    Wi' his hautboy.

The Holy Fair they sit and read,
And wi' twa pipes blaw anet-seed,
And cracks o' mony a maiden head,
    O'Tam and Sue;
Then off they come, as clean's a bead,
    Adieu, adieu!

C. THE LEASE ON THE FARM OF ELLISLAND

From the original in the collection of Mr. Oliver R. Barrett

The lease occupies three and one half pages of a folio of stamped paper. At the bottom of each page the two principals signed their names, as well as at the conclusion of the document. The last half of page 4 is occupied by Burns's renunciation of the lease, written in his own hand. Inasmuch as this lease does not seem to have been published, it is here reprinted entire by the courteous permission of the owner, Mr. Oliver R. Barrett.

It is contracted and agreed between the parties following viz. Patrick Miller of Dalswinton Esqr. on the one part, and Robert Burns late in Mossgavill in the parish of Mauchline in Airshire on the other part in manner and to the effect underwritten; that is to say, the said Patrick Miller by these presents sets and in tack and assedation Lets to the said Robert Burns, his heirs and assignees whatsoeuer but secluding sub-tenants in all events, and also secluding assignees during the natural life of the said Robert Burns, but reserving to him power to assign by any deed to take effect after his death, all and whole that part of the lands of Elliesland lying on the South side of the riuer Nith in the parish of Dunscore and Sheriffdom of Dumfries, and that for the space of four nineteen years and crops from and after his entry thereto which is hereby

APPENDIX

declared in every respect to commence at the term of Martinmas next seventeen hundred and eighty eight; Reserving expressly from the lands above mentioned two acres of any part or parts thereof which the said Patrick Miller pleases, for the purpose of planting, the planting and inclosing which two acres to be at the said Patrick Miller's sole expence, and reseruing also to be planted and inclosed a Belt of twenty yards in breadth along the march which divides the aboue mentioned lands from those of Captain Riddel of the Carse, the expence of planting said belt to be defrayed by the said Patrick Miller, but the expense of inclosing the same to be disbursed by the tenant out of the three hundred pounds after mentioned, And reserving further for planting the Bank along the riuer side, the expence of planting which shall be defrayed by the said Patrick Miller. And, In respect that it is agreed upon between the said parties that the said Robert Burns shall build a dwelling house, Barn, byre and stable on the said farm, on a plan to be approuen of by the said Patrick Miller, and shall inclose the said lands. For these purposes the said Patrick Miller Binds and obliges him and his heirs and successors to pay to the said Robert Burns the sum of Three hundred pounds Sterling; of which sum he is, in the course of the ensuing summer, to advance him

[signed]	PATRICK MILLER
[signed]	ROBERT BURNS

(Page second)

him one hundred and fifty pounds Sterling, on condition of at least building a dwelling house in the course of the said summer; and to pay to him the remaining one hundred and fifty pounds afterwards in whole or in parts as the said Robert Burns shall find it necessary to receive it, upon the said Robert Burns always giuing the said Patrick Miller euidence that he has expended, in carrying on the building and inclosing, sums equal to those which he shall from time to time ask and claim; and also vouching to him that he has laid out one hundred pounds of the sum first stipulated for the purposes for which he received it. And it is also prouided that, should the said Robert Burns get the buildings and inclosures completed for less than three hundred pounds, then the remainder of the said sum given to the said Robert Burns shall be laid out by him in the improvement of the farm as to him shall seem most expedient; Which tack aboue written, with and under the reservations foresaid the said Patrick Miller binds and obliges himself and his foresaids to warrant to the said Robert Burns and his aboue written at all hands and against all deadly (?) as his will. For which causes and on the other part The said Robert Burns Binds and obliges himself and his heirs, Executors, and successors whomsoeuer to content and pay to the said Patrick Miller and his heirs or assignees the sum of Seuenty pounds Sterling yearly in name of tack duty, but to be restricted for the first three years and crops to fifty pounds Sterling yearly payable at two terms in the year Whitsunday and Martinmas by equal portions, beginning the first payment of the said tack duty at the term of Whitsunday seventeen hundred and eighty nine and the next term's payment at Martinmas thereafter for the first crop and year of his said possession, and so on thereafter during the currency of this lease, with a fifth part more of each of said termly payments in liquidate penalty in case of faillie and the legal interest thereof from the respective terms when the same became due and during the not payment of the same. And further, as it is agreed by the said parties that the

[signed]   PATRICK MILLER
[signed]   ROBERT BURNS

(Page third)

the said Robert Burns shall be allowed to make use of the houses and pasture the grass of the said farm from Whitsunday to the said term of Martinmas next, which is aboue declared to be the commencement of this lease, therefore the said Robert Burns hereby Binds and obliges him and his foresaids to pay to the said Patrick Miller and his foresaids, for the said houses and grass, so to be used by him, such a sum as shall at the time be agreed upon by the said parties, and, failing such agreement, then the said Robert Burns and his foresaids shall pay for the same such sum as shall be fixed upon by an Arbiter mutually chosen by the parties. And also the said Robert Burns Binds and obliges him and his foresaids to labour and manure the lands hereby let in a proper manner during the currency of this lease; and, during the last six years thereof, not to keep more than one third of the said lands in crop each year, and during that period to use a sufficient quantity of manure with whatever crop he lays down the lands. Moreouer he binds and obliges himself and his foresaids to build and complete the aforesaid dwelling house and the other buildings and execute the inclosing on this said farm in manner aboue mentioned, and particularly of the Belt of planting aboue specified, Declaring always that the inclosures to be made on said farm shall consist of Six—in number, or of any other number which the said parties shall afterwards agree upon, the said Robert Burns and his foresaids being always obliged to make the said inclosures sufficient and to leaue the same in that state at the issue of the lease; and which dwelling house the said Robert Burns becomes bound to finish and complete during the course of the ensuing summer. And further that he or his foresaids shall make no encroachments on the said riuer Nith, by making any Caul, pier, or embankment, throwing in stones or rubbish, or by driuing piles or in any other manner of way whateuer. And the said Robert Burns Binds and obliges himself and his foresaids to remoue himself, his family, servants, goods and gear forth of the

[signed]	PATRICK MILLER
[signed]	ROBERT BURNS

(Page fourth)

the said lands at the expiry of this lease without any previous warnings or process of remouing to that effect, and to leaue the houses and offices in a tenantable condition at his said remoual; And further, Both parties Bind and oblige themselues and their foresaids to implement and perform their respective parts of the premises to each other under the penalty of one hundred pounds Sterling to be paid by the party failing to the party performing or willing to perform ouer and above performance, And they consent to the registration hereof in the books of Council and session or any other Competent that letters of horning on six days charge and other necessary execution may pass on evidence to be Interponed hereto in form as offers and to that effect they Constitute————— their pro [manuscript illegible] &c

In witness whereof they haue subscribed these presents consisting of this and the three preceding pages and likewise a duplicate hereof all written on stampt paper by Thomas Walker Baird Clerk to John Gordon Writer to the Signet at Edinburgh this Eighteenth day of March one thousand seven hundred and eighty eight years before these witnesses the said Thomas Walker Baird and John Murray one of the Clerks in the Bank of Scotland's office.

[signed] JOHN MURRAY Witness   [signed] PATRICK MILLER
[signed] THOS. W. BAIRD Witness   [signed] ROBERT BURNS.

Whereas, I have paid the rents of the farm of Ellisland to the term of Martinmas first, & settled my accounts relating thereto with Mr Miller of Dalswinton the proprietor of said farm, & have agreed to give up my tack of the said farm at Martinmas first I accordingly hereby give up and renounce for ever the said Tack; in witness whereof I write and subscribe these presents at Dalswinton, this tenth of September, in the year one thousand, seven hundred and ninety one—

ROBT BURNS

D. BURNS'S EXCISE COMMISSION

From the original in the collection of Mr. John Gribbel

This interesting document, here reprinted by the courteous permission of Mr. John Gribbel, the owner, occupies one printed sheet (16 by 13 inches). In it Burns is designated as "Robert Burns, Gentleman"—a fact which must have given a certain amount of satisfaction to the person who found himself thus characterized. The signatures of the three Commissioners appear in the left-hand margin; each was originally accompanied by a seal. These seals, and the great seal, which appeared in the upper left hand corner, have been removed. The date is of interest—July 14, 1788, an indication that the machinery of the Board moved slowly, for Burns had qualified for the commission some time before.

TO ALL TO WHOM these Presents shall come, Greeting. Know Ye, That we, whose Hands and Seals are hereunto set, being the major Part of the chief Commissioners and Governors for the Management of the Receipt of the Excise; that is to say, the Duties upon

APPENDIX

making and importing Beer, Ale, Spirits, and other Exciseable Liquors, in that Part of *Great Britain* called Scotland, and in all and every of the Islands and Territories thereunto belonging; and of the Duties upon making Candles, and of the Duties upon Hops growing, and to grow, within the Limits aforesaid: And we also, being the major Part of the Commissioners and Governors for the Receipt and Management of the several and respective Duties herein after mentioned within the Limits aforesaid; that is to say, of the several and respective Duties upon making of Soap, Paper, Pasteboard, Millboard, and Scaleboard, respectively; and upon printing, painting, or staining of Paper; and upon printing, painting, staining, or dying of Silks, Callicoes, Linens, and Stuffs respectively; and upon the making of Starch, and of Gilt and Silver Wire respectively; and upon tanning, tawing, or dressing of Hides and Skins, and Pieces of Hides and Skins; and upon the making of Vellum and Parchment respectively; and upon Silver-plate and Manufactures of Silver respectively; and of the Inland Duties upon Coffee, Tea, and Chocolate respectively; and upon making Malt, and making and importing Mum, Cyder, and Perry respectively; and of the Duties upon Glass, and all the Materials or Metal, or other Preparations made use of in the making of Glass; and upon every Coach, Berlin, Landau, Chariot, Calash, Chaise-marine, Chaise, Chair, and Caravan, or by what Name soever such Wheel Carriages now are or hereafter may be called or known, that shall be kept by or for any Person for his or her own Use, or to be let out to hire respectively; and of the Duties payable by all Persons and Bodies Politick or Corporate, owning, using, having or keeping, certain Quantities of Silver-plate, arisen or accrued, or to arise or accrue in SCOTLAND aforesaid, and in all and every of the Islands and Territories thereunto belonging, reposing especial Trust and Confidence in the Knowledge, Skill, Industry, Integrity, Fidelity, and Circumspection of *Robert Burns Gentleman* [written] HAVE (pursuant to the several and respective Powers to us given and granted, in and by the several and respective Statutes relating to the said several and respective Duties, and in and by our several and respective Commissions, Constitutions, and Appointments) nominated, constituted, and appointed, and, for His Majesty's Service, DO nominate, constitute, and appoint him, the said *Robert Burns* [written] to be One of the Surveyors, Messengers, Gaugers, and Officers, of and for the said several and respective Duties before mentioned, all and every of them respectively; and of all other Duties that shall or may be put under the Management of us the

[508]

said present Commissioners, or of the like Commissioners for the Time being; and for the measuring and attending Malt that shall be shipped for Exportation; and for the seizing of all Brandy, Arrack, Rum, Spirits, Strong Waters, Coffee, Tea, Chocolate, and Cocoa Nuts, which shall be unlawfully imported or carried within the Limits aforesaid: AND do hereby impower and require him, the said *Robert Burns* [written] that, pursuant to the Powers and Authorities in and by the said several and respective Statutes relating to the said several and respective Duties, he shall and do, from Time to Time, by gauging, weighing, Measuring, and otherwise take, and also do enter into a Book and Books, to be from Time to Time delivered to him for that Purpose, full and true Accounts of the Quantities, Qualities, Natures, and Kinds, of all and every the several and respective Goods, Commodities, and Manufactures respectively, chargeable with, and liable to, the said several and respective Duties, which he, from Time to Time, shall or may find out or discover; and thereof respectively shall and do, from Time to Time, make and deliver to us the present Commissioners, and to the Commissioners for the said Duties for the Time being, or to the major Part of us or them respectively, or to such as we, or the Major part of us, have appointed, or as we, or the Commissioners for the said Duties for the Time being, or the major Part of us or them respectively, shall nominate and appoint for such Purpose, full and true Returns, Reports, Registers, Vouchers, and Accounts in Writing, of the full and true Quantities, Qualities, Natures, and Kinds, of all and every the said several and respective Goods, Commodities, and Manufactures before mentioned, chargeable with or liable to the said several and respective Duties, by him from Time to Time found out or discovered; and that he shall and do exercise, execute, and perform, all and every the Powers and Authorities in and by the several and respective Statutes given and granted, or enacted to be done, exercised, executed, and performed by such Surveyor, Messenger, Gauger, or Officer, according to the true Intent and Meaning of such Statutes respectively; To HOLD, exercise, execute, and perform, the said Office of such Surveyor or Messenger, Gauger and Officer, as aforesaid, during the Pleasure of us the said present Commissioners, and during the like Pleasure of the Commissioners for the said Duties for the Time being, or of the major Part of us or them respectively. AND all Sheriffs, Bailies, Justices of the Peace, Magistrates of Burghs, Constables, and other Officers of the Peace, and all and every other Person and Persons whatsoever, is and

APPENDIX

are hereby prayed and required to be aiding and assisting unto him the said *Robt. Burns* [written] in the due Execution hereof, as he or they will answer the contrary at his or their utmost Peril. GIVEN under our Hands and Seals at the Chief Office of Excise, and for the said Duties, in EDINBURGH, this *Fourteenth* [written] Day of *July* [written] in the *Twenty eighth* [written] Year of the Reign of our Sovereign Lord *George the Third* [written] by the Grace of GOD, of *Great Britain, France,* and *Ireland,* KING, Defender of the Faith, and so forth; and in the Year of our LORD One thousand seven hundred and *Eighty eight* [written].

[Signatures:]

> J. WHARTON
> GEO. BROWN
> JAS. STODDARD

[1] *Memoir of . . . James Currie,* by W. W. Currie, I, 271. London, 1831. 2 vols.
[2] Peterkin's 1815 reprint of Currie's first edition; I, 214.
[3] *Ibid.,* p. ciii.
[4] J. De Lancey Ferguson, "In Defence of Richard Hartley Cromek;" *Philological Quarterly,* IX, 239 ff. (1930).
[5] *Op. cit.,* p. 30.
[6] *Ibid.,* p. 34. For an interesting criticism of Jeffrey's and Scott's articles on Burns, see the "Remarks on two late Reviews of the Works of Burns," in *Poems by Robert Burns,* II, 265 ff. (Edinburgh, 1811, 2 vols.) "These strictures," says the anonymous writer, "are so acrimonious and exaggerated, that one really cannot speak of them without some danger of being tainted by that spirit of harshness which pervades them."
[7] *Op. cit.,* p. xlii.
[8] Ibid., p. xl.
[9] Lockhart's *Life of Burns,* ed. W. S. Douglas, p. 295, n. London, 1892.
[10] *Op. cit.,* I, vii. (Quoted from New York edition, 1859.)
[11] *Op. cit.,* I, vii.
[12] *Op. cit.,* I, iii ff.

INDEX

An entry composed of an Arabic numeral alone refers to the indicated page of the volume; *e.g.*, 423 (page 423 of the text).

An entry composed of a Roman numeral followed by an Arabic numeral refers to a footnote in the designated chapter; *e.g.*, VII, 23 (note no. 23 at close of chapter VII).

A

Adair, Dr. James, 250–253; 279.
"Adam Armour's Prayer," 157.
Adam, James, X, 53.
Addison, Joseph, 43; 44; 59.
"Address to a Haggis," 192; 223; 229.
"Address to Beelzebub," 158; 159; 166; 168.
"Address to Edinburgh," 192; 217; 229; 230.
"Address to the Deil," 169; 170; 171.
"Address to the Scottish Distillers," 342.
"Address to the Unco Guid," 87; 158; 159–160; 229.
Adventurer, The, 336.
"Ae Fond Kiss," 273; 436; 449; 473.
Afton MSS, The, V, 12.
"Ah Woe is Me," III, 62.
Aiken, Robert, 114; 129; 135; 141; 150; 151; V, 20; 196; 274.
Ainslie, Rachel, 238.
Ainslie, Robert, 211–213; 215; 235; 236; 237; 241; 256; 271; 276; 280; 283; 289; 311; 319; 359; 361; 455.
Akenside, Mark, 44; 59.
Alexander, George; Fourth Duke of Gordon, 196–197; 247.
Alexander, Jane Maxwell; Duchess of Gordon, 196–197; 219; 247; 444.
Allardyce, Alexander, 498.
Alloway, Burns's birthplace in, 13–14.
"Altho' Thou Maun Never be Mine," 385.
"A Man's a Man for A' That," 421–423.
American Congress of 1776, The, 341.

Anderson, Dr. Harry B., II, 67; 435.
"And I'll Kiss Thee Yet," 414.
Angellier, Auguste, II, 8; on Highland Mary, 139; 477; 492; 498.
Angus, W. Craibe, 477.
Arabian Nights, The, 336.
Armour, Jean, 23; 107; 108; 111; 112; 114; birth, 120; meets Burns, 121; "marriage", 121; disapproval of family, 122; called before Session, 123; "desertion" of Burns, 123–124; rebuked by Auld, 126; warrant against Burns, 127; birth of twins, 128; 135; 141; 143; 150; 151; 230; renewed intimacy with Burns, 239; 250; 270; 275; parents reconciled to Burns, 282; second pregnancy, 282; takes refuge in Tarbolton, 283; returns to Mauchline, 283; birth of second twins, 284; marriage to Burns, 287–289; Kirk sanctions marriage, 302–303; joins Burns at Ellisland, 305; bears Francis Wallace, 306; bears William Nicol, 308; 348; moves to Dumfries, 359; bears James Glencairn, X, 48; bears Elizabeth Riddell, 363; 430; 433; bears Maxwell, 437; death, 437; 447; 450.
Arnold, Matthew, 162.
Arnot, John, 135.
Associate Synod, The, 21.
Athole, Duke of, 246; 485.
"Auld Farmer's Salutation to his Mare, The," 4; 171; 174.
"Auld Lang Syne," 329; 350; 421.
Auld, William ("Daddy"), 23; 103;

104; 107; 108; 125; 170; 302; 303; 304; 455; 498.

"Author's Earnest Cry and Prayer, The," 136.

Autobiographical Letter to Dr. Moore, Burns's, quoted, *passim*.

Ayr, 4; description of, 8; 9.

Ayrshire, Description of, 4; population, 4; map of, 5; chief towns, 6; economic conditions in, 13–15; agriculture in, 15–17; climate, 16; roads, 17; religious establishments, etc., 19–28 (see Presbyterianism); educational system, 29–30; casual allusions to, *passim*.

Ayrshire Garland, The, 338.

B

Bachelor's Club, The Tarbolton, 70–71.

Back Causeway, The, Drawing of, 285.

Ballantine, John, 151; 222; 275; 278.

Bannockburn, 38; 244; 419.

"Bard's Song, The," 465.

Barrett, Oliver R., *Preface*; 503.

Bastille, fall of, 342.

Bayne, Allan, 140.

Beattie, James, 216; 221; 260.

Begbie, Ellison, 71–73.

Begg, Isabella Burns (the poet's sister), 136; 490.

Begg, Isabella (the poet's niece), 83; 84.

Beugo, John, 231.

"Birks of Aberfeldy, The," 246.

Blacklock, Dr. Thomas, 141; 153; 154; 191; 203; 207–209; 260.

Blair, Dr. Hugh, 113; 154; 163; 191; 203–205; 215; 252; 336.

"Bonie Peggy Alison," III, 62.

Border Tour, The, 211; Burns begins tour, 235–236; Coldstream, 236; welcomed by Masons at Eyemouth, 237; Dunbar, 237; Newcastle, 238; Carlisle, 238; Dumfries, 238; return to Mossgiel, 239.

Boswell, James, 198.

Bothwell Bridge, Battle of, 11; 37.

Brand, Isbel (the poet's aunt), 249.

Brand, William (the poet's uncle), 249.

Brice, David, 124; 125; 135.

"Brigs of Ayr, The," 229; 230.

Broun, Gilbert (the poet's grandfather), 37.

Broun, Samuel (the poet's uncle), 56.

Brown, Richard, 6; 75; suggests poetry as Burns's vocation, 76; 267; 270; 284; 485.

Browning, Robert, 472.

Bruce, Michael, 50.

Bruce, Robert the, 8; 252; 356; 419; 420.

Buchan, John, 495.

Burke, Edmund, 362; 375.

Burn, Robert (architect), 193.

Burnes, Agnes Broun (the poet's mother), 32; marriage, 37; birth, 37; family history, 37; education, 38; later life, 38; assists at birth of Francis Wallace Burns, 306.

Burnes, Jean (the poet's aunt), 249.

Burnes, Robert (the poet's cousin), 248.

Burnes, Robert (the poet's uncle), 34; 305.

Burnes, Robert (the poet's grandfather), 32; 33.

Burnes, William (the poet's father), 12; 32; early life, 33–37; cottage at Alloway, drawing of 35; marriage, 37; 38; removal to Mount Oliphant, 45; 53; 55; 58; removal to Lochlie, 64; 65; illness and bankruptcy, 78–79; death, 81; epitaph, 81; 82; 364; Tait's poem on, 499.

Burness, James (the poet's cousin), 249; 305; 427; XI, 2.

Burns, Agnes (the poet's sister), 40; II, 10.

Burns, Anabella (the poet's sister), 40; II, 10.

Burns, Calendar, The Kilmarnock, II, 10.

Burns Chronicle, The, quoted in footnotes, *passim*.

Burns, Elizabeth Riddell (the poet's daughter), birth, 363; bad health, 366; death, 372.

Burns, Francis Wallace (the poet's son), birth, 306; 359; death, X, 163.

Burns, Gilbert (the poet's brother), 14; 34; 39; 40; 46; 47; 48; 50; 51; 60; 67; 82; 83; 98; 100; 151; 218; 249; debt to Robert, 257 and VIII, 1; 305; 326; 329; 344; 347; 359; 446; 448;

453; 480; 486; his edition of Currie, 487–488.

Burns, James Glencairn (the poet's son), 381; birth, X, 48; death, X, 163; 437.

Burns, John (the poet's brother), birth, II, 10; death, 102.

Burns, Maxwell (the poet's son), birth, 437; X, 48; death, X, 163.

Burns, Robert (the poet's son), birth, 128; 270; 298; 359; 365; 414; 437; death, IV, 61.

Burns, Robert (the Poet), record of birth, 32; early surroundings and education, 41–60; life at Mount Oliphant, 45–55; Kirkoswald, 56–58; Nellie Kilpatrick, 54; overtasks his strength, 55; Peggy Thompson, 56, 57; life at Lochlie, 64–93; dancing school, 67; Tarbolton Bachelor's Club, 70–71; Ellison Begbie, 71–73; flax-dressing experiences, 73–74; first connection with Masonry, 74; friendship with Richard Brown, 75–76; return to Lochlie, 77; leases Mossgiel, 82; affair with Elizabeth Paton, 83–84; birth of "Dear-bought Bess", 84; *First Commonplace Book*, 85–89; poems composed at Lochlie and Irvine, III, 62; removal to Mossgiel, 96; life at Mossgiel, 96–146; Elizabeth Paton, 118–120; Jean Armour, 120–129; Mary Campbell, 129–145; publishes Kilmarnock volume, 149.

Leaves Mauchline for Edinburgh, 186; popularity, 192–193; new friends in Edinburgh, 194–220; the 1787 Edinburgh edition, 220–231; sale of copyright to Creech, 224; leaves Edinburgh for Border tour, 232.

Border tour, 235–239; return to Mossgiel, 239; renewed intimacy with Jean Armour, 239–240; second vacation tour (West Highlands), 241–243; the Highland tour, 243–249; return to Edinburgh, 250; fourth tour, 250–252; return to Edinburgh, 254; lends money to Gilbert, 257, and VIII, 1.

Work for *Scots Musical Museum*, 258–263; Clarinda, 263–271; visit to Mauchline, 270–271; birth of Jean's second twins, 284; Clarinda again, 271–274; efforts to secure Excise appointment, 274–278; leases Ellisland, 278–281; the return to Jean, 282–288; marriage, 287–289; summary of Edinburgh experiences, 289–291.

Arrival at Ellisland, 297; house-building, 299–301; ecclesiastical sanction of his marriage, 302–303; birth of Francis Wallace, 306; Anne Park, 307; birth of daughter to Anne Park, 308; birth of William Nicol, 308; relations to William Burns, 310–314; goes on duty in the Excise, 317; promotion in the Excise, 319; friendship with Robert Riddell, 321–328.

Monkland Friendly Society, 324–325; "Tam o' Shanter," 326–328; relations to Mrs. Dunlop, 328–334; liberalism, 337–341; health, 343–346; financial failure of Ellisland, 346; sale of lease to landlord, 347; sale of goods, 348; summary of Ellisland experiences, 348–350.

Removal to Dumfries, 355; birth of Elizabeth Riddell, 363; visit to Mossgiel, 363; schooling for his children, 364; moves to house in Mill Vennel, 365; work on Thomson's *Select Scotish Airs*, 365; offer of newspaper position, 369; vacation tour to Galloway, 369; Jean Lorimer, 370; appointed acting Supervisor of Excise, 370; connection with Dumfries Volunteers, 371; death of daughter Elizabeth Riddell, 372.

Serious illness, 372; Dumfries friendships, 373–387; relations to Mrs. Walter Riddell, 387–394; Excise experiences, 394–406; political views, 399–401; acting Supervisor, 403; on sick leave in Excise, 404; work for Johnson and Thomson, 407; publication of Edinburgh two-volume edition (1793), 407–410; Thompson's *Select Scotish Airs*, 410–423; journalistic connections, 423–424; *Merry Muses of Caledonia*, 424–426.

INDEX

Financial difficulties, 426; tradition of bankruptcy, 428; tradition of social ostracism, 429; death, 430; funeral, 436; traditions concerning alcoholism and venereal infection, 431–433; summary of life, 442–444.

His personality, 444–445; sense of humor, 445; pride, 445; recklessness, 446–447; affection, 448; sentimentality, 449–450; religious views, 450–452; intellectual power, 452–453; business ability, 454; ambition, 455–456; disappointment, 457–458; accomplishment, see *Burns, Robert, Poetry of*, below.

Burns, Robert, children of
Elizabeth Paton (Dear-bought Bess), by Elizabeth Paton, birth of, 84; III, 53; baptism, 119; subsequent history of, IV, 40.
Robert and Jean, twins, by Jean Armour; birth of, 128; death, IV, 61.
Campbell, Mary, possible child by, 142–145.
May Cameron, child by, 219.
Jennie Clow, child by, 219.
Second twins, by Jean Armour, 284.
Francis Wallace Burns, by Jean Armour, birth, 306; death, X, 163.
Elizabeth Park, by Anne Park, 308; IX, 36.
William Nicol Burns, by Jean Armour, birth, 308; death, X, 163.
Elizabeth Riddell Burns, by Jean Armour, birth, 363; death, 372.
James Glencairn Burns, by Jean Armour, birth, X, 48; death X, 163.
Maxwell Burns, by Jean Armour, birth, 437; death, X, 163.

Burns, Robert, as Exciseman, first allusion to Excise, 274; takes steps to secure appointment, 275–278; 280; instruction, 314; receives commission, 315; requests assignment to a district, 316; sworn into service, 317; on active duty, 316; salary, 317; duties, 317–318; promotion, 319; applies for Port Division, 320; transferred to Dumfries third division, 395; assigned to Port Division, 397; denounced as unpatriotic, 397–401; proposals concerning revenues, 402;

serves as acting supervisor, 403; on sick leave, 404; his "character" in Excise records, 406; copy of his commission, 507.

Burns, Robert, health of, early overtasks his strength, 55; illness at Irvine, 73; physical breakdown, 99; 100; hypochondria, 256; injury to knee, 265; overtasks his strength at Ellisland, 343; influenza, 343; nervous breakdown and heart trouble, 344; breaks his arm, 345; 358; hypochondria, 366; rheumatism, 392; Mrs. Riddell's comment on his appearance, 393; sick leave from Excise, 404; rheumatic fever, 429; sea-bathing at Brow, 430; traditional explanations of his early death, 431–433; recent medical diagnosis, 434–435.

Burns, Robert, letters of, quoted *passim*.

Burns, Robert, poetry of, "love, labor, and song," 54; encouragement from Richard Brown, 76; 89; 90; interest in Scottish song, 89; metrical skill, 91, 92; Dr. Blacklock's comment on, 153–154; Sibbald's criticism of, 155; Mackenzie's criticism of, 155; Dr. Moore's criticism of, 156; "Holy Willie's Prayer," 160–161; "The Jolly Beggars," 162–165; "The Cotter's Saturday Night," 171–173; use of Spenserian stanza, 172; anticipation of Wordsworth's *Preface*, 173; "Auld Farmer's Salutation to his Mare," 174; "The Holy Fair," 175–178; narrative skill, 178; "To a Mouse," 178–181; harbinger of the "Romantic Movement," 181; relation to Scottish vernacular tradition, 182; technical skill, 184.

No growth in power in Edinburgh edition, 230; adaptation of songs for *Museum*, 258–263; interest in music, 413–414; "A Man's a Man for A' That," 421–422; lyrics composed at Dumfries, 436; his poetic vision, 460–466; the supernatural, 460; nature, 461; man, 462–466; the farmer, 462; the seeker for liberty, 463; the hypocrite, 464; the lover, 464–466.

His imagination, 466–468; his power of expression, 468–473;

INDEX

metrical skill, 468–469; memorable phrases, 470; tone color, 470; narrative skill, 470–471; descriptive power, 471; apt characterizations, 471; intellectual honesty, 472; lyric technique, 472–473; imitators, 473; summary of his poetical genius, 474–475.

Burns, Robert, reading of, books in average Ayrshire home, 15; list of early school books, 44; fairy tales, 45; books borrowed by William Burnes for his sons, 47–49; *Titus Andronicus*, 50; study of French and Latin, 52; *Manual of Religious Belief*, 53; *Collection of Letters*, 58; reading during early years, 59, 60; reading at Lochlie, 85; knowledge of Scottish song, 161; 216; books ordered for Monkland Society, 324; 325; 334; personal orders from Peter Hill, 335; political reading, 362; study of song collections, 407; 408; 409; X, 20; 452; 453; 459.

Burns, William (the poet's brother), II, 10; 305; 310–312; death of, 313; IX, 42; 449.

Burnside, Dr. William, 356; 358.

C

Cadell and Davies, Messrs., 231; 408; 409; 479; 487.

Caird, John (the poet's uncle), 249.

Caledonian Hunt, The, 192; 195.

Caledonian Mercury, The, 192.

"Calf, The," 229.

Calvin and Calvinism, 22; 24; 25–28; 53; early satires on, 116; 269; 450; 451.

Cameron, May, 142; 212; bears a child to Burns, 219; 238; 241; 250; 308; X, 12; 447.

Campbell, Dr. Alexander, 37.

Campbell, (the poet's first schoolmaster), 41; 59.

Campbell, Mary (Highland Mary), confusion of legend and fact concerning, 129–130; her monument, 130; her Bible, 131; date of her parting from Burns, 133; letter announcing her death, 136; death, 139;

tradition of spiritual love, 139–140; hostility of her family to Burns, 141; record of infant's coffin in her grave, 142; summary and suggested solution of the problem, 143–145; 230; 241; possible visit of Burns to her grave, 242; 274; 275; 308; "Thou Lingering Star," 309; 344; 419; 447; 450; 468; 493.

Candlish, James, 51.

"Canst Thou Leave me Thus," 391.

Carfrae, Patrick, 413.

Carlyle, Thomas, 175; 295; 296; 321; 354; 419; 455; 472; review of Lockhart's *Life of Burns*, 489.

Carswell, Catherine, 139; IV, 47; IV, 87; comment on her *Life of Burns*, 495.

"Cauld Kail," 456.

Cervantes, Miguel, *Don Quixote*, 336; 445.

Chalmers, Margaret, 219–220; 225; 245; 250; 251; 277; 281; 287; 288; VIII, 34.

Chamberlayne, Edward, 496.

Chambers, Robert, 163; 242; 432; 478; 482; 490–491; 492; 493.

Chambers-Wallace Edition of Burns, quoted *passim*; 492–493.

Chaucer, Geoffrey, 175; 445; 462; 464; 470.

Churchill, Charles, 216.

Church of Scotland, The, see Calvinism and Presbyterianism.

Cibber, Colley, 335; 336.

"Clarinda" (Mrs. Agnes M'Lehose), 226; 257; early life, 264; children, 264; arranges first meeting, with Burns, 265; beginning of Sylvander-Clarinda correspondence, 265; love, 266; religion, 267; second interview with Burns, 268; learns of Jean, 268; troubled conscience, 268–269; letter of reproof to, 269; learns of Burns's marriage, 271; breaks with Burns, 271; correspondence renewed, 272; sails for Jamaica, 273; final interview with Burns, 273; 277; 280; 287; 289; 311; 330; 360; 361; 383; 387; 394; 450.

Clark, John, 430.

Clarke, James, 339; 340; 426.

INDEX

Clarke, Stephen, 258; 259; 261.

Claverhouse, John Graham of, 20; 37; 246.

Cleghorn, Robert, 343.

Clow, Jennie, 142; bears child to Burns, 219; 273; 360; 361; 383; IX, 15; X, 12; 447; 448.

Cockburn, Mrs. Allison, 90; 197.

Coleridge, Samuel Taylor, 459; 466; 470; 471.

"Collier's Lassie, The," 414.

Collins, William, 216.

Colman, George, 335.

Commonplace Book, The First, 85–89; 100; 159; 161; 258; 449; 455.

Commonplace Book, The Second, (Edinburgh), 195; 200; 207; 287; 424.

Congreve, William, 335.

Conrad, Joseph, 475.

Constable, Lady Winifred Maxwell, 33.

Cook, Davidson, 134; VIII, 13; X, 100.

Corbet, William, 320; IX, 65; 395; 397; 401.

Corneille, Pierre, 335.

"Cotter's Saturday Night, The," 114; comments on, 171–173; 236; 411; 413; 462.

"Court of Equity, The," 157.

Covenanters, The, 11; 19; 20; 26; 296; 356.

Cowper, William, 174; 181; 335.

Crabbe, George, 174.

Craig, Lord, 264; 269.

Craigenputtock, 295; 321.

"Craigieburn Wood," 383; 384.

Crawford, Superintendent, 395.

Creech, William, 17; 114; 188–190; 210; 218; selected as agent for 1787 edition, 221–223; buys copyright, 224; financial dealings with Burns, 225–228; 237; 243; 250; 254; 256; 257; 274; 284; 362; 364; 407; 408; 409.

Crichton-Browne, Sir James, II, 67; 434.

Crochallan Fencibles, The, 190; 192; 209.

Cromek, Robert Hartley, 134; 263; 482–484.

Cromwell, Oliver, 238.

Cruikshank, William, 251; 254; 270; 343.

Cullie, David, 298.

Culloden, Battle of, 11; 33; 247.

Cunningham, Alexander, 198; 299; 362; 366; 374; 376; 380; 381; 405; 430; 450; 480.

Cunningham, Allan, 99; 244; 281; 299; 307; 318; 327; 338; 372; 454; 478; 488; 489.

Cunningham, James, Earl of Glencairn, 191; 194–196; 275.

Cunningham, Lady Elizabeth, 195.

Cunninghame, Sir William, 153.

Currie, Dr. James, 39; 70; 130; 134; 142; 145; 200; 227; 247; 250; 251; 323; 354; 370; 372; 374; 375; 378; 382; 431; 433; 434; 435; 478; account of his *Life and Works of Burns*, 479–482; 484; 487; 488.

Currie, William Wallace, 323.

D

Dalrymple, James, of Orangefield, 191.

Dalrymple, Dr. William, 9; 32; 39; 53; 66; 337; 498.

Dalzel, Andrew, 196.

Dalziel, Alexander, 195.

Dalziel, (or Dalzell) General Thomas, 11.

Davidson, Betty, 40; 45; 60.

"Death and Dr. Hornbook," 158; 159; 203; 229.

"Death and Dying Words of Poor Mailie, The," III, 62; 170; V, 34.

"Dedication to Gavin Hamilton, A," 109; 471.

"Deil's Run Awa' wi' the Exciseman, The," 396.

De Lolme, John, 365; X, 20.

Derham, William, 47; II, 33; 48.

"Despondency," 128.

Dick, James C., 134; 263; 477; 483.

Dickens, Charles, 445.

"Does Haughty Gaul Invasion Threat," 372.

Douglas, William Scott, 137; 480; 491–492; his *Works of Robert Burns* quoted, *passim*.

"Dream, A," 166.

Dryden, John, 44; 59; 335; 464.

Dumfries, History of, 356; trades in, 357; churches, 357; schools, 358;

INDEX

theatre, 358; climate, 358; casual allusions to, *passim*.

Dunbar, William, 182.

"Duncan Gray," 419.

Dundas, Henry, Lord Melville, 18.

Dunlop, David, Preface.

Dunlop, Mrs. Francis, 34; 116; 136; 137; 139; 186; 192; 213; 216; 222; 228; 239; 270; 287; 299; 302; 306; 309; 316; 320; 321; birth and early life, 328; delight in Kilmarnock edition, 329; beginning of correspondence with Burns, 329; a critic of Burns's work and conduct, 330; a defender of Burns, 331; estrangement from Burns and reconciliation, 332–334; 340; 344; 345; 349; 363; 383; 394; 395; 398; 431; 450; *Robert Burns and Mrs. Dunlop*, 494.

E

Edgar, Andrew, IV, 14, 15, and 55; 498.

Edinburgh, 186; description of, 187–188; life in, 188–190; distinguished citizens of, 191; Burns's first winter in, 186–232; his second winter in, 256–291; casual allusions to, *passim*.

Edinburgh Edition of Burns's *Poems*, The 1787, 156; 160; 161; 194; 195; 207; 210; 220–231; advertised by Creech, 222; two forms of, 223; published, 223; copyright sold to Creech, 224; Burns's profits from, 228; description of, 229; comparison with Kilmarnock edition, 229; new poems in, 229–230; makes Burns widely known, 231; 243; 289.

Edinburgh Edition of Burns's *Poems*, The 1793, 407–410; publication of, 409.

Edinburgh Gazetteer, The, 362.

Edinburgh Magazine, The, 141; 154; 191; 327.

Elders of the Church of Scotland, 22; 23.

"Election Ballad for Westerha'," IX, 118.

"Elegy on Willie Nicol's Mare," VI, 61.

Ellisland, 13; 214; 278; 279; 280; 281; Burns's life at, 294–350;

location of, 294; description of parish, 294–296; description of farm itself, 296; terms of lease, 297; 298; 453; transcript of lease, 503–510; casual allusions to, *passim*.

Emerson, Ralph Waldo, 70; 179; 296.

English Review, The, 156; V, 19; VI, 64.

"Epistle from Esopus to Maria," 391.

"Epistle to a Young Friend," 120; 169.

"Epistle to Davie," 100; 169.

"Epistle to Davie, Second," 157.

"Epistle to James Smith," 150.

"Epistle to J. Lapraik," 167; 168.

"Epistle to John Goldie," 115; 157; 158.

"Epistle to John Kennedy," 157.

"Epistle to John Rankine," 118; 119.

"Epistle to the Rev. John M'Math," 157; 158.

Erskine, Andrew, 411.

Erskine, Henry 113; 191; 197–198.

Erskine, John, IV, 46.

Erskine, John, of Mar, 400.

Ewing, J. C., Preface; III, 51; III, 53; VII, 20; VII, 22; X, 72; 477.

Excise, Burns's connection with, see Burns, Robert, as Exciseman.

F

"Fair Empress of a Poet's Soul," 271.

"Fairest Maid on Devon Banks," X, 127.

Fenelon, François de, 52.

Ferguson, Adam, 191; 202–203.

Ferguson, J. De Lancey, Preface; 134; 163; V, 27; VI, 33, 35, and 36; VIII, 13; 332; 333; IX, 65; IX, 137; X, 75; X, 86; 483; his *Letters of Robert Burns,* quoted *passim*; comments on his *Letters,* 495–496.

Fergusson, Provost, 45; 58.

Fergusson, Robert, 85; 88; 90; 92; 149; 175; 182; 193; 194; 459; 469.

Fielding, Henry, 336.

Findlater, Alexander, 320; 370; 376–378; defence of Burns, 378; 379; 384; 394; 401; 403; 405; 406; 417; 431; 486.

Findlay, James, 68; 314.

Fisher, A. (Mrs. Slack), 44; II, 22.

Fisher, E., I, 11; 336.

INDEX

Fisher, William ("Holy Willie"), 108–109; 161; 468; 471; see also "Holy Willie's Prayer."

"Five Carlins, The," IX, 118.

Flax-dressing, Burns's experience at, 73–77.

Fontanelle, Louisa, 363.

"Fornicator, The," IV, 38.

Fourth Vacation Tour, Burns's, 250; Linlithgow, Sterling, and Harvieston, 250; Margaret Chalmers, 251; visits Ramsay and Murray, 251; meets Mrs. Bruce, 252; visits grave of Robert Bruce, 252; 253.

Franklin, Benjamin, 153; 207.

G

Gairdner, John, IV, 18.

Galloway, Burns's tour through, 369–370.

Garrick, David, 335; 336.

Geddes, Dr. John, 253; VII, 49.

General Assembly of the Church of Scotland, The, 21; 24–25; 338.

Gentleman's Magazine, The, 131–132.

Gibson, Agnes ("Poosie Nansie"), 103; 104.

Gibson, James, 477.

Gladstone, Hugh, X, 63.

Glasgow Faculty of Physicians, The, 264.

Glasgow Faculty of Procurators, The, 264.

Glencairn, Earl of, The, see Cunningham, James, Earl of Glencairn.

Glendriddell MSS, The, 57; II, 2; V, 14; 322–324; 328; IX, 71.

"Go Fetch to me a Pint of Wine," 350; 470.

Goldie, John, 115; 157; 158.

Gordon, Duchess of, The, see Alexander, Jane Maxwell, Duchess of Gordon.

Gordon, Duke of, The, see Alexander, George, Duke of Gordon.

Gordon, William, Earl of Kenmure, 370.

Government of Scotland, The, 18–19.

"Gowden Locks of Anna, The," 307.

Gracie, James, 382; X, 28.

Graham, Henry Gray, 498.

Graham, Mrs. Robert, 409.

Graham, Robert, of Fintry, 247; 257;

VIII, 1; 275; 276; 277; 315; 316; 335; 343; 346; 395; 398; 400; 402; 405; 406; X, 74.

Gray, James, 378–379; 431; X, 40; 486.

Gray, Thomas, 44; 59; 216.

Greenfield, William, the Reverend, 205–206; VI, 39; VI, 40.

"Green Grow the Rashes, O," VIII, 3; 161; 217; 230.

Greenock Burns Club, The, 130; 142.

Gribel Collection, The, 241.

Gribbel, John, Preface; 323; IX, 71; 507.

Grose, Captain Francis, 326–327.

Guthrie, William, 48; II, 32; 324; 336.

H

Hadden, J. Cuthbert, X, 108.

"Had We Never Lov'd sae Kindly," 270; 484; see also "Ae Fond Kiss."

Haliburton, Hugh (pseud. for J. L. Robertson), II, 23.

"Hallowe'en," 45; 217; 460.

Hamilton, Captain John, 359; 365; 371; 428.

Hamilton, Charlotte, 245; 251.

Hamilton, Gavin, 23; 24; 82; 96; 98; 99; 104; 109–111; 113; 114; 121; 145; 151; 154; 195; 196; 219; 239; 245; 287; 338.

Hamlet, 179.

"Handsome Nell," 386.

Hannibal, Life of, 43.

Hariot, Lady, 237.

Harvieston, Burns's visit to, see Fourth Vacation Tour, Burns's.

Hay, James, 247.

Hay, Lewis, 220.

Health, Burns's, see Burns, Robert, health of.

Hecht, Hans, 425; 494.

Henley, W. E., 355; 406; 454; 494.

Henley, W. E., and Henderson, T. F., *The Poetry of Roert Burns;* quoted, *passim;* comments on, 493–494.

"Here's a Health to Them that's Awa'," 401.

Heron, Patrick, 429

Heron, Robert, 130; 152; 227; 354; 479; 481.

Herrig's Archiv, X, 140.

INDEX

"Highland Mary," 136; 139; 419.
See also Campbell, Mary.
Hill, Peter, 193; 210; 221; 257; 298;
320; 324; 334; 335; 336; 347; 366;
380.
History of Sir William Wallace, The,
43; 59; II, 18.
Hogg, James, 489.
"Holy Fair, The," 108; 157; 175–178;
204; 229; 252; 337; 464; 469; 470;
471.
"Holy Willie's Prayer," 23; 108; 114;
115; 158; 160–161; 175; 307; 464;
471; 485; 486.
Holyrood Palace, 188.
Huber, Marie, 336.
"Humble Petition of Bruar Water, The,"
246.
Hume, David, 28; 85; 190.
Hutcheson, Francis, 27; 28.
Hyslop, John, 382.
Hyslop, Meg, 382.

I

"I Hae a Wife o' my Ain," 350; 473.
"I Hold it, Sir, my Bounden Duty,"
157.
Idler, The, 336.
"Inventory, The," 157.
Irvine, 6; 7; Burns's life at, 73–77.
Irving, David, 482.

J

Jeffrey, Francis, 191; 483.
"John Anderson, my Jo," 174–175;
350; 473.
"John Barleycorn," III, 62; 203.
Johnson, James, 89; 161; 197; 226;
231; 250; Burns's connection with
the *Museum,* 258–263; 369; 372;
407; 410; 412; 415; 455; 456; 469;
493.
Johnson, Samuel, 153; 192; 198; 207;
335.
Johnstone, Sir James, 342.
"Jolly Beggars, The," 161; 162–165;
168; 203; 422; 458; 465; 471;
484; 485.
Jolly, William, IV, 2; IV, 13.
Jonson, Ben, 335.

Journal of the Border Tour, Burns's,
235–238.
Journal of the Highland Tour, Burns's,
244–249.
Juvenal, 464.

K

Kames, Lord, 190.
Keats, John, 472.
Kemp, the Reverend John, 264; 269;
271.
Kennedy, John, 151.
Ker, Robert, X, 63.
Kilmarnock, population of, 9; description of, 10; history of, 11; casual
references to, *passim.*
Kilmarnock Edition of Burns's *Poems,*
The, 57; 102; 109; 111; 113; 114;
129; 135; 141; 143; 145; 149–185;
proposals for publishing, 150; cost
of, 151; popularity of, 152; early
comments on, 153–156; omissions
from the volume, 157–165; the
published poems, 166–181; estimate
of volume as a whole, 181–184; 199;
204; compared to the 1787 Edinburgh
edition, 229–231; 258; 365; 417;
446; 456; 462.
Kilpatrick, Nelly, 54; 72; 386.
"Kind Sir, I've Read your Paper
Through," 341.
Kirkoswald, 55; 56; 57; 58; 59.
Kirkpatrick, the Reverend Joseph, 294;
296; 337; 340; 355.
"Kirk's Alarm, The," 107; 114; 338;
485.
Kirk Session, The, the institution, 22;
23; at Mauchline, 110; 111; 114;
122; 123; 303.
Knox, John, 11; 19; 20; 25; 26; 27;
188; 324; 339.
Koch, Theodore W., Preface.

L

"Laddie, Lie Near Me," 456.
"Lament, The," 128.
Langhorne, John, 202.
"Lass of Cessnock Banks, The," III, 62.
"Lassie wi' the Lint-white Locks," 384.

[519]

Lawrie, the Reverend George, 141; 153; 154; 208; 290.

Letter from a Blacksmith to the Ministers and Elders, A, 175; 176.

Letters by the Wits of Queen Anne's Reign, 58; 72.

Lewars, Jessie, 383; 385–387.

Lewars, John, 334; 382; 385; 397; 406.

"Lines Pinned to Mrs. Riddell's Coach," 391.

Lochlie, 7; 13; Burns's life at, 64–93; description of farm, 65; dancing school, 67; Burns's friends at, 68–70; Bachelor's Club, 70–71; courtship of Ellison Begbie, 71–73; flax-dressing experience, 73–74; Masonic affiliations, 74; Richard Brown, 75–76; economic distress, 77–79; bankruptcy of William Burnes, 79; death of William Burnes, 81; Elizabeth Paton, 83–84; reading done at, 85; writing done at, 85–92; casual allusions to, *passim.*

Locke, John, 85; 266.

Lockhart, John G., 131; 202; 244; 295; 309; 310; 327; 354; 372; 395; 397; 428; 429; 478; comments on his *Life of Robert Burns,* 488–489.

Logan, John, 151; 338.

London Morning Chronicle, The, 423; 424.

Lorimer, Jean ("Chloris"), 370; 383; 384; X, 53.

Lorimer, William, 377; 384.

Loudon, Earl of, The, 98; 109.

Lounger, The, 155; 191; 199; 324.

Lowe, David, III, 14; III, 16.

Lowes, John L. (*The Road to Xanadu*), 466.

M

Macfadzean, R. W., 317.

Mackenzie, Dr. John, 113–114; IV, 30; 199; VI, 27; 283; 284; 445; 502; 503.

Mackenzie, Henry, 85; 155; 191; 198–199; 221; 224; 503.

Mackinley, the Reverend William, 194.

Macphail, Archibald, 142.

Macunn, Professor John, 421.

Manual of Religious Belief, A, 53; II, 47.

"Man was Made to Mourn," 45; 161.

Mark Twain (pseud. for S. L. Clemens), 445.

"Marrow men," 27; I, 11.

Marshall, James, VI, 10.

Marshall, William, 335; IX, 101.

Masson, Arthur, 43; 44; II, 22.

Mauchline, the town and its inhabitants, 102–117; map of, 105; casual references, to, *passim;* see also Mossgiel.

Maxwell, Dr. William, 369; 374; 375; 376; 381; 480.

Maxwell, Provost, 334.

M'Bain, James, I, 3; III, 28.

McAdam, John, 153.

McCandlish, James, 495.

McIlraith, John, X, 50.

McNaught, Duncan, IV, 17; IV, 56.

McMinn, Ney, Preface.

M'Diarmid, John, 309; 348; 359.

M'Diarmid, William, X, 43.

Merry Muses of Caledonia, The, 190; 424–426.

M'Gill, Dr. William, 9; 337; 338; 339.

Miller, Patrick, 225; 238; 250; 257; 271; 274; 278; 281; 295; 296; 297; 347; 409; 424; 503; 504; 505; 506.

Miller, Peter, 342.

Mill Vennel, The, Dumfries, drawing of, 367.

Milton, John, 44; 59; 239; 475.

Mirror, The, 324.

Mitchell, John, 318; 395; 396; 398; 426.

M'Lehose, Mrs. Agnes, See Clarinda.

M'Lure, David, 64; 78; 79; 500.

M'Math, The Reverend John, 115; 157; 158.

M'Murdo, John, 425.

Moliere, Jean, 335.

Monkland Friendly Society, The, 324–325; 334; 336; 349.

"Monody on a Lady Famed for her Caprice," 391.

"Montgomerie's Peggy," III, 62.

Monthly Review, The, 155.

Moore, Dr. John, 33; 57; 215–219; 227; 228; 242; 243; 268; 323; 331.

Morin, John, 347; 348.

INDEX

Morrison, Matthew, 300.

Morris, William, 470.

Mossgiel, Burns's life at, 96–146; terms of Burns's lease, 96; outlook from, 97; the farmhouse, 96–97; Burns's responsibilities, 99; Masonic affiliations, 100; literary ambitions, 100–101; death of John Burns, 102; the town of Mauchline, 102–117; church and churchyard, 104; "Daddy Auld," 107–108; William Fisher, 108–109; Gavin Hamilton, 109–111; John Richmond, 111–112; James Smith, 112–113; Dr. John Mackenzie, 113; Robert Aiken, 114; other friends, 114–117; Elizabeth Paton, 118–120; birth of her daughter, 119; Jean Armour, 120–129; Mary Campbell, 129–145; casual references to, *passim*.

Motherwell, William, 489.

Mount Oliphant, Burns's life at, 45–61; terms of the lease, 45–46; family life at, 46–48; books in the home, 47–50; schooling, 51–52; religious education, 52–53; first love affair, 53–54; study of surveying, 55–57; love affair with Peggy Thompson, 57; summary of Mount Oliphant years, 59–61; casual references to, *passim*.

Muckle, Archibald, 283.

Muir, Robert, 115; 116; 151; 270; 280.

Muir, William, 283.

Murdoch, John, 30; 41; 42–43; 47; 50; 51; 53; 59; II, 15; II, 41; II, 47; 75; 80; 199; 313; IX, 51.

Murray, Sir William, 251.

Museum, The Scots Musical, see *Scots Musical Museum, The.*

M'Whinnie, David, 151.

"My Father was a Farmer," III, 62.

"My Highland Lassie," 133.

N

Nasmyth, Alexander, 231.

National Council of Learned Societies, The, Preface.

New Lights, The, 21; casual references to, *passim*.

"New Psalm, A," 342.

Nicol, John, 354.

Nicol, William, 213–215; casual references to, *passim*.

Nimmo, John, 257; 265.

Nimmo, Miss, 265.

"Nineteenth Psalm Versified, The," V, 21.

Nisbet, John, 11.

Niven, William, 65.

"Now Westlin Winds," III, 62.

O

"Occasional Address, An," 363.

"Ode for General Washington's Birthday," X, 85.

"Ode to the Departed Regency Bill," 342; 401.

"Of A' the Airts," 307.

Old Lights, The, 21; casual references to, *passim*.

"On William Creech," VI, 77.

"Ordination, The," 158; 160; 194; 229.

"O Saw ye Bonny Lesley," 413.

Ossian, 85; 249; 336.

Otway, Thomas, 335.

"O Wert Thou in the Cauld Blast," 386.

P

Paine, Thomas, 362; 363; 421; 422.

"Paraphrase of the First Psalm," V, 21.

Parish, The, 22.

Park, Anne, 141; 142; 307; bears child to Burns, 308; 310; IX, 36; 363; 382; 383; 447; 448.

Park, Elizabeth (daughter of preceding), birth, 308; subsequent history, IX, 36; 359; 363; 437; 448.

Paton, Elizabeth, 68; bears child to Burns, 84; 108; 118–120; 121; 447; 448.

Paton, Elizabeth (daughter of preceding), birth, 84; III, 53; 119; subsequent history, IV, 40; VIII, 1; 359; 437; 448.

Paul, Hamilton, the Reverend, 486–487.

Peebles, Dr. William, 337.

"Penitential Thought in the Hour of Remorse," 87.

INDEX

Pentland Hills, Battle of, 11.
Peterkin, Alexander, 378; 485–486.
Pindar, Peter (pseud. for John Wolcott), 415; 416; 417.
Pitt, Septimus, Preface.
Pleyel, Joseph, 411.
"Ploughman's Life, The," III, 62.
Poe, Edgar Allan, 470.
Poems, Chiefly in the Scottish Dialect, see Kilmarnock Edition of Burns's *Poems,* The, see also Edinburgh Edition, The 1787, see also Edinburgh Edition, The 1793.
"Poet's Welcome to his Love Begotten Daughter, A," 75; IV, 9; 119.
"Poor Mailie's Elegy," 91; 170;
Pope, Alexander, 216; 453, 462.
"Prayer under Pressure of Violent Anguish," 74; V, 21.
Prentice, Archibald, 186.
Presbyterianism; the Presbyterian Church in Scotland, 19; history of, 19–22; "Old Lights" and "New Lights," 21; organization, 22–25; creed, 25–28; democracy of, 28; casual allusions to, *passim.*
Presbytery, The, place in church organization, 23; number of, 23; function of, 23–24; 110; 338.
"Prophet and God's Complaint, The," 163.

R

Racine, Jean, 335.
Ramsay, Allan, 85; 88; 90; 149; 182; 459; 469.
Ramsay, John, 33; 251; 252; 498.
Rankine, John, 68; 118; 157.
"Rattlin', Roarin' Willie," 414.
Ray, John, 47; 49.
Rebellion of 1715, The, 3; 33; 341; 400.
Rebellion of 1745, The, 3; 33; 34; 341.
Red Comyn, The, 356.
"Red, Red Rose, A," 436; 470.
Reformation, The, 149.
Reid, George, 186.
"Reply to an Announcement by John Rankine," 157.
Revolution, the American, 401.

Revolution, the French, 342; 375; 383; 399.
Richardson, Gabriel, 382.
Richardson, Samuel, 85; 450.
Richmond, John, 107; 111; 113; 125; 127; 128; 152; 163; 164; 187; 191; 209; 241; 242; 243; 307.
Riddell, Elizabeth Kennedy (Mrs. Robert), 322; 363; 390; 391.
Riddell, Maria (Mrs. Walter), 369; 370; 383; 387–394; 425; 430; 444; 455; 478; 479; 480.
Riddell, Robert, of Glenriddell, 134; 135; 263; 295; 321–328; 349; 390; 400; 409; 417; 482; 504.
Riddell, Walter, 387; 390; 417.
"Rights of Woman, The," 363.
"Rigs o' Barley, The," III, 62.
Ritter, Dr. Otto, 90; III, 63.
Robertson, Principal William, 190.
Robinson, Edwin Arlington, 472.
Rodger, Hugh, 56.
"Ronnals of the Bennals, The," III, 62.
Rosamond, the brig, 395–397.
Ross, John, 10.
Ross, John D., IV, 86; V, 17; 494.
Rowe, Mrs. Elizabeth, 44.
Royal Dumfries Volunteers, The, 371; 372; 373; 376; 429; 436.
Ruddiman, Thomas, 52.
Russell, John, the Reverend, 160; 170.

S

Saint Giles's Cathedral, 188.
Salmon, Thomas, 47; 497.
Schaff, Philip, I, 9; I, 10.
"Scotch Drink," 170.
Scots Musical Museum, The, 133; 197; 209; 226; 250; 254; 258–263; 280; 289; 322; 334; 342; 349; 385; 410; 412; 416.
Scots Musical Museum, The, Riddell's interleaved copy of, 263; 407; 482.
"Scots Wha Hae," 419–421; 436; X, 136.
Scots Worthies, The, 336.
Scott, Sir Walter, 191; 202–203; 374; 444; 483; 484.
Second vacation tour, to the West Highlands, 241–243.
Select Collection of Original Scotish

INDEX

Airs, A, 132; 138; 365; 385; 407; 410–423.

Selkirk, Earl of, The, 370.

Sempill, Robert, 92.

Sempills of Beltrees, The, 459.

Shakespeare, William, 59; 175; 335; 336; 379.

Sharp, Lauriston, Preface.

Shelley, Percy Bysshe, 423; 466; 472.

Shenstone, William, 44; 59; 85; 216.

Sheridan, Richard, 335.

Shields, John, 11.

Shirley, G. W., Preface; VII, 9; 317; and all notes signed "G.W.S."

Shirrefs, Andrew, 248.

Sibbald, James, 154; 155.

Sillar, David, 66; 68; 69; 70; 90; 485.

Simson, John, 27.

Sinclair, Sir John, I, 5; 103; 295; 325; 356; *The Statistical Account*, 497–498.

Sinton, John, IX, 62; X, 84; X, 90.

Skinner, John, the Reverend, 248; 259.

Sloane, Thomas, IX, 138.

Smellie, William, 114; 190; 209–210; 228; 256; 336; X, 63.

Smith, Adam, 27; 190.

Smith, James, 111; 112–113; 127; 151; 163; 209; 240; 241; 288; 303; 307; 455.

Smollett, Tobias, 335; X, 20.

Snyder, F. B., X, 91; X, 98; X, 152.

Society of Improvers of Knowledge of Agriculture, The, 16.

Solemn League and Covenant, The, 26.

Sommerville, John, 226.

Spectator, The, 324.

Spottiswoode, John, 496.

Stackhouse, Thomas, 48; 49; II, 37.

Staig, David, 402.

Stair MSS, The, 153; V, 12.

"Stanzas of Psalmody," 401.

"Stanzas Written in Prospect of Death," V, 21.

Sterne, Laurence, 85; 450.

Stewart, Mrs. Alexander, 153.

Stewart, Professor Dugald, 113; 154; 191; 199–202; 215; 455; 480.

Stobbie, Adam, 405; 406.

Stoddart, James, 186.

"Strictures on Scottish Songs and Ballads," 482; 483.

Stuart, Peter, 341; 342; 423.

Stuart, Prince Charles, 11; 236; 341.

Stuart, the House of, 340; 341.

Sutherland, George, 335; 363.

Synod, The, 24.

T

Tait, Alexander (Saunders), 69; 79; 499–503.

Tait, Crauford, 345.

"Tam Glen," 473.

"Tam o' Shanter," 326–328; 350; 364; 409; 410; 420; 460; 461; 470–471.

"Tam Samson's Elegy," 229.

Tarbolton Bachelor's Club, The, 70–71; 102.

Tea Table Miscellany, The, 59.

Tennant, John, 53; 280; 281; 336.

Tennyson, Alfred, 171; 470.

Third Vacation Tour, to the Central Highlands, 243–249; Bannockburn, 244; Linlithgow, 245; Killiekrankie, 246; Blair Castle, 246; Inverness, 247; Aberdeen, 248; Edinburgh, 249.

Thompson, H. W., VI, 27.

Thomson, James, 44; 59; 85; 216; 450; 453.

Thomson, George, 132; 134; 138; 139; 161; 162; 307; 362; 363; 369; 372; 383; 384; 385; 404; 407; 410–423; 427; 436; 455; 456; 457; 469; 486; 493.

Thomson, Peggy, 56; 57; 72; 119.

"Thou Lingering Star," 136; 139; 309; 350.

Tinnock, Nanse, 107.

Titus Andronicus, 50.

"To a Daisy," 170; V, 34; 231.

"To a Louse," V, 34.

"To a Mouse," V, 34; 170; 171; 178–181; 449.

"To Chloris," 385.

"To Hugh Parker," 298.

"To John Rankine in Reply to an Announcement," 118.

"To Major Logan," IV, 93.

"To Mary in Heaven," see "Thou Lingering Star."

"To Robert Graham on Receiving a Favor," 316.

"To Ruin," 128; 161.

INDEX

"To the Reverend John M'Math," IV, 32.

Tours, Vacation, Burns's, First tour, see Border Tour; Second tour, see Second Vacation Tour; Third tour, see Third Vacation Tour; Fourth tour, see Fourth Vacation Tour; Fifth tour, see Galloway, Burns's tour through.

"To William Simpson," 167.

Train, Joseph, 112; 396.

"Twa Dogs, The," 55.

"Twa Herds, The," 158; 160; 485.

Tytler, Alexander Fraser, 409; 410.

Tytler, Sarah, VI, 23.

U

Union of 1707, The, 3; 18; 19.

V

Vanbrugh, Sir John, 335.

"Verses Intended to be Written Below a Noble Lord's Picture," 195.

"Verses Written near Loch Ness," VII, 48.

Violin, Burns's attempt to play the, 90.

"Vision, The," 100; 229.

Voltaire, Jean de, 236; 328; 335.

W

Waddell, P. Hately, IX, 139; X, 8.

Walker, Josiah, 113; 246; 433; 485.

Wallace, Sir William, 8; 88; 296; 328.

Wallace, William, 141; 328; the Chambers-Wallace *Burns*, quoted, *passim*; reviewed, 492–493; *Robert Burns and Mrs. Dunlop*, quoted 81–94; 328; 332; reviewed, 494.

Wardlaw, Lady, 90.

Watson, J. L., VI. 23.

Westminster Confession of Faith, The, 26; 336.

"When Guilford Good our Pilot Stood," 229.

White, Thomas, 378; 379; X, 43.

Whitefoord, Sir John, 113; 275.

Whitman, Walt, 467.

Whittier, John G., 4; 171.

Will, William, X, 31; X, 36.

Williamson, David, 427.

"Willie Brew'd a Peck o' Maut," 350.

"Willie's Awa'," 237.

Wilson, John (of Kilmarnock), 12; 151; 152; 161.

Wilson, John (of Tarbolton), 68; 159.

"Winter, a Dirge," 74; 88.

"Winter Night, A," 217.

Wodrow, Dr. Patrick, 66; 115.

Wodrow, Dr. Robert, 66; 496.

Wood, J. Maxwell, IX, 67.

Wood, Dr. Alexander, 265; 276.

Woodley, William, 387.

Wordsworth, William, 97; 171; 173; 174; 181; 182; 183; 246; 362; 459; 467; 470.

World, The, 336.

Wright, Dudley, III, 31.

Wycherley, William, 335.

Y

"Ye Banks and Braes o' Bonie Doon," 436; 473.

"Young Peggy Blooms our Bonniest Lass," VIII, 3.